The **Rough Guide** to

Croatia

written and researched by

Jonathan Bousfield

NEW YORK • LONDON • DELHI

www.roughguides.com

Contents

◄◄ Split harbour ◄ Dubrovnik

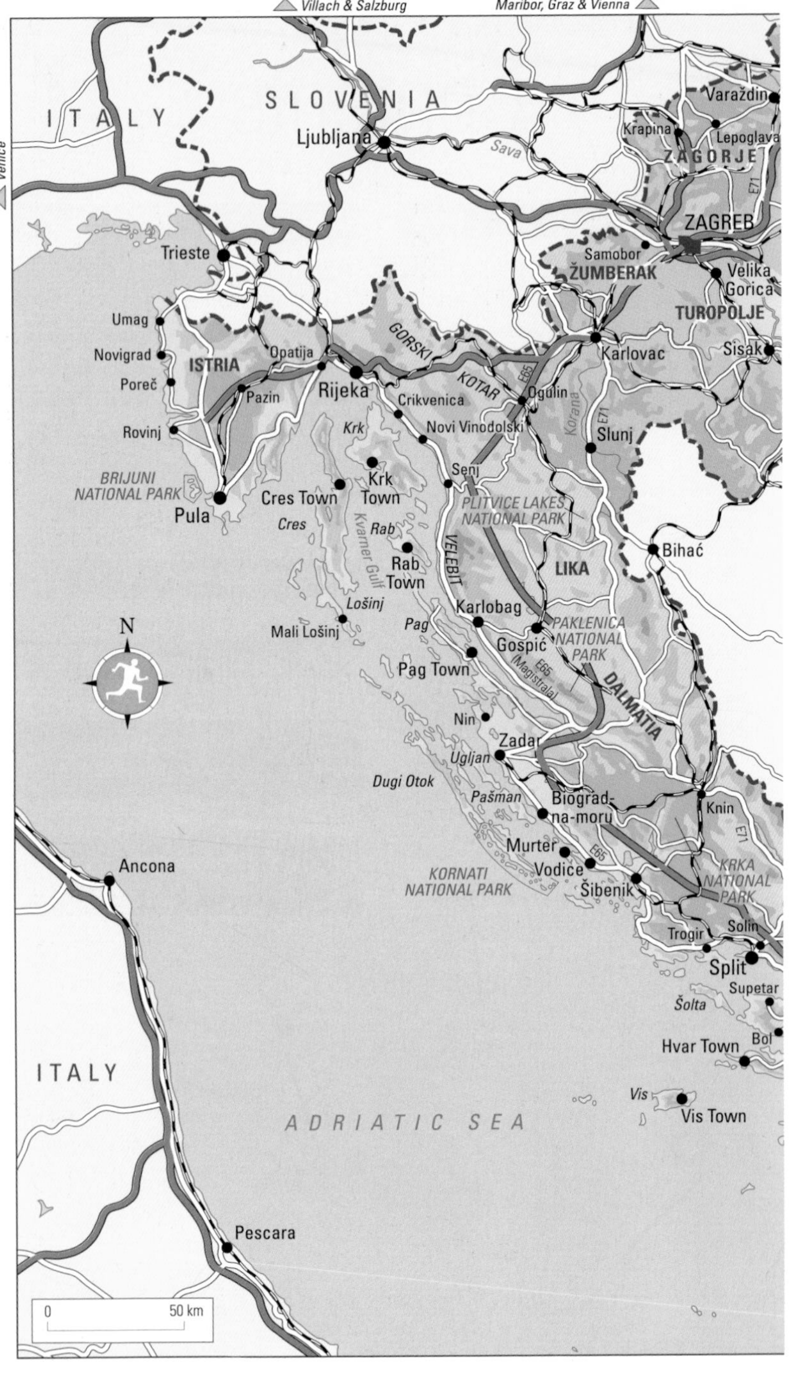
Villach & Salzburg
Maribor, Graz & Vienna
Venice
SLOVENIA
ITALY
Ljubljana
Sava
Varaždin
Krapina
Lepoglava
ZAGORJE
ZAGREB
Samobor
ŽUMBERAK
Velika Gorica
TUROPOLJE
Trieste
Umag
Novigrad
Poreč
ISTRIA
Opatija
Pazin
Rijeka
GORSKI KOTAR
Karlovac
Sisak
Ogulin
Crikvenica
Novi Vinodolski
Korana
Slunj
Rovinj
Krk
Krk Town
Senj
BRIJUNI NATIONAL PARK
Pula
Cres Town
Cres
Kvarner Gulf
Rab
Rab Town
PLITVICE LAKES NATIONAL PARK
VELEBIT
LIKA
Bihać
Lošinj
Mali Lošinj
N
Karlobag
Pag
PAKLENICA NATIONAL PARK
Gospić
E65 (Magistrala)
Pag Town
DALMATIA
Nin
Zadar
Ugljan
Dugi Otok
Pašman
Biograd-na-moru
Knin
Murter
Vodice
Šibenik
KORNATI NATIONAL PARK
KRKA NATIONAL PARK
Ancona
Trogir
Solin
Split
Supetar
Šolta
Hvar Town
Bol
Vis
Vis Town
ITALY
ADRIATIC SEA
Pescara
0
50 km

Budapest
Budapest
Metres
1500
1000
500
200
100
0
Čakovec
Koprivnica
PODRAVINA
Drava
HUNGARY
Pécs
Danube
Bjelovar
Virovitica
LONJSKO POLJE NATURE PARK
Slatina
SLAVONIA
Drava
KOPAČKI RIT NATURE PARK
Kutina
Daruvar
Našice
Osijek
Sava
Novska
Požega
Đakovo
Vukovar
Bačka Palanka
Slavonski Brod
Vinkovci
Danube
E70
E70
Belgrade
Banja Luka
BOSNIA - HERCEGOVINA
Tuzla
Sava
SERBIA
Travnik
Zenica
Bugojno
Sarajevo
Sinj
Cetina
Imotski
Omiš
Brela
Makarska
BIOKOVO NATURE PARK
Brač
Mostar
Međugorje
Hvar
Korčula
Ploče
Vela Luka
Korčula Town
Pelješac Peninsula
Ston
MONTENEGRO
Lastovo
Mljet
E65 (Magistrala)
Dubrovnik
Cavtat
Podgorica
ALBANIA

Introduction to Croatia

With nearly 2000km of rocky, indented shore and more than a thousand islands, many blanketed in luxuriant Mediterranean vegetation, Croatia boasts one of the most dramatic stretches of coastline that Europe has to offer. Despite the region's popularity as a package destination for more than four decades, exploitation of the coastal settlements has been kept in check, and there are still enough off-the-beaten-track islands, quiet coves and stone-built fishing villages to make you feel as if you're visiting one of southern Europe's most unspoilt areas. As a bonus, many of Croatia's coastal towns and cities are living museums of Mediterranean culture, generously endowed with historical remains from Roman times onwards. Inland, a varied profusion of mountains, lakes and bird-inhabited wetlands provide plenty of interest for the nature lover.

The country has come a long way since the early 1990s, when within the space of half a decade – almost uniquely in contemporary Europe – it experienced the collapse of communism, a war of national survival and the securing of **independence**. Croatia is now once again an optimistic, welcoming and safe destination, and visitors will be struck by the tangible sense of pride that independent statehood has brought. National culture is a far from one-dimensional affair, however, and much of the country's individuality is due to its geographical position straddling the point at which the sober central European virtues of hard work and order collide with the

▲ Decorated church spire, Zagreb

spontaneity, vivacity and taste for the good things in life that characterizes the countries of southern Europe – a cultural blend of **Mitteleuropa** and **Mediterranean** that gives Croatia its particular flavour. Not only that, but the country also stands on one of the great faultlines of European civilization, the point at which the Catholicism of Central Europe meets the Islam and Orthodox Christianity of the East. Though Croats traditionally see themselves as a Western people, distinct from the other South Slavs who made up the former state of Yugoslavia, many of the hallmarks of Balkan culture – patriarchal families, hospitality towards strangers and a fondness for grilled food – are as common in Croatia as in any other part of

Fact file

- Croatia (**Hrvatska** in Croatian) is a crescent-shaped country of 4.5 million people. Roughly 85 percent of the population are **Croats**, who speak a Slavic language akin to Serbian and Bosnian, and practise the **Catholic Christian** faith. There is also a sizeable **Serbian** population (about thirteen percent of the total), who belong to the **Orthodox Church** and are concentrated along Croatia's borders with Bosnia-Hercegovina and Serbia.
- Croatia is a **parliamentary democracy** with a directly elected – though nowadays largely ceremonial – president as head of state. The Croatian parliament, the **Sabor**, is made up of two houses – the 151-member Zastupnički dom (House of Representatives), from which the prime minister and most of his cabinet are usually chosen; and the 68-member Županijski dom (House of Regional Representatives).
- **Tourism** is Croatia's most important industry and is increasingly seen as the cash cow that will support all other branches of the economy. The prime exports are textiles, pharmaceuticals and agricultural products. Croatia's heavy industries have not found the transition from state ownership to a market economy easy. Shipbuilding, which was one of Croatia's prime earners in the 1970s and 1980s, almost totally collapsed in the 1990s.

▼ Zlatni rat, Brač

southeastern Europe, suggesting that the country's relationship with its neighbours is more complex than many Croats will admit.

National sensitivity about such matters has its roots in Croatia's troubled relationship with the **Serbs**, who arrived in southeastern Europe at around the same time, some fifteen hundred years ago, and whose language is almost identical to Croatian. Historical circumstances later drove the two groups psychologically and culturally apart, even though they often continued to live together – the fact that so many areas of Croatia and Bosnia-Hercegovina were ethnically mixed is one reason why the break-up of Yugoslavia was such a tragically messy affair. Despite the events of recent years, however, the destinies of Croats and Serbs look set to remain intertwined: there's still a sizeable Serb minority within Croatia, and Serbs who fled the country in the wake of the Croatian army's campaigns in 1995 are (officially, at least) being encouraged to return.

▲ Agave plant, Hvar

Bringing life back to war-damaged areas and resettling both Croatian and Serbian refugees is just one of the problems faced by a country that continues to suffer many of the ills experienced by post-communist societies in general: the collapse of outdated industries, high unemployment, low wages for the majority, and the rise of a new entrepreneurial class which is often flamboyantly corrupt. Tourism was always Croatia's biggest source of income before the war, and the return of holiday-makers to the Adriatic coast has been eagerly welcomed by the Croats. Unlike many of her Eastern European neighbours, however, Croatia was initially slow to receive aid and investment from the West, until elections in January 2000 removed a nationalist, anti-Western government from office. Since then, Croatia has regained its place in the wider European family, and looks likely to join the EU before the decade is out.

Where to go

Croatia's underrated capital **Zagreb** is a typical Central European metropolis, combining elegant nineteenth-century buildings with plenty of cultural diversions and a vibrant café life. It's also a good base for trips to the undulating hills and charming villages of the rural **Zagorje** and **Žumberak** regions to the north and west, and to the well-preserved Baroque town of **Varaždin** to the northeast.

The rest of **inland Croatia** provides plenty of opportunities for relaxed exploring. Stretching east from Zagreb, the plains of **Slavonia** form

▲ Folk festival, Rijeka

Religious feast days

As befits a devoutly Catholic country, the Croatian year is peppered with religious feasts and holidays. The pre-Lenten carnival (*karneval*; often known as *fašnik* in inland Croatia, *pust* on the Adriatic) reaches a climax on Shrove Tuesday or the weekend immediately preceding it, when there are processions and masked revelry in towns all over Croatia. Easter week is characterized by solemn processions in many places, especially Hvar and Korčula. More important still is the Assumption (Aug 15), when churches throughout the country hold special services and large pilgrimages are made to Marian shrines such as Marija Bistrica near Zagreb, Sinj in the Dalmatian hinterland, and Trsat near Rijeka. The Birth of the Virgin (Sept 8) is only slightly less important in the Catholic calendar, and is celebrated in similar fashion.

the richest agricultural parts of Croatia, with seemingly endless corn and sunflower fields fanning out from handsome, Habsburg-era provincial towns such as **Osijek** and **Vukovar** – although the latter was almost totally destroyed in a notoriously bitter siege during the 1991–95 war and will take time to rebuild. Inland Croatia also offers numerous **hiking** opportunities: **Mount Medvednica**, just above Zagreb, or the **Samoborsko gorje** just to the west of the capital are good for gentle rambling, while the mountains of the **Gorski kotar** between Zagreb and the sea offer more scope for strenuous hikes. Also lying between Zagreb and the coast, and easily visited from either, are the deservedly hyped **Plitvice Lakes**, an enchanting sequence of forest-fringed turquoise pools linked by miniature waterfalls.

Croatia's lengthy stretch of coastline, together with its islands, is big enough to swallow up any number of tourists. At the northern end, the peninsula of **Istria** contains many of the country's most developed resorts, along with old Venetian towns like **Poreč** and **Rovinj**, rubbing shoulders with the raffish port of **Pula**, home to some impressive Roman remains. Inland Istria is characterized by sleepy hilltop villages, often dramatically situated, such as **Motovun**, **Grožnjan**, **Roč** and **Hum** – each mixing medieval architecture with rustic tranquillity.

The island-scattered **Kvarner Gulf**, immediately south of Istria, is presided over by the city of **Rijeka**, a hard-edged industrial centre and the Adriatic's most important transport hub. Close by are a clutch of resorts that were chic high-society hangouts in the late nineteenth century and retain a smattering of *belle époque* charm: quaint, diminutive **Lovran**, and the larger, more developed **Opatija** and **Crikvenica**. Not far offshore, the Kvarner islands of **Cres**, **Lošinj** and **Krk** have long been colonized by the package-holiday crowds, although each has retained its fair share of quiet seaside villages and tranquil coves, while the capital of **Rab**, south of Krk, is arguably the best-preserved medieval town in the northern Adriatic.

Beyond the Kvarner Gulf lies **Dalmatia**, a dramatic, mountain-fringed stretch of coastline studded with islands. It's a stark, arid region where fishing villages and historic towns cling to a narrow coastal strip rich in figs, olives and subtropical vegetation. Northern Dalmatia's main city is **Zadar**, whose busy central alleys are crammed with medieval churches. From here, ferries

▲ Windsurfing off Brač

serve a chain of laid-back islands such as **Silba**, **Ugljan**, **Pašman** and the ruggedly beautiful **Dugi otok** – none of them sees many package tourists, and they're enticingly relaxing as a result. Despite being the site of an unmissable Renaissance cathedral, middle Dalmatia's main town, **Šibenik**, is the least compelling of the region's urban centres, but makes a good staging post en route to the waterfalls of the **River Krka** just inland, and the awesome, bare islands of the **Kornati archipelago**.

Croatia's second city, **Split**, is southern Dalmatia's main town, a vibrant and chaotic port with an ancient centre moulded around the palace of the Roman emperor, Diocletian. It's also the obvious jumping-off point for some of the most enchanting of Croatia's islands. The closest of these to the city is **Brač**, where you'll find lively fishing villages and some excellent beaches, while nearby **Hvar** and **Korčula** feature smallish towns brimming with Venetian architecture and numerous beaches. Slightly further afield,

▲ Korčula

National parks

If an unending display of natural riches is what you're after, then Croatia certainly offers variety, with stark mountains, forest-cloaked islands, and wildfowl-infested wetlands all vying for your attention. Several unique locations enjoy national park protection: most celebrated of these is Plitvice, a descending sequence of clear blue lakes punctuated by a stunning series of terraced waterfalls and foaming cataracts.

One must-visit offshore attraction is the Kornati archipelago, an extraordinarily beautiful group of largely uninhabited islands whose sparse covering of shrubs and sage produces an unearthly palette of grey, green and purple shades. A major target for yachting folk, the Kornati can also be reached on day-excursions from the mainland.

Sweeping views of the coastal islands can be enjoyed from the desolate grey slopes of the Velebit mountains, where the Paklenica National Park offers everything from cliff-enclosed gorge trails to scenic ridge-top hikes.

Those who make it to the far east of the country will be rewarded with a glimpse of the mysterious sunken forests of Kopački rit, a renowned haven for wading birds.

the islands of **Vis** and **Lastovo**, which were closed to tourists until the late 1980s, remain particularly pristine.

South of Split lies the walled medieval city of **Dubrovnik**, site of an important arts festival in the summer and a magical place to be whatever the season. Much of the damage inflicted on the town during the 1991–95 war has been repaired, and tourists have been quick to return. Just offshore lie the sparsely populated islands of **Koločep**, **Lopud** and **Šipan** – oases of rural calm only a short ferry ride away from Dubrovnik's tourist bustle. Also reachable from Dubrovnik is one of the Adriatic's most beautiful islands, the densely forested and relaxingly serene **Mljet**.

Most Adriatic **beaches** are pebbly or rocky affairs, and on some parts of the coast man-made concrete bathing platforms make up for the lack of a proper strand. The most attractive sweeps of pebble beach are at **Bol**, on the island of Brač, and at the towns lining the **Makarska Riviera** south of Split. Sandy beaches are rare, though glorious examples can be found at **Baška** on the island of Krk, the **Lopar peninsula** on Rab, or **Lumbarda** on Korčula.

▲ Hvar Town

When to go

Croatia's climate follows two patterns: **Mediterranean** on the coast, with warm summers and mild winters, and **continental** inland – slightly hotter during the summer, and extremely cold in winter, with average daily temperatures barely scraping freezing from December to February. **July and August** constitute the peak season on the Adriatic, and this is definitely the time to visit if busy beaches and lively café society are what you're looking for. Many Croats make their way to the coast at this time, and social and cultural activity in the inland cities tends to dry up as a result. Peak-season daytime temperatures can be roasting, both on the coast and inland, and dawn-to-dusk sightseeing can be a gruelling experience at the height of summer. Hotel accommodation soon fills up in the peak season, and it may be more relaxing to travel in **June and September**, when there is significantly less pressure on facilities. From October to May the coast can be very quiet indeed, and many hotels and tourist attractions may well shut up shop for the winter. **Autumn** is a good

Club culture

Combining central European artiness, Mediterranean style, and anarchic Balkan unpredictability, Croatia's club scene is currently the most vibrant in south-eastern Europe. Zagreb is the year-round focus of activity, offering everything from mainstream weekend partying to off-the-wall underground happenings of a chin-stroking nature. Long-established venues like cutting-edge DJ temple Aquarius, live rock and jazz club KSET, and alternative-music mecca Močvara, are regular stop-offs for international performers.

Encouraged by the boom in Adriatic tourism, Zagreb's club culture is migrating to the coast in a big way. Several DJ bars set up summer camp on Zrće beach on the island of Pag, creating an easygoing, hype-free Adriatic alternative to Ibiza. Elsewhere, dance clubs up and down the coast are hosting the kind of international DJs who wouldn't have been able to find Croatia on a map until a few years ago.

time to enjoy inland Istria and national park areas like the Plitvice Lakes and the River Krka, when the woodland colours produced by the mixture of deciduous and evergreen trees are at their best. Given the innocuous winters on the Adriatic coast, urban sightseeing in historic centres such as Zadar, Split and Dubrovnik can be enjoyable at any time of year. It's also worth bearing in mind that hotel prices on the Adriatic may be up to fifty percent cheaper in winter than they are in peak season. Winters in inland Croatia are a different kettle of fish entirely: snow is common here over this period, and can be a picturesque backdrop to sightseeing, although transport in highland areas is frequently disrupted as a result. **Spring** is well into its stride by mid-March, and in southern Dalmatia the sea might be warm enough to swim in by mid- to late May.

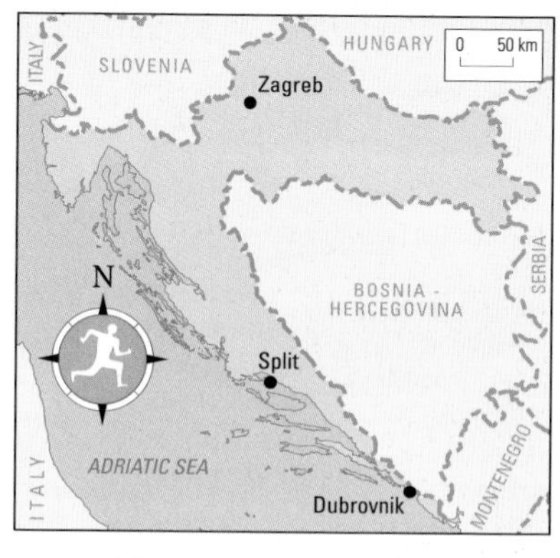

Average temperatures (°C)

	Jan	Feb	Mar	Apr	May	June	July	Aug	Sept	Oct	Nov	Dec
Dubrovnik												
	8.3	9.1	11.2	13.9	17.8	22.2	25.6	25.0	22.3	17.8	12.9	10.2
Split												
	7.5	8.5	11.5	12.8	18.9	23.9	26.7	26.1	22.8	16.7	12.5	9.5
Zagreb												
	0	1.2	5.5	11	16	18.7	22.3	21.8	15.6	12.3	5.4	2.3

30 things not to miss

It's not possible to see everything Croatia has to offer in one trip – and we don't suggest you try. What follows is a selective and subjective taste of the country's highlights, from Baroque palaces to perfect grilled fresh fish. They're arranged in five colour-coded categories to help you find the very best things to see, do and experience. All entries have a page reference to take you straight into the guide, where you can find out more.

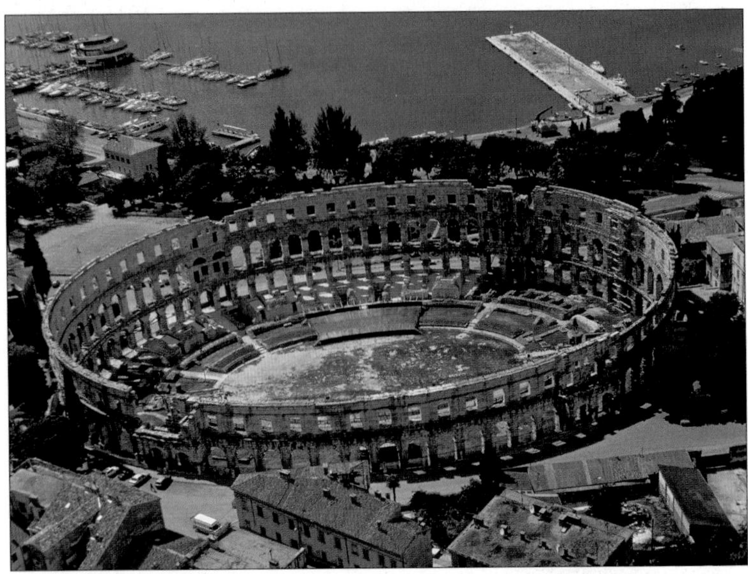

01 **Amphitheatre, Pula** Page **182** • Imperial Rome's greatest gift to the eastern Adriatic, this awesome arena still serves as the venue for pack-'em-in summertime concerts.

02 Sea kayaking Page **56 & 450** • The Dalmatian coast is often best enjoyed from the water, and what better way to see it than by taking a leisurely paddle.

03 Café society Page **48** • Pavement cafés play a key social role in this nation of gregarious coffee-gluttons.

04 Varaždin Page **128** • A postcard-perfect Baroque town, complete with crumbling palaces, ornate churches and a unique garden cemetery.

05 Skradinski buk Page **339** • Head for Krka National Park to admire this stunning series of waterfalls.

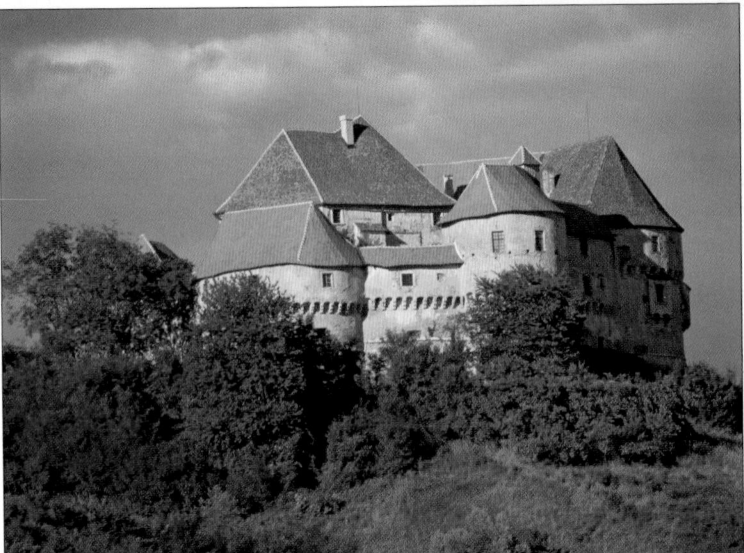

06 **The Zagorje** Page **117** • In Zagreb's rural hinterland, hilltop castles such as Veliki Tabor and Trakošćan perch decoratively above vineyards, cornfields and turkey-filled farmyards.

07 **Boat trips to the Kornati islands** Page **328** • These stark, sparsely populated islands, now a national park, form the target of spectacular boat excursions from the mainland.

08 Peljesac peninsula Page **431** • Explore rugged mountain scenery, quiet coves and unspoilt seaside villages in a region renowned for its robust red wines and fantastic seafood.

09 Hvar Page **398** • The swankiest resort on the Adriatic is also one of the most evocative, offering a welter of Renaissance palaces and churches.

11 Diocletian's palace, Split Page **360** • Taken over by the townsfolk centuries ago, the Roman emperor's pied-à-terre now forms the chaotic heart of the modern city.

10 Čigoć Page **153** • This bucolic timber-built village in the Lonjsko polje wetlands is the famed nesting ground of white storks.

12 Plitvice Lakes Page **148** • A bewitching sequence of foaming waterfalls and turquoise lakes, hemmed in by forest-clad hills.

13 Lošinj island Page 247 • Unhurried atmosphere, unspoilt fishing ports and lush Mediterranean vegetation make this one of the most charming spots in the northern Adriatic.

14 Folk festivals Page 50 • Croatia's busy calendar of folk gatherings provides ample opportunity to sample the country's rich heritage of traditional music and dance.

15 The coastal ferry Page 38 • Wending its way from Rijeka in the north to Dubrovnik in the south, and passing some spectacular maritime scenery on the way, this is Croatia's one must-do journey.

16 Trsteno Page **466** • Relax in Renaissance gardens, in a beautiful coastal village just north of Dubrovnik.

17 Rovinj Page **194** • Riviera-town chic collides with fishing-port charm in the most Italianate of Istria's coastal resorts.

18 Paklenica National Park Page **274** • A hiker's paradise, combining craggy limestone gorges, dense pine forests and meadow-carpeted alpine uplands.

19 Tvrdalj Page **407** • Tucked away in the alleyways of Stari Grad, this Renaissance nobleman's house is as restful a spot as you will find on the Dalmatian coast.

20 Scuba diving Page **55** • Fast becoming the number-one activity on the coast, offering the perfect opportunity to get up close to Croatia's colourful undersea world.

21 Trogir cathedral Page **345** • This venerable monument to medieval Christianity bears the most spectacular stone carvings in the country.

22 Zadar Page **306** • Vibrant peninsula town packed with Roman ruins, Romanesque churches and café-crowded alleyways.

23 Istrian hill towns Page **211** • The weatherbeaten, brown-stone settlements of Motovun, Oprtalj and Grožnjan provide the perfect vantage points from which to survey the lush landscape of central Istria.

24 Walking the Lungomare, Opatija Riviera Page **238** • This eight-kilometre-long promenade takes you past a rock-scattered shoreline, subtropical vegetation and a string of Habsburg-era coastal villas.

25 Gradec, Zagreb Page **83** • Stately ensemble of historic buildings, terracotta tiles and leafy backstreets squatting unobtrusively above the noise and bustle of the capital's modern centre.

26 The Elaphite islands Page **471** • These easy-to-explore, largely car-free islands offer great hiking and sandy beaches.

27 Truffle Days, Istria Page **215** • The start of the truffle-hunting season is marked by festivities throughout Istria in September – especially in Buzet, where the world's largest truffle omelette is eagerly scoffed by an army of celebrants.

28 Fresh seafood Page **46** • The rich waters of the Adriatic produce enough varieties of fish to fill an aquatic encyclopedia; expertly grilled, they're the perfect centrepiece to any meal.

29 The Dominican monastery, Dubrovnik
Page **456** • The quiet cloister provides a perfect home for a small but superb collection of Renaissance paintings.

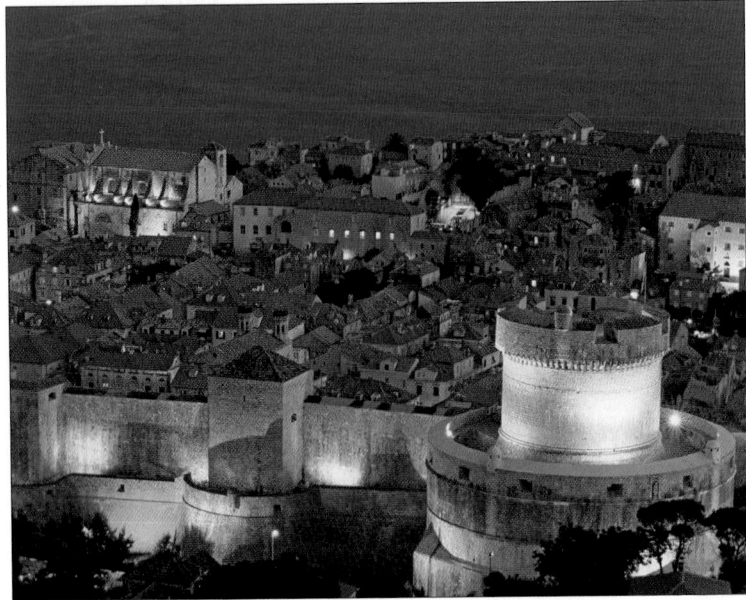

30 Walking Dubrovnik's walls Page **449** • The briefest of trots round the battlements will serve as a breathtaking introduction to this ancient city.

Basics

Basics

Getting there

The easiest way to get to Croatia is by air, though fares from outside Europe can be expensive; a cheaper option may be to pick up a flight to a city outside Croatia (such as Trieste or Venice in Italy, Salzburg or Graz in Austria) and continue by train or bus.

Travelling **overland from Britain** is a moderately long haul, and you'll save little, if anything, by taking the train, although with a rail pass you can take in Croatia as part of a wider European trip. **Driving** there from Britain will involve a journey of at least 1400km, best covered over two days.

Airfares always depend on the **season**, with the highest fares in July and August, when the weather is finest; you'll get the best prices during the low season, October to April (excluding Christmas and New Year when prices are hiked up and seats are at a premium). Note also that flying on weekends may add a small premium to the round-trip fare; price ranges quoted below assume midweek travel.

You can often cut costs by going through a **specialist flight agent** – either a consolidator, who buys up blocks of tickets from the airlines and sells them at a discount, or a **discount agent**, who in addition to dealing with discounted flights may also offer special student and youth fares and a range of other travel-related services such as travel insurance, rail passes, car rentals, tours and the like.

You may even find it cheaper to pick up a bargain **package deal** from one of the tour operators listed below. The main advantage of package holidays is that hotel accommodation is much cheaper than if you arrange things independently, bringing mid-range hotels well within reach and making stays in even quite snazzy establishments a fraction of the price paid by walk-in guests. The season for Adriatic packages runs from April to October; city breaks in Zagreb and Dubrovnik are available all the year round. Croatia is also the venue for an increasing number of **maritime packages** – ranging from sailing courses for beginners to boat charter for the experienced (see p.36).

Many airlines and discount travel websites offer you the opportunity to book your tickets, hotels and holiday packages **online**, cutting out the costs of agents and middlemen; these are worth going for, as long as you don't mind the inflexibility of non-refundable, non-changeable deals. Almost all airlines have their own websites, offering flight tickets that can sometimes be just as cheap, and are often more flexible

Flights from the UK and Ireland

Flying from the UK to Croatia takes between two and a quarter and two and three quarter hours. Direct **scheduled flights** are operated by Croatia Airlines, which flies from London Heathrow to Zagreb and to Split throughout the year, and in the summer season (May–Oct) from London Gatwick to Dubrovnik, Split and Pula; London Heathrow to Rijeka; and Manchester to Dubrovnik and Split. British Airways run year-round direct flights from London Gatwick to Split and Dubrovnik. As for **budget carriers**, Wizzair operates from London Luton to Zagreb and Split, Ryanair flies from Dublin to Pula and London Stansted to Pula, and easyJet goes from London Gatwick to Split, London Luton to Rijeka, and Bristol to Rijeka.

Expect to pay around £150 return low season, £200–250 return high season if travelling with Croatian Airlines or British Airways, although bear in mind that prices rise drastically if you don't book well in advance. Tickets with budget carriers can be significantly cheaper – again, you have to book well in advance to take advantage of the lowest fares.

Most package-tour operators use **charter flights** to Croatia, and sell discounted tickets on services which aren't full. Although rare in

July and August, cheap seats do crop up in the shoulder season (May, June, September and October) from a variety of Irish and UK airports – look for press advertisements or contact your local travel agent for details.

If it's difficult to find a ticket to Croatia at an affordable price, you could consider a one-stop flight with a major European carrier such as Alitalia (to Croatia from London or Dublin via Milan), CSA (from various UK airports via Prague), KLM (from Dublin and UK regional airports via Amsterdam) or Lufthansa (various UK airports via Frankfurt).

Finally, you could consider flying to a **nearby** country and continuing your journey overland or by ferry. EasyJet and Ryanair both fly from London Stansted to Venice; Ryanair also flies to Trieste, Ancona, Klagenfurt, Graz and Salzburg; while easyJet, Wizzair and SkyEurope serve Budapest. The relative convenience of the above destinations largely depends on which part of Croatia you're aiming for: Venice, Trieste, Klagenfurt, Graz, Salzburg and Budapest all have direct train connections with Zagreb; Trieste also enjoys daily bus connections with Istrià and the Dalmatian coast. If it's Dalmatia you're aiming for, bear in mind that Ancona has numerous ferry links with Split and Zadar (see box on p.32 for details). You could also fly with either easyJet or the Slovene airline Adria from London Gatwick to Ljubljana, from where there are rail connections to Zagreb.

Package deals

The **resorts** most frequently offered by British companies are in Istria (Poreč and Rovinj), Dalmatia (Hvar, Korčula and Makarska) and Dubrovnik (either in Dubrovnik itself or in the Mlini-Cavtat area just to the south). Some of the hotels in Poreč and Dubrovnik are a bus ride away from their respective towns (check before you commit yourself to a particular holiday), but almost everywhere else your accommodation will be within walking distance of an attractive town or fishing port of some sort. The frequency of public transport makes it easy to explore further.

The widest range of resorts is offered by **Croatia specialists** such as Bond Tours, Holiday Options and Europa Skylines, who can put together customized flight-plus-accommodation deals in low season (April, May, late Sept & Oct), with prices beginning at about £400 for seven days, rising to £500–550 for two weeks. In high season (July & Aug) expect to pay from around £550 for a week, and from £750 for two weeks. As for **city breaks**, a three-day stay in Zagreb or Dubrovnik will cost £350–500 per person depending on which grade of hotel you choose. **Coach holidays** to Croatia work out slightly cheaper than those involving flights, although the length of the journey can be a disadvantage – out of a nine-day holiday, you only get to spend seven nights in Croatia. A few specialist operators offer **naturist holidays** in the self-contained mega-resorts of Istria.

Motorsailer cruises in Dalmatia start at around £560 for seven days. To learn the rudiments of sailing, you can arrange a one-week **beginner's course** – prices start at about £600 per person. The cheapest seven-day holiday in an eight-berth yacht is typically around £500–600 per person (rising to £700–800 in a two-berth yacht), depending on the season. Prices rise steeply for fancier yachts. You won't be able to charter a smallish three- to four-berth bareboat yacht for much under £600 per week, while prices for larger craft can run into thousands; a skipper will cost upwards of £90 a day extra.

Flights from the US and Canada

There are currently no direct flights from North America to Croatia, though most major airlines offer one- or two-stop flights via the bigger European cities, often in conjunction with Croatia Airlines, the national carrier. **From the US**, a midweek round-trip fare to Zagreb in low season starts at $800 from New York ($1050 from US West Coast cities), rising to $1300 ($1800 from the West Coast) during high season. **From Canada**, round-trip fares start at Can$1350 from Toronto and Can$1800 from Vancouver during the low season, rising to Can$1600 and Can$2100 respectively during high season. Note that the above prices are for tickets bought from airlines directly, and the pricing varies hugely depending on the route

Sailing and yachting packages

Croatia's island-scattered littoral is the perfect place for sailing and yachting, the season usually lasting from early May to early October. The most basic form of sailing holiday, for which you need no nautical experience, is a cruise in a motorsailer – basically a large, engine-powered yacht with simple bunk accommodation and a crew to do the work. If you already know the ropes you might consider flotilla sailing, in which a group of yachts with an expertly crewed lead boat embarks on a set seven- or fourteen-day itinerary. Flotilla yachts usually range from two-berth to eight-berth, so per-person prices decrease according to the size of your group. At least one of your party will have to have sailing experience – exactly how much differs from one travel company to the next.

Yacht charter can either be "bareboat" (meaning you have to sail it yourself) or "skippered" (which means you pay for the services of a local captain). Prices are subject to many variables, the most important being the model of yacht and the number of berths. For bareboat charter, at least one member of the party has to have about two years' sailing experience – again, precise requirements differ from company to company. To find out more, you can contact a specialist agency in your home country – see the relevant listings on p.36.

and the carrier combination; discount agencies usually have lower fares.

Specialist travel agents such as TravelTime and Atlas offer air-inclusive independent **packages**. Expect to pay about $1100 for eight days in Dubrovnik or Dalmatia in low season, $1650 in high season. Atlas has an extensive selection of adventure tours (cycling, sea kayaking, canoeing and rafting trips), as well as Adriatic cruises and flotilla-sailing trips. There are also several North American tour operators offering escorted and independent tours to Croatia – a number of which also include Slovenia in their itinerary. A list of tour operators is given on pp.34–36.

If you just want to book accommodation and transport within Croatia, contact Atlas Travel Agency, TravelTime or the Croatian National Tourist Board (see p.64). If you're planning to visit Croatia as part of a wider trip across Europe, you may want to get the cheapest transatlantic flight you can find, and continue your journey overland – in which case it's worth considering a **Eurail pass** for train travel; see p.31 for details.

Flights from Australia and New Zealand

The cheapest flights to Zagreb from Australia and New Zealand usually involve a combination of two airlines and two stops en route. For example, a common combination **from Australia** would get you to Zagreb via first Singapore, then Frankfurt or Zürich. Fares on these routes range from Aus$1700 in low season to Aus$2450 in high season. You can restrict your journey to one change of plane by opting for a slightly more expensive combination – flying Sydney to Zagreb via Vienna, Frankfurt or even London will add another Aus$100–200. Flights **from New Zealand** will involve at least two stops and cost NZ$2250 in low season, rising to NZ$3000 in high season. Alternatively, you might be able to save a little money by flying to, say, Vienna and continuing overland to Croatia; if you want to see the country as part of a wider trip across Europe, it might be worth considering a European rail pass (see p.31).

A small number of **package-tour operators** offer holidays in Croatia from Australia and New Zealand, including accommodation, cruises along the Dalmatian coast, sightseeing packages and rail passes.

Flights from South Africa

There are no direct flights to Croatia **from South Africa**, but plenty of airlines offer one-stop flights via European hubs such as London, Frankfurt or Paris. Flying with an airline such as Lufthansa from Johannesburg to Zagreb via Frankfurt costs around ZAR9200

Fly less – stay longer! Travel and climate change

Climate change is the single biggest issue facing our planet. It is caused by a build-up in the atmosphere of carbon dioxide and other greenhouse gases, which are emitted by many sources – including planes. Already, flights account for around 3–4 percent of human-induced global warming: that figure may sound small, but it is rising year on year and threatens to counteract the progress made by reducing greenhouse gas emissions in other areas.

Rough Guides regard travel, overall, as a global benefit, and feel strongly that the advantages to developing economies are important, as are the opportunities for greater contact and awareness among peoples. But we all have a responsibility to limit our personal "carbon footprint". That means giving thought to how often we fly and what we can do to redress the harm that our trips create.

Flying and climate change

Pretty much every form of motorized travel generates CO_2, but planes are particularly bad offenders, releasing large volumes of greenhouse gases at altitudes where their impact is far more harmful. Flying also allows us to travel much further than we would contemplate doing by road or rail, so the emissions attributable to each passenger become truly shocking. For example, one person taking a return flight between Europe and California produces the equivalent impact of 2.5 tonnes of CO_2 – similar to the yearly output of the average UK car.

Less harmful planes may evolve but it will be decades before they replace the current fleet – which could be too late for avoiding climate chaos. In the meantime, there are limited options for concerned travellers: to reduce the amount we travel by air (take fewer trips, stay longer!), to avoid night flights (when plane contrails trap heat from Earth but can't reflect sunlight back to space), and to make the trips we do take "climate neutral" via a carbon offset scheme.

Carbon offset schemes

Offset schemes run by **climatecare.org, carbonneutral.com** and others allow you to "neutralize" the greenhouse gases that you are responsible for releasing. Their websites have simple calculators that let you work out the impact of any flight. Once that's done, you can pay to fund projects that will reduce future carbon emissions by an equivalent amount (such the distribution of low-energy lightbulbs and cooking stoves in developing countries). Please take the time to visit our website and make your trip climate neutral.

www.roughguides.com/climatechange

in low season, ZAR10720 in high season, and takes around eighteen hours. Flying to Split or Dubrovnik usually involves one more stop and costs ZAR1500–2500 extra.

Trains

Travelling to Croatia **by train** from the UK is unlikely to save money compared with flying, but can be a leisurely way of getting to the country if you plan to stop off in other parts of Europe on the way. It's certainly simpler and more cost-effective to buy a rail pass, invest in an international rail timetable (see opposite) and plan your own itinerary than to try and purchase a rail return ticket to Croatia: most ticket agents deal exclusively with premier express services, and fares often work out more expensive than flying – a London–Zagreb return will set you back something in the region of £200–260. The high cost is at least partly explained by the fact that almost all through-tickets from London to European destinations now use Eurostar trains, which go through the Channel Tunnel, rather than the (traditionally cheaper) ferries. It's still possible to travel by rail from London to the continent via ferry, but (unless you have a rail pass) you'll probably have to buy individual tickets for each stage of the journey.

There are two main **London–Zagreb** rail itineraries: the first is via Paris, Lausanne, Milan, Venice and Ljubljana; the second via Brussels, Cologne, Salzburg and Ljubljana. The total journey time on either route is around thirty hours, depending on connections – considerably longer if you cross the Channel by ferry rather than taking the Eurostar. If you're making a beeline for Dalmatia, consider heading for Ancona in Italy (16hr from Paris), the departure point for ferries to Zadar, Split and Dubrovnik.

Rail passes

If you're travelling across Europe by train, it's worth considering the huge array of **rail passes** available, covering regions as well as individual countries. Some have to be bought before leaving home, others can only be bought in the country for which they're valid.

Inter-Rail passes are only available to European residents, and you'll be asked to provide proof of residency before being allowed to purchase one. They come in over-26 and (cheaper) under-26 versions, and cover 28 European countries (including Turkey and Morocco) grouped together in **zones**:

A Republic of Ireland/Britain
B Norway, Sweden, Finland
C Germany, Austria, Switzerland, Denmark
D Bosnia-Herzegovina, Czech Republic, Slovakia, Poland, Hungary, Croatia
E France, Belgium, Netherlands, Luxembourg
F Spain, Portugal, Morocco
G Greece, Turkey, Slovenia plus some ferry services between Italy and Greece
H Bulgaria, Romania, Serbia & Montenegro, Macedonia

As Croatia is in zone D, you'll need a global pass valid for one month and covering all zones (£405; £285 for under-26s) to get there from Britain or Ireland. Inter-Rail passes do not include travel between Britain and the continent, although Inter-Rail pass holders are eligible for discounts on rail travel in the UK and cross-Channel ferries. The Inter-Rail pass also gives a discount on the London–Paris Eurostar service.

Eurail passes

Non-European residents qualify for the **Eurail Pass**, which must be purchased before arrival in Europe (or from RailEurope in London by non-residents who were unable to get it at home). The pass allows unlimited free first-class train travel in sixteen European countries, but not in Croatia or neighbouring Slovenia – so you'll have to buy a regular ticket to cover the last leg of the journey. The pass is available in increments of 15 days, 21 days, one month, two months and three months. If you're under 26, you can save money with a **Eurail Youthpass**, which is valid for second-class travel or, if you're travelling with up to four other companions, a joint **Eurail Saverpass**, both of which are available in the same increments as the Eurail Pass. You stand a better chance of getting your money's worth out of a Eurail Flexipass, which is good for ten or fifteen days' travel within a two-month period. This, too, comes in first-class and under-26/second-class.

Further details of these passes and other Eurail permutations, and prices, can be

Useful rail publications

The red-covered **Thomas Cook European Timetable** details schedules of over 50,000 trains in Europe, as well as timings of over 200 ferry routes and rail-connecting bus services. It's updated and issued every month; the main changes are in the June edition (published end of May), which has details of the summer European schedules, and the October one (published end of Sept), which includes winter schedules; some have advance summer/winter timings also. The book can be purchased online (which gets you a ten-percent discount) at Ⓦwww.thomascooktimetables.com or from branches of Thomas Cook (see Ⓦwww.thomascook.co.uk for your nearest branch), and costs £11.50. Their useful **Rail Map of Europe** (regular price £8.95) also comes with an online discount.

found on ⓦ**www.raileurope.com**, and the passes can be purchased from one of the agents listed on pp.36–37.

Euro Domino passes

Only available to European residents, **Euro Domino passes** are individual country passes which provide unlimited travel in 28 European and North African countries. They are available for between three and eight days' travel within a one-month period; prices vary depending on the country, but include most high-speed train supplements. There is a discounted youth price for those under 26, and a half-price child (age 4–11) fare. A Euro Domino pass covering Croatia itself costs around £45 for three days, £72 for seven days – a worthwhile buy if you're doing a lot of travelling in central and eastern Croatia, but not much use on the coast.

By car from the UK

Driving to Croatia is straightforward. The most direct route from the UK is to follow motorways from the Belgian coast via Brussels, Cologne, Frankfurt, Stuttgart, Munich, Salzburg and Villach as far as the Slovene capital Ljubljana, from where you can continue by ordinary road south to Rijeka on the Adriatic coast or south-east to Zagreb. An alternative approach is through France, Switzerland and Italy as far as **Ancona** on Italy's Adriatic coast, from where there are ferries to various points on the Dalmatian coast. Farther down towards the heel of Italy there are ferries from **Bari** to Dubrovnik.

Note that if you're driving through Austria you'll have to buy a **vignette** (a windscreen sticker available at border crossings and petrol stations) in order to use the motorway system. The cheapest version is valid for ten days and costs €7.60.

Italy–Croatia ferries

Ferry services from Ancona, Bari, Pescara, Rimini and Venice in Italy to Croatia are run by Azzurra Line, Jadrolinija, Split Tours,

Italy–Croatia ferry timetables

Azzurra Line

Ferries	Bari–Dubrovnik (2 weekly July & Aug).

Jadrolinija

Ferries	Ancona–Split–Hvar Stari Grad–Korčula (4–6 weekly June–Sept). Ancona–Split (3 weekly rising to 5 weekly July & Aug). Ancona–Zadar (3 weekly June–Sept rising to 7 weekly July & Aug). Bari–Dubrovnik (2 weekly rising to 6 weekly July & Aug).

Split Tours

Ferries	Ancona–Split (2 weekly rising to 7 weekly July & Aug).

SNAV

Ferries	Ancona–Zadar (July & Aug daily). Ancona–Split (mid-June to mid-Sept 1 daily). Pescara–Hvar–Split (mid-June to mid-Sept 1 daily).

Venezia Lines

Ferries	Rimini–Pula (2 weekly June–Sept). Rimini–Poreč (1 weekly June–Sept) Venice–Mali Lošinj (1 weekly June–Sept) Venice–Opatija (1 weekly June–Sept) Venice–Poreč (4 weekly June–Sept) Venice–Pula (3 weekly June–Sept) Venice–Rabac (1 weekly June–Sept) Venice–Rovinj (2 weekly June–Sept)

SNAV and Venezia Line. Foot passengers can usually buy tickets on arrival at the relevant ferry port, but if you're travelling with a vehicle it's wise to book in advance, especially in July and August. Services between the central Italian ports and Split usually take eight to nine hours. The fastest crossings are with SNAV's Croazia Jet and Pescara Jet high-speed ferries (4hr 30min), which operate the Ancona–Split and Pescara–Split routes. An additional number of swift hydrofoil and catamaran services are laid on between Italian ports and Split or Zadar in season, but these services are passenger-only. For ferries, simple deck passage between the Italian and Croatian ports costs about £33/€50/$60 (payable in local currency), but as most crossings are overnight, consider investing an additional €30/£20/$36 for a bed in a basic cabin. Pushbikes are free, motorcycles cost about €30/£20/$36, cars €50/£33/$60. Return tickets are usually twenty percent cheaper than two singles.

By bus from the UK

The **bus** journey from London to Zagreb (changing in Frankfurt) takes just under 34 hours and is only slightly cheaper than the train, with a return costing £180 (£170 for under-26s and seniors).

Airlines, agents and operators

Online booking

Ⓦ **www.expedia.co.uk** Discount airfares and daily deals. Search and book flights, hotels, cars and packages worldwide (UK only; for US Ⓦ www.expedia.com; for Canada Ⓦ www.expedia.ca).
Ⓦ **www.lastminute.com** Offers good last-minute holiday package and flight-only deals (UK only; for Australia Ⓦ www.lastminute.com.au).
Ⓦ **www.opodo.co.uk** UK site offering flight, hotel and car deals, as well as city breaks and last-minute deals.
Ⓦ **www.orbitz.com** US site with packages, and individual trips, flights and hotel deals worldwide.
Ⓦ **www.travelocity.co.uk** Destination guides and deals on car rental, accommodation and lodging, as well as fares. Provides access to the travel agent system SABRE, the most comprehensive central reservations system in the US (UK only; for US Ⓦ www.travelocity.com; for Canada Ⓦ www.travelocity.ca).
Ⓦ **www.zuji.com.au** Australian website searching airlines, hotels and package deals for the best prices. (Australia only; for New Zealand Ⓦ www.zuji.co.nz).

Airlines

Adria Airways UK Ⓣ 020/7734 4630 or 7437 0143, Ⓦ www.adria-airways.com.
Aer Lingus US and Canada Ⓣ 1-800-IRISH-AIR, UK Ⓣ 0870/876 5000, Republic of Ireland Ⓣ 0818/365 000, Ⓦ www.aerlingus.com.
Aeroflot US Ⓣ 1-888-340-6400, Canada Ⓣ 1-416-642-1653, Australia Ⓣ 02/9262 2233, UK Ⓣ 0207/355 2233, Ⓦ www.aeroflot.co.uk, Ⓦ www.aeroflot.com.
Air Canada Ⓣ 1-888-247-2262, UK Ⓣ 0871/220 1111, Republic of Ireland Ⓣ 01/679 3958, Ⓦ www.aircanada.com.
Air France US Ⓣ 1-800-237-2747, Canada Ⓣ 1-800-667-2747, UK Ⓣ 0870/142 4343, Australia Ⓣ 1300/390 190, SA Ⓣ 0861/340 340, Ⓦ www.airfrance.com.
Air New Zealand Australia Ⓣ 13 24 76, New Zealand Ⓣ 0800/737 000, Ⓦ www.airnz.co.nz.
Alitalia US Ⓣ 1-800-223-5730, Canada Ⓣ 1-800-361-8336, UK Ⓣ 0870/544 8259, Republic of Ireland Ⓣ 01/677 5171, New Zealand Ⓣ 09/308 3357, SA Ⓣ 11/721 4500, Ⓦ www.alitalia.com.
American Airlines Ⓣ 1-800-433-7300, UK Ⓣ 0845/7789 789, Republic of Ireland Ⓣ 01/602 0550, Australia Ⓣ 1300/650 747, New Zealand Ⓣ 0800/887 997, Ⓦ www.aa.com.
Austrian Airlines US Ⓣ 1-800-843-0002, UK Ⓣ 0870/124 2625, Republic of Ireland Ⓣ 1800/509 142, Australia Ⓣ 1800/642 438 or 02/9251 6155, Ⓦ www.aua.com.
bmi US Ⓣ 1-800-788-0555, UK Ⓣ 0870/607 0555 or Ⓣ 0870/607 0222, Ireland Ⓣ 01/407 3036, Ⓦ www.flybmi.com.
bmibaby UK Ⓣ 0871/224 0224, Republic of Ireland Ⓣ 1890/340 122, Ⓦ www.bmibaby.com.
British Airways US and Canada Ⓣ 1-800-AIRWAYS, UK Ⓣ 0870/850 9850, Republic of Ireland Ⓣ 1890/626 747, Australia Ⓣ 1300/767 177, New Zealand Ⓣ 09/966 9777, Ⓦ www.ba.com.
Cathay Pacific US Ⓣ 1-800-233-2742, UK Ⓣ 0208/834 8888, Australia Ⓣ 13 17 47, New Zealand Ⓣ 09/379 0861, Ⓦ www.cathaypacific.com.
Continental Airlines US and Canada Ⓣ 1-800-523-3273, UK Ⓣ 0845/607 6760, Republic of Ireland Ⓣ 1890/925 252, Australia Ⓣ 02/9244 2242, New Zealand Ⓣ 09/308 3350, International Ⓣ 1800/231 0856, Ⓦ www.continental.com.

Croatia Airlines US ⓣ1-973-884-3401, UK ⓣ0208/563 0022, Australia ⓣ03/9699 9355, New Zealand ⓣ09/838 7700, ⓦwww.croatiaairlines.hr.
CSA (Czech Airlines) US ⓣ1-800-223-2365, Canada ⓣ416-363-3174, UK ⓣ0870/444 3747, Republic of Ireland ⓣ0818/200 014, ⓦwww.czechairlines.co.uk
Delta US and Canada ⓣ1-800-221-1212, UK ⓣ0845/600 0950, Republic of Ireland ⓣ1850/882 031 or 01/407 3165, Australia ⓣ1300/302 849, New Zealand ⓣ09/379 3370, ⓦwww.delta.com.
easyJet UK ⓣ0905/821 0905, ⓦwww.easyjet.com.
Garuda Indonesia US ⓣ1-212-279-0756, UK ⓣ020/7467 8600, Australia ⓣ1300/365 330 or 02/9334 9944, New Zealand ⓣ09/366 1862, ⓦwww.garuda-indonesia.com.
KLM (Royal Dutch Airlines) See Northwest/KLM. US ⓣ1-800-225-2525, UK ⓣ0870/507 4074, Republic of Ireland ⓣ1850/747 400, Australia ⓣ1300/767 310, New Zealand ⓣ09/921 6040, SA ⓣ11/961 6767, ⓦwww.klm.com.
Lufthansa US ⓣ1-800-645-3880, Canada ⓣ1-800-563-5954, UK ⓣ0870/837 7747, Republic of Ireland ⓣ01/844 5544, Australia ⓣ1300/655 727, SA ⓣ0861/842 538, ⓦwww.lufthansa.com.
Malaysia Airlines US ⓣ1-212-697-8994, UK ⓣ0870/607 9090, Republic of Ireland ⓣ01/676 2131, Australia ⓣ13 26 27, New Zealand ⓣ0800/777 747, ⓦwww.malaysia-airlines.com.
Malev Hungarian Airlines ⓣ1-212-566-9944, Canada ⓣ1-800-665-6363, UK ⓣ0870/909 0577, Republic of Ireland ⓣ01/844 4303, ⓦwww.malev.hu.
Northwest/KLM US ⓣ1-800-225-2525, UK ⓣ0870/507 4074, Australia ⓣ1300-767-310, ⓦwww.nwa.com
Qantas Airways US and Canada ⓣ1-800-227-4500, UK ⓣ0845/774 7767, Republic of Ireland ⓣ01/407 3278, Australia ⓣ13 13 13, New Zealand ⓣ0800/808 767 or 09/357 8900, SA ⓣ11/441 8550, ⓦwww.qantas.com.
Ryanair UK ⓣ0871/246 0000, Republic of Ireland ⓣ0818/303 030, ⓦwww.ryanair.com.
Singapore Airlines US ⓣ1-800-742-3333, Canada ⓣ1-800-663-3046, UK ⓣ0844/800 2380, Republic of Ireland ⓣ01/671 0722, Australia ⓣ13 10 11, New Zealand ⓣ0800/808 909, SA ⓣ11/880 8560 or 11/880 8566, ⓦwww.singaporeair.com.
SkyEurope UK ⓣ0905/722 2747, ⓦwww.skyeurope.com.
South African Airways US and Canada ⓣ1-800-722-9675, UK ⓣ0870/747 1111, Australia ⓣ1800/221 699, New Zealand ⓣ09/977 2237, SA ⓣ11/978 1111, ⓦwww.flysaa.com.
Swiss US ⓣ1-877-FLY-SWIS, UK ⓣ0845/601 0956, Republic of Ireland ⓣ1890/200 515, Australia ⓣ1300/724 666, New Zealand ⓣ09/977 2238, SA ⓣ0860/040 506, ⓦwww.swiss.com.
Thai Airways US ⓣ1-212-949-8424, Canada ⓣ1-416-971-5181, UK ⓣ0870/606 0911, Australia ⓣ1300/651 960, New Zealand ⓣ09/377 3886, ⓦwww.thaiair.com.
United Airlines US ⓣ1-800-UNITED-1, UK ⓣ0845/844 4777, Australia ⓣ13 17 77, ⓦwww.united.com.
Virgin Atlantic US ⓣ1-800-821-5438, UK ⓣ0870/380 2007, Australia ⓣ1300/727 340, SA ⓣ11/340 3400, ⓦwww.virgin-atlantic.com.
Wizzair Poland ⓣ +48 22 500 9499, ⓦwww.wizzair.com.

Agents and operators

ebookers UK ⓣ0800/082 3000, Republic of Ireland ⓣ01/488 3507, ⓦwww.ebookers.com. Low fares on an extensive selection of scheduled flights and package deals.
North South Travel UK ⓣ01245/608 291, ⓦwww.northsouthtravel.co.uk. Friendly, competitive travel agency, offering discounted fares worldwide. Profits are used to support projects in the developing world, especially the promotion of sustainable tourism.
Trailfinders UK ⓣ0845/058 5858, Republic of Ireland ⓣ01/677 7888, Australia ⓣ1300/780 212, ⓦwww.trailfinders.com. One of the best-informed and most efficient agents for independent travellers.
STA Travel US ⓣ1-800-781-4040, Canada ⓣ1-888-427-5639, UK ⓣ0870/1630 026, Australia ⓣ1300/733 035, New Zealand ⓣ0508/782 872, SA ⓣ0861/781 781, ⓦwww.statravel.com. Worldwide specialists in independent travel; also student IDs, travel insurance, car rental, rail passes and more. Good discounts for students and under-26s.

Tour operators

Abercrombie & Kent US ⓣ1-800/554-7016, ⓦwww.abercrombiekent.com. Customized upmarket tours to Croatia.
Adriatic Adventures Australia ⓣ02/9823 0011, ⓦwww.adriatictours.com.au. Croatian travel specialists offering packages to Adriatic resorts such as Bol, Brela and Dubrovnik.
Adriatica.net UK ⓣ0207/183 0437, CRO +385 1 241 5611, ⓦwww.adriatica.net. Enormous range of accommodation-only deals and activity holidays throughout Croatia, from Croatia's biggest online travel agent.
Adventure World Australia ⓣ02/8913 0755, ⓦwww.adventureworld.com.au. Accommodation, sailing, hiking tours and more.

Adventures Abroad US ⓣ1-800/665-3998, ⓦwww.adventures-abroad.com. Thirteen-day guided tours of coastal Croatia; also Slovenia and Croatia, as well as Albania and Croatia packages.

Atlas Travel Agency CRO ⓣ+385 20 442 222, ⓦwww.atlas-croatia.com. Croatian firm with a wide range of holidays including bus tours, sailing holidays, adventure tours (such as diving, canoeing and rafting) and programmes for senior citizens.

Bond Tours UK ⓣ01372/745 300, ⓦwww.bondtours.com. Package operator specializing in the Dalmatian coast and islands, with accommodation ranging from private apartments to smart hotels. Also holidays in Kornati island cottages, sailing holidays and city breaks in Zagreb.

Bosmere Travel UK ⓣ01473/834 094, ⓦwww.bosmeretravel.co.uk. Small, family-run hotels outside the major resorts. Also scuba-diving, sailing and accommodation-only deals.

Concorde Ireland ⓣ01/872 7822, ⓦwww.concordetravel.ie. Holidays in Dalmatia, and charter flights from Dublin and Cork, from an operator with long-time Croatian experience. They also deal with accommodation, flights and car rental.

Cottages to Castles UK ⓣ01622/775 236, ⓦwww.cottagestocastles.com. Villa holidays in Istria and Dalmatia.

Croatia Tours Ireland ⓣ01/878 0800, ⓦwww.croatiatours.ie. Destinations in Istria, Dalmatia and the Dubrovnik region, plus tailor-made itineraries, from a specialist operator.

Croatia for Travellers UK ⓣ0207/226 4460, ⓦwww.croatiafortravellers.co.uk. Tailor-made packages using a wide range of hotel and apartment accommodation along the Adriatic coast and to Zagreb and the Plitvice Lakes. Can also arrange "Robinson Crusoe" holidays in Kornati island cottages, fly-drive deals and Adriatic cruises in motorsailers.

Croatia Travel Agency US ⓣ1-800/662-7628, ⓦwww.croatiatravel.com. New York-based agency specializing in all things Croatian, including packages, airfare, cruises and car rental.

Croatian Affair UK ⓣ0207/385 7111, ⓦwww.croatianaffair.com. Flights plus accommodation in apartments along the Adriatic coast. Also yachting holidays.

Croatian Villas UK ⓣ0208/888 6655, ⓦwww.croatianvillas.com. Tasteful apartments and holiday houses throughout Dalmatia and the Kvarner region, with a particularly good choice of properties in Lovran and on the island of Veli Brijun.

Cross-Culture Journeys US ⓣ1-800/491 1148, ⓦwww.ccjourneys.com. Cultural tours of Istria and the Dubrovnik region.

Dalmatian and Istrian Travel UK ⓣ0208/749 5255. Tailor-made package deals throughout Croatia, plus Jadrolinija ferry reservations.

Discover Croatia Holidays Australia ⓣ1300/660 189, ⓦwww.discovercroatia.com.au. Dedicated specialists offering packages and tailor-made arrangements to pretty much everywhere in the country.

Eastern Eurotours Australia ⓣ07/5526 2855 or 1800/242 353, ⓦwww.easterneurotours.com.au. Holidays in Dubrovnik, Split and Zagreb, plus multi-centre Adriatic tours and sea cruises.

Elderhostel US ⓣ1-800/454-5768, ⓦwww.elderhostel.org. Specialists in educational and activity programmes, cruises and homestays for senior travellers, including Croatia, Hungary and Slovenia combo packages.

Exodus UK ⓣ0208/675 5550, ⓦwww.exodus.co.uk. Adventure tour operators taking small groups to Plitvice, Brač and other destinations.

Explore Worldwide UK ⓣ01252/760 000, ⓦwww.exploreworldwide.com. Cultural tours and Adriatic cruises.

Gate1Travel US ⓣ1-800/682-3333, ⓦwww.gate1travel.com. Worldwide group and independent packages, including the escorted ten-day "Affordable Croatia" and twelve-day "Dalmatian Coast" tours, plus Croatia-Slovenia combinations.

Headwater Holidays UK ⓣ01606/720 033, ⓦwww.headwater.com. Light walking tours taking in nature and culture in Dalmatia.

Hidden Croatia UK ⓣ0871/208 0075, ⓦwww.hiddencroatia.com. Big range of destinations in all parts of the country, alongside tailor-made arrangements, sailing, kayaking and gourmet holidays, and flights from several UK airports.

Holiday Options UK ⓣ0870/420 8386, ⓦwww.holidayoptions.co.uk. Packages to a large range of destinations in Dalmatia and the islands, plus a choice of two-centre holidays, including Croatia-Slovenia combinations, and seven-day Dalmatian cruises in motorsailers.

Kompas US ⓣ1-800/233-6422, ⓦwww.kompas.net. Various packages including city breaks in Dubrovnik, Split and Zagreb and customized tours.

Martin Randall Travel UK ⓣ0208/742 3355, ⓦwww.martinrandall.com. Upmarket escorted art and culture tours taking in the best of Dalmatia and Dubrovnik.

My Croatia UK ⓣ0118/961 1554, ⓦwww.mycroatia.co.uk. Gourmet tours and cookery courses in Istria.

Page & Moy UK ⓣ0870/010 6373, ⓦwww.page-moy.co.uk. Escorted cultural tours in Dubrovnik.

Palmair UK ⓣ01202/200 700, ⓦwww.palmair.co.uk. Packages to the Dubrovnik region with direct flights from Bournemouth.

Ramblers Holidays UK ⓣ01707/331 133, ⓦwww.ramblersholidays.co.uk. Cultural tours with a bit of easy walking, centring on Split and Dubrovnik.

Russian Gateway Australia 02/9745 3333, ⓦwww.russian-gateway.com.au. Flight-plus-accommodation deals, and cultural tours of the Adriatic coast.

Saga UK ⓣ0800/096 0074, ⓦwww.saga.co.uk. Holidays for the older traveller throughout Istria, Dalmatia and the Dubrovnik region.

Scuba-en-Cuba UK ⓣ01895/624100, ⓦwww.scuba-en-cuba.com. Diving holidays on Korčula.

Simply Travel UK ⓣ0208/541 2214, ⓦwww.simply-travel.com. Upmarket tour company specializing in charming villas and hotels in the less touristy parts of Croatia.

Skedaddle UK ⓣ0191/265 1110, ⓦwww.skedaddle.co.uk. Biking tours in Istria, staying in rural accommodation.

TravelTime US ⓣ1-800/354-8728, ⓦwww.traveltimeny.com. The main Croatian specialist operator in the US, with a wide range of packages including guided tours, city breaks, kayaking, wine-tasting and culinary tours, and programmes for senior citizens.

Vintage Travel UK ⓣ0845/344 0460, ⓦwww.vintagetravel.co.uk. Apartment holidays with small-town Istria a speciality.

Wilderness Travel US ⓣ1-800/368-2794, ⓦwww.wildernesstravel.com. Tours focusing on culture, hiking and sailing.

Naturist holidays

Peng Travel UK ⓣ0845/345 8345, ⓦwww.pengtravel.co.uk. Packages in the major Istrian naturist resorts.

Sailing holidays and yacht charter

Activity Yachting UK ⓣ01243/641 304, ⓦwww.activityyachting.com. Learn-to-sail packages, flotilla sailing and bareboat charter out of Murter in central Dalmatia.

Backpacker Croatia Sailing UK ⓣ0845/257 8289, ⓦwww.sail-croatia.com. Motorcruiser tours of Dalmatia.

Cosmos Yachting UK ⓣ0800/376 9070, ⓦwww.cosmosyachting.com. Individual yacht charter or skippered charter out of Zadar, Pula, Split, Dubrovnik and other ports.

Global Yachts UK ⓣ0207/193 1676, ⓦwww.global-yacht-charters.com. Flotilla holidays, sailing schools and individual charter from various Adriatic marinas.

Interpac Yachts US ⓣ888/99-YACHT, ⓦwww.interpacyachts.com. Yacht-charter specialists offering customized Adriatic cruises.

Nautilus Yachting UK ⓣ01732/867445, ⓦwww.nautilus-yachting.com. Learn-to-sail packages based in Murter, plus bareboat yacht and motor-yacht charter from various Dalmatian ports.

Neilson UK ⓣ0870/333 3356, ⓦwww.neilson.co.uk. Flotilla sailing in Dalmatia.

Sail Croatia UK ⓣ0871/733 8686, ⓦwww.sailcroatia.net. Skippered and bareboat charter from a wide range of Dalmatian island bases.

Sailing Holidays UK ⓣ0208/459 8787, ⓦwww.sailingholidays.com. Two-week flotilla sailing holidays in the central Dalmatia and Kornati areas.

Seafarer UK ⓣ0871/423 5547, ⓦwww.seafarercruises.com. Bareboat charters and flotilla sailing based in Dalmatia.

Setsail Holidays UK ⓣ01787/310 445, ⓦwww.setsail.co.uk. Bareboat charter, and two-week flotilla sailing in Dalmatia.

Sunchaser Yachting UK ⓣ0208/768 3858, ⓦwww.sunchaseryachting.com. Bareboat and skippered yachts in all sizes and for all pockets, from various Dalmatian marinas.

Sunsail UK ⓣ023/9222 2300, ⓦwww.sunsail.com. One- and two-week flotilla sailing trips, and bareboat charter in Dalmatia and the Dubrovnik region.

Templecraft Yacht Charters UK ⓣ01273/867 445, ⓦwww.templecraft.com. Individual yacht charter out of Pula, Zadar and Split.

Tenrag UK ⓣ01227/721 874, ⓦwww.tenrag.com. Yacht charter out of Pula, Zadar Biograd, Split and Dubrovnik.

Top Yacht Charter UK ⓣ01243/520 950, ⓦwww.top-yacht.com. Individual yacht charter out of Pula, Zadar and Split.

Rail contacts

CIT World Travel Australia ⓣ02/9267 1255 or 03/9650 5510, ⓦwww.cittravel.com.au. Eurail, Europass and Italian rail passes.

Europrail International Canada ⓣ1-888/667-9734, ⓦwww.europrail.net. European rail passes.

Eurostar UK ⓣ0870/518 6186, ⓦwww.eurostar.com. Passenger train which currently goes from Waterloo International in London to Paris (2hr 40min) or Brussels (2hr 20min); from autumn 2007 a new high-speed link should reduce the journey time further, and trains will leave from London St Pancras rather than Waterloo. You can get through-tickets – including the tube journey to the London terminal – from Eurostar itself, from most travel agents or from mainline train stations in Britain. Inter-Rail passes give discounts on the Eurostar service.

Rail Europe US ⓣ1-877/257-2887, Canada ⓣ1-800/361-RAIL, UK ⓣ0870/837 1371, ⓦwww.raileurope.com. Eurail agent; also sells

Europasses, multinational passes and most single-country passes.

Rail Plus Australia ⓣ1300/555 003 or 03/9642 8644, ⓦwww.railplus.com.au, NZ ⓣ09/377 5415, ⓦwww.railplus.co.nz. European rail passes.

The Man in Seat 61 ⓦwww.seat61.com. Enthusiast-run site packed with information on all aspects of international rail travel. Far more reliable than many "official" sites.

Trailfinders UK ⓣ0845/058 5858, Republic of Ireland ⓣ01/677 7888, Australia ⓣ1300/780 212, ⓦwww.trailfinders.com. All Europe passes.

Trainseurope UK ⓣ0900/195 0101, ⓦwww.trainseurope.co.uk. Inter-Rail passes and through-tickets on European routes.

Ferry contacts

Azzurra Line IT ⓣ+39 80 528 35 75, ⓦwww.azzurraline.com. Bari to Dubrovnik.

Direct Ferries UK ⓣ0871 222 3312, ⓦwww.directferries.co.uk. Online booking for Italy–Croatia ferries.

Jadrolinija CRO ⓣ+385 51/666-111, ⓕ+385 51/213-116, ⓦwww.jadrolinija.hr. Italy–Croatia ferries.

P&O Ferries UK ⓣ0870/600 0600, ⓦwww.poferries.com. Dover to Calais.

Sea France UK ⓣ0870/571 1711, ⓦwww.seafrance.com. Dover to Calais.

Split Tours CRO ⓣ+385 21/352-533, ⓦwww.splittours.hr. Italy–Croatia ferries.

SNAV IT ⓣ+39 71 207 6116 ⓦwww.snav.it. Italy–Croatia ferries.

Viamare UK ⓣ0207/431 4560, ⓦwww.viamare.com. UK agent for SNAV.

Bus contacts

Eurolines UK ⓣ0870/580 8080, ⓦwww.nationalexpress.co.uk/eurolines, Republic of Ireland ⓣ01/836 6111, ⓦwww.eurolines.ie.

Getting around

Croatia's indented coastline and mountainous topography conspire to make travel a scenic but time-consuming experience, although a growing network of toll motorways has sped up journey times for drivers. Croatia's train system covers the north and east pretty well, but is little use on the coast, where the country's extensive and reliable bus network comes into its own. As well as providing the only route to the islands, ferries offer a leisurely way of getting up and down the coast, and travelling the length of the Adriatic by boat is one of the most memorable journeys Croatia has to offer.

Trains

Croatian Railways (Hrvatske željeznice; ⓦwww.hznet.hr) run a smooth and efficient service, and it is slightly cheaper than using buses in those areas where routes overlap. Around Zagreb and in the north the network is pretty dense, and you can use trains to visit most places of interest in inland Croatia. Trains also run from Zagreb to Pula, Rijeka and Split on the Adriatic, but there are no rail lines running up and down the coast. The **Inter-Rail** pass is valid for Croatia (which is in zone D along with the Czech and Slovak republics, Poland and Hungary), but **Eurail** is not. If you're resident in Europe, you could buy a **Euro Domino** pass for Croatia itself, but this is hardly worth it unless you're in constant transit from one end of the country to the other. For more on train passes, see p.31.

There are two types of train (*vlak*, plural *vlakovi*): **putnički** (slow ones which stop at every halt) and **IC** (inter-city trains which are faster and more expensive). **Tickets** (*karte*) are bought from the ticket counter at the station (*kolodvor*) before travel; those bought from the conductor on the train are subject to a surcharge unless you've joined the train at an insignificant halt that doesn't have a ticket counter. On some inter-city routes, buying a return ticket (*povratna karta*) is cheaper than buying a single ticket (*karta u jednom pravcu*) twice, although it often makes no difference. Seat reservations (*rezervacije*) are obligatory on some inter-city services. The only journey on which sleeping car (*spalnica*) or couchette (*kušet*) accommodation is available is the overnight service between Zagreb and Split.

Timetables (*vozni red* or *red vožnje*) are usually displayed on boards in station departure halls – *polasci* or *odlasci* are departures, *dolasci* are arrivals. The timetable for the whole network is in theory available in a compact paperback from most larger train stations (40Kn), although it sells out fast. Timetable information is also available on Croatian Railways' website.

Buses

Croatia's **bus** network is run by a confusing array of local companies, but services are well integrated and bus stations are generally well organized, with clearly listed departure times and efficient booking facilities. Buses (*autobusi*) operating inter-city services are usually modern air-conditioned coaches, and travelling large distances is rarely uncomfortable – stops of ten minutes or more are made every ninety minutes or so. The buses operating shorter routes on the islands or in the provinces are more likely to be ageing and uncomfortable vehicles which can get unbearably stuffy in summer – but you're unlikely to be spending a long time in them.

There are few places in the country that you can't get to by bus, and departures on the principal routes are usually hourly (Zagreb to the coast, and routes up and down the coast). Rural areas, however, may only be served by one or two buses a day, and maybe none at all at weekends. Out in the sticks, the bus timetable is much more likely to correspond to the needs of the locals: there'll be a flurry of departures in the early morning to get people to work, school or market, and a flurry of departures in mid-afternoon to bring them back again, but nothing in between.

If you're at a big city bus station, **tickets** must be obtained from ticket windows before boarding the bus, and will bear the departure time (*vrijeme polaska*), platform number (*peron*) and a seat number (*sjedalo*). Your ticket will also carry the name of the bus company you're travelling with: two different companies might be running services to the same place at around the same time. If you're not getting on at the start of the route, tickets might not go on sale until the bus actually arrives. If there's nowhere to buy a ticket, sit on the bus and wait for the conductor to sell you one. It's a good idea to buy tickets a day or two in advance in summer if you can, especially for any services between Zagreb to the coast – though bear in mind that you can only buy advance tickets from the city where the bus originates rather than from some point along the route.

Fares are a little cheaper than in Western Europe, although costs differ slightly according to which company you're riding with and what part of the country you're in. Generally speaking, you get more kilometres for your money in inland Croatia than you do on the coast. Long inter-city trips like Rijeka–Zadar or Split–Dubrovnik weigh in at around 120Kn one-way; Split–Zagreb will cost around 160Kn. **Return tickets** are sporadically offered by some companies on a selection of their inter-city routes – they'll work out slightly cheaper then buying two one-way fares. On bus journeys that involve a **ferry crossing** (such as Rijeka–Lošinj or Rijeka–Rab), the cost of the ferry will be included in the price. You'll be charged extra for rucksacks and suitcases (7–10kn per item).

Tickets for **municipal buses** in towns and cities should usually be bought in advance from newspaper kiosks and then cancelled by punching them in the machine on board. You can buy tickets from the driver, as well, in most cases, although this might be slightly more expensive and you may have to provide the correct change.

Ferries

A multitude of **ferry services** link the Croatian mainland with the Adriatic islands. Most of them are run by **Jadrolinija** (see p.32), the main state ferry firm, although private operators such as Split Tours are beginning to offer competition.

Short hops to islands **close to the mainland** – such as Brestova to Porozina on Cres, Jablanac to Mišnjak on Rab, or Orebić to Dominće on Korčula – are handled by simple roll-on-roll-off ferries, which either operate a shuttle service or run every thirty minutes or so. Prices for foot passengers on such routes rarely exceed 20Kn (this will usually be incorporated into your fare if you're crossing by bus). A car will cost about 80Kn extra; a motorbike, 30Kn.

Departures to destinations slightly **farther offshore** run to a more precise timetable. The ports offering access to the most important groups of islands are Zadar (Ugljan, Dugi otok), Split (Šolta, Brač, Hvar, Vis and Lastovo) and Dubrovnik (Koločep, Lopud, Šipan and Mljet). **Fares** for foot passengers are low: approximate prices are Zadar–Sali (Dugi otok) 20Kn, Split–Hvar 32Kn, Split–Lastovo 42Kn, Split–Supetar (Brač) 25Kn, Split–Vis 36Kn, and Dubrovnik–Mljet 40Kn. On these routes you'll pay 200–300Kn for a car, 70–100Kn for a motorbike. If you're travelling without a vehicle, look out for summer-only **hydrofoils and catamarans** linking Split with destinations on Šolta, Brač, Hvar and Vis. Although slightly more expensive than ferries, they'll be twice as fast.

Jadrolinija also operates a **coastal service** from Rijeka to Dubrovnik, calling at Zadar, Split, Stari grad (Hvar) and Korčula on the way, and sometimes continuing to Bari in Italy and Igoumenitsa in Greece in the summer. This runs at least once a day in both directions in summer, twice a week in winter. Travelling from Rijeka to Dubrovnik takes twenty hours and always involves one night on the boat. Prices (often quoted in euros but payable in kuna) vary greatly according to the level of comfort you require. The cheapest Rijeka–Dubrovnik fare (which involves spending the journey either on the open deck or in smoky bar areas) is 230Kn; you'll pay double that for a couchette-style bunk bed and three times as much for a bed in a well-appointed cabin. Taking a car on the same journey will cost an extra 620Kn, a motorbike or bicycle 200Kn. Return tickets are twenty percent cheaper than the price of two singles, and prices fall by up to twenty percent in winter. **Tickets** are sold at offices or kiosks near the departure dock. For longer journeys, book in advance wherever possible; Jadrolinija addresses and phone numbers are given in the text where relevant.

All ferries, apart from simple shuttle services, will have a **buffet** where you can buy a full range of drinks, although food may consist of crisps and unappetizing sandwiches, so it's best to bring your own. The main coastal ferry has a restaurant with a full range of reasonably priced food; breakfast is included if you book a cabin.

Flights

The obvious attraction of flying is the time it saves: the plane journey from Zagreb to Dubrovnik takes an hour, compared to a whole day to get there overland. **Croatia Airlines** (Ⓦwww.croatiaairlines.com) operates domestic services between Zagreb and Pula (1 daily), Split (summer 4 daily; winter 3 daily), Zadar (summer 2 daily; winter 1 daily) and Dubrovnik (summer 3 daily; winter 2 daily). Between May and October there are flights (weekends only) to Bol on the island of Brač. A Zagreb–Dubrovnik return costs about 1000Kn. There's not normally any point in booking internal flights from Croatia Airlines offices in your home country – they invariably work out twice as expensive as buying them in Croatia, unless they're bought in conjunction with an international flight to Croatia.

By car

Croatia's **road system** is comprehensive, but not always of good quality once you get beyond the main highways. Major additions to the motorway (*autocesta*) network in recent years ensure that it's now much easier to get across country from east to west. The main stretches run from Zagreb to Županja near the Serbian border, Zagreb to Goričan on the Hungarian border, and Zagreb to Krapina on the way to Slovenia and Austria. The Zagreb–Zadar–Split motorway, the main link between inland Croatia and the coast, is complete save for some short stretches, and is due to be extended southwards to Dubrovnik in the next few years. There's also a serviceable two-lane highway from

Croatia distance chart(in km)

	Dubrovnik	Karlovac	Osijek	Pula	Rijeka
Dubrovnik		526	521	711	601
Karlovac	526		336	236	126
Osijek	521	336		572	462
Pula	711	236	572		110
Rijeka	609	126	462	110	
Šibenik	305	282	494	406	296
Slavonski Brod	472	246	91	482	372
Split	216	309	505	503	393
Varaždin	630	154	236	390	280
Zadar	377	232	559	334	224
Zagreb	572	56	280	292	182

Zagreb to Rijeka. All the above are subject to **tolls** – take a ticket as you come on and pay as you exit. Elsewhere, the main routes (especially the coast-hogging Magistrala) are single carriageway and tend to be clogged with traffic – especially in summer, when movement up and down the coast can be time-consuming. Note that everywhere in Croatia, roads in off-the-beaten-track areas can be badly maintained.

To drive in Croatia, you'll need a driving licence, registration documents and a Green Card. **Speed limits** are 50kph in built-up areas, 80kph on minor roads, 100kph on main roads, 130kph on motorways. It is illegal to drive with any alcohol whatsoever in your bloodstream. **Petrol stations** (*benzinska stanica*) are usually open daily 7am–7pm, although there are 24-hour stations in larger towns and along major international routes. If there's anything wrong with your vehicle, petrol stations are probably the best places to ask where you can find a mechanic (*automehaničar* or *majstor*) or a shop selling spare parts (*rezervni dijelovi*). A tyre repair shop is a *vulkanizer*. If you **break down**, the Croatian Automobile Club (HAK; ⓦwww.hak.hr) has a 24-hour emergency service (ⓣ987); their website is also a good source of **traffic news**.

Finding **parking** spaces in big cities can be a nightmare, and illegally parked vehicles will be swiftly removed by tow-truck (known locally as the *pauk*, or "spider") and impounded until payment of a 500Kn fine. Most cities have garages where you can leave your car for a small fee.

Car rental in Croatia is pricey, at around £45/€67/$80 a day and £200/€300/$370 a week for a small hatchback with unlimited mileage, depending on the season. The major rental chains have offices in all the larger cities and at Zagreb airport; addresses are detailed in the "Listings" sections at the end of city accounts throughout the Guide. Most travel agents in Croatia will organize car rental through one of the big international firms or a local operator. It's usually cheaper if you arrange rental in advance, either through one of the agents listed below or with specialist tour operators like Croatia for Travellers or Holiday Options (see p.35).

Car rental agencies

Alamo US ⓣ1-800-462-5266, ⓦwww.alamo.com.
Avis US ⓣ1-800-230-4898, Canada ⓣ1-800-272-5871, UK ⓣ0870/606 0100, Republic of Ireland ⓣ021/428 1111, Australia ⓣ13 63 33 or 02/9353 9000, New Zealand ⓣ09/526 2847 or 0800/655 111, ⓦwww.avis.com.
Budget US ⓣ1-800-527-0700, Canada ⓣ1-800-268-8900, UK ⓣ0870/156 5656, Australia ⓣ1300/362 848, New Zealand ⓣ0800/283 438, ⓦwww.budget.com.
Europcar US & Canada ⓣ1-877-940-6900, UK ⓣ0870/607 5000, Republic of Ireland ⓣ01/614 2800, Australia ⓣ393/306 160, ⓦwww.europcar.com.
Hertz US & Canada ⓣ1-800-654-3131, UK ⓣ0207/026 0077, Republic of Ireland ⓣ01/870

Šibenik	Slavonski Brod	Split	Varaždin	Zadar	Zagreb
305	472	216	630	377	582
282	246	309	154	232	56
494	91	660	236	559	282
406	482	503	390	334	292
296	372	405	280	280	175
	97	436	72	338	
403		448	239	468	190
97	448		463	169	378
436	239	463		386	98
72	468	169	386		253
338	190	365	98	288	

5777, New Zealand ⓣ0800/654 321, ⓦwww.hertz.com.

Holiday Autos UK ⓣ0870/400 4461, Republic of Ireland ⓣ01/872 9366, Australia ⓣ299/394 433, ⓦwww.holidayautos.co.uk. Part of the LastMinute.com group.

National US ⓣ1-800-CAR-RENT, UK ⓣ0870/400 4581, Australia ⓣ0870/600 6666, New Zealand ⓣ03/366 5574, ⓦwww.nationalcar.com.

SIXT Republic of Ireland ⓣ1850/206 088, UK ⓣ0800/4747 4227, US ⓣ1-877-347-3227, ⓦwww.irishcarrentals.ie.

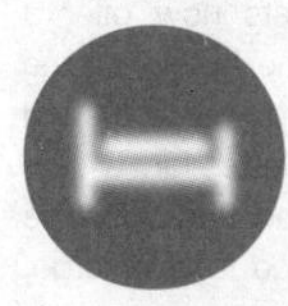

Accommodation

The tourism boom of the 1960s and 1970s gave Croatia an impressive number of large beachside hotels, while small B&Bs and pensions are on the increase. For the moment, though, the inexpensive private rooms and apartments offered by families up and down the coast still represent the country's best-value accommodation. The Adriatic coast is well provided with campsites, but hostels only exist in a handful of major centres.

Hotels

Most Croatian **hotels** are multistorey affairs providing modern comforts with little atmosphere; far more interesting are the handful of stately, early twentieth-century establishments in major cities and in resorts which were originally patronized by the Habsburgs. Most of the hotels used by Western European package holidaymakers have been expensively renovated since the end of the 1991–95 war, bringing them up to contemporary international standards. Hotels that see more in the way of Croatian or East European guests have generally received less investment, and often still sport worn carpets and garish 1970s wallpaper – although they're perfectly clean and comfortable in all other respects.

Most Croatian hotels have been classified according to the international **star grading** system, although some of the grades awarded might seem a little generous – some of Croatia's five-star hotels would only qualify for four stars elsewhere, and so on down the scale. Generally speaking, one-star hotels

Accommodation price codes

The accommodation in this guide has been graded using the following price codes, based on the cost of each establishment's **least expensive double room** in high season (July & Aug), excluding special offers. Where single rooms exist, they usually cost 60–70 percent of the price of a double.

- 1 Less than 250Kn
- 2 250–350Kn
- 3 350–450Kn
- 4 450–600Kn
- 5 600–800Kn
- 6 800–1100Kn
- 7 1100–1400Kn
- 8 1400–1800Kn
- 9 More than 1800Kn

have rooms with shared WC and bathroom; two-star hotels have rooms with en-suite facilities; three-stars have slightly larger en-suite rooms and, most probably, a television; four-stars correspond to comfy business class; and five-stars are in the international luxury bracket. Not many hotels fall into the one-star category, however, you're much more likely to come across two-star establishments, for which you can expect to pay 450–600Kn for a double, but it's worth bearing in mind that the better categories of private rooms and apartments offer similar comforts for less money. Three-star hotels are the hardest to predict, both in terms of quality and price, and you'll pay anything between 600Kn and 1000Kn, depending on whether it's just a glorified two-star with an extra lick of paint, or a genuinely comfortable and well-managed outfit that meets international standards. Any four-star hotel will have plush carpets, bathtubs in most rooms and a range of other facilities (such as gym or swimming pool) for around 800–1400Kn. There's an increasing number of five-star hotels in Croatia, most of which are in Zagreb or in and around Dubrovnik (1200Kn a double upwards).

Hotels in inland Croatia charge the same price all year round, but on the coast rates vary widely according to season, with July and August proving the most expensive months in which to travel. Prices drop by ten to twenty percent in the shoulder season (May, June and Sept), and may be as much as fifty percent cheaper in winter. Dubrovnik and Hvar are currently the most fashionable – and consequently most expensive – parts of the country, while hotels in areas such as northern and mid-Dalmatia can work out significantly cheaper.

Some hotels in resort areas **close** between November and April, although most moderate-sized Adriatic towns will have at least one mid-range hotel open all year.

There's a growing number of small **family-run hotels** aiming to conquer the mid-range market, offering the comforts and level of service of a good three-star hotel, but in cosy, informal surroundings and at a slightly cheaper price. They don't crop up in all parts of the country, but we've recommended them throughout the Guide wherever they exist.

Hotel prices almost invariably include **breakfast**. At its most basic, this will feature rolls with butter, jam, and some ham and cheese, although the majority of hotels hosting Western package guests now offer a buffet selection. Many of the hotels on the Adriatic also offer full-board (*pansion*) and half-board (*polupansion*) deals for a few extra kuna, but bear in mind that you'll be eating bland, internationalized food in large, institutional dining rooms.

Private rooms and apartments

Private **rooms** (*privatne sobe*) are available everywhere in Croatia where there are tourists. They're offered by locals eager to rent out unoccupied space in their homes – many Croats on the coast have enlarged or modernized their houses to provide extra rooms. Standards vary widely, but rooms are usually grouped into three categories by the tourist association in each area. **Category I** rooms are simple affairs furnished with a couple of beds, a wardrobe and not much else, and you'll be using your host's bathroom. **Category II** rooms have en-suite bathrooms, and **category III** rooms will probably come with TV and plusher furnishings, as well as en-suite facilities. In July and August **prices** start at around 150/200/250Kn (❶) for a category I/category II/category III double in a smallish resort, rising to about 250/330/400Kn (❷–❸) in relatively expensive places like Dubrovnik and Korčula. Prices in the shoulder season (April–June & Sept–Oct) can be ten to twenty percent cheaper. Many families don't let out rooms over the winter, although local travel agencies will probably come up with something, providing you contact them a week or so in advance. Prices are subject to a thirty- to fifty-percent surcharge if you stay for fewer than three nights. Single travellers usually pay about seventy percent of the price of a double except in July and August, when the full double price might have to be paid to secure a room.

Bookings are administered by local travel agencies; where there's no established travel agency, the local tourist office will handle the job. Agencies are usually open daily from 8am to 8pm or later in July and August; they may take a long afternoon break on Sundays. In May, June and September opening hours will include longish afternoon breaks Monday to Friday, and hours will be shorter (often mornings only) at weekends. When paying for a private room, you'll be charged a fee of about 10Kn to cover the cost of registering you with the police (see p.59), and a residence tax (*boravišna pristojba*) of 7–10Kn each per night, which is the local tourist association's main source of funding.

If you can't find a tourist agency or tourist office, it's usually very easy to turn up a private room by asking around or looking for "sobe" or "Zimmer frei" signs posted up outside local houses. You may also be offered rooms by landladies waiting outside train, bus and ferry stations, especially in Split and Dubrovnik – be sure to establish the location of the room and agree a price before setting off. Rooms obtained in this way sometimes work out significantly cheaper than the agency-approved ones, but equally leave you prone to rip-offs. There's little chance that your hosts will be passing on registration fees or tourist tax to the relevant authorities (they'll charge you for them, then pocket the cash themselves), and they may exploit your naivety by inflating these additional costs, or inventing new ones of their own. However you find a room, it's acceptable to have a look at it before committing yourself.

Apartments

Rented out in the same way as private rooms, **apartments** (*apartmani*) usually consist of a self-contained unit or floor of a house with its own kitchen and bathroom, maybe a small lounge and possibly a terrace for sitting outside. Two-person apartments often provide much more convenience, comfort and value for money than a double room in a hotel, and even single travellers – who will have to pay the price of a double – may find apartments favourably priced compared to bland hotel rooms. For those travelling as a family or in a group, apartments offer excellent value, providing that sleeping quarters are not too cramped – check how many beds are crammed into a single bedroom before accepting.

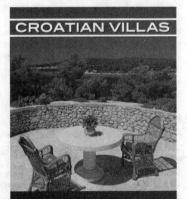

Two-person apartments – for which we've given price codes in the Guide – generally cost around 350–500Kn per night (❸–❹). Where available, four-person apartments cost around 450–800Kn; six-person apartments 600–900Kn. The higher the price, the more likely you are to get a central location, TV and a parking space, should you need it. Prices fall by ten to twenty percent in April, May, June, September and October. As with private rooms, you should contact a local travel agent well in advance if you want to book an apartment over the winter.

Rural homestays

In northern Croatia attempts are being made to encourage the development of **rural homestays** under the banner of *agriturizam* or "agricultural tourism". The idea is to encourage people in the countryside to offer farmhouse-style accommodation and locally produced food and drink. This is at its most developed in inland Istria, where the regional tourist association (Turistička zajednica istarske županije; Forum 3, 52100 Pula, ⓣ052/452-797, ⓦwww.istra.com) publishes an annually updated *agriturizam* booklet detailing all the rural homestay possibilities. The other areas in which the concept has made significant inroads is the Zagorje, north of Zagreb; the region around the Plitvice National Park; and the Slavonian village of Bilje near the Kopački rit Nature Park.

Room quality varies from place to place, although most village homestays offer neat little en suites, often with a rustic feel to the furnishings. Prices are roughly equivalent to those in private rooms and apartments, and usually include breakfast; half- or full-board arrangements featuring tasty home-cooked food are often available for an extra cost.

Hostels

HI-affiliated **youth hostels**, run by the Croatian Hostelling Association (Hrvatski ferijalni i hostelski savez; Dežmanova 9, 10000 Zagreb; ⓣ01/48-47-474, ⓦwww.hfhs.hr), are thin on the ground, although those that do exist (in Zagreb, Pula, Zadar, Dubrovnik, Krk and Punat) are usually habitable and friendly. Prices vary according to season: around 70–90Kn for a bed in winter, rising to 90–120Kn in July and August. Breakfast costs 20–30Kn. Half-board and full-board deals are also offered at very reasonable prices, although the food may not be particularly special. Most hostels close during the day, and you're expected to check in either in the morning (around 8–9am) or in the evening (typically 5–10pm). If you're doing a lot of hostelling, it's worth joining the hostelling organization of your home country to qualify for the member's rate, which is about fifteen percent cheaper than the standard.

Youth hostel associations

UK and Ireland

YHA England & Wales ⓣ0870/770 8868, ⓦwww.yha.org.uk.
Hostelling International Northern Ireland ⓣ028/9032 4733, ⓦwww.hini.org.uk.
Irish Youth Hostel Association ⓣ01/830 4555, ⓦwww.irelandyha.org.
Scottish Youth Hostel Association ⓣ01786/891 400, ⓦwww.syha.org.uk.

US and Canada

Hostelling International-American Youth Hostels ⓣ1-301/495-1240, ⓦwww.hiayh.org.
Hostelling International Canada ⓣ1-800/663-5777 or 613/237-7884, ⓦwww.hihostels.ca.

Australia and New Zealand

Australia Youth Hostels Association ⓣ02/9565 1699, ⓦwww.yha.com.au.
Youth Hostelling Association New Zealand ⓣ0800/278 299 or 03/379 9970, ⓦwww.yha.co.nz.

Campsites

Campsites (*autokamp*) abound on the Adriatic coast, ranging from large-scale affairs with plentiful facilities, restaurants and shops to small family-run sites squeezed into private gardens or olive groves. Some major centres – notably Split – are currently without campsites, but almost everywhere else is catered for. Sites are generally open from May to September and charge 30–60Kn per person, plus 30–60Kn per pitch and 30–50Kn per vehicle. Prices are significantly higher in fashionable destinations such as Dubrovnik. Electricity in the bigger sites costs a few extra kuna. Bear in mind that the stony ground of the Adriatic coast often makes it difficult to hammer in tent pegs – spare rope comes in handy to fasten your canvas home to nearby rocks and trees. Camping rough is illegal, and the rocky or pebbly nature of most Croatian beaches makes them uncomfortable to sleep on anyway.

Naturist campsites are a common feature of the northern Adriatic resorts, with big, self-contained complexes outside Rovinj, Poreč and Vrsar in Istria, and Krk, Baška and Punat on the island of Krk.

Eating and drinking

There's a varied and distinctive range of food on offer in Croatia, largely because the country straddles two culinary cultures: the seafood-dominated cuisine of the Mediterranean and the filling schnitzel-and-strudel fare of central Europe. Drinking revolves around a solid cross-section of wines and some characterful, fiery spirits.

Main meals are eaten in a **restoran** (restaurant, sometimes also called a *restauracija*) or a **konoba** (tavern) – the latter is more likely to have folksy decor but essentially serves the same range of food. A **gostiona** (inn) is a more rough-and-ready version of a *restoran*. For Croatians the most important meal of the day is lunch (*ručak*) rather than dinner (*večera*), although restaurants are accustomed to foreigners who eat lightly at lunchtime and more copiously in the evening, and offer a full range of food throughout the day. Throughout the Guide, we've given **phone numbers** for those restaurants where it may be worth **booking in advance**.

Because many Croatians eat lunch relatively late in the afternoon, restaurants frequently offer a list of **brunch-snacks** (called *marende* on the coast, *gableci* inland) between 10.30am and noon. These are usually no different from main meat and fish dishes, but come in slightly smaller portions, making an excellent low-cost midday meal. Details are often chalked up on a board outside rather than written on a menu. Most restaurants **open** at 10.30 or 11am and close at around 11pm; on Sundays, they tend to close earlier, apart from in resort areas.

No Croatian town is without at least one **pizzeria**, where the price of a filling meal will be significantly cheaper than in a standard meat-and-fish Croatian restaurant. Most of these establishments serve Italian-style, thin-crust pizzas made to reasonably authentic recipes, and seafood pizzas are quite a feature on the coast. Pizzerias tend to serve larger and more imaginative salads than the standard Croatian restaurant, and are often the best places to eat pasta. Again, Croatian pasta dishes are normally authentic, cheap and filling. Look out also for **slastičarnice** (patisseries), the traditional place for buying eat-in or take-away cakes, pastries and ice cream.

What to eat

Any list of **starters** should begin with *pršut*, a home-cured ham from Istria and Dalmatia, which, at its best, is a real melt-in-the-mouth delicacy. It's often served on a platter together with cheese: *paški sir* from the island of Pag is the most famous – a hard, piquant cheese with a taste somewhere between parmesan and mature cheddar; *sir sa vrhnjem* (cream cheese) is a milder alternative. *Kulen*, a spicy, paprika-laced sausage from Slavonia, is also worth trying.

For a comprehensive list of Croatian food and drink terms, see pp.525–529.

Soups (*juha*) are usually clear and light and served with spindly noodles, unless you opt for the thicker *krem-juha* (cream soup).

One starter that is stodgy enough to serve as a main course is *štrukli*, a pastry and cheese dish, which is common to Zagreb and the Zagorje hills to the north. It comes in two forms: *kuhani* (boiled) *štrukli* are enormous ravioli-like pockets of dough filled with cottage cheese; for *pečeni* (baked) *štrukli* the dough and cheese are baked in an earthenware dish, resulting in a cross between cheese soufflé and lasagne.

Meat dishes

Main **meat dishes** normally consist of a grilled or pan-fried *kotlet* (chop) or *odrezak* (fillet or escalope). These are usually either **pork** or **veal**, and can be prepared in a variety of ways: a *kotlet* or *odrezak* cooked *na žaru* will be a simple grill, *bečki odrezak* (Wiener schnitzel) comes fried in breadcrumbs, *pariški odrezak* (Pariser schnitzel) is fried in batter, and *zagrebački odrezak* (Zagreb schnitzel) is stuffed with cheese and ham. *Miješano meso* (mixed grill) appears on all menus and will usually consist of a pork or veal *kotlet*, a few *ćevapi* (rissoles of minced beef, pork or lamb), a *pljeskavica* (a hamburger-like mixture of the same meats) and maybe a spicy *kobasica* (sausage), served alongside a bright-red aubergine and pepper relish known as *ajvar*.

Lamb is usually prepared as a spit-roast. In sheep-growing regions (Cres, Rab, the hinterland of Zadar and Split) it's quite common to see roadside restaurants where a whole sheep is being roasted over an open fire in the car park to tempt travellers inside. One way of preparing diced lamb that's typical of Istria and the Adriatic islands is to cook it *ispod peke* –placed under a metal lid that is covered with hot embers and slowly baked. Stewed meats are less common than grilled or baked ones, although goulash (*gulaš*) is frequently employed as a sauce served with pasta. A main course associated with Dalmatia (where it's traditionally considered a special-occasion food eaten on the big holy days, although it's perfectly common in restaurants) is *pašticada* (beef cooked in vinegar, wine and prunes). The most common **poultry** dish is *purica z mlincima* (turkey with baked pasta slivers), which is indigenous to Zagreb and the Zagorje. Other meaty mains include *punjene paprike* (peppers stuffed with rice and meat) and *sarma* (cabbage leaves filled with a similar mixture). *Arambašica*, a version of *sarma* found in the Dalmatian hinterland, contains more meat and less rice.

Seafood dishes

On the coast you'll be regaled with every kind of **seafood**. Starters include *salata od hobotnice* (octopus salad) and the slightly more expensive *salata od jastoga* (nibble-size portions of lobster flesh seasoned with olive oil and herbs). **Fish** can come either *na žaru* (grilled), *u pečnici* (baked) or *lešo* (boiled). Grilling is by far the most common way of preparing freshly caught fish, which is sold by weight (the best fish starts at about 220Kn per kilo in cheap and mid-range restaurants, 350Kn per kilo in top-class establishments). Waiting staff will tell you what fish they have in stock, or will show you a tray of fish from which to choose. A decent-sized fish for one person usually weighs somewhere between a third and half a kilo, although you can always order a big fish and share it between two people.

Among the tastiest white fish are *komarča* (gold bass), *kovač* (John Dory), *list* (sole), *lubin* (sea bass), *orada* (giltheaded seabream) and *škrpina* (scorpion fish), although the range of fish caught in Adriatic waters is almost limitless. *Oslić* (hake) is slightly cheaper than the others, and is often served sliced and pan-fried in batter or breadcrumbs rather than grilled – when it will be priced per portion rather than by weight. Cheaper still is so-called *plava riba* (oily fish), a category that includes anchovies and mackerel. Another budget choice is *girice*, tiny fish similar to whitebait, which are deep fried and eaten whole. Inexpensive main courses that crop up almost everywhere on the coast are *brodet* (boiled fish accompanied by a hot peppery sauce), *lignje na žaru* (grilled squid) and *crni rižot* ("black risotto"; made from pieces of squid with the ink included).

The more expensive or specialist establishments will have delicacies such as crab, oysters, mussels and lobster. Scampi usually come as whole prawns which you have to crack open with your fingers, rather than the sanitized, breadcrumbed variety found in northwestern Europe. They're often served with a *buzara* sauce, made from garlic and white wine.

Salads, accompaniments and desserts

You'll usually be offered a choice of accompaniments with your main course: boiled potatoes, chips, rice and gnocchi are the most common. Indigenous forms of **pasta** include *fuži* in Istria, *šurlice* on the island of Krk and *mlinci* in Zagreb and the Zagorje – the last are lasagne-thin scraps of dough which are boiled, then baked. Additional vegetables can be ordered as items from the menu. Croatians eat an enormous amount of **bread**, and you'll be expected to scoff a couple of large slices with your meal regardless of whatever else you order.

The most common **salads** are *zelena salata* (green salad) and *miješana salata* (mixed salad). Other popular side dishes are gherkins (*krastavci*) and pickled peppers (*paprike*). Fish dishes are usually accompanied by *blitva* (mangelwurzel), a spinach-like plant indigenous to Dalmatia, served with boiled potatoes and garlic.

Typical restaurant **desserts** include *sladoled* (ice cream), *torta* (cake) and *palačinke* (pancakes), which are usually served *sa marmeladom* (with marmalade), *s čokoladom* (with chocolate sauce) or *s oresima* (with walnuts). In Dubrovnik, try *rožata*, the locally produced version of crème caramel. A *slastičarnica* is another place to find ice cream, cakes and pastries, including *baklava*, the syrup-coated pastry indigenous to the Balkans and Middle East.

Breakfast and snacks

Unless you're staying in a private room or a campsite, **breakfast** will almost always be included in the cost of your accommodation. At its simplest it will include a couple of bread rolls, a few slices of cheese and/or salami, and some butter and jam. Mid- and top-range hotels will offer a buffet breakfast, complete with a choice of cereals, scrambled eggs and bacon. Few Croatian cafés serve breakfast of any kind, and they don't usually mind if you bring along bread buns or pastries bought from a nearby bakery and consume them alongside your coffee.

Vegetarians in Croatia

Vegetarian cuisine has never been one of Croatia's strong points, but there's usually enough to choose from on restaurant menus if you look hard enough. Strict vegetarians should exercise caution however: many items that look like good vegetarian choices – the various bean soups and the ratatouille-style **đuveč** – are invariably made with meat stock. Even in well-meaning restaurants, it's not uncommon to find dishes advertised as "vegetarian" but that turn out to have ham or chicken in them. Yummy-looking grilled vegetables may have been cooked on the same grill as the meat dishes (so be sure to ask).

If you eat fish, you'll find excellent seafood available almost everywhere. Even in inland Croatia restaurants will feature at least one fish or squid dish. Vegetarians can often construct a handsome meal from the meat-free dishes listed as starters or side dishes. Pastas with various sauces, mushroom dishes, and sizeable salads are rarely hard to find. Mushroom omelettes (*omlet sa gljiivama*) and cheese fried in breadcrumbs (*pohani sir*) are fairly ubiquitous. Italian-influenced pizzerias and spaghetterias are perhaps the best bet: most pizzerias offer a **pizza vegeterijanska** featuring a selection of seasonal vegetables, and there's usually a choice of meatless pasta dishes including, if you're lucky, a vegetarian lasagne. One traditional meat-free dish is the cheesy *štrukli*, although this is a north Croatian speciality which can rarely be found on the coast.

Ja sam vegeterijanac (*vegeterijanka* is the female form of the noun) means "I am a vegetarian." To ask "Have you got anything which doesn't contain meat?", say **Imate li nešto bez mesa**?

Basic self-catering and picnic ingredients like cheese, vegetables and fruit can be bought at a supermarket (*samoposluga*) or an open-air market (*tržnica*). **Markets** often open early (about 6am) and begin to pack up in the early afternoon, though in well-touristed areas they sometimes keep going until late evening. Bread can be bought from either a supermarket or a *pekarnica* (bakery). Small outlets may offer a simple white loaf and little else, although you'll usually be offered a wide choice of breads, ranging from French sticks through wholemeal loaves to pumpernickel-style black breads. You'll have to point at what you want though: names of different loaves differ from one place to the next. A *pekarnica* may often sell sandwiches – filled most commonly with ham, cheese or *pršut*, Croatia's excellent home-cured ham.

For **snacks**, look out for *slastičarnice* selling *burek*, a flaky pastry filled with cheese; it's delicious when fresh, although it can be stodgy and greasy if left standing for too long. For a more substantial snack, try the traditional southeast European repertoire of grilled meats: *ćevapi*, *ražnjići* (shish kebab) or *pljeskavica*, all of which are often served in a *somun* – a flat bread bun which is rather larger than a standard Western-style burger bun. Although these basic grill snacks will be on the menu of all but the grandest restaurants, they're at their best in the unpretentious fast-food places you'll find clustered around markets and bus stations. For an excellent light lunch, look out for the traditional working-man's food of inland Croatia, **grah** (or *fažol* in Dalmatia), a delicious soup of paprika-spiced haricot beans (*grah* literally means "beans") with bits of sausage or *pljeskavica* added. While in Istria, look out for *maneštra*, a rich bean and vegetable soup which often includes sweetcorn.

Drinking

Drinking takes place in a *kavana* (café) – usually a roomy and comfortable place with plenty of outdoor seating and serving the full range of alcoholic and non-alcoholic drinks, as well as pastries and ice creams – or in a *kafić* (café-bar), essentially a smaller version of the same thing, although usually catering to a younger clientele. The word "pub" is frequently adopted by café-bars attempting to imitate British, or more often Irish, styles; these places will probably have Guinness adverts on the walls and a familiar range of Irish brews on tap. Both cafés and café-bars open extraordinarily early (sometimes as early as 6am) in order to serve the first espresso to those going to work, although alcohol isn't served until 9am. Closing time is usually 11pm, although regulations are often relaxed in summer, when café-bars stay open much later. You can also find coffee and soft drinks in a *slastičarnica* (often also the best place to find freshly made lemonade), although they're often less atmospheric than a *kavana* or a *kafić* and may close earlier in the evening. Few Croatian cafés of any kind serve substantial food except for the odd sandwich.

Most Croatian **beer** is of the light lager variety. Karlovačko and Ožujsko are the two most common brands, although the less widespread Velebit from Gospić is probably the best. Domestic dark beers include Tomislav from Zagreb and Osiječko Crno from Osijek. Certain foreign brands – Stella Artois, Tuborg and Laško (from Slovenia) – are made in Croatia under licence. Guinness and Kilkenny are the most common foreign beers you're likely to find served on tap in café-bars and pubs. Whether you're drinking beer in bottles or on tap, a *malo pivo* (small beer) usually means 30cl and costs 12–15Kn, a *veliko pivo* (large beer) is a half-litre and will set you back 15–25Kn. Bottled beers are slightly more expensive.

Croatia produces an impressive range of red and white **wines**, few of which find their way onto Western supermarket shelves. Among the dry and medium-dry whites, look out for Vrbnička Žlahtina from Vrbnik on Krk; Vugava from Vis; Semion and Malvazija from Istria; and Kaštelet, Grk and Pošip from Korčula. Of the reds, the dark heady Dingač from the Pelješac peninsula has the best reputation and is the most expensive, although Babić from Primošten and Viški plavac from Vis are frequently as good, as is Teran, a fresh, light red from Istria. In shops and supermarkets table wine sells for about 25–50Kn per litre bottle, while a decent Dingač will set you back about 90Kn. Popular wine-derived drinks include *bevanda* (white or red wine mixed with plain water), *gemišt* (white wine and fizzy mineral water), *špricer* (white wine and soda water) and the eternally popular summer tipple *bambus* (red wine mixed with cola).

Local **spirits** (*žestoka pića*) are commonly consumed as an aperitif before meals and are usually produced from grapes (in which case they're called *loza* or *lozovača*) or from other fruits – the most common of these being plum brandy (*šljivovica*) and pear brandy (*vilijamovka*). Grape-based spirits are often given additional flavours and have health-giving properties, notably as *travarica* (herb brandy), *medovina* (honey brandy) and *orahovača* (walnut brandy). *Pelinkovac* is a juniper-based spirit similar to Jaegermeister, *vinjak* is locally produced cognac, and *maraskino* is a cherry liqueur from Zadar in Dalmatia. *Biska* is a mistletoe-flavoured aperitif from inland Istria. Foreign brandies and whiskies are available pretty much everywhere.

Apart from the vast urns of overstewed brown liquid served up by hotels at breakfast time, **coffee** is usually of a high quality. It is served as a strong black espresso unless specified otherwise – *kava sa mlijekom* comes with a drop of milk, *kava sa šlagom* comes with cream, and *bijela kava* (white coffee) is usually like a good *caffè latte*. Cappucino is also fairly ubiquitous. **Tea** is usually of the herbal variety; ask for *indijski čaj* (Indian tea) if you want the English-style brew. *Čaj sa limunom* is with a slice of lemon, *sa mlijekom* comes with milk.

In the best cafés coffee is served with an accompanying glass of water; otherwise feel free to ask for one. **Mineral water** and other soft drinks are often served in multiples of 10cl or *dec* (pronounced "dets"). If you want 20cl of mineral water ask for *dva deca*, 30cl is *tri deca*. If you want fruit juice, note that the word *đus* ("juice") usually means orange juice.

The media

Having enjoyed a lively media scene in the 1980s and 1990s, when political and social changes were reflected in a startling array of opinionated and often subversive newspapers and magazines, Croatia has settled down to something approaching central European sobriety.

The most prestigious national **daily newspaper**, *Vjesnik* (Ⓦwww.vjesnik.com), has a reputation for stodgy reporting and obsequiousness to whichever government happens to be in power. In comparison, the other national daily, *Jutarnji List*, is breezy and populist, contains much more showbiz gossip and is more independent politically. Closest to Western tabloids in style is the evening paper *Večernji List* (Ⓦwww.vecernji-list.hr), which nevertheless includes good cultural coverage buried among the human interest stories.

The most influential of the **weeklies** is *Globus*, a glossy news magazine that reflects the broadly pro-Western, pro-liberal attitudes of Zagreb's emerging business class. However, it fails to inspire the love and respect enjoyed by Split's *Feral Tribune* (Ⓦwww.feral.hr), an irreverent cross between serious news magazine and counter-cultural youth rag, which began life as a humorous and satirical supplement of *Slobodna Dalmacija* (Dalmatia's leading regional newspaper) in the late 1980s. *Feral* was an important source of opposition to the HDZ during the 1990s, offering a vibrant alternative to the stuffy and uninspiring political analysis served up by other papers and frequently ridiculing Franjo Tuđman. Tuđman took it personally and attempted a number of ruses to have *Feral* shut down – having it classified as a pornographic publication in order to qualify it for a higher tax rate, taking its editor to court for defaming the office of the president and threatening its staff with military call-up being just three. Now that Tuđman is no longer around, *Feral* has lost much of its bite, but remains the main anti-establishment voice in the country.

An increasing range of **foreign-language newspapers** is available from news kiosks in Zagreb and on the coast. Many of the best-known English, German and Italian dailies are on sale within 24 hours of publication, and are usually two or three times more expensive than in their home countries. International fashion, lifestyle and computer magazines are fairly ubiquitous. Best of the tourist-oriented publications are the informative, A5-sized city guides published by **In Your Pocket** (ⓦwww.inyourpocket.com), available free from tourist offices, hotels and some restaurants. As well as *Zagreb in your Pocket* (published six times a year), there are seasonally updated guides to the cities of Rijeka, Zadar, Dubrovnik and Osijek.

TV and radio

Like some of Croatia's newspapers, the two main **national television channels**, both run by state-owned HRT (Hrvatski radio i televizija), have a history of deference to successive governments, although they're now far from being the blatant propaganda tools they were under the communists and then the HDZ. Current output tends towards the didactic, dominated by plodding documentaries about Croatian history and culture, although HRT1 produces plenty of lavish shows featuring Croatian pop stars, especially in the summer when outdoor concerts are screened. **Privately owned stations** RTL and Nova TV have more in the way of imported soaps and dramas. In summer, **Croatia Radio** (92.1Mhz), along with numerous local stations on the coast, puts out regular English-language news bulletins.

With a shortwave radio, you can pick up the broadcasts of the BBC World Service (ⓦwww.bbc.co.uk/worldservice), Voice of America (ⓦwww.voa.gov) and Radio Canada (ⓦwww.rcinet.ca) among others; check their respective websites for frequencies and schedules.

Festivals

As befits a devoutly Catholic country, the Croatian year is peppered with feast days and religious holidays, featuring church processions and celebratory masses. In addition, each town or village has its own patron saint, whose feast day becomes the excuse for a communal knees-up – a selection is included below.

The church calendar frequently dovetails with an older pagan one, corresponding to the changing seasons and the agricultural cycle. The most important event in the early part of the year is the pre-Lenten **carnival** (*karneval*; often known as *fašnik* in inland Croatia, *pust* on the Adriatic), which actually begins before Christmas but does not reach a climax until Shrove Tuesday or the weekend immediately preceding it, when there are processions and masked revelry in towns all over Croatia. A lot of places organize parades with floats, the participants donning disguises which frequently satirize local politicians or comment on the events of the past year. Rijeka, Samobor and Velika Gorica (just south of Zagreb) host the biggest events. The amount of post-parade hedonism differs from place to place, although the recently revived carnival in Split has already earned a reputation for its relaxed party atmosphere. Carnival processions are repeated in summer in some Adriatic resorts – a fun fancy-dress affair aimed at children and tourists. In smaller places carnival practices are still linked to pre-Christian fertility rites: in the villages near Rijeka groups of men (called *zvončari* or "ringers") don sheepskins and ring bells to drive away evil spirits, while in many areas a doll known as *pust* (or *poklad* in Lastovo) is ritually burned in order to cleanse the coming agricultural year of bad luck.

The next big event is **Easter week**, characterized by solemn processions in many towns, especially Hvar, Korčula and Vodice. Traditionally, the beginning of the summer agricultural cycle was marked by **St George's Day** (Jurjevo; April 23), when a villager clad in branches and known as Zeleni Juraj (Green George) went from house to house accompanied by local children performing songs and dances. He received a gift from each household and in return presented them with a fertility charm in the form of a twig. Sadly, you'll see references to Jurjevo in ethnographic museums more often than in real life, although it's still celebrated in the villages of the Stubica valley north of Zagreb, and at Donja Lomnica, Gradići, Hrašće and Lukavac just south of Zagreb (the Zagreb county tourist office will have details of many of these; Ⓦwww.tzzz.hr).

Another celebration with distinct pagan undertones is **St John's Day** (June 24), when local youths jump over bonfires (*Ivanjski krijes*) in a typical summer-solstice celebration. It's still practised in many places, especially in Karlovac. High summer is characterized by a sequence of important Christian holidays. **Our Lady of the Snows** (Aug 5) is celebrated with processions to churches associated with "miraculous" summer snowfalls, most famously at Kukljica on the island of Ugljan, where the procession takes the form of a flotilla of small boats. More important still is the **Assumption** (Aug 15), when churches throughout the country hold special services, and large pilgrimages are made to Marian shrines such as Marija Bistrica near Zagreb, Krasno near Senj, Ludbreg between Varaždin and Koprivnica, Sinj in the Dalmatian hinterland, and Trsat near Rijeka. The **Birth of the Virgin** (Sept 8) is only slightly less important in the Catholic calendar, and is celebrated in similar fashion.

All Saints' Day (Nov 1) is one of the most important Catholic feasts of the autumn, when families visit graveyards to pay their respects to the departed. By the evening, many big-city cemeteries are transformed into a sea of candles. **St Martin's Day** (Nov 11) is traditionally the day when the year's wine is first tasted, and is often used as an excuse for revelry in wine-producing areas. In accordance with a widespread central European tradition, St Martin's Day is also marked by the slaughter and roasting of a goose. A slaughter of a more widespread kind takes place at the end of November, when many rural families (especially in Slavonia and the Dalmatian hinterland) set aside a weekend in order to carry out the annual **pig slaughter** (*svinokolja* or *kolinja*), and begin preparation of the sausages and hams which will be consumed over the next year.

On **St Nicholas's Day** (Dec 6) children leave out stockings and are rewarded with small presents if they're good. They also receive a gold- or silver-painted twig (*šiba*) – a symbol of the beating they will receive should they misbehave. Children are also threatened by visits from the monster Krampus, a kind of St Nicholas in reverse, who takes away bad children in his bag. **Christmas** itself is much the same as anywhere else in Europe, with presents laid out under the family Christmas tree. The main family meal is eaten on Christmas Eve (Badnja večer), and traditionally consists of fish (often carp), after which everyone attends midnight mass.

The country's main **folk festival** is the International Folklore Festival, held in Zagreb on the last weekend of July and traditionally the best place to see songs and dances from all over the country. The tradition of the Dalmatian *klapa* (male-voice choir) is preserved in numerous festivals up and down the coast, the biggest being the one held in Omiš in July. The remaining big folk events are all in Slavonia and have a more regional character, although the Brodsko Kolo Festival in Slavonski Brod (mid-June), Vinkovci Autumn (late Sept) and Đakovo Folk Festival (end Sept) are all worthwhile shindigs. Guests in Adriatic hotels will be treated to folklore shows, often over dinner, throughout the summer season. Local songs and dances are performed outside the church in Čilipi, near Dubrovnik, every Sunday morning.

Feast days and folkloric events

Feb 2 Kumpanjija Sword Dance, Korčula.
Feb 3 Feast of St Blaise, Dubrovnik.
Sunday before Shrove Tuesday Carnival Procession, Rijeka.
Shrove Tuesday Carnival Procession, Split.
Good Friday Procession of the Religious Brotherhoods, Korčula.
April 23 St George's Day (Jurjevo).
May 7 Feast of St Domnius, Split.
May 8 Birthday of Cardinal Stepinac, Krašić.
Second weekend in May Roč Accordion Festival.
June Festival of Međimurje songs (Međimurske popevke), Nedelišće, midway between Varaždin and Čakovec.
Mid-June Brodsko Kolo Folklore Festival, Slavonski Brod.
June 24 St John's Day (Ivanje).
July Susret sopaca (Meeting of Sopila Players), Pinezići, Krk. A festival of *sopila* (a sort of shrill oboe).
July Klapa Festival, Omiš.
Mid-July Summer Carnival, Novi Vinodolski.
July 25 Feast of St James. Performances of the Kumpanjija Sword Dance, Korčula.
July 27 St Christopher's Day. Crossbow Tournament, Rab.
July 29 Feast of St Theodore. Performance of the Moreška Sword Dance, Korčula.
July 30 Day of Susak. The island of Susak celebrates itself, with many Susak exiles and their descendants returning for the occasion.
Late July Carnival, Iž.
Late July International Folklore Festival, Zagreb.
July or August Krk Folklore Festival.
Early Aug Fešta od srdela (Anchovy Festival), Fažana. Food and folklore.
Early Aug Sinjska Alka, Sinj. A sort of medieval joust held in celebration of the 1715 victory over the Turks.
Early Aug Saljske užance, Sali. Folk festival and town carnival.
Aug 5 Feast of Our Lady of the Snows (Madona od snijega/sniga). Boat procession on Ugljan; and performance of the Kumpanjija Sword Dance, Korčula.
Aug 8 Feast of St Lawrence.
Mid-Aug Tilting at the Ring (Trka na prstenac), Barban. Competition in which horsemen attempt to spear a ring on the end of a lance.
Aug 15 Assumption (Velika Gospa). Large gatherings at Marija Bistrica, Trsat, Sinj and Aljmaš.
Aug 16 Feast of St Rock. Performance of the Moštra Sword Dance at Postrana and the Kumpanjija Sword Dance at Korčula.
Aug 27–29 Feast of St Pelagius, Novigrad.
Late Aug/early Sept Kaj su jeli naši stari (What our forefathers ate), Vrbovec, just east of Zagreb. Traditional food and folklore festival.
Mid-Sept Vinkovačka Jesen (Vinkovci Autumn), Vinkovci. Folklore Festival.
Sept 8 Birth of the Virgin (Mala Gospa).
Last weekend in Sept Đakovački vezovi (Đakovo Embroidery), Đakovo. Folklore festival with singing and dancing.
Last weekend in Sept Grape Harvest Festival, Pregrada, Zagorje.
Oct 8 Feast of St Simeon, Zadar. Religious procession and opening of St Simeon's coffin.
Nov 1 All Saints' Day (Svi sveti).
Nov 11 Feast of St Martin (Martinje). Celebrations at Dugo Selo, Tar, Vrsar and Buzet.
Dec 6 Feast of St Nicholas (Sveti Nikola). Presents are given to children and a fishing boat is burnt outside the Benedictine monastery at Komiža, Vis.
Dec 25 Christmas (Božić).

Cultural festivals

Every Adriatic town organizes cultural events of some sort over the summer, usually featuring outdoor concerts of pop, classical music or folk. The most important of these is the **Dubrovnik Summer Festival**, six weeks of classical music and drama beginning in early July, much of which is performed in the squares and courtyards of the old town. The Dubrovnik Festival's only real rival in the high-culture stakes is the **Split Summer**, which offers a varied diet of top-notch music and theatre. Historical buildings also form the backdrop for a number of other classical music events, including the Osor Music Evenings on the island of Cres; summer concerts in the half-abandoned hill village of Lubenice, also on Cres; the Musical Summer in the Istrian hill town of Grožnjan; summer recitals in St Donat's Church in Zadar; and the Varaždin Festival of Baroque Music, which uses many of the city's fine churches.

Zagreb has a full roster of festival events, the most prestigious being the Biennale of New Music, a festival of cutting-edge contemporary classical work held in odd-numbered years. Challenging new work also crops up at the Contemporary Dance Week in early June; Eurokaz European Theatre Festival in late June, and PIF international puppet festival in late August.

Avant-garde traditions elsewhere in the country are showcased at the Požega festival of one-minute films, the Zadar Dreams festival of new theatre, the Split Festival of Creative Disorder and Split's Festival of New Film and Video.

Outdoor rock concerts and dance events take place all over the Adriatic coast in summer. The Valkana Beach Festival near Pula in August is one of the better established rave and techno extravaganzas, although new ones are emerging all the time.

Croatian arts festivals

March Test! Festival of Student Theatre, Zagreb. Ⓦ www.test.hr.

March Žedno Uho (Thirsty Ear), Zagreb. Alternative music festival. Ⓦ www.sczg.hr.

Late April Biennale of New Music, Zagreb (odd-numbered years only).

May Festival of the European Short Story, Zagreb.

May Festival of One-Minute Films, Požega.

Early June Contemporary Dance Week (Tjedan suvremenog plesa), Zagreb.

Late June Eurokaz Festival of Contemporary Theatre, Zagreb.

Late July International Folklore Festival, Zagreb. Ⓦ www.msf.hr.

Late June to early Aug Zadar Theatrical Summer (Zadarsko kazališno ljeto), Zadar. Contemporary drama and dance from Croatia and abroad.

Late June to July Rijeka Summer Nights (Riječke ljetne noći), Rijeka. International theatre and music. Ⓦ www.rijeckeljetnenoci.com.

Late June to late Aug Kastav Cultural Summer (Kastafsko kulturno leto). Concerts in the streets and squares of Kastav, near Rijeka. Ⓦ www.kkl.hr.

Early July Split Jazz Festival.

Early July to late Aug Dubrovnik Summer Festival (Dubrovačke ljetne igre). Ⓦ www.dubrovnik-festival.hr.

Early July to late August Lubenice Music Nights (Lubeničke glazbene večeri). Chamber concerts and solo recitals in the village of Lubenice, Cres.

Early July Podravski motivi Local arts and crafts, Koprivnica.

July Osor Music Evenings (Osorske večeri), Osor, Cres. International chamber music festival.

July Zagreb Baroque Festival (Zagrebački barokni festival) Ⓦ www.zabaf.hr.

July Istria Ethno Jazz, Pula, Pazin and Svetvinčenat.

Mid- to late July Festival of Dance and Non-verbal Theatre (Festival plesa i neverbalnog kazališta), Svetvinčenat.

Mid-July to mid-Aug Zadar Theatrical Summer (Zadarsko kazališno ljeto).

July to early Aug Concerts in the Church of St Donat (Glazbene večeri u sv. Donatu), Zadar. Top-class chamber musicians from around the world. Ⓦ www.donat-festival.com.

Mid-July to mid-Aug Split Summer (Splitsko ljeto), Split. Music and drama staged in what was once Diocletian's Palace. Ⓦ www.splitsko-ljeto.hr.

Late July Diocletian Night (Noć Dioklecijana), Split. Locals dress up as ancient Romans for a night of city-centre partying, symbolically welcoming third-century Emperor Diocletian back into town.

Late July to early Aug Grožnjan Jazz Festival.

Early Aug Valkana Beach Festival, Pula. DJs and club culture.

Aug Ethno Ambient Live, Salona, near Split. World music.

Aug Croatian Film Festival, Pula.

Aug International Film Festival, Motovun. Ⓦ www.motovunfilmfestival.com

Aug Zadar Dreams (Zadar snova). Festival of alternative drama and performance art.

Aug Festival of Creative Disorder (Festival kreativnog nereda), Split. Alternative art, music and performance.

Aug Kamplin Jazz Festival, Krk.

Aug Musical Summer (Glazbeno ljeto), Grožnjan.

Late Aug Pontes Literature Festival, Krk. Ⓦ www.pontes.com.

Late Aug to early Sept PIF International Festival of Puppet Theatre (Međunarodni festival kazališta lutaka), Zagreb.

Late Aug to early Sept Špancirfest, Varaždin. Open-air music in all genres. Ⓦ www.spancirfest.com.

Sept Festival of World Theatre (Festival svijetskog kazališta), Zagreb. Prestigious event attracting big names in European drama; the likes of Peter Brook and Oskaras Koršunovas have directed here in recent years. Ⓦ www.zagrebtheatrefestival.hr.

Mid-Sept International Festival of Experimental Film and Video (Internacionalni festival eksperimentalnog filma i videa), Zagreb. Projections of weird and wonderful films in the Students' Centre. Ⓦ www.25fps.hr.

Late Sept to early Oct Split Film Festival, Split. Shorts, documentaries and art-house films. Ⓦ www.splitfilmfestival.hr.

Late Sept to early Oct Varaždin Festival of Baroque Music. Performances in Varaždin cathedral and other city churches.

Oct Zagreb Film Festival, Zagreb.

Oct or Nov Nebo World Music Festival, Zagreb.

Nov Earwing No Jazz Festival, Zagreb. Sonic weirdness. Ⓦ www.sczg.hr.

Sports and the outdoors

Croatia is an increasingly versatile destination for adventure tourism, with numerous outdoor activities on offer, from hiking in the hills of the interior to scuba-diving in the Adriatic. Sailing is best organized before you arrive (see p.29). Croatian team and individual sports occupy an important position in society, not least because of the significant role they have played in enhancing national prestige abroad – the outstanding example of course is former Wimbledon champion Goran Ivanišević, whose face you'll see on billboards advertising everything from bank accounts to beer.

Spectator sports

Football (*nogomet*) has come a long way in Croatia since it was introduced to the country in 1893 by the crew of a British frigate who took on a team of locals just outside Trogir's main town gate. Croatian footballers formed an important part of the Yugoslav sides of the 1960s and 1970s, whose reputation for skill and audacity earned them the tag of "the Brazilians of Europe", although few imagined the impression the Croats would make on the international scene in the 1990s. Resting on a backbone of talented individuals including Zmonimir Boban, Robert Prosinečki, Davor Šuker, Alen Bokšić, Slaven Bilić and Igor Štimac, the Croatian team finished third in the 1998 World Cup, beating Germany 3–0 in the quarter-finals before narrowly succumbing in the semis to host nation France. However, Croatia performed poorly in the 2002 and 2006 World Cups, leading many to believe that the golden age of Croatian football is over.

The domestic league is hampered by a lack of real competition. The big teams Dinamo Zagreb and Hajduk Split have more or less monopolized domestic honours since 1991, occasionally challenged by the likes of NK Zagreb, Rijeka and Osijek. Both Hajduk and Dinamo (under their previous name of Croatia Zagreb) have performed creditably in the UEFA Champions' League, although both teams are hamstrung by the fact that their best players invariably leave to play abroad as soon as they've made a name for themselves. Matches between the big two can attract big crowds, but otherwise attendances are all too often in the low thousands, with most fans content to follow the game on TV instead.

The football season lasts from mid-August to late May, with a two-month winter break in January and February. Matches usually take place on Saturdays or Sundays, with extra games scheduled for Wednesday evenings as the season draws to a climax in April/May. The cheapest seats rarely cost more than 30Kn. Tickets for all but the biggest matches can be bought at the ground before the game. For international matches (usually played at Dinamo Zagreb's Maksimir stadium) or European ties, purchase tickets from the stadium box office as far in advance as possible.

After football, the most popular sport is **basketball** (*košarka*), with teams like Split, Zadar and Cibona Zagreb enjoying large followings and a Europe-wide reputation. It's another sport in which Croatia exports its best players, with performers like Tony Kukoč, Dino Rađa and the late Dražen Petrović (see p.93) finding big-time success in the NBL. **Handball** (*rukomet*), **volleyball** (*odbojka*) and **waterpolo** (*vaterpolo*) all get a good deal of newspaper and television coverage. One sport which is definitely not televised – although you'll see a lot of it in Dalmatia and Istria – is a form of **bowls** known as *bočanje* (derived from the Italian *boccie*), which is played in villages on a sandy outdoor rectangle by local men on summer evenings. Finally, no discussion of Croatian sport would be complete without mention of the skiing phenomenon and all-round national treasure **Janica Kostelić**, who returned from the 2002 and 2006 Winter Olympics with a record-breaking haul of gold medals, sending the nation into jubilant celebrations on both occasions.

You can bet on most kinds of sports in one of the betting shops (*sportska kladionica*) which have sprung up all over Croatia in recent years – nowadays there's hardly a single high street without one.

Hiking

Hiking was first popularized in Croatia in the late nineteenth century, when the exploration of the great Croatian outdoors was considered a patriotic duty as well as a form of exercise. It's still a popular weekend activity, especially in spring and early summer, before the searing Mediterranean heat sends people scurrying for the beaches.

Easy rambling territory in inland Croatia is provided by wooded **Mount Medvednica** and the **Samobor Hills** (Samoborsko gorje), both close to Zagreb and criss-crossed by well-used trails. Higher altitudes and longer walks can be found in the **Gorski kotar** region, between Karlovac and the coast: the main targets here are Risnjak in the north of the range, best reached from Rijeka, and Klek and Bijele stijene in the south. On the Adriatic coast, **Učka**, immediately above Opatija and Lovran, is one of the most easily accessible mountains, and can be safely bagged by the moderately fit hiker. Farther south, the more challenging **Velebit** range stretches for some 100km along the eastern shore of the Kvarner Gulf; its main hiking areas are around the Zavižan summit, near Senj, and the Paklenica National Park at Velebit's southern end. In Dalmatia, the principal peaks are **Kozjak** and **Mosor** (immediately west and east of Split respectively) and, most challenging of all the Adriatic mountains, **Biokovo**, above the Makarska Riviera.

Ranges such as Gorski kotar and Velebit seem to invite extended expeditions, but unfortunately hut-to-hut walking in Croatia is still in its infancy, and no local travel agencies organize it. Mountain refuges (*planinarski dom*) run by local hiking associations do exist, but they're usually only open at the weekend, making anything longer than a 36-hour trek unfeasible.

Detailed **hiking maps** are published by the Croatian Hiking Association, Kozarčeva 22, Zagreb (Hrvatski planinarski savez; Mon 8am–6pm, Tues–Fri 8am–3pm; ⓣ01/4823-624, ⓦwww.plsavez.hr/hps), although they're only sporadically available in bookshops and you'll have to visit the association in person to inspect the full range. Tourist offices sometimes sell hiking maps of their own area (for instance the tourist information centre in Zagreb sells maps of Mount Medvednica), but don't bank on it.

Rafting

In Zagreb, many of the bigger travel agents (see "Listings", p.110) offer weekend **white-water rafting** trips to the Kupa, Dobra and Mrežnica rivers from early July until late October. On the coast, tourist agencies organize trips down the River Cetina, south-east of Split, and the River Zrmanja, just east of Zadar; you'll find contact details in the relevant sections of the Guide. The rafting season usually runs from May to September, although trips on the Zrmanja may be suspended in July owing to low water levels. Prices vary according to the duration of the trip – expect to pay 250–350Kn per person for a day's excursion.

Diving

Thanks to the crystal-clear waters of the Adriatic and the diversity of the local marine life, Croatia has become one of the most popular **scuba-diving** venues in the Mediterranean over the last few years. There's a growing number of diving centres along the Adriatic coast offering lessons, guided expeditions and equipment rental. Most resorts will have somewhere offering one-day introductory courses for 250–350Kn, as well as a range of other courses for all abilities. If you already hold a diving certificate, you need to pay a registration fee (100Kn), available from registered diving centres or from the local harbour master's office (*lučka kapetanija*), before being allowed to dive in Croatia.

Two of the most rewarding areas for diving, with clear waters and rich marine life, are the **Kornati islands** in mid-Dalmatia and the island of Mljet near Dubrovnik. Both have National Park status and diving here can only be arranged through officially sanctioned operators – see the relevant sections of the Guide for details. For general information, contact the Croatian Diving Federation at Dalmatinska 12, 10 000 Zagreb (Ⓣ01/48-48-765, Ⓕ48-49-119, Ⓦwww.diving-hrs.hr).

Windsurfing

There are really only two places to go in Croatia for serious windsurfers. The best is **Bol** on the island of Brač, which stands on the northern side of the narrow channel dividing Brač from Hvar, providing calm waters and channelling the right kind of winds. Second-best is the **Kučište-Viganj** area just west of Orebić, which occupies a similar position on the Pelješac channel dividing the mainland from Korčula. Bol is a fully developed package resort with all the accommodation and nightlife opportunities one would expect; Kučište and Viganj on the other hand are unspoilt villages equipped with a few private rooms and campsites. Whichever you choose, you'll find plenty of people renting out gear (boards 200–250Kn per day) and offering courses (about 600Kn for 8hr tuition).

Sea kayaking

Sea kayaking is an increasingly popular way of exploring the coast around Dubrovnik, the Elaphite Islands and Korčula. It's extremely easy to organize, with several Dubrovnik-based travel agents (see p.450) arranging half- or full-day tours around the city walls or the nearby islands. Kayakers are led in a small flotilla by the tour leader, and apart from the few short minutes required to learn how to use a paddle, no training or previous experience is required.

Skiing

Croatia has two main skiing areas: **Sljeme** on Mount Medvednica, just outside Zagreb, and **Bjelolasica** in the Gorski Kotar between Zagreb and Rijeka. Although both are fun venues for occasional skiing if you're already visiting Croatia, neither is worth planning a holiday around. Altitudes (1035m and 1533m respectively) are too low to guarantee long periods of adequate snow cover, and most Croats treat skiing trips as spur-of-the-moment events if the weather is right. You can rent gear and sign up for lessons at either place.

Travel essentials

Addresses

The Croatian word for street, *ulica*, is either abbreviated to *ul*. or omitted altogether if the meaning is clear enough without it. The street name always comes before the number. Buildings that don't have a street number are often designated by the letters "bb", meaning *bez broja* or "without a number".

Costs

Croatia is by no means a bargain destination, and the cost of accommodation is on par with Western European countries. Eating and drinking, however, remains reasonably good value.

Accommodation will be your biggest single expense, with the average private room weighing in at around £20/€30/$36 for a double, rising to £35/€50/$60 in fashionable places like Dubrovnik. In high season the cheapest doubles in hotels hover around the £50–70/€75–100/$90–125 mark, although they can be significantly cheaper in spring or autumn.

As for **transport**, short journeys by ferry and bus (say from Split to one of the nearby islands) cost in the region of £3/€4.50/$5.50, while moving up and down the country will naturally be more expensive (a Zagreb–Split bus ticket, for instance, costs upwards of £16/€24/$28).

About £10/€15/$18 per person per day will suffice for **food and drink** if you're shopping in markets for picnic ingredients, maybe eating out in inexpensive grill-houses and pizzerias once a day, and limiting yourself to a couple of drinks in cafés; £45/€65/$85 a day will be sufficient for breakfast in a café, a sit-down lunch and a decent restaurant dinner followed by a couple of night-time drinks. The prices of accommodation, ferry tickets, international bus tickets and tourist excursions are often quoted in **euros**, although you can pay in kuna.

Prices often include a **sales tax**, known locally as PDV, of up to 22 percent. Foreign visitors can claim a PDV tax refund at the Croatian Customs Service for goods over 500Kn (around £50/€75/$90), as long as they have kept all original invoices – though the refund can take up to a year to arrive.

Crime and personal safety

The crime rate in Croatia is low by European standards. Your main defence against petty theft is to exercise common sense and refrain from flaunting luxury items. Take out an insurance policy before you leave home (see p.60) and always carry a photocopy of the crucial information-bearing pages of your passport with you – this will enable your consulate to issue you swiftly with new travel documents in the event of your passport being stolen.

Croatian police (*policija*) are generally helpful and polite when dealing with foreigners, and usually speak some English. Routine police checks on identity cards are common in Croatia: always carry your passport or driving licence. If you get into trouble with the authorities, wait until you can explain matters to someone in English if at all possible. The police are not allowed to search your car or place of abode without a warrant.

Should you be arrested, you can be held in a police station for 24 hours without charge. The police are supposed to notify your consulate of your arrest automatically, but often fail to do so.

Emergency numbers

Police ⓣ92
Ambulance ⓣ94
Fire ⓣ93
Sea rescue and diving alert ⓣ9155

Sexual harassment

Croatia is a patriarchal society in which many women find themselves holding down a full-time job while simultaneously managing the household on behalf of their menfolk. However, there are few specific situations in which female travellers might feel uncomfortable and no real no-go areas, although some of the more down-at-heel café-bars can feel like male-only preserves. By Western standards, Croatia's streets are relatively safe at night, even in the cities.

Croatian men like to regard the annual deluge of foreign female tourists as fair game, but any display of Mediterranean machismo tends to be leavened by genuine attempts at gallantry and charm. A suitably firm response should be enough to cope with unwanted attentions. Alternatively, try to imitate the repertoire of stony silences and withering looks employed by the local women.

The aftermath of war

Almost a third of Croatia was occupied by Serb forces between 1991 and 1995, and although you shouldn't have any qualms about visiting these areas now, a few precautions should be borne in mind. Almost all frontline areas were heavily **mined** during the war, and few of these minefields have been fully cleared. Most are well marked with signs bearing the skull-and-bones symbol and the word "mine", although it would be unwise to trust this marking system one hundred percent – some mined areas may not be as well labelled as others. Basically, any abandoned village or stretch of agricultural land which looks as if it has been left uncultivated since 1995 is potentially dangerous. If you're travelling to eastern Slavonia (Beli Manastir, Vukovar, Ilok), western Slavonia (Jasenovac, Novska, Pakrac), the area between Karlovac and Split (Slunj to Knin) and the Zadar hinterland, stick to roads and pavements and don't go wandering off into the countryside unsupervised.

Travellers exploring the above itineraries are likely to see **war damage** in the shape of shelled buildings and burned-out houses, but also a great deal of energetic building and reconstruction. Both Croats and Serbs are returning to areas where they once lived side by side, and outbreaks of inter-communal violence are now few and far between. However, the casual visitor will probably miss the nuances of Croat–Serb relations: tension still exists, many refugees continue to occupy houses claimed by others, and each community tends to stick to its own cafés and bars. Exercise discretion therefore before embarking on historical or political discussions with the locals.

Culture and etiquette

Tips (*napojnice*) are not obligatory, and wait staff don't expect them if you've only had a cup of coffee or a sandwich. If you've had a round of drinks or a full meal, it's polite to round up the bill by ten percent or to the nearest convenient figure.

Smoking is more widespread in Croatia than in Western Europe and North America, and bars are not always well ventilated. Croatian restaurants and cafés are required by law to provide **no-smoking areas**, but these are rarely sufficiently isolated for them to make much difference.

Public toilets (*zahod* or *WC*) are rare outside bus or train stations, although every restaurant and café-bar will have one.

Wearing skimpy **beachwear** is OK on the beach itself, but you're advised to cover up if entering bars or restaurants, or catching a bus back to your hotel.

Topless bathing is acceptable almost anywhere, but entering cafés or buses in your beachwear is strongly disapproved of. Naturism (denoted locally by the German acronym "FKK") has a long history on the Adriatic coast. There are self-contained naturist holiday villages in Istria (the biggest are just outside Poreč, Rovinj and Vrsar), and naturist campsites in Istria and the island of Krk. Throughout Croatia, you'll find isolated coves or stretches of beach which have been set aside for naturists, at a discreet distance from the main family-oriented sections.

Disabled travellers

More attention has been paid to Croatians with disabilities since the 1991–95 war, in view of the large number of wounded and disabled veterans it created. Many public places in Croatia are wheelchair accessible, especially in larger cities, though in general, access to public transport and tourist sites still leaves a lot to be desired.

There's a growing number of **wheelchair-accessible hotels**, though these tend to be in the more expensive price brackets. Some areas of the country seem slower to adapt than others – at the last visit, the fashionable town of Hvar didn't have a single hotel with wheelchair access.

Tourist offices throughout Croatia will usually find out whether there are any suitable accommodation facilities in their region if you ring in advance, but be sure to double-check the information they give you – some tourist office listings optimistically state that a place has disabled facilities, when in fact it doesn't.

The Association of Organizations of Disabled People in Croatia (Savez Organizacija Invalida Hrvatske) Savska cesta 3, 10 000 Zagreb ⓣ01/48-29-394, ⓦwww.soih.hr publishes informative guides – though in Croatian only – for disabled travellers to Zagreb, Pula, Split, Varaždin and Rijeka.

Electricity

Wall sockets in Croatia operate at 220 volts and take round, two-pin plugs. A standard continental adaptor allows the use of 13-amp, square-pin plugs.

Entry requirements

Citizens of EU countries, the US, Canada, Australia and New Zealand are allowed to enter Croatia without a visa for stays of up to ninety days. If you want to stay longer, it's easier to leave the country and re-enter than to go through the hassle of applying for an extension at the local police station.

Visitors to Croatia are required by law to **register** with the local police within 24 hours of arrival. If you're staying in a hotel, hostel or campsite, or if you've booked a private room through a recognized agency, the job of registration will be done for you. If you're staying with friends or in a room arranged privately, your hosts are supposed to register you. In practice however, they very rarely do so. This only becomes a problem if the police have reason to question you about where you're staying, which in well-touristed areas is very rare. Even if they do, official attitudes to registration are flexible: the police often turn a blind eye to tourists and hosts alike if you're merely enjoying a short holiday on the coast, but can throw you out of the country if you've been staying in Croatia unregistered for a long period of time.

There are no **customs** restrictions on the kind of personal belongings that you need for your holiday, although you are limited to 200 cigarettes, one litre of spirits and 500g of coffee. It's a good idea to declare major items – laptop computers, televisions and other electronic equipment, boats – to ensure that you can take them out of the country when you leave. Pets are allowed in, providing you have a recent vaccination certificate. Note that when leaving you can only take 2000Kn of currency with you.

Croatian embassies and consulates

Australia 14 Jindalee Crescent, O'Malley, Canberra ACT 2606 ⓣ02/6286 6988, ⓕ6286 3544, ⓔcroemb@bigpond.com. Also consulates in Sydney, Melbourne and Perth.
Canada 229 Chapel Street, Ottawa, ON K1N 7Y6 ⓣ613/562-7820, ⓕ562-7821, ⓦwww.croatiaemb.net.
Ireland Adelaide Chambers, Peter St, Dublin 8 ⓣ01/476 7181, ⓔcroatianembassy@eircom.net.
New Zealand 131 Lincoln Rd, Henderson, PO Box 83-200 Edmonton, Auckland ⓣ09/836 5581, ⓕ836 5481, ⓔecro-consulate@xtra.co.nz.
UK 21 Conway St, London W1P 5HL ⓣ0870/005 6709, ⓦhttp://croatia.embassyhomepage.com.
US 2343 Massachusetts Ave NW, Washington, DC 20008 ⓣ202/588-5899, ⓕ588-8936, ⓦwww.croatiaemb.org. Also consulates in New York, Chicago and Los Angeles.

Gay and lesbian travellers

Although homosexuality has been legal in Croatia since 1977, it remains something of an underground phenomenon, and public displays of affection between members of the same sex may provoke hostility, especially outside big cities. The younger generation is more liberal in its attitudes to homosexuality, and though there are few recognized gay hangouts, some of the more alternative clubs in Zagreb have a reputation for attracting a tolerant, mixed crowd. Adriatic beaches where same-sex couples will feel comfortable include those around the Istrian resorts of Rovinj and Poreč, on Sveti Jerolim near Hvar, and on Lokrum near Dubrovnik.

The website ⓦhttp://travel.gay.hr offers useful travel tips on various Croatian destinations. The main organization for the advancement of gay and lesbian rights in Croatia, Iskorak (ⓦwww.iskorak.hr), has a site with some general English language information.

Health

No inoculations are required for travel to Croatia. Standards of public health are good, and tap water is safe everywhere. However, anyone planning to spend time walking in the mountains should consider being inoculated against tick-borne encephalitis.

Minor complaints can be treated at a **pharmacy** (*ljekarna*); in cities, many of the staff will speak some English, while even in places where the staff speak only Croatian, it should be easy enough to obtain repeat prescriptions if you bring along the empty pill container. A rota system ensures that there will be one pharmacy open at night-time and weekends – details are posted in the window of each pharmacy.

For serious complaints, head for the nearest **hospital** (*bolnica* or *klinički centar*), or call an **ambulance** (ⓣ94). Hospital treatment is free to citizens of most EU countries, including the UK and Ireland, on production of a valid passport; nationals of other countries should check whether their government has a reciprocal health agreement, or ensure they have adequate insurance cover. Conditions in Croatian hospitals are generally good, although expensive western drugs are sometimes in short supply, and you might have to buy your own.

Insurance

You'd do well to take out an **insurance policy** before travelling to cover against theft, loss and illness or injury. A typical travel insurance policy usually provides cover for the loss of baggage, tickets and – up to a certain limit – cash or cheques, as well as cancellation or curtailment of your journey. Most of them exclude so-called dangerous sports unless an extra premium is paid: in Croatia this can mean scuba-diving, whitewater rafting, windsurfing and trekking, though probably not kayaking or jeep safaris. If you need to make a claim, you should keep receipts for medicines and medical treatment, and in the event you have anything stolen, you must obtain an official statement from the police.

Internet

Internet cafés are well established in Croatia's cities, and are increasingly common in the Adriatic resorts as well. Prices are generally reasonable: expect to pay around 20–30Kn per hour online. Some Internet cafés require customers to register as members (usually free of charge) before allowing use of the computers – so you might want to keep a passport or other form of ID handy.

Laundry

Self-service launderettes are hard to come by in Croatia, although most towns have a laundry (*praonica*) where you can leave a service wash.

Living in Croatia

High levels of unemployment in Croatia ensure that work is not that easy to find, and local wages are in any case pretty low – anything above £500/€725/$950 a month is generous indeed. All foreigners need a work permit in order to be employed in Croatia: few employers actually enjoy this kind of paperwork and are even less likely to take you on as a result.

Teaching English has traditionally been the main opportunity for work in Croatia, though even here jobs aren't always easy to come by: the standard of local English teaching is reasonably high and few schools specifically seek out native English speakers. Vacancies are unlikely to be advertised anywhere; most people find work through personal contacts rather than official channels. If you're determined to get a teaching job, consider getting a CELTA (Certificate in English Language Teaching to Adults) qualification before you leave home. Strictly speaking, you don't need a degree to do the course, but you'll certainly find it easier to get a job with the degree/certificate combination. The British Council in the UK (Ⓣ0161/957 7755, Ⓦwww.britishcouncil.org) recruits TEFL teachers for posts worldwide and occasionally has placements in Croatia; check the website for a current list of vacancies.

Voluntary work helping to protect the griffon vultures on the island of Cres can be arranged through ECCIB (Eco-centre Caput Insulae in Beli), Beli 4, Cres (Ⓣ051/840-525, Ⓦwww.caput-insulae.com). Dolphin monitoring is another possibility, with volunteer programmes organized by Blue World on the island of Lošinj (Ⓣ+385 51 604-666, Ⓦwww.blue-world.org). If you speak some Croatian, you could approach Suncokret, Avenija Dubrovnik 10, 10 000 Zagreb (Ⓣ01/655-1715, Ⓦwww.suncokret.hr), a non-governmental organization which provides help for socially needy Croatians and organizes programmes working with people traumatized by war. They run a couple of summer camps around the country, at which you're expected to pay for your own food and accommodation.

A number of **language schools** now offer courses in Croatian to the growing number of foreigners eager to learn it. In Zagreb, the Foreign Language Centre (Centar za strane jezike), Vodnikova 12 (Ⓣ+385 1 4829-222, Ⓦwww.vodnikova.hr) organizes regular courses and one-on-one tuition, as well as one- to four-week summer courses in Dubrovnik. Tuition in Zagreb can also be arranged by APLO, Trg bana Jelačića 1/111 (Ⓣ+385 1 4835-863, Ⓦwww.aplo-centar.com). As well as organizing tuition in London, the Croatian Language School, 65 St Mary's Rd, London W5 5RG (Ⓣ0208/948 5771, Ⓦwww.easycroatian.com) organizes summer schools in Croatia.

The Croatian Heritage Foundation (Hrvatska Matica Iseljenika) organizes summer courses on various aspects of **Croatian culture and language**, including folk music workshops. They also organize academic courses at the University of Zagreb in conjunction with American and Canadian universities. Full details can be obtained from Hrvatska Matica Iseljenika, Odjel za školstvo, Trg Stjepana Radića 3, 10 000 Zagreb (Ⓣ01/611-5116, Ⓦwww.matis.hr). For students from the USA, another resource to investigate is Ⓦwww.studyabroad.com, which carries listings of study and work programmes worldwide, including some in Croatia.

Mail

Most **post offices** (*pošta* or *HPT*) are open Monday to Friday from 7 or 8am to 7 or 8pm, and Saturday 8am to 1 or 2pm. In villages and on islands, Monday to Friday 8am to 2pm is more common, though in big towns and resorts some offices open daily, sometimes staying open until 10pm.

Airmail (*zrakoplovom*) takes about three days to reach Britain, and eight to ten to reach North America; surface mail takes at least twice as long. **Stamps** (*marke*) can be bought either at the post office or at newsstands. If you're sending parcels home, don't seal the package until the post office staff have had a look at what's inside: customs duty is charged on the export of most things, although newsprint and books are exempt. **Post restante** services are available at the main post office (*glavna pošta*) in every sizeable town – mail should be addressed to Poste Restante, followed by the name of the town. Mail sent to poste restante in Zagreb (the official address is Poste Restante, 10 000 Zagreb) is held at the post office next to the train station, which is open round the clock. American Express customers can use the mailing addresses of any branch of the Atlas travel agency – they represent American Express in Croatia and will hold your mail for two months.

Maps

The biggest range of maps covering Croatia is by Freytag & Berndt, which produces a 1:600,000 map of Slovenia, Croatia and Bosnia-Hercegovina, a 1:300,000 map of Croatia, a 1:250,000 map of Istria and northern Croatia and 1:000,000 regional maps of the Adriatic coast.

City and town plans are more difficult to come by, although tourist offices often give away (or sell quite cheaply) serviceable maps of their town or island. In addition, Freytag & Berndt publishes city plans of Zadar, Split and Dubrovnik. The best map of Zagreb is the 1:20,000 plan prepared by the Geodetski zavod Slovenije (Slovene Geodesic Institute), available in three versions: one published by a local firm in Zagreb, a second published by the Hungarian firm Cartographia and the third by Freytag & Berndt. All the above are available from shops in Croatia.

Money

Croatia's unit of currency is the **kuna** (Kn; the word kuna, meaning "marten", recalls the days in medieval Croatia when taxes were paid for in marten pelts), which is divided into 100 lipa. Coins come in denominations of 1, 5, 10, 20 and 50 lipa, and 1, 2 and 5 kuna; notes come in denominations of 5, 10, 20, 50, 100, 500 and 1000 kuna. At the time of writing, the exchange rate was reasonably stable at 11Kn to £1, 7.4Kn to €1, and 5.8Kn to US$1.

The best place to change money is at a bank (*banka*) or exchange bureau (*mjenjačnica*). **Banks** are generally open Monday to Friday 8am to 5pm, and Saturday 8am to 11am or noon, although summer opening hours often come into effect in the Adriatic, when an afternoon break is introduced and hours are lengthened to 8pm or even 10pm in the evenings to compensate. In smaller places banks normally close for lunch on weekdays year round, and aren't open at all on Saturdays. **Exchange bureaux** are often found inside travel agencies (*putničke agencije*) and have more flexible hours, remaining open until 9 or 10pm seven days a week in summer if there are enough tourists around to justify it. The larger post offices also have exchange facilities, offering rates similar to those in banks (for post office opening times, see p.61). Exchange rates in hotels usually represent extremely poor value for money.

It's relatively hard to get rid of kuna once you've left Croatia, although exchange offices in neighbouring countries such as Slovenia and Hungary often accept it. The best advice is to spend up, or change the leftovers back to hard currency before you quit the country (some banks may ask to see your exchange receipts before doing this, so keep them safe).

Traveller's cheques are the safest way to carry money, and can be exchanged in almost all banks and exchange bureaux in Croatia for a one to two percent commission. The cheques can be in US dollars, pounds sterling or euros – all are accepted with equal enthusiasm. American Express cheques can also be exchanged at any office of the Atlas Travel Agency.

Credit cards are accepted in most hotels and in the more expensive restaurants and shops, and can be used to get cash advances in banks (note that these can incur high rates of interest). You can use **credit and debit cards** to withdraw cash from ATMs, found in all Croatian town centres and at most points of arrival in the country.

Opening hours and public holidays

Shops in Croatia are usually open Monday to Friday from 8am to 8pm, and on Saturdays from 8am to 2 or 3pm. City supermarkets often stay open until about 6pm on Saturdays, and open on Sunday mornings, as well. On the coast, during summer, shops introduce a long afternoon break and stay open later in the evenings to compensate. Office hours are generally Monday to Friday 8am to 3 or 4pm.

Tourist offices, travel agents and tourist attractions often change their opening times as the year progresses, generally remaining open for longer during the summer season (usually June–Sept).

On the coast, **museums and galleries** are often open all day every day (sometimes with a long break in the afternoon) in July and August, and closed altogether in the depths of winter. At other times, things can be unpredictable, with attractions opening their doors when tourist traffic seems to justify it. In big cities and inland areas, museums and galleries are more likely to have regular opening times year round, and are often closed on Mondays.

Churches in city centres and well-touristed areas usually stay open daily between 7am and 7pm or later, but many in smaller towns and villages only open their doors around Mass times. Churches or chapels which are known for being architecturally unique or which contain valuable frescoes may have set opening times (in which case we've mentioned them in the Guide); otherwise you'll have to ask around to establish which of the locals has been nominated as holder of the key (*ključ*).

Monasteries are often open from dawn to dusk to those who want to stroll around the cloister, although churches or art collections belonging to the monasteries conform to the opening patterns for museums and churches outlined above. Accessibility often depends on the number of monks in residence and the regulations governing the monastic order itself – Benedictines, for example, have strict rules governing how much of the day should be set aside for prayer, and Benedictine nuns traditionally shun contact with the outside world, thereby limiting opportunities for members of the public to visit.

Phones

Croatian **phone booths** use magnetic cards (*telekarta*), which you can pick up from post offices or newspaper kiosks.

Public holidays

All shops and banks are closed on the following public holidays:
January 1 New Year
January 6 Epiphany
March or April Easter Monday
May 1 Labour Day
May Corpus Christi
June 22 Day of the 1941 Anti-Fascist Uprising
June 25 Day of Croatian Statehood
August 5 National Thanksgiving Day
August 15 Assumption
October 8 Independence Day
November 1 All Saints' Day
December 25 & 26 Christmas

They're sold in denominations of 25, 50, 100, 200 and 500 units (*impulsa*). Generally speaking, a single unit will be enough for a local call, and the 25-unit card (costing around 13Kn) will be sufficient for making a few longer-distance calls within the country or a short international call. For international calls of longer duration, invest in a higher-value card, or head for the post office, where you're assigned a cabin from which to phone and given the bill afterwards – either way, rates are cheapest Monday to Saturday 10pm to 7am, and all day Sunday. It's best to avoid making international calls from your hotel room: charges are extortionate, and seem to rise in proportion to the star-rating of the hotel.

If you want to use your **mobile phone** abroad, you should contact your service provider to ensure that your international roaming facility is switched on (often entailing the payment of a hefty deposit); travellers from North America will also need to ensure they have a triband phone. Bear in mind that you are likely to be charged extra for incoming calls when abroad. If you want to retrieve messages while you're away, you'll have to ask your provider for a new access code, as your home one is unlikely to work abroad.

Both of Croatia's mobile phone operators, T-Com and VIP, operate schemes whereby it's possible to buy a local SIM card that you can use in your GSM phone, allowing you to make calls within the country at local rates, and to be called within Croatia without the caller incurring international charges. However you'll first need to check that you have a phone which isn't automatically blocked by your home operator when you insert a "foreign" SIM card. It will cost you around 200Kn to get on the scheme (although a certain amount of this fee is in the form of pre-payment for your future calls), after which you can purchase pre-payment top-ups in increments of 50Kn and upwards – so it's worth doing a few sums to see whether it's going to be worthwhile signing up.

Photography

Most Croatian high streets will have a photo shop where both digital and film photographers can get their holiday prints instantly developed. Film for black-and-white prints or colour transparencies is hard to get hold of outside major resorts, and you won't be offered the range you're used to at home – it's best to stock up before you leave.

Shopping

Many of Croatia's best souvenir ideas involve food and drink. Top Croatian wines can generally be picked up at high-street supermarkets, although a specialist wine shop (*vinoteka*) will stock a broader choice. Bottles of herb-flavoured *rakija*, often featuring fragments of herb in the bottle, also make good gifts. Widely available delicatessen products include truffle-based sauces and pâtées, *pršut*, figs in honey and other fruit-based preserves. Extra-virgin olive oil is as good as any in Europe. Soaps made from olive oil and fragranced with local herbs are also a good buy, as are bags of lavender, harvested on the island of Hvar.

Intricate embroidery featuring folk motifs is still produced in many areas of inland Croatia, and in the Konavle region south of Dubrovnik. Even the smallest pieces make gorgeous souvenirs, but can be very expensive. Lacemaking is still a traditional occupation in the Adriatic town of Pag, where lacemakers are frequently encountered selling their wares from doorways and living-room windows. Flea and bric-a-brac markets are a major feature in Zagreb, but are thin on the ground elsewhere.

Time

Croatia is always one hour ahead of the UK (except for one week at the end of September when the time is the same), six hours ahead of US Eastern Standard Time, nine hours ahead of Pacific Standard Time, ten hours behind Australian Eastern Standard Time, and twelve hours behind New Zealand.

Tourist information

The best source of general information on Croatia is the **Croatian National Tourist Office** (Ⓦwww.croatia.hr), but note that most of their offices abroad prefer to deal with the public by telephone rather than admit personal callers – ring ahead and check before trying to visit them in person. The staff are generally very helpful and can usually supply brochures, accommodation details and maps of specific towns and resorts. There are no Croatian tourism offices in Ireland, Canada, Australia or New Zealand – in those countries you can either contact the Croatian embassy or consulate (see p.59) or the tourist offices in London or Washington.

All towns and regions within Croatia have a tourist association (*turistička zajednica*), whose job it is to promote local tourism. Many of these maintain tourist offices (*turistički ured* or *turistički informativni centar*), although they vary a great deal in the services they offer. All can provide lists of accommodation or details of local room-letting agencies, but only some of them (usually in areas lacking a recognized accommodation agency) will book a room on your behalf. English is widely spoken, and staff in coastal resorts invariably speak German and Italian as well. Opening times vary according to the amount of tourist traffic. In July and August they might be open daily from 8am to 8pm or later, while in May, June and September, hours might be reduced to include an afternoon break or earlier closing times at weekends. Out of season, tourist offices on the coast tend to observe normal office hours (Mon–Fri 8am–3pm) or close altogether – although there's usually someone on hand to respond to faxes or email messages.

You can also get English-language information on the Croatian Angels telephone line (May–Sept: Ⓣ062 999 999), operated by the national tourist office.

Croatian tourist information offices abroad

UK Croatian National Tourist Office, 2 The Lanchesters, 162–164 Fulham Palace Rd, London W6 9ER Ⓣ0208/563 7979, Ⓕ563 2616, Ⓦwww.gb.croatia.hr.

US Croatian National Tourist Office, 350 Fifth Ave, Suite 4003, New York, NY 10118 Ⓣ212/279-8672, Ⓕ279-8683, Ⓦwww.us.croatia.hr.

Guide

Guide

1

Zagreb

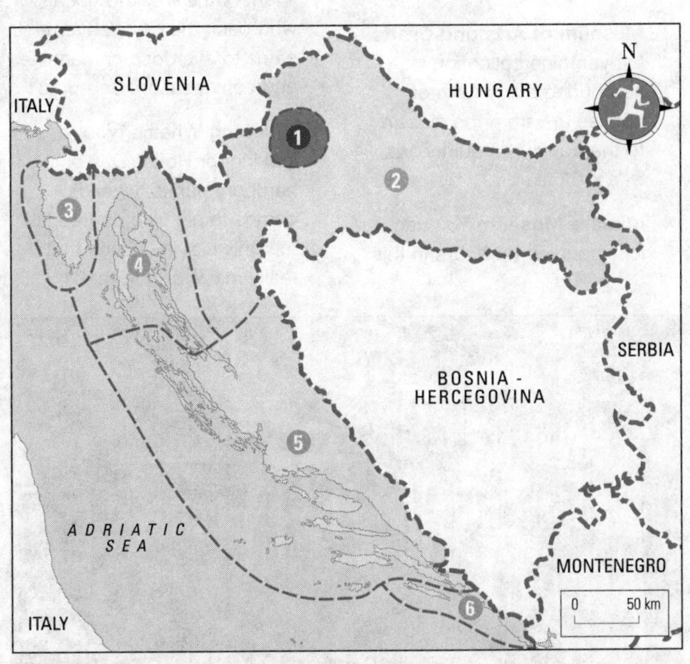
SLOVENIA
HUNGARY
ITALY
N
1
2
3
4
5
6
SERBIA
BOSNIA - HERCEGOVINA
ADRIATIC SEA
MONTENEGRO
0 50 km
ITALY

CHAPTER 1

Highlights

* **Tkalčićeva ulica** This pedestrianized strip of cafés and bars is the perfect venue for night-time promenading, people-watching or just posing. See p.80

* **Gradec** Relaxing Baroque quarter, nestling unobtrusively in the heart of the modern city. See p.83

* **Museum of Arts and Crafts** Labyrinthine collection harbouring every form of applied art, from the classic to the downright quirky. See p.89

* **Mimara Museum** You can lose yourself for hours in this vast collection of painting and sculpture from all over the world. See p.89

* **Mount Medvednica** The mountain ridge on Zagreb's doorstep is a paradise for woodland walkers. See p.96

* **Saturday morning coffee** The most important social event of the week for locals, who pack the city's pavement cafés to overdose on caffeine and conversation. See p.101

* **Clubbing** Whether you're looking for House DJs or hardcore punks, when it comes to nightlife Zagreb is the only city in Croatia that really matters. See p.104

△ Tram, Zagreb

1

Zagreb

Although the capital of an independent nation for less than two decades, **ZAGREB** has been the cultural and political focus of Croatia since the Middle Ages. Now home to almost a quarter of the country's population, the city grew out of the medieval communities of Kaptol and Gradec, which began life as separate fortified settlements but gradually grew to identify themselves as a single city. However, the present-day appearance of Zagreb owes most to the rapid growth of the nineteenth century, and many of the city's buildings are grand, peach-coloured monuments to the self-esteem of the Austro-Hungarian Empire. Outwardly, at least, Zagreb still shares the refined urban culture of Mitteleuropa – public transport is well organized, the streets are clean, the parks impeccably manicured – but behind the city's genteel facade teems a complex blend of central European, Mediterranean and Balkan cultures.

In recent years the city's **population** has edged towards the million mark, fed in part by an influx of migrants from areas of Croatia and Bosnia-Hercegovina affected by the conflicts of the 1991–95 period. Those families that have been resident here for a few generations are proud to call themselves *purgeri*, a term derived from the same Germanic root as the English word "burgher" and which harks back directly to the city's Habsburg past. True "purgerism" in all its heel-clicking, hand-kissing extravagance may have died out, but the name lives on as an important badge of **Zagreb identity** and, inevitably, is used pejoratively by outsiders to describe the snobbish urban pretensions of the capital.

With most travellers to Croatia heading straight for the coast, Zagreb is rarely overrun by foreign tourists, encouraging visitors to adapt to the unhurried rhythms of local life rather than trawling from one tourist trap to another. Sight-seeing is a low-key affair – museums are frequently absorbing but rarely spectacular – and a couple of days will be enough to give you a good taste of what the capital offers, unless you get sucked in by the city's burgeoning nightlife, in which case a somewhat longer sojourn may well be in order.

By day, Zagreb functions best as an outdoor city. The alleyways of the Baroque **Kaptol** and **Gradec** districts are atmospheric places for a wander whatever the season, while in spring and summer downtown streets that can seem oppressively sombre during the winter suddenly become clogged with café tables as soon as the weather improves, and popular strolling areas such as **Tkalčićeva** and **Preradovićev trg** take on a languorous Mediterranean glamour.

Urban attractions aside, you shouldn't leave Zagreb without exploring at least some of the city's attractive rural hinterland. To the north, the ridge of **Mount Medvednica** and its peak, **Sljeme**, provide the city with a year-round recreation area, and much of inland Croatia (see Chapter 2) is within day-trip range.

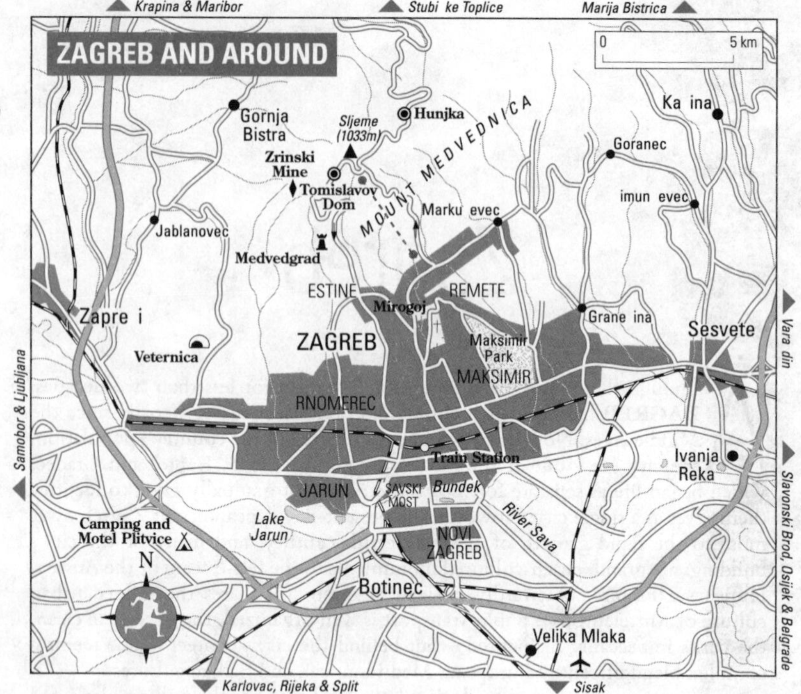

Some history

Despite evidence of Iron Age settlements on top of Gradec hill, the history of Zagreb doesn't really start until 1094, when Ladislas I of Hungary established a bishopric here in order to bring the northern Croatian lands under tighter Hungarian control. A large ecclesiastical community grew up around the cathedral and its girdle of episcopal buildings on **Kaptol** (which roughly translates as "cathedral chapter"), while the Hungarian crown retained a garrison opposite on **Gradec**. Both were significantly damaged during the Mongol incursions of 1240–42, prompting King Bela IV of Hungary to rebuild the settlement on Gradec and accord it the status of a royal free town in order to attract settlers and regenerate urban life. The settlements prospered from their position on the trade routes linking Hungary to the Adriatic, despite the growing Ottoman threat that began to emerge in the fifteenth century.

The communities of Kaptol and Gradec rarely got on – control of the watermills on the river dividing them was a constant source of enmity. The biggest outbreak of intercommunal fighting occurred in 1527, when the throne of Croatia was disputed by the Habsburg emperor Ferdinand II (supported by Gradec) and the Hungarian noble Ivan Zapolyai (supported by Kaptol), a conflict which culminated in the sacking of Kaptol by Habsburg troops. Henceforth the separate identities of Kaptol and Gradec began to disappear, and the name **Zagreb** (meaning, literally, "behind the hill" – a reference to the town's position at the foot of Mount Medvednica) entered popular usage as a collective name for both.

By the end of the sixteenth century the Ottoman Empire was in control of much of inland Croatia, reducing the country to a northern enclave with Zagreb at its centre. Despite continuing to host sessions of the (largely ceremonial) Croatian Sabor or parliament, Zagreb increasingly became a provincial outpost of the Habsburg Empire, and the Croatian language was displaced by German, Hungarian and Latin. It wasn't until the mid-nineteenth century that the growth of a Croatian national consciousness confirmed Zagreb's status as guardian of national culture. The establishment of an academy of arts and sciences (1866), a philharmonic orchestra (1871), a university (1874) and a national theatre (1890) gave Zagreb a growing sense of cultural identity, although ironically it was a German, the architect Hermann Bollé (1845–1926), creator of the School of Arts and Crafts, Mirogoj Cemetery and Zagreb Cathedral, who contributed most to the city's new profile.

With the creation of **Yugoslavia** in 1918, political power shifted from Vienna to Belgrade – a city that most Croats considered an underdeveloped Balkan backwater. Things improved marginally after World War II, when Croatia was given the status of a socialist republic and Zagreb became the seat of its government, but the city still resented the extent to which it was overshadowed by Belgrade. A major period of architectural change came in the 1950s and 1960s, when ambitious mayor Većeslav Holjevac presided over the city's southward expansion, and the vast concrete residential complexes of **Novi Zagreb** were born.

Zagreb survived the **collapse of Yugoslavia** relatively unscathed, despite being hit by sporadic Serbian rocket attacks. Life in post-independence Zagreb was initially characterized by economic stagnation and post-communist corruption, but in recent years the capital has benefitted from an upsurge in business activity and as a result has acquired a stylish, prosperous and optimistic sheen.

Arrival, information and city transport

Zagreb is a disarmingly easy place to find your way around, with almost everything of importance revolving around the city's central square, **Trg bana Jelačića**. From here most attractions are within walking distance, although many of the cheaper accommodation options, along with a number of museums, restaurants, bars and clubs, lie 2–3km (a short tram ride) away from the square. North of the main square, Zagreb is an attractively hilly place, merging with the slopes of **Mount Medvednica**; elsewhere the terrain is unremittingly flat, with grid-plan suburbs stretching south to the broad **River Sava**, 3km from the square, with the concrete-and-steel settlement of **Novi Zagreb** on the opposite bank.

Arrival

Zagreb's **airport**, situated around 10km southeast of the city, is connected with the bus station by half-hourly buses (30Kn; 40min) between 7.30am and 8pm; after that time buses run only to connect with Croatia Airlines flights. A taxi from the airport to the centre costs about 200–250Kn. Zagreb's central **train station** is on Tomislavov trg, on the southern edge of the city centre, ten minutes' walk from Trg bana Jelačića. The main **bus station** is about ten minutes' walk east of the train station at the junction of Branimirova and Držićeva. Tram #6 (destination Černomerec) runs from here to Trg bana Jelačića, stopping at the train station on the way.

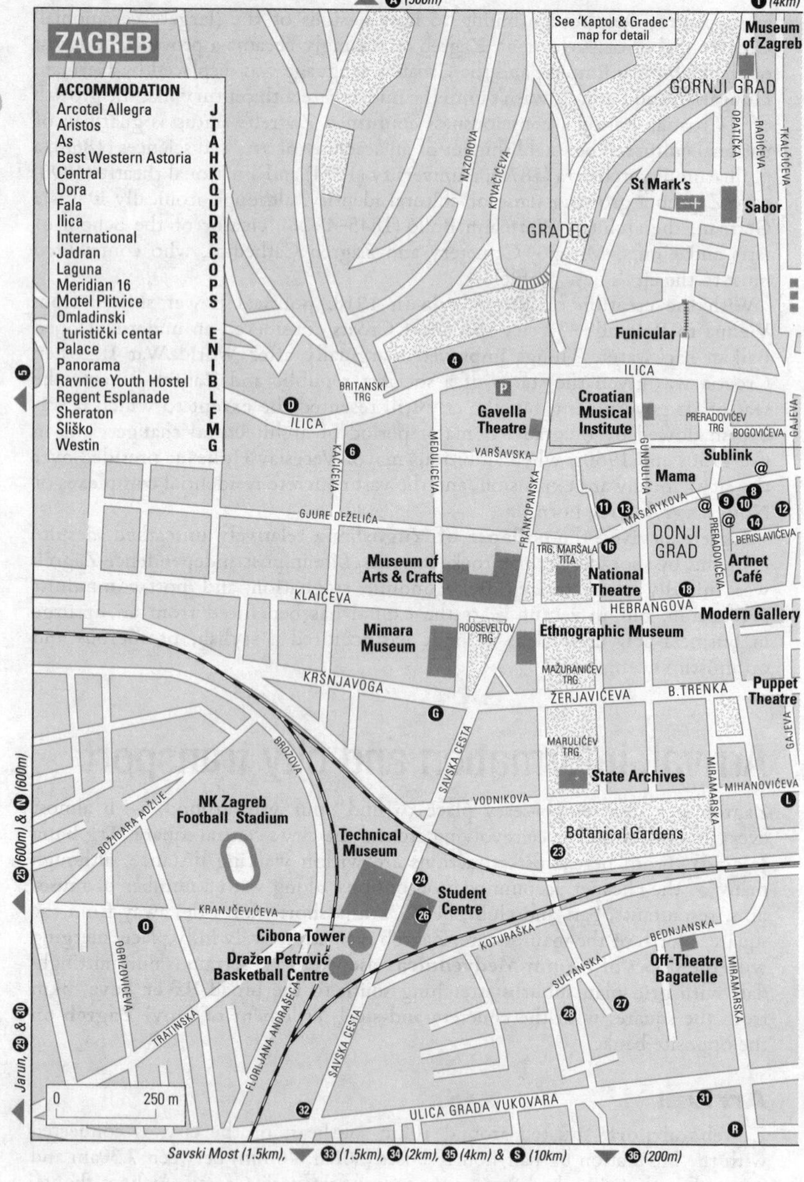

Information

There are two main **tourist offices** (*turistički informativni centar*; TIC) in central Zagreb, one at Trg bana Jelačića 11 (June–Sept Mon–Fri 8am–8pm, Sat & Sun 9am–6pm; Oct–May Mon–Fri 8.30am–8pm, Sat 10am–5pm, Sun 10am–2pm; ⓣ01/48-14-051 or 48-14-052, ⓦwww.zagreb-touristinfo.hr), and another a

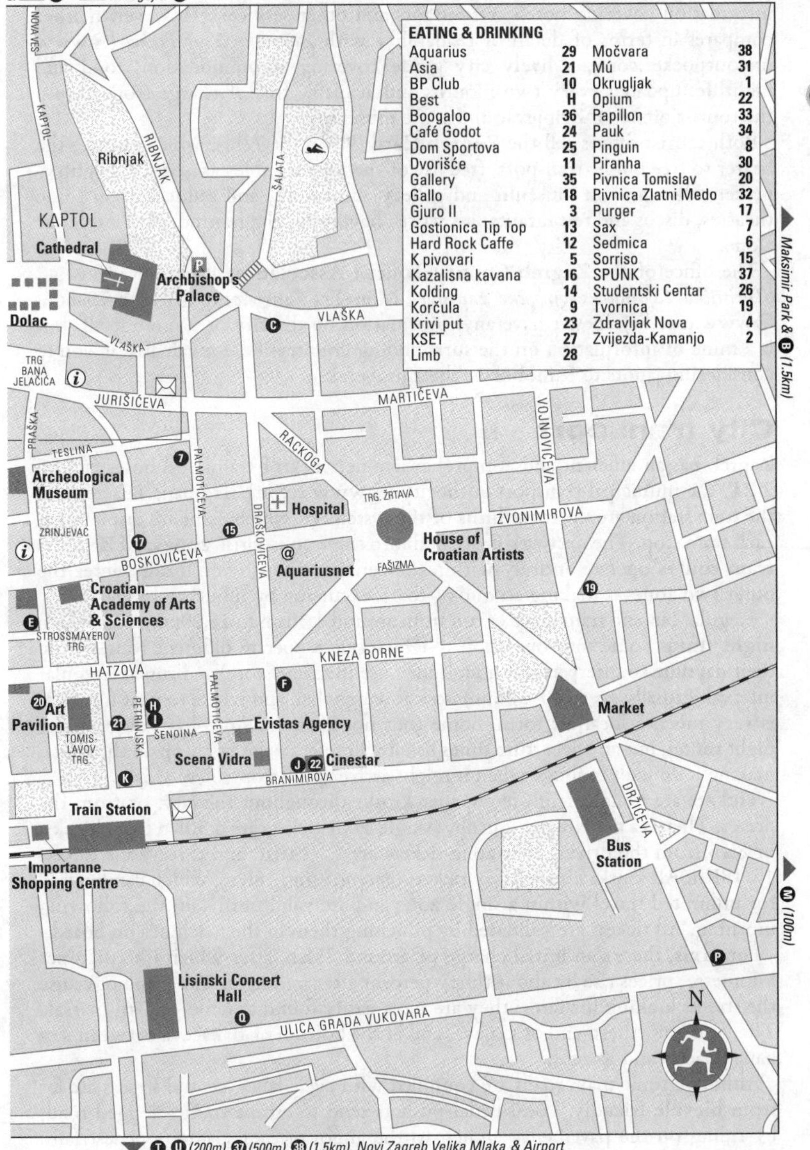

few hundred metres to the south at Zrinjevac 14 (June–Sept Mon–Fri 8am–8pm, Sat & Sun 9am–6pm; Oct–May Mon, Wed & Fri 9am–5pm, Tues & Thurs 9am–6pm; ⓣ01/49-21-645). Both offices have free city maps and can recommend accommodation options, although neither will book rooms.

Free **booklets** available from the tourist offices include *Events and Performances* (providing monthly concert listings) and *Zagreb A–Z* (Yellow Pages-style information covering hotels, restaurants and other services). However, neither compares in terms of detail or readability with *Zagreb in Your Pocket* (Ⓦwww.inyourpocket.com), a lively city guide covering accommodation, food and nightlife, updated every two months and available free of charge from hotels, the tourist office on Zrinjevac and some museums.

Both tourist offices sell the **Zagreb Card** (90Kn for 72hr), which entitles the bearer to free public transport, free use of the Sljeme cable car (see p.97), a fifty-percent discount on museum and gallery admissions, and reductions in some theatres, discos and restaurants; it's worth having for the transport and cable car alone.

The office of the **Zagreb County Tourist Association** at Preradovićeva 42 (*Turistička zajednica zagrebačke županije*; Mon–Fri 8am–4pm; Ⓣ01/48-73-665, Ⓦwww.tzzz.hr) doesn't have any information on the city of Zagreb itself, but is a mine of information on the surrounding countryside – invaluable if you're considering jaunts to Samobor or the Žumberak.

City transport

Zagreb has an efficient and comprehensive network of trams and buses run by **ZET**, the municipal transport authority (Ⓦwww.zet.hr). Trg bana Jelačića and the train station are the main **hubs** of the system, of which maps are displayed at each tram stop. The network is divided into three concentric **zones**; all Zagreb's **tram routes** operate entirely within the central zone, so you'll only enter the outer two zones if making an out-of-town excursion by suburban bus.

Regular bus and tram services run from around 4.30am to 11.20pm, after which **night trams** come into operation. Night services operate different routes from their daytime counterparts (although they use the same stops) and run at irregular intervals (usually every 40–50min), so knowing when and where to wait for them is very much a local art form. Some (but not all) tram stops have diagrams of night routes, but any departure times listed will refer to the first stop on the route, making it difficult to judge when it might arrive at the stop you're at.

Tickets are bought from newspaper kiosks throughout the city, or from the driver. There's a flat fare per journey: single-zone tickets are 6.50Kn from kiosks, or 8Kn from the driver; two-zone tickets are 12/14Kn; and three-zone tickets 17/18Kn. All kiosks also sell day tickets (*dnevne karte*; 18Kn), which can be used for unlimited travel within a single zone and are valid until 4am the following morning. All tickets are validated by punching them in the machines on board.

For **taxis**, there's an initial charge of around 25Kn, after which it's 10Kn per kilometre; prices rise by about thirty percent after midnight. Taxis do not cruise the streets looking for fares: they are most easily found at ranks on Trg maršala Tita, at the northern end of Gajeva, and at the bottom of Bakačeva between Trg bana Jelačića and Kaptol.

Although some main roads are equipped with cycle lanes, central streets are far from **bicycle**-friendly. Local pedal-pushers tend to escape traffic-clogged roads by riding on the pavement – much to the annoyance of Zagreb's pedestrians. There are a couple of locations where you can rent bikes (see "Listings"; p.109).

Accommodation

While Zagreb is reasonably well served with medium- and top-range **hotels**, budget choices are relatively thin on the ground and should be reserved at least a

Zagreb street names

The flexible nature of Croatian grammar means that there are often two ways of saying a **street name**, and the version you hear in the spoken language may not be the same one you see on street signs. Maps tend to feature the versions of names used in the spoken language, although be prepared for inconsistencies. Thus "Nikola Tesla Street" in the centre of Zagreb can be rendered as either ulica Nikole Tesle ("street of Nikola Tesla") or Teslina ulica ("Tesla's street"). The latter is more common in everyday speech and on maps, although the word ulica ("street") is usually dropped. Similarly, ulica Pavla Radića becomes Radićeva, and ulica Ivana Tkalčića becomes Tkalčićeva.

To complicate matters further, a couple of Zagreb's best-known squares have colloquial names which differ from their official ones. Trg Nikole Šubića Zrinskog usually goes under the name of Zrinjevac; and Trg Petra Preradovića is almost universally referred to as Cvjetni trg ("Flower Square"), because it has long been the venue of a florists' market.

Version seen on street signs	Version used in spoken language and on maps
Trg svetog Marka	Markov trg
Trg Marka Marulića	Marulićev trg
Trg braće Mažuranića	Mažuranićev trg
Trg Petra Preradovića	Preradovićev trg/Cvjetni trg
Trg Josipa Jurja Strossmayera	Strossmayerov trg
Trg kralja Tomislava	Tomislavov trg
Trg Nikole Šubića Zrinskog	Zrinjevac
Ulica kneza Branimira	Branimirova
Ulica Ljudevita Gaja	Gajeva
Ulica Janka Draškovića	Draškovićeva
Ulica Andrije Hebranga	Hebrangova
Ulica Junije Palmotića	Palmotićeva
Ulica Pavla Radića	Radićeva
Ulica Augusta Šenoe	Šenoina
Ulica Nikole Tesle	Teslina
Ulica Ivana Tkalčića	Tkalčićeva

few days in advance. Apart from the handful of places that measure up to international five-star standards, Zagreb's downtown hotels don't offer a great deal of choice: rooms are pretty much the same wherever you go, and few places have a distinct character. There are better deals either in the **suburbs**, or 20km north of town near the Sljeme summit of Mount Medvednica (for directions on how to get there, see p.96), an idyllic spot if you like woodland walks, but hardly the ideal base for urban sightseeing. All hotels include breakfast in the price unless otherwise stated.

Zagreb's stock of **youth hostel** beds is on the increase, but is still inadequate for a city of this size. Private **rooms** can be arranged through Evistas, midway between the train and bus stations at Šenoina 28 (Mon–Fri 9am–8pm, Sat 9am–5pm; Ⓣ01/48-39-554, Ⓔvistas@zg.t-com.hr, Ⓦwww.travel-tourist.com; ❷), which will place you with a local family in the town centre or in the suburbs of Novi Zagreb or Jarun. They also offer two-person apartments with bathroom and kitchenette (❸–❹), although you have to stay at least three days – note that they don't accept credit cards. Short-term apartment rental (400–600Kn/night) can also be arranged in advance through the Never Stop/Nemoj stati agency, Boškovićeva 7a (Ⓣ091 63-78-111, Ⓦwww.nest.hr).

The nearest **campsite** (May–Sept) is 10km southeast of town at the *Motel Plitvice* in Lučko (Ⓣ01/65-30-444, Ⓕ65-30-445, Ⓔmotel@motel-plitvice.hr), a grassy spot right beside the highway that runs round the southern side of the city, with self-service restaurants and shops on site. There's no direct public transport to the site.

All accommodation is marked on the map on pp.72–73 unless otherwise noted.

Hostels

Hostel Fulir Radićeva 3a Ⓣ01/48-30-882 or 098 193 0552, Ⓦwww.fulir-hostel.com.See map on p.79. Small but cheery 14-bed hostel, occupying the first floor of a galleried courtyard a stone's throw from the main square. There's bunk-bed accommodation in attic-ceilinged rooms, adequate locker space, and reasonably new furnishings and fittings. There's also a small kitchen where you can make tea or coffee, and an Internet terminal is available for a few extra kuna. Dorm beds 150Kn.

Omladinski turistički centar Petrinjska 77 Ⓣ01/48-41-261 or 48-47-267, Ⓦwww.hfhs.hr. Grotty two-hundred-bed hostel five minutes' walk north from the train station, offering beds in four- or six-bed dorms, and a handful of en-suite doubles. May close down for complete renovation in the near future – ring in advance to check. Dorm beds 110Kn, doubles ❷

Ravnice Youth Hostel 1. Ravnice 38d Ⓣ01/23-32-325, Ⓦwww.ravnice-youth-hostel.hr. Privately owned, easy-going and friendly hostel 4km east of the centre, in a large modern house just behind Croatia's biggest confectionery factory – which produces a pleasant chocolatey aroma whenever the wind's in the right direction. They offer bright, pastel-coloured bunk-bed rooms, plus a couple of doubles; there's no breakfast, but you get free use of a kitchen and there are plenty of neighbourhood shops. There are Internet terminals in the common room, and you can also get your washing done for a nominal fee. Take either tram #4 (direction Dubec) from the train station, tram #7 (direction Dubrava) from the bus station, or trams #11 (direction Dubec) and #12 (direction Dubrava) from Trg bana Jelačića, and get off at Ravnice (the second stop after Maksimir soccer stadium). The hostel is well signposted, five minutes' walk down 1. Ravnice. Dorm beds €15 (or kuna equivalent), doubles ❷

Hotels

Central Zagreb

Arcotel Allegra Branimirova 29 Ⓣ01/46-96-000, Ⓦwww.arcotel.at. A perfect pied-à-terre for the design-conscious, with rooms featuring snazzy minimalist decor, large-screen TVs and proper bathtubs. The bed linen is decorated with pictures of Sigmund Freud, which may put a damper on your nocturnal activities. Guests have free use of gym and sauna. Handy for the train station and a fifteen-minute walk from the main square. ❻

Best Western Astoria Petrinjska 71 Ⓣ01/48-08-900, Ⓔinfo@hotelastoria.hr, Ⓦwww.bestwestern.com. Snug, central hotel with arty prints in the hallways and warm red, green and yellowish hues in the rooms – each of which comes with TV, mini-bar and a/c. Bathrooms are neat and modern but not all of them have a full-sized tub. ❻

Central Branimirova 3 Ⓣ01/48-41-122, Ⓦwww.hotel-central.hr. Rooms here are smart and comfortable, if a little small and cramped, with en-suite facilities and TV. Diagonally opposite the train station. ❺–❻

Dubrovnik Gajeva 1 Ⓣ01/48-73-555, Ⓦwww.hotel-dubrovnik.htnet.hr. See map on p.79. Dependable four-star comprising a 1920s main building overlooking Trg bana Jelačića, and an angular glass-and-steel annexe stretching along Gajeva to the south. Expect smart pastel-coloured rooms (doubles have baths, singles come with showers); those in the older half of the hotel have rather dowdy furnishings but many have the compensation of main-square views. ❼

Ilica Ilica 102 Ⓣ01/37-77-522, Ⓦwww.hotel-ilica.hr. Family-run hotel featuring tidy en-suite rooms with TV and phone. Room sizes range from small to tiny, and the interiors are either winningly eccentric or overpoweringly kitsch, depending on one's taste. It's still good value for the price range, so reserve well in advance and, if possible, ring to reconfirm the day before your arrival. It's in the courtyard of a low-rise residental block 1500m west of Trg bana Jelačića; take tram #6 from the bus or train station (destination Černomerec) until you see the hotel on your right. ❹

Jadran Vlaška 50 ⓣ01/45-53-777, ⓦwww.hup-zagreb.hr. Medium-rise hotel just east of the city centre, a fifteen-minute walk from the train station. Dingy from the outside, it's quite pleasant within, and has modest en-suite rooms with TV and phone. Take tram #4 (destination Dubrava) from the train station or tram #8 (destination Mihaljevac) from the bus station to Draškovićeva, after which it's a short walk east along Vlaška. ❺

Palace Strossmayerov trg 10 ⓣ01/48-99-600, ⓦwww.palace.hr. Attractive turn-of-the-century pile between the train station and Trg bana Jelačića, preserving a few period fittings in the hallways and reception areas. Most rooms are modern, plush affairs with a/c, minibar and bathtub, although there's still a handful of frumpy unrenovated rooms due to be refurbished in 2007/8. ❼

Pension Jägerhorn Ilica 14 ⓣ01/48-33-877, ⓦwww.hotel-pansion-jaegerhorn.hr. See map on p.79. In a courtyard just off the main shopping street, just 500m from Trg bana Jelačića. Rooms come with shower, TV and a/c; atmospheric top-floor doubles have sloping attic ceilings. Take tram #6 (destination Černomerec) from the bus or train station to Trg bana Jelačića, then walk west. ❻

Regent Esplanade Mihanovićeva 1 ⓣ01/45-66-666, ⓦwww.esplanade.tel.hr or ⓦwww.regenthotels.com. Luxurious outpost of Mitteleuropa next to the train station, with marble-clad Art Deco lobby plus an opulent café and function rooms. The repro furniture in the rooms may be a bit over the top for some tastes, but the marble-floored bathrooms with big tubs represent a major plus. Good views of downtown Zagreb from north- and west-facing rooms. ❽–❾

Sheraton ul. Kneza Borne 2 ⓣ01/45-53-535, ⓦwww.sheraton.com/zagreb. Plush rooms and attentive service in a convenient downtown location. There's a small indoor pool, too. ❼

Westin Kršnjavoga 1 ⓣ01/48-92-000, ⓦwww.westin.com/zagreb. Modern 335-room hotel handily located close to the theatres and museums around Trg maršala Tita. All rooms come with bathtub, deep-mattressed beds piled high with pillows, and tea and coffee-making facilities. The indoor swimming pool is on the small side but has a lovely palm-court atmosphere. ❼–❽

The suburbs

Aristos Cebini 33, Buzin ⓣ01/66-95-900, ⓦwww.hotel-aristos.hr. Businesslike four-star located 10km southeast of the centre in an anonymous area of offices and showrooms. It offers all the creature comforts but its proximity to the airport is the main selling point. The #268 Zagreb-Velika Gorica bus trundles past. ❼

As Zelengaj 2a ⓣ01/46-09-111, ⓕ46-09-303. Four-star comforts 2km northwest of the centre in the leafy suburb of Zelengaj, in a curvy-roofed contemporary building that blends rather well with its woodland surroundings. The roomy doubles offer classy nineteenth-century-style furnishings, TV, minibar and big bathtubs, and there's a formal, top-notch restaurant on site. You can walk down into the city through a belt of suburban forest. ❼

Dora Trnjanska 11e ⓣ01/63-11-900, ⓦwww.zeljeznicko-ugostiteljstvo.hr. Railway-owned former workers' hostel, transformed into an unpretentious medium-sized hotel, offering simple but neat en-suite rooms with TV. Somewhat unromantically situated beside a busy multi-lane highway, but handily placed for both bus and train stations, and the city centre is only a twenty-minute walk away. It's very popular with both tourists and businessmen on a budget, so ring in advance. ❺

Fala 11.Trnjanske ledine 18 ⓣ01/61-11-062, ⓦwww.hotel-fala-zg.hr. Despite being next to a four-lane road, this small-scale family-run hotel has a peaceful, suburban backstreet feel. En-suite rooms are bright and pleasant, and the hallways are packed with houseplants. It's a 25-minute walk south of the centre: from the bus station, take tram #5 (destination Jarun) to the Lisinski stop. ❹

International Miramarska 24 ⓣ01/61-08-800, ⓦwww.hotel-international.hr. Bland ten-storey building offering Eighties-style beige-brown rooms with TV and bathtub. It's in a modern area of government offices and grey residential blocks, a ten-minute walk south of the train station. On the characterless side, but perfectly comfortable and well run. Walkable from the train station: from the bus station, take tram #5 (destination Jarun) to the Miramarska stop. ❻

Laguna Kranjčevićeva 29 ⓣ01/38-20-222, ⓦwww.hotel-laguna.hr. Five-storey concrete affair opposite the NK Zagreb football stadium and a stone's throw from the Dražen Petrović basketball centre – which probably explains why it's so popular with visiting sports teams. Rooms are on the small side, but come with TV, bathtub and standard-issue socialist-era furniture. From the train station, tram #9 (direction Ljubljanica) to the Tehnički muzej stop. ❺

Meridijan 16 ul. grada Vukovara 241 ⓣ01/60-65-200, ⓦwww.meridijan16.com. Attractively priced, medium-sized hotel a few steps south of the bus station, offering creamy-coloured rooms with laminated floors, a/c, flat-screen TV, WC/shower and a small desk. Buffet breakfast, and secure car-parking space in the back yard complete the picture. ❺

Panorama Trg sportova 9 ⓣ01/36-58-333, ⓦwww.fourpoints.com/zagreb. High-rise hotel 2km east of the centre, recently renovated to provide four-star levels of comfort. Rooms have warm colour schemes and most come with proper-sized bathtubs and tea and coffee-making facilities (some don't; so be sure to ask when booking). North-facing rooms on the higher floors come with spellbinding views of the city. Take tram #9 (destination Ljubljanica) from the train station to Trešnjevački trg, then turn right onto Trakošćanska and after five minutes you'll see the hotel looming up on your left. ❺–❻

Sliško Supilova 13 ⓣ01/61-84-777, ⓦwww.slisko.hr. Medium-sized hotel in a residential street 50m from the bus station. Some of the rooms are a tight squeeze, but they all come with modern furnishings, TV and a/c. Ask about cash discounts. ❹

Mount Medvednica

Hunjka Sljemenska cesta bb ⓣ01/45-80-397, ⓕ45-52-185. See map on p.70. Medium-sized hotel on the eastern shoulder of Mount Medvednica, offering simple but smart en-suite rooms with pine floors and furnishings, plus an on-site restaurant. Situated in a lovely meadow encircled by forest, about 23km out of Zagreb on the road to Donja Stubica; the nearest public transport is the top station of the Sljeme cable car, a forty-minute walk away. ❸

Tomislavov dom Sljeme ⓣ01/45-55-833, ⓦwww.sljeme.hr. See map on p.70. Large mountaintop hotel surrounded by woodland, with chic, newly furnished en suites. There's a well-equipped fitness centre and funky amoeba-shaped pool. It's just below the summit of Sljeme, a five-minute walk from the cable car station, or 21km from the centre of Zagreb by road. ❺

The City

Central Zagreb divides into three distinct areas, joined by the main square, **Trg bana Jelačića**. Occupying the high ground north of the square are the two oldest parts of the city, **Kaptol** and **Gradec**, the former the site of the cathedral, the latter a peaceful district of ancient mansions and quiet squares. Beneath them spreads the nineteenth- and twentieth-century **Donji grad**, or "Lower Town", a bustling area of prestigious public buildings and nineteenth-century apartment blocks.

Beyond the centre, there's not much of interest among the broad boulevards and bland modern buildings which extend south to the River Sava and, beyond that, to the suburb of **Novi Zagreb**. Aside from the artificial lake at **Jarun**, southwest of the city, and the leafy park of **Maksimir** to the east, the most obvious target is the nearby ramblers' paradise of **Mount Medvednica**, served by cable car from suburban Zagreb and an easy trip out from the centre.

Trg bana Jelačića and around

A broad, flagstoned expanse flanked by cafés and hectic with the whizz of trams and hurrying pedestrians, **Trg bana Jelačića** ("Governor Jelačić Square") is as good a place as any to start exploring the city, and is within easy walking distance of more or less everything you're likely to want to see. It's also the biggest tram stop in Zagreb, standing at the intersection of seven cross-town routes, and the place where half the city seems to meet in the evening – either beneath the ugly clock mounted on metal stilts on the western side of the square, or at the Znanje bookshop (colloquially known as "Krleža" after Croatia's greatest twentieth-century writer, Miroslav Krleža) on the corner of the square and Gajeva. The square is traditionally the venue for mass outbreaks of Croatian solidarity, most recently on December 5, 2005, when almost 100,000 people turned out to greet the Davis Cup-winning tennis team of Goran Ivanišević, Ivo Karlović, Mario Ančić and Ivan Ljubičić.

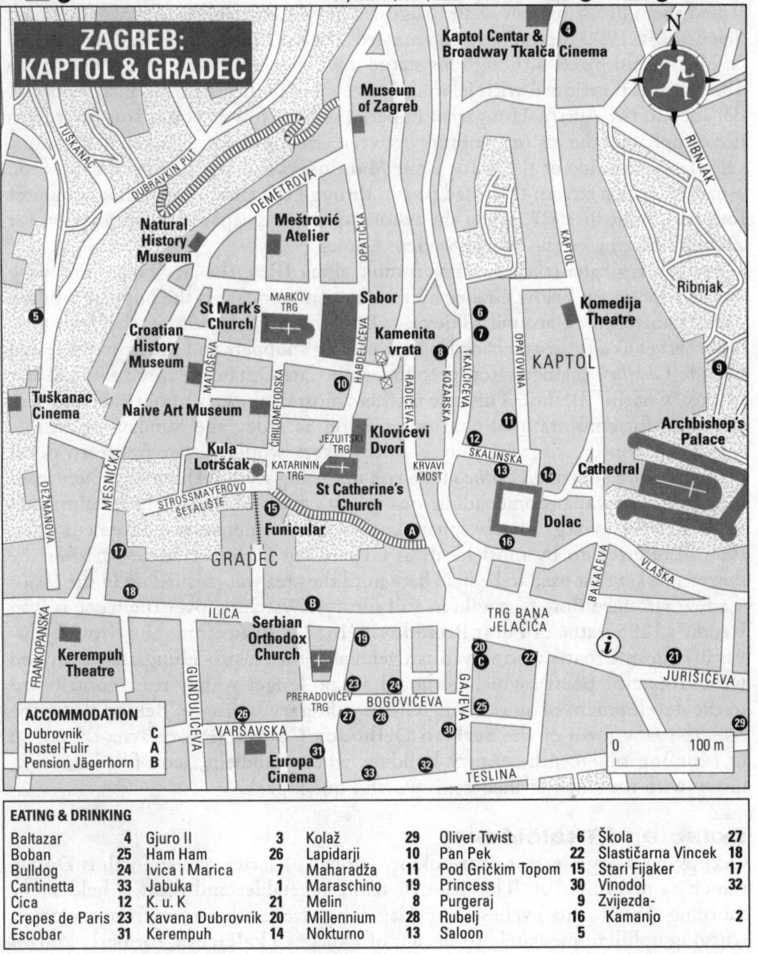

Originally a vast open space known as "Harmica" owing to its use as a collection point for local taxes (after the Hungarian word *harmincad*, meaning a thirtieth), Trg bana Jelačića was laid out as the city's main square in the 1850s and has been Zagreb's focal point ever since. The elegant pastel blues and pinks of its surrounding buildings provide a suitable backdrop for the attention-hogging equestrian statue of the nineteenth-century Ban of Croatia, **Josip Jelačić**, completed in 1866 by the Viennese sculptor Fernkorn just as the Habsburg authorities were beginning to erode the semi-autonomy which Jelačić had won for the nation. The square was renamed Trg republike in 1945 and the statue – considered a potential rallying point for Croatian nationalism – was concealed behind a wooden shell covered with communist propaganda slogans. Party agitators finally dismantled the statue on the night of July 25, 1947, although its constituent parts were saved from destruction by a local museum curator, who stored them in a basement of the Yugoslav (now Croatian) Academy of Arts and Sciences. In 1990 the square was renamed Trg bana Jelačića and Jelačić restored to his rightful place, although his statue now faces a different direction. In the 1860s it was positioned with Jelačić's drawn sabre pointing north, in a gesture of defiance to the Austro-Hungarian imperial order. Now it points southwards, as if to emphasize the historic rupture between Croatia and her Balkan neighbours. On the eastern side of the statue is the **Manduševac**, a small, stepped depression – named after a stream that used to run through the area – concealing a modest fountain, built in 1987, when the whole square was repaved in preparation for Zagreb's hosting of the World Student Games.

West of Trg bana Jelačića, trams rumble along **Ilica**, the city's main shopping street, which runs below Gradec hill. South of the square is the popular modern pedestrianized area around **Gajeva**, where the glass facade of the *Dubrovnik* hotel serves as a futuristic backdrop for passing shoppers and the drinkers seated outside *Charlie's* (named after its founder, the late Dinamo Zagreb football star Mirko "Charlie" Braun). This café is where most of the city's political elite seem to gather for conspiratorial chin-wagging on Saturday and Sunday lunchtimes – even in winter, Zagreb's movers and shakers would rather freeze to death drinking coffee outside *Charlie's* than risk not being seen. A sharp right here leads into **Bogovićeva**, a promenading area full of cafés and shops which culminates in **Preradovićev trg**, a lively square known for its cinemas and pavement cafés. It's still referred to by most locals as Cvjetni trg ("Flower Square"), after the flower market that used to be held here until the area was cleaned up in the 1980s – a few sanitized florists' pavilions still survive. Watching over the scene is Ivan Rendić's 1895 statue of **Petar Preradović** (1818–72), an ethnic Serb from Bjelovar in eastern Croatia who served as a general in the Austro-Hungarian army and wrote romantic poetry which, although it's no longer widely read, contributed to the development of an evolving Croatian literary language. Behind the statue rises the grey form of the **Serbian Orthodox Church** (Pravoslavna crkva), an unassuming nineteenth-century building whose candlelit, icon-filled interior, heavy with the smell of incense, is worth a quick peek.

Dolac and Tkalčićeva

Occupying a large terrace overlooking Trg bana Jelačića to the north is **Dolac**, the city's main market. This feast of fruit, vegetables and meat is held every morning, but is at its liveliest on Friday, when fresh fish arrives from the coast. Curving uphill immediately to the left of Dolac is **Tkalčićeva**, formerly known as Potok ("Stream") owing to its position on the dried-up watercourse that once separated Kaptol from Gradec. Probably the prettiest single street in the city, Tkalčićeva preserves a neat ensemble of the one- and two-storey, steep-roofed nineteenth-century houses that have largely disappeared elsewhere. There's a smattering of boutiques and art galleries tucked into the street's low-ceilinged mansions, although most of these are now occupied by the youthful café-bars which have transformed Tkalčićeva into the city's prime area for drinking on warm summer evenings. In the first half of the twentieth century the whole area had a somewhat darker reputation, when Kožarska, the alleyway which runs parallel to Tkalčićeva to the west, served as the city's red-light district, "reeking of debauchery, adultery, crime, drunkenness, and promiscuity", in the words of diarist and novelist Miroslav Krleža. It was so popular with Hitler's soldiers in World War II that the city authorities had to put up signs in German banning military personnel from entering. Also leading off to the west of Tkalčićeva is **Krvavi most** ("Bloody Bridge" – a reminder of the often violent disputes between Gradec and Kaptol), a street that links up with Radićeva, offering a short cut up to Gradec.

Kaptol

Northeast of Trg bana Jelačića, the filigree spires of Zagreb's cathedral mark the edge of the district known as **Kaptol**, home to the city's Catholic institutions and still patrolled by pious citizens and nuns of various orders. The area consists of little more than one long street – initially called Kaptol, later becoming Nova ves in its northern reaches – and the **cathedral** itself, at its southern end, the district's only arresting feature. Ringed by the ivy-cloaked turrets of the eighteenth-century **Archbishop's Palace** ("a southern Kremlin", fancied the archeologist Arthur Evans), the cathedral is almost wholly neo-Gothic, having been rebuilt by Viennese architects Friedrich von Schmidt and Hermann Bollé

△ Zagreb cathedral

Archbishop Alojzije Stepinac

For many, **Alojzije Stepinac** (1898–1960) personifies the link between the Croatian nation and the Catholic Church. Branded a quisling by the communists, but regarded by most ordinary Croats as a martyr and patriot, he has assumed immense symbolic importance since his death in 1960. It's a development which has been broadly encouraged by the Vatican: Stepinac was beatified by Pope John Paul II on his visit to Croatia in October 1998.

Born into a relatively prosperous peasant family in the village of Krašić, 50km southwest of Zagreb, Stepinac was initially dissuaded from entering the priesthood by his parents, who were eager for him to manage the family farm. During World War I he served with the Yugoslav Legion, a body assembled by the Allies to fight for a united South Slav state. After the war he briefly studied agronomy in Zagreb, but soon returned to Krašić, dismayed by the immoral lifestyles of his fellow students. Settling back into village life he got engaged to girl-next-door Marija Horvat, who addressed him as "my dear ice-cold betrothed" and eventually broke off the relationship, realizing that his mind was focused on more spiritual matters.

Having opted for the Church, Stepinac ascended through the priestly ranks at great speed, becoming **Archbishop of Zagreb** in 1937. Stepinac's rise was promoted by the government in Belgrade, which still viewed him as pro-Yugoslav – although Stepinac, like many Croats, had by this stage lost his faith in South Slav unity. Stepinac had little enthusiasm for Nazism, but initially instructed Croatian priests to support the German-imposed NDH, the "Independent State of Croatia" proclaimed in April 1941. Once the true nature of the NDH became apparent, however, Stepinac began to change tack. By June 1941 he was already protesting to Pavelić about the inhuman treatment of Serbian deportees, though he initially thought the crimes committed in the name of the NDH were the work of individual hotheads rather than the regime itself – according to the memoirs of the sculptor Ivan Meštrović, the archbishop burst out crying when he finally realized that Pavelić himself was giving the orders. Stepinac consequently stepped up his criticism of the regime as the war went on, and used his personal authority to save many individuals who would otherwise have faced execution.

As the war neared its end, Stepinac's profound hostility to the communist partisans prevented him from reaching an understanding with Croatia's new masters. Eager to demoralize the anti-communist opposition, Yugoslavia's new strongman Josip Broz Tito (see box on pp.124) decided to make an example of the archbishop, and had him **arrested** in May 1945. After a preposterous trial in which the Catholic hierarchy was accused of working in tandem with foreign intelligence services, Stepinac was found guilty of "anti-national activities" in December 1946 and sentenced to sixteen years' imprisonment.

Stepinac spent five years in **Lepoglava jail** (see p.127) before being allowed home to Krašić, where he occupied a modest two-room apartment in the house of the local priest. Stepinac's release was presented to the world media as an example of the communist regime's leniency, although he was effectively under house arrest until his death. Foreign journalists who tried to see the archbishop were told that a constant police guard was needed to protect Stepinac from the wrath of the working class. Made a **cardinal** by the pope in 1952, Stepinac was the subject of quiet admiration among those Croats who remained unconvinced by government propaganda, and his grave in Zagreb cathedral became an unofficial shrine long before the collapse of communism in 1990.

after a catastrophic earthquake in 1880. Most of the money and creative endeavour were invested in the two spires – the big architectural statement it was felt a growing city like Zagreb needed. The interior is high and bare – only four

Renaissance choirstalls from the early sixteenth century and the faded remains of some medieval frescoes survive from before the quake. The modest main altar, bearing a copy of the statue of the Madonna and Child in the church at Maria Bistrica, stands in front of a glass casket holding an effigy of Archbishop Alojzije Stepinac (see box opposite), head of the Croatian Church during World War II and imprisoned by the communists immediately afterwards. Stepinac's grave, near the altar on the north wall of the church, is marked by a touching relief by Ivan Meštrović in which the archbishop kneels humbly before Christ. There's another statue by Fernkorn in front of the cathedral, depicting a richly gilded Madonna surrounded by four angels, which provides a beckoning sparkle as you approach Kaptol from the south.

Descending from the cathedral onto Vlaška and turning left brings you to **Ribnjak**, a small, shady park situated on the site of a former fishpond, and overshadowed on one side by the crumbling remains of Kaptol's erstwhile fortifications. One of the city's most charming open spaces, the park was reserved for Kaptol's priests until 1947, when the railings surrounding it were demolished by the same communist activists who put paid to the statue of Jelačić on Trg bana Jelačića.

Gradec

Uphill to the northwest of Trg bana Jelačića, **Gradec** (known colloquially as "Grič") is the most ancient and atmospheric part of Zagreb, a leafy, tranquil area of tiny streets, small squares and Baroque palaces, whose mottled brown roofs peek out from the hill. The most leisurely approach is to take the **funicular** (*uspinjača*; daily 6.30am–9pm; every 10min; 3Kn each way), which ascends from Tomićeva, an alleyway about 200m west of Trg bana Jelačića; alternatively, wander up the gentle gradient of Radićeva towards the **Kamenita vrata**, or "stone gate", which originally formed the main eastern entrance to the town. Inside Kamenita vrata – actually more of a long curving tunnel than a gate – lies one of Zagreb's most popular shrines, a simple sixteenth-century statue of the Virgin in a grille-covered niche. Miraculous powers have been attributed to the statue, largely on account of its surviving a fire in 1731 – a couple of benches inside the gate accommodate passing city folk eager to offer a quick prayer.

Katarinin trg and around

Just to the south of Kamenita vrata, Jezuitski trg is flanked on the east side by **Klovićevi dvori**, a seventeenth-century former Jesuit monastery now used for temporary art exhibitions (Tues–Sun 11am–7pm; admission price varies according to what's on display; Ⓦ www.galerijaklovic.hr); it also houses a small café and courtyard which hosts concerts during the Zagreb Summer Festival (see box on p.105). Beyond here, where Jezuitski trg opens out onto the next square, **Katarinin trg**, is **St Catherine's Church** (Crkva svete Katerine; daily 10am–1pm), built by the Jesuits in the 1620s and containing one of the most delightful Baroque interiors in Croatia, with its lacework pattern of pink-and-white stucco whorls executed by Antonio Quadrio in the 1720s. Francesco Robba's delicate portrayal of the Jesuit order's founder, St Ignatius of Loyola, to the right of the main altar, is the outstanding piece of statuary, portraying the saint in a typically Baroque swoon of spiritual ecstasy.

On the south side of the square, Dverce leads both to the top station of the funicular down to Ilica and to **Kula lotršćak**, or "Burglars' Tower" (May–Oct Tues–Sun 11am–8pm; 10Kn), another remnant of the upper town's fortifications, from which a bell was once sounded every evening before the city gates were closed (to keep out burglars, hence the name). An energetic tramp up a tightly wound spiral staircase brings you out onto a wooden terrace, with superb views of Zagreb's red-tiled roofs below. On the way up you'll pass the window through which a small cannon is fired every day at noon, a practice begun in 1877 to coordinate the city's bell-ringers. On either side of the tower stretches **Strossmayerovo šetalište**, a promenade which follows the line of Grädec's former south-facing fortifications – again, the views over the city and plains beyond are terrific.

The Naive Art Museum

About fifty metres north of Katarinin trg at Ćirilometodska 3, the **Naive Art Museum** (Muzej naivne umjetnosti; Tues–Fri 10am–6pm, Sat & Sun 10am–1pm; 20Kn; Ⓦwww.hmnu.org) provides an excellent introduction to the work of Croatia's village painters. The development of a school of painting inspired by peasant craft traditions was largely the work of an academically trained outsider, **Krsto Hegedušić**, who had been impressed by the work of untutored painters like Henri "Le Douanier" Rousseau while studying in Paris. Visiting family in the Slavonian village of Hlebine in the 1930s, Hegedušić discovered that the paintings of local men Ivan Generalić and Franjo Mraz displayed much of the style and verve he had seen in the work of other European non-academic artists, and took them under his wing, encouraging them to exhibit more widely. The work of Generalić dominates the first of the gallery's six rooms, with his early watercolours of Croatian village life reflecting a Brueghelesque fascination with rural festivities. His pictures soon developed a more fairytale, symbolic style, however – his numerous pictures of stags in forests resemble the illustrations in medieval manuscripts. Subsequent rooms deal with later generations of naive painters from across Croatia, with highlights including Ivan Lacković-Croata's scenes of villages in winter, crowded with spindly, stylized trees and snow-laden houses; Emerik Feješ's kaleidoscopic cityscapes; and Ivan Rabuzin's meditative, almost abstract visions of rural harmony. The final room concentrates on Josip Generalić (son of Ivan), who painted like a comic-strip artist on acid, deserting rural themes in favour of subjects like war, actresses and the mass suicides of cult members.

Markov trg and around

It's a short walk north up Ćirilometodska to the heart of Gradec, **Markov trg**, a restrained square of golden-brown buildings which serves as the symbolic heart of Croatia. Though it's not obvious from their modest facades, the buildings on the western side of the square house the Croatian cabinet offices, while those on the east include the **Sabor** (national parliament) and the so-called **Banski dvor** (Ban's Palace), originally the seat of the Habsburg-appointed governor and now the seat of Croatia's government. Markov trg has always been an important focus of government ceremonial: rulers of Croatia were sworn in here from the mid-sixteenth century onwards, a tradition renewed by President Tuđman in the 1990s, while in 1573 peasant leader Matija Gubec was executed here in a parody of such ceremonies – he was seated on a throne and "crowned" with a band of red-hot iron. Nowadays, you're unlikely to come across any signs of political activity aside from the occasional purr of a ministerial Mercedes or the furtive glances of sharp-suited security men.

St Mark's Church

The main focus of the square is the squat **St Mark's Church** (Crkva svetog Marka), a much-renovated structure whose multicoloured tiled roof displays the coats of arms of Zagreb and Croatia to the sky – and, it would seem from opening any book on Zagreb, dozens of photographers. The emblems adorning the Croatian coat of arms (the one on the left as you face it) symbolize the three areas which originally made up the medieval kingdom: north-central Croatia is represented by the red-and-white chequerboard known as the *šahovnica* – a state symbol since the Middle Ages; Dalmatia by three lions' heads; and Slavonia by a running beast (the *kuna*, or marten, Croatia's national animal) framed by two rivers – the Sava and Drava. The church itself is a homely Gothic building, originally constructed in the fourteenth century but since ravaged by earthquake, fire and nineteenth-century restorers, though some parts – including the south portal – are original. The Baroque bell tower was added in the seventeenth century, while the interior decorations, by the painter Jozo Kljaković and the sculptor Ivan Meštrović, date from the 1930s. Kljaković's frescoes are imposing but rigid, portraying huge, muscle-bound Croatian kings caught in dramatic mid-gesture; Meštrović's *Crucifixion* is more sensitive, merging sympathetically with the rest of the church.

The Croatian History Museum and the Natural History Museum

Slightly downhill to the west of Markov trg at Matoševa 9, the **Croatian History Museum** (Hrvatski povijesni muzej; Mon–Fri 10am–5pm, Sat & Sun 10am–1pm; 20Kn; Ⓦwww.hismus.hr), in one of the more crumbly of Gradec's Baroque mansions, houses prestigious temporary exhibitions. A few steps to the north at Demetrova 1, the **Natural History Museum** (Hrvatski prirodoslovni muzej; Tues–Fri 10am–5pm, Sat & Sun 10am–1pm; 15Kn; Ⓦwww.hpm.hr) is remarkable as much for the style of the displays as for the exhibits themselves, with objects laid out in a succession of old-fashioned cabinets that haven't been significantly reorganized in more than half a century. The history of the world's fauna on the second floor is particularly atmospheric, with visitors proceeding through a narrow corridor lined with corals, skeletons and creatures in bottles. There's an impressive range of stuffed mammals at the end – although pride of place goes to the eight-metre-long basking shark caught in the north Adriatic in 1934.

The Meštrović Atelier

Just north of Markov trg, at Mletačka 8, the **Meštrović Atelier** (Tues–Fri 10am–6pm, Sat & Sun 10am–2pm; 10Kn) occupies the house where Croatia's foremost twentieth-century sculptor, Ivan Meštrović, lived between 1924 and 1942. This is a delightful museum – one which you don't have to be a Meštrović fan to enjoy – with an intimacy that's lacking in the artist's other former home and museum, in Split (see p.368). Featuring wooden panelling and ceramic stoves ordered by Meštrović himself, the place still feels like a thoughtfully designed family abode rather than a reverential gallery. On display are sketches, photographs and small-scale studies for creations such as the giant *Grgur Ninski* in Split and the *Crucifixion* in St Mark's Church, along with some lovely female statuettes in the small atrium.

The Museum of Zagreb

Beyond the Atelier, Mletačka leads into Demetrova and from there to Opatička. Turn left here to the **Museum of Zagreb** at no. 20 (Muzej grada Zagreba; Tues–Fri 10am–6pm, Sat & Sun 10am–1pm; 20Kn; Ⓦwww.mdc.hr/mgz), undoubtedly the city's best, telling the tale of Zagreb's development from medieval times to the present day, with the help of snazzy presentation and

English-language texts. Approached through the courtyard of the former Convent of the Poor Clares, the museum occupies a complex of buildings tacked on to the thirteenth-century **Popov toranj** (Priests' Tower), which was built to provide the clerics of poorly defended Kaptol with a refuge in case of attack. Inside the museum, scale models of Zagreb through the ages reveal the changing face of the city, and there's a modest but well-chosen selection of weaponry, furnishings and costumes. Sacral art taken from local churches includes an expressive seventeenth-century sculptural ensemble depicting Jesus flanked by the apostles, which originally stood above the portal of Zagreb cathedral. Upstairs, political posters, photographs of political leaders and ideological slogans help to breathe life into the turbulent history of the twentieth century; one of the final rooms contains an unintentionally surreal display of the furniture destroyed by the JNA (Yugoslav People's Army) rocket attack on Gradec in October 1991, with smashed crockery and splintered furniture arranged as if part of some contemporary art exhibit.

The Gliptoteka

A staircase leads downhill from Opatička to the east, finishing up at the northern end of Tkalčićeva. A left turn up Tkalčićeva soon brings you to the **Gliptoteka** at Medvedgrasdska 2 (Tues–Fri 11am–7pm, Sat & Sun 10am–2pm; 20Kn), a collection of plaster copies of famous sculptures which is more interesting than it sounds – partly because of the atmospheric red-brick factory building in which it's housed. Things get under way with an impressive assemblage of replica *stećci* (medieval gravestones) from Bosnia-Hercegovina. Decorated with floral swirls, sun symbols and hunting scenes, they're a striking example of indigenous folk art. A collection of Croatian sculpture follows (comprising some originals among the copies), with twentieth-century greats Antun Augustinčić and Ivan Meštrović particularly well represented. The Gliptoteka also hosts seasonal architecture, design and photography exhibitions – the tourist office (see p.72) will tell you what's on.

Donji grad

South of Gradec, the modern **Donji grad** ("Lower Town") sprawls out in all its grey, grid-patterned glory. Breaking the urban uniformity is a series of interconnected garden squares, laid out from the 1870s onwards, which gives the downtown area a U-shaped succession of promenading areas and parks. Known as Lenuci's Horseshoe (Lenucijeva podkova) after Milan Lenuci, the city planner responsible for its layout, this was a deliberate attempt to give Zagreb a distinctive urban identity, providing it with public spaces bordered by the set-piece institutions – galleries, museums, academies and theatres – that it was thought every modern city should have. The horseshoe was never entirely finished, though, and it's unlikely you'll follow the full U-shaped itinerary intended by Lenuci. The first of the horseshoe's two main series of squares starts with Trg Nikole Šubića Zrinskog – usually referred to as **Zrinjevac** – which begins a block south of Trg bana Jelačića; to the west of Zrinjevac is the second line of squares, culminating with **Trg maršala Tita**. To the south are the **Botanical Gardens**, which were intended to provide the final green link between the two arms of the horseshoe, but didn't quite manage it: several characterless downtown blocks prevent it from joining Tomislavov trg to the east. The set-piece buildings on and around both Zrinjevac and Trg maršala Tita wouldn't look out of place in such bastions of Mitteleuropa as Graz or Linz, giving this part of Zagreb a prosperous, dignified air, although Donji grad's other structures are mostly offices, ministry headquarters or apartments, and there's not much in the way of shopping or café life in this part of town.

Zrinjevac

South of Trg bana Jelačića, the first section of Lenuci's Horseshoe, **Zrinjevac**, is a typical late nineteenth-century city park, featuring shady walks, a bandstand and a fountain which was designed by the ubiquitous Herman Bollé and looks like a bizarre cross between a cake-stand and a toadstool. Until 1873, when it was first laid out as a park, this area marked the southern boundary of the city: the muddy site of fairs and markets where peasants from the surrounding countryside gathered to trade cows and horses.

The Archeological Museum

The most eye-catching of the nineteenth-century buildings flanking the square is the beige Neoclassical structure at no.19, now home to the **Archeological Museum** (Arheološki muzej; Tues–Fri 10am–5pm, Sat & Sun 10am–1pm; 20Kn; ⓦwww.amz.hr). The three-floor collection gets off to a colourful start with a collection of Greek vases amassed by nineteenth-century Habsburg army officer Laval Nugent, before moving on to pottery and inscriptions recalling the Greek settlements on the Adriatic coast. Presiding over a room of Roman-period heads and torsos is a third-century relief of the goddess Nemesis, portrayed here as a frowny-faced woman dismounting from her chariot. Among the most striking of the museum's exhibits is the collection of ancient pottery – decorated with zigzags and chequer patterns – produced during the so-called Vučedol period, which saw an upsurge in crafts and agriculture and is named after the Bronze Age settlement at Vučedol, near Vukovar. The star exhibit here is the famous **Vučedol Pigeon** (Vučedolska golubica), the three-legged zoomorphic pouring vessel pictured on the 20Kn banknote. There are also two rooms of Egyptian mummies, mostly dating from the Ptolemaic period, one of which has a climate-controlled chamber all to itself. This last was found wrapped in a linen shroud (now displayed on the wall beside it) bearing ancient Etruscan writing – the longest known text in this as yet untranslated language.

The Modern Gallery

A block south of the Archeological Museum, on the corner of Strossmayerov trg and Hebrangova, another imposing nineteenth-century pile provides a home for the **Modern Gallery** (Moderna galerija; Mon–Sat 10am–6pm, Sun 10am–1pm; 20Kn), an all-embracing collection of Croatian art from 1850 to World War II. It's a well-presented display that includes something for everybody. Highlights of the nineteenth-century section include Vlaho Bukovac's sensuous *Gundulić Imagining Osman*, in which Dubrovnik poet Ivan Gundulič is surrounded by cavorting nymphs; and the moody Symbolist paintings of contemporaries Bela Čikoš-Sesija and Mirko Rački. Socially committed twentieth-century artist Krsto Hegedušić is represented by canvases depicting life in the village of Hlebine in the 1930s, while the photographs of Tošo Dabac provide a visual urban safari through the Zagreb of the inter-war years.

A few metres south of the Modern Gallery, an anonymous-looking doorway at Strossmayerov trg 12 leads to the Croatian Academy's **Graphic Art Gallery** (Kabinet grafike; Mon–Sat 10am–6pm; admission varies depending on what's on display), which hosts an absorbing variety of temporary exhibitions.

The Strossmayer Gallery of Old Masters

Immediately opposite the Modern Gallery, occupying the leafy centre of **Strossmayerov trg**, the Croatian Academy of Arts and Sciences was founded as the "Yugoslav" Academy of Arts and Sciences by **Bishop Juraj Strossmayer** in 1866. Based in the cathedral town of Đakovo in eastern Slavonia, Strossmayer was a leading light in the current of nineteenth-century Croatian nationalism that regarded Yugoslavism – the drawing together of all southern Slavs – as the best way of offering resistance to Croatia's traditional enemies – Hungarians, Austrians and Italians; he's still a hugely respected figure, regardless of what may have happened in the intervening hundred years.

The second floor of the academy building is taken up by the **Strossmayer Gallery of Old Masters** (Strossmayerova galerija starih majstora; Tues 10am–1pm & 5–7pm, Wed–Sun 10am–1pm; 20Kn; Ⓦwww.mdc.hr/strossmayer), a sumptuous collection of paintings from the fourteenth century onwards, which starts with two rooms of Renaissance Madonnas cradling chubby-cheeked babes. In the following room, a turbulent *Engagement of St Catherine* by Tintoretto stands next to a depiction of the same subject by fellow Venetian Veronese. Look out, too, for a small *Mary Magdalene* by El Greco, some early Flemish canvases by Joos van Cleve, the anonymous *Master of the Virgin among Virgins*, and French paintings by the likes of Fragonard, Boucher, Claude Lorrain and Poussin. Crouched in the lobby of the building is the **Baška Tablet** (Bašćanska ploča), an eleventh-century inscription from the island of Krk bearing the oldest-known example of Glagolitic (see p.266), the archaic script used by the medieval Croatian Church.

A statue of Strossmayer by Ivan Meštrović sits among the trees behind the building, a curiously gangling piece of sculpture that makes the bishop look more like a hyperactive conjurer than a dignified cultural leader.

Tomislavov trg and the Art Pavilion

South of the Croatian Academy, Strossmayerov trg merges into **Tomislavov trg**, the northern boundary of which is marked by the early twentieth-century **Art Pavilion** (Umjetnički paviljon; Mon–Sat 11am–7pm, Sun 10am–1pm; Ⓦwww.umjetnicki-paviljon.hr; 20Kn; free on Mondays). Resplendent in the bright-yellow paint job beloved of Habsburg-era architects, the pavilion hosts regular temporary art exhibitions in its gilded stucco and mock-marble interior.

Beyond the pavilion lie the immaculate lawns and flowerbeds of Tomislavov trg, its name taken from the tenth-century Croatian king, Tomislav, whose equestrian statue stands at the square's southern end, greeting travellers emerging from the Neoclassical portals of Zagreb's main train station.

Trg žrtava fašizma

East of Zrinjevac and Strossmayerov trg, all roads seem ultimately to lead to **Trg žrtava fašizma** (Victims of Fascism Square), a large traffic roundabout which was renamed **Trg hrvatskih velikana** (Square of Great Croatians) in 1990 – until anti-fascist groups complained vociferously enough to have the old name returned. The square is dominated by the **House of Croatian Artists** (Dom hrvatskih likovnih umjetnika; Tues–Fri 11am–7pm, Sat & Sun 10am–2pm; admission varies depending on what's on), an arresting circular pavilion designed as an art gallery by Ivan Meštrović in the 1930s, but converted into a mosque in August 1944 by the NDH in an attempt to cultivate Bosnian Muslim support for their pro-Nazi regime. It's still colloquially referred to as the *džamija* (mosque), though its three minarets were demolished in 1947, after which it was press-ganged into use as a museum of the socialist revolution. Consisting of a domed central space surrounded by long, curving galleries, it's a wonderfully atmospheric venue in which to enjoy the top-notch contemporary art exhibitions held here.

Trg maršala Tita

Heading westwards from Zrinjevac along either Teslina or Hebrangova, it's a five-minute walk to **Trg maršala Tita** (Marshal Tito Square), a grandiose open space dominated by the lemon-meringue-pie-coloured pile of the **Croatian National Theatre**. Opened by Emperor Franz Josef in 1890 and boasting a Neoclassical portal topped by a trumpet-blowing muse, it's a vivacious statement of late nineteenth-century Croatia's growing cultural self-confidence. In front of the theatre, in a circular concrete pit, is yet another work by Meštrović, the tenderly erotic *Well of Life* (1905), while in the southwestern corner of the square, somewhat overshadowed by a trio of pines, is a sculpture by Fernkorn, showing St George on a rearing horse laying into a snarling dragon.

The Museum of Arts and Crafts

A long gabled building on the western side of Trg maršala Tita houses the **Museum of Arts and Crafts** (Muzej za umjetnost i obrt; Mon 1–7pm, Tues, Fri & Sat 10am–7pm, Wed 10am–9pm, Sun 10am–2pm; 20Kn; Ⓦwww.muo.hr), a huge collection of furniture and textiles from the Middle Ages to the present day – anybody interested in the history of interiors will have a field day here. The interior is impressive in itself, with gilt lion heads gazing down from cast-iron balustrades above the central atrium. The first floor kicks off with a fifteenth-century Virgin and Child altarpiece of Tyrolean origin, continues with a parade of furniture and porcelain through the ages, and culminates in a hall of religious art with restored wooden altarpieces from churches all over northern Croatia. Most striking is the seventeenth-century altar of St Mary from the village of Remetinec, northeast of Zagreb, showing a central Madonna and Child flanked by smaller panels in which a whole panoply of saints bend in a stylized swoon of spiritual grace. There's a fine selection of seventeenth-century paintings in the first-floor ambulatory, most notably Charles Lebrun's fleshily sensuous *Bacchanal*, and Guido Reni's *Aeneas and Dido*, in which the love-struck pair fix each other with puppy-like gazes.

Objects on the second floor reflect Zagreb's status at the turn of the twentieth century as a prosperous outpost of Mitteleuropa, with locally produced ceramics from Zagreb's School of Applied Art (which has been nurturing innovative design ever since its foundation in 1882), as well as imported furnishings – notably Tiffany and Gallé glassware, and a plant-pot stand by doyen of the Viennese arts and crafts scene prior to World War I, Josef Hoffmann.

The stairs leading up to the third floor are lined with examples of 1960s poster art, including several geometric designs produced by the Croatian abstract art pioneer Ivan Picelj. At the top lie an array of clocks, a lot of silverware and a collection of early twentieth-century stained glass produced by local firm Koch & Marinković. Among the last, look out for Vilko Gecan's *Life of the Woodcutter* (*Život drvosječe*) from 1924, five idealized panels illustrating the life cycle of the Croatian peasant, depicted here with the kind of reverence one would normally expect from a church altarpiece.

The Mimara Museum

Lying just southwest of Trg maršala Tita on Rooseveltov trg is the most prestigious – and controversial – museum in Zagreb, the **Mimara Museum** (Muzej

Mimara; Tues, Wed, Fri & Sat 10am–5pm, Thurs 10am–7pm, Sun 10am–2pm; 25Kn; ⓦwww.mimara.hr). Housed in an elegant neo-Renaissance former high school, the museum is made up of the bequest of **Ante Topić Mimara** (1899–1987), a native of Dalmatia who grew rich abroad and presented his vast art collection to the nation. No one really knows how he amassed his wealth, how he came by so many prized objects, or indeed whether he was even the real Ante Topić Mimara – some maintain that he was an impostor who, in the chaos of a World War I battlefield, stole the identity tags of a fallen comrade. What's more, doubts have been raised about the attributions given to some of the paintings in Mimara's collection – many are labelled "workshop of . . ." or "school of . . ." in order to keep the art historians happy.

Whatever the truth, Mimara's tastes were nothing if not eclectic. There's a bit of everything here, and the collection can easily take up a couple of hours' viewing time. On the **ground floor** are exhibits of ancient glassware from Egypt, Greece, Syria and the Roman Empire, together with later examples of glass from Venice and the rest of Europe. Close by are Persian carpets from the seventeenth to the nineteenth centuries. Among the Far Eastern artefacts are Ming vases decorated with bendy-bodied dragons and a monumental bronze Head of Buddha. The **first floor** gets under way with a collection of European applied art, including Carolingian reliquary boxes, an extraordinary thirteenth-century enamelled crucifix from Limoges bearing a skinny, bulbous-headed Jesus (room 16), and an exquisitely carved English ivory hunting horn from the 1300s (room 17). Next come several rooms of religious sculpture – among the finer pieces is a fifteenth-century Flemish Archangel Gabriel with beautifully rendered wing feathers (room 20). The **second floor** presents a chronological trot through the history of European painting, beginning with Byzantine icons and several outstanding Renaissance altarpieces, the most arresting of which is Bicci di Lorenzo's *Virgin and Child* (room 31), in which a rosy-cheeked infant enthusiastically sucks away at an aubergine-shaped breast. A lavishly decorated ceremonial hall (room 35) provides a suitable home for many of the collection's larger-format canvases – Rubens' *Virgin with the Innocents* is a riot of pink puppy fat, while the sitter for Rembrandt's *Portrait of a Lady* appears to be in the process of being suffocated by her enormous ruff. Among the nineteenth-century French paintings in the final room (no. 40), you'll find an effortlessly light *Bather* by Renoir and a brace of small-format still lifes by Manet.

The Ethnographic Museum

South of Trg maršala Tita, the horseshoe continues with Mažuranićev trg, an unspectacular quadrangle of administrative buildings, including the **Ethnographic Museum** (Etnografski muzej; Tues–Thurs 10am–6pm, Fri–Sun 10am–1pm; 10Kn; ⓦwww.etnografski-muzej.hr), a rewarding collection which deserves rather more visitors than it currently receives. Before passing through the main entrance take a look at the cupola above, where an Art-Nouveau-influenced sculptural ensemble by Rudolf Valdec features an allegorical figure of Croatia embracing craftsmanship and commerce – a reminder that the building served as Zagreb's Chamber of Applied Arts and Trade when first built in 1903. Inside, the collection of costumes from every corner of Croatia is as complete as you'll find, displaying numerous examples of the embroidered aprons and tunics that are found throughout the country. Downstairs lies an engaging jumble of artefacts brought back from the South Pacific, Asia and Africa by intrepid Croatian explorers.

Marulićev trg and the State Archives

Marulićev trg, the next square to the south, is named after – and boasts a statue of – the Renaissance writer and father of Croatian literature **Marko Marulić** (1450–1524), author of *Judita*, the first narrative poem in the Croatian language. A reworking of the biblical tale of Judith, who killed the Assyrian general Holofernes, Marulić's poem was taken to be an allegory of Croatia's struggles against the Turks. The square was controversially – some say tastelessly – modernized in the late 1990s, when the lawn was lowered and the statue

△ A detail from the State Archives

surrounded by what look like rows of airport landing lights, illuminating the bard in a manner not entirely in keeping with the restrained nineteenth-century apartment houses on either side.

The bottom end of Maruličev trg is dominated by Zagreb's finest example of Art Nouveau architecture, the **State Archives** (Državni arhiv; Mon–Fri noon–2pm). Designed by local architect Rudolf Lubynski in 1913 to serve as the University Library, its pale sandstone exterior is covered with eccentric ornamental details, with reliefs by Robert Frangeš Mihanovič just above head height and globe-wielding owls roosting at roof level. Exhibitions relating to Croatian history are held in the lobby, but to appreciate the full splendour of the interior you should arrive in time for a guided tour of the former library reading rooms (Mon–Fri noon, 1pm & 2pm; 20Kn). The richly ornamented interiors feature stained glass, Art Nouveau desk lamps, ornate chandeliers, and frescoes by Croatia's leading artists of the day – Vlaho Bukovac's *Evolution of Croatian Culture* in the main reading room shows the nation's greatest artists and poets queueing up to receive garlands from the goddess Athena.

The Botanical Gardens

On the far side of the library, just across Mihanovićeva, beside the railtracks, lie the city's tranquil **Botanical Gardens** (Botanički vrt; April–Oct Tues–Sun 9am–7pm; free), where a colourful array of well-tended flowerbeds, rose gardens and rockeries fade into wilder areas of long grass and semi-forest. Despite being described as a "boring second-rate cemetery" by the novelist Miroslav Krleža, who used to sit here writing his diary during World War I, the place is nowadays an utterly charming island of city-centre tranquillity and relaxation – the perfect place to take some time out after a couple of hours' sightseeing.

The Technical Museum and beyond

South of the Mimara Museum, **Savska cesta** heads southwest towards the concrete-and-steel confections of twenty-first-century Zagreb, passing the **Technical Museum** (Tehnički muzej; Tues–Fri 9am–5pm, Sat & Sun 9am–1pm; 20Kn; Ⓦwww.mdc.hr/tehnicki), one of the city's more entertaining collections, at no. 18. The displays begin with a set of historic fire engines, followed by a jumble of wooden watermills and steam turbines. Steam- and diesel-powered machinery comes next: the line-up of disembodied plane engines (including a Rolls-Royce Merlin II from 1938, used to power the Spitfire aircraft) has the abstract dignity of a sculpture gallery. A central hall holds buses, cars, trams and aeroplanes, as well as a World War II Italian submarine captured by the Partisans in 1943 and drafted into the Yugoslav navy under the name *Mališan* ("The Nipper"). Other attractions include a small planetarium with regular showings (Tues–Fri 4pm, Sat noon; 10Kn); a reconstruction of a mine shaft (guided tours only: Tues–Fri 3pm, Sat 11am; 10Kn); and the reconstructed laboratory of Croatian-born inventor **Nikola Tesla** (guided tours only: Tues–Fri 3.30pm, Sat 11.30am; 10Kn), who pioneered the development of alternating current, radio transmission and electric lighting (to name but three of his obsessions; see box opposite).

Over the road lies the **Student Centre** (Studentski centar), where a theatre, cinema and several function rooms occupy the pavilions of the former Zagreb Fair. Further south along Savska cesta, trams rattle on towards the River Sava, passing an important Zagreb landmark en route: the cylindrical **Cibona Tower**, a 1980s office block whose highly reflective surface exudes a silvery, futuristic haughtiness. Zagreb's main basketball team (also called Cibona) play immediately

Nikola Tesla (1856–1943)

Born the son of a Serbian Orthodox priest in the village of Smiljan, just outside Gospić, Nikola Tesla went on to become the Leonardo da Vinci of the electronic age.

He studied in Graz and Prague before working for telephone companies in Budapest and Paris. In 1884 he emigrated to the US and found work with Thomas Edison – the pair allegedly fell out when Edison promised to reward Tesla with a $50,000 bonus for improving his electricity generators, then failed to pay up.

After working for a time as a manual labourer, Tesla set up his own company and dedicated himself to generating and distributing electricity in the form of alternating current – a system which is now standard throughout the world. With financial support from American company Westinghouse, Tesla demonstrated his innovations at the Chicago World Fair in 1893, becoming an international celebrity in the process.

In 1899 Tesla moved to Colorado Springs, where he built an enormous high-frequency current generator (the "Tesla Coil"), with which he hoped to transmit electric energy in huge waves around the earth. Photographs of Tesla's tall, wiry figure using the coil to produce vast electronic discharges helped turn the inventor into one of the iconic figures of modern science.

Tesla also pioneered the development of long-range radio-wave transmissions, but failed to demonstrate his innovations publicly and was scooped by Giuglielmo Marconi, who successfully sent wireless messages across the Atlantic in 1902. The US patent office credited Marconi as the inventor of radio – a decision overturned in Tesla's favour in 1943.

Official recognition was something that eluded Tesla throughout his career. In 1915 the Nobel committee considered awarding their science prize jointly to Tesla and Thomas Edison, but abruptly changed their mind on discovering that the pair were too vain to share it.

Tesla's failure to capitalize on his inventions owed a lot to his secretive nature. His habit of announcing discoveries without providing any supporting evidence led many to see him as a crank. During his period at Colorado Springs, he claimed to have received signals from outer space. In later life, he claimed at various times to be working on a death ray, and an "egeodynamic oscillator" whose vibrations would be enough to destroy large buildings, On Tesla's death in 1943, the FBI confiscated some of the scientist's papers, prompting all kinds of speculation about the secret weapons that Tesla may or may not have been working on.

During the Yugoslav period, Tesla's genius was proudly remembered by both the Technical Museum in Zagreb and the Tesla Museum in Belgrade. In the 1990s however, independent Croatia didn't quite know how to celebrate the achievements of a Croatian-born Serb like Tesla, but the scientist's 150th birthday provided an opportunity for Croatia to start treating the Tesla legacy seriously. With 2006 officially declared "The Year of Tesla" and billboards bearing his distinctive mustachioed visage going up all over the country, the great inventor was finally re-embraced by the land of his birth.

next door in the **Dražen Petrović Basketball Centre**, named after the player whose career was cut short by a fatal car crash in 1993. The best European player of his generation, Petrović led Cibona to the European championships in 1985 and 1986, and went on to play for Real Madrid, Portland and the New Jersey Nets before posthumously making it into the NBA's Hall of Fame in 2002. A museum celebrating Petrović's life is due to open in the basketball centre in the near future – the tourist office (see p.72) can provide details. In the meantime, you can always pop into the next-door *Amadeus* café, whose walls are covered with photographs of Petrović in action.

The suburbs

Zagreb's sightseeing potential is largely exhausted once you've covered the compact centre, although there are a few worthwhile trips into the suburbs – all of which are easily accessible by tram or bus. **Maksimir, Jarun** and **Mirogoj cemetery** are the park-like expanses to aim for if you want a break from the downtown streets, while the peaceful village-suburb of **Remete** provides the setting for a celebrated pilgrimage church.

Mirogoj

Ranged across a hillside just over 2km northeast of the centre, the main city cemetery of **Mirogoj** was laid out by Hermann Bollé in 1876. The main (western) entrance to the graveyard is in many ways his most impressive work: an ivy-covered, fortress-like wall topped by a row of greening cupolas. The cemetery serves all Zagreb's citizens regardless of faith, so alongside the Catholic gravestones you'll find Orthodox memorials bearing Cyrillic script, Muslim graves adorned with the crescent of Islam, and socialist-era tombstones boasting the *petokraka*, or five-pointed star. Head round the back of the chapel just inside the main entrance to find the grave of independent Croatia's first president Franjo Tuđman, a black reflective-surfaced slab that draws its fair share of patriotic pilgrims.

The most evocative parts of this vast necropolis are the arcades running either side of the main entrance, containing work by some of Croatia's best late nineteenth-century sculptors, with rows of elegantly rendered memorials overlooked by spindly cast-iron lanterns. If you head right from the entrance, it's difficult to miss Ivan Rendić's grieving female figures atop the graves of Petar Preradović and Emanuel Priester; slightly farther on, Robert Frangeš Mihanović's extraordinary bleak relief of stooping bearded figures decorates the tomb of the Mayer family. Head left from the entrance to find the Miletić tomb, where Rudolf Valdec's fine *Angel of Death* is framed on either side by outstretched sculpted hands, into which descendants of the family still place roses.

Bus #106 heads up to Mirogoj from Kaptol every fifteen minutes or so; otherwise, take tram #14 (direction Mihaljevac) from Trg bana Jelačića to Gupčeva Zvijezda, then walk the remaining ten minutes up to the cemetery via Mirogojska cesta.

Maksimir

Three kilometres east of the centre is Zagreb's largest and lushest open space, **Maksimir**, reached by trams #11 or #12 (direction Dubrava) from Trg bana Jelačića. Named after Archbishop Maximilian Vrhovac, who in 1774 established a small public garden in the southwestern corner of today's park, Maksimir owes much to his successors Aleksandar Alagović and Juraj Haulik, who imported the idea of the landscaped country park from England. It's perfect for aimless strolling, with the straight-as-an-arrow, tree-lined avenues at its southwestern end giving way to more densely forested areas in its northern reaches. As well as five lakes, the park is dotted with follies, including a mock Swiss chalet (Švicarska kuća) and a recently spruced-up belvedere (*vidikovac*), now housing a café which gets mobbed on fine Sunday afternoons. The eastern end of the park holds the city's **zoo** (daily: May–Sept 9am–8pm; Oct–April 9am–4pm; 20Kn; Ⓦ www.zoo.hr), shaded by trees and partly situated on a small island; it's a pleasant place to stroll whether or not you're taken with the animals. On the opposite side of the road to the park stands the Maksimir football stadium, home to both Dinamo Zagreb and the national side.

Remete

From the western side of Maksimir park, Bukovačka cesta threads its way uphill through increasingly affluent hillside residential districts before arriving at **Remete**, a village suburb some 6km north of the city centre. Crouched in a grassy vale below Mount Medvednica, the village was chosen by Pauline monks as the site for their monastery in the thirteenth century, and, despite the dissolution of the order in the 1790s, the monastery's **Church of St Mary** (Crkva svete Marije) remains an important focus for pilgrims on Marian feast days – especially August 15 (Assumption) and September 8 (Birth of the Virgin). Essentially a Gothic structure with a tacked-on Baroque facade, the church maintains its popularity with the faithful thanks to the presence of a tender fifteenth-century wooden statue of the Madonna on the main altar, to which miracle-working properties are ascribed. More powerful still are the richly coloured Baroque frescoes which swirl around the ceiling, most likely the work of **Ivan Ranger**, the widely travelled painter-monk from Lepoglava. Many of the scenes show locals in traditional north Croatian costume thanking the Virgin of Remete for her assistance in alleviating the effects of fires, floods or famines. Outside stands a pillar topped with a suitably ascetic-looking statue of Simeon the Stylite, a fifth-century saint who spent 36 years living on top of a pole in the Syrian desert. You can get to Remete on bus #226 (every 35–45min) from either Kaptol or Svetine, just west of Maksimir stadium.

Jarun

On sunny days, city folk head out to **Jarun**, a two-kilometre-long artificial lake encircled by footpaths and cycling tracks 4km southwest of the city centre. Created to coincide with Zagreb's hosting of the 1987 World Student Games, it's an important venue for rowing competitions, with a large spectator stand at the western end, although most people come here simply to stroll or sunbathe. The best spot for the latter is **Malo jarunsko jezero** at Jarun's eastern end, a bay sheltered from the rest of the lake by a long thin island. Here you'll find a shingle beach, several outdoor cafés (which remain open well into the night) and grassy, partly shaded areas of park. This is a good place from which to clamber up onto the dyke that runs along the banks of the **River Sava**, providing a good vantage point from which to survey the cityscape of Novi Zagreb beyond.

The best way of getting to the lake is to catch tram #17 from Trg bana Jelačića (direction Prečko) to the Staglišće or Jarun stops, either of which is a ten-minute walk north of the water's edge.

Novi Zagreb

Spread over the plain on the southern side of the River Sava, **Novi Zagreb** (New Zagreb) is a vast grid-iron of housing projects and multi-lane highways that nowadays looks much less attractive than its utopian planners intended. Thrown up in the 1960s in order to accommodate the stream of migrants drawn by the booming economy of the big city, it's a true melting pot of Croatia's population. The central part of Novi Zagreb is not that bad a place to live: swaths of park help to break up the architectural monotony, and each residential block has a clutch of bars and pizzerias in which to hang out. Outlying areas have far fewer facilities, however, and possess the aura of half-forgotten dormitory settlements on which the rest of Zagreb has turned its back.

The main reason to visit this part of town is the **Museum of Contemporary Art** (Muzej suvremene umjetnosti); due to open in late 2007, it's a purpose-built structure hogging the corner of Avenija Dubrovnik and Avenija Većeslava

Holjevca. To get there from Trg bana Jelačića, take tram #14 (destination Zaprude) as far as the Siget stop.

A kilometre west of the museum along Avenija Dubrovnik, the huge complex of pavilions comprising the **Zagreb Fair Grounds** (Zagrebački velesajam) is the city's main venue for trade exhibitions, although major art shows and fashion events occasionally add a touch of glamour to the proceedings – the Zagreb tourist office will have details of what's on.

Five hundred metres north of the museum, the **Bundek** is a kidney-shaped lake surrounded by woodland and riverside meadow. Recently re-landscaped and bestowed with foot- and cycle-paths, it's an increasingly popular strolling and picnicking venue.

Velika Mlaka

Five kilometres beyond the southern boundaries of Novi Zagreb, the road to Zagreb airport passes **VELIKA MLAKA**, a former village and now a prosperous dormitory suburb of Zagreb. In the centre, about ten minutes' walk north of the main road, an enclosure shaded by pine trees provides the setting for **St Barbara's Church** (Crkva svete Barbare), one of the most outstanding examples of traditional architecture in the region. To gain access to the church you'll have to phone the tourist office in the nearby town of Velika Gorica (Mon–Fri 7am–3pm; ⓣ01/62-21-666) to find out which of the villagers is currently in charge of the key.

A seventeenth-century timber construction covered in small wooden shingles and topped by a jaunty spire, it was substantially rebuilt in 1912, when the porch – decorated with sun symbols and squiggle patterns – was added. Inside, the walls, ceiling and main altar are covered with seventeenth- and eighteenth-century paintings telling the tale of St Barbara in comic-strip style; her life story is not for the squeamish – she was decapitated by her dad for refusing an advantageous marriage. Towards the rear of the nave, look out for a scene involving St Kummernis (a female saint, known as St Wilgefortis in Germany and St Uncumber in England, who was divinely granted a beard in order to ward off worldly suitors) throwing her golden slipper to a fiddle-playing beggar while being crucified.

To get to Velika Mlaka, catch the #268 Zagreb-Velika Gorica bus from ulica Paromlinska (at the south end of the underpass next to Zagreb train station).

Mount Medvednica

The wooded slopes of **Mount Medvednica**, or "Bear Mountain" (also known as the Zagrebačka Gora, or "Zagreb uplands"), offer the easiest escape from the city, with the range's highest peak, **Sljeme** (1033m), accessible by cable car and easily seen on a half-day trip. The mountain slopes are densely forested and the views from the top are not as impressive as you might expect, but the walking is good and there's a limited amount of skiing in winter, when you can rent gear from shacks near the summit. Driving, you can reach Sljeme by heading north out of central Zagreb along Ribnjak, and taking a well-signed right turn after about 3km – the hairpin ascent through forest is an exhilarating experience. On public transport, take tram #14 from Trg bana Jelačića to the Mihaljevac terminus, followed by #15 to the Dolje terminus, from where it's a ten-minute walk via pedestrian tunnel and woodland path to the cable car station (*žičara*; daily 8am–8pm; departures on the hour; 11Kn one way, 17Kn return). From here it's a stately twenty-minute journey to the top, with expansive views of greater Zagreb opening up as you ascend. When the cable car isn't running because of maintenance work or bad weather a small yellow sign reading *žičara ne vozi* is posted at the Mihaljevac tram terminus.

Slijeme

However you arrive, Slijeme's main point of reference is the **TV transmission tower** just above the cable car station, built on the summit in 1980. The tower's top floor originally housed a restaurant and viewing terrace, but the lifts broke down after three months and it's been closed to the public ever since. A north-facing terrace near the foot of the tower provides good views of the low hills of the Zagorje, a rippling green landscape broken by red-roofed villages. A left turn out of the cable car station brings you to the *Tomislavov Dom* hotel (see p.78), home to a couple of cafés and a restaurant, below which you can pick up a trail to the medieval fortress of **Medvedgrad** (2hr; see below). Alternatively you can follow signs southwest from Tomislavov Dom to the *Grafičar* mountain hut, some twenty minutes away, where there's a café serving basic snacks. From the path outside the hut it's a five-minute walk to the **Zrinski Mine** (Rudnik Zrinski; Sat & Sun 10am–3.30pm; 20Kn), where you can explore several hundred metres of sixteenth-century silver workings to the accompaniment of atmospheric sound effects – dripping water, clinking hammers, and an actor's voice reading out the roll-call of miners.

A right turn from the cable car station leads after ten minutes to **Činovnička livada**, a sloping meadow popular with picnickers. The path carries on over the meadow towards the **Chapel of Our Lady of Sljeme** (Majke Božje Sljemenske; Thurs, Sat & Sun 10am–6pm), built in 1932 to commemorate the one-thousandth anniversary of Croatia's conversion to Christianity. Ostensibly inspired by Croatian medieval architecture, it's actually a highly idiosyncratic modern building, featuring elegantly sloping buttresses and an obliquely angled bell tower. Paths continue east along the ridge, emerging after about twenty minutes at the **Puntijarka** mountain refuge, a popular refreshment stop whose cafeteria serves excellent *grah* (bean soup) and grilled meats. Another twenty minutes along the ridge brings you to the *Hunjka* hotel (see p.78), where there's another small restaurant and several more trails leading off into the woods covering Medvednica's eastern flanks.

Hunjka is the jumping-off point for a path that leads to **Horvat's Steps** (Horvatovih stuba), a north-bound downhill trail comprising five hundred steps prepared by walking enthusiast Vladimir Horvat between 1946 and 1956. The trail provides a good taste of the stark limestone landscape that characterizes the northern face of the mountain. Follow the steps all the way down and you'll hit a trail that descends to the Zagorje village of Stubičke Toplice (see p.118), a three-hour walk in total.

Medvedgrad

Commanding a spur of the mountain 4km southwest of Sljeme is the fortress of **Medvedgrad**. It was built in the mid-thirteenth century at the instigation of Pope Innocent IV in the wake of Tatar attacks, although its defensive capabilities were never really tested and it was abandoned in 1571. Then, in the 1990s, it was decided to rebuild the fortress as a monument to the Croatian nation. Walls and towers were swiftly reconstructed, and an **Altar of the Homeland** (Oltar domovine), an eternal flame surrounded by stone blocks and glass sculptures in the form of tears, was placed at the fortress's eastern rim. Conservationists were dismayed by the altar's failure to blend in with its historic surroundings, but it has quickly assumed an important role in state ceremonial, with the president of the republic and other dignitaries laying wreaths here on national holidays. You can roam the castle's south-facing ramparts, which enjoy panoramic views of Zagreb and the plain beyond, and there's a restaurant in a subterranean hall serving traditional north Croatian favourites like *grah*, *štrukli* and *štrudl*.

Unless you're walking here from Sljeme, via the marked paths that slant down from the *Tomislavov dom* hotel, Medvedgrad is best approached from the suburb of **Šestine**, 5km northwest of central Zagreb, which can be reached by bus #102 from Mihaljevac or Britanski trg (400m west of Trg bana Jelačića along Ilica). Get off when you see the bright yellow Šestine church 4km out of the centre and walk north past the church towards the *Šestinski Lagvić* restaurant 1km uphill. About 80m beyond the restaurant, a path – initially difficult to spot – darts into the woods on the left; look out for the red and white waymarkings painted onto a nearby tree. From here it's a straightforward forty-minute ascent through oak forest to the fortress.

Veternica Cave

A popular weekend destination at the southwestern end of Medvednica is the **Veternica Cave** (špilja Veternica; April–Oct Sat & Sun 10am–3.30pm; 20Kn), a limestone cavern located amid attractive woodland just above the west Zagreb suburb of Stenjevec. Once you've entered the gaping mouth of the cavern, a path cut into the limestone floor passes through an increasingly atmospheric sequence of fissures and chambers, the walls and ceilings of which are studded with seashell fossils – a reminder of the time millennia ago when the flatlands of Croatia formed a huge inland sea. Alas, summertime visitors are unlikely to experience a face-to-face encounter with the cave's bats, which hibernate here in large numbers during the winter months.

If you're driving to Veternica, take the Samobor road west out of Zagreb and then the (signed) right-hand turn in Stenjevec. After ten minutes' gentle ascent you'll arrive at a broad meadow known as Ponikve; from here a gravel road heads west to the *Glavica* **Hut**, where there's a café-restaurant (Tues–Sun). From the hut, a footpath descends through forest to the cave itself. To get there by bus, take #124 from Černomerec to Gornji Stenjevec then follow the marked path uphill to the cave.

Eating

Whatever your budget, there's no shortage of **places to eat** in Zagreb, although the range of food on offer is pretty much the same wherever you go. The majority of **restaurants** concentrate on the pork- and veal-based central European dishes indigenous to northern Croatia, and there are several excellent fish restaurants as good as anything you'll find on the coast. The number of ethnic restaurants in Zagreb is still quite modest, but decent Italian pasta is widely available, and there's a surfeit of pizzerias around Trg bana Jelačića and Tkalčićeva. Some of the best restaurants for **traditional food** are to be found in the northern suburbs – worth the trek out if you want to observe the local bigwigs at play. Naturally, **prices** vary according to what you're eating: pizzas, pasta and grills are cheapest, fresh fish the most expensive, and standard Croatian meat dishes fall somewhere in between.

Picnic supplies can be purchased from the stalls of **Dolac market**, just above the main Trg bana Jelačića, or from **supermarkets**: Konzum, in the subterranean

Importanne shopping centre in front of the train station has the longest opening hours (Mon–Sat 6am–midnight, Sun 7am–8pm).

Fast food

Crepes de Paris corner of Margaretska and Bogovičeva. Hole-in-the-wall serving sweet and savoury pancakes and toasted sandwiches. Daily until 11pm.

Ham Ham Varšavska 8. Fast-food joint which looks like a lounge bar, offering a range of salads, sandwiches, pasta dishes and risottos which you order at the counter. Portions are on the small side, but the swanky interior design will probably take your mind off such shortcomings. Mon–Sat until 11pm.

Pan Pek Trg bana Jelačića. Bakery outlet selling takeaway sandwiches, pizza slices, muffins, and rack upon rack of fresh bread, right on the main square. Mon–Sat until 9pm.

Pingvin Teslina 7. Courtyard kiosk with a few bar stools scattered outside, offering sandwiches with traditional Croatian ingredients such as *pršut* (home-cured ham) and *kulen* (spicy Slavonian salami). Daily until 3am.

Rubelj Dolac Market. Steer clear of the international burger franchises and head instead for this Balkan-style grill serving up *ćevapi* (mincemeat rissoles), *ražnjići* (skewered chunks of meat) and *pljeskavica* (mincemeat pattie), which is best enjoyed when garnished with *kajmak* (a cross between cream cheese and yoghurt) or *ajvar* (red pepper and aubergine puree). Sit-down or takeaway. Daily until midnight.

Restaurants

The restaurants below are graded according to the following ranges: **inexpensive** (40–80Kn), **moderate** (80–150Kn) and **expensive** (over 150Kn), based on the average cost of a basic meal (main course, salad and a drink). Indulging in aperitifs, bottles of wine and desserts will, of course, push the bill up considerably. Unless otherwise stated, restaurants are usually **open** daily from around 11am until 11pm or midnight. If it's advisable to **book** a table in advance, we've included a telephone number.

Kaptol and Gradec

The restaurants below are shown on the map on p.79.

Baltazar Nova ves 4. A five-minute walk north of the cathedral along Kaptol, this is one of the best venues in the city for the standard north Croatian repertoire of veal cutlets and pork fillets, all expertly grilled. There's a pleasant courtyard and service is attentive. Moderate to expensive.

Ivica i Marica Tkalčićeva 64. Housed in the back room of the café of the same name, this health-food restaurant is probably the best place in town to fill up on *štrukli* (the cheesy pastry indigenous to northern Croatia). In addition you can choose between filling soups and salads, risottos and fresh trout; just remember to leave room for the delicious sweets. The decor, employing natural materials like wood and stone, completes the wholesome picture. Moderate.

Kerempuh Dolac bb. Often overlooked because it's hidden away behind the main fruit-and-veg market, this is one of the best places in town to fill up on traditional Croatian pork-based favourites. The cheap lunchtime dishes draw a regular stream of local office workers. Daily until 4pm. Inexpensive to moderate.

Maharadža Opatovina 19. A familiar range of satisfyingly spiced curries, or pizzas for the unadventurous, served up in a relaxing ambience. Handily placed just round the corner from Tkalčićeva, the city's main bar-crawling area. Moderate.

Nokturno Skalinska 4. In a side street just off Tkalčićeva, offering serviceable pizzas, a varied choice of lasagnes, simple pasta dishes, good salads and an outdoor terrace in one of Zagreb's most attractive alleyways. Daily until 1am. Inexpensive.

Pod Grićkim Topom Zakmardijeve stube 5 ⓣ01/48-33-607. Good Croatian food in a cosy restaurant on the steps leading down from Strossmayerovo šetalište to Trg bana Jelačića, with a nice garden terrace overlooking the lower town. Mon–Sat until midnight, Sun until 4pm. Moderate to expensive.

Zvijezda-Kamanjo Nova ves 84 ⓣ01/46-67-171. Balkan grill-food elevated to the level of haute cuisine, with succulent *ćevapi*, *ražnjići* and *vješalice* (thin strips of pork wrapped round a skewer) served up alongside other south European standbys such as baked peppers and *pečeni grah* (baked beans). There's a generous salad bar, too.

Cosy interior with folksy touches, and a pleasant shaded courtyard. A ten-minute walk north of the Cathedral. Moderate.

Donji grad

Unless otherwise stated, the restaurants below are shown on the map on pp.72–73.

Asia Augusta Šenoe 1. Best and longest-established of the city's modest handful of Chinese restaurants, offering authentic food and formal service. A place in which to savour a relaxing evening meal rather than wolf down a budget feed. Moderate to expensive.

Boban Gajeva 9 ⓦ www.boban.hr. See map on p.79. Owned by the family of football star Zvonimir Boban, this popular and central pasta restaurant with breezy service is located in the vaulted cellar of the café of the same name. Inexpensive to moderate.

Cantinetta Teslina 14. See map on p.79. Good-quality Croatian, Italian and modern European food, conveniently located just south of Trg bana Jelačića. A stylish place with warm decor and a few snazzy interior design touches, but not too formal. Closed Sun. Moderate to expensive.

Dvorišće Obrtnički prolaz 7 ⓣ 48-11-400. Hidden away in an alleyway between Masarykova and Varšavska, the "Backyard" is a bit more elegant than the name suggests, with classy Croatian-European food served up in a brickwork and pastel interior. A choice of fish and pasta dishes help to broaden out the menu, although it's the hearty meat dishes that deserve most attention – flagship main courses like steak with blackberry sauce or wild boar with cherries are unlikely to disappoint. Mon–Sat until 11pm, Sun until 5pm. Expensive.

Gallo Hebrangova 34 ⓣ 01/48-14-014, ⓦ www.gallo.hr. Meaty European dishes with an Italian twist, plus a sizeable international wine list. Smart and chic, it's popular with businessmen and the expat community. Expensive.

Gostionica Tip Top Gundulićeva 18. Like *Korčula* just up the street, *Tip Top* (still popularly referred to by its former name of *Blato*) has for years been a byword in tasty, affordable Dalmatian cooking, and has a loyal local clientele as a result. The interior is engagingly strange, with 1970s-vintage wood panelling and lampshades in the form of jellyfish. Lunchtime staples like *crni rižot* (squid risotto) and *pašticada* (beef in prune sauce) might run out by evening, but there's plenty in the way of fish and seafood on the menu: *lignje* (squid) with boiled potatoes and *blitva* comes particularly recommended. Wash it all down with wines and spirits from the island of Korčula. Closed Sun. Moderate.

Korčula Teslina 17 ⓦ www.restoran-korcula.hr. Dalmatian restaurant of many years' standing with nautical knick-knacks scattered throughout the interior and a trusty seafood menu that's popular with lunching office workers. You'll find good-quality grilled fish alongside slightly cheaper items such as fried tuna fillets, pan-fried squid (*lignje*) and fried octopus (*hobotnica*) with potatoes. Mon–Sat until 11pm, Sun until 4pm. Moderate.

Opium Branimirova 29 ⓦ www.opium.hr. Flavoursome Thai food at bearable prices, in the shopping centre next door to the *Arcotel Allegra*. Not the most atmospheric of locations, but handy if you're heading for the Cinestar multiplex (see p.108). Moderate.

Pivnica Tomislav Trg kralja Tomislava. This semi-submerged beer hall near the train station is unlikely to be your venue of choice for a romantic candlelit dinner. If you want cheap and filling portions of *grah* (bean stew with pork), grilled pork or sausage, however, then you need look nowhere else; look out for set lunchtime menus chalked up on the board outside. Not to be confused with the similarly-named *Restoran Tomislav* just round the corner on Baruna Trenka. Inexpensive.

Purger Petrinjska 33. Don't be put off by the rather anonymous interior; this restaurant is one of the most reliable sources of inland Croatian cooking in the capital. Staple dishes like goulash or *grah* will sort you out at lunchtime, while the more substantial dishes on the menu include just about every form of grilled meat and schnitzel you might wish for. Cutlets prepared *na samoborski način* ("in Samobor style", with generous amounts of garlic) come especially recommended. Outdoor seating in the courtyard, and a solid list of Croatian wines. Moderate. Closed Sun.

Sorriso Boškovićeva 11 ⓦ www.sorriso.hr. Well-prepared, well-presented Italian food and a pretty good wine list too, in a moody, brick-lined subterranean space. Closed Sun. Moderate to expensive.

Stari Fijaker Mesnička 6, about 300m west along Ilica from Trg bana Jelačića. See map on p.79. Charmingly old-fashioned downtown restaurant with barrel-roofed interior, lampshades in the shape of carriages and an exemplary line in standard Croatian meat dishes. Good place for a slap-up evening meal, although inexpensive standbys such as *punjene paprike* (stuffed peppers) are also available. Mon–Sat until 11pm, Sun until 10pm. Moderate to expensive.

Vinodol Teslina 10. See map on p.79. Handily placed a block away from the central square, with tables ranged across an enormous covered courtyard. Famous for its spit-roast lamb, but most other central European meat dishes are available, too. Moderate.

Zdravljak Nova Ilica 72 ⓦwww.biovega.hr. A friendly, unfussy vegetarian restaurant in a cramped but cosy upstairs room, sharing the same building as Zagreb's premier health food shop. Tofu stews, bean soups and salads, and a choice of daily lunchtime specials. Closed Sun. Inexpensive.

Farther afield

K Pivovari Ilica 222. See map on pp.72–73. Large, modern beerhall-cum-restaurant attached to the Zagrebaćka pivovara brewery (which makes the mass-market Ožujsko lager as well as the more interesting porter-style Tomislav). The meat-heavy fare on offer is dependably satisfying, and it's one of the few places in the city that always has old-fashioned staples like *buncek* (pork knuckle with sauerkraut) on the menu. Three stops away from Trg bana Jelačića on a Černomerec-bound #6 or #11 tram. Mon–Sat until midnight, Sun until 5pm. Moderate.

Mú ul. grada Vukovara 72 ⓣ01/63-10-080. See map on pp.72–73. Exquisitely grilled T-bones, Chateaubriands and other beefy cuts in Zagreb's premier temple to the art of the steak. Grilled vegetables and baked polenta dishes offer some hope for herbivores. With floor-to-ceiling windows and contemporary furnishings, it's a chic spot too. A short walk south of the train station, it's squeezed between a bank and the DM supermarket and is easy to miss from the street. Mon–Sat till midnight, Sun till 6pm. Expensive.

Okrugljak Mlinovi 28 ⓣ01/46-74-112. See map on pp.72–73. Traditional Croatian food in rustic surroundings, with wood-panelled booths indoors, plenty of seating outside, and regular live music – popular tunes from classical to folk – on violin and piano. It's a popular venue for business meetings and family celebrations. Take tram #14 to the Mihaljevac terminus, from where it's a ten-minute walk north on the road to Šestine. Daily until 1am. Expensive.

Drinking

There's a wealth of **café-bars** with outdoor seating in central Zagreb, especially in the pedestrianized section around Bogovićeva and Preradovićev trg. The other main strolling district is Tkalčićeva, just north of Trg bana Jelačića, which, with a watering hole every few metres, looks like one vast outdoor bar. In these central areas, there's often little difference between individual establishments when it comes to the kind of music they play or the range of drinks on offer: it's really just a question of finding a free table from which to watch the world go by. Saturday morning is the traditional time for meeting friends and lingering over a coffee, although downtown areas remain busy day and night, seven days a week, if the weather is good enough for alfresco drinking. Things quieten down as soon as the weather gets cold, although the more characterful café-bars retain their clientele through the winter.

The cafés and bars listed below are **open** daily from early in the morning until 11pm or midnight unless stated otherwise. Larger cafés may offer a range of pastries, ice creams and cakes, but the smaller establishments focus squarely on drinking – so don't expect to find much in the way of food.

Patisseries and ice-cream parlours

The patisseries and ice-cream parlours below are shown on the map on p.79.

Ivica i Marica Tkalčićeva 64. This deservedly popular café and cake shop successfully mixes folksy traditions (wooden benches, waiting staff dressed in regional costume) with a thoroughly modern commitment to healthy living. All of their genuinely irresistible cakes are made from wholemeal flour and other natural ingredients. The *Međimurska gibanica* (layered cake from Međimurje incorporating cheesecake, apple and poppy seeds) is a masterpiece in itself. No smoking.

Kavana Dubrovnik Trg bana Jelačića. Zagreb's main square offers three or four staid cafés where you might want to take your aunt, and this is probably the best of them. The furnishings are contemporary rather than kitsch, the staff impeccably polite, and the ice creams, gateaux and pancakes go down a treat. The floor-to-ceiling windows offer good views of the world outside.

Millennium Bogovićeva bb. Swanky ice-cream parlour situated right in the centre of Zagreb's principal pavement-café strip; as good a place as any to sit and observe promenading city-dwellers.

Princess Gajeva 4. On the small side and with limited seating, *Princess* nevertheless offers an unparalleled range of cakes and exotic sweets, and a handful of intriguing savoury snacks: a slice of their *pita sa zeljem* (vegetable pie) or *zagorski strukli* (cheesy pastry) will keep the vegetarian in you satisfied.

Slastičarna Vincek Ilica 18. A long-standing favourite of the sweet-toothed, *Vincek* offers some of the best ice cream in the city, alongside a hard-to-take-your-eyes-away selection of cakes and pastries. There's a take away counter at the front, if you fancy eating on your feet, and a sit-down area offering coffee and other hot drinks towards the back. Mon–Fri until 11pm, Sat until 4pm. Closed Sun.

Cafés and bars

Boban Gajeva 9. See map on p.79. Perpetually busy café-bar in prime city-centre position, with a roomy, vaulted interior, low-key lighting and loungey corners equipped with sofas – the kind of place where drinkers of all descriptions feel at home.

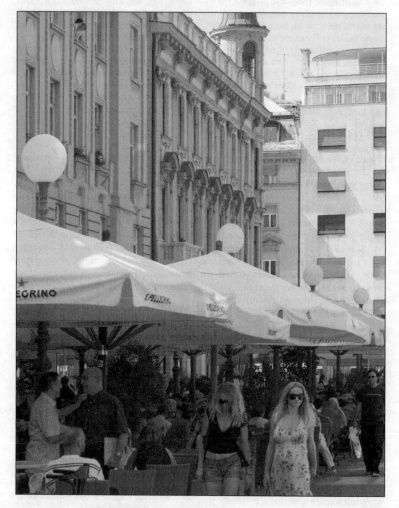

△ Zagreb café

Bulldog – Belgian Beer Café Bogovićeva 6. See map on p.79. This elegant split-level bar and pavement café is one of the most popular meeting places in town, especially on Saturday mornings, when the whole of Zagreb seems to insist on sipping coffee here.

Café Godot Savska 23. See map on pp.72–73. A cosy and relaxing place, somewhere between a European café and an Irish pub in feel. Convenient place for a drink after visiting the Technical Museum.

Cica corner of Tkalčićeva and Skalinska. See map on p.79. Arguably the most charming spot on Zagreb's most charming street, the cramped but cosy *Cica* features distressed secondhand furniture, vases your grandma would like and other bits of intriguing jumble. The coffees and hot chocolates are first-rate, and there's an entire menu devoted to traditional Croatian *rakija* – with carob (*rogač*), honey (*medica*) and walnut (*orahovača*) flavours particularly recommended.

Escobar Preradovićeva 4. See map on p.79. Excellent coffee and cookies in lounge-bar surroundings make this one of the best places in the Donji grad to dawdle over a brew.

Gallery Aleja mira bb, Jarun. See map on pp.72–73. Of the numerous places lining the northern shores of Lake Jarun (see p.95) this is one of the more worthwhile; a glass-and-timber pavilion serving expensive international beers and cocktails to a youngish feel-good crowd. Cultivates a loungey café vibe during the daytime, then turns into a frenetic pack-'em-in club on weekend nights. Daily until 3 or 4am.

Hard Rock Caffe Gajeva 10. See map on pp.72–73. Not part of the international chain, but with a similarly raucous, memorabilia-crowded ambience. In summer the *Caffe* sets out tables in the garden of the Archeological Museum just across the road – an excellent place to enjoy a coffee amid Roman gravestones.

Kazališna Kavana Trg maršala Tita. See map on pp.72–73. Zagreb's only surviving Viennese-style coffee house, though it's been modernized many times over the years, and the literary and artistic set who used to hang out here have moved on. A good place to recharge your batteries after a visit to the Mimara Museum.

Kolaž Amruševa. See map on p.79. This semi-submerged box of a place is only a short stroll from the main square but seems to be in another world. The bare-brick interior, low-key lighting and warm fabrics create the ideal ambience for a long night of alcohol-oiled conversation. It's a small place, and the DJ events held here at weekends produce an enjoyable crush.

Kolding Berislavićeva 8, three blocks south of Trg bana Jelačića. See map on pp.72–73. A civilized cellar bar with vaguely turn-of-the-century furnishings, *Kolding* is elegant but easy-going with it. It's a nice place for an intimate drink, and there's plenty of outdoor seating in the covered, winter-garden-effect courtyard.

Krivi put Runjaninova. See map on pp.72–73. Housed in an old warehouse just behind the Botanical Gardens, the "Wrong Direction" is a functional rectangular space with a live-music stage at one end and a bar at the other. A wall full of bright, dauby paintings helps to create an appropriately bohemian atmosphere. Patrons spill out into the large courtyard when it becomes too sweaty, noisy and smoky inside.

K. u. K Jurišićeva. See map on p.79. One of the cosiest places for a coffee break that central Zagreb has to offer, this charming two-level café is decked out with pictures of Zagreb old and new. Closed Sun.

Limb Plitvička. See map on pp.72–73. Friendly neighbourhood bar which has become something of a cult destination owing to its cartoonish wall paintings of can-can dancers, eccentric choice of background CDs and late opening hours. Proximity to the *KSET* club (see p.106) ensures its popularity as the venue of choice for impromptu after-gig partying.

Maraschino Margaretska 1. See map on p.79. Comfy, relaxing and chic café-bar on the corner of Cvjetni trg. It's named after the cherry-based liqueur from the Adriatic city of Zadar, hence the collection of Zadar-themed photographs covering the walls.

Melin Kožarska. See map on p.79. For years, the *Melin* has been attracting a wide-ranging crowd with its inexpensive drinks, post-industrial grunge decor and eclectic mix of sounds. About the only bar in Zagreb in which you are ever likely to hear a Captain Beefheart record, this is a terrific alternative to some of the posier establishments nearby.

Oliver Twist Tkalčićeva 36. See map on p.79. One of the prime places to see and be seen in a street that's full of bars, serving up a generous selection of local and imported beers in a two-level wood-panelled interior, with a big outdoor terrace. Daily until 2am or later.

Papillon north bank of the River Sava, near the Savski most bridge. See map on pp.72–73. Housed in a boat stranded on the grassy flood plain which borders the river, this is one of the best places in Zagreb for a laid-back night of mildly alternative weirdness, with off-the-wall DJs, stand-up comedy and the occasional live band providing the entertainment. It's the perfect place to end up after a late-afternoon riverside stroll, and the summertime outdoor reggae picnics should not be missed. Take tram #4 from the train station to the Savski most terminus and head east along the dyke above the river.

Pivnica Zlatni Medo Savska 56. See map on pp.72–73. If you like cavernous spaces with wooden benches piled high with students, then this is well worth the short trip south of the centre. The beers (a light lager-type beer and a dark porter) are brewed on the premises, and there's an extensive range of pork-and-potatoes Croatian food.

SPUNK Hrvatske bratske zajednice bb. See map on pp.72–73. An inconvenient 2km south of the centre, this memorably monikered bar (inspired by a 1970s comic-strip character, apparently) is in the same building as the National University Library, and fills up with students and alternative types from the early evening until the early hours. Offbeat DJs, regular live bands, and fantastic sci-fi murals by madcap artist Igor Hofbauer, provide three great reasons to visit. Handy for a pre-club drink if you're on the way to *Moćvara* (see p.106).

Sedmica Kačićeva 7. See map on pp.72–73. Frequently crowded place ten minutes' walk west of the main square with tiny bar area, mezzanine and a bar stool-scattered covered passageway. Popular with a slightly older crowd, with a higher than average sprinkling of arty and literary types. The aphrodisiac *rakija od mirte* (misletoe brandy) is a popular order.

Škola Bogovićeva. See map on p.79. Located on the floor above the Profil Megastore, this centrally located lounge bar is usually too packed with trendy bodies to provide any room for actually lounging around in. It's slightly pricier than most downtown drinking dens, but the dazzling white designer interior, funky vibes and commendable cocktail list make it well worth the splash-out.

Nightlife and entertainment

Zagreb offers the rich and varied diet of **entertainment** that you would expect from a metropolis of a million people. With international performers increasingly drawn to the city by regular concert seasons and an ever-expanding range of high-profile arts **festivals**, Zagreb is no longer the culturally isolated place it was in the 1990s. Note that arts events tend to thin out in August, when many of Zagreb's inhabitants head for the coast.

Extensive entertainment **listings** appear in the free monthly English-language pamphlet *Events and Performances*, available from the Zagreb tourist office (or on their website, ⓦwww.zagreb-touristinfo.hr); or in the bi-monthly *Zagreb In Your Pocket*, available from hotels and the tourist information centre on Zrinjevac. There's also daily listings information in the back pages of Croatian-language newspapers like *Jutarnji List*, *Novi List* and *Vjesnik*, the last of which has cinema and theatre schedules on its website at ⓦwww.vjesnik.hr.

Clubs

Despite a lean period during the war years, the emergence of a vibrant rave, techno and house scene in the mid-1990s revived the city's fortunes, and today Zagreb nightlife centres around a growing contingent of characterful and informal **discos** and **clubs**, many of which present the only real opportunities for catching **live rock** and **jazz**. The student year (which roughly runs from late September to late June) is the period that sees most activity in the clubs. Conversely, things quieten down significantly in July and August – some clubs may close up completely for a few weeks over the summer. Venues tend to be **open** from about 10pm to 3am or 4am unless stated otherwise. **Admission charges** for clubs and gigs range between 30Kn and 80Kn – more for big, one-off events. To find out about forthcoming gigs, check the posters plastered liberally around the city centre or pick up flyers from record shops (see "Shopping", p.108).

Zagreb festivals

Zagreb's impressive menu of cultural events includes a range of **festivals** that attract prestigious international participants. Many of these have their own web pages; otherwise, advance information can be obtained from the Zagreb tourist office.

Test! mid-March. Annual review of top international student theatre (Ⓦwww.test.hr).

Thirsty Ear (Žedno uho) April/May. Long-established alternative rock fest with guests from home and abroad, run by the Student Centre (Ⓦwww.sczg.hr).

Music Biennale (Glazbeno biennale) April. Highly rated festival of contemporary classical music held every odd-numbered year.

Festival of the European Short Story (Festival Evropske kratke priče) May. Readings, panel discussions and drink-fuelled party evenings involving top authors from Croatia and abroad. Some readings are in English; others come with big-screen English translation.

Contemporary Dance Week (Tjedan suvremenog plesa) late May/early June. Varied, often challenging programme of modern choreography from around the globe, taking place in Gavella (see p.107) and other city-centre theatres.

Cest is de best late May/early June. Week-long festival of street performers augmented by a big range of live music, taking place on outdoor stages positioned throughout the city centre (Ⓦwww.kraljeviulice.com).

Eurokaz Theatre Festival late June. Challenging avant garde drama with an impressive roster of international guests.

International Folklore Festival (Međunarodna smotra folklora) last weekend in July. Highly enjoyable display of ethnic music and dance from all over Croatia, plus a range of international guests. Performances take place on the central Trg bana Jelačića and in venues all over town (Ⓦwww.msf.hr).

Zagreb Summer Festival (Zagrebački ljetni festival) mid-July to mid-Aug. Festival of orchestral and chamber music, which brings together many of the international performers appearing at the Dubrovnik festival the same year.

International Festival of Puppet Theatre (Međunarodni festival kazališta lutaka) late Aug. A great chance to catch some of the best puppet productions from all over central and eastern Europe, with shows for both kids and adults (Ⓦhttp://public.srce.hr/pif-festival).

World Theatre Festival (Festival svjetskog kazališta) mid-Sept. Big names in international drama.

Zagreb Film Festival Oct. Initiated in 2003 and already attracting documentaries and art movies from around the world (Ⓦwww.zagrebfilmfestival.com).

Nebo Oct or Nov. Week-long world music festival attracting local and international names (Ⓦwww.nebofestzagreb.com).

Earwing No Jazz Festival Nov. Worldwide music from the no-man's land between jazz, experimental rock and the classical avant-garde, with concerts taking place at the Student Centre (Ⓦwww.sczg.hr).

City centre

Unless otherwise stated, the clubs below are shown on the map on pp.72–73.

BP Club Teslina 7 Ⓦwww.bpclub.hr. Basement bar and jazz club featuring frequent live music, owned by the godfather of the Croatian jazz scene, vibe-player Boško Petrović. A convivial late-night drinking haunt with waiter service for the smart set, and a long, thin, standing-only bar area for the hoi polloi. Gets crowded on gig nights, but well worth the squeeze.

Gjuro II Medveščak 2. Cult nightspot just north of the centre, incorporating a long, narrow, bar area with a frequently packed dancefloor at the far end. Fills up with younger disco-pop fans on Friday and Saturday, with a more discerning older crowd midweek. Closed Sun & Mon.

KSET Unska 3 ⓦwww.kset.org. See map on p.79. Small, intimate, student-run club and concert venue, concentrating on rock, jazz and experimental music. Notoriously difficult to find: from Savska head east along Koturaška, turn right into Unska, then go straight over the crossroads and take the first dingy alley on the left. Daily until midnight, Sept–June only.

Purgeraj Ribnjak 1 ⓦwww.purgeraj.hr. Pavilion in the park behind the cathedral, hosting either DJs or live music most nights of the week (mostly rock, jazz or blues). Pick up the monthly schedule from the bar.

Saloon Tuškanac 1a ⓦwww.nightclubsaloon.com. Legendary Zagreb meeting-place in a leafy corner of town 500m west of the centre, with a warren of stylish, wood-panelled rooms inside and a large terrace outside. A moderately dressy clientele includes a sprinkling of beautiful people and showbiz personalities, but it's not dishearteningly exclusive by any means. The music is an enjoyable mishmash of commercial disco, except on Tuesdays, when you'll hear pop-rock nostalgia for thirty-, forty- and even older-somethings.

Sax Palmotićeva 22 ⓦwww.hgu.hr/sax. Large, comfortable basement club run by the Croatian Musicians' Union, with live music (mostly jazz, rock and cabaret) most nights. Plenty of seating, Western beers on tap and a range of cocktails.

Studentski Centar (Student Centre) Savska Cesta 25 ⓦwww.sczg.hr. Rambling cultural centre incorporating several sit-down and standing-room-only venues, with frequent club nights and gigs (often featuring alternative acts of international stature). Look for posters or check the website. Closed July & Aug.

Tvornica Šubićeva 1 ⓦhttp://tvornica-kulture.hr. Former ballroom just north of the bus station, currently serving as a venue for live rock, club nights and theatre. It's not open every night of the week, so check listings info or posters before setting out.

Out of town

Unless otherwise stated, the clubs below are shown on the map on pp.72–73.

Aquarius Jarun ⓦwww.aquarius.hr. This waterfront pavilion at the eastern end of Lake Jarun, 4km southwest of the centre, is the city's main venue for electronic dance music – most of the big American house DJs have played here at least once over the last ten years. Expect commercial-ish house and techno on Friday and Saturday, and more experimental stuff on Thursdays and Sundays. Big-name Croatian pop-rock stars perform on the outdoor terrace in summer. Usually closed Mon & Tues unless live gigs are scheduled. Tram #17 to Jarun.

The Best Mladost Sports Centre, Jarunska 5 ⓦwww.bestclubbing.hinet.hr. Everything from run-of-the-mill discos to big-name international techno DJs, attracting a youngish crowd looking for uncomplicated hedonistic fun. Tram #17 (destination Jarun) from Trg bana Jelačića to the Stjepan Radić stop, then a short walk down Jarunska.

Boogaloo Vukovarska 68 ⓦwww.otv-club.com. Sparsely decorated, but roomy club occupying a former cultural centre and TV studio, a ten-minute walk south of the train station. They hold themed DJ nights aimed at the cooler end of dance culture, plus occasional gigs.

Dom Sportova Trg sportova 1 ⓦwww.dom-sportova.hr. Cavernous sports-hall-type venue for major gigs, with poor acoustics and long lines for beer, though the enthusiasm of a big Zagreb crowd usually makes up for any inherent lack of atmosphere. Touring Western rock bands frequently end up here. Take tram #3, #9 or #12 (direction Ljubljanica) to Trešnjevački trg, then turn right up Trakosćanska.

Jabuka Jabukovac 28 ⓦwww.nofad.info. See map on p.79. Cult alternative club which had its heyday in the 1980s and seems to be enjoying a new lease of life, playing predominantly retro sounds to a coterie of ageing goths and new-wavers. Housed in the building that once served as Nazi puppet Ante Pavelić's private bowling alley in the 1940s, in the Tuškanac suburb, a twenty-minute walk northwest of the centre. Open Fri & Sat.

Močvara Jedinstvo factory, Trnjanski nasip bb ⓦwww.mochvara.hr. Magnet for non-mainstream music fans, run by independent art cooperative URK in an old factory on the northern banks of the River Sava. Live gigs (by established foreign performers as well as Croatian indie bands) at least twice weekly, arthouse film shows, theatre and club nights (anything from world music to Seventies funk) on other evenings, along with cheap drinks and a friendly atmosphere. It's about 3km south of the centre: take bus #219, #220 or #221 from the southern end of the train station underpass, get off at the second stop and walk south towards the riverbank – once you get there, the club is away to your right. Closed at least one night a week, and most of July and August.

Pauk Jarunska 2 ⓦwww.sczg.hr. Spaceship-sized auditorium (a brief glance at the ribbed ceiling will tell you why it's called *pauk*, or "spider"), located amid the dorms of the Stjepan Radić student village. Gigs and themed DJ nights on weekends from October through to June, organized by the Student Centre. Tram #17 (direction Prečko) from Trg bana Jelačića to the Stjepan Radić stop.

Piranha Bar Jarunska obala bb ⓦwww.piranha.com.hr. One of the prime weekend drinking and dancing venues on the shores of Lake Jarun, attracting a steady stream of dressed-up kids and twentysomethings with a well-chosen mix of commercial dance music. Big-name DJs and live Croatian pop-rock acts occasionally perform on stage. Tram #17 to Jarun.

Classical music, drama and ballet

Theatre and concert **tickets** are usually easy to come by, and tend to be about half the price of those in Western Europe. Performances, including opera, are almost invariably in Croatian, unless you happen to be in town during one of the major festivals, when international groups are invited.

Croatian Musical Institute (Hrvatski glazbeni zavod) Gundulićeva 6 ⓣ01/48-30-822. Main city venue for chamber music, just west of the main square. Box office Mon–Fri 10am–noon, and 1hr prior to performances.

Croatian National Theatre (Hrvatsko narodno kazalište; HNK) Trg maršala Tita 15 ⓣ01/48-28-532, ⓦwww.hnk.hr. Zagreb's cultural flagship, this sumptuous Neoclassical building provides the city's main venue for prestige classical drama, as well as opera and ballet. Box office Mon–Fri 10am–7.30pm, Sat 10am–1pm, and 1hr 30min before performances.

Exit Ilica 208 ⓣ01/37-04-120. Studio theatre serving up a stimulating mixture of contemporary drama and cabaret. Some 2km west of the main square; take tram #6 or #11 (direction Černomerec) to the Republike Austrije stop. Box office Tues–Sat 4.30–8pm.

Gavella Frankopanska 8 ⓣ01/48-48-552, ⓦwww.gavella.hr. Second only to the Croatian National Theatre in terms of prestige, this is an elegant, medium-sized auditorium hosting leading local and foreign theatre companies, plus occasional concerts. Box office Mon–Sat 9.30am until performance time.

Kerempuh Ilica 31 ⓣ01/48-33-347. Offers a mixture of serious theatre, satire and comedy. Box office Tues–Sun 10am–8pm.

Komedija Kaptol 9 ⓣ01/48-14-566, ⓦwww.komedija.hr. Musicals, operettas and occasional heavyweight drama. Box office opens 1hr 30min prior to performances.

Off Theatre Bagatelle Bednjanska 13 ⓣ01/61-70-423. Fringe productions, theatre workshops and cabaret in a tiny theatre that looks from the outside like a suburban house. Box office opens 4hr prior to performances.

Scena Vidra Draškovićeva 80 ⓣ01/48-10-111. Small studio theatre housed in a former cinema, with a functional auditorium and a funky pre-show bar. Box office Tues–Sun 10am–3pm, and 2hr prior to performances.

Studentski Centar/&TD Savska 25 ⓣ 01/45-93-510, ⓦwww.sczg.hr. Home to leading contemporary theatre company &TD, with repertoire ranging from the populist to the experimental. You'll find the theatre at the far end of the complex, behind a derelict semicircular pavilion. Box office Mon–Sat 11am–1pm, and 2hr prior to performances.

Vatroslav Lisinski Concert Hall (Koncertna dvorana Vatroslav Lisinski) Trg Stjepana Radića 4 ⓣ01/61-21-166, ⓦwww.lisinski.hr. Just south of the train station, this modern complex is Zagreb's main venue for serious music, with both the Zagreb Philharmonic and the Croatian Radio Symphony Orchestra performing regularly in the main auditorium, and chamber music in the small hall. Box office Mon–Fri 9am–8pm, Sat 9am–2pm.

Zagreb Puppet Theatre (Zagrebačko kazalište lutaka) Baruna Trenka 3 ⓣ01/48-78-445, ⓦwww.zkv.hr. Imaginatively designed puppets, wonderful stage sets, and a repertoire strong in traditional fairytales. Performances start at noon or 6pm. Box office 1hr prior to performances.

Zagreb Youth Theatre (ZeKaeM) Teslina 7 ⓣ01/48-72-544, ⓦwww.zekaem.hr. Top-quality work by leading youth theatre groups, in a modern mid-sized auditorium bang in the city centre. Box office Mon–Fri 10am–8pm, Sat 5–8pm, Sun 1hr prior to performances.

Cinemas

Zagreb's cinemas show a wide range of recent releases from the West; they're shown in the original language with Croatian subtitles.

Broadway Tkalča Nova ves 14 ⓣ01/46-67-686, ⓦwww.broadway-kina.com. Plush, modern multi-screen in the Kaptol Centar shopping and entertainment complex north of the cathedral.
Cinestar Branimirova 29 ⓣ01/46-86-600, ⓦwww.blitz-cinestar.hr. State-of-the-art, if soulless, multiplex, with plenty of drinking and snacking opportunities in the adjoining shopping mall.
Tuškanac Tuškanac 1 ⓣ01/48-48-771, ⓦwww.filmski-programi.hr. Repertory cinema showing non-mainstream movies and classics.

Spectator sports

Football remains the city's principal sporting preoccupation, with the big teams playing matches on Saturday afternoons between August and May (with a mid-season break in Jan & Feb). Tickets rarely exceed 30Kn for league matches, when they can be bought from kiosks near the turnstiles. Prices go up for European matches or internationals, when tickets are best bought in advance from the relevant stadium. **Dinamo Zagreb** (and the Croatian national team) play at the Maksimir stadium, Maksimirska 128 (tram #1 or #17 from Trg bana Jelačića or #9 from the train station to the Borongaj terminus). The rather basic stadium at Kranjčevićeva 4 is home to the city's other major team, **NK Zagreb**. Take tram #3, #9 or #12 (direction Ljubljanica) to the Cibona Tower, then head west under the railway bridge. Few other spectator sports attract sizeable crowds save **basketball**, with Zagreb's top team, Cibona, playing at the Dražen Petrović Basketball centre, Savska 30 (ⓣ01/48-43-333, ⓦwww.cibona.com); matches take place on Saturdays from September to late April.

Shopping

Zagreb's principal high-street shopping areas are **Ilica**, the long, sinuous street running west from the main square; the **Importanne Galleria**, a multistorey mall just east of the main square on Vlaška; and **Kaptol Centar**, a smart shopping centre complete with cafés and a cinema, north of the cathedral at Nova ves 17. **Radićeva**, running uphill from the main square, harbours a growing number of antique shops and kooky designer boutiques. To see what mainstream Croatian **clothes** designers are churning out these days, head for Heruc Galerija, Ilica 26; or Image Haddad, Ilica 6.

There are some tacky **souvenir** outlets near the cathedral, but there's little in the way of locally made products that you would actually want to take home with you – unless you seek out some of the delicatessen stores we've listed under "Croatian specialities" below.

Antique and flea markets

Britanski trg Sundays 8am–2pm. Enjoyable open-air market 1km west of the main square, featuring household bric-a-brac, old postcards, folksy textiles and the occasional genuine antique. Central location and a decent choice of nearby cafés make this a popular spot with the locals. Two stops from Trg bana Jelačića on trams #6 and #11 (direction Černomerec).
Hrelić Sunday morning. Huge flea market occupying waste ground at the southeastern end of the city, offering row upon row of secondhand clothes, domestic knick-knacks, objets d'art and utter rubbish. Largely unshaded, so take a hat in summer. Tram #6 (direction Sopot) from Trg bana Jelačića to the Most mladosti stop (on the south side of Most mladosti bridge), followed by a twenty-minute walk eastwards along the south bank of the river.

Croatian specialities

Bakina kuča Strossmayerov trg 7. "Grannies House" offers a sumptuous range of upmarket alcoholic drinks, foodstuffs and fragrant herbs. Mon–Sat 8am–8pm.
Bolero Ilica 47. Speciality sweet shop overflowing with delicious homemade chocolates. There

are chocolate hearts in abundance, but also chocolate spanners and screws for the mechanic in your life.

Bornstein Kaptol 19 ⓦwww.bornstein.hr. Upmarket wine shop selling domestic tipples with a strong Istrian slant. Mon–Fri 9am–7pm, Sat 2–7pm.

Franja Vlaška 62 and Ilica 24. Coffee shop which also sells the kind of fancy food products that make perfect presents, including Croatian wine, *rakija*, olive oil and fig jam. Mon–Fri 7am–8pm, Sat 7am–5pm.

Ivić Vlaška 64. Fresh Dalmatian produce, and plenty of bottled and tinned goodies from olives to truffles. Mon–Fri 8am–9pm, Sat 8am–3pm.

Natura Croatica Pod Zidom 5 and Preradovićeva 8 ⓦwww.naturacroatica.com. Wine, *rakija*, olive oil and speciality biscuits. On the pricey side but very classy all the same. Mon–Fri 9am–9pm, Sat 9am–3pm.

Pršut Galerija Vlaška 7. Lots of lovely *pršut* (Croatia's delectable home-cured ham; see Croatian Cuisine color insert, sold by the gram or by the leg. Mon–Fri 8am–8pm, Sat 8am–2pm.

Books

Algoritam Gajeva 1, next to the *Hotel Dubrovnik*. Large, up-to-date selection of foreign-language publications, including lots in English. International magazines are sold on the ground floor; books in the basement below. Mon–Fri 8.30am–9pm, Sat 8.30am–3pm.

Jesenski and Turk Branches at Vukotinovićeva 4 and Preradovićeva 5. Browser-friendly secondhand bookseller with a small selection of foreign-language paperbacks and plenty of large-format international art books.

Profil Bogovićeva 7. Three-storey multimedia store with a decent selection of English-language fiction, tourist-oriented coffee-table titles, and guidebooks. Mon–Sat 9am–9pm.

CDs and records

Aquarius Vlaška 48 and corner of Varšavska and Gundulićeva. Retail offshoot of the club of the same name (see p.106), specializing in dance music but carrying a good selection of everything else as well.

Croatia Records Bogovićeva bb. Biggest of the high-street CD stores, run by Croatia's biggest record label – this is the best place for commercial rock-pop.

Dancing Bear Gundulićeva 7. Wide range of both domestic and international releases in all genres.

Dinaton Preradovićeva 12. Specialists in jazz and classical CDs.

Dobar Zvuk Preradovićeva 24. Secondhand store hidden away in a courtyard, much loved by vinyl junkies.

Kovač Masarykova 14. Another treasure trove of old vinyl and second-hand CDs, with obliging staff. Off the main street, in a courtyard.

Listings

Airlines Adria, Praška 9 ⓣ01/48-10-011, ⓦwww.adria.si; Aeroflot, Varšavska 13 ⓣ01/48-72-055, ⓦwww.aeroflot.ru; Air France, *Hotel Westin*, Kršnjavoga 1 ⓣ01/48-37-100, ⓦwww.airfrance.com; Austrian Airlines, at the airport ⓣ01/62-65-900, ⓦwww.aua.com; Bosna Air, airport ⓣ01/45-62-672, ⓦwww.airbosna.ba; Croatia Airlines, Zrinjevac 17 ⓣ01/48-19-633, ⓦwww.croatiaairlines.hr; CSA, Zrinjevac 17 ⓣ01/48-73-301, ⓦwww.csa.cz; LOT, Generalturist, Zrinjevac 18 ⓣ01/48-73-123, ⓦwww.lot.com; Lufthansa, Generalturist, Zrinjevac 18 ⓣ01/48-73-123, ⓦwww.lufthansa.com; Malev, *Hotel Westin*, Kršnjavoga 1 ⓣ01/48-36-936 ⓦwww.malev.com.

Airport Enquiries ⓣ01/62-65-222, ⓦwww.zagreb-airport.hr.

Bus station Enquiries on ⓣ060/313-333, or check ⓦwww.akz.hr.

Car rental Avis, *Hotel Sheraton*, Kneza Borne 2 ⓣ062-222-226, ⓦwww.avis.com.hr; Budget, *Hotel Sheraton*, Kneza Borne 2 ⓣ01/45-54-943, ⓦwww.budget.hr; Dollar & Thrifty, at the airport ⓣ01/62-65-333, ⓦwww.subrosa.hr; Hertz, Vukotinovićeva 4 ⓣ01/48-46-777, ⓦwww.hertz.hr; Sixt, *Hotel Panorama*, Trg sportova 9 ⓣ01/30-15-303, ⓦwww.sixt.hr.

Embassies and consulates Australia, 3rd floor, Kaptol Centar, Nova ves 11 ⓣ01/48-91-200, ⓦwww.auembassy.hr; Bosnia-Hercegovina, Torbarova 9 ⓣ01/46-83-761; Canada, Prilaz Gjure Deželića 4 ⓣ01/48-81-200; Czech Republic, 8th floor, Savska cesta 41 ⓣ01/61-77-246, ⓦwww.mzv.cz; Germany, ul. grada Vukovara 64 ⓣ01/63-00-100, ⓦwww.deutschebotschaft-zagreb.hr; Ireland, Turinina 3 ⓣ01/66-74-455; Netherlands, Medvešćak 56 ⓣ01/46-84-880, ⓦwww.netherlandsembassy.hr; New Zealand, Trg S. Radića 3 ⓣ01/61-51-382; Serbia and Montenegro, Pantovčak 245 ⓣ01/45-79-067; UK, Ivana Lučića 4 ⓣ01/60-09-100, ⓦwww.britishembassy.gov.uk/croatia; US, 10km south of the centre at Thomasa Jeffersona 2 ⓣ01/66-12-200, ⓦwww.usembassy.hr.

Exchange There are exchange counters (*mjenjačnica*) at all banks, travel agents and post offices. Outside regular office hours, try the exchange counter at the bus station (24hr), or at the post office next to the train station at Branimirova 4 (24hr).

Ferry bookings Jadrolinija tickets can be bought from Marko Polo, Masarykova 24 ⓣ01/48-15-216.

Hospital The main casualty department is at Draškovićeva 19.

Internet Cafés The number of cybercafés in Zagreb is on the increase. Most insist on registering you as a member before letting you loose on the computers, so bring your passport. Membership is usually free; expect to pay 20–30Kn per hour online. *Aquarius.net* (ⓣ01/46-18-873, ⓦwww.aquariusnet.hr), at Držislavova 4, just west of Trg hrvatskih velikana, is small, dark and functional; enter via the *Plava Ptica* café next door. *Art.net café*, Preradovićeva 25 (ⓣ01/45-58-471, ⓦwww.haa.hr; closed Sun), is roomy, very plush and rather formal in atmosphere, with occasional live music and literary evenings. An alternative cultural centre, where you can hang out, drink coffee and listen to chill-out beats as well as send emails, is *Mama*, at Preradovićeva 18 (ⓣ01/48-56-400, ⓦwww.mi2.hr). In the courtyard of Teslina 12, *Sublink* (ⓣ01/48-11-329, ⓦwww.sublink.hr) was Croatia's first cybercafé and is still a cult Zagreb meeting point – it's friendly and relaxed, if cramped at times.

Laundry Service washes and dry cleaning at Petecin, Kaptol 11 (Mon–Fri 8am–8pm, Sat 8am–2pm), and Dorateus, Draškovićeva 31 (Mon–Fri 7am–7pm, Sat 8am–noon).

Left luggage At the bus station (daily 6am–10pm) and train station (24hr).

Libraries British Council, Ilica 12 (Mon & Fri 11am–5pm, Tues, Wed & Thurs 1.30–7.30pm, Sat 10am–8pm; ⓣ01/48-99-500); French Cultural Institute, Preradovićeva 40 (Mon–Fri 9am–5pm; ⓣ01/48-55-222); Goethe Institute, ul. grada Vukovara 64 (Mon–Thurs 9.30am–5pm, Fri 9.30am–3.30pm; ⓣ01/61-95-000); Italian Cultural Institute, Preobraženska 4 (Mon–Thurs 8.30am–1pm, Fri 8.30am–2.30pm; ⓣ01/48-30-208).

Parking Free parking spaces in the city centre are hard to find, so it's best to head for one of the main garages, the handiest central ones being on Ilica and Langov trg (both 5Kn/hr).

Pharmacy corner of Trg bana Jelačića and Radićeva (24hr).

Photographic supplies Foto Studio Zagreb, Praška 2.

Post offices Jurišićeva 13 (Mon–Fri 7am–9pm, Sat 7am–7pm, Sun 8am–2pm); Branimirova 4 (24hr).

Sporting equipment Elan, Draškovićeva 25, sells equipment for all manner of winter sports; for snowboarding gear specifically, you can also try Extreme Sport, Mesnička 3.

Swimming For an outdoor swim, you can choose between the beach at Jarun or the more central outdoor pool at Šalata, ten minutes' walk north-east from Trg bana Jelačića at the top end of the Schlosserove stube steps (June–Sept Mon–Fri 1.30–6pm, Sat & Sun 11am–7pm). The best of the indoor pools is the Bazen Utrine in Novi Zagreb at Balotin prilaz bb (tram #6 or #14 to Utrina; Tues & Thurs 9am–7pm, Wed & Fri 9am–8pm, Sat 1–5pm, Sun 3–8pm).

Taxis There are taxi ranks on Trg maršala Tita and on the corner of Teslina and Gajeva. To book, call ⓣ970, or 01/66-82-505 or 66-82-558.

Telephones National and international calls can be made from the metered booths at the post offices on Jurišićeva or Branimirova.

Train enquiries Information on ⓣ060/333-444 (domestic services) and ⓣ01/37-82-532 (international).

Travel agents Atlas, Zrinjevac 17 ⓣ01/48-73-064, ⓦwww.atlas.hr; Croatia Express, Teslina 4 ⓣ01/48-11-842, ⓦwww.zug.hr; Generalturist, Praška 5 ⓣ01/48-05-555, ⓦwww.generalturist.com; Globtour, Zrinjevac 1 ⓣ01/48-10-021, ⓦwww.globtour.hr; STA Travel, Krvavi most 3, ⓦwww.sta-zagreb.com.

Travel details

Trains

Zagreb to: Čakovec (6 daily; 2hr 20min–3hr 20min); Delnice (6 daily; 2hr 30min–3hr 20min); Karlovac (14 daily; 35–50min); Koprivnica (10 daily; 1hr 15min–1hr 30min); Kutina (16 daily; 1hr–1hr 40min); Našice (4 daily; 3hr 30min); Novska (18 daily; 1hr 30min–2hr); Osijek (4 daily; 4hr 15min); Rijeka (6 daily; 3hr 45min–4hr 20min); Savski Marof (every 30min–1hr; 30min); Sisak (hourly; 1hr); Skrad (5 daily; 2hr 20min–3hr); Split (4 daily; 5hr 30min–8hr); Varaždin (10 daily; 2hr 10min–3hr); Vinkovci (10 daily; 2hr 30min–5hr).

Buses

Zagreb to: Čakovec (10 daily; 2hr 30min); Cres (2 daily; 6hr 30min); Delnice (12 daily; 1hr 30min);

Desinić (Mon–Sat 8 daily, Sun 4 daily; 2hr); Dubrovnik (4 daily; 9–11hr); Karlovac (every 30min; 50min); Korčula Town (1 daily; 13hr); Krapina (Mon–Fri 8 daily, Sat & Sun 2 daily; 1hr 10min–1hr 30min); Krapinske Toplice (Mon–Fri 12 daily, Sat 10 daily, Sun 7 daily; 1hr 20min); Kutina (10 daily; 1hr 45min); Marija Bistrica (Mon–Fri 17 daily, Sat 9 daily, Sun 6 daily; 1hr 15min); Osijek (Mon–Sat 8 daily; Sun 6 daily; 5hr 30min); Pag Town (5 daily; 5hr); Plitvice (7 daily; 2hr 30min); Poreč (6 daily; 4hr–5hr 30min); Požega (5 daily; 2hr 45min); Pula (10 daily; 4hr–6hr 30min); Rijeka (20 daily; 2hr 30min); Rovinj (6 daily; 4hr–5hr 40min); Samobor (Mon–Sat every 20–30min, Sun hourly; 40min); Split (8 daily; 5–9hr); Varaždin (12 daily; 2hr); Zadar (hourly; 5hr).

Domestic flights

Zagreb to: Bol (April–Sept 1 or 2 weekly; 50min); Dubrovnik (April–Sept 3 daily, Oct–March 2 daily; 50min); Pula (1 daily; 50min); Split (April–Sept 4 daily, Oct–March 3 daily; 45min); Zadar (1 daily; 45min).

International trains

Zagreb to: Belgrade (4 daily; 6hr 30min); Budapest Keleti (2 daily; 5hr 40min–7hr 20min); Graz (2 daily; 4hr); Ljubljana (6 daily; 2hr 20min); Maribor (2 daily; 2hr 30min); Salzburg (1 daily; 7hr); Sarajevo (1 daily; 10hr); Vienna (2 daily; 6hr 30min); Venice (2 daily; 7–8hr).

International buses

Zagreb to: Belgrade (1 daily; 10hr); Frankfurt (2 daily; 14–16hr); Graz (2 daily; 4hr); Munich (2 daily; 10hr); Sarajevo (1 daily; 10hr); Stuttgart (1 daily; 14hr).

2

Inland Croatia

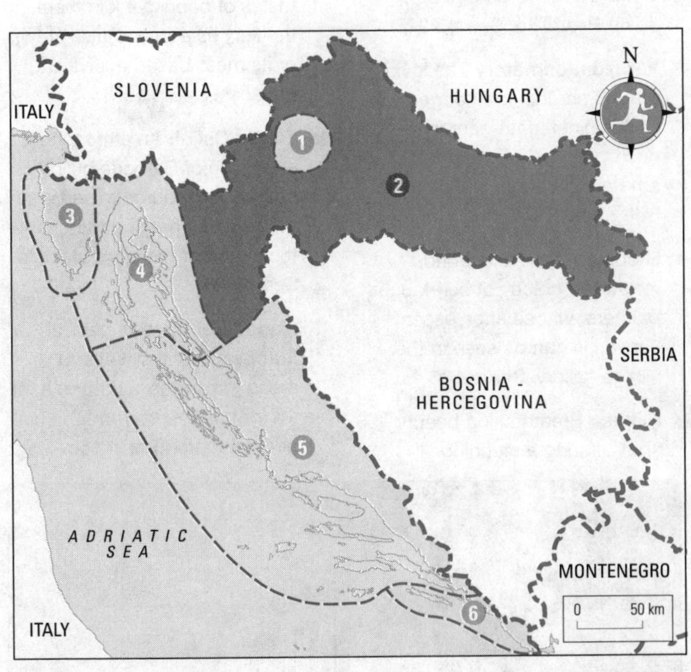

CHAPTER 2 # Highlights

* **Gingerbread hearts** (*licitarska srca*) Garish, tacky and totally inedible, these heart-shaped biscuits remain a must-buy souvenir for any visitor to the Zagorje region. See p.117

* **Kumrovec** Beautifully preserved Zagorje village which is also the birthplace of Croatia's most famous son, Josip Broz Tito. See p.122

* **Varaždin cemetery** The lovingly tended shrubs and hedgerows of this nineteenth-century necropolis will excite the amateur gardener in everyone. See p.132

* **Hlebine** Home to a world-renowned colony of self-taught painters, whose effervescent canvases can be seen in the village gallery. See p.136

* **Plitvice** Breathtaking beauty spot offering a stunning profusion of forest-fringed lakes, waterfalls and rapids. See p.148

* **Lonjsko polje** Enchantingly archaic timber-built villages, frequented by storks, wild horses and spotty-hided pigs. See p.152

* **Slavonian food** Slavonians will eat anything as long as it tastes of paprika – join them in the fiery *fiš paprikaš* (fish stew), or its meat-based equivalent, *čobanac*. See p.158

* **Tvrđa, Osijek** An atmospheric ensemble of Baroque buildings built by Habsburgs to serve as their military headquarters, now the centre of the city's nightlife. See p.165

* **Kopački rit** One of central Europe's premier wetland areas, providing a natural habitat for herons, cormorants and birdwatchers. See p.168

△ Waterfalls at Plitvice

2

Inland Croatia

The jumble of geographical regions that make up inland Croatia seem, on the face of it, to have little in common with one another. Historically, however, the Croats of the interior were united by a set of cultural influences very different from those that prevailed on the coast. After the collapse of the medieval Croatian kingdom in the early part of the twelfth century, inland Croatia fell under the sway of first Hungary, then the Habsburg Empire, increasingly adopting the culture and architecture of central Europe. All this has left its mark: sturdy, pastel-coloured farmhouses dot the countryside, while churches sport onion domes and Gothic spires, providing a sharp contrast with the pale stone houses and Venetian-inspired campaniles of the coast.

The main appeal of inland Croatia lies in its contrasting landscapes. It's here that the mountain chains which run from the Alps down to the Adriatic meet the Pannonian plain, stretching all the way from Zagreb to eastern Hungary. The **Zagorje** region, just north of Zagreb, resembles southern Austria with its mixture of knobbly hills, vineyards and compact, busy villages, while southwest of Zagreb are the slightly wilder uplands of the **Žumberak** and the smoother, pastoral hills of the **Lika**. Nestling among the latter are the **Plitvice Lakes**, a sequence of pools linked by picturesque mini-waterfalls – Croatia's most captivating, and most visited, natural attraction. Much less touristed but equally rewarding are the misty, marshy flatlands southeast of the capital, with the **Lonjsko polje Nature Park** offering a mixture of archaic timber-built villages and birdwatching opportunities. The eastern provinces of **Podravina** and **Slavonia**, watered by the rivers Drava and Sava respectively, are classic corn-growing territory: broad expanses of flat, chequered farmland only partially broken up by low green hills.

There are worthwhile urban centres here too, with several well-preserved Baroque towns in which something of the elegance of provincial Habsburg life has survived. The most attractive of these is **Varaždin**, northeast of Zagreb, although **Karlovac**, to the southwest, and **Požega**, to the southeast, are also worth a look. There's little in the way of big-city thrills except in **Osijek**, inland Croatia's main urban centre after Zagreb, and the most convenient place from which to explore eastern Slavonia.

Eastern Slavonia apart, much of inland Croatia is within day-trip range of **Zagreb**, from where road and rail routes fan out in all directions: north through the Zagorje towards Slovenia, northeast via Varaždin to Hungary, and east across the Slavonian plain towards Serbia. Busiest of all is the route southwest towards the coast, which runs through Karlovac before splitting two ways – straight on across the Gorski kotar hills towards Rijeka, or south across the Lika towards

INLAND CROATIA

Vienna
Lake Balaton & Budapest
Budapest
0 50 km
N
Maribor
SLOVENIA
Ptuj
MEĐIMURJE
Čakovec
Nagykanisza
HUNGARY
Varaždin
Trakošćan
ZAGORJE
Lepoglava
Celje
Pregrada
Krapina
Krapinske Toplice
Kumrovec
Koprivnica
Hlebine
Drava
Pécs
Mohács
Danube
Zabok
Marija Bistrica
Križevci
Gornja Stubica
PODRAVINA
E59
E71
ŽUMBERAČKO-SAMOBORSKO GORJE NATURE PARK
ZAGREB
Bjelovar
Bregana
Dugo Selo
Virovitica
Beli Manastir
Batina
SERBIA
Japetić (879m)
Samobor
Zmajevac
ŽUMBERAK
Ivanić Grad
Slatina
Donji Miholjac
BARANJA
Velika Gorica
Kršić
Jastrebarsko
LONJSKO POLJE NATURE PARK
KOPAČKI RIT NATURE PARK
RISNJAK NATIONAL PARK
Ozalj
Crna Mlaka
TUROPOLJE
Papuk (953m)
Bizovac
Bilje
Kopačevo
Daruvar
Karlovac
Donja Kupčina
Jelisavac
Kupa
SLAVONIA
Kutina
E661
Osijek
Skrad
Gorski Kotar
Petrinja
Sisak
Velika
Kutjevo
Našice
E73
Duga Resa
Čigoć
Pakrac
Delnice
Lonja
Kula
Vukovar
Glina
Požega
Klek (1187m)
Mužilovčica
Ogulin
Novska
Đakovo
Danube
Šarengrad
Bjelolasica
Krapje
Nova Gradiška
Vinkovci
Jasenovac
Slavonski Brod
Ilok
Bapska
Josipdol
E70
Šid
Novi Vinodolski
Slunj
Sava
Oštarski Stanovi
Senj
Rakovica
Županja
Lipovac
Grabovac
Sava
LIKA
Korana
Prijedor
BOSNIA-HERCEGOVINA
Rastovača
PLITVICE NATIONAL PARK
Bihać
Ljubljana & Salzburg
Ljubljana & Salzburg
Rijeka
Rijeka
Novi Sad
Novi Sad
Belgrade
Zadar, Dubrovnik & Split
Korenica & Knin
Sarajevo
Banja Luka
Tuzla

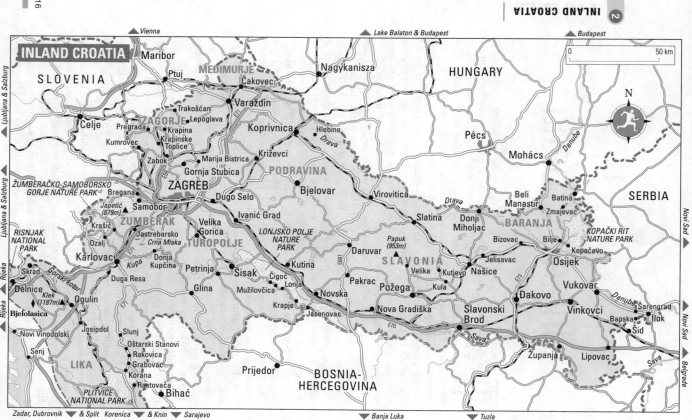

Zadar and Split, passing near the Plitvice Lakes on the way. Travellers making forays south or east of Zagreb will almost certainly cross parts of former war zones, and visitors to war-affected areas will see evidence of the recent conflict in the shape of burned-out houses and large signs warning of uncleared minefields. There's no reason to be wary of travelling in the region, however: life has returned to the towns, public transport runs smoothly, and the majority of accommodation is back in business.

The Zagorje

Spread out between Zagreb and the Slovene border, the **Zagorje** is an area of chocolate-box enchantment: miniature wooded hills are crowned with the castles they seem designed for, and streams tumble through lush vineyards. Almost every hillock is crowned by a so-called *klet*, a small, steep-roofed structure traditionally used for storing wine (nowadays they're more often put to use as weekend cottages). Although the area is covered with a dense patchwork of villages, human beings seem outnumbered by the chickens, geese and turkeys that scavenge between the cornfields and vegetable plots. The museum-village of **Kumrovec**, the pilgrimage church at **Marija Bistrica** and the castles at **Veliki Tabor** and **Trakošćan** are the main targets for visitors, although there's any number of Baroque churches and attractive rural villages awaiting the attentions of those who wish to explore further. If you have a car, it's feasible to visit three or four of these attractions in the course of a single day-trip from Zagreb; for those dependent on public transport, one destination in the Zagorje per day is more realistic.

Denizens of the Zagorje speak **kajkavski**, a dialect named after the distinctive local word for asking "what?" (*kaj*), and whose grammatical idiosyncrasies fall somewhere between modern Croatian and Slovenian. Local delicacies include *štrukli* (pockets of dough filled with cottage cheese) and the ubiquitous *purica z mlincima*, or turkey served with *mlinci* (baked pasta noodles which look like scraggy bits of pastry).

Most towns in the Zagorje have direct **bus** links with Zagreb, but you'll need your own transport if you want to explore the region in depth. The **road** from Zagreb via Krapina to Maribor in Slovenia is the most direct route into the region, although all the interesting touring itineraries lie on the minor roads to either side. **Trains** offer a dependable, if slow, way of getting to Krapina, Stubičke Toplice and Gornja Stubica.

Gingerbread hearts

One souvenir you'll come across again and again in the Zagorje is the *licitar*, the icing-covered pepper-flavoured biscuit that often takes the form of a big red heart (*licitarsko srce*; invariably translated as "**gingerbread heart**" even though there's rarely any ginger in them) and can sometimes assume enormous proportions. A popular holiday gift ever since the Middle Ages, the *licitar* is still considered an essential purchase for anyone visiting the Zagorje pilgrimage centre of Marija Bistrica (see p.119), where almost every bakery window displays gaudily decorated hearts, horses and other forms. *Licitari* are usually baked rock-hard and are supposed to be treasured as an ornament rather than eaten: sweet-toothed travellers may have better luck with the locally made *medenjaci*, melt-in-the-mouth biscuits made from honey dough.

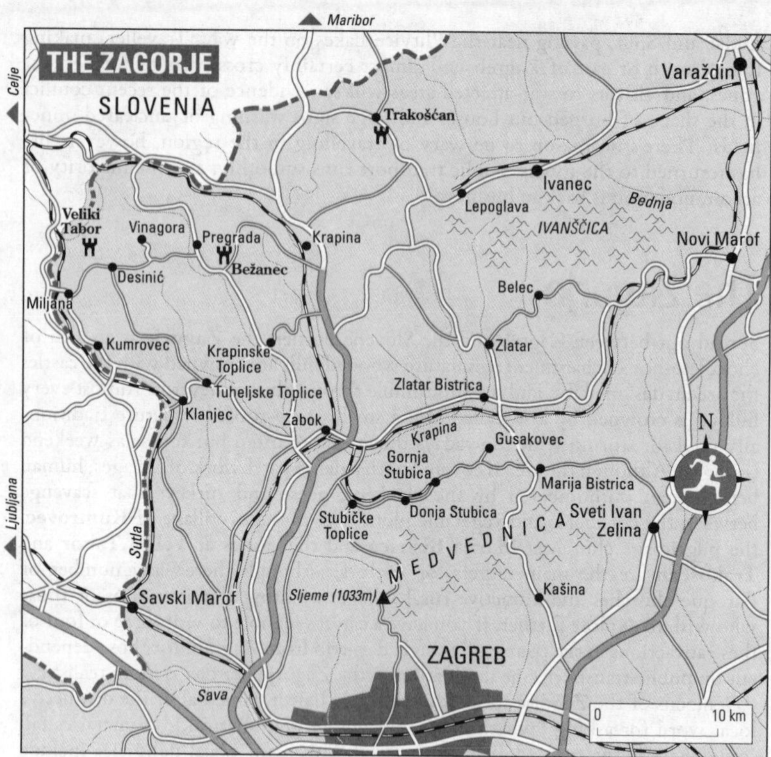

The Stubica valley

The part of the Zagorje most easily accessible from Zagreb is the gently undulating Stubica valley, spread out below the northern slopes of Mount Medvednica, which provides a lush agricultural backdrop for the long, straggling settlement of **Stubica** – really three villages, Stubičke Toplice, Gornja Stubica and Donja Stubica. Coming by public transport from the capital, you'll have to endure the notoriously slow Zagreb-Varaždin train to **Zabok**, where you change for the train to Gornja Stubica. By car, the most impressive approach is along the road over Mount Medvednica via Sljeme (see p.97): the views from the northern flanks of the mountain are breathtaking.

Stubičke Toplice

Emerging from a rustic patchwork of green, the small spa resort of **STUBIČKE TOPLICE** is a relaxing place; there's nothing much here apart from a cluster of sanatoriums, and an open-air swimming pool complex (*kupalište*; June–Sept daily 7am–7pm; 20Kn) behind a screen of trees in the centre of the village. The **tourist office** on the main street at Viktora Šipeka 24 (Mon–Fri 8am–3pm, Sat 10am–3pm; ⓣ049/282-727, ⓕ283-404) can provide addresses of local private **rooms** (❶); the *Matija Gubec*, close by at Viktora Šipeka 27 (ⓣ049/282-501, ⓦwww.hotel-mgubec.com; ❹), has bland, modern en-suite rooms and a large indoor swimming pool. For **eating**, *Slamasti krovovi*, just west of the tourist office, is the place to dine on local staples like *purica z mlincima* and *zagorski štrukli* in a folksy, embroidered-tablecloth interior. The vineyard-encircled *Zagorski klet*, a well-signed twenty-minute walk uphill from the main street, is more down to earth in style, but boasts sweeping views south towards the slopes of Mount Medvednica.

Gornja Stubica

Six kilometres east of Stubičke Toplice, beyond the undistinguished settlement of Donja Stubica, lies **GORNJA STUBICA**, a village famous for its role as the launching place of the **Peasants' Revolt** of 1573. The inhabitants of sixteenth-century Zagorje were overloaded with feudal obligations, while their proximity to the frontline in the war between the Habsburg and Ottoman empires landed them with the additional burden of supplying the war effort with food and manpower. To make matters worse, the Protestant leanings of local landowners offended the staunchly Catholic sensibilities of an already disgruntled peasantry. Ironically, it was the big Catholic magnates of Croatia who put the rebellion down, with the Bishop of Zagreb, Juraj Drašković, routing a badly armed peasant army at the Battle of Stubičko Polje on February 9, 1573. Drašković deliberately spread rumours that peasant leader **Matija Gubec** had been elected "king" by his co-conspirators, an accusation which served both to discredit the rebels and to provide the excuse for a fiendishly appropriate punishment – Gubec was executed in Zagreb by being "crowned" with a red-hot ring of iron.

The stirringly named **Museum of Peasant Uprisings** (Muzej seljačkih buna; April–Sept daily 9am–7pm; Oct–March Tues–Sun 9am–5pm; 20Kn), in the Orsić Palace, 2km north of the village (and behind Antun Augustinčić's vast hilltop statue of Gubec), brings the period to life with a well-presented collection of armour and weaponry, and English-language texts. The palace chapel is a minor Baroque delight, with illusionist ceiling paintings by Anton Lehringer offering a perspective-bending copy of the dome of St Peter's in Rome.

A smaller hillock just southwest of the village is crowned by the stout lime tree known as **Gubčeva Lipa**, where the peasants supposedly met to launch the insurrection. The adjacent *Birtija Pod Lipom*, decked out with rustic furnishings and embroidered tablecloths, is a good place for a **drink**, while the *Puntar* **restaurant**, just downhill from here on triangular Trg svetog Jurja, doles out *grah*, grilled meats and other filling standards. The *Puntar* also offers a handful of simply decorated **rooms** (Ⓣ049/289-286, Ⓕ290-997; ❶).

Marija Bistrica and around

Located below the northeastern spur of Mount Medvednica, some 37km from Zagreb and 11km east of Gornja Stubica, the town of **MARIJA BISTRICA** is home to the most important Marian shrine in Croatia. It's a popular destination for pilgrims year round, though things can get particularly crowded on August 15 (Assumption) and on the Sunday preceding St Margaret's Day (July 20), when the shrine is traditionally reserved for the city folk of Zagreb.

The town itself is a small, rustic place onto which modern coach-party tourism has been rather unceremoniously grafted. It's dominated totally by the **Pilgrimage Church of St Mary of Bistrica** (Hodočasnička crkva Marije Bistričke), which perches on a hillock in the centre of town, and has been rebuilt on numerous occasions to accommodate ever-growing numbers of visitors. The current structure, put together between 1880 and 1884 by the architect of Zagreb cathedral, Hermann Bollé, is a remarkably eclectic and playful building (unlike the comparatively stern cathedral). It features a jumble of Baroque and Neoclassical detail, crowned by a hulking black-and-red chevroned steeple, which is flanked by castellated red-brick turrets.

The principal object of popular veneration is the **Black Madonna**, a fifteenth-century statue of the Virgin set into the main altar. According to tradition, the statue was bricked into a church wall in 1650 to prevent it from falling into the hands of marauding Turks, and here it remained for 34 years until (it is said) a miraculous beam of light revealed its hiding place. News of the Madonna was spread by the then Bishop of Zagreb, Martin Borković, who was eager to promote Marija Bistrica as a spiritual centre at a time when pilgrimages in general were being encouraged throughout the Habsburg lands – popular religion was seen as a useful way of getting the masses behind the Catholic regime. The Madonna subsequently survived a fire in 1880 that destroyed almost everything else in the church, thereby adding to its aura.

The vast outdoor amphitheatre at the back of the church was built for the pope's visit here in October 1998, an occasion marked by the beatification of Archbishop Alojzije Stepinac (see box on p.82). Behind the amphitheatre, paths lead up the Calvary Hill (Kalvarija) past sculptures of the Stations of the Cross, culminating in a fine view back towards the town.

Practicalities

Marija Bistrica is served by numerous buses from Stubičke Toplice to the west and Zagreb to the south – the latter route following a scenic road which crawls over the eastern shoulder of Medvednica via the villages of Kašina and Las. Buses stop on the main street immediately below the church, from where the pedestrianized Zagrebačka leads up to the **tourist office** at no. 66 (Tues–Fri 7am–3pm, May–Sept also Sat & Sun 8am–2pm; ⓣ & ⓕ049/468-380, ⓦwww.marija-bistrica.hr). They can provide the addresses of a handful of local families offering private **rooms** (❶), but otherwise accommodation in town is limited to the church-owned *Salve Regina* **hotel** just down the hill (ⓣ049/469-026; ❸), with acceptable but charmless en-suite rooms in a modern two-storey building. Far preferable if you have your own transport is *Lojzekova hiža* (ⓣ049/469-325 or 461-949; ❶), near the village of **Gusakovec**, a well-signposted six-kilometre drive west of town – from Marija Bistrica, follow signs to Stubičke Toplice and look for a signed right turn after 5km. This traditional farmhouse offers tiny but cosy en-suite attic rooms (including some with bunks for children) in a delightful spot bordered by woods on one side and livestock-filled meadows on the other.

Lojzekova hiža is the best place locally to **eat and drink**, although numerous cafés and bistros near Marija Bistrica's church serve the usual refreshments and snacks. *Grozd*, just outside the church entrance, serves up exemplary *štrukli* and has the customary range of Croatian meat dishes. On big pilgrimage days, several establishments along the main street offer grills and spit-roasts cooked on outdoor barbecues. Marija Bistrica is also famous for the large number of local **bakeries** churning out *licitari* and *medenjaci*; almost every shop in the town centre is overflowing with them.

North of Marija Bistrica

The road heading north out of Marija Bistrica descends towards the broad Krapina valley before rising again into the foothills of the next ridge to the north, wooded Mount Ivanščica. After 12km you hit the small market town of **Zlatar**, unremarkable in itself, but a useful jumping-off point for the nearby village of **BELEC**, accessible by a minor road that runs northeast out of Zlatar.

Standing beside Belec's main street is the **Church of Our Lady of the Snow** (Crkva svete Marije Snježne; Masses Sun at 8am & 11am; walk past the church gate and knock on the door of the first farmhouse on the right in order to find the keyholder), deceptively ordinary from the outside, but containing a fantastic riot of frothy Baroque furniture and ornaments within. Countess Elisabeth Keglević-Erdödy had the church built in 1675 after hearing that a miraculous apparition of the Virgin Mary had occurred in nearby Kostanjek. It soon became a popular pilgrimage site, especially among Croatian nobility, who stumped up the cash for a thorough redecoration in the 1740s. Resplendent in pinks, eau-de-nil greens and luxurious gilt, the resulting ensemble of altars and wall-paintings is designed to be viewed as a single work of art, although several individual details stand out. The most important of these is the wooden pulpit from which statuettes of prophets seem poised to leap, above a relief of revellers dancing around the golden calf. It was carved by Josip Schokotnigg of Graz, who was also responsible for the altars of St Barbara and St Joseph, which stand on either side of the main altar of the Holy Trinity, a swirling mass of cherubs and gesticulating saints.

Klanjec, Kumrovec and around

One of the most picturesque routes into the western Zagorje follows the valley of the Sutla, a river scenically framed by woodland and cornfields, which marks the boundary between Croatia and Slovenia for a thirty-kilometre stretch north of Savski Marof. The biggest of the villages along the way is **KLANJEC**, 30km northwest of Zagreb, whose red-roofed houses huddle around the dogtooth-patterned spire of an eighteenth-century **Franciscan church**. Inside, there's a lovely Rococo altar on the left-hand side of the nave. Delights of a more sepulchral nature are to be found in the red-brick **burial vault of the Erdödy family** (Mon–Fri 9am–3pm; donation requested), entered from around the side of the former monastery buildings next door to the church. If there's no one in attendance at the vault, enquire at the local library (*knjižnica*) diagonally opposite the church. One of the most powerful clans in Croatia in the late-sixteenth and early-seventeenth centuries, the Erdödys were generous patrons of the Franciscans of Klanjec, and were in turn granted use of this vault as a personal mausoleum. Inside lies a splendid pair of Baroque sarcophagi fashioned from pewter: the first, decorated with golden lions' heads and bell flowers, belongs to Sigismund Erdödy, seventeenth-century Governor of Croatia; the second, spectacularly mounted on a quartet of supine stags, contains the remains of Sigismund's son Emerik.

A few steps away from the vault on the northern side of the square stands the **Antun Augustinčić Gallery** (April–Sept daily 9am–5pm; Oct–March Tues–Sun 9am–3pm; 20Kn), a large, modern pavilion honouring the local-born artist (1900–79) who became one of twentieth-century Croatia's most prolific sculptors. An imposing display of busts and torsos is topped off by two huge plaster replicas of horse sculptures – one designed in 1940 to serve as a monument to King Aleksandar of Yugoslavia, the other made in 1954 for the UN building in New York.

There are four daily buses and five daily trains (the last leg of the train journey is on a Croatian Railways-operated bus) to Klanjec from Zagreb. The nearest **accommodation** to Klanjec is at the *Tuheljske Toplice* spa hotel (Ⓣ049/556-224, Ⓦwww.terme-tuhelj.hr; ④), 4km east on the road to Zabok, which offers recently refurbished en suites with TV, along with the chance to rest your weary bones in the mineral-water-fed swimming pools. There's a smart **restaurant** behind the hotel in the nineteenth-century **Mihanović Palace** (Dvorac Mihanović), so-called because the poet Antun Mihanović – responsible, among other things, for the words to Croatia's national anthem – was a frequent guest here in the 1850s.

Kumrovec

About 10km upriver from Klanjec, the village of **KUMROVEC** is renowned both as the best of Croatia's museum-villages and as the birthplace of the

△ Statue of Josip Broz Tito

father of communist Yugoslavia, **Josip Broz Tito**. The simple peasant house in which Tito was born was turned into a museum during his own lifetime, while the surrounding properties were rebuilt and restored in the ensuing decades to provide an example of what an early twentieth-century Zagorje village looked like. Those who remember Tito with affection still collect here on May 4, the anniversary of his death, and on the weekend preceding May 25, Tito's official birthday.

The museum complex

Set back from the main road behind a large car park, the **"Old Village" Museum** (Muzej "staro selo"; daily: April–Sept 9am–7pm; Oct–March 9am–4pm; 20Kn; ⓦwww.mdc.hr/kumrovec) consists of a collection of pastel-coloured houses and farmsteads ranged alongside a gurgling brook. Tito's birthplace, a few steps beyond the entrance, is marked by a trademark statue of the Marshal by Anton Augustinčić – blown up by right-wing hooligans on Boxing Day 2004, it has now been restored to its rightful place. Inside, life-like re-creations of the 1890s rooms contain a restrained collection of photos and mementos, including the uniform worn by Tito while leading the Partisan struggle from the island of Vis in 1944. The other buildings are each devoted to a particular rural craft, with displays of blacksmithing, basket-weaving and toy-making – the last featuring dainty, brightly painted wood-carved horses and other animals. One house is given over to a series of tableaux illustrating a traditional wedding feast, and is crowded with costumed mannequins and tables decked with imitation food.

Practicalities

Getting to Kumrovec is easy enough, with commuter trains from Zagreb to Savski Marof connecting with five daily Savski Marof–Kumrovec buses (the buses are run by Croatian Railways, so you can buy a through ticket). The buses terminate at the semi-derelict Kumrovec train station, a twenty-minute walk north of the village itself.

There's no **accommodation** in Kumrovec itself, but *Pansion Zelenjak*, set amid wooded riverside scenery 3km south of the village (ⓣ049/550-747, ⓦwww.zelenjak.com; ❸), is a good base from which to explore the area if you have your own transport, offering smart rooms with shower and TV. It also has a classy **restaurant** with a strong line in freshwater fish.

For **eating** in Kumrovec, *Kod starog*, within the museum complex, offers local staples such as cheese, sausage and *štrukli*, while *Stara Vura*, 100m east of the museum complex in the new part of the village, serves the full range of grilled pork, poultry and fish dishes.

Miljana and beyond

Nine kilometres beyond Kumrovec, the village of **MILJANA** is overlooked by the best-preserved Renaissance palace in the Zagorje, built in the early 1600s by the Rafkay family and painstakingly restored by private owners in the 1970s. The palace isn't open to the public, but you're free to admire the ochre facade, and may be allowed to peek inside the asymmetrical arcaded courtyard.

The hills rearing up behind Miljana harbour one of the few local sources of **accommodation** in the shape of the *Masnec family*, Luka Poljanska 41 (ⓣ049/552-133; ❶), a modern farmhouse with prim, balconied en suites affording views over the vineyards; home-produced wine is on offer in the ground-floor restaurant. It's reached by driving towards the Slovene border and making a right turn 50m before the frontier post – from here the *Masnec* is a well-signed

Josip Broz Tito (1892–1980)

Josip Broz was born on May 7, 1892, the seventh son of peasant smallholder Franjo Broz and his Slovene wife Marija Javeršek. After training as a blacksmith and metal-worker, Josip Broz became an officer in the Austrian army in World War I, only to be captured by the Russians in 1915. Fired by the ideals of the Bolshevik Revolution, he joined the Red Army and fought in the Russian Civil War before finally heading for home in 1920. Some believe that the man who came back to Croatia with a discernible Russian accent was a Soviet-trained impostor who had assumed the identity of the original Josip Broz – an appealing but unlikely tale. Whatever the truth, on his return Broz found himself in a turbulent Yugoslav state in which the Communist Party was soon outlawed, and it was his success in reinvigorating demoralized party cells that ensured his rise through the ranks.

Broz took the pseudonym **Tito** in 1934 upon entering the central committee of the Yugoslav Communist Party (he became leader in 1937). Nobody really knows why he chose the name: the most frequently touted explanation is that the nickname was bestowed on him by colleagues amused by his bossy manner – "*ti to!*" means "you [do] that!" in Croatian – although it's equally possible that he took it from the eighteenth-century Croat writer Tito Brezovacki.

Tito's finest hour came following the German invasion of Yugoslavia in 1941, when he managed to take control of the anti-fascist uprising, even though it wasn't initially inspired by the communists. Despite repeated (and often very successful) German counteroffensives, he somehow succeeded in keeping the core of his movement alive – through a mixture of luck, bloody-mindedness and sheer charisma rather than military genius. He also possessed a firm grasp of political theatre, promoting himself to the rank of marshal and donning suitably impressive uniforms whenever Allied emissaries were parachuted into Yugoslavia to meet him. The British and Americans lent him their full support from 1943 onwards, thereby condemning all other, non-communist factions in Yugoslavia to certain political extinction after the war.

Emerging as dictator of Yugoslavia in 1945, Tito showed no signs of being anything more than a loyal Stalinist until the Soviet leader tried to get rid of him in 1948. Tito's survival – subsequently presented to the world as "Tito's historic 'no' to Stalin" – rested on his innate ability to inspire loyalty among the tightly knit circle of former Partisans who, by and large, surrounded him until his death. Flushed with the prestige of having resisted Soviet pressure, Tito concentrated on affirming Yugoslavia's position on the world stage and increasingly left the nitty-gritty of running the country

three-kilometre drive through hilltop villages. Once settled in, you can hike to Veliki Tabor along farm tracks, or walk down into the Slovenian spa town of **Atomske Toplice** (keep your passport handy), which spreads over the opposite bank of the Sutla river.

Veliki Tabor and around

It's just 6km from Miljana to the most impressive of the Zagorje castles, **Veliki Tabor** (daily: April–Sept 10am–6pm; Oct–March 10am–3pm; 20Kn), whose imposing barrel-shaped bastions look down on the road from a grassy hilltop. Built in the twelfth century to guard the lands of the counts of Celje (a Slovenian town 50km to the west), it acquired its present shape in the fifteenth and sixteenth centuries, when its characteristic semicircular towers were grafted onto the earlier pentagonal shell. Inside, the courtyard contains three tiers of galleries, added in the sixteenth century by the Rattkays, one of northern Croatia's most to others. Forming the **non-aligned movement** with Nehru and Nasser after 1955 provided a platform which allowed him to travel the world, giving Yugoslavia an international profile yet to be regained by any of its successor republics. In domestic affairs he contrived to present himself as the lofty arbiter who, far from being responsible for the frequent malfunctions of Yugoslav communism, emerged to bang heads together when things got out of control. Thus, his decision to bring an end to the Zagreb-based reform movement known as the Croatian Spring in 1971 was sold to the public as a Solomonic intervention to ensure social peace rather than the authoritarian exercise it really was.

A vain man who loved to wear fancy uniforms and medals, dyed his hair and used a sun lamp, Tito enthusiastically acquiesced to the **personality cult** constructed around him. May 25 was declared his official birthday and celebrated nationwide as "Dan mladosti" ("Day of Youth"), enhancing Tito's aura as the kindly father of a grateful people. He was also a bit of a ladies' man, marrying four times and switching partners with a speed that dismayed his more puritanical colleagues. During the war, he negotiated an exchange of prisoners with the Ustaše in order to secure the release of his second wife, Herta Hass, from a concentration camp. On her arrival at Tito's Partisan HQ, Hass was informed by bemused aides that she'd already been supplanted by wireless operator Zdenka Paunović.

Affection for Tito in Yugoslavia was widespread and genuine, if not universal. There's no doubt that Titoist communism was "softer" than its Soviet counterpart after 1948: many areas of society were relatively free from ideological control and, from the 1950s onwards, Yugoslavs were able to travel and work abroad.

For most Croats nowadays, Tito's legacy is ambiguous. Tito was fortunate enough to die before Yugoslavia's economy went seriously wrong in the 1980s, and for many he remains a symbol of the good old days when economic growth (paid for by soft Western loans) led to rising living standards and a consumer boom. However, the authority of the party – and Tito's leadership of it – was never to be questioned, and many dissenting voices ended up in prison as a result. Tito is also seen as the man responsible for the **Bleiburg massacre** of 1945 (when thousands of Croatian reservists were put to death by avenging Partisans), the repression of Croatia's Catholic Church, and the crackdown on the Croatian Spring. Despite keeping national aspirations on a tight leash, however, Tito's Yugoslavia ensured Croatian territorial continuity by establishing borders still in existence today. For this reason alone, many streets and squares in Croatia continue to bear Tito's name.

powerful landowning families. With long-term renovation currently under way, it's difficult to predict which parts of the interior you can visit: expect to see a reasonable handful of rooms filled with pikes, maces, knightly tombstones and other medieval oddments. The most theatrical of the exhibits is the (supposed) skull of Veronika of Desinić, a medieval maiden who was bricked into the walls of the castle after spurning the advances of the local lord.

There are eight **buses** daily from Zagreb to the village of **Desinić**, to the east of the castle, from where it's a three-kilometre walk to the castle access road and a further 2km uphill to the site. About 1km east of the castle, a well-signed turn-off leads up to the *Grešna Gorica* farmhouse **restaurant**, a popular venue for long weekend lunches. With a traditionally furnished dining room and splendid views of Veliki Tabor, it does a full range of Croatian cuisine, including Zagorje specialities such as *štrukli*, *purica z mlincima* (turkey with baked strips of pasta) and *srneći gulaš* (venison goulash). There's a small playground and a farmhouse zoo outside.

Masnec apart, the nearest **accommodation** to Veliki Tabor is the delightfully rustic *Seljački Turizam Trsek* ("Village Tourism Trsek"; ⓣ049/343-464; ❶), 2km beyond Desinić at Trnovec Desinički 23 – to get there, take the main road east out of Desinić and turn left when you see the sign. If you're hankering after cosy en-suite rooms in a hilltop farmstead surrounded by vineyards, then this is the place to be. With tasty traditional meals served up in a dining room hung with rustic knick-knacks, half-board is well worth considering.

Krapina

Squeezed among lumpish, vine-covered hills midway between Zagreb and Maribor in Slovenia, the busy little town of **KRAPINA** is famous for its connections with so-called "Krapina Man" (*krapinski čovjek*), a type of Neanderthal who lived in caves hereabouts some thirty thousand years ago. The bones of several such hominids were discovered by Dragutin Gorjanović Kramberger in 1899 on Hušnjakovo hill, a short walk west of the town centre on the far side of the River Krapinica. The find is commemorated by a wedge-shaped glass-and-concrete **museum** plugging a cleft in the hillside where the remains were found (daily: June–Sept 9am–5pm; Oct–May 8am–3pm; 20Kn); the multimedia display inside provides an entertaining insight into the lifestyles of Krapina's stone-age inhabitants. Outside, a pathway leads up through the woods to the exact spot where the bones were found, nowadays marked by life-size statues of a Neanderthal family.

The other main attraction hereabouts is 2km east of town in the hillside suburb of Trški Vrh, where the arcaded **Church of St Mary of Jerusalem** (Crkva svete Marije Jeruzalemske) provides the Zagorje faithful with another important pilgrimage destination. Inside lies an exemplary riot of eighteenth-century religious fervour, although the gilded altarpieces and pink-blue frescoes work better as an integrated whole rather than as individual works of art. The church is usually closed outside Mass times, but a local keyholder (check with the Krapina tourist office) will open up for you.

Practicalities

Krapina's **train station** and main **bus station** lie five minutes south of the town centre, although some bus services terminate at a new terminal 1km further south. Krapina's **tourist office**, centrally located at Magistratska 11 (Mon–Fri 8am–3pm, Sat 8am–noon; ⓣ049/371-330, ⓔtzg-krapina@kr.t-com.hr), can provide advice on **accommodation**, although there are no private rooms in the immediate vicinity of town. Luckily, there's a cosy well-run pension in the form of the *Gostionica pod Starim Krovovima*, right on the main square at Trg Ljudevita Gaja 15 (ⓣ049/370-536, ⓕ370-594; ❸), offering a handful of bright, clean en-suite rooms with TV – the most atmospheric of which are the attic rooms, with sloping ceilings – and a couple of three- and four-bed rooms for families. On the eastern side of town, the thirteen-room *Croatia* motel lies right beside the Maribor–Zagreb road at Antuna Mihanovića 1 (ⓣ049/370-547, ⓕ300-146; ❸), and has simple no-frills en suites and a fast-food canteen. The **restaurant** at *Gostionica pod Starim Krovovima* is an informal place in which to tuck into a filling repertoire of grilled pork chops, schnitzels and freshwater fish. The *Neanderthal Pub*, just below the prehistoric man museum, is nowhere near as primitive as its name suggests, serving up set lunches and pasta dishes in the daytime, and dispensing a comfortingly wide choice of beers and spirits in the evening.

Lepoglava

Twenty kilometres northeast of Krapina, the bland town of **LEPOGLAVA** is dominated by the dour facade of the country's largest **prison**, occupying the former buildings of a Pauline monastery. The list of those who have passed through its gates reads like a *Who's Who* of twentieth-century Croatian politics. Numerous communists, Josip Broz Tito included, languished here during the 1930s, only to turn Lepoglava to their own uses once they came to power. Archbishop Stepinac was here for five years after World War II, and subsequent internees included many who went on to play a prominent role in post-independence Croatia – President Tuđman, Dražen Budiša (leader of the Social Liberal Party), Vlado Gotovac (leader of the Liberal Party) and Ivan Zvonimir Čičak (founder of the Croatian branch of the Helsinki Committee on Human Rights) among them.

Lepoglava's only other claim to fame is the Gothic chapel of the **monastery church** (Sun 9am–noon), which stands beside the prison entrance on the main street. The lozenge-shaped gaps between the rib-vaulting were filled in with exuberantly colourful frescoes by local monk Ivan Ranger in the sixteenth century, and an imposing Baroque altar was installed around a much older, Byzantine-style painting of the Madonna. There are a couple of daily **buses** to Lepoglava from Zagreb and more frequent train and bus services from Varaždin, 30km to the northeast.

Trakošćan

Of all the Zagorje castles, **Trakošćan**, sitting on a hilltop 11km northwest of the town of Lepoglava, is the most visited. The sturdy thirteenth-century citadel was rebuilt in neo-Gothic style by Count Juraj Drašković in the 1850s, and the sight of Trakošćan's jaunty turrets and custard-coloured battlements is one of the Zagorje's most famous. With a well-organized museum inside and a landscaped park with boating lake outside, you could easily spend a good half-day or longer here.

△ Trakošćan castle

The **interior** (daily: April–Sept 9am–6pm; Oct–March 9am–3pm; 20Kn) is a tribute to the medieval tastes of its nineteenth-century owners, full of extravagantly pinnacled door frames, elaborate woodcarving and monumental stone fireplaces. Hunting trophies, suits of armour and portraits of the Drašković family throughout the ages all add to the Gothic film-set effect. The first-floor Hunting Room (*lovačka dvorana*) boasts a rib-vaulted ceiling seemingly supported by stone lions, and a ceramic oven decorated with sundry animal heads. In addition, there's a fascinating display of weaponry through the ages, and a big collection of aristocratic portraits on the upper floors.

There are currently no direct **buses** to Trakošćan from Zagreb, although the ten daily services (six at weekends) from Varaždin ensure that you can just about tackle the castle as a long day-trip from the capital. The *Coning Trakošćan* **hotel** (Ⓣ042/796-224, Ⓦwww.hotel.hr/coning; ④), situated in meadows below the castle, has rather drab en-suite rooms with TV, along with a sauna, gym and tennis courts. Despite its rather sterile appearance, the hotel's restaurant is a great place to try local specialities such as *Zagorska juha* (creamy soup with chunks of meat and veg).

Varaždin and the northeast

Northeast of Zagreb, road and rail lines to Budapest cross an outlying spur of the Zagorje hills before descending towards the lush farmlands bordering the River Drava, which for much of its length forms Croatia's border with Hungary. In the midst of this green, agricultural region lies **Varaždin**, mainland Croatia's best-preserved Habsburg-era town, and well worth a day-trip from Zagreb. Other settlements in the region are very much in Varaždin's shadow, although **Čakovec**, thirty minutes northeast, is worth a stop-off if you're in the area. It serves as the centre of the **Međimurje**, a rustic frontier province, totally flat and traditionally isolated, which stretches out between the Mura and Drava rivers.

Southeast of Varaždin, roads run parallel to the Drava through prosperous rural **Podravina**, an area whose neat villages, orchards and maize fields exude an air of bucolic plenty. Fringed by gentle hills raked by the occasional vineyard, it's a pretty area to drive through once you get onto the country roads, although specific attractions are thin on the ground save for the village of **Hlebine**, a renowned centre of naive art just outside Podravina's main market town, **Koprivnica**. From Koprivnica, road and rail routes continue southeast through the Podravina towards the Slavonian towns of Našice and Osijek, passing through the dusty and uninspiring towns of Virovitica and Slatina en route.

Varaždin

Seventy kilometres northeast of Zagreb, **VARAŽDIN** occupied a key position on the medieval Hungarian kingdom's route to the sea and became an important military stronghold for successive Hungarian and Habsburg rulers in their struggle against Ottoman expansion. Varaždin grew fat on the profits of the Austrian–Turkish wars of the late 1600s and early 1700s, encouraging many noble families to build houses here – from 1765 to 1776 it was actually Croatia's capital, until a disastrous fire (allegedly started by a pipe-smoking local youth who fell over while chasing a pig) forced the relocation of the capital to Zagreb. Following the fire, life slowly returned to the town's opulent **Baroque palaces**, many of which, following restoration, are resplendent in their original cream, ochre, pink and pale-blue colours. Most now do duty as apartment blocks, offices and banks, so there's a limit to the number of places you can actually visit. There's also a postcard-perfect **castle**, now home to northeastern Croatia's most worthwhile museum, and a quite a few churches – many of which survived the fire – all crammed within the compact and still relatively untouristed old town. An additional reason to visit is provided by Varaždin's **graveyard**, famous

△ Varaždin

throughout Croatia for its towering topiary and strollable park-like feel. A large student population ensures that modern Varaždin has a vivacious, youthful edge – the presence of an information technology faculty has made the town into one of the most prestigious places to study outside the capital. Varaždin's one remaining claim to fame is the extraordinarily high incidence of **bicycle use** among its inhabitants, giving it the air of a prosperous provincial town in the low countries.

Arrival, information and accommodation

Varaždin's **bus station** is a five-minute walk southwest of the town centre, which is reached by crossing the modern, flagstoned Kapucinski trg. The **train station** is slightly farther out, on the eastern fringes of the town centre at the far end of Kolodvorska. The friendly staff at the **tourist office**, near the castle at Padovčeva 3 (April–Oct Mon–Fri 8am–6pm, Sat 9am–1pm; Nov–March Mon–Fri 8am–4pm; ⓣ042/210-987, ⓦwww.tourism-varazdin.hr), can provide advice and a free town map, while T-tours, Gundulićeva 2 (Mon–Fri 8.30am–7.30pm, Sat 8.30am–12.30pm; ⓣ042/210-989, ⓔt-tours@vz.tel.hr), handle bookings of private **rooms** (❶–❸) in the town and outlying villages.

Accommodation

BBC/Sobe Kutnjak Radićeva 7 ⓣ042/210-671, ⓔkutnjak@vz.hinet.hr. Four-room bed-and-breakfast (two singles, one double and one triple) located above the *BBC* café, just north of the bus station. Rooms come with WC/shower and TV. ❸

Pansion Garestin Zagrebačka 34 ⓣ042/214-314, ⓦwww.gastrocom.hr. Popular city-centre restaurant with ten rooms above, each featuring private facilities, a/c and TV. ❹

Pansion Maltar Prešernova 1 ⓣ042/311-521, ⓕ211-190. A cosy, informal B&B, five minutes' walk south of the main square. ❸

Turist Aleja Kralja Zvonimira 1 ⓣ042/395-395, ⓦwww.hotel-turist.hr. Centrally located, one-hundred-room three-star, with comfortable en-suite rooms each with satellite TV. "Business class" rooms come with minibar and a bit more desk space. The international cuisine in the *Turist*'s restaurant is well above the usual standard of hotel food in inland Croatia. ❹–❺

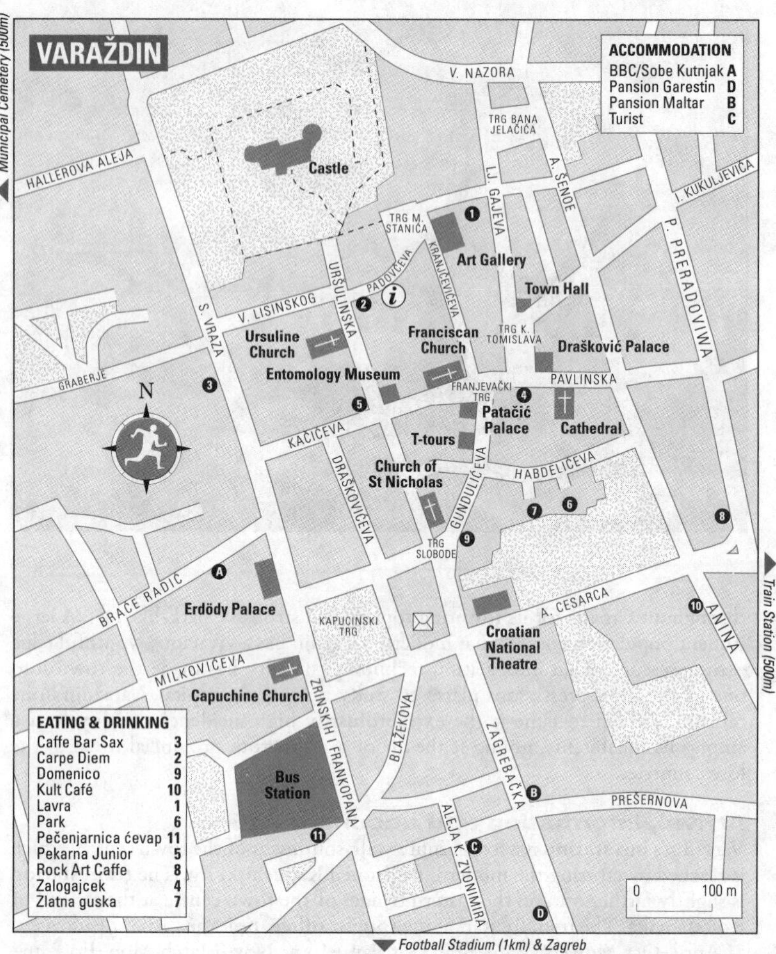

The Town

The heart of old Varaždin is largely pedestrianized, with modern boutiques and cafés hidden behind the shuttered windows and carved doorways that embellish the former town houses of the nobility. The sturdy grey-and-yellow tower of the **Church of St Nicholas** (Crkva svetog Nikole), one of the town's few surviving Gothic monuments, presides over the small, triangular **Trg slobode** (Freedom Square), your likely starting point if arriving from the bus or train stations.

Franjevački trg and around

From Trg Slobode, Gundulićeva leads north to **Franjevački trg** (really a broad street rather than a square), which is flanked by the mansions of wealthy merchants, their ostentatious arched portals surmounted by family crests and heavy stone balconies. Grabbing most of the attention is the cream-and-beige **Patačić Palace** (Palača Patačić), with Rococo mouldings writhing their way across its facade and a huge oriel window hovering above the corner of Franjevački trg and Gundulićeva. Now occupied by an Austrian bank, the palace was built for Franjo Patačić and his poetess wife, and became the centre of salon society in late eighteenth-century Varaždin. On the square's northern side is the seventeenth-century **Franciscan Church of St John the Baptist** (Crkva svetog Ivana Krstitelja), boasting a soaring belfry and an extravagantly gilded main altar. A scaled-down copy of Ivan Meštrović's *Grgur Ninski* statue, the original of which is in Split, stands outside.

A few steps west of the statue, the Neoclassical **Herczer Palace** at Franjevački trg 6 houses the **Entomology Museum** (Entomološki muzej; Tues–Fri 10am–5pm, Sat & Sun 10am–1pm; 20Kn). It features a display of more than 4500 insects based on the collection of local biologist Franjo Košćec (whose study is also re-created here), arranged thematically according to habitat – forest, meadow, riverbank and so on. Modern display cases and imaginative lighting lend the collection the character of a contemporary art installation. North of the museum, Ursulinska leads up to the castle via the **Ursuline Church** (Ursulinska crkva), the recent recipient of a bright-pink makeover and whose soaring onion-topped tower is one of the most distinctive features of the Varaždin skyline. Inside is a pleasing array of both Gothic and Baroque fittings, with a late-medieval sculpture of Madonna and Child catching the eye to the left of the main altar, and an eighteenth-century organ above the entrance door encrusted with harp-twanging statuettes.

Trg kralja Tomislava and around

Franjevački trg's eastern end opens out onto **Trg kralja Tomislava**, the main town square, surrounded by balustraded palaces and overlooked by the sky-rocketing clock tower of the sixteenth-century **town hall** (*vijećnica*). Arrive outside the town hall between 11am and noon on a Saturday and you'll witness the changing of the **town guard** (*građanska garda*); this ritual, enacted by volunteers clad in original nineteenth-century uniforms, is in memory of the (largely ceremonial) units which were a major source of civic pride during the Habsburg era. Hugging the eastern side of the square is the coffee-coloured **Drašković Palace** (Palača Drašković), once home to the renowned eighteenth-century beauty Suzana Drašković. When her husband died in 1765, the viceroy of Croatia, Franjo Nadasdy, moved his entire court to Varaždin in order to be near her, turning the town into the de facto capital of Croatia in the process.

Just off the main square to the east, the **Church of the Ascension** (Crkva Marijinog Uznesenja) was originally built by the Jesuits in the 1640s. Now the town's cathedral, it stands on the cusp of the Baroque and Rococo eras, with most of the interior decorations, including the main altar, having been added in the 1730s. The plain, whitewashed interior provides the perfect setting for a no-holds-barred display of gilded statuary on the high altar and in the side chapels. A block north of Trg kralja Tomislava on Trg M. Stančića, the bright-orange exterior of the seventeenth-century Palača Šermage conceals the town's **art gallery** (Galerija starih i novih majstora; Tues–Fri 10am–5pm, Sat & Sun 10am–1pm; price depends on what's on). The permanent collection is currently in storage, but the gallery's seasonal art and history exhibitions are well worth a look.

The castle and cemetery

Immediately opposite the art gallery, a wooden drawbridge and gatehouse mark the entrance to the **Castle** (*stari grad*), an irregular rectangle surrounded by two concentric moats divided by grassy earthworks. Dating from the mid-1500s, when Varaždin was in the front line against the advancing Turks, it was eventually transformed into a stately residence by the powerful Erdödy family, who lorded it over the region for several centuries. The courtyard, with its three tiers of balustrades, has been beautifully restored; the **museum** within (Tues–Fri 10am–5pm, Sat & Sun 10am–1pm; 20Kn) contains an engrossing display of weaponry, local crafts and furniture throughout the ages, much of it accompanied by English-language captions. Located at the end of a first-floor corridor is the **Chapel of St Lawrence** (Kapelica svetog Lovre), built by Toma Bakač Erdödy in thanks for his victory over the Ottomans at Sisak in 1593, and an adjoining circular sacristy, squeezed into a defensive tower.

About 500m west of the castle, down Hallerova aleja, Varaždin's **Municipal Cemetery** (*gradsko groblje*) is a minor horticultural masterpiece. Laid out in 1905 by public-spirited tailor Hermann Haller, it's as much a public park as a graveyard, with row upon row of conifers carefully sculpted into tall hedges and pillars, these stately green monoliths seeming to swallow up the graves themselves.

The Erdödy Palace and Capuchine Church

Returning from the castle or cemetery to the bus station via Stanka Vraza, you'll pass the **Erdödy Palace** (Palača Erdödy) at no. 8, another peach-coloured testament to Varaždin's dominant architectural style. Built by the Erdödys to provide themselves with a cosy downtown alternative to the draughty medieval rooms they had to put up with at the castle, it's now the seat of the city's prestigious music school (Glazbena škola) and the venue for occasional chamber concerts. A few steps further south, the eighteenth-century **Capuchine Church of the Holy Trinity** (Kapucinska crkva svetog Trojstva) is worth a quick peek for its organ, embellished with a delightful pair of angels tooting away on heavenly trumpets.

Eating and drinking

There's a good range of places to **eat** in the centre. For eating on the move, *Pekarna Junior*, at Kačićeva 2, doles out a good selection of sandwiches and pastries until 10pm (1pm on Sun). As you would expect from a town with a large student population, there's no shortage of central places to **drink**. The terrace cafés on Trg kralja Tomislava and Trg M. Stančića are the places to go on warm summer evenings; otherwise, head for one of the characterful indoor drinking dens listed below.

Restaurants

Domenico Trg slobode 7. The classiest of several central pizza outlets, occupying a wooden-beamed pavilion with views of the town park. Also offers a choice of moderately priced pasta dishes and a serviceable seafood risotto.

Park Habdelićeva 6. Dependable range of typically central European veal- and pork-based fare in a plain modern building. The outdoor terrace, jutting out into the town park, is a wonderful place to sit in summer.

Pečenjarnica ćevap Vidovski trg 17. The tastiest grilled-meat dishes in town, in an unpretentious sit-down snack bar just round the corner from the bus station.

Zalogajček Trg kralja Tomislava. Smart, cosy health-food shop and veggie canteen, located at the end of an arcade just off the main square. Each day there's a different choice of freshly made soups, tofu dishes, salads and other savoury concoctions, all of which are very reasonably priced. Daily until 8pm.

Zlatna guska Habdelićeva 4 ⓣ042/213-393. Housed in a seventeenth-century palace on the fringes of the town park, the "Golden Goose" is one of the most acclaimed restaurants in the region, serving up succulent steaks, freshwater fish and a handful of vegetarian dishes in a barrel-vaulted cellar. Reckon on 200–300Kn per person for a three-course meal with drinks. Reservations advised at weekends.

Cafés and bars

Caffe Bar Sax Vraza 15. A relaxing and comfy corner café decorated with antique furnishings, old posters and photographs, with a small outdoor terrace.

Carpe Diem Ivana Padovca 5. Deep wicker armchairs, loungey decor and a fair-sized cocktail menu make this one of the most stylish watering holes in the centre.

Kult Café Anina 2. Minimally decorated, mildly arty café-bar with a sporadic programme of small-scale concerts and spoken-word events. It's round the back of the Kult multimedia centre, basically a boutique cinema showing a mixture of mainstream and art movies.

Lavra Gajeva 17. Snug, soothing cellar bar suitable for a daytime coffee or a longer evening drink. Stone-lined, barrel-vaulted interior, with outdoor seating in the yard.

Rock Art Caffe Petra Preradovića 24. Roomy bar decorated with old guitars, album covers and the like. Big conservatory and plentiful outdoor seating make this a relaxing place to hang out whatever the time of day or night.

Festivals and entertainment

Varaždin is at its liveliest during the **Špancirfest** (late August/early September; Ⓦwww.spancirfest.com), a week-long arts festival featuring street theatre, open-air rock, world music and jazz gigs, and carnivalesque costume parades. During the last two weeks of September the town's churches and palaces provide suitably ornate venues for the **Varaždin Baroque Evenings** (Varaždinske barokne večeri; Ⓦwww.varazdin.hr/barokneveceri.htm), with international conductors and soloists performing a rich repertoire of early classical music.

Chamber music **concerts** and solo recitals take place throughout the year at either the Erdödy Palace (see opposite; events are advertised on a billboard outside; pay on the door) or the Croatian National Theatre (Hrvatsko narodno kazalište or HNK) at Augusta Cezarca 1 – programme details and tickets are available from the Concert Office (Koncertni ured; in the same building as the theatre; Ⓣ042/212-907, Ⓦwww.concertni-ured.com.hr).

Varaždin can also boast a moderately successful first-division **football** team, Varteks (Ⓦwww.nk-varteks.hr), who play in an all-seater stadium 1km south of town on the Zagreb road.

Čakovec

Northeast of Varaždin, the main road to Hungary crosses the River Drava and traverses the flatlands of the Međimurje before arriving at **ČAKOVEC**, some 15km beyond. A relaxing if unspectacular provincial town, it centres on a largely modern area around Trg kralja Tomislava. The western end of the square features one of the finest Secession-era buildings in Croatia, the **Casino**;

Travelling on to Hungary

Crossing Croatia's long border with Hungary is relatively straightforward. If you're **driving**, the speediest route between Zagreb and Budapest is the toll motorway which passes just to the south of Varaždin and Čakovec before crossing the border at **Goričan**. There are also road crossings at **Gola** (between Koprivnica and Nagyatad), **Terezino Polje** (between Virovitica and Barcs), **Donji Miholjac** (between Našice and Pécs) and **Kneževo** (between Osijek and Szekszárd).

The most direct approach to the Hungarian capital by public transport is by **train**, with three daily services from Zagreb to Budapest Keleti station – two of these call at Koprivnica en route, while the other stops off at Varaždin and Čakovec.

Osijek is a useful starting point for heading into southern Hungary **by bus**, with three daily services to Pécs and one to Mohács.

The Zrinskis

From the sixteenth century onwards, eastern Croatia's status as a borderland disputed by the Habsburg and Ottoman empires led to the rise of a new breed of warrior aristocrats, whose power rested on their military prowess on the battlefield and unswerving loyalty to the Habsburg dynasty. One of the most influential Croatian families of the time was the Zrinskis, four of whom were elected Ban of Croatia between the mid-sixteenth and mid-seventeenth centuries.

The first of these was **Nikola Šubić Zrinski** (1508–66), who was awarded the castle of Čakovec by Habsburg Emperor Ferdinand I in 1546 – an acknowledgement of his financial contribution to the war against the Turks. When Suleyman the Magnificent advanced into Habsburg territory in 1566, Nikola Šubić led the defence of the fortress of **Szigetvár** in southern Hungary (about 100km southeast of Čakovec). Faced by overwhelmingly superior forces, he led his men on a doomed attempt at breakout from the fortress. They perished to the last man. Nikola Šubić's exploits were immortalized by his great-grandson, **Nikola VII** (1620–64), whose epic Hungarian-language poem *Szigeti Veszedelem* ("Sziget in Peril") was to become a standard text for Hungarian patriots.

The Zrinskis continued to flourish as long as the Habsburg court valued their role as frontier barons, but the relationship became strained after the **Treaty of Vásvár** in 1664, which many Hungarian and Slavonian aristocrats felt made too many territorial concessions to the Turks. By the late 1660s **Petar Zrinski** (1621–71) and brother-in-law **Fran Krsto Frankopan** had assumed leadership of an anti-Habsburg revolt by Croatian and Hungarian aristocrats. Petar even opened negotiations with the Turks, promising to make Hungary-Croatia a vassal state of the Ottoman Empire in return for help against the Austrians. Such help never materialized, and Habsburg Emperor Leopold I had both Zrinski and Frankopan **executed** in Wiener Neustadt on April 30, 1671.

The Zrinskis and Frankopans remain important symbols of Croatia's unfulfilled destiny in central Europe. Neither were ever Croatian patriots in the modern sense: they belonged to a cosmopolitan aristocracy which invested most of its political energies in the defence of family privileges. However, the ending of both the Zrinski and Frankopan dynasties in 1671 dealt Croatian culture a serious blow; both families supported the publishing of Croatian-language books, and Fran Krsto Frankopan was himself an able poet. Once they had been replaced by nobles solidly oriented towards Vienna and Budapest, Croatia was deprived of an upper class with any real enthusiasm for national culture.

designed by Hungarian architect Henrik Böhm in 1904, it's a vivacious red-brick structure whose mushroom-shaped protuberances look like a deliberate affront to its po-faced neighbouring buildings.

Čakovec's main draw, however, is its seventeenth-century **castle**; in a park just west of the centre, it's the former home of the powerful Zrinski family (see box, above). Beyond the moat and surviving western wall, the two-storey Baroque palace in the heart of the fortress now houses the **Museum of the Međimurje** (admittance on the hour; Tues–Fri 10am–3pm, Sat & Sun 10am–1pm; 20Kn). Objects connected with the Zrinskis, including the fine Renaissance tombstone of Nikola Šubić Zrinski, are complemented here by two rooms of Iron Age finds from nearby Goričan, including several big urns decorated with geometric patterns, and an enormous drinking vessel whose handle is adorned with pictures of horned beasts. The ethnographic section contains a colourful collection of women's shawls, decorated with embroidered roses and other vivacious blooms.

Practicalities

Čakovec's **bus station** is a block north of Trg kralja Tomislava, while the **train station** is slightly farther out to the southwest. There's a helpful **tourist office** at Trg kralja Tomislava 2 (Mon–Fri 8am–4pm, Sat 8am–1pm; ⓣ040/310-969, ⓦwww.tourism-cakovec.hr). Čakovec's proximity to the Hungarian border ensures that there's a number of decent **accommodation** options: *Hotel Aurora*, behind the bus station at Franje Punčeca 2 (ⓣ040/310-700, ⓕ310-787; ④), has a handful of bright en-suite rooms with TV and sloping attic ceilings. Just north of the castle and a few steps west of the bus station, *Pansion kod Jape* at Zrinsko-Frankopanska bb (ⓣ040/310-238 or 310-243; ③) offers similarly cosy rooms with private facilities on the top floor of a brand-new office block.

Downtown **eating** options include fish specialities at the *Riblji Restoran* and cheaper Italian fare at *Pizzeria Pipo*, both occuping different halves of the same building on Ulica kralja Tomislava 2. *Gradska kavana*, just off Ulica kralja Tomislava at Matice Hrvatska 2, is a good place to enjoy a daytime **drink** and slice of cake; while *Arcus*, down from the tourist office at Strossmayerova 8, is an elegant café-bar with a youngish clientele.

The weekend preceding Shrove Tuesday sees the traditional **Međimurje carnival** (Međimurski fašnik) parades in the town, when villagers from the surrounding area converge on the Čakovec, sporting, among other things, wild animal masks and imitation storks' heads on sticks; more information about the festivities can be obtained from the tourist office.

Koprivnica and Hlebine

Southeast of Varaždin and Čakovec extends the **Podravina**, a ribbon of maize- and sunflower-covered flatlands running between the River Drava to the northeast and the Bilogora highlands to the south. Most routes pass through the agribusiness centre of **KOPRIVNICA**, where the rail lines from Zagreb to Osijek and Budapest part company. Useful as a jumping-off point for the village of **Hlebine** and the nearby Hungarian border, it's a neat and prosperous provincial town, laid out around an attractive central square next to a well-tended municipal park. The **Town Gallery** (Gradska galerija; Tues–Fri 10am–1pm & 5–8pm, Sat & Sun 10am–1pm), on the north side of the park at Zrinski trg 9, doesn't have a permanent collection but the temporary exhibitions of contemporary work are usually worth a look. Over on the south side of the park at Trg dr. Leandera Brozovića 1, the **Koprivnica Museum** (Muzej grada Koprivnice; Mon–Fri 8am–2pm, Sat 10am–1pm; 10Kn) is strong on nineteenth-century furniture, and has a sizeable photographic display devoted to the 1991–1995 war.

Practicalities

Koprivnica's **bus** and **train** stations lie next to each other, ten minutes' walk west of the main square. The **tourist office** lies 100m northeast of the square at Trg bana Jelačića 7 (Mon–Fri 9am–4pm, Sat 10am–2pm; ⓣ048/621-433, ⓦwww.koprivnicatourism.com). As far as **hotels** are concerned, you can choose between the *Podravina*, an unatmospheric but comfortable concrete structure south of the square at Hrvatske državnosti 9 (ⓣ048/621-025, ⓦwww.hotel-podravina.hr; ④); and its sister establishment *Bijela kuća*, a slightly smarter option beside the train station at Kolodvorska 12 (ⓣ048/240-321, ⓦwww.hotel-podravina.hr; ④).

For **eating**, *Pivnica Kraluš* at Zrinski trg 7 offers local staples such as *grah* (bean stew) and *buncek* (pork knuckle) washed down with locally brewed Pan beer, in a wonderfully weird interior featuring a black cobblestone floor, stained-glass windows and a mushroom-shaped central fireplace. Several parkside **cafés** on Zrinski trg provide opportunities for lingering over coffee and ice cream. Late-night drinkers gravitate towards *Nautilus*, five minutes' south on Ulica Taraščice, or the next-door *Kugla* (weekends only), which offers the best programme of live music and club nights east of Zagreb.

One annual **festival** worth looking out for is **Motifs of Podravina** (Podravski motivi; usually the first or second weekend of July), when there's a big display of local arts and crafts – most notably the delicate local embroidery known as *Ivanečki vez* – together with folkloric performances on the main square.

Hlebine

Sixteen kilometres southeast of Koprivnica, the one-street village of **HLEBINE** has been associated with naive art since the 1930s, and is still

Naive art in Croatia

The emergence of a group of untutored painters in rural Croatia owes a great deal to the trained artist **Krsto Hegedušić** (1901–75) who, while studying in Paris, became an admirer of "naive" (self-taught) artists such as Henri "Le Douanier" Rousseau and the Georgian painter of Tbilisi streetlife, Niko Pirosmani. Returning to Hlebine, Hegedušić was amazed to find that village youths such as **Ivan Generalić** (1914–92) and **Franjo Mraz** (1910–81) seemed to possess the same talent for rendering the world around them in a fresh and vivid style. He encouraged the young artists to adopt the traditional craft of painting in oil or tempera on glass, a technique which gave their colourful scenes of village life an added luminescence.

Hegedušić was a left-leaning intellectual who believed that rural life should be depicted in a non-idealized way to show people how the Croatian peasant really lived. The early works of Generalić and Mraz were grittily documentary in conception, although for gutsy realism even they couldn't compare with the images of peasant toil being produced by **Mirko Virius** (1889–1943), a self-taught painter from Đelekovec, north of Koprivnica, who sought to present a true picture of rural poverty to the urban public. Hegedušić invited Generalić, Mraz and Virius to exhibit with Zemlja ("Earth"), a group of socialist artists from Zagreb, giving naive painting a respectability which has endured ever since. However, Croatian naive art became less politically engaged as the years went on: Zemlja was outlawed in 1935, Virius was killed in a World War II Ustaše concentration camp, and the social concerns of the original Hlebine painters fell into the background. Ivan Generalić entered his magic-realist phase, and the second generation of Croatian village painters, such as **Ivan Rabuzin** (b. 1921) and **Josip Generalić** (son of Ivan), increasingly used the naive style to paint the world inside their heads rather than the world outside the garden gate.

After World War II the tradition of village painting was encouraged all over Yugoslavia by a new regime eager to promote a type of people's art free of Western "decadence", and in both communist Yugoslavia and post-independence Croatia, naive art has been hailed as an authentic expression of indigenous peasant culture. Most of the work produced by today's naive artists tends towards the decorative and the kitsch, largely because there's such a big market for homely rustic themes. Hlebine remains the only village in Croatia where naive art is regarded as a legitimate local craft passed from one generation to the next; if you don't make it here, the best place to view the works of Croatia's rural painters is the **Gallery of Naive Art** in Zagreb (see p.84).

home to an estimated two hundred self-taught painters and sculptors. The **Galerija Hlebine** (Mon–Fri 10am–4pm, Sat 10am–2pm; 10Kn), a modern pavilion which you'll pass on your left as you enter the village from the Koprivnica, documents the work of the Hlebine school, with changing exhibitions chosen from their extensive archive collection. There's a special room devoted to Ivan Generalić, whose personal brand of magical realism had an enormous impact on successive generations, and helped make Hlebine painters so popular with the buying public. Generalić's rather jolly, bucolic vision of peasant life is showcased here with portraits of local characters, fanciful visions (as in *The Eiffel Tower in Hlebine*) and examples of one of his favourite subjects, the crucified rooster or *raspeti petao* – not the mock-religious image you might imagine, but the artist's revenge on the beast that used to wake him up every morning when he was a child. Ten minutes' walk farther down the village's main street, the **Galerija Josip Generalić** (pre-arranged visits only; Ⓣ048/836-430, Ⓦwww.generalic.com) occupies the former studio of both Ivan Generalić and his son Josip, and holds examples of their work, alongside paintings by Ivan's grandson Goran Generalić.

Hlebine is served by six daily **buses** from Koprivnica on weekdays, but services are few and far between at weekends, when you'll need your own transport to visit. Opposite the main art gallery are a **café** and a small store where you can buy food.

Samobor

Nestling beneath the eastern spur of the wooded Samobor hills around 25km west of Zagreb, **SAMOBOR** is every Croat's idea of what a provincial inland town should look like, a tidy, prosperous agglomeration of pastel-coloured houses, largely unsullied by industry and modern architecture, and with an abundance of hilly woodland on the doorstep. Samobor rivalled Zagreb as a trade and craft centre in the Middle Ages, though it's nowadays very much a dormitory suburb of its big neighbour, attracting a smattering of day-trippers keen to explore the woods above the town or sample the local delicacy, *samoborska kremšnita*, a wobbly mass of vanilla custard squeezed between layers of flaky pastry. Other local goodies worth stocking up on include *samoborski bermet*, a brownish, stomach-settling spirit that tastes like cough mixture, and the sharply flavoured *samoborska muštarda* (mustard).

The best time to be in Samobor is immediately preceding Lent, during the **Samobor carnival** (Samoborski fašnik; Ⓦwww.fasnik.com). One of Croatia's best-known and most authentic festivals, it dates from the early 1820s and – apart from a short period in the wake of World War II, when it was suspended – has been a permanent fixture in the town calendar ever since. On the weekend before Shrove Tuesday floats rumble through the streets in lively parades and hedonistic locals run around in masks, creating an impromptu party atmosphere. On Shrove Tuesday itself an effigy named Princ Fašnik ("prince of the carnival") is blamed for everything that has gone wrong over the previous twelve months and is ritually burned on the main square.

Arrival, information and accommodation

Samobor's **bus station**, five minutes' walk north of the main square, Trg kralja Tomislava, is served by buses run by the local Samoborček company, from both Zagreb's main bus station and the Černomerec tram terminal (at the end of tram

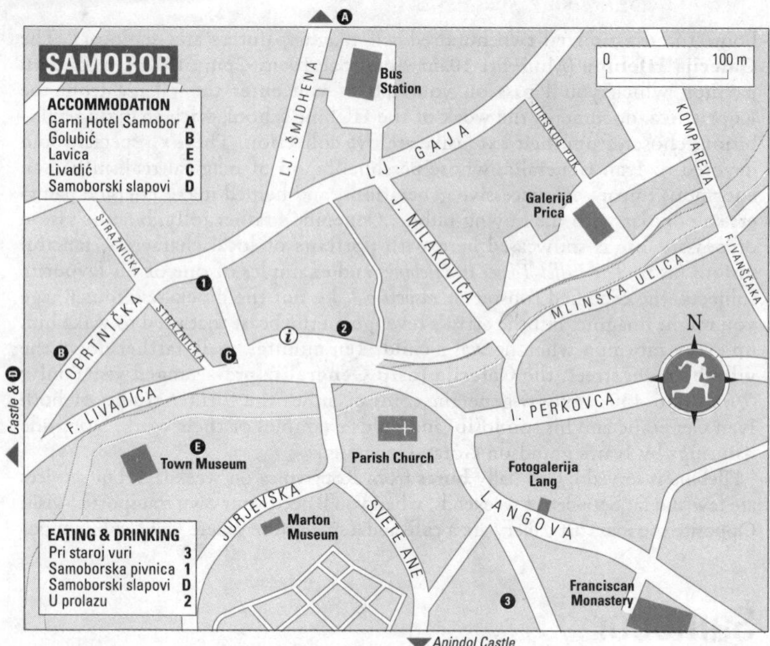

lines #2, #6 and #11). The **tourist office**, at Trg kralja Tomislava 5 (Mon–Fri 8am–7pm, Sat 9am–7pm, Sun 10am–7pm; ⓣ01/33-60-044, ⓦwww.samobor.hr), hands out brochures, sells a town map and can help book accommodation.

Hotels and pensions

Garni Hotel Samobor Josipa Jelačića 30 ⓣ01/33-66-971, ⓦwww.hotel-samobor.hr. Comfortable doubles and triples in a suburban house in the leafy outskirts of town, about 800m northeast of the square. ❷

Golubić Obrtnička 12 ⓣ01/33-60-937, ⓕ33-60-030. Family-run pension just behind the main square, offering a handful of unfussily decorated en-suite rooms with TV and fridge. The couple don't speak much English but they'll make you feel at home all the same. ❷

Lavica Livadićeva 5 ⓣ01/33-68-000, ⓦwww.lavica-hotel.hr. Town-centre establishment with neat en suites (some with bathtub, some with shower) above a restaurant. Not as atmospheric as the other places, but perfectly serviceable. There are some triples and quads, but they're a tight squeeze. ❷

Livadić Trg kralja Tomislava 1 ⓣ01/33-65-850, ⓦwww.hotel-livadic.hr. Medium-sized, friendly, family-run hotel in a 150-year-old house. All rooms are slightly different: some have parquet floors and retro-style furnishings, while others come with modern designer fittings. All have reasonably-sized TVs and bathrooms – if you want a full-size bathtub you'll have to ask for one of the atmospheric attic suites. ❹–❺

Samoborski slapovi Hamor 16 ⓣ01/33-84-059 or 33-84-061, ⓕ33-84-062. Three kilometres northwest of town on the Lipovec road and a good option for those with their own transport, this place has small, neat en-suite rooms with TV, but the real attraction is the location in a narrow wooded valley. ❸

The Town

The town centre revolves around the long, extended triangle of **Trg kralja Tomislava**, beside which flows the Gradna – a minor tributary of the Sava, and here more of a swollen brook than a river – spanned by a succession of slender bridges. Lined by sober, beige town houses and overlooked by a canary-yellow parish church, the square has a character that's overwhelmingly Baroque, which renders the Art Nouveau pharmacy at no. 11 all the more striking – note the haughty, starch-winged angels high up on the facade.

Heading south uphill from Trg kralja Tomislava towards the parish church and bearing right into Jurjevska soon brings you to a handsomely restored granary at no. 7, now home to one of Croatia's best collections of applied art, the **Marton Museum** (Muzej Marton; Sat & Sun 10am–1pm & 3–6pm, Tues–Fri by arrangement; Ⓣ01/3364-160, Ⓦwww.muzej-marton.hr; 20Kn). Based on the private collection of local businessman Veljko Marton, the museum presents an entertaining jaunt through the history of glass and porcelain production, with Meissen tableware, Sèvres figurines and the Eastertide dinner plates of Russian Tsar Nicholas I jostling for attention. Antique furniture and nineteenth-century portrait paintings round off a beautifully presented display.

As you return to the square and head southeast, Langova curls its way up past suburban houses, passing **Fotogalerija Lang** at no. 15 (Sat & Sun 11am–1pm & 4–7pm, Mon–Fri by arrangement; Ⓣ01/33-62-884); this small, privately owned space stages some of the best contemporary photography exhibitions in the country. At the end of the street, the eighteenth-century church of Samobor's **Franciscan Monastery** contains some worthwhile Baroque art by two of the most prolific local painters of the period: a monumental *Dormition of the Virgin* by France Jelovšek and altar paintings by Valentin Metzinger.

A couple of hundred metres beyond the northeastern end of the square, beside a riverside park, the second floor of the town cinema provides a home for the **Galerija Prica** at Trg Matice Hrvatske 3 (Tues–Thurs 9am–3pm, Fri 1–7pm, Sat & Sun 10am–1pm; 15Kn), which is devoted to the zestful, colour-charged canvases of local painter Zlatko Prica (1916–2003) and the significantly more sombre work of his photographer daughter Vesna (1947–96).

The Town Museum

At the square's western end is the **Town Museum** (Gradski muzej; Tues–Fri 9am–3pm, Sat & Sun 9am–1pm; 12Kn), housed in Livadićev dvor, the nineteenth-century home of composer Ferdinand Weisner (1799–1879), whose enthusiasm for the liberation of the Slavs from the Habsburg yoke led him to change his name to the more Croatian-sounding Ferdo Livadić. An important meeting place for the leaders of the Illyrian movement in the 1820s and 1830s, his home now contains a modest collection of furniture, ceramics and fusty portraits of local burghers. More interesting is the ethnographical section in an adjacent outbuilding, where a smattering of English-language texts help to tease significance out of the rough wooden agricultural implements on display.

Anindol

Uphill from Samobor's parish church, Svete Ane climbs past the town graveyard towards **Anindol**, a wooded hillside criss-crossed by paths. After about ten minutes, tracks lead off to the right towards the forest-bound Chapel of St Anne (Crkvica svete Ana), from where you can choose between a steep route uphill to the Chapel of St George (Crkvica sveti Jure) or a lateral path to Samobor's medieval **castle**. Both chapels are closed except for special Masses, and the castle is

Hiking in the Samoborsko gorje

Samobor is the obvious base for hiking trips into the **Samoborsko gorje**, a ravine-scarred upland region which rises suddenly to the east of town, and backs directly onto the hills of the Žumberak. Both ranges fall within the boundaries of the **Žumberak-Samoborsko gorje Nature Park** (Park prirode Žumberak-Samoborsko gorje; ⓦwww.ppzsg.org), which begins 5km west of Samobor and stretches 30km farther west towards Ozalj. An area of deep forest interspersed with sub-alpine meadows, the eastern end of the park is perfect for gentle uphill hikes, and is correspondingly busy with local families on summer weekends. The 1:50 000 *Žumberak-Samoborsko gorje* **map** published by the Nature Park is a useful aid to exploration; Samobor tourist office or the Eco Centre at Slani Dol (see below) may have copies for sale.

The best starting point for walks is **Šoićeva kuća**, a timbered cottage (closed Mon) serving refreshments at the western end of the village of **Veliki Lipovec**, which is 9km west of Samobor along the road passing the (signposted) *Samoborski slapovi* hotel and restaurant. Samobor–Lipovec **buses** ply this route 8–10 times daily. The most popular walk from Šoićeva kuća is the ascent of wooded **Japetić** (879m), the Samoborsko gorje's highest point (1hr 30min–2hr). Two hundred metres southwest of Šoićeva kuća, a road ascends steeply to the right, leading past cottages until the asphalt gives way first to gravel track, then to footpath. After a steady climb through the woods you reach a plateau, where fairly obvious signs direct you either to Japetić's summit, or to the Japetić mountain hut (weekends only) just to the south, which serves excellent *grah* and has good views of the Kupa valley to the southwest, with the forest-enclosed lakes of Črna Mlaka over to the left.

An alternative hike from Šoićeva kuća leads to the 752-metre peak of **Oštrc**, ninety minutes' walk to the south. Directly opposite Šoićeva kuća a marked path heads uphill into the woods, passing through the ruins of the medieval Lipovec castle, continuing along a steep up-and-down path through the woods before eventually emerging onto the Preseka ridge, which runs above lush pastures. At the northeastern edge of the ridge lies Oštrc mountain hut (weekends only), serving good *grah* and simple cuts of meat. From here it takes only twenty minutes to reach the summit of Oštrc itself, where there are more fine views. From Oštrc you can either return to Šoićeva kuća the way you came, or follow a marked path to Japetić via a wooded saddle known as Velika vrata (the Oštrc–Japetić leg takes 1hr 30min), although the ascent of Japetić from Velika vrata is much steeper than the direct route from Šoićeva kuća.

An alternative access point to the hills is the ridge-top village of **Slani Dol**, 10km west of Samobor, reached by leaving town along the Veliki Lipovec road but forking right after about 3km instead of carrying on to Šoićeva kuća; the village is served by 11 **buses** daily from Samobor (fewer at weekends). Occupying the village's highest point is the **Eco Centre** (Eko centar; Mon–Fri 8am–4pm, Sat & Sun 9am–5pm; ⓣ01/33-27-660), maintained by the Žumberak-Samoborsko gorje Nature Park and housing an informative display devoted to local flora and fauna – there's also a spectacular view of the surrounding vineyard-covered hills from the centre's forecourt. Slani Dol is also the start of a long-distance hiking trail known as **Queen Beech Way** (Put kraljice bukve), a two- to three-day trek that leads to Sošice, in the heart of the Žumberak. Recreational ramblers with limited time to spare can attempt the first leg, which ascends from Slani Dol through meadows and beech forest to the Sveti Bernard hut (2hr), where there's a good view and the chance of refreshments at weekends.

no more than an overgrown ruin, but the tranquillity of the surrounding woods makes a walk here worthwhile. It was on Anindol that Josip Broz Tito (see p.124) organized the founding congress of the Croatian Communist Party on August 1, 1937, in an attempt to persuade the Croats that Yugoslav communists shared their nationalist aspirations. With communist organizations outlawed in the Yugoslavia of the time, the gathering had to be organized in secret. An annual hiking festival was used as a cover: with the whole area filling up with weekend visitors, party activists could infiltrate without arousing suspicion. Only sixteen communist agents actually made it to the "congress", and Tito was reduced to scratching the resolutions of the meeting on the back of a calendar with a penknife – or so the story goes.

Eating and drinking

For **food and drink**, *Samoborska pivnica*, a barrel-vaulted beer cellar just off the main square at Šmidhenova 3, serves up cheap staples like pork knuckle (*koljenica*), *štrukli*, tasty local sausages and a full range of meat dishes. Slightly more upmarket, *Pri staroj vuri*, in a suburban street five minutes' walk above the square at Giznik 2 (go up Langova behind the parish church and bear right), specializes in traditional north Croatian cuts of meat, and is one of the best places in the region to tuck into local specialities such as *lungić* (lean pork fillet) and *pačja prsa* (breast of duck). Farther afield, the restaurant of the *Samoborski slapovi* hotel (see p.138) dishes up excellent trout and other freshwater fish from their own pond. The best **cafés** in which to linger over coffee and cake are those on the main square: *U prolazu* is said to offer the best *samoborske kremšnite*, although the *Livadić* runs it a close second and offers a chloresterol-raising range of other home-baked desserts. The narrow streets leading east from the square are well supplied with **bars** overlooking the River Gradna.

Specialist **shops** offering locally made liquor, mustard, salami and other delicacies include *Samoborske delicije*, a well-stocked and rather upmarket delicatessen just off the main square at Šmidhenova 2; and *Filipec*, Stražnička 1a, which sells *bermet* (a sticky brown *digestif* of local manufacture) and *muštarda* from a hole-in-the-wall shop next to a cellar where the latter is made.

Karlovac

Less than an hour west from Zagreb, **KARLOVAC** hides its provincial charms behind a screen of high-rise suburbs and light industry. The centre, however, is a minor delight: a compact grid of crumbling old houses which still preserves the street plan bequeathed to it by Habsburg planners. Initially a purely military settlement, Karlovac was built from scratch in 1579 in order to strengthen Austria's southern defences against Ottoman encroachment. It was deliberately sited between two rivers (the Kupa and the Korana) which had slightly different water levels, therefore providing a constant flow of water for the town's moat. Initially commanded by Archduke Karl of Styria and named Karlstadt in his honour, Karlovac gradually lost its strategic importance as Habsburg forces drove the Ottomans southwards in the late seventeenth century, and life within the fortress walls began to develop a civilian character. The town walls were demolished in the nineteenth century, but their shape – that of a six-pointed star – is still discernible in the earthworks and moats (now drained and transformed into parks) that surround the centre.

Karlovac is an easy day-trip from Zagreb, and onward connections to Rijeka, Zadar and Split are plentiful. A good time to be in town is for the **St John's Day Bonfire** (Ivanjski krijes) on June 23, when the inhabitants of two riverside suburbs, Gaza and Banija, stage competing bonfires and firework displays on either side of the Kupa.

The Town

A good way to start exploring the town is simply to follow the course of the old fortifications, nowadays marked by an almost unbroken circuit of tree-lined promenades surrounding the centre. Within lies a fine ensemble of eighteenth- and nineteenth-century town houses, although damage sustained in 1991 (when the front line was only about 5km away) is still painfully visible. The main square, Trg bana Jelačića, looks particularly shell-scarred and empty; that said, it's worth calling in at the **Holy Trinity Church** (Crkva presvetog Trojstva) on the corner, which has an unusually low barrel-vaulted ceiling decked out with bright Baroque frescoes. A block north of here on Strossmayerov trg, a small **Town Museum** (Gradski muzej; Tues–Fri 7am–3pm, Sat & Sun 10am–noon; 10Kn), set in the Baroque-style Frankopan winter palace, features scale models of old Karlovac and traditional costumes from the surrounding area.

Following first Klaićeva, then Ruski put, southeast of the main square for ten minutes will bring you to the banks of the **River Korana**, site of a leafy riverside park, a weirside café, and a stretch of pebbly beach periodically invaded by inquisitive swans. Out of town in the opposite direction, the medieval stronghold of **Dubovac** can be reached by following Ulica Vladka Mačeka west from central Karlovac before heading uphill to the left – a walk of about thirty minutes. Once held by the Frankopans, feudal lords of the island of Krk who extended their power to the Croatian mainland, it's a compact but well-preserved structure, surrounding a triangular courtyard overlooked by three tiers of galleries. The grassy terrace outside affords an excellent view of Karlovac stretched out on the plain below.

If you're driving out of town in the Plitvice direction you'll pass the **Museum Collection of the Homeland War** (Muzejska zbirka naoružanja domovinskog rata; dawn–dusk; free), 4km south of town in the village of Turanj. An open-air display of tanks, armoured cars and artillery pieces parked outside a (now ruined) Habsburg barracks, it marks the spot where Karlovac's Croatian defenders halted the Serbian advance in 1991.

Practicalities

Karlovac's **bus station** is about 500m southwest of the centre on Prilaz Vece Holjevca, the main north–south route through the town; the **train station** is 1.5km north of the centre along the same road. Tomislavova, next to the bus station, presents the most direct route into town, crossing the line of the former moat before arriving at the central square. There's a left-luggage office (daily 6am–8pm) in the bus station, useful if you're just passing through, and a helpful **tourist office** just east of the centre at Petra Zrinskog 3 (Mon–Fri 8am–3pm, Sat 9am–noon; ⓣ047/615-115, ⓦwww.karlovac-touristinfo.hr). Your choice of **hotels** is limited to the *Carlstadt* at Vraniczanyeva 2 (ⓣ047/611-111, ⓦwww.carlstadt.hr; ④), which has plain but comfortable rooms with TV and en suite, and provides a reasonable buffet breakfast, and the rather more upscale *Korana Srakovčić*, by the river at Perivoj Josipa Vrbanića 8 (ⓣ047/609-090, ⓦwww.hotelkorana.hr; ⑤), right beside the tennis club and waterside paths. There's an attractive **campsite**, the *Slapić*, 12km southwest of town in the village of **Belavići** (beyond Duga Resa on the road to Josipdol; ⓣ047/854-700), reached via an old wooden bridge beside a converted mill. You can swim in the Mrežnica river, and Belavići train station (served by Zagreb–Karlovac–Rijeka trains) is 300m away.

Back in town, snack **food** is plentiful around the bus station, and there's a reasonable pizzeria, *Bastion*, just west of the central square on Stjepana Radića, which also does tasty sweet and savoury pancakes. For a serious sit-down meal, try the *Kerempuh* restaurant, a little way east of the bus station at Vladimira Nazora 4, where you can tuck into substantial veal, pork and turkey dishes in brick-lined rooms. There's a generous sprinkling of cafés just west of the centre around Petra Zrinskog: *Drmeš*, up a side street at Šebetićeva 3, is a brash, raucous place extravagantly decked out in pub bric-a-brac; *River Pub*, Preradovićeva 10, is a spacious bar bustling with young drinkers at weekends, when cover bands or karaoke sessions may well be laid on.

The Žumberak

North of Karlovac lies the **Žumberak**, an enchanting area of steep, vineyard-clad hills and wooded vales punctuated by small plots of sheep-pasture and corn. The region's main appeal lies in its scenery – rather like a wilder version of the Zagorje, with denser forests, faster-flowing rivers and a higher degree of rural depopulation. Primarily given over to ageing smallholders and weekending city folk, the area's scattered **villages** – some of them so isolated that they're only connected to the outside world by gravel track – boast a high proportion of rickety half-timbered houses and open-sided wooden barns full of drying hay. Much of the local population is made up of so-called **Greek Catholics** (Grkokatolici), Orthodox Slavs who migrated to the area in the sixteenth and seventeenth centuries in the wake of Ottoman advances and were offered lands and security by the Habsburg court in return for accepting the primacy of the pope.

The central area of the Žumberak falls within the boundaries of the **Žumberak-Samoborsko gorje Nature Park** (Park prirode Žumberak-Samoborsko gorje; Ⓦwww.ppzsg.org), who maintain **information kiosks** at Medvenova Draga and Grdanjci on the main roads leading into the Žumberak, and also run the Eco Centre at Slani Dol near Samobor (see p.140). All of the above are likely to stock copies of the 1:50,000 *Žumberak-Samoborsko gorje* **map**, the only reliable guide to the region's roads and tracks.

The main **road** into the Žumberak from Karlovac passes through the villages of **Ozalj**, **Krašić** and **Pribić** before working its way round the massif, close to the Slovenian border, and joining up with the other principal road to the region at Bregana, just north of Samobor. There's little **public transport** into the Žumberak proper, although Ozalj and Krašić are reachable from Karlovac by train and bus respectively. Beyond here you really need a car, and it's a delightful and rewarding region to drive through if you have a decent road map and a reasonable dose of patience – the Žumberak's minor roads provide excellent opportunities for getting lost. **Accommodation** is thin on the ground, although well worth seeking out if you're looking for a rural break: you'll find rooms in Čunkova Draga (p.144), Kostanjevac (p.144), *Eko-selo Žumberak* (p.145) and *Divlje Vode* (see p.145).

Ozalj

Straddling the River Kupa some 16km north of Karlovac, **OZALJ** is a small rural spot located at the point where the green limbs of the Žumberak descend to meet the plain below. Just west of the village centre, **Ozalj Castle** is a Colditz-like lump of crumbling grey stone featuring temporary history exhibitions in its **museum** (Mon–Fri 7am–3pm; 10Kn). Returning to the centre of Ozalj, the main road to Krašić heads east over the Kupa, providing a fine view of the weirside **Munjara** (the "lightning factory"), a hydro-electric power station built in 1908; it's a charming Gothic-romantic folly whose crenellated turrets seem to echo the architecture of the castle above. Ten minutes' walk out of town to the east along the road to the village of Trg, the **Ozalj Ethno-Village** (Etno selo) comprises a couple of lovingly-restored nineteenth-century thatched-roof farmhouses together with their outbuildings. You can wander freely around the small complex, although the simple peasant interiors are open only sporadically – ask at the museum in the castle.

Krašić and around

Ten kilometres northeast of Ozalj, the equally rustic village of **KRAŠIĆ** is fast emerging as one of Croatia's most important pilgrimage centres thanks to its status as the birthplace of **Alojzije Stepinac**, archbishop of Zagreb during World War II. After being imprisoned by the communists on trumped-up charges of collaboration, Stepinac lived out the last years of his life under house arrest in Krašić, where he was cared for by a pair of nuns and accompanied by a pet sheep – given to him by a kindly local and obviously intended as food, though Stepinac couldn't bear to have it slaughtered. Stepinac's two-room apartment, located in the parish priest's home just behind the village church, is now preserved as a **Memorial Museum** (Spomen-muzej; open Mon–Sat whenever the priest is around; donation requested), although the ascetic archbishop was not a great hoarder of personal effects – bedstead, writing table and church vestments are about all he left behind. The squat ochre **church** in which the ailing archbishop said Mass was largely rebuilt in neo-Gothic style in 1913, by an architect who obviously had Art Nouveau tastes – note the caryatids peering down from the exterior walls. There's not much to see inside save for a side chapel which preserves some original chunks of medieval masonry.

There are a couple of **cafés** on the main square in front of the church, where you'll also find a small **tourist office** (Wed, Sat & Sun 9am–4pm; Ⓣ01/62-70-910, Ⓔkrasic@tzzz.hr), which has information on the Žumberak region and sells Stepinac-related souvenirs.

Pribić

Beyond Krašić, the road heads through a series of villages sunk deep in wooded valleys. First up is **PRIBIĆ**, an important centre of Greek Catholic culture, where the splendid neo-Byzantine **Church of the Annunciation** (Crkva svetog Blagovijesta) rises up from a reedy islet at the entrance to the village. The interior is half derelict and rarely accessible, but the exterior presents a fine blend of Orthodox architecture and Art Nouveau, with fanciful eagles and gargoyles emerging from its domes.

The Northern Žumberak

Smothered in forest 5km northwest of Pribić, the hamlet of **Medvenova Draga** marks the main southern entrance to the nature park – a small **information centre** beside the road (usually open mornings) may have maps and English-language leaflets for sale. Immediately beyond, **ČUNKOVA DRAGA** is the site of the best **accommodation** in this part of the Žumberak, in the shape of *Seoski turizam Medven* (Ⓣ01/62-70-665; ➊), a converted farmhouse with cosy self-catering apartments, idyllically situated beside an old watermill. A few twists and turns later the road arrives in **KOSTANJEVAC**, where the friendly *Seljačko*

Domaćinstvo Podžumberak (Ⓣ01/62-71-254, Ⓔgoran.klanfar@inet.hr; ❶) offers more modest accommodation in attic rooms above a working farmhouse.

Ten kilometres farther on, a left turn after the village of **Kostanjevac** leads you past wooden barns and ancient, tumbledown houses to the village of **SOŠICE**, grouped around two churches standing side by side, one Catholic and one Greek Catholic – the latter is the one with the taller, rocket-like belfry. Just downhill from the churches is a small **Ethnographic Collection** (Etnografska zbirka; Mon–Sat 9am–5pm; donation requested), run by local Greek Catholic nuns, who preside over a smartly arranged collection of farm implements, antiquated looms and traditional costumes. Of the female attire on display, the rich red-and-blue-striped aprons of the local Greek Catholics contrast sharply with the simpler whites of their Catholic neighbours, demonstrating how the two communities preserved separate traditions despite centuries of coexistence. The homely *Gostionica Ilas*, towards the northern end of the village, is as good a place as any for a **drink** stop, and serves up **snack food** at weekends.

Back on the main northbound route, the road forges an ever more lonely path through thickening forest before climbing onto a mountain ridge and wheeling eastwards roughly parallel to the Croatian–Slovene frontier. It's an exhilarating drive, taking you through the bucolic, half-abandoned hill villages of Budinjak, Poklek and Stojdraga, with panoramic views of forest-covered highlands opening up at frequent intervals. Two kilometres beyond Stojdraga, a right turn – which rapidly deteriorates into a gravel track – leads deep up a narrowing side valley, arriving after 8km at one of the region's most popular weekend destinations, **Eko-selo Žumberak** (Žumberak Eco-Village), a bizarre cross between a Wild West homestead and a nineteenth-century Croatian village complete with riding stables, a "cowboy saloon" and an excellent **restaurant**. The *Eko-selo* also offers **rooms** (Ⓣ01/33-87-472 or 098 900 9824, Ⓦwww.eko-selo.hr; ❷), some in traditional wooden houses built from recycled timber taken from collapsing buildings throughout the region.

Back on the Bregana route, you'll soon pass the popular recreation spot of *Divlje Vode*, a fish farm overlooked by an excellent **restaurant**, where you can eat fresh trout and frogs' legs (*žablji kraci*) on a shady terrace. The complex also offers **accommodation** (Ⓣ01/33-87-623, Ⓦwww.karlo.hr; ❸) in the form of bright, newly furnished en suites. From here it's another 4km to the village of **Grdanjci**, where there's a small **information kiosk** for the benefit of those entering the nature park from the northeast. Shortly afterwards the road arrives in **Bregana**, where it meets up with the main route southeast to Samobor and Zagreb.

West of Karlovac: the Gorski kotar

Road and rail routes from Karlovac to Rijeka follow a scenic route through the hills and mountains of the **Gorski kotar** (literally "wooded district"; Ⓦwww.gorskikotar.com), a spectacular landscape of green river valleys and forested hillsides. Given its proximity to the Zagreb-Rijeka transport routes, it is a surprisingly untouristed area, although there's a nascent winter sports scene at the region's main holiday centre, **Bjelolasica**, and numerous summer hiking opportunities. Both Bjelolasica and the nearby town of **Ogulin** are good starting points for walks in the nearby mountains, with the landmark peak of **Klek** providing the obvious target for day-trip hikers. Farther north, the workaday town of **Delnice** is the main staging post en route to both the **Risnjak National**

Park and the ravine-top village of **Skrad**, where numerous woodland beauty spots await inspection.

The Karlovac–Rijeka highway forges straight through the northern Gorski kotar, passing near Delnice on the way, while the Karlovac–Split motorway skirts the region's southeastern side, providing easy access to Ogulin. The Zagreb–Rijeka railway also provides good access to the region, wheeling south through Ogulin before turning north towards Delnice.

The southern Gorski kotar

Fifty-five kilometres southwest of Karlovac, **OGULIN** is an untidy small town built around a **castle** founded by the Frankopans around 1500, and subsequently used as a prison. The structure still boasts an impressively turreted pair of towers, but the **museum** within (Mon–Fri 8am–2pm, Sat 9am–noon; 10Kn) is disappointing, with displays on the history of hiking in the region and a rather bare memorial cell where Josip Broz Tito was interned in 1932. Opposite the castle, a small viewing platform overlooks a dramatic canyon-scape, where the River Dobra flows into an underground passage, re-emerging several kilometres to the east before joining the River Kupa near Karlovac.

Ogulin is easily reached by **train** from Zagreb with six services a day, although for sheer convenience you can't beat the *Karlek* tourist train (mid-June to late Aug), which runs from Zagreb on Saturday mornings, and is met by connecting minibuses to Bjelolasica, Klek and other local recreation spots. Ogulin's **train** and **bus stations** are ten minutes' walk from the centre (turn right outside the stations and follow the main road). The **tourist office** on the main street at Bernardina Frankopana 2 (Mon–Fri 8am–3pm; Ⓣ & Ⓕ 047/532-278, Ⓦ www.tz-grada-ogulina.hr) can help with local hiking information and can fix you up with private **rooms** (❶) in surrounding villages. There are a few **cafés** along the main street, but no decent places to eat unless you count the *Sabljaci* restaurant, which offers both freshwater fish and a water side location on the eastern shores of Lake Sabljak, a five-kilometre drive south of town. The nearest **hotel** accommodation is in Bjelolasica.

Klek

Seven kilometres due west of Ogulin, the 1187-metre **Klek** is not the highest of the Gorski kotar mountains, but is undoubtedly one of the most dramatic. Its summit – a tall rocky cylinder rising out of a forested ridge – dominates the local landscape for miles around and, somewhat appropriately given its menacing appearance, is said to be the place where local witches and demons meet on the eve of May 1 (a date that has always been associated with the supernatural in central Europe). Klek has been one of inland Croatia's most important targets for hikers ever since 1838, when the future governor of Croatia, Josip Jelačić, scaled it in the company of King Friedrich August II of Saxony, adding a dash of aristocratic glamour to a pastime then in its infancy.

You can walk to Klek and back from Ogulin by following the Bjelolasica road west of town, although it's easier to drive (or catch one of four daily buses) as far as the village of **Bijelsko**, 8km west of Ogulin, thereby cutting a good ninety minutes off your journey. Arriving in the village from the direction of Ogulin, you'll see a house on your right with the legend "Klek: 1hr" helpfully painted on the wall. From here a well-marked trail ascends steadily through the woods, arriving at the Klek mountain hut (drinks and snacks available at weekends) after about 45 minutes. The path then coils its way round the stone barrel of Klek's upper reaches towards the summit, which should take you about another 25 minutes to negotiate, though a couple of steep, rope-assisted sections on the way up may deter those who lack a good head for heights. The views from Klek's broad, flat top are magnificent.

Bjelolasica

Seventeen kilometres beyond Bijelsko, a right turn in the village of **Jasenjak** leads up a narrow wooded valley to the **Bjelolasica Olympic Centre** (Olimpijski centar Bjelolasica; ⓣ047/562-118, ⓦwww.bjelolasica.hr; ❸–❹), some 5km beyond. Laid out on meadows below steep, pine-covered slopes, this is a year-round tourist resort made up of several chalet-style accommodation blocks set beside a central administration and café-restaurant pavilion. As the name suggests, it's also a training camp for serious sportspeople, with numerous professional teams making use of its athletics track and indoor sports halls. Bjelolasica is also Croatia's only real skiing resort, although the season is unpredictable and short (Dec–Feb, snowfalls allowing), so most winter sports fans tend to arrange ad hoc weekend breaks here rather than book skiing holidays in advance. Chairlifts run up the flanks of **Mount Bjelolasica**, immediately west of the resort, where there are slopes for beginners and intermediates, plus a single, five-hundred-metre run for advanced skiers; ski rental can be arranged on arrival. In spring and summer Bjelolasica is a good base for medium-to-strenuous hiking, with the primary target being the 1531-metre peak of Bjelolasica itself (3–4hr each way). Basic hiking maps can be picked up at the centre.

The northern Gorski kotar

The main urban centre of the northern Gorski kotar is **DELNICE**, a rather featureless town 60km west of Karlovac and a handy jumping-off point for both the Risnjak National Park and the wooded ravines of Skrad. The town lies 2km to the north of the main Karlovac–Rijeka highway, and most Zagreb–Rijeka trains and buses stop off here. There's a string of cafés and shops along the main street, but no other inducements to hang around save for the local **tourist office**, also on the main street (Mon–Fri 8am–3pm; ⓣ051/812-156, ⓦwww.tz-delnice.hr), which can provide maps, advice on exploring the region, and details of private rooms (❶) in local villages.

The Risnjak National Park

From Delnice, a minor road (served by two daily buses) runs 10km northwest to the village of **CRNI LUG**, the starting point for explorations of the **Risnjak National Park** (Narodni park Risnjak), which covers a group of rugged, forest-covered mountains centred on the 1528-metre Veliki Risnjak. **Food** and **accommodation** are available in Crni Lug's *Nacionalni park Risnjak* motel (ⓣ051/836-133; ❷), where you can pick up hiking maps and information before setting out for the **park** entrance, 2km west of the village in the hamlet of Bijela Vodica. There's a range of walking possibilities; the easiest excursion for day-trippers is the **Leska Educational Trail** (Poučna staza Leska), a 4.5-kilometre circuit which starts in Crni Lug and leads through a variety of forest environments, with signboards alerting the visitor to local flora and fauna. Rather more taxing is the assault on the summit of Veliki Risnjak itself (allow 3–4hr each way), a steep but rewarding trek which offers expansive views of the surrounding countryside once you get beyond the treeline, with the Kvarner Gulf stretching out to the west and a huddle of Gorski kotar peaks to the south.

Another worthwhile excursion for those with their own transport is the trip to the village of **Razloge**, 12km north of Crni Lug, from where a well-marked path winds its way down towards the **source of the River Kupa** (izvor Kupe). A karstic spring which takes the form of a two-hundred-metre-long turquoise lake, it's the perfect place for nature-aided meditation.

Skrad and around

Fifteen kilometres northwest of Delnice, the hillside village of **SKRAD** is at first sight a drab little place – formerly an important way-station on the Zagreb–Rijeka road, it was left high and dry by the construction of the new highway a few kilometres to the south. However, there are some wonderful **walks** in the vicinity, most notably in the deep wooded valley downhill to the west, a defile carved by the rushing waters of the Jasle, a tributary of the Kupa.

Skrad is easy to get to: most Zagreb–Rijeka **trains** stop at the station just downhill from the village centre, and there are three daily **minibuses** from Delnice. The train station is the main starting point for trails into the canyon, with a path on the opposite side of the tracks winding its way through dense (and often muddy) forest. After a steep descent of some thirty minutes, a left-hand fork leads to **Zeleni vir** (Green Whirlpool), where two majestic waterfalls tumble over a seventy-metre-high cliff, screening a cave whose mouth often fills with turquoise-green water – hence the place's name. From here, paths lead south towards the so-called **Vražji prolaz** (Devil's Passage), where the waters of the young Jasle force their way between sheer cliffs, forming a ravine which in places is scarcely two metres wide. Wooden walkways take you above the frothing waters, emerging after some fifteen minutes near the mouth of a small cave known as Muževa hiža. From here you can either return the way you came, or follow paths uphill through the woods to the northeast, eventually re-emerging at the back of the train station – a circuit of two-and-a-half hours in total.

South of Karlovac: the Plitvice Lakes

Beyond Karlovac, southbound travellers have a choice of two routes: either the new Zagreb–Split toll motorway which heads southeast across the Gorski kotar, or the old, single-lane road to Split, which forges due south across the upland pastures of the **Kordun** and **Lika** regions. Despite being somewhat slower, the latter route offers plenty in terms of natural beauty and historical resonance, passing through a series of villages that are slowly returning to normality after wartime occupation by the Serbs. It's a busy road, choked with crawling coast-bound cars on summer weekends, and you'll come across innumerable roadside **restaurants** serving up spit-roast lamb or suckling pig to hungry travellers. Owing to the large volume of tourist traffic, an increasing number of local villagers are advertising private **rooms** for rent – hence the slightly surreal spectacle of newly renovated houses with cheery signs offering vacancies in a multitude of languages standing right next door to bombed-out homes whose owners have yet to return.

Perched on a hilltop 50km south of Karlovac, the small town of **SLUNJ** is unremarkable save for the confluence of the Korana and Slunjčica rivers just below, with the rushing waters of the latter dropping into the Korana gorge through a series of small waterfalls and burbling rapids. In times past this natural power source led to the development of a riverside watermilling settlement known as **Rastoke**. Several traditional millers' buildings still survive, solid structures with stone lower floors and timber upper storeys. It's a delightful area for a stroll, with excellent views of the gorge from the path above the north bank of the Korana, and everything is relatively easy to find: you'll glimpse Rastoke down to the right when entering the town by road from the north (buses stop 800m further uphill on Slunj's main square).

There's no other reason to hang around in Slunj, but the helpful **tourist office** just down from the square at Zagrebačka 12 (Mon–Fri 8am–3pm; ⓣ047/777-630, ⓦwww.slunj.hr) can point you in the direction of private **rooms** (❶) in Slunj and outlying villages.

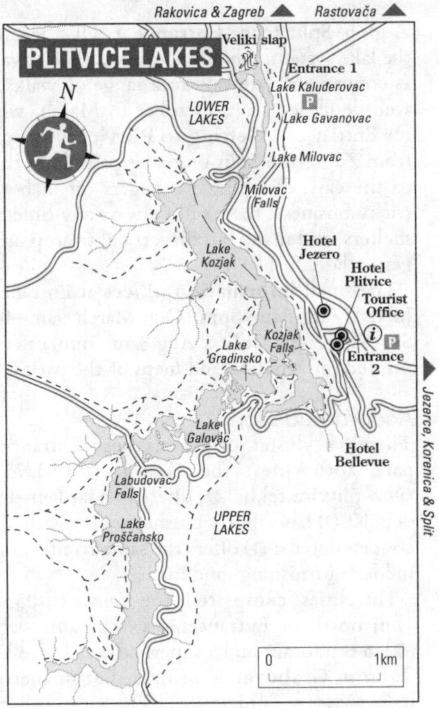

Plitvice Lakes National Park

Forty kilometres south of Slunj, the **PLITVICE LAKES NATIONAL PARK** (Nacionalni park plitvička jezera; ⓦwww.np-plitvicka-jezera.hr) is the country's biggest single natural attraction, and with some justification. The eight-kilometre string of sixteen lakes, hemmed in by densely forested hills, presents some of the most eye-catching scenery in mainland Croatia, with water rushing down from the upper lakes via a sequence of waterfalls and cataracts. This unique landscape came into being as a result of the action of travertine, calcium-rich material picked up by the river and then deposited downstream – a process which, when repeated over the course of several millennia, produced a terraced sequence of barriers behind which lakes formed. Nowadays these lakes – a bewitching turquoise when seen from a distance – teem with fish and watersnakes, while herons frequent the shores of the quieter, northern part of the system, and deer, bears, wolves and wild boar throng the wooded heights above.

Despite being occupied by Serb forces from 1991 to 1995, the park is remarkably well organized: paths are easy to follow, regular shuttle buses and boats ferry visitors to major trailheads, and English-speaking staff are on hand with advice at the park's two major entry points. All this ensures that you can see a great deal in a short space of time, although keen walkers could easily spend a day or two exploring the whole area.

Arrival, information and accommodation

The park (daily: May–Sept 8am–7pm; Oct–April dawn–dusk; July & Aug 120Kn; rest of year 90Kn) can be entered from two points on the main

Zagreb–Split road: **Entrance 1** (Ulaz jedan) is at the northern (lower) end of the lake system, while **Entrance 2** (Ulaz dva) is 2.5km further south. Both serve as convenient gateways to a range of walks, but be aware that Entrance 2 may well be closed from October to March, when it makes sense to head directly for Entrance 1. **Getting to Plitvice** is straightforward: many (but not all) buses from Zagreb to Split or Zadar pass along the main road which fringes the park to the east, dropping passengers off at both entrances. **Moving on** can be a tricky business: there's not always any timetable information at the roadside bus shelters, and many bus drivers fail to stop unless you jump out into the road and gesticulate.

The small **information offices** at Entrance 1 (April–June & Sept 9am–5pm; July & Aug 8am–8pm; Oct–March 9am–4pm) and Entrance 2 (April–June & Sept 9am–5pm; July & Aug 8am–7pm) offer a wealth of advice, but are short on printed information and maps of the park.

Accommodation

There's a cluster of **hotels** near Entrance 2, all of which are run by the park authorities: the *Bellevue* (Ⓣ053/751-015, Ⓕ751-013, Ⓔnp-plitvice@np-plitvice.tel.hr; ❹) offers standard en-suite rooms; the *Plitvice* (same contact details; ❹) has slightly plusher rooms with TV and minibar; and the *Jezero* (same contact details; ❺) offers the same comforts as the *Plitvice* but with slightly more modern furnishings and fittings.

The closest **campsite** is the *Korana* (Ⓣ053/751-879), on the main road about 7km north of Entrance 1, a large and well-organized place with bungalows (❷), a restaurant and a supermarket. Three kilometres further on, the *Autokamp Turist* in **Grabovac** is a similar but smaller place with more trees (Ⓣ047/784-077, Ⓦwww.slunjcica.hr). The same village is home to the roadside **motel** *Grabovac* (❸), which offers sparsely furnished but habitable rooms and a big self-service restaurant.

There are private **rooms** (❶) in the nearby villages of **Rastovača** (close to Entrance 1) and **Jezerce** (just south of Entrance 2); vacancies are handled by the kiosks run by the park authorities at both entrances, but they may only operate in July and August – at other times you should apply to the **tourist office** in the centre of **Korenica**, a small town 7km south of the lakes (Ⓣ053/776-798, Ⓦwww.tzplitvice.hr).

The string of villages along the main road north of the park have an increasing number of private rooms, especially **Korana** (7km distant), **Grabovac** (9km), **Rakovica** (12km) and **Oštarski Stanovi** (18km). The **tourist office** in Rakovica, at no. 6 in the village's only street (Ⓣ047/784-450, Ⓦwww.rakovica.hr), handles information and reservations for private rooms (❶) in these villages, as does a kiosk by the roadside in Grabovac (June–Sept; Ⓣ047/784-300 or 098 170 4746, Ⓦwww.ais-tours.com), run by the AiS agency. The majority of houses offering rooms are well signed from the main road though, so if you're travelling through the area by car you shouldn't have too much difficulty tracking down vacancies. Inter-city buses pick up and drop off in these places too, but owing to the paucity of on-the-spot timetable information, you can't rely on them to shuttle you in and out of the park once you've arrived.

The Lakes

Entrance 1, situated at the point where the lake waters flow off into the Korana gorge, is ten minutes' walk away from **Veliki slap** (literally "the big waterfall"), a high wall of water that is the park's single most dramatic feature. Paths lead to the foot of the waterfall, passing alongside the top of the smaller **Sastavci** fall, which empties into the cliff-lined Korana gorge. From Veliki slap you can proceed south on foot towards the lower group of cataracts, where wooden walkways traverse the foaming waters. Beyond lies **Kozjak**, the largest of Plitvice's lakes. By sticking to the western side of Kozjak you'll eventually emerge at the northern terminus of the **shuttle ferry** service (included in entrance ticket), which will take you south towards Entrance 2. Otherwise you can walk to Entrance 2 along the eastern bank of Kozjak, or take the bus from the road just above the lakeside path.

Entrance 2 is the best jumping-off point for the biggest group of cataracts, where waters from the highest of the Plitvice lakes, **Prošćansko**, tumble down into a succession of smaller pools and tarns before reaching Kozjak lower down. Exploring this part of the system can easily absorb at least half a day; to save time, you can take the **shuttle bus** (cost included in entrance ticket) to the southernmost stop (Labudovac) and take a stroll around the upper cataracts from there.

Eating

Entrance 2 has a **supermarket** opposite, and both entrances have **snack bars** offering a range of drinks and basic food. For more substantial fare, it's best to head for the *Lička kuća* **restaurant** opposite Entrance 1, a large, touristy place decked out with folksy wooden fittings and serving traditional Lika food such as spicy sausages, *đuveđ* (a paprika-flavoured ratatouille with rice) and roast lamb; the hotel restaurants at Entrance 2 are a bit bland. Look out for local women selling homemade cheese (the mild yellow *škripavac*) along the roadside. It's usually sold in large circular pieces weighing over a kilo, but you can ask for a half (*polovina*) or quarter (*četvrtina*) if you don't think you can manage a whole one.

The Lonjsko polje and around

The area **southeast of Zagreb** is characterized by unbroken green flatlands watered by the Sava and its tributaries. As you travel away from the city, the region is dotted with modern villages that serve as dormitory suburbs of the capital, but the farther south you go, the more examples of ancient timber houses and rustic lifestyles you'll come across. **Sisak** is the rather characterless main town in the region, and is really just a staging point on the way to more enticing rural destinations. South of Sisak on the banks of the River Sava, the area of wetland known as the **Lonjsko polje** is justly famous for its wooden village architecture and nesting storks. Marking the Lonjsko polje's southern end, the town of **Jasenovac** was the site of a notorious concentration camp in World War II and is now home to a dignified memorial park. The beautifully decorated Baroque church at **Kutina**, just east of the Lonsko polje, rounds off a tour of the region.

Zagreb is the best base from which to explore the area, with road and rail routes heading southeast towards Sisak, and the Autocesta (the Zagreb–Belgrade highway) skirting the region to the east.

Sisak

The obvious northern gateway to the region is **SISAK**, a dreary, medium-sized town 22km west of the Popovača exit of the Autocesta. Sited near the junction of the Sava, Odra and Kupa rivers, Sisak has served successive rulers as a strategic strongpoint, beginning with the Romans, who named it Siscia and used it as a base for their river fleet. Fragments of Roman glassware and pottery are displayed in a small **municipal museum** (Gradski muzej; Tues–Fri 9am–5pm, Sat 10am–1pm; 10Kn), east of the tourist office at Kralja Tomislava 10, but there's little else to captivate you in town save for the sixteenth-century **castle**, 3km farther south. Watching over the confluence of the Sava and Kupa, it's a splendid triangular structure protected by a barrel-shaped bastion at each corner. The castle interior remains boarded up for the time being, but its riverside setting makes a visit worthwhile – and there's a fine **restaurant** in one of the outbuildings. To get to the fortress from central Sisak, drive or walk southeast along Kralja Tomislava until you get to the River Sava, where you turn right onto the riverside Obala T. Bakača – the fortress is clearly visible straight ahead.

Practicalities

Sisak is connected to the capital by bus and train; the **bus** and **train stations** stand next to each other on Trg republike, 500m north of the **tourist office** (Mon–Fri 8am–5pm; ⓣ044/522-655, ⓦwww.sisakturist.com), which is on the western fringe of the town centre in a seventeenth-century riverside granary known as the Mali Kaptol, Rimska bb. If you need to use Sisak as a base for exploring the Lonjsko polje, careworn but habitable en-suite rooms are available at the *Panonija* **hotel**, a concrete structure right in the centre at I. K. Sakcinskog 21 (ⓣ044/515-600, ⓦwww.hotel-panonija.hr; ❸). The *Cocktail* **restaurant** at Ante Starčevića 27 is the best place in the centre for hearty local food, while the *Siscia Jazz Club* – in the same building as the tourist office – is a relaxing, brick-vaulted café-bar with live music in the evenings.

The Lonjsko polje

Stretching southeast of Sisak, the **Lonjsko polje** contains more in the way of nineteenth-century wooden architecture than any other region of Croatia. The other main characteristic of the *polje* (which literally means "field") are the swamplands and riverine forest which appear in spring and autumn, when the tributaries of the River Sava habitually break their banks and the area is colonized by spoonbills, herons and storks. The oak forests and pastures of the *polje* are also home to the Posavlje horse (Posavski konj), a stocky, semi-wild breed, and the spotty-hided Turopolje pig (Turopoljska svinja), which lives off acorns. The area between Sisak and Jasenovac was designated the **Lonjsko polje Nature Park** (Park prirode Lonjsko polje; ⓦwww.pp-lonjso-polje.hr) in 1990, although the development of tourism in the area is still in its infancy – there's precious little accommodation in the Lonsko polje, and only a couple of places to eat. Public transport is meagre, so it's best to come by car if you can.

From Sisak it's an easy if inadequately signed drive to the villages of the Lonjsko polje: leave town on the road to Popovača and turn right after 5km when you see a sign reading "Lonja". Travelling by public transport, there are four daily buses to Čigoć (of which two carry on to the village of Lonja, calling at Mužilovčica on the way), 28km from Sisak. However you approach the region, you'll find yourself on a badly surfaced road which winds its way southeast along the banks of the River Sava, passing through a sequence of single-street villages characterized by their chicken-choked yards and the kind of tumbledown, timber-built houses that seem to have jumped straight out of an illustrated book of fairy stories.

△A nineteenth-century wooden house in Lonjsko polje

Čigoć

Located 30km southeast of Sisak, the village of **ČIGOĆ** is a world-renowned collection point for migrating white storks, who head here every spring (usually arriving late March or early April) ready to feast on the *polje*'s abundant supply of insects, fish and frogs. The storks nest on chimneys and telegraph poles throughout the village. You stand a good chance of seeing baby storks during the hatching season, which falls in late April or May. According to tradition, the storks leave Čigoć for the wintering grounds of southern Africa (an eight- to twelve-week journey) on St Bartholomew's Day (August 24), although a handful of creatures stay in the village all year, their migratory instincts weakened by food handouts by soft-hearted locals. Most of the houses in Čigoć are traditional two-storey structures with thatched roofs, overhanging eaves, and a main entrance on the first floor, reached by a covered outside staircase known as a *ganjak*; many also have elaborately carved porches or balconies. One of these structures midway through the village houses a **park information point** (daily 8am–4pm; ⓣ044/715-115), which sells tickets (20Kn) to the park on an honour-based system (many people simply drive through), along with a map. They can also advise on trails leading east from Čigoć, and the other villages, out into the countryside, parts of which might be under water depending on the time of year.

Continuing along the main street from the information point you'll soon come across the **Čigoć Tourist Association** (Turistička družba Čigoć), really a small private museum (daily whenever the family is in residence; 5Kn), consisting of an upstairs room crammed with traditional textiles and colourful embroidery. Four doors on, the Sučić family's **ethnographical collection** (Etnografska zbirka Sučić; daily whenever the family is in residence; donation requested) features more of the same, plus a rickety barn filled with just about every outmoded agricultural implement that Mr Sučić could lay his hands on. Towards the eastern end of the village, the *Stara hiža* **restaurant** offers drinks, snacks and occasionally more substantial dishes, depending on what they have in stock.

Croatia's borderlands

Croatia's long border with Bosnia and Serbia has long been ethnically mixed, a legacy of the population movements caused by Ottoman advances into the central Balkans. Christians of various creeds who had been displaced from their homes by the Turks were settled here by the Habsburgs to man the so-called **Military Frontier**, a wedge of land along the border with Ottoman-controlled territory, which was placed under direct rule from Austria and organized along military lines. Established in the sixteenth century as a belt of territories running through the north of present-day Croatia, the Military Frontier gradually moved southwards as Austrian armies threw the Ottomans back, until by the early 1700s it had stabilized into the wishbone-shaped frontier with Ottoman-controlled Bosnia which is still reflected in the modern-day border. Many of the people who settled here were migrants from the southern Balkans, a mixture of Slavs and Vlach shepherds who – owing to the fact that they were Orthodox Christians, and therefore subject to the Serbian patriarchate – developed a Serbian national consciousness as the centuries passed. The waning of Ottoman power in the 1700s meant that the Military Frontier lost its use as a defensive cordon, although the Habsburgs kept it as a way of maintaining a permanently armed and drilled population for use in the empire's wars in other parts of Europe. This provided the Serbs and Croats of the region with powerful national myths: both communities came to consider themselves the most war-like, noble and masculine expressions of their respective peoples, and by the early twentieth century many Serbs regarded the Military Frontier region – or simply **Krajina** ("border land"), as they now called it – as the heartland of martial Serb values.

The Military Frontier was abolished in 1881, but the region's ethnically mixed character remained. The so-called **Independent State of Croatia** (NDH), created by Nazi Germany after the fall of Yugoslavia in 1941, tried to "cleanse" Croatia of its Serbian population by violent means – hundreds of thousands of Croatian Serbs in the border regions were either driven from their homes, forcibly converted to Catholicism, or killed. Memories of the NDH period had a profound effect on Serbian attitudes in the years leading up to the collapse of communist Yugoslavia, and with the victory of the pro-independence HDZ in the Croatian elections of April 1990, Serbian propagandists in Belgrade deliberately played on the fears of Serbs living in Croatia by suggesting that the dark days of the NDH were about to return. In an atmosphere of inter-ethnic mistrust generated in large part by the Belgrade media, Serbs living in the border regions of Croatia launched a **rebellion** from the town of Knin (northwest of Split) in September 1990, which later developed into all-out war following Croatia's declaration of independence in June 1991. Supported by the Yugoslav People's Army, Serbian insurgents took control of a swath of territory stretching from Slavonia in the east to the Knin region in the west, which they planned to detach from the nascent Croatian state. Croat settlements within these

Mužilovčica and beyond

Beyond Čigoć lies a succession of villages similar in appearance but without as many storks. First you come to **MUŽILOVČICA**, where you'll find a small, private ethnographic **museum** at *Seoski turizam Mužilovčica* (Rural tourism Mužilovčica) and the beautifully preserved timber house of Jakša and Zlata Ravlić at no. 72, on the village's only street. The Ravlićes offer simple bunk-bed **accommodation** in the refurbished barn (Ⓣ044/710-151, Ⓔjaksa.ravlic@sk.t-com.hr; ❶) and, even if you're not staying, will serve up excellent home-cooked **food** (especially locally caught fish) if you give them advance warning of your arrival.

A dirt road at the southern end of Mužilovčica leads northeast to the so-called **Retencisko polje**, an area of pastureland bordered by dykes which

Serb-controlled areas were ethnically cleansed, while the east Slavonian town of **Vukovar**, one of the places that stood in the way of the Serbian land grab, was almost totally destroyed in the autumn of 1991. Other inland towns such as Osijek, Vinkovci, Slavonski Brod and Karlovac found themselves at the heart of Croat resistance to further Serbian expansion and, although all were subjected to heavily shelling, they remained in Croatian hands.

By the end of 1991 large chunks of inland Croatia were under the control of the Serbs, who proceeded to organize the breakaway territory as the **Serbian Republic of the Krajina** – a nominally independent state which was in practice heavily dependent on Belgrade. The deployment of UN peacekeepers to the front line after March 1992 temporarily brought the conflict to an end, but only seemed to confirm Serb gains. Aware that international diplomacy was unlikely to secure a return of the Serb-occupied territories, the Croatian government re-equipped its armed forces and prepared to take them back by force. In May 1995 the **Blijesak** ("Flash") offensive cleared Serbian forces from western Slavonia, a pocket of land midway between Zagreb and Slavonski Brod. In August of the same year **Oluja** ("Storm") resulted in the collapse of Krajina forces around Knin. Flushed with military success, the Croats were able to negotiate a peaceful transfer of power in the one remaining area of Croatia under Serb control, eastern Slavonia. Local Serbs opted to surrender the territory without a struggle: according to the terms of the 1995 **Erdut Agreement**, eastern Slavonia was to be governed by the UN for two years before returning to Croatian sovereignty in January 1998. The changeover took place relatively peacefully, and despite an initial exodus of local Serbs, most chose to stay and accept the new administration.

Croats who had been forced out of Serb-controlled areas in 1991 were now free to return, although war damage and the lack of a functioning economy meant that many stayed away. The situation was complicated by the position of the local Serb population, who had fled in their thousands in the wake of Blijesak and Oluja – the right of all refugees, regardless of ethnicity, to return to their prewar homes was one of the key elements of the 1995 **Dayton Accord**, which was designed to bring a definitive end to the conflicts in Croatia and Bosnia. As a result, both Croatian and Serbian returnees are competing for an insufficient number of homes and jobs, and tensions between the two communities remain. Returning Croats are understandably suspicious of Serbian neighbours against whom they were fighting a few years before, while those Serbs who have chosen to stay feel they are being made to bear a collective guilt for the actions of a few. The question of **war crimes** remains ever-present: mass graves of Croats who disappeared in 1991 are still being uncovered, while a true picture of the excesses committed by Croatian irregulars in the wake of Blijesak and Oluja is yet to be established.

becomes a huge lake in the wake of rainy periods, attracting numerous species of waterfowl.

Returning to the road and continuing southeast brings you after 6km to **Lonja**, another strung-out, tumbledown village, followed after 12km by **Krapje**, whose rather better-preserved wooden houses sit in a neat row, spaced at regular intervals – the orderly result of strict regulations introduced by the Habsburgs to control house-building in the settlements of the Military Frontier.

Jasenovac

Fifteen kilometres beyond Krapje and 10km south of the Novska exit of the Autocesta is **JASENOVAC**, the site of a notorious World War II concentration camp. Established in autumn 1941, this was the largest in an archipelago of camps stretching from Krapje in the north to Stara Gradiška in the south. It was here that the pro-Nazi puppet state, the NDH (Nezavisna Država Hrvatska or "Independent State of Croatia"), incarcerated Serbs, Jews, Gypsies and anti-fascist Croats and set them to work producing bricks and metal chains. Unproductive or unwanted prisoners were murdered in cold blood, while overwork, malnourishment and a succession of cold winters took their toll on countless thousands of others. When Jasenovac was finally wound up in April 1945, the Ustaše attempted to murder the remaining inmates, six hundred of whom staged a mass breakout – a total of 91 got away.

The camp was razed in 1945 and turned into a **memorial park** (*spomen-park*) two decades later. Situated beside the road into town from Novska, it is centred on a striking modern sculpture described as a "melancholy lotus" by its creator, Serbian architect and politician Bogdan Bogdanović (who, as the liberal mayor of Belgrade in the 1980s, was purged by Slobodan Milošević's hardliners). The **museum** (ⓦ www.ushmm.org/jasenovac) at the park entrance is in the throes of major long-term reorganization, and it's not known when it will reopen to the public. In the meantime you can wander from the site

Jasenovac and its legacy

Alojzije Stepinac, the archbishop of Zagreb during World War II, was so shamed by the concentration camp at **Jasenovac** that he likened it to the mark of Cain, to be worn by the Croatian nation for ever. Since then, the failure of first Yugoslav, then Croatian, officialdom to come to terms with what really happened at Jasenovac has only served to prove the wisdom of Stepinac's words. Initially, there was a tendency among post-war Yugoslav historians to inflate the numbers of the camp's victims, and an estimate of 700,000 to 1,000,000 dead came to be officially accepted, despite the lack of research to back it up. Croatian historians, led by **Franjo Tuđman**, asserted that the death toll at Jasenovac could not have exceeded 30,000–40,000. They felt that the circulation of such high figures was exploited by official circles in Yugoslavia to blacken the reputation of the whole Croatian nation and render feelings of Croatian patriotism impossible for future generations. The lack of unbiased research makes all figures questionable, although outside observers nowadays consider 85,000–90,000 to be a fair estimate – the majority of the victims are likely to have been Serbs. With Tuđman's controversial writings fuelling the debate, Jasenovac became a political football during the dying days of Yugoslavia, with the Serbian media whipping up anti-Croatian feeling by harking back to the crimes of World War II, and the Croats minimizing the importance of Jasenovac in an attempt to sweep the excesses of the Nazi period under the carpet.

Even after Croatian independence, Jasenovac lost none of its power to divide opinion. Faced with the question of what to do with the site once it was returned to Croatian control, President Tuđman suggested turning Jasenovac into a memorial to all the victims of World War II by burying the remains of casualties from both sides in one **common grave**. The idea that bones of the Ustaše might be mixed together with those of their victims shocked liberal opinion, as well as outraging Jewish organizations worldwide and souring Croatia's relations with Israel. Not surprisingly, the idea was swiftly dropped. Jasenovac was in the news again in May 1998, with the extradition from Argentina of one of the camp's former commanders, **Dinko Šakić**. The decision to charge Šakić with "crimes against humanity", but not with full-blown genocide, merely led to further accusations that the trial was another attempt to lessen the significance of Jasenovac rather than recognize the horrors that took place there. Šakić was found guilty and given a twenty-year sentence in October 1999.

entrance to the concrete lotus and back, passing a restored stretch of railtrack where a cattle-truck train (on which inmates were delivered to the camp) is permanently parked.

The rest of Jasenovac still bears the scars of a more recent war: the centre of town was cleared of Croats in 1991, and its church dynamited (the local Serbs suffered a similar fate when the Croats returned in May 1995). There's little to do in town except call in at the **Lonjsko polje Nature Park administration office**, housed in local government buildings opposite the (now rebuilt) church on the main square, Trg kralja Petra Svačića (Mon–Fri 8am–3pm; Ⓣ044/672-080, Ⓦwww.pp-lonjsko-polje.hr), where you can pick up maps and advice on exploring the park. The **tourist office**, in the municipal library building behind the church (Mon–Fri 7.30am–3.30pm; Ⓣ044/672-587, Ⓔtz_opcine_jasenovac@net.hr), can help you book a room at the *Gostiona kod Ribića* (Ⓣ044/672-066; ❷), a simple **pension** just up the road; the owner doesn't speak English, but the **restaurant** here serves up delicious, paprika-laden stews of fish caught in local rivers. There are four **trains** a day from Zagreb to Jasenovac (changing at Sunja), but they take over three hours to get here, so it's better to come by car if at all possible.

Kutina

If you're looking for somewhere to rest up in the Lonjsko polje region, then the sleepy town of **KUTINA**, 36km east of Sisak and 36km northwest of Jasenovac, is as good a place as any. It's easy to get to, lying 2km off the main Zagreb–Belgrade motorway, and has regular public transport connections with the Croatian capital. Five minutes' north of the **bus** and **train stations**, an architecturally undistinguished town centre is enlivened by a nineteenth-century Neoclassical mansion on Trg kralja Tomislava, built for the landowning Erdödy family and now home to the **Moslavina Regional Museum** (Muzej moslavine; Mon–Fri 10am–1pm; 10Kn). The archeological collection is filled with eye-pleasing detail – notably the surprisingly contemporary-looking geometric designs etched onto neolithic pots and plates – and the explosively embroidered bed linen and headscarves in the ethnographic section will postively knock you out. From here, Crkvena leads uphill past Kutina's only remaining ensemble of traditional wooden houses, towards the most celebrated ecclesiastical structure in the region, the **Church of Our Lady of the Snows** (Crkva Marije Snježne). Commissioned by the Erdödy family in the mid-eighteenth century, it's lavishly decorated with late Baroque frescoes, with a zestful sequence of biblical scenes flowing over ceiling and walls. Even more spectacular are the sculptures – mostly the work of the Straub family from Bavaria – including an extravagantly carved pulpit, and animated portrayals of saints Ladislaus, George, Emeric and Martin flanking a graceful Madonna and Child on the main altar. The church is sporadically open during the daytime: if it's locked, ask for the key at the parish office (župni ured; the pale grey building at the top of Crkvena) or contact the Kutina **tourist office**, back in the centre at Hrvatskih branitelja 2 (Mon–Fri 9am–3pm; Ⓣ044/681-004, Ⓦwww.turizam-kutina.hr).

Accommodation is limited to the *Hotel Kutina*, centrally placed at Dubrovačka 4 (Ⓣ044/692-400, Ⓦwww.hotel-kutina.hr; ❸–❹ depending on stage of renovation), which offers box-like but comfortable en suites, some with new furnishings and TV. Inside the hotel, the *Moslavačka hiža* **restaurant** serves up tasty local fare and is decked out in the style of a nineteenth-century wood-panelled living room.

Slavonia

Stretching from the Lonjsko polje to the Danube, which forms Croatia's border with Serbia, the rich agricultural plain of **Slavonia** has an unjust reputation as the most scenically tedious region of the country. All that most visitors ever see of it is the view from the Autocesta – the highway originally built to link Zagreb with Belgrade, and still the main route into the eastern corner of the country – as it forges across unbroken flatlands. The effects of war, Serbian occupation and the painfully slow pace of reconstruction have left their mark, but the region has its attractions, not least a distinctive and often captivating rural landscape, characterized in summer by a seemingly endless carpet of corn and sunflowers, with vineyards on the low hills to the north.

Slavonia's main urban centre is **Osijek**, a former Austrian fortress town which retains a dash of Habsburg-era elegance. It's around Osijek that the best of Slavonia's scenery lies, a patchwork of greens and yellows dotted with dusty, half-forgotten villages, where latticed wooden sheds groan under the weight of corncobs and, in the autumn, strings of red paprikas hang outside to dry. Just north of Osijek, the **Kopački rit Nature Park**, with its abundant birdlife, is Croatia's most intriguing wetland area, while in the far southeast the siege-scarred town of **Vukovar** is slowly regaining its provincial Baroque charm. Elsewhere in Slavonia there's a relative dearth of urban sights, save in the pleasant provincial towns of **Požega**, **Našice** and **Đakovo**.

Slavonian **cuisine** is characterized by a rich variety of fresh fish from the Sava and Drava rivers, notably carp, catfish and pike. A mixture of these are stewed together to produce *fiš paprikaš*, the spicy, soupy mainstay of most restaurant menus around Osijek and in the southeast. The meat-eater's alternative to this is *čobanac*, a goulash-esque paprika-laden stew which is served up in vast tureens. Many Slavonian families keep a pig or two, traditionally slaughtered towards the end of November in the annual *kolinje*, or pig cull. The main pork-based delicacy is *kulen*, a rich, paprika-flavoured sausage served as a snack or hors d'oeuvre.

Požega

Some 150km east of Zagreb, at the **Nova Gradiška** exit, a minor road heads north from the Autocesta to **POŽEGA**, an appealing market town lying amid the small lumpish hills of the **Babja Gora**. The town was occupied by the Turks between 1536 and 1691, but today the look of the place is overwhelmingly Baroque, its main square, Trg svetog Trojstva, surrounded by yellow, arcaded buildings, two-storey monuments to provincial contentment.

On the southern side of the square, the Gothic Franciscan **Church of the Holy Spirit** (Crkva svetog Duha) was used as a mosque by the Turks and has recently been spruced up, while the older **St Lawrence's Church** (Crkva svetog Lovre) contains some fine Gothic frescoes, though it's currently undergoing restoration and is inaccessible. The **Town Museum** (Gradski muzej; Mon–Fri 9am–3pm; 10Kn), at the west end of the main square, has a limited display of local archeological finds, and a small ethnographic section featuring some incandescent hand-woven rugs with vegetal and bird designs. There's also a small display devoted to local-born nineteenth-century adventurer Dragutin Lehrman, who served the King of Belgium as colonial administrator of the Congo. He helped found Požega museum by donating many of the artefacts he brought back with him. A few steps north along Županijska lies the most eye-catching of Požega's nineteenth-century civic buildings, the

County Hall (Zgrada Županije), its avocado-coloured facade topped by a trio of clock towers.

Down an alleyway at the eastern end of the square, the lemon-yellow belfry of **St Theresa's Church** (Crkva svete Terezije) overlooks a statue commemorating Luka Ibrišimović Sokol, a Franciscan warrior-monk who won a famous victory over the Turks at nearby Sokolovec on March 12 1688, liberating Požega in the process. It's a strikingly militant piece of anti-Ottoman propaganda, portraying the priest with sword unsheathed, trampling on a crescent symbolizing Islam.

Practicalities

Both the **bus** and the **train stations** are at the northern end of town; a ten-minute walk down Stjepana Radića will get you to the centre. Požega's **tourist office**, at Trg svetog Trojstva 3 (Mon–Fri 8am–3pm, Sat 8am–1pm; ⓣ034/274-900, ⓦwww.pozega-tz.hr), can point you in the direction of a couple of **pensions** (❶–❸) in the suburbs. There are a pair of smallish **hotels** in the shape of *Grgin Dol* (ⓣ034/273-222, ⓔpozeska-dolina@po.t-com.hr; ❸), just east of the main square at Grgin Dol 20, with poky but smart en-suite rooms; and *Vila Stanišić*, midway between the stations and the main square at Dr Franje Tuđmana 10 (ⓣ034/312-168; ❸), its cosy en-suite rooms above a restaurant. There are loads of **cafés** and simple **restaurants** tucked away in the streets just north of the main square: *Pečenjarnica Kamenita Vrata*, Kamenita Vrata, is a no-frills snack stop offering filling bowls of *čobanac* and *grah*, as well as basic grilled meats; *Tomislav*, round the corner at Babukićeva 25, offers more in the way of sit-down restaurant fare, with a range of hearty pork and chicken dishes; while the **patisserie** at *Vila Stanišić* is perfect for picking up pastries and cakes.

Požega is the unlikely setting for one of Croatia's strangest cultural events, the **Festival of One-Minute Films** (Revija jednominutnih filmova; ⓦwww.crominute.hr). Held over a weekend towards the end of May, it attracts largely amateur and avant-garde work from around the world; the tourist office will have details.

Northeast from Požega

If you're heading for Đakovo, Vinkovci or Belgrade from Požega, your best option is to rejoin the Autocesta at Slavonski Brod and continue eastwards from there. Travellers bound for Osijek, however, would do best to follow the minor road **northeast from Požega**, which crosses the low-lying limbs of wooded **Papuk** – which at 953m is Slavonia's only "mountain" – before dropping down towards the Drava basin at Našice. The route takes you through some of the best of Slavonia, with lush green tobacco plantations breaking up the more familiar vineyards and cornfields.

Našice and beyond

Forty-five kilometres from Požega, the small town of **NAŠICE** is a typical Slavonian one-street settlement, with all its principal buildings laid out in a single strip. Midway along this main street at Pejačevićev trg stands the former palace of the Pejačević family, built in the early nineteenth century in fanciful neo-Renaissance style and now sporting an eye-catching ochre paint job. Inside, an elegant double staircase sweeps you up to the **Našice Regional Museum** (Zavičajni muzej Našice; Mon & Fri 9am–3pm, Tues–Thurs 9am–6pm, Sat 9am–noon; 12Kn), which celebrates Croatia's first female composer Dora Pejačević (1885–1923) with a room full of family photographs and mementoes

– a CD selection of Pejačević's compositions usually plays in the background while you browse. There's also a room full of works by local-born sculptor Hinko Juhn (1891–1940), and a ravishing display of traditional embroidery. Behind the palace, the tree-filled Pejačević park descends towards a small serpentine-shaped lake.

Požega–Osijek **buses** pick up and drop off outside the museum before continuing to the bus station, 1km away on the northeastern side of town. There's a comfortable if unexciting two-star **hotel**, the *Park*, virtually next door to the palace at Pejačevićev trg 4 (ⓣ031/613-822, ⓦwww.hotel-park.hr; ③); the hotel's restaurant serves up solid meat-and-two-veg fare in a vast impersonal dining room.

Beyond Našice, the road heads across arable flatlands towards Osijek, passing through a string of villages stocked with narrow, nineteenth-century houses with wooden porches. Most attractive of these is probably **Jelisavac**, 7km out of Našice, a predominantly Slovak settlement which has bilingual street signs. The Habsburgs encouraged peasants from all over central Europe to re-populate Slavonia after its re-conquest from the Turks, creating an ethnic patchwork which to a certain extent still survives today.

Slavonski Brod

Roughly 200km southeast of Zagreb, **SLAVONSKI BROD** is a largely modern town whose high-rise suburbs were built to house workers drawn by the local Đuro Đaković engineering works, although a smattering of Habsburg-era buildings in the centre – including an eighteenth-century fortress – may tempt you to take a breather here before pressing on. The town hardly merits an overnight stop unless you're in town for the **Brodsko Kolo Folklore Festival** (mid-June), which features songs, dance and horse-and-trap displays from all over Slavonia. Details are available from the Slavonski Brod tourist association (ⓣ & ⓕ035/447-721, ⓦwww.tzgsb.hr).

The main square, **Trg I. B. Mažuranić**, faces the broad sweep of the River Sava, from where there are views of Slavonski Brod's sister town, Bosanski Brod (in the Serbian-controlled half of Bosnia-Hercegovina), on the opposite bank. From the square, Šetalište braće Radić follows the river eastwards to the eighteenth-century **Franciscan monastery** (Franjevački samostan), which features a nice colonnaded courtyard and a church rich in wooden Baroque altarpieces. Just north of the monastery, a modern pavilion hosting temporary exhibitions is the only currently functioning part of the **Museum of the Brod-Posavlje Region** (Muzej brodskog posavlja; Mon–Fri 9am–3pm; 10Kn), the main building being in the throes of a major reconstruction. Heading back to the main square and then continuing west, you can't miss the grassy earthen ramparts of **Brod Fortress** (Brodska tvrđava; Jan–May & Oct–Dec 8am–5pm; June–Sept 7am–9pm; free), a huge star-shaped citadel built in 1715 to protect Slavonia from Ottoman-controlled Bosnia on the other side of the river. A gravel path on the south side of the fortress leads past a surviving stretch of moat and into a central quadrangle lined with red-brick barracks, stables and storehouses. Most are in an atmospheric state of semi-ruin, although a restored section of barrack buildings on the western side now serves as the **Ružić Gallery** (Galerija Ružić; May–Sept Tues–Fri 9am–1pm & 5–8pm, Sat & Sun 10am–2pm; Oct–April Tues–Fri 10am–2pm & 4–7pm, Sat & Sun 10am–2pm; 10Kn), housing works by local sculptor Branko Ružić and a representative selection of post-World War II Croatian painting.

Practicalities

Both **bus** and **train stations** are ten minutes' walk north of Trg I. B. Mažuranić. Brod Turist, just north of the main square at Trg Pobjede 30 (Mon–Fri 7am–7.30pm, Sat 7am–1pm; ⓣ035/445-765), acts as an **information point** on behalf of the local tourist association, handing out leaflets and selling town maps. Functional en-suite **rooms** are available at the *Brod*, in a greying modern block just round the corner at Petra Krešimira IV 3 (ⓣ035/440-515; ❸). Far preferable if you have your own transport is the *Zdjelarević*, 17km west of town in the village of Brodski Stupnik at Vinogradska 102 (ⓣ035/427-775, ⓦwww.zdjelarevic.hr; ❹–❺), a family-run fifteen-room hotel situated at the foot of the owner's vineyard (which is the source of some highly regarded Graševinas and Chardonnays). Rooms are charmingly decorated, while the hotel restaurant serves some of the best traditional cuisine in the region – including some meat dishes that might dismay horse lovers.

Best of the **restaurants** back in Brod is the *Slavonski podrum*, just east of the Franciscan Monastery at A. Štampara 1, which serves up substantial cuts of pork and veal in a half-timbered house with wooden beams and benches. *Zvonimir*, between the main square and the fortress at Trg Stjepana Miletića 11, is a good place to tuck into a bowl of *ćobanac*. *Kavana Mala*, Trg I. B. Mažuranić, is the best place for a relaxing **drink**, otherwise head for the *Iguana Bar* at Šetalište braće Radića 15, which has a river-facing terrace and is a popular, raucous place by night.

Đakovo

Beyond Slavonski Brod, the Autocesta forges ever eastwards towards the frontier with Serbia, some 95km distant. After 35km, a secondary route breaks off northwards towards the neat and tidy plains town of **ĐAKOVO**, which is served by regular buses from both Slavonski Brod and Osijek, as well as occasional trains on the Vrpolje–Osijek branch line. Whatever your point of arrival, you'll be guided into the centre by the skyline-hogging, 84-metre-high twin towers of Đakovo's neo-Gothic, red-brick **Cathedral** (daily 7am–noon & 3–7pm). This vast building, constructed between 1862 and 1882 by the Viennese Gothic Revival architect Baron Frederick Schmidt, was commissioned by Bishop Josip Juraj Strossmayer, who used Đakovo as a base from which to promote a Croatian – and indeed south-Slav – cultural renaissance, promoting native-language book production and facilitating contacts between Croatian and Serbian intellectuals. Despite its initially austere appearance, the cathedral is decorated with a wealth of intriguing detail, from the beehive-like cones which stand guard on either side of the entrance, to the pinnacled cupola which rises above the main transept. Inside, walls and ceilings are decorated with uplifting biblical scenes, painted in the style of the Nazarenes (German contemporaries of the Pre-Raphaelites) by the father-and-son team of Alexander and Ljudevit Seitz.

Immediately north of the cathedral, a squat, custard-coloured building houses the **Strossmayer Museum** (Spomen-muzej Biskupa Josipa Jurja Strossmayera; Tues–Fri 8am–7pm, Sat 8am–2pm; 5Kn), with a few of Strossmayer's personal effects and copies of his writings. Beyond lies the café-lined Korzo, a pedestrianized main street at whose far end stands one further curiosity – a dainty **parish church**, occupying the shell of a sixteenth-century mosque. Ten minutes' walk from the centre (follow Matije Gupca eastwards from the cathedral), the **Lippizaner stud farm** (Ergela) at Augusta Šenoe 47 (ⓦwww.ergela-djakovo.hr) is another legacy of the Strossmayer period, and still enjoys a Europe-wide reputation for rearing and training the famous white horses. The stud farm occasionally puts on shows for coach parties, but individual visitors might see the horses being put through their paces if they turn up on weekdays between 9am and 3pm.

Practicalities

Đakovo's **train station** is 1km east of the centre at the far end of Kralja Tomislava, while the **bus station** is five minutes' walk east of the cathedral along Splitska. The **tourist office** at Kralja Tomislava 3 (Mon–Fri 8am–3pm, Sat 8am–noon; ⓣ031/812-319, ⓦwww.tz-djakovo.hr) has free town maps, but you may not always find an English speaker there. *Hotel Blaža*, fifteen minutes' walk north of the centre at A. Starčevića 158 (ⓣ031/816-760, ⓕ816-764; ❸), is a medium-sized **hotel** whose en-suite rooms have TV. The more central *Croatia Turist*, at Preradovićeva 25 (ⓣ031/813-391, ⓕ814-063; ❸), has smallish rooms with TV and bathroom, and a decent **restaurant** that offers a range of classic pork and veal dishes (including *šumski odrezak*, a rolled pork fillet stuffed with mushrooms), washed down with local wines. *Gradski podrum*, on the Korzo, offers a slightly cheaper range of grills and does a satisfying *čobanac*.

Đakovo is the scene of one of Croatia's most important **festivals** of authentic folk culture, **Đakovački vezovi** (literally "Đakovo embroidery"; last weekend in Sept), which features a weekend-long series of song and dance performances by folkloric societies from throughout eastern Croatia. This provides the excuse for a grand open-air party, with each evening culminating in gigs by Croatian pop bands.

Vinkovci

Thirty kilometres due east of Đakovo, **VINKOVCI** was once the most important rail junction in the region, standing at the crossroads of lines linking Zagreb to Belgrade and Budapest to Sarajevo. You might still find yourself changing buses or trains here, as there are good onward connections to Osijek and Vukovar, and there's a sufficiently large clutch of eye-catching nineteenth-century buildings in the town centre to make a fleeting visit worthwhile.

Occupying an arcaded building on the main Trg bana Šokčevića, the **Town Museum** (Gradski muzej; Tues–Fri 10am–1pm & 5–7pm, Sat & Sun 10am–1pm; 10Kn) has a well-presented collection of archeological finds, with 8000-year-old storage jars decorated with zigzag patterns bearing witness to Vinkovci's ancient origins. The Romans established a trading post named Cibalia here in the first century AD, leaving a wealth of ceramics and amphorae in their wake. A sizeable ethnographic collection upstairs concentrates on the crafts and costumes of the Šokci, Croats who migrated from Turkish-controlled Bosnia to Austrian-ruled Slavonia in the late-seventeenth and early-eighteenth centuries and still form the bedrock of the local population. Their embroidered blouses and coats display a stunning diversity of colour and form – on the Ottoman–Habsburg borderlands each village had a trademark pattern of its own, enabling locals to identify each other more easily.

Practicalities

Vinkovci's **bus** and **train stations** stand next to each other 1km north of the town centre – head down Starčevićeva and bear right onto Nazorova to reach the main square, at the far end of which you'll find the **tourist office** at Trg bana Šokčevića 3 (Mon–Fri 9am–5pm; ⓣ032/334-653, ⓦwww.tz-vinkovci.hr). There's a run-of-the-mill high-rise **hotel**, the *Slavonija*, just west of the square at Duga ulica 1 (Ⓣ032/342-777, Ⓦwww.son-ugo-cor.com; ❸), although the plush modern *Cibalia*, near the stations at Starčevićeva 51 (Ⓣ032/339-222, Ⓦwww.hotel-cibalia.com; ❹) has more going for it in the style stakes. The *Terme* **restaurant**, near the *Slavonija* hotel at Genscherova 2, offers a choice of flavoursome local meat and fish dishes, and *Kavarna Art*, next door to the museum, is the most relaxing place for a **drink**.

Osijek

Tucked into the far northeastern corner of Slavonia, 30km from the Hungarian border and just 20km west of the Serbian province of Vojvodina, **OSIJEK** is the undisputed capital of the region. An easy-going, park-filled city hugging the banks of the River Drava, Osijek has a relaxed spaciousness – owing in large part to its being spread out across three quite separate town centres. The oldest of these, **Tvrđa**, retains the air of a living museum; originally a Roman strongpoint, it was subsequently fortified by the Ottomans and then finally rebuilt in Baroque style by the Austrians, who kicked the Turks out in 1687. The Austrians were also responsible for the construction of **Gornji grad** (Upper Town – so called because it's upriver from Tvrđa), the nineteenth-century area which still exudes a degree of *fin-de-siècle* refinement and now serves as the administrative heart of the modern city. At the eastern end of town, **Donji grad** (Lower Town) is a relatively quiet residential district, developed at around the same time as Gornji grad in order to accommodate economic migrants from the surrounding plains.

After the fall of Vukovar in November 1991, the Yugoslav People's Army and Serb irregulars laid siege to Osijek and subjected the town to a nine-month bombardment. Osijek survived, but the sense of economic stagnation that followed the conflict is only just beginning to lift.

Osijek has enough in the way of sightseeing and nightlife to detain you for a day or two, and the city's proximity to the **Kopački rit Nature Park** provides the perfect excuse to lengthen your stay.

Arrival, information and public transport

Osijek's **bus** and **train stations** are next to each other on Trg L. Ružička, on the south side of the town centre. From here it's a ten-minute walk – first up Radićeva, then left into Kapucinska – to reach Trg Ante Starčevića, the heart of Gornji grad (alternatively, travel three stops on tram #2). The helpful staff at the **tourist office**, a few doors up from the cathedral at Županijska 2 (Mon–Fri 7am–4pm, Sat 8am–noon; Ⓣ031/203-755, Ⓦwww.tzosijek.hr), provide *Gradski vodič*, a free monthly events guide in Croatian, and *Osijek In Your Pocket* (Ⓦwww.inyourpocket.com), a lively and informed source of English-language listings information which is also available free from hotels and restaurants. Cetratour, at Ružina 16 (Ⓣ031/37-920, Ⓦwww.cetratour.hr), organizes bike and canoe expeditions to the Kopački rit Nature Park.

Osijek has two **tram lines**: tram #2 operates a circular route between the train and bus stations and Trg Ante Starčevića; while tram #1 runs from west to east linking Gornji grad, Tvrđa and Donji grad. Single-journey tickets cost 7Kn and are bought from newspaper kiosks.

Accommodation

There's a dearth of private rooms in Osijek, although OK Tours at Trg slobode 7 (Mon–Fri 9am–5pm, Sat 9am–noon; Ⓣ031/212-815, Ⓔok-tours@os.t-com.hr)

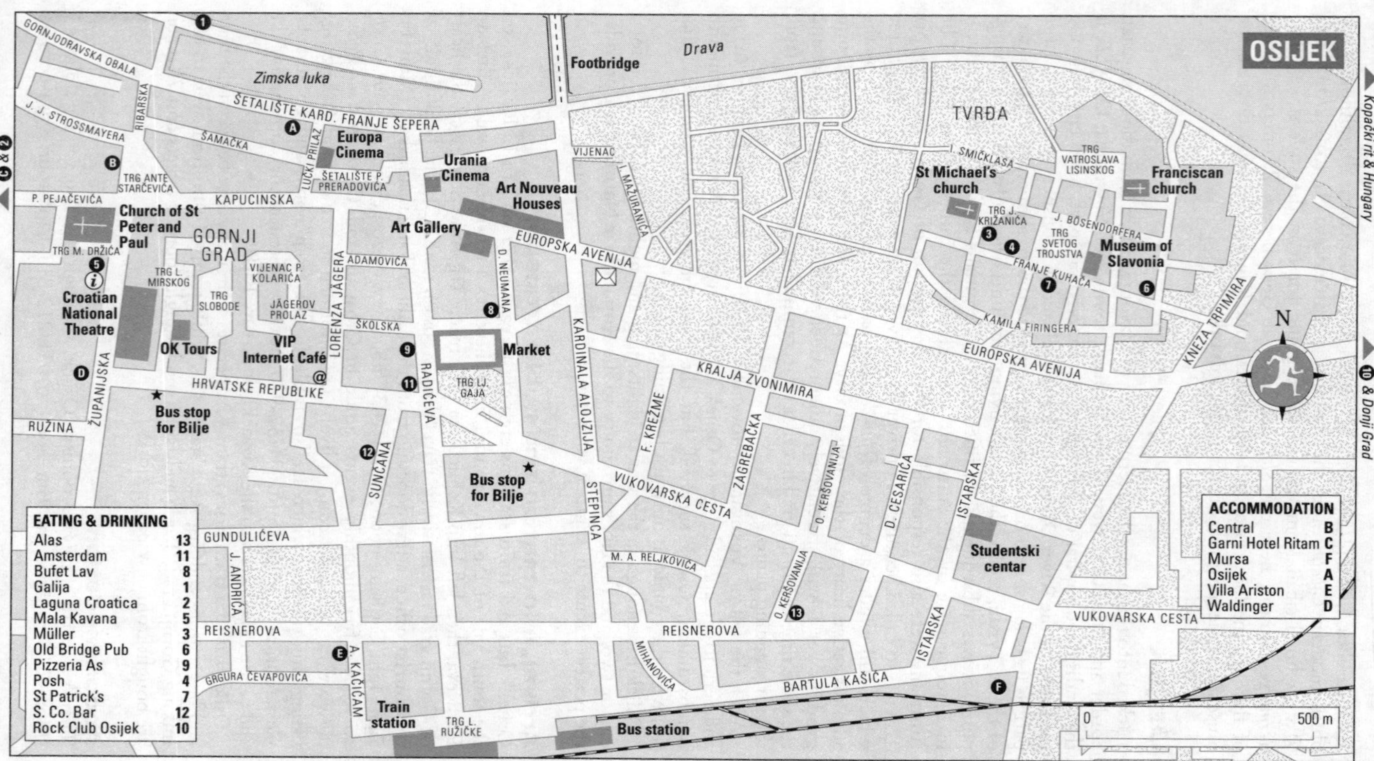
OSIJEK
Kopački rit & Hungary
10 & Donji Grad
G & 2
N
Drava
Footbridge
Zimska luka
TVRĐA
GORNJI GRAD
GORNJODRAVSKA OBALA
ŠETALIŠTE KARD. FRANJE ŠEPERA
J. J. STROSSMAYERA
RIBARSKA
ŠAMAČKA
LUČKI PRILAZ
Europa Cinema
ŠETALIŠTE P. PRERADOVIĆA
Urania Cinema
Art Nouveau Houses
VIJENAC
I. MAŽURANIĆA
I. SMIČKLASA
St Michael's church
TRG J. KRIŽANIĆA
TRG VATROSLAVA LISINSKOG
Franciscan church
J. BÖSENDORFERA
TRG SVETOG TROJSTVA
Museum of Slavonia
FRANJE KUHAČA
KAMILA FIRINGERA
KNEZA TRPIMIRA
EUROPSKA AVENIJA
TRG ANTE STARČEVIĆA
P. PEJAČEVIĆA
KAPUCINSKA
Church of St Peter and Paul
TRG M. DRŽIĆA
Croatian National Theatre
TRG L. MIRSKOG
TRG SLOBODE
VIJENAC P. KOLARIĆA
JÄGEROV PROLAZ
OK Tours
VIP Internet Café
LORENZA JÄGERA
ADAMOVIĆA
ŠKOLSKA
Art Gallery
D. NEUMANA
Market
TRG LJ. GAJA
RADIĆEVA
KARDINALA ALOJZIJA
STEPINCA
HRVATSKE REPUBLIKE
ŽUPANIJSKA
RUŽINA
Bus stop for Bilje
Bus stop for Bilje
SUNČANA
KRALJA ZVONIMIRA
F. KREŽME
ZAGREBAČKA
O. KERŠOVANIJA
D. CESARIĆA
ISTARSKA
VUKOVARSKA CESTA
Studentski centar
M. A. RELJKOVIĆA
MIHANOVIĆA
GUNDULIĆEVA
J. ANDRIĆA
REISNEROVA
GRGURA ČEVAPOVIĆA
A. KAČIĆAM
Train station
TRG L. RUŽIČKE
Bus station
BARTULA KAŠIĆA
0
500 m
ACCOMMODATION
Central B
Garni Hotel Ritam C
Mursa F
Osijek A
Villa Ariston E
Waldinger D
EATING & DRINKING
Alas 13
Amsterdam 11
Bufet Lav 8
Galija 1
Laguna Croatica 2
Mala Kavana 5
Müller 3
Old Bridge Pub 6
Pizzeria As 9
Posh 4
St Patrick's 7
S. Co. Bar 12
Rock Club Osijek 10

can reserve **B&B** accommodation in the village of **Bilje**, a twenty-minute bus ride to the north (see p.168).

Hotels and pensions

Central Trg Ante Starčevića 6 ⓣ031/283-399, ⓦwww.hotel-central-os.hr. Nineteenth-century place bang on Gornji grad's main square, with charmless but serviceable en-suite rooms. ❺

Garni Hotel Ritam Kozjačka 76 ⓣ031/310-310, ⓦwww.hotel-ritam.hr. Big suburban house 1.5km west of Gornji grad, with bright, comfortable en suites. ❸

Mursa Bartula Kašića 2a ⓣ031/283-399. Concrete lump that looks like a grain silo, a short distance east of the train and bus stations. Sparsely furnished but habitable en-suite rooms with TV. ❸

Osijek Šamačka 4 ⓣ031/230-333, ⓦwww.hotel-osijek.hr. Another concrete lump, this time on the Drava waterfront. The hotel has been recently renovated to four-star standard, and the quality of service is everything you would expect from this price range. The north-facing rooms have superb views of the river. ❻–❼

Villa Ariston Kačićeva 6 4 ⓣ031/251-351, ⓕ031/251-350, ⓔaristonmr@ehotelier.comhr. Small and intimate three-star located in a quiet street near the railway station, offering plush rooms with a/c and TV. Regular rooms come with shower, apartments come with bathtub. Apartments ❼, rooms ❻

Waldinger Županijska 8 ⓣ031/250-450, ⓦwww.waldinger.hr. Peaceful, sixteen-room four-star housed in a nineteenth-century building. High-ceilinged, tastefully furnished rooms come with TV, desk space and bathtub. The three-star annexe in the back yard is billed as a "pension" and offers simply furnished en suites overlooking a neat patch of garden. Main building ❺, pension ❹

The Town

Modern Osijek centres on the neat, triangular **Trg Ante Starčevića** in Gornji grad. Bordered by stout nineteenth-century buildings, it's overlooked by the rocketing ninety-metre spire of the town's red-brick, neo-Gothic **Parish Church of St Peter & Paul** (Župna crkva svetog Petra i Pavla). Commissioned in the 1890s by the energetic bishop of Đakovo, Josip Juraj Strossmayer, the church is filled from floor to ceiling with bible-story frescoes by leading twentieth-century painter Mirko Rački, all executed in engagingly simple and colourful style.

Heading east from Trg Ante Starčevića, Kapucinska brings you to the broad, tree-lined sweep of Europska avenija, site of the most spectacular group of **Art Nouveau** houses in Croatia. Commissioned by rich local lawyers and merchants in the years before World War I, each is richly decorated with reliefs of caryatids, nymphs, herculean hero figures and other motifs typical of the period. For a more modernist take on pre-World War I architecture, nip down Stjepana Radića to the **Urania cinema** (built in 1912), where you'll encounter a monumental, grill-like facade that brings to mind the open jaws of an enormous whale.

If you return to Europska avenija and cross the road you'll come to the **Art Gallery** at no. 9 (Galerija likovnih umjetnosti; Tues–Fri 10am–6pm, Sat & Sun 10am–1pm; 10Kn); it houses an eye-catching collection of nineteenth-century portraits by local Slavonian painters, and a cross-section of work by twentieth-century artists from across Croatia.

Tvrđa

Two kilometres west from Gornji grad along Europska avenija – also reachable on tram #1 from Trg Ante Starčevića or by walking along Šetalište Kardinala Franje Šepera, the broad flagstoned path alongside the Drava – lies the complex of Baroque buildings known as **Tvrđa** (literally "citadel"), a collection of military and administrative buildings thrown up by the Austrians after the destruction of the earlier Ottoman castle. Tvrđa's grid of cobbled streets zeros in on Trg svetog Trojstva, a broad expanse bearing a **plague column**, built in 1729 with funds donated by the local fortress commander's wife to give thanks for deliverance from a particularly devasting outbreak of plague which is thought to have killed a third of Osijek's population. The column is surrounded by faded, ochre administrative buildings from which Habsburg commanders organized the defence of the southern frontier. Many of these are now occupied by high schools or university faculties, and the square is busy with scurrying students on weekdays. Occupying the former city magistrate's office on the southeast corner of the square, the **Museum of Slavonia** (Muzej slavonije; Tues–Sun 8–11am & 11.30am–2pm; 13Kn) hosts temporary themed exhibitions on local history, and displays pottery and sculptural fragments recovered from Roman Mursa, Osijek's distant forerunner – look out for the exquisitely carved gravestone in the ground-floor lapidarium, with its portrayal of a satyr derobing a nymph. Off the square to the west, the double onion-dome frontage of the former Jesuit **St Michael's Church** (Crkva svetog Mihovila) lords it over a knot of narrow alleys, although it's relatively bare inside save for an ornate cherub-encrusted pulpit. A few steps northeast of Trg svetog Trojstva, on Lisinskog, the eighteenth-century **Franciscan church** (Franjevačka crkva) features a much-venerated Gothic statue of the Virgin and Child on the high altar.

The riverfront

Alleys descend from Tvrđa towards the riverfront, where you can follow Šetalište Kardinala Franje Šepera back towards Gornji grad, passing a pedestrian bridge which crosses the Drava towards ritzy-sounding **Copacabana** on the opposite bank – a grassy bathing area with an open-air pool, a waterslide and a couple of cafés. Back on the south side of the river, Šetalište Kardinala Franje Šepera arrives eventually at the **Zimska luka** ("winter harbour"), a dock for small pleasure craft protected by a breakwater from the strong currents of the Drava, and another popular spot for lounging around in cafés.

Eating

Good **restaurants** are sprinkled rather sparingly through the city. Once you locate them, however, you'll find the range of fish dishes and paprika-flavoured stews generally excellent. There are plenty of good-value snack possibilities on the way into town from the bus and train stations, with a string of plainly decorated bistro-type places offering grilled food and pizzas.

Restaurants

Alas Reisnerova 12a. One of the best places in the city for sampling freshwater fish – either fried in breadcrumbs or stewed in traditional Slavonian, paprika-laden style. The speciality of the house is *perkelt od soma* (big chunks of catfish swimming in spicy goulashy soup), usually served with delicious homemade noodles. Prices are moderate too, with mains costing around 60–70Kn.

Bufet Lav Trg Ljudevita Gaja 5. If you want good home cooking and don't mind a few rough edges, then this basic but friendly place near the market will sort you out with a filling bowl of *grah* (beans with pork), *čobanac* (beefy goulash) or *fiš paprikaš* – a great place for a quick cheap lunch.

Galija Gornjogradska obala. Decent pizzas, pasta dishes and salads on a boat moored just round the corner from the Zimska luka. Floor-to-ceiling windows make this a great spot from which to observe life on the riverbank. Prices are on the moderate side.

Laguna Croatica Dubrovačka 13 ☎031/369-203. This smart, brick-lined cellar is an elegant location in which to sample freshwater fish, with trout, pike-perch and catfish served either pan-fried, baked or in a variety of sauces. There's also grilled fish from the Adriatic and a broad range of wines from across the country. Three courses and a drink will set you back around 200–250Kn per person. It's ten minutes' walk west of Gornji grad: head along Pejačevića behind the cathedral, and turn left into Dubrovačka after about five minutes.

Müller Križanićev trg 9 ☎031/204-770. Unfussy Tvrđa restaurant with a satisfying if unspectacular range of Croatian cuisine – from freshwater fish through grilled steaks to Adriatic-influenced seafood dishes. Prices are moderate, and there's a reasonable list of local Slavonian wines, too.

Pizzeria As Radićeva 16. Generous thin-crust pizzas with a reasonably authentic range of Italian toppings, served in a comfortable and relaxing brick cellar. Also offers decent pasta dishes and risottos.

Drinking and nightlife

The biggest concentration of **drinking venues** are on and around Trg svetog Trojstva in Tvrđa. It's also worth checking out the Zimska luka, with its string of summer-only cafés below the *Hotel Osijek*, and the stretch of Radićeva between Hrvatske republike and Gundulićeva, where there's an enjoyable café-bar every twenty metres or so. Places in Gornji grad tend to close at 11pm; in Tvrđa opening hours are somewhat more elastic.

The main venue for **classical music** and **theatre** is the Croatian National Theatre (Hrvatsko narodno kazalište; ⓣ031/220-700) at Županijska 9. Osijek has two **cinemas**: the Europa, near the *Hotel Osijek* on Lučki Prilaz, and the Urania, just east at the junction of Europska and Radićeva.

Bars

Amsterdam Radićeva 18, Gornji grad. Cramped but civilized subterranean bar with a laid-back clientele, classic rock tracks on the CD player, and an appetizing range of bottled beers.

Mala Kavana Trg Marina Držila, Gornji grad. Plush coffee-supping venue next to the cathedral that's ideal for a break from daytime sightseeing, and has an outdoor terrace that remains lively until well into the evening.

Old Bridge Pub Kuhača 4, Tvrđa. Roomy drinking palace with a pub-style space on the ground floor, lounge-bar furnishings in the attic above, and a stone-lined cellar below. The Croatian, German and Irish beers on tap attract a mixed clientele ranging from suits to students.

Tufna Kuhaća 10, Tvrđa. If you like quirky interiors then this is a real collector's piece, comprising a series of first-floor rooms that seem to have sprung from the imaginings of a deranged lounge-bar designer. DJ-driven party nights at weekends, when there's an entrance fee.

Rock Club Osijek Trg bana Jelačića 12, Donji grad. Donji grad's only worthwhile night-time destination features a post-industrial interior with the front half of an automobile stuck to the wall (the rear half is in the back of the main room). Rock and blues usually plays on the sound system, with live music of the same persuasion at weekends.

St Patrick's Trg svetog Trojstva, Tvrđa. Most enjoyable of the Tvrđa café-bars, with a large outdoor terrace facing the best of Osijek's Baroque buildings, and a comfy interior featuring (for some perverse reason) a shrine to Chelsea football club. Mainstream Irish beers on tap, as well as the locally brewed Osiječko pivo.

S. Co. Bar Sunčana 6, Gornji grad. Formerly known as Voodoo, this studenty, alternative meeting-place is something of an Osijek institution. Pop-art frescoes on the walls, cool sounds and a friendly vibe.

Listings

Books Algoritam, at Trg Slobode 7 (Mon–Fri 9am–9pm, Sat 9am–3pm), has English-language paperbacks and guide books.

Exchange The nearest bank to the bus and train stations is Privredna Banka Zagreb, Radićeva 19 (Mon–Fri 7am–7pm, Sat 7am–noon).

Internet *VIP Internet Café*, L. Jägera 24 (8am–11pm).

Pharmacy Ljekarna Centar, Trg A. Starčevića 7 (Mon–Fri 7am–8pm, Sat 8am–3pm). Night counter open 8pm–7am (ring the bell for service).

Post and telephone The main post office is on the corner of Europska avenija and Kardinala Stepinca (Mon–Sat 7am–8pm).

Taxi There are ranks outside the train station; otherwise ring ⓣ031/200-100.

The Baranja

North of Osijek, the main road to Hungary forges through the pastel-coloured villages and corn-rich fields of the **Baranja**, a fertile extension of the Slavonian plain which fills the triangle formed by the Drava to the west, the Danube to the east, and the low hills of southern Hungary to the north. Despite having spent the years from 1991 to 1998 first under Serbian occupation, then UN control, Baranja is getting back to normal life with remarkable speed. The tourist potential of its wine-growing areas, natural wetlands and rustic settlements is yet to be fully exploited, making it ripe for discovery. The main attraction of the Baranja is the **Kopački rit Nature Park**, although the region possesses enough in the way of picturesque villages and wine cellars to justify a more extensive tour.

Kopački rit Nature Park

Eight kilometres out of Osijek the road passes through the village of **Bilje**, the main gateway to the **Kopački rit Nature Park** (Park prirode Kopački rit; Ⓣ031/750-855, Ⓦwww.kopacki-rit.vip.hr). The park covers an area of marsh and partly sunken forest just north of the point where the fast-flowing River Drava pours into the Danube, forcing the slower Danube waters to back up and flood the plain. The resulting wetland is inundated from spring through to early autumn, when fish come here to spawn and wading birds congregate to feed off them. At this time you'll also see cormorants, grey herons and, if you're lucky, black storks, which nest in the oak forests north of Bilje. Autumn sees the area fill up with migrating ducks and geese, while the surrounding woodland provides a year-round home for deer and wild boar. Some of the fields and country lanes surrounding the park are yet to be cleared of **mines** – anyone walking or driving through the area should stick to the roads, and remain on the lookout for local "mine" signs.

Arrival, information and accommodation

To get to Kopački rit from Osijek **by car**, take the northbound road to Beli Manastir as far as the village of Bilje, where you take the right turn to Kneževi vinogradi. About 500m farther on, take another right to Kopačevo. At the entrance to Kopačevo village, a left turn to Tikveš brings you to the **visitor centre** (Prijemni centar), which serves as the main gateway to the park. Coming by public transport, catch one of the half-hourly Osijek–Bilje **buses** from either Hrvatske republike or Trg Ljudevita Gaja, getting off in the centre of Bilje and following the directions above on foot (40–50min).

The visitor centre sells **tickets** (May–Sept 30Kn; Oct–April 10Kn), offers advice on how to explore the park and doles out English-language leaflets and a map. Individual tourists can then drive, cycle or walk into the park, but the best way to explore is to join one of the hour-long park-operated **boat trips** (tickets from the visitor centre; 80Kn), so you can navigate some of the wildfowl-rich waterways that can't be accessed by car or on foot. The trips set out from Lake Sakadaš (see opposite); there are usually about three boat trips a day at weekends, fewer on weekdays – ring the park in advance to make sure you don't miss out.

There's a handful of very comfortable **pensions** in Bilje, each offering bed and breakfast with the option of additional meals for a modest extra fee. One of the most welcoming is *Crvendać*, at Biljske satnije ZNG RH 5 (Ⓣ031/750-264, Ⓦwww.crvendac.com; ❶), which has neat, newly furnished rooms with shared bathroom and quirky red colour schemes throughout; the similarly cosy *Mazur*, Kneza Branimira 2 (Ⓣ031/750-294 or 098 897-649, Ⓔkresimir.mazur@os.t-com.hr; ❶), has rooms with old-fashioned furnishings – some en suite, others sharing facilities in the hallway. *Sandrina*, at Strossmayerova 4b (Ⓣ031/751-326, Ⓔzeljko.pavlovic@os.t-com.hr, Ⓦwww.zpavlo.hr; ❷), is much more like a small hotel in style, offering rooms with air-conditioning and satellite TV in a large modern house.

The Reserve

The main route into the reserve is along the dyke-top road which heads north from the visitor centre, separating a series of commercial fishponds on the left-hand side from the magisterial sunken forest of **Lake Sakadaš** on the right, where wading birds stalk their prey among a tangle of white willows. North of here, tracks continue through **Tikveš**, an area of oak forest where you stand a good chance of spotting wild pigs and deer. Josip Broz Tito used the fine villa of **Dvorac Tikveš** as a hunting lodge; it was neglected during the Serb occupation (when most of the furnishings disappeared), but you can still see the balcony where Tito and guests waited, rifle in hand, while servants drove forest beasts out onto the lawn in front of them. Some of the outbuildings are being transformed into an international ecology centre, and the villa itself is earmarked for luxury hotel development.

It's worth taking a look at the village of **Kopačevo** itself, immediately east of the visitor centre. Home to a mixed Croatian–Hungarian population, it contains some of the best traditional architecture in eastern Slavonia, with the kind of houses you'll see all over the Hungarian plain, southeastern Croatia and the Serbian Vojvodina laid end-on to the road, with long verandas facing in onto secluded courtyards.

Eating

For **eating**, the *Varge* **restaurant**, at the southern end of Bilje, serves up a superbly spicy *čobanac*; the *Zelena Žaba* in Kopačevo offers equally enticing local fare in the shape of *fiš paprikaš* and *fiš perkelt* (Hungarian fish casserole). Inside the park, on the road towards Tikveš, the *Kormoran* restaurant is a good place to sample the local carp, which is toasted on the end of a stick beside an open fire.

Onwards into the Baranja

There's plenty more to see in the Baranja beyond Kopački rit, although sights are of a disparate nature and you really need a car to get around. Twenty-five kilometres north of Bilje, the Baranja's main market centre, **BELI MANASTIR**, is an unexciting little place, and you'd be better off heading for smaller villages like **KARANAC**, 8km east of Beli, where you'll see streets lined with traditional one-storey farmhouses, their south-facing verandas draped with drying paprikas and other vegetables. If **staying the night** in this rural environment appeals you can try the *Sklepić* farmstead, at no. 58 on Karanac's main street (Ⓣ031/750-243, Ⓔdenis.sklepic@inet.hr; ❷), a nineteenth-century building featuring traditionally furnished rooms (including embroidered pillowcases and tablecloths) alongside reassuringly modern bathrooms. Further up the same street, *Baranjska kuća* at no. 99 is a friendly **bar-restaurant** serving up exemplary *čobanac* and *fiš paprikaš* to an appreciative local crowd.

Northeast of Beli Manastir, the monotony of the Slavonian–Baranjan plain is broken by the **Banska kosa**, a ridge of sandy hills covered with vineyards. The most interesting of the settlements here is the long, straggling village of **ZMAJEVAC**, whose wine cellars cut into the southern slopes of the Banska kosa are increasingly noted for their Graševina, Riesling and other whites. Most of the cellars occupy man-made caverns on the hilly north side of the village:

should you wish to down a glass or even buy a few bottles, several cellars are open to the public and are signed from the main road.

The easternmost extremity of the Banska kosa, overlooking the River Danube at the frontier town of **BATINA**, provides a suitably dramatic perch for one of Croatia's most imposing **communist-era memorials**. Taking the form of a monumental female statue brandishing a five-pointed star, it was built to commemorate the Soviet Red Army, who crossed the river here in November 1944 in the face of fierce German resistance. It's an outstanding example of ideological sculpture, and well worth visiting for the views you get from its concrete plinth, with the wooded shores of the Danube down below, and the Serbian province of Vojvodina stretching out on the opposite bank.

Vukovar

Regular buses from Vinkovci and Osijek run through the wheat- and cornfields to the once-beautiful town of **VUKOVAR**, 35km to the southeast. Hugging the west bank of the Danube, Vukovar was until 1991 one of Yugoslavia's more prosperous towns, with a quaint Baroque centre, a successful manufacturing industry based around the Borovo tyre and footwear factory, and an urban

The siege of Vukovar

Inter-ethnic tension flared in Vukovar in April 1991, when barricades went up between the Croatian-controlled town centre and the Serb-dominated suburbs. The firing of a rocket at the Serb district of **Borovo Selo** by Croat extremists was a calculated attempt to raise the stakes. Croatian policemen patrolling Borovo Selo were shot at by Serbian snipers on May 1, and when a bus-load of their colleagues entered the suburb the following day, they were met by an ambush in which twelve of them lost their lives. The JNA (Yugoslav People's Army) moved in, ostensibly to keep the two sides apart, digging into positions that were to serve them well with the breakout of all-out war in the autumn.

On September 14, 1991, the Croatian National Guard surrounded the JNA barracks in town. Serb irregulars in the outlying areas, supported by the JNA, responded by launching an attack. Croatian refugees fled the suburbs, crowding into the centre. Aided by the fact that many of the outlying villages were ethnically Serb, the JNA swiftly encircled the town, making it all but impossible to leave (the only route out was through sniper-prone cornfields), and subjecting the population to increasingly heavy shelling. By the beginning of October the people of Vukovar were living in bomb shelters and subsisting on meagre rations of food and water, their plight worsened by the seeming inactivity of the government in Zagreb. The commander of the town's defence, Mile Dedaković Jastreb, accused President Tuđman of sacrificing Vukovar in order to win international sympathy for the Croatian cause. Vukovar finally fell on November 18, with most of the inhabitants fleeing back to the town hospital or making a run for it across the fields to the west. Of those who fell into Yugoslav hands, the women and children were usually separated from the men – many of the latter simply disappeared.

The worst atrocities took place after Yugoslav forces reached the **hospital**, which they proceeded to evacuate before the agreed arrival of Red Cross supervisors. Those captured here were bundled into trucks and driven away to be murdered, finishing up in a mass grave near the village of Ovčara, 7km southeast. About two thousand Croatian soldiers and civilians died in the defence of Vukovar, and a further two thousand are still missing, although the recovery of bodies from mass graves is going on all the time.

culture that was lively, open and tolerant. However, the town's proximity to the Serbian border and an ethnically mixed population (of whom 44 percent were Croat and 37 percent Serb) conspired to place Vukovar at the sharp end of the Croat-Serb conflict. The resulting **siege** and capture of Vukovar by the Yugoslav People's Army and Serbian irregulars left the centre of town in ruins, and did untold emotional damage to those lucky enough to escape. In January 1998 the town was returned to Croatia as part of the Erdut Accord, though Croats driven from Vukovar seven years before were initially slow to return, either because their homes were still in ruins or because the local economy wasn't yet strong enough to provide sufficient jobs. There are currently about eighteen thousand Croats and nine thousand Serbs living in Vukovar – about two thirds of the original population – although social contact between the two communities is virtually nonexistent.

Entering Vukovar by road from the north, you'll first pass through the suburb of **Borovo**, built as a model workers' settlement by Czech shoe manufacturer Bata in the 1930s. With a huge red-brick factory at its centre, and smaller red-brick housing units scattered among the surrounding pine trees, it's an enduring – if somewhat under-appreciated – monument to inter-war urban planning.

The Town

Vukovar's bus station lies on the fringes of the twentieth-century town, opposite the main market. Walk through the market and turn left onto the town's main street, Strossmayerova, to reach the **Eltz Palace** (Dvorac Eltz), an imposing aristocratic seat built for a local landowning family in the early eighteenth century. Badly damaged in the siege but still standing, the palace is home to the **Town Museum** (Gradski muzej; Mon–Sat 7am–3pm; 10Kn), whose collections were expropriated by the Serbs in 1991. An agreement to return them was signed in 2001, and they've begun to trickle back, although it remains to be seen what will go on permanent display in the palace's surviving barrel-vaulted rooms.

Strossmayerova leads in the opposite direction towards the old town proper, crossing the River Vuka (which flows into the Danube a couple of hundred metres downstream) on the way. The first of the once-impressive civic buildings you come across on the opposite bank is the bombed-out shell of the **Radnički Dom** ("House of the Workers"), where the Yugoslav Socialist Party met to transform itself into the Yugoslav Communist Party in June 1920, only to be banned by the government five months later. Beyond lies the town's main street, lined with late Baroque buildings with arcaded lower storeys – some of which have already been tastefully restored. On high ground to the southeast stands the eighteenth-century **Franciscan monastery** (Franjevački samostan), faithfully reconstructed after almost total destruction. Beyond the monastery, the ice-cream-cone-shaped **water tower** thrusts skywards, still displaying dramatic signs of shell damage – although plans for its restoration are afoot.

Practicalities

The **tourist office** is on the way to the Eltz Palace at Strossmayerova 15 (Mon–Fri 7am–3pm; ⓣ032/442-889, ⓔturisticka-zajednica-grada-vukovara@vk.htnet.hr). Roughly opposite the tourist office at Strossmayerova 18, the four-star *Hotel Lav* (ⓣ032/445-100, ⓦwww.hotel-lav.hr; ❻) provides plush **rooms** with warm colour schemes, air conditioning, desk space and minibar. Overlooking the confluence of the Danube and the Vuka, the two-star *Dunav*

Crossing into Serbia

Crossing from eastern Croatia **into Serbia** shouldn't present too many problems. At the time of writing, citizens of EU countries, Australia, Canada, New Zealand and the United States are allowed to enter Serbia on production of a valid passport. Citizens of other countries should check current visa regulations before setting out.

The main road crossing points are at **Lipovac**, on the Županija–Sremska Mitrovica stretch of the Autocesta, **Tovarnik** on the Vinkovci–Šid road, **Ilok** on the Vukovar–Novi Sad road, **Erdut** on the Osijek–Novi Sad road, and **Batina** on the Beli Manastir–Sombor road. Crossing the border can be an unpredictable process, with Serbian border guards subjecting travellers they don't like the look of to thorough searches, while waving others straight through.

There's an increasing number of public transport links between the two countries, with four daily **trains** from Zagreb to Belgrade – which pass through Slavonski Brod and Vinkovci on the way – and several daily Zagreb–Belgrade **buses**. If you're heading for Novi Sad, capital of the Serbian Vojvodina, then make your way to Vukovar and catch one of the seven daily buses from there.

(Ⓣ032/441-285, Ⓕ441-762; ❸–❹) has plainer, functional en-suite rooms, although many come with appetizing river views. There aren't many **eating** and **drinking** opportunities aside from the cafés and restaurants in the two hotels, and a few basic places offering grills and pizzas around the market.

Travel details

Trains

Karlovac to: Ogulin (6 daily; 1hr); Ozalj (6 daily; 20min); Rijeka (6 daily; 3hr 20min); Split (2 daily; 7hr); Zagreb (hourly; 40min).
Slavonski Brod to: Zagreb (8 daily; 2–3hr).
Zabok to: Gornja Stubica (8 daily; 30min); Krapina (9 daily; 25min); Stubičke Toplice (8 daily; 20min); Zagreb (14 daily; 40min–1hr); Zlatar Bistrica (14 daily; 20min).
Zagreb to: Čakovec (6 daily; 2hr 30min–3hr); Jasenovac (4 daily; change at Sunja; 3hr 10min); Karlovac (hourly; 40min); Klanjec (5 daily; change in Savski Marof; 1hr 30min); Koprivnica (8 daily; 1hr 30min); Kumrovec (5 daily; change in Savski Marof; 2hr); Ogulin (6 daily; 1hr 40min); Osijek (4 daily; 5hr); Savski Marof (20 daily; 35min); Sisak (hourly; 1hr); Slavonski Brod (8 daily; 2–3hr); Varaždin (12 daily; 2hr–2hr 30min); Zabok (14 daily; 40min–1hr); Zlatar Bistrica (14 daily; 1hr–1hr 20min).

Buses

Đakovo to: Osijek (Mon–Sat hourly, Sun 8 daily; 45min); Slavonski Brod (10 daily; 1hr 15min); Vinkovci (Mon–Sat 8 daily, Sun 5 daily; 45min); Zagreb (Mon–Sat 6 daily, Sun 4 daily; 4hr 30min).
Delnice to Skrad (3 daily; 25min).
Karlovac to: Krašić (Mon–Fri 4 daily, Sat 2 daily; 35min); Ozalj (Mon–Fri 2 daily; 25min); Plitvice (hourly; 1hr 40min); Rijeka (20 daily; 2–3hr); Split (4 daily; 8hr); Zadar (4 daily; 4hr); Zagreb (every 30min; 50min).
Koprivnica to: Hlebine (Mon–Fri 6 daily, Sat 2 daily; 30min); Osijek (Mon–Fri 1 daily; 4hr); Varaždin (Mon–Fri 10 daily, Sat 8 daily, Sun 4 daily; 45min–1hr 10min).
Marija Bistrica to: Stubičke Toplice (Mon–Sat 6 daily, Sun 4 daily; 35min); Zagreb (Mon–Fri 15 daily, Sat 8 daily, Sun 6 daily; 1hr 15min).
Osijek to: Batina (7 daily; 1hr 10min); Bilje (every 30min; 10min); Đakovo (Mon–Sat hourly, Sun 10 daily; 45min); Ilok (Mon–Fri 7 daily, Sat 6 daily, Sun 1 daily; 1hr 45min); Požega (Mon–Fri 6 daily, Sat 3 daily, Sun 1 daily; 2hr); Slavonski Brod (10 daily; 2hr); Vinkovci (Mon–Sat hourly, Sun 5 daily; 1hr); Vukovar (Mon–Sat hourly, Sun 8 daily; 45min); Zagreb (6 daily; 5hr 30min).
Požega to: Našice (Mon–Fri 6 daily, Sat 3 daily, Sun 1 daily; 1hr); Osijek (Mon–Fri 6 daily, Sat 3 daily, Sun 1 daily; 2hr); Slavonski Brod (4 daily;

1hr); Velika (Mon–Fri 9 daily, Sat 5 daily, Sun 1 daily; 30min); Zagreb (5 daily; 2hr 45min).
Samobor to: Lipovec (Mon–Fri 12 daily, Sat 10 daily, Sun 8 daily; 30min); Slani dol (Mon–Fri 11 daily, Sat 5 daily, Sun 3 daily; 30min); Zagreb (every 20–30min; 40min).
Sisak to: Čigoć (4 daily; 45min); Lonja (2 daily; 1hr 15min); Zagreb (Mon–Sat 24 daily, Sun 18 daily; 1hr 10min).
Slavonski Brod to: Đakovo (10 daily; 1hr 15min); Osijek (10 daily; 2hr); Požega (5 daily; 1hr); Vukovar (3 daily; 2hr); Zagreb (12 daily; 3hr).
Varaždin to: Čakovec (every 30 min; 20min); Koprivnica (Mon–Fri 10 daily, Sat 8 daily, Sun 4 daily; 45min–1hr 10min); Krapina (Mon–Sat 2 daily, Sun 1 daily; 1hr); Osijek (Mon–Fri 1 daily; 5hr); Split (2 daily; 9hr); Trakošćan (Mon–Fri 10 daily, Sat 7 daily, Sun 3 daily; 50min); Vukovar (Mon–Fri 1 daily; 5hr 40min); Zagreb (every 30min; 1hr 40min–2hr).
Vinkovci to: Đakovo (Mon–Sat hourly, Sun 3 daily; 45min); Ilok (Mon–Sat 6 daily, Sun 3 daily; 1hr 50min); Osijek (Mon–Sat hourly, Sun 5 daily; 1hr); Vukovar (Mon–Sat 12 daily, Sun 5 daily; 50min).
Vukovar to: Ilok (Mon–Fri 20 daily, Sat & Sun 8 daily; 45min); Osijek (Mon–Sat hourly, Sun 8 daily; 45min); Slavonski Brod (3 daily; 2hr); Vinkovci (Mon–Sat 24 daily, Sun 8 daily; 50min); Zagreb (5 daily; 6hr 30min).
Zagreb to: Čakovec (10 daily; 2hr 30min); Delnice (hourly; 2hr 20min); Desinić (Mon–Sat 8 daily, Sun 4 daily; 2hr); Karlovac (every 30min; 50min); Klanjec (4 daily; 1hr 10min); Krapina (Mon–Fri 8 daily, Sat & Sun 2 daily; 1hr 10min–1hr 30min); Krapinske Toplice (Mon–Fri 12 daily, Sat 10 daily, Sun 7 daily; 1hr 20min); Kumrovec (Mon–Fri 4 daily, Sat 3 daily; 1hr); Marija Bistrica (Mon–Fri 15 daily, Sat 8 daily, Sun 6 daily; 1hr 15min); Osijek (6 daily; 5hr 30min); Plitvice (hourly; 2hr 30min); Požega (5 daily; 2hr 45min); Samobor (every 20–30min; 40min); Sisak (Mon–Sat 24 daily, Sun 18 daily; 1hr 10min); Slavonski Brod (12 daily; 3hr); Varaždin (12 daily; 1hr 40min–2hr).

International trains

Čakovec to: Budapest Déli (1 daily; 5hr); Budapest Keleti (1 daily; 5hr).
Varaždin to: Budapest Déli (1 daily; 5hr 20min).

International buses

Osijek to: Belgrade (5 daily; 4hr); Mohács (1 daily; 2hr 30min); Novi Sad (3 daily; 3hr 30min); Pécs (3 daily; 3hr).
Slavonski Brod to: Tuzla (5 daily; 5hr).
Varaždin to: Maribor (1 daily; 1hr 50min).
Vukovar to: Belgrade (5 daily; 3hr); Novi Sad (6 daily; 2hr 30min); Sombor (2 daily; 2hr 30min).

3

Istria

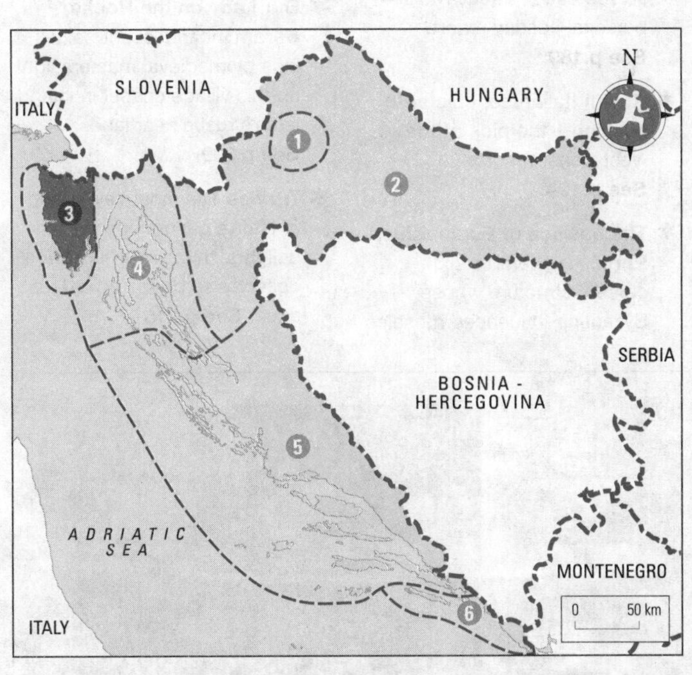

SLOVENIA
HUNGARY
ITALY
N
1
2
3
4
5
6
SERBIA
BOSNIA - HERCEGOVINA
ADRIATIC SEA
MONTENEGRO
0 50 km
ITALY

CHAPTER 3 Highlights

* **Pula amphitheatre** The Romans built things to last, and this 2000-year-old monument is still the dominating feature of Pula's landscape. See p.182

* **Brijuni islands** An idyllic offshore paradise that once served as President Tito's personal holiday resort. See p.189

* **Rovinj** Italianate, chic and bustling – the pick of the west-coast resorts. See p.194

* **The basilica of Euphrasius, Poreč** A venerable sixth-century structure whose Byzantine-influenced mosaics are as good as any around the Mediterranean. See p.203

* **Hill towns** Rich in historical resonances, mellow towns like Motovun and Oprtalj seem a world away from the heavily touristed coast. See p.207

* **Our Lady on the Rocks, Beram** Incandescent paintings by medieval masters light up this village chapel in inland Istria's rustic heartlands. See p.209

* **Truffles** The most celebrated of Istria's gastronomic delights, this smelly fungus deserves to be tasted at least once. See p.215

△ Grožnjan

3

Istria

A large, triangular peninsula pointing down into the northern Adriatic, **Istria** (in Croatian, "Istra") represents Croatian tourism at its most developed. In recent decades the region's proximity to Western Europe has ensured an annual influx of sun-seeking package tourists, with Italians, Germans, Austrians and what seems like the entire population of Slovenia flocking to the mega-hotel developments that dot the coastline. Istrian beaches – often rocky areas that have been concreted over to provide sunbathers with a level surface on which to sprawl – do tend to lack the appeal of the out-of-the-way coves that you'll find farther south in Dalmatia or the Adriatic islands, yet the modern hotel complexes and rambling campsites have done little to detract from the region's essential charm: development has left many of the Italianate coastal towns relatively unspoiled, while the interior, with its medieval hilltop settlements pitched high in the mountains, still preserves an off-the-beaten-path feel despite its rising popularity.

Istria draws on a rich cultural legacy. A borderland where Italian, Slovene and Croatian cultures meet, the region endured more than four hundred years of Venetian rule before its incorporation into first the Austro-Hungarian Empire, then Fascist Italy, the Yugoslav Federation, and finally independent Croatia. Historically, an Italian-speaking population lived in the towns (most of which still bear Italian names – or at least Croatianized versions thereof), while Croatian-speakers occupied the rural areas. Despite post-World War II expulsions, there's still a fair-sized Italian community, Italian is very much the peninsula's second language, and the local dialect of Istria's Croats contains a liberal sprinkling of Italian words.

With its amphitheatre and other Roman relics, the port of **Pula**, at the southern tip of the peninsula, is Istria's largest city and a rewarding place to spend a couple of days – rooms are relatively easy to come by and many of Istria's most interesting spots are only a short bus ride away. On the western side of the Istrian peninsula are pretty resort towns like **Rovinj** and **Novigrad**, with their cobbled piazzas, shuttered houses and back alleys laden with laundry. Poised midway between the two, the mammoth resort of **Poreč** has much less in the way of authentic Mediterranean charm, but offers everything in the way of tourist facilities. Inland Istria couldn't be more different – historic hilltop towns like **Motovun**, **Grožnjan**, **Oprtalj** and **Hum** look like leftovers from another century, half-abandoned accretions of ancient stone poised high above rich green pastures and forests.

Regular **buses** connect Pula with Zagreb; otherwise, the city of Rijeka (in the Kvarner Gulf; see p.228) is the most convenient gateway to the region. There

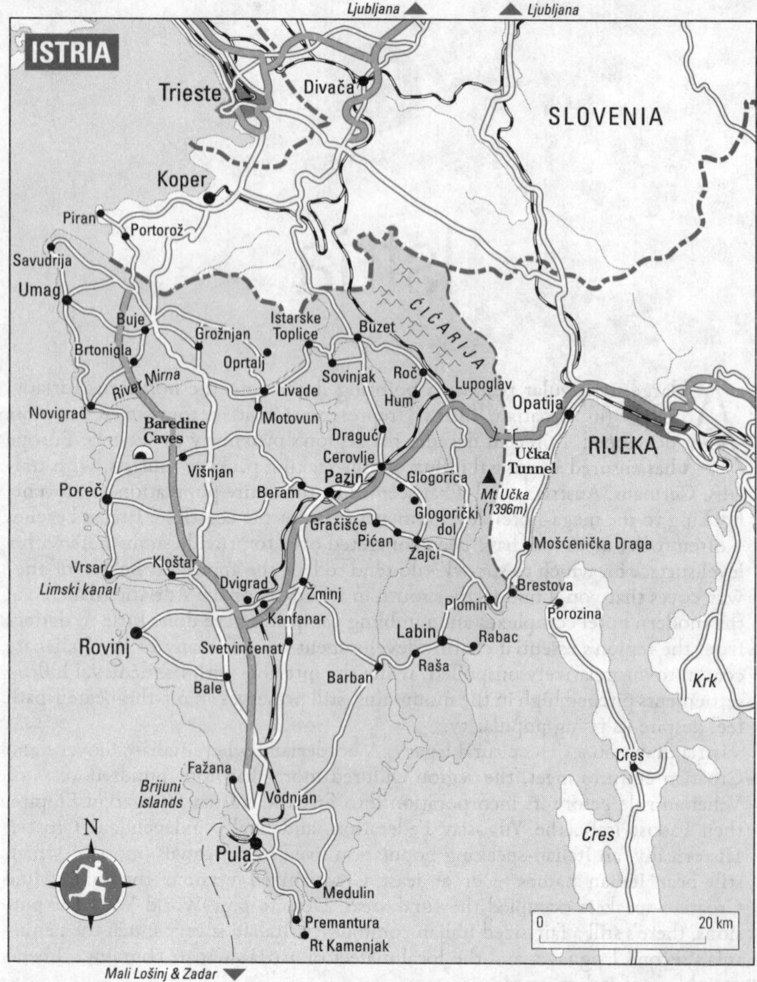

are also buses from Pula and Poreč to the Italian city of Trieste, and the Slovene resorts of Portorož and Piran on the north side of the peninsula. There's also a summer-only **train** from the Slovene capital Ljubljana to Pula, while **ferries** connect Pula with Mali Lošinj in the Kvarner and Zadar in Dalmatia. In summer, weekly **catamarans** ply the route between Istrian coastal towns and Venice and Trieste (the latter only from Poreč and Rovinj). Once you stray from these major routes, getting around Istria without a **car** can be quite difficult, especially in the interior where erratic buses are the only means of transport.

Some history

Istria gets its name from the **Histri**, an Illyrian tribe which ruled the region before succumbing to the **Romans** in the second century BC. The invaders left a profound mark on Istria, building farms and villas, and turning Pula into a major urban centre. **Slav tribes** began settling the peninsula from the seventh century onwards, driving the original Romanized inhabitants of the peninsula towards the coastal towns or into the hills.

Istria became a province of the Frankish Empire in 1040, but maritime and inland Istria began to follow divergent courses as the Middle Ages progressed. Most of the interior was presented as a feudal dependency to the Patriarchate of Aquileia – a virtually independent ecclesiastical city-state owing nominal fealty to Byzantium – in the twelfth century, while the coastal towns survived as independent communes until, one by one, they adopted **Venetian suzerainty** from the thirteenth century onwards. The lands of the Aquileian Patriarchs subsequently came under **Habsburg control**, ushering in centuries of intermittent warfare between Austrians and Venetians for control of the peninsula. The fall of Venice in 1797 left the Austrians in control of the whole of Istria. They confirmed Italian as the official language of the peninsula, even though Croats outnumbered Italians by more than two to one. Istria received a degree of autonomy in 1861, with Poreč becoming the seat of a regional diet, but only the property-owning classes were allowed to vote, thereby excluding many Croats and perpetuating the Italian-speaking community's domination of Istrian politics.

Austrian rule ended in 1918, when **Italy** – already promised Istria by Britain and France as an inducement to enter World War I – occupied the whole peninsula. When Mussolini's Fascist Party came to power in October 1922, prospects for the Croatian majority in Istria worsened still further: the Croatian language was banished from public life, while a law of 1927 decreed that Slav surnames were henceforth to be rendered in Italian. During World War II, however, opposition to fascism united Italians and Croats alike, and Tito's Partisan movement in Istria was a genuinely multinational affair, although this didn't prevent outbreaks of inter-ethnic violence and tit-for-tat killings. The atrocities committed against Croats during the Fascist period were avenged indiscriminately by the Partisans, and the *foibe* of Istria – limestone pits into which bodies were thrown – still evoke painful memories for Italians to this day.

After 1945 Istria became the subject of bitter wrangling between Yugoslav and Italian governments, with the Yugoslavs ultimately being awarded the whole of the peninsula. Despite promising all national minorities full rights after 1945, the Yugoslav authorities actively pressured Istria's Italians into leaving, and the region suffered serious **depopulation** as thousands fled. In response, the Yugoslav government encouraged emigration to Istria from the rest of the country, and today there are a fair number of Serbs, Macedonians, Albanians and Bosnians in Istria, many of whom were attracted to the coast by the **tourist industry**, which took off in the 1960s and, despite a few lean years during the war-ridden 1990s, has never looked back.

Geographically distant from the main flashpoints of the Serb-Croat conflict, Istria entered the twenty-first century more cosmopolitan, more prosperous and more self-confident than any other region of the country. This state of affairs was not without its problems, however, with local Istrian politicians tending to regard Zagreb as the centre of a tax-hungry state which took money out of the region without putting anything back in. Growing regionalist sentiment in the early 1990s led to the rise of the **Istrian Democratic Party** (Istarska demokratska stranka, or IDS), a moderate, centrist party which has remained the peninsula's most influential political force ever since. One consequence of Istria's new-found sense of identity has been a reassessment of its often traumatic relationship with Italy, and a positive new attitude towards its cultural and linguistic ties with that country. Bilingual road signs and public notices have gone up all over the place, and the region's Italian-language schools – increasingly popular with cosmopolitan Croatian parents – are enjoying a new lease of life.

Pula

Once the Austro-Hungarian Empire's chief naval base, **PULA** (in Italian, Pola) is an engaging combination of working port and brash Riviera town. The Romans put the city firmly on the map when they arrived in 177 BC, bequeathing it an impressive **amphitheatre** whose well-preserved remains are the city's single greatest attraction. Pula is also Istria's commercial heart and transport hub, possessing its sole airport, so you're unlikely to visit the region without passing through at least once. There's also an easily accessible cluster of **Classical** and **medieval** sights in the city centre, while the rough-and-ready atmosphere of the crane-ringed **harbour** makes a refreshing contrast to the seaside towns and tourist complexes farther along the coast. Central Pula doesn't boast much of a seafront, but there's a lengthy stretch of rocky **beach** about 3km south of the city centre, leading to the hotel complex on the **Verudela peninsula**, built in the 1980s to accommodate package-holidaying Brits.

Arrival, transport and information

Pula's **airport** is 5km northeast of the centre, just off the main Rijeka road, but there's no bus link; a taxi into town will set you back 100–120Kn. The **train station** is a ten-minute walk north of the town centre at the far end of Kolodvorska; the main **bus station**, serving both local and inter-city destinations, is on Trg 1 Istarske brigade, 1km northeast of the amphitheatre. **City buses** use the same terminal, although most of them also run through the central street, Giardini. Single-journey tickets for city buses cost 10Kn and are bought from the driver.

The **tourist office** at Forum 3 (June–Sept daily 8am–midnight; Oct–May Mon–Fri 9am–7pm; ⓣ052/219-197, ⓦwww.pulainfo.hr) offers a wealth of practical advice, free maps and brochures, and events information.

Accommodation

There's a number of private **rooms** (❶–❷) in the centre, as well as holiday **apartments** (two-person ❷–❸, four-person 470–600Kn) in the beachside suburbs of **Stoja** and **Verudela**. The most conveniently located room **agencies** are Atlas, just north of the amphitheatre at Starih Statuta 1 (ⓣ052/393-040, ⓦwww.atlas-croatia.hr), and A-Turizam, in the old town centre at Kandlerova 24 (ⓣ & ⓕ052/212-212, ⓦwww.a-turizam.com).

Hostels

Hostel Pula Valsaline ⓣ052/391-133, epula@hfhs.hr. A sizeable place comprising several accommodation blocks on Valsaline Bay, 4km south of the centre. Offers four- and six-bed rooms, a self-service restaurant, a diving school and its own stretch of shingle beach; it gets booked up fast in the summer, so it's best to reserve in advance. To get there, take bus #2 or #2A (both Verudela direction) from Giardini and get off at Vila Idola, a pre-World War I villa which comes into view on your right as you leave suburban Pula – the hostel itself is across fields to the right on the cusp of the bay. Beds with breakfast 110Kn.

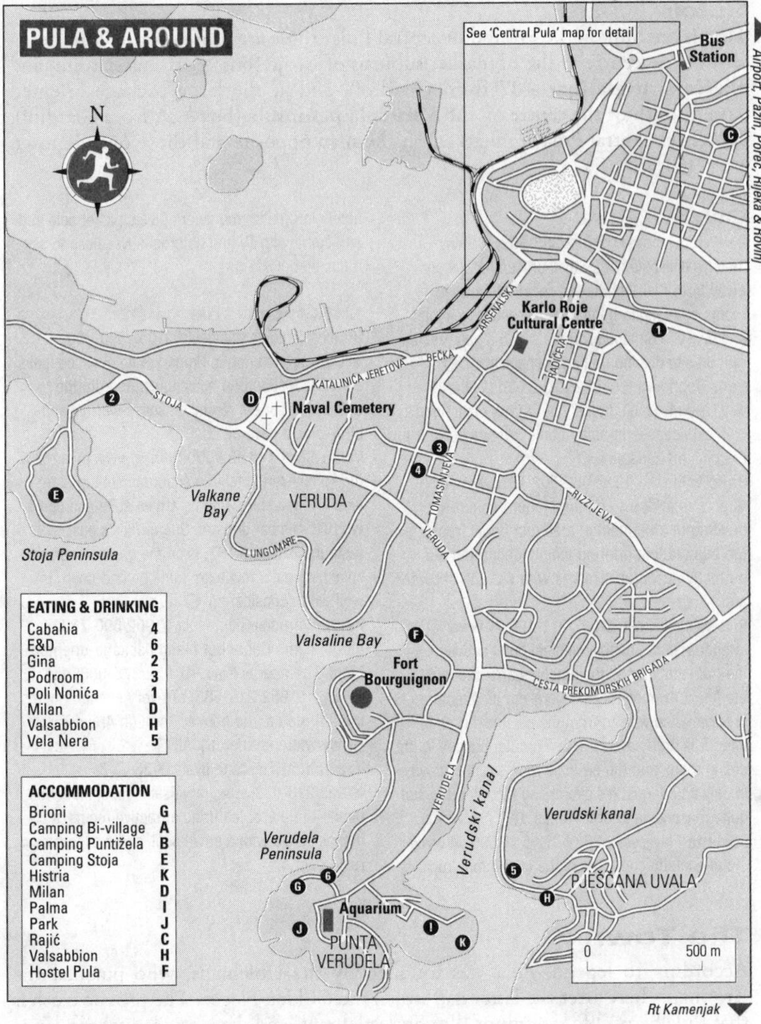

Campsites

Bi-village Valbandon ⓣ052/380-700, ⓦwww.bivillage.com. Ten kilometres out from Pula on the road to Fažana, this huge site occupies a grassy, part-shaded position with its own stretch of gravelly beach. Well equipped, and well placed for excursions to Brijuni, it's the most expensive site in the Pula region, and can resemble a camper van city in high season. Pula–Fažana buses pass by. Open all year.

Camping Puntižela Puntižela 155 ⓣ052/517-490, ⓦwww.puntizela.hr. Seven kilometres north-west of town on the Puntižela peninsula, this is a big wooded site with modest facilities and its own, often crowded, beach. Bus #5 (direction Štinjan) from the main bus station, followed by a five-minute walk west. April–Oct.

Stoja Stoja 37 ⓣ052/387-144, ⓦwww.arenaturist.hr. The nearest site to central Pula, with a wooded rocky peninsula all to itself some 3km southwest of town in the suburb of Stoja. The surroundings are idyllic, but it can get noisy and dirty at the height of summer. Bus #1 from Giardini stops outside the entrance. April–Oct.

Hotels

Hotels are thin on the ground in central Pula; there are more rooms 5km south-east of the centre in the upmarket suburbs of **Stoja** (bus #1 from Giardini) and **Pješčana uvala** (bus #27 from Giardini), and at the large package-oriented hotels south of the centre on the **Verudela peninsula** (bus #2A from Giardini). Hotels in central Pula are marked on the map opposite and those outside town on p.181.

Central Pula

Galija Epulonova 3 ⓣ052/383-802, ⓦwww.hotel-galija-pula.com. Small private hotel steps away from Giardini; the ten colourful en-suite rooms have modern interiors, TV, phone, minibar and dial-up connection. There's also a good restaurant on site dishing up Istrian specialities. ❺

Omir Dobrićeva 6 ⓣ052/210-614 or 218-186, ⓕ213-944. Small, friendly but rather plain hotel with serviceable en-suite rooms, slightly uphill from Giardini, off Zadarska. ❹

Rajić Valturska 12 ⓣ052/502-815, ⓕ544-530, ⓔpero.rajic@pu.t-com.hr. Modern concrete building in a residential area just uphill from the bus station, offering plainly decorated but perfectly acceptable rooms with WC and shower and TV. ❹

Riviera Splitska 1 ⓣ052/211-166, ⓦwww.arenaturist.hr. Shabbily genteel hotel between the train station and the amphitheatre. Probably the finest example of Habsburg-era architecture in Istria when viewed from the outside, but the interior is drab save for a few ornate touches in the dining room, and the en-suite rooms rather dowdy. In July and August it's overpriced for what it is, but quite reasonable at other times. ❺

Scaletta Flavijevska 26 ⓣ052/541-599, ⓦwww.hotel-scaletta.com. One of the best family-run hotels in Croatia; rooms are plush, pastel-coloured and come with TV and bathroom. Needless to say, it fills up quickly. ❻

Out from the centre

Histria Verudela peninsula ⓣ052/590-000, ⓦwww.arenaturist.hr. Upmarket hotel which looks a bit like a suburban housing estate from the outside, but offers roomy en suites with TV and bath, plus a covered pool. ❼

Milan Stoja 4 ⓣ052/300-200, ⓦwww.milan1967.hr. Family-run hotel in a suburban setting 2km west of the centre. Rooms are en suite and come with TV, minibar and a/c. One of Pula's best restaurants (see p.187) is on the ground floor, so splashing out a few extra kuna on half-board is well worth considering. ❻

Palma Verudela peninsula ⓣ052/590-760. Large, comfortable but bland package-oriented hotel. The nearby **Park** (ⓣ052/375-000) and **Brioni** (ⓣ052/215-585) are very similar. Rooms in all three can be booked through Arena Turist (ⓦwww.arenaturist.hr). All ❻

Valsabbion Pješčana uvala IX/26 ⓣ & ⓕ052/218-033, ⓦwww.valsabbion.hr. Modern family-run place, featuring attractive rooms, a fitness studio with a small pool, and a superb restaurant. ❻

The Town

According to legend, Pula was founded by the Colchians, who pursued the Argonauts here after the latter had stolen the Golden Fleece. The prosaic truth is that Pula began life as a minor Illyrian settlement, and there's not much evidence of a significant town here until 177 BC, when the Romans arrived and transformed Pula into an important commercial centre endowed with all the imperial trimmings – temples, theatres and triumphal arches – appropriate to its status.

The amphitheatre

The chief reminder of Pula's Roman heritage is the immense **amphitheatre** (*amfiteatar* or *arena*; daily: June–Sept 8am–8pm; Oct–May 9am–5pm; 20Kn) just north of the centre, a huge grey skein of connecting arches whose silhouette dominates the city skyline. Built towards the end of the first century BC, it's the sixth largest amphitheatre in the world, with space for 22,000 spectators, although why such a capacious theatre was built in a small Roman town of only five thousand inhabitants has never been properly explained.

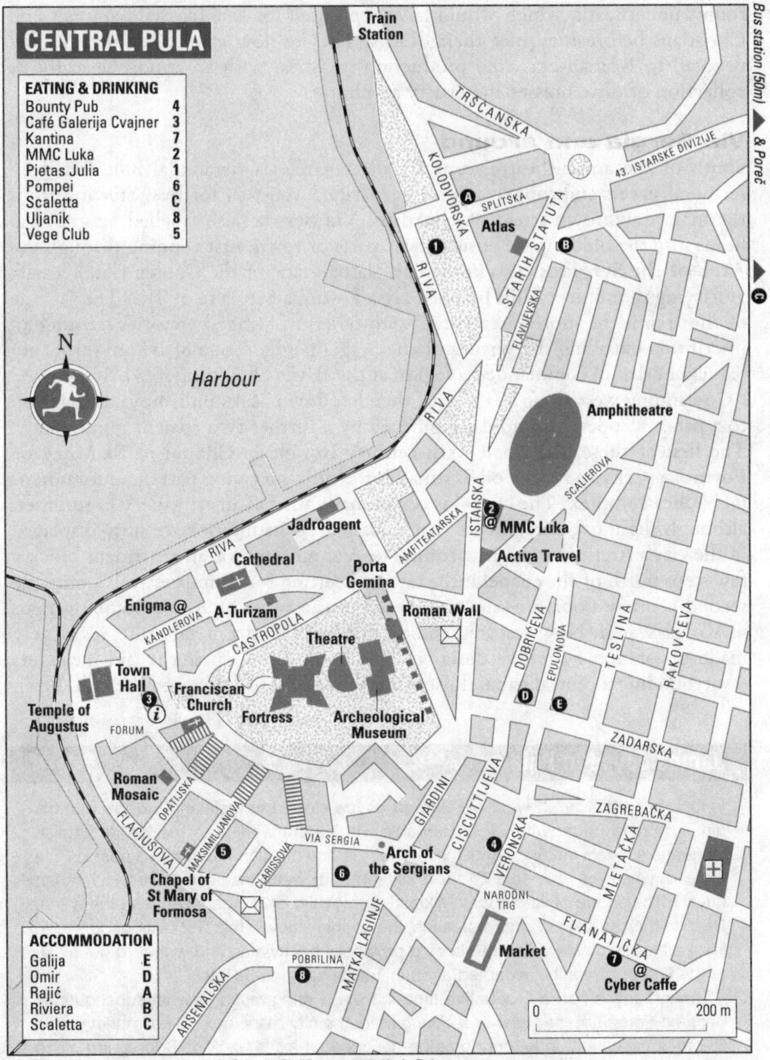

The outer shell is remarkably complete, although only a small part of the seating remains anything like intact; the interior tiers and galleries were quarried long ago by locals, who used the soft limestone to build their own houses. It is, in fact, lucky that the amphitheatre survives here at all: overcome by enthusiasm for Classical antiquities, the sixteenth-century Venetian authorities planned to dismantle the whole lot and reassemble it piece by piece in their own city; they were dissuaded by one of their more enlightened patricians, Pula-born Gabriele Emo, whose gallant stand is remembered by a plaque on one of the amphitheatre's remaining towers. Once inside, you can explore some of the cavernous rooms underneath, which would have been used for keeping wild animals and Christians before they met their deaths. They're now given over to a display devoted to Roman-era wine production in Istria, with an atmospherically lit collection of olive presses and crusty amphorae.

Via Sergia and around

South of the amphitheatre, central Pula encircles a pyramidal hill, scaled by secluded streets and topped with a star-shaped Venetian fortress. Starting from the main downtown street of **Giardini**, **Via Sergia** (also labelled Sergijevaca) heads into the older, more atmospheric parts of town, first running through the **Arch of the Sergians** (also known as Zlatna vrata, or the Golden Gate), a self-glorifying monument built by one Salvia Postuma Sergia in 30 BC. The far side of the arch is the more interesting, with reliefs of winged victories framing an inscription extolling the virtues of the Sergia family – one of whom (probably Salvia's husband) commanded a legion at the Battle of Actium in 31 BC.

Continuing west along Via Sergia, then left down Maksimilijanova, brings you to a patch of open ground distinguished by a further two ancient monuments. The first of these, the small sixth-century Byzantine **Chapel of St Mary of Formosa** (Crkvica Marije od Trstika), is the only surviving part of a monumental basilica complex. The chapel is occasionally used as an art gallery in summer, although the mosaic fragments that once graced its interior are now displayed in the city's Archeological Museum. The rear entrance of an apartment block a few steps north of the chapel is the unlikely setting for an impressively complete second-century floor **mosaic**, uncovered in the wake of Allied bombing raids in World War II. Now restored and on display behind a metal grille, it's largely made up of non-figurative designs – geometric flower-patterns and meanders – surrounding a central panel illustrating the legend of Dirce and the bull. From

James Joyce in Pula

In October 1904 the 22-year-old **James Joyce** eloped to mainland Europe with his girlfriend (and future wife) Nora Barnacle. He sought work with the Berlitz English language schools in Zürich and Trieste, but the organization found him a post in Pula instead, where he was paid £2 for a sixteen-hour week teaching Austro-Hungarian naval officers (one of whom was Miklos Horthy, ruler of Hungary between the wars). Despite their straitened circumstances, the couple enjoyed this first taste of domestic life – although Joyce viewed Pula as a provincial backwater, and, eager to get away at the first opportunity, accepted a job in Trieste six months later.

Though Joyce had a productive time in Pula, writing much of what subsequently became *Portrait of the Artist as a Young Man*, the city made next to no impact on his literary imagination. In letters home he described it as "a back-of-God-speed place – a naval Siberia", adding that "Istria is a long boring place wedged into the Adriatic, peopled by ignorant Slavs who wear red caps and colossal breeches".

There are few places in modern Pula which boast Joycean associations: a wall plaque on an apartment block opposite the Arch of the Sergians marks the site of the language school where Joyce taught, and the *Café Miramar*, where Joyce went every day to read the newspapers, survives as a furniture store – it's opposite the entrance to the Uljanik shipyard on the Riva. You can also enjoy a drink in the café-bar *Uliks* ("Ulysses" in Croatian), situated on the ground floor of the apartment block which once housed the language school; the terrace boasts a life-size bronze sculpture of the artist himself sitting on one of the chairs, but a disappointing lack of Joyce memorabilia inside.

here it's worth making a brief detour southwards to the main **post office** on Trg Danteov, an ambitious modern structure designed in 1933 by Angiolo Mazzoni – whose Futurist leanings are evinced by the staircase spiralling awesomely upwards from the dark red vestibule.

At the western end of Via Sergia, stepped streets lead uphill onto the city's central mound, one of them – Balde Lupetine – passing the severe, unadorned form of the thirteenth-century **Franciscan Monastery** (Franjevački samostan) on the way. There's a delightful **museum** in the adjoining cloister (mid-June to mid-Sept daily 10am–1pm & 4–7pm; 5Kn), in which you'll find all kinds of stonework dating from Roman to late medieval times, and a display of Roman mosaic fragments in a couple of side rooms. A doorway leads from the cloister into the monastery **church**, home to an attention-grabbing fifteenth-century altarpiece featuring two tiers of gilded saintly figurines presided over by a severe-looking Virgin with Child.

The Forum and the cathedral

Via Sergia finishes up at the ancient Roman **Forum**, nowadays the old quarter's main square. On the far side is the **Temple of Augustus**, built between 2 BC and 14 AD to celebrate the cult of the emperor and one of the finest Roman temples outside Italy, with an imposing facade of high Corinthian columns. Inside, there's a permanent exhibition (mid-June to mid-Sept Mon–Fri 9am–8pm, Sat & Sun 9am–3pm; 10Kn) of the best of Pula's Roman finds, including the sculpted torso of a Roman centurion found in the amphitheatre, and a figure of a slave kneeling at the sandalled feet (more or less all that's left) of his master. The building next door began life as a Temple of Diana before being modified and rebuilt as the **Town Hall** (Gradska vijećnica) in the thirteenth century – a Renaissance arcade was added later.

Heading northeast from the Forum along Kandlerova brings you to Pula's simple and spacious **Cathedral of St Mary** (Katedrala svete Marije; daily 7am–noon & 4–6pm), a compendium of styles with a dignified Renaissance facade concealing a Romanesque modification of a sixth-century basilica, itself built on the foundations of a Roman temple. There's a great deal of interest inside: the stately pillars running either side of the nave are topped by ornately carved sixth-century capitals, while fragments of original floor mosaic can still be made out just in front of the high altar. The altar itself consists of a third-century marble sarcophagus that's said to have once contained the remains of the eleventh-century Hungarian King Solomon.

The fortress and Archeological Museum

From almost anywhere along Kandlerova you can follow streets up to the top of the hill, the site of the original Roman Capitol and now the home of a mossy seventeenth-century **fortress** (*kaštel*), built by the Venetians in the form of a four-pointed star. It houses the sparse and uninformative **Historical Museum of Istra** (Povijesni muzej Istre; June–Sept daily 8am–5pm; Oct–May by appointment ⓣ052/211-566; 10Kn), with scale models of vessels built in local shipyards and a cabinet of Habsburg-era souvenir mugs decorated with the whiskery visage of Emperor Franz Josef and his World War I ally Kaiser Wilhelm II of Germany. The museum's real appeal is the chance it gives you to ramble around the fortress's ramparts, which provide commanding views of Pula and its environs – you can see the cranes of the Uljanik shipyard clustered over to the west and the spire of Vodnjan church, a distant but discernible presence 12km away to the north.

A path leads round the south wall of the fortress towards the other side of the town centre, passing the remains of a second-century **Roman Theatre** en route to the **Archeological Museum** (Arheološki muzej; May–Sept Mon–Sat 9am–8pm, Sun 10am–3pm; Oct–April Mon–Fri 9am–2pm; 12Kn). The greater part of Pula's movable Roman relics have finished up in this rather old-fashioned museum, with room upon room of unimaginatively displayed ceramics, brooches and oil lamps; English-language labelling helps to ease your progress from one display case to the next. Highlights include the Roman gravestones arranged in the hallways and stairwells, many of which feature sensitive portraits of the deceased, and the pre-Roman artefacts from the Illyrian settlement of Nesactium – especially the enigmatic, squiggle-embellished tombstones, one of which takes the form of a man riding a horse, upon whose flanks an image of a fertility goddess has been carved. Just by the museum is the second-century AD **Porta Gemina**, smaller and plainer than the Arch of the Sergians, whose two arches give it its name: the Twin Gate.

South of the centre

Immediately **south of Pula**, the city's dusty high-rise suburbs suddenly give way to a series of rocky promontories and forest-fringed inlets, culminating, 6km away, in the Verudela peninsula. You can get to Verudela, where the city's package hotels are located, on a direct bus#3A or #2A from Giardini, but a more leisurely approach will take you past several interesting sights on the way. You could quite feasibly spend a pleasant afternoon walking all or part of the way to Verudela if the weather is not too hot; otherwise, a more selective approach to the itinerary described below is advised.

Three kilometres southwest of the centre along Arsenalska (subsequently Bečka and then Katalinića Jeretova) lies Pula's finest graveyard, the Habsburg-era **Naval Cemetery** (Mornaričko groblje). Planted with dark cypresses and incongruously jaunty palms, this is a wonderfully strollable park as much as anything else, although there's a good deal of funerary sculpture to enjoy too, with some imposing nineteenth-century memorials recalling Austrian sailors, and a civilian section where many of the Italian-speaking inhabitants of inter-war Pula were buried. From the cemetery, Stoja descends to the concrete bathing platforms of **Valkane** bay, the nearest beach to the centre. A stylish seaside rendezvous in the inter-war years, it nowadays has a grubby, unkempt look about it, and it's far better to head left along the **Lungomare**, the road running southeast along the coast towards **Valsaline** bay, passing a succession of broad rock slabs which provide perfect spots for bathing. Heading uphill near the *Hotel Splendid*, just beyond Valsaline, brings you to a gravel track which leads to **Fort Bourguignon** (Mon 7–9pm, Tues–Fri & Sun 11am–1pm & 7–9pm, Sat 11am–1pm; 10Kn), an enormous doughnut-shaped lump of stone built in 1861–66 and named after an Austrian Admiral. Visitors can wander the galleries and peruse a display documenting the eleven other forts built around the city by the Habsburgs, turning Pula into an impregnable fortress in the process. Farther south is the wooded **Verudela peninsula**, bordered to the east by the lovely Verudski kanal inlet, home to Pula's marina. The southern extremity of the peninsula, **Punta Verudela**, is home to a couple of good shingle beaches, of which the Havajka, on the west side of the peninsula behind the *Park* hotel, and the Ambrela, northwest of the *Brioni* hotel, are the most popular. The beaches are deluged with vacationing city folk during the summer, and remain a popular strolling area throughout the year. Another Habsburg fortress, on high ground near the tip of the peninsula, now houses an **aquarium** (daily: June–Sept 9am–9pm;

Oct–May 10am–5pm; Ⓦwww.aquariumpula-istra.hr; 20Kn), with an assortment of water-bound creatures gazing out of their tanks, and displays devoted to local marine ecology.

South of Pula: Cape Kamenjak

Some of the most spectacular **beaches** in the Pula region can be found on **Cape Kamenjak** (Rt Kamenjak), some 13km beyond the city limits at the southernmost tip of the Istrian peninsula. They're reachable by the main road from Pula to Premantura, from where a marked turn-off takes you 3km along a dirt road. This area, which makes for a wonderful day-trip from Pula, is protected as a **Nature Park** (15Kn entrance fee at the barrier) and boasts a variety of secluded coves and beaches. *Safari Club*, a fantastical bamboo- and straw-covered hodgepodge of organic materials, bizarre objects and sculptures made of recycled stuff, is the only place inside the park to get food and refreshments; they do a mean sangria and a range of health-food sandwiches.

Eating and drinking

There's a good supply of serviceable **restaurants** in the centre of Pula, although – as so often in Croatia – the really outstanding eating places are in the suburbs. For snacks and supplies, the covered **market** and the surrounding cafés on Trg Narodni, about 100m east of the Arch of the Sergians, are the best place for buying provisions or picking up sandwiches and pastries. Just north of the Forum, the Pekarna Jozef at Kandlerova 17 is a good place to stock up on bread and cakes.

Although the alfresco cafés and ice cream parlours around the Forum provide plenty of opportunities for daytime **drinking**, central Pula doesn't really lend itself to a night-time bar-crawl. Most of the characterful hostelries popular with Puležani are spread throughout the city rather than concentrated in one central promenading area, and you'll have to be prepared to venture beyond the tourist-trodden areas in order to enjoy the city at its best.

Restaurants

Gina Stoja 23 ⓣ052/387-943, Ⓦwww.gina-restaurant.com. Three kilometres west of the centre in the suburb of Stoja, this charming family-run place offers the standard Adriatic repertoire of shellfish, grilled white fish and breaded squid – all of which is exceedingly well executed and reasonably priced to boot. Wooden ceiling beams and slightly distressed furniture create a relaxing semi-rustic atmosphere. Bus #1 from Giardini.

Kantina Flanatićka 18 ⓣ052/214-054. Central lounge-bar-cum-restaurant just beyond the city market, set in a stylishly furnished stone-clad cellar. The menu sticks to the tried-and-tested grilled fish and steaks repertoire you'll find elsewhere, but quality and presentation are a cut above the average. Big salads and meatless pasta dishes provide vegetarians with something to get their teeth into.

Milan Stoja 4 ⓣ052/300-200. A family-run restaurant in a modern suburban pavilion just opposite the Naval Cemetery, offering supremely good seafood (especially the shellfish) and high-class service at above-average prices. Known also for its cakes, and an extensive international wine list. Bus #1 from Giardini.

Poli Nonića Vrtlarska 1 ⓣ052/211-754. "Chez Grandad" offers traditional food at moderate prices in a suburban house ten minutes' walk east of the centre, popular with locals and well away from the main tourist trail. Friendly service and excellent Istrian fare such as *kobasice* (sausages) and *ombolo* (smoked pork chops cooked on the hearth). Specialities such as *hobotnica pod pekom* (octopus baked under an ember-covered lid) should be ordered a day in advance.

Pompei Clarissova 1. Serviceable pizzas, excellent pasta dishes and generous salads, on a city-centre side street perfectly placed for a mid-sightseeing break.

Scaletta Flavijevska 26. A swish, expensive, intimate place attached to the hotel of the same name, with top-quality seafood and meat dishes – try the *istarski odrezak* (veal stuffed with *pršut* and figs).

Valsabbion Pješčana uvala bb ⓣ052/218-033. Upmarket restaurant with a nationwide reputation for its fresh seafood and extravagant desserts, and a nouvelle cuisine approach to presentation. Bus #27 from Giardini.

Vege Club Maksimijanova 19. Popular city-centre lunching place serving veggie risottos, couscous, soya-based stews and salads. Mon–Fri until 5pm, Sat until 3pm. Closed Sun.

Vela Nera Marina Veruda ⓣ052/219-209. Chic, expensive restaurant on a terrace overlooking the marina, with the usual range of fish and shellfish, plus Istrian specialities like *rezanci sa tartufima* (noodles with truffles), or a very rich stewed *kunić* (rabbit). Bus #27 from Giardini.

Cafés and bars

Bounty Pub Veronska 8. An animated place with plenty of outdoor seating, two blocks east of the Arch of the Sergians. Popular with the daytime coffee crowd as well as night-time revellers.

Cabahia Širolina bb. Mildly bohemian drinking den on a side street 3km southwest of the centre, with a cosily eccentric interior and an outdoor terrace that falls somewhere between Spanish hacienda and Saharan oasis.

Café Galerija Cvajner Forum 2. The prime people-watching venue on the main square, next to the tourist office. Comfy sofas and contemporary art exhibits dominate inside.

E&D Verudela 22. If this roomy place has a lounge-bar feel on the inside, then it's a garden-bar on the outside, with clipped lawns, shrubs, a water feature, and views towards the open sea. If you happen to be on the Verudela peninsula, this is the perfect coffee-break venue in the daytime, and in the evening you can plough your way through the cocktail menu. Bus #2A to the end of the line.

MMC Luka Istarska 30. Contemporary art gallery, café and Internet café just a stone's throw from the Arena.

Pietas Julia Riva bb. This magnet for weekend hedonists is just west of the amphitheatre. Choose between the standing-room-only bar area or the lounge-style terrace, from where you can gaze out towards a typical Pula landscape of palm trees and shipyard cranes.

Podroom corner of Tomasinijeva and Budicinova. Lounge around on designer banquettes in Pula's funkiest interior, or mingle with a fun-seeking crowd on the outdoor terrace. Handily situated round the corner from *Cabahia*.

Entertainment and festivals

Pula's **amphitheatre** hosts large-scale opera and pop performances in the summer, often featuring major international stars – check ⓦwww.histriafestival.com or the tourist office for schedule details. The only reliable central **club** is *Uljanik*, at Dobrilina 2 (ⓦwww.clubuljanik.hr), which hosts DJ nights (anything from commercial techno to alternative rock) throughout the year, as well as live gigs on a big open-air terrace in summer – posters in town will provide an idea of what's on. Off-beat gigs and counter-cultural happenings occasionally take place at Karlo Rojc, Gajeva (ⓦwww.rojcnet.hr), a huge former technical school (and subsequently a barracks) built by the Habsburgs and currently occupied by alternative cultural organizations and NGOs. It's located just off Radićeva, a ten-minute walk south of the centre.

Pula's main **cinema** is the Zagreb, bang in the centre at Giardini 1; there's also an art cinema at the Istrian National Theatre on Laginjina 5. Ever since 1953 the amphitheatre has hosted the Pula **Film Festival** (early Aug; ⓦwww.pulafilmfestival.hr), which traditionally premieres the year's crop of domestic feature films. Back in the days when the Yugoslav film industry produced several big-budget features a year, the Pula Film Festival was a major international glam-fest which attracted big name stars – along with guest-of-honour President Tito, who revelled in the opportunity to be photographed next to actresses like Gina Lollobrigida, Elizabeth Taylor and Sophia Loren. Now that Croatia only produces a handful of (largely low-budget) films a year the festival has rather lost its way, but attempts have been made to breathe new life into the event by including more international films. Another annual event is the **IstriaEtnoJazz** (usually in late June & early July; ⓦwww.istraetnojazz.com), exploring the boundaries between traditional music and more contemporary styles, with concerts in Pula, Svetvinčenat and Pazin.

Listings

Airlines Croatia Airlines, Carrarina 8 (Mon–Fri 8.30am–4pm, Sat 9am–noon; ⓣ052/218-909).
Airport enquiries ⓣ052/530-105.
Bank Zagrebačka banka, M. Laginje 1 (Mon–Fri 7.30am–7pm, Sat 7.30am–noon). There's an ATM outside.
Books and magazines Algoritam, just off Sergijevaca on prolaz kod Kazališta, sells English-language magazines, novels and guidebooks.
Car rental Budget, Carrarina 7 ⓣ052/218-252; Hertz, *Hotel Histria* ⓣ052/210-868.
Ferry tickets Jadroagent, Riva 14 (Mon–Sat 8am–4pm, Sun 12.30–3.30pm; ⓣ052/210-431, ejadroagent-pula@pu.t-com.hr).
Fleamarket Ciscuttijeva ulica, near the main market, hosts an antique and bric-a-brac fair every Saturday (8am–2pm).
Hospital Gradska Bolnica, Zagrebačka 30 ⓣ052/376-500.
Internet access *Cyber Caffe*, Flanatička 14; *Enigma*, Kandlerova 19; *MMC Luka*, Istarska 30.
Left luggage At the bus station on Trg 1 Istarske brigade (daily 4.30–9.30am, 10am–6pm & 6.30–11.30pm).
Mail and telephones The main post office is at Trg Danteov 4 (daily 8am–9pm), and there's a smaller branch just south of the amphitheatre at Istarska 7 (Mon–Sat 8am–3pm).
Pharmacy Ljekarna centar, Giardini 15 (24hr).
Police Trg republike 2 ⓣ92.
Taxis Try the rank on Giardini or call ⓣ052/223-228.
Travel agents GeneralTurist, Carrarina 4 (ⓣ052/218-487), sells international airline tickets; Activa Travel, Scalierova 1 (ⓣ052/215-497, ⓦwww.activa-istra.com), offers truffle-picking, biking tours and accommodation in stone houses in Istria's interior.

The west coast

Istria's **west coast** represents the peninsula at its most developed. In itself it's attractive enough, with fields of rich red soil and pine woods sloping gently down to the sea, but a succession of purpose-built resorts has all but swallowed up the shoreline. Inland, the coastal strip fades imperceptibly into conifer-studded heathland and fields bounded by dry-stone walls and dotted with *kažuni*, the characteristic stone huts with conical roofs traditionally used by Istrian shepherds for shelter when overnighting with their flocks. North of Pula, **Rovinj** is Istria's best-preserved old Venetian port; farther north, beyond the picturesque fishing village of **Vrsar** and the **Limski kanal**, spreads the large resort of **Poreč** – package-holiday-land writ large, although it does boast the peninsula's finest ecclesiastical attraction in the shape of the mosaic-filled Basilica of St Euphrasius. The mega-hotels around the town offer undoubted comforts, but with a lot of concrete on the side.

The Brijuni Islands

North of Pula lie the **Brijuni** (in Italian, Brioni), a small archipelago of fourteen islands that became famous as the private retreat of Tito before being accorded **national park** status and opened to tourists in 1983 – visitors are still only allowed on two of the islands, **Veli Brijun** and **Mali Brijun**, and travel here remains strictly controlled.

You can visit the Brijuni on an organized day-trip – which usually involves a tour of Veli Brijun by tourist train – or book into one of the two upmarket hotels on Veli Brijun, in which case you'll have freedom to stroll around parts of the island unsupervised.

Fažana

The obvious gateway to the islands is the small fishing village of **FAŽANA**, 8km northwest of Pula (reachable from the city on bus #18). The Brijuni National Park office on Fažana's harbourfront square (July & Aug daily 8am–10pm; June & Sept daily 8am–8pm; Oct–April Mon–Sat 8am–3pm; ⓣ052/525-882, ⓦwww.brijuni.hr) sells tickets for day-trips to the biggest island and main tourist draw, Veli Brijun, as well as arranging transport to the hotels.

Fažana's **tourist office**, right on the waterfront at Riva 2 (June–Aug daily 8am–10pm; May–Sept Mon–Fri 8am–3pm; ⓣ052/383-727, ⓔtz-fazana@pu.t-com.hr), provides local information, maps and brochures, while Stefani Trade at Župni trg 3 (mid-June to mid-Sept daily 8.30am–11pm; ⓣ052/521-910, ⓔstefani@pu.t-com.hr) doles out **private rooms** (❶–❷) and apartments (❷–❸) on the mainland.

The importance of Tito to Brijuni and Fažana is remembered during the **Tito Days** (Titovi dani) **festival** in Fažana, a tongue-in-cheek affair involving folk

The presidential playground

Although the islands were a popular rural retreat for wealthy Romans, the Brijunis' history as an offshore paradise really began in 1893, when they were bought by Austrian industrialist **Paul Kupelwieser**, owner of a steel mill in the Czech town of Vitkovice. Kupelwieser, whose aim was to turn the islands into a luxury resort patronized by the cream of Europe's aristocracy, brought in Nobel Prize-winning bacteriologist Robert Koch, who rid the islands of malaria by pouring petroleum on the swamps. Smart hotels and villas were built on Veli Brijun, and the Mediterranean scrub was cleared to make way for landscaped parks. The Brijunis' heyday was in the period immediately before World War I: Archduke Franz Ferdinand and Kaiser Wilhelm II both stayed on the islands, and struggling English-language teacher James Joyce came here to celebrate his 23rd birthday on February 2, 1905.

Following World War I, the development of Brijuni as a golf and polo-playing resort helped preserve the islands' reputation as a key venue for aristocratic fun and games. Running costs proved high however, and Kupelweiser's son Karl committed suicide here in 1930 when it became clear that this elite paradise would never turn a profit.

After World War II, **Tito** decided to make Veli Brijun one of his official bases, planting much of the island's subtropical vegetation and commissioning a residence (the White Villa, or "Bijela Vila") in which he was able to entertain visiting heads of state in the style to which they were accustomed. It was here that Tito, Nehru and Nasser signed the Brioni Declaration in 1956, which paved the way for the creation of the **Non-Aligned Movement** (which nowadays consists of 114 nations). Far away from prying eyes, the islands were the perfect spot from which to conduct secret diplomacy – Yugoslav-sponsored terrorist Abu Nidal was a house guest in 1978. Tito himself contrived to spend as much time here as possible, conducting government business when not busy hunting in his private game reserve or pottering about in his gardens and orchards (tangerines from which were traditionally sent to children's homes throughout Yugoslavia as a new year's gift). International stars attending the Pula Film Festival (see p.188) stayed here as Tito's personal guests, bestowing his regime with a veneer of showbiz glamour.

After Tito's death in 1980 the islands were retained as an official residence, and a decade later became the favoured summer destination of President Tuđman. Tuđman's rank ineptitude as a world statesman ensured that no foreign leader ever came to visit him here, and with Tuđman's successor Stipe Mesić declining to make use of the islands, it looks like the Brijuni will lose their mythical status in Croatian politics.

concerts, brass bands, and locals dressed up as communist young pioneers – it takes place on and around May 25, Tito's official birthday. Despite his status as the architect of a flawed Yugoslav state, Tito is remembered with much fondness in Istria – not least because he brought an end to Italian rule over the peninsula.

Getting to the islands

There are about eight excursions daily from Fažana from May to mid-October and one daily the rest of the year, apart from January, when no services run (4hr; July & Aug 180Kn, June & Sept 170Kn, April, May & Oct 150Kn, Feb, March, Nov & Dec 100Kn). Tickets are sold at the Brijuni National Park office on the Fažana quayside. If you're staying in a package hotel in Istria you'll probably pay around 250Kn for a Brijuni excursion, with transport to Fažana – and possibly lunch – thrown in. Trips to Brijuni are also offered by boats in Pula harbour (from around 200–250Kn per person), although they don't always give you the full tour provided by the national park.

If you want to **stay on the islands**, be warned that the hotels, next door to each other on Veli Brijun's main bay, are deliberately overpriced in order to cultivate an aura of exclusivity. The *Neptun-Istra* (Ⓣ052/525-807; ❼) is a standard three-star whose rooms come with TV, minibar and bath; the quieter and marginally plusher *Karmen* (Ⓣ052/525-807; ❼) offers pretty much the same. If you want a real taste of luxury then consider staying in one of the island's stylish historic villas (booked through the national park office in Fažana), located in secluded coastal spots towards the southern end of Veli Brijun: there's the eight-person *Primorka* (1200/8800kn per day), the four-person *Dubravka* (600/4400kn per day), or the five-person *Lovorka* (600/4400Kn per day). It's the *Lovorka* that has most in the way of an aristocratic pedigree, having served as the summer home of the polo-playing party animal that was the Duke of Spoleto, between the two world wars.

If you are staying on the island, the best way to get around is to hire a golf cart (500Kn/5hr) or bicycle (100Kn/day) from the sports centre just along from the *Neptun-Istra* hotel.

There's a 22-hole **golf course** just north of the hotels, designed along ecological lines in order to reduce the amount of watering and pesticides required for its upkeep. The fairways are nibbled by deer rather than mown, and the greens are made from compacted sand. You can rent golf gear and pay green fees at the sports centre.

Food and drink is available from the café-restaurants of the *Neptun-Istra* and the *Karmen* hotels.

Veli Brijun

After a fifteen-minute crossing of the Brijuni Channel, excursion craft from Fažana arrive at Kupelwieser's hotel complex on **Veli Brijun**'s eastern shore. From here a miniature train with an English-speaking guide heads north through the golf course towards a **safari park** at the northern tip of the island. This was originally stocked with beasts given to Tito as presents by world statesmen – elephants Sonny and Lanka (presented by Indira Gandhi in 1975) are still happy to pose for photographs, and you can also see zebras, antelopes and indigenous long-horned cattle (*boškarin*) from the Istrian interior. The train continues along the western side of the island to the **White Villa** and other official residences, including the Villa Jadranka, where guests have included Queen Elizabeth II and Gina Lollobrigida. The train stops at the southwestern corner of the island to allow exploration of a ruined **Byzantine fortress**; the fortress's stark grey walls

△ Zebra in Veli Brijuni's safari park

make a bleak contrast to the green paradise it was built to defend. The train then returns to the hotel complex via the scant remains of a first-century BC Roman villa at Veriga Bay.

Tito on Brijuni

At the end of the tour, day-trippers are free to explore an additional group of sights beside the hotel complex before returning to the mainland. Most prominent of these is a fifteenth-century **Gothic church**, restored by Kupelweiser prior to World War I and ceremonially reopened by ill-fated Archduke Franz Ferdinand.

Nearby, an exhibition hall entitled **Tito on Brijuni** (Tito na Brijunima; July & Aug daily 8am–8pm; June & Sept daily 8am–7pm; May & Oct daily 8am–6pm; opens for excursion boats only at other times of year; free with excursion ticket) starts, on the ground floor, with a display of the animals given to Tito as presents and stuffed after their death, including four seven-week-old giraffes poisoned by salmonella soon after their arrival from Africa. Upstairs is a fascinating exhibition of photos documenting Tito's various personae: one moment a man of the people talking to Fažana fisherfolk, the next, sharing jokes with jet-setting house guests such as Sophia Loren, Elizabeth Taylor and Richard Burton, who played the part of Tito in the epic war film *Sutjeska* in 1970. Look out for a photograph of Tito taking Ho Chi Minh for a spin in a motorboat, both men sporting raffish panama hats – an experience which the Vietnamese leader appears to be enjoying somewhat less than the Marshal.

Across the lawn from the exhibition building, a large cage serves as the summer residence of one of Tito's favourite pets, **Koki the parrot**. Koki still likes to chirrup the banal phrases learnt from its erstwhile master, and it's strange to think that the voice of the Yugoslav leader still lives on via the beak of his sociable white-feathered friend.

Vodnjan

Heading up the west coast from Pula, the main road runs inland through the historic town of **VODNJAN** (in Italian, Dignano), 11km north of Pula, with its warren of weather-beaten alleys gathered tightly around a time-worn main square. Vodnjan is famous for two things: the enduring presence of a large Italian-speaking community, and the well-preserved **Vodnjan mummies** – the desiccated bodies of various saints stored in the eighteenth-century **St Blaise's Church** (Crkva svetog Blaža; June–Sept Mon–Sat 9am–7pm & Sun 2–7pm; Oct–May open only when the priest is around; 35Kn). Built in imitation of Palladio's San Pietro in Castello, Venice, its soaring campanile is the highest in Istria. Inside, the mummies are kept behind a burgundy-coloured curtain to the rear of the main altar. Originally stored in the church of San Lorenzo in Venice, they were brought to Vodnjan in 1818 for safekeeping after the monastic order that originally looked after them had been dissolved. Three complete and well-preserved bodies are laid out in glass cases, with a range of smaller relics in a series of containers above – one of which holds a twisted brown form reputed to be the torso and arm of St Sebastian. The most revered of the bodies is that of Leon Bembo the Blessed, a twelfth-century Venetian cleric and diplomat who gave up worldly pleasures for the monastic life, developing a reputation as a faith healer and sage. Beside him lie St Nikoloza of Koper (with a still-fresh-looking garland of flowers round her head) and St Ivan Olini of Venice, both renowned medieval healers – popular belief maintains that there's a link between the saints' healing powers and the subsequent failure of their bodies to decompose. Note that the priest enforces the decent clothing policy very fiercely – no sleeveless shirts or shorts are allowed inside the church.

The **Collection of Sacral Art** (Zbirka sakralne umjetnosti; same times as the church; 10Kn; 38Kn with the mummies) in the sacristy has innumerable smaller relics, including one glass jar which is claimed to contain the lower jaw and tongue of St Mary of Egypt, a sixth-century Alexandrian courtesan who converted to Christianity and thereafter opted for a life of asceticism in the desert. The star exhibit, however, is Paolo Veneziano's early fourteenth-century polyptych of St Bembo the Blessed, a wooden board which originally served as the lid of Bembo's coffin. A series of scenes show Bembo exercising his healing powers, mighty bishops and nobles visiting Bembo's deathbed, and pilgrims paying homage to Bembo's miraculously preserved body.

Practicalities

Buses (local Pula-Vodnjan services #22 and #41, as well as inter-city buses from Pula to Pazin, Rovinj and Poreč) all pick up and drop off on the western edge of town, a short walk from the main square, where you'll find Vodnjan's **tourist office** at Narodni trg 3 (summer daily 8am–noon & 5–8pm; ⓣ052/511-672, ⓔtz-vodnjan-dignano@pu.t-com.hr). The cosiest place **to stay** in town is the garish pink *Pansion San Rocco* at Sveti Roko 41 (ⓣ052/512-011, ⓕ052/394-529; ❷), which has small, sprucely furnished en-suite rooms with TV. For those with their own transport, *Stancija Negričani*, 8km north of Vodnjan and well signed from the northern end of town (ⓣ052/391-084, ⓦwww.stancijanegricani.com; ❹–❺ depending on room size), is one of the best rural hotels in the whole of Croatia. Set in a large stone farmhouse surrounded by forest and fields (with a swimming pool and volleyball court), the en-suite rooms are all decorated in nineteenth-century style, with old wooden bedsteads and rustic furniture – but pristine modern bathrooms and TV.

The *Stancija Negričani*'s pricey **restaurant**, which serves up delicious homemade specialities, is open to non-residents; advanced reservations are required. Back in town, you can tuck into hearty Croatian food at *Pansion San Rocco*, or at the superior *Vodnjanka*, on the main Pula–Pazin road at Istarska bb (ⓣ052/511-435; closed Sun). The latter, whose interior is a cross between a nineteenth-century barn and a kooky art gallery, serves up the best in local cuisine, including spicy Istrian sausages and some divine homemade pasta dishes.

Bale

Ten kilometres beyond Vodnjan, **BALE** (in Italian, Valle) occupies a hilltop site typical of the peninsula, with houses built in a defensive circle – it's a good example of a town abandoned by its Italian population after 1945 and never properly lived in since. The most arresting edifice here is the **Soardo-Bembo Palace**, a fifteenth-century Venetian Gothic building with an elegant balcony built into its towered facade. It's currently being restored and will probably house a local history museum at some point in the future. Beside the palace, an arch topped by a clumsily rendered Venetian lion leads into the core of the old town, which amounts to little more than a circular alleyway spanned by small arches, with rough stone buildings on either side. Follow this round in either direction to reach **St Elizabeth's Church** (Crkva svete Elizabete) in the central square, a largely nineteenth-century neo-Baroque building, although it preserves a Romanesque campanile and fragments from earlier sixth- and eighth-century churches in the crypt. Just outside the old town beside the road to Rovinj, the smaller, simpler, fifteenth-century **Church of the Holy Spirit** (Crkva svetog Duha) contains late Gothic frescoes and doubles sporadically as a gallery in the summer months. It also houses a lapidarium in the basement (mid-June to mid-Sept daily 9am–1pm & 5–8pm; 10Kn), with a small collection of ancient stones found in churches around Bale.

Pula–Rovinj buses stop on the main road just below the entrance to the old town, Trg palih boraca, where there's a small seasonal **tourist office** (mid-June to Aug daily 8am–2pm & 3–9pm; ⓣ052/824-270, ⓦwww.bale-valle.hr). A limited number of **private rooms** (❶–❷) are available from Amfora, La Musa 3 (ⓣ052/841-773), although they disappear fast in summer. *Kamene Priče*, just above the Soardo-Bembo palace at Kaštel 57 (ⓣ052/824-231, ⓔtomislav.pavleka@pu.t-com.hr; ❸), offers **lodging** in an atmospheric old stone house; there are only three en-suite rooms with kitchenettes, so you'll need to ring well in advance. About a kilometre northwest of town, just off the Rovinj road and worth a stop, the *Sweet Bar* **café** is renowned for its excellent homemade cakes and biscuits.

Rovinj

There are few more pleasant towns in Istria than **ROVINJ** (in Italian, Rovigno). Delicately poised between medieval port and modern tourist resort, it has managed to preserve its character better than anywhere else along the peninsula's west coast, by keeping major development well away from its historic centre: the harbour is a likeable mix of fishing boats and swanky yachts, while the quaysides are a blend of sunshaded café tables and fishermen's nets. Spacious Venetian-style houses and elegant piazzas lend an overridingly Italian air to the town, and the festive mood the tourists bring only adds to the atmosphere. Rovinj is also the most Italian town on this coast: there's an Italian high school, the language is widely spoken, and street signs are bilingual.

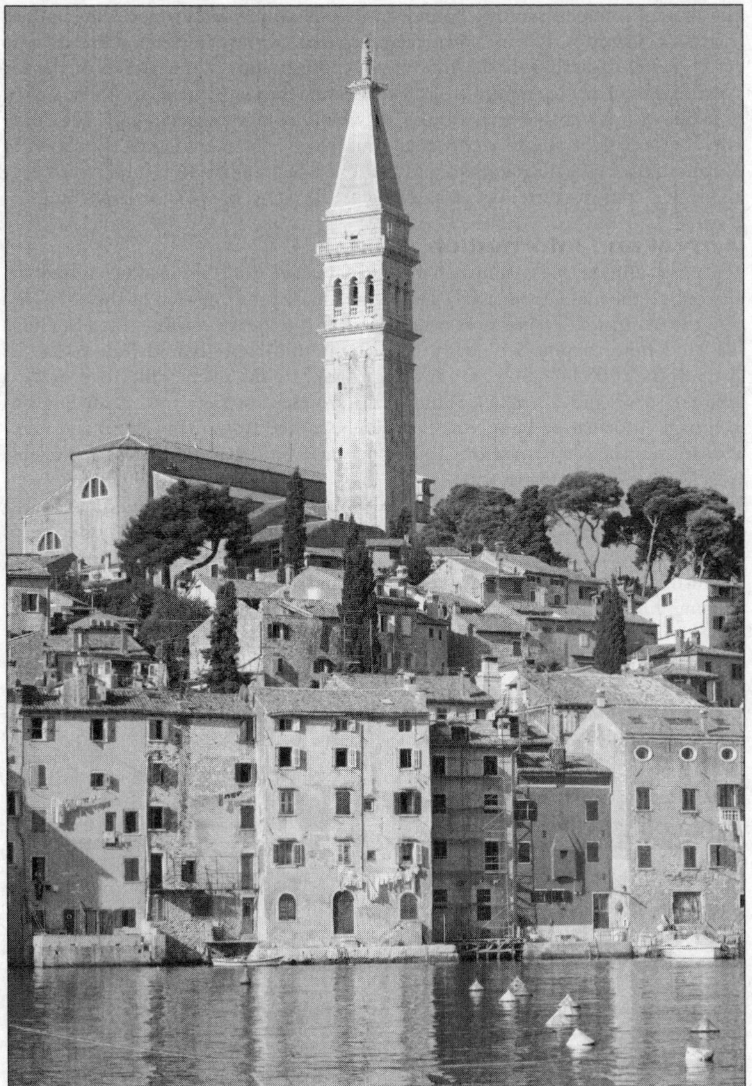

△ Rovinj

Rovinj's urban core is situated on what was formerly an island. The strait separating it from the coast was filled in during the mid-eighteenth century, after which the town expanded onto the mainland, until then the site of a separate settlement of Croat farmers. Initially, the urban Italian culture of Rovigno assimilated that of the mainland Slavs, until industrial development in the late nineteenth century encouraged a wave of economic migrants, tipping the demographic scales in the Croats' favour. Playing a leading role in this was the Rovinj **tobacco factory**, founded in 1872, which still produces the bulk of Croatia's cigarettes. Rovinj's other claim to fame is the painters and **artists** who have gravitated here since the 1950s and whose studios fill the streets of the old town. For one day in August (usually the second Sunday), the main street, Grisia, is taken over by an open-air display in which anyone can take part, providing they register their works at the town museum on the morning of the show. **St Euphemia's Day** (Blagdan svete Eufemije) on September 16 – Euphemia being the town's patron saint – provides an excuse for another week of happenings.

Arrival and information

It's a five-minute walk from Rovinj's **bus station** along the pedestrianized Via Carrera to the main Trg maršala Tita, which marks the junction of the old island and the mainland. The **tourist office**, just off the square at Obala Pina Budičina 12 (mid-June to mid-Sept daily 8am–9pm; mid-Sept to mid-June Mon–Sat 8am–3pm; ⓣ052/11-566, ⓦwww.tzgrovinj.hr), should be able to provide a free city map and a map of biking trails around town, as well as an English-language information booklet. **Bikes** can be rented from many shops and agencies around the old town from 100Kn per day, and **Internet access** is available at @Mar–com, Via Carrera 26.

Kompas-Istra at Trg maršala Tita 5 (ⓣ052/813-187) and Generalturist at Trg maršala Tita 2 (ⓣ052/811-402, ⓔgeneralturist@generalturist.com) offer heaps of **day-trips**, including a four-hour fish picnic to the Limski kanal for 220Kn, an all-day excursion to Plitvice for 500Kn and a day-trip to Brijuni for 295Kn. During high season, Venezia Lines runs a weekly **catamaran service** from Rovinj to Trieste and Venice.

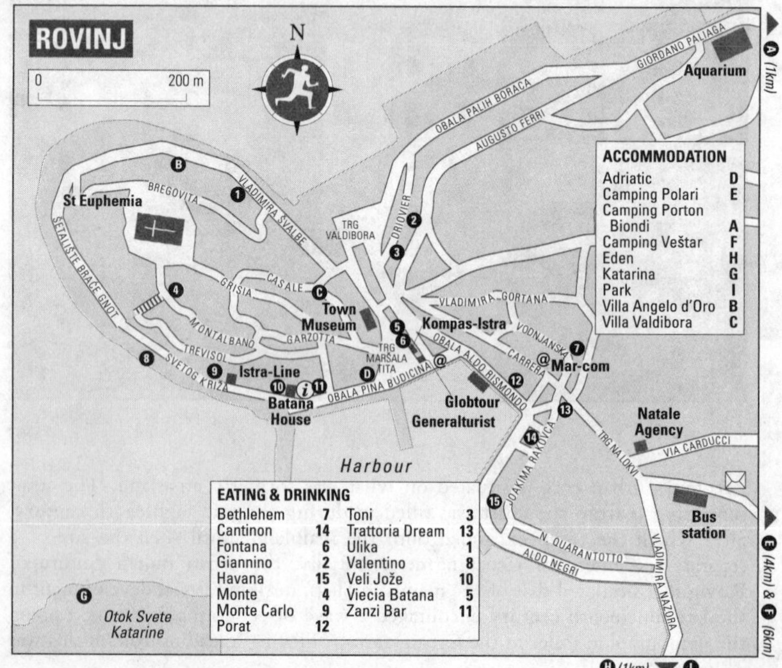

Accommodation

There's a smattering of private **rooms** (❶–❷) and **apartments** (❷–❹) in the old town, although most are in the more modern areas. They can be booked through numerous **agencies** (usually open daily 8am–10pm in July and August, but may take an afternoon break in the shoulder season); try Natale, opposite the bus station at Carducci 4 (ⓣ052/13-365, ⓦwww.rovinj.com); Istra-line, near the tourist office at Vrata na obali 1 (ⓣ052/811-209, ⓦwww.country-club.hr); or Globtour, at Obala A. Rismondo 2 (ⓣ052/814-130, ⓦwww.globtour-turizam.hr). Note that most agencies won't take a booking for one night only and, if they do, it might incur a hefty one hundred percent surcharge.

With so many well-appointed private rooms and apartments, Rovinj's mainstream package **hotels** are not worth the price unless you go slightly upmarket – luckily, a number of characterful places rise above the crowd. Note that many hotels are block-booked by package companies in July and August, when independent travellers will have to ring well in advance to secure a room.

The nearest **campsite** is the *Porton Biondi* (ⓣ052/813-557), which occupies a roomy, pine-shaded site right by the sea 1km north of town. An alternative if you have your own transport is *Veštar* (ⓣ052/829-150, ⓦwww.maistra.hr), on its own secluded bay 6km to the south. *Polari*, occupying a rocky cove 4km south of town, is a naturist camp (ⓣ052/801-501, ⓦwww.maistra.hr).

Hotels

Adriatic Corner of Trg maršala Tita and P. Budičina ⓣ052/815-088, ⓦwww.istra.com/jadranturist. Venerable establishment right on the harbour, offering en-suite rooms with a/c, phone and TV. Most are comfortable, although there are a couple of poky doubles with courtyard-facing views. With only 27 rooms it has an intimate, almost genteel feel – so book very, very early. ❻

Eden L. Adamovića bb ⓣ052/800-400, ⓦwww.istra.com/jadranturist. A kilometre south of town along a pretty coastal path, this is a vast modern four-star complex backed by forest, with an outdoor pool and generous buffet breakfast. Closed Nov–March. ❼

Katarina just offshore on the island of Sveta Katarina ⓣ052/804-100, ⓦwww.hotelinsel-katarina.com. An early twentieth-century villa-hotel with modern annexes either side, whose recently modernized rooms have TV, a/c and their own bathroom. There's also an outdoor pool and plenty of wooded parkland at the back. Linked to town by half-hourly taxi-boat. Closed Nov–March. ❼

Park Ronjgova bb ⓣ052/811-077, ⓦwww.istra.com/jadranturist. Recently renovated mega-resort 1km south of town along a forested seafront promenade. Bland but functional rooms overlook the sea or the forest, and there are three swimming pools and a fitness centre. ❼

Villa Angelo d'Oro Via Švalba 38–42 ⓣ052/840-502, ⓦwww.rovinj.at. Superbly restored town house on the north side of the peninsula; the luxurious rooms are decorated with antique furnishings, and there's a charming rooftop terrace, a sauna and a solarium. Closed Jan & Feb. ❽

Villa Valdibora S. Chiurco 8 ⓣ052/845-040, ⓦwww.valdibora.com. Luxury apartments in a seventeenth-century stone house, with repro furniture and beautiful fabrics. Two-person apartments ❽, four-person apartments 2500Kn.

The Town

Northwest of the main square, **Trg maršala Tita**, the narrow pedestrianized alleyway of **Grisia** passes through a cute Baroque archway before climbing steeply through the heart of the old town to the eighteenth-century **St Euphemia's Church** (Crkva svete Eufemije; May–Sept daily 10am–6.30pm; Oct–April open for Mass only), whose 58-metre high tower – said to be modelled on that of St Mark's in Venice – dominates Rovinj from the top of its stumpy peninsula. Topping the tower is a statue of St Euphemia, a Christian from Chalcedon in Asia Minor who was martyred during the reign of Diocletian – she was supposedly thrown to the lions in the Constantinople hippodrome after having survived various other tortures, symbolized by the wheel which leans against her flanks. The church itself is a roomy three-aisled basilica with a Baroque altarpiece at the end of each. The altar of St Euphemia is the one furthest to the right, behind which is a small sanctuary containing Euphemia's sixth-century sarcophagus. A bare stone box, it was brought to Rovinj in 800 AD to keep it safe from the Iconoclasts, who were in the process of smashing up all the relics they could find in Constantinople.

It's below the church, and on either side of Grisia, that Rovinj's most atmospheric streets are to be found – narrow, cobbled **alleyways** packed with tiny craft shops, overlooked by high shuttered windows, spindly TV aerials and the thin, thrusting **chimneys** that have become something of a Rovinj trademark. Pressure on housing forced married sons to set up home in a spare room of their parents' house, and before long every house in town accommodated several families, each with its own hearth and chimney.

Back on Trg maršala Tita, the **Town Museum** at no. 11 (Zavičajni muzej Rovinj; May–Sept Tues–Sun 9am–noon & 7–10pm; Oct–April by appointment, ⓣ052/840-471; 15Kn) has archeological oddments, model ships and antique furniture, although it's the wide-ranging art collection that stands out. Among the numerous Madonna and Childs are several imposing Baroque works by anonymous Venetian artists, including a dignified *Deposition of St Sebastian*, and some older, Byzantine-influenced works, including the colourful pageantry of Bonifazio de Pitati's *Adoration of the Magi* (1430) and Leandro Bassano's vibrant *Madonna with Child, St John and the Angels* (early seventeenth century). Works by local contemporary artists are also on display.

On the southern side of the peninsula at Obala Pina Budicina 2, **Batana House** (Kuća o batani; daily: June–Sept 10am–3pm & 5–10pm; March–May & Oct–Nov 10am–1pm & 3–5pm; 10Kn) honours the tiny, flat-bottomed fishing boats in which Rovinj fishermen used to ply their trade. Featuring old photographs, videos and artfully arranged fishing tackle, it's a visually arresting display.

Over towards the northern side of the peninsula, Trg maršala Tita opens out onto **Trg Valdibora**, site of a small fruit-and-veg **market**. A road leads east from here along the waterfront to the Marine Biological Institute at Obala Giordano Paliaga 5, home to an **aquarium** (daily: June–Sept 9am–9pm; April, May & Oct 10am–4pm; 15Kn) dating back to 1891 – it's one of the oldest in Europe – and featuring tanks of Adriatic marine life and flora.

Beaches and islands around Rovinj

Paths on the south side of Rovinj's busy harbour lead beyond the *Hotel Park* towards **Zlatni Rt**, a densely forested cape criss-crossed by numerous paths and fringed by rocky **beaches**. Other spots for bathing can be found on the two islands just offshore from Rovinj – **Sveta Katarina**, the nearer of the two, and **Crveni otok** (Red Island), just outside Rovinj's bay, both of which can be reached by ferries from the harbour (every 30–45min). Neither is exactly deserted (there's a hotel on each), but the combination of pine-shaded shores and ultra-clean waters beats anything else the coast around Rovinj has to offer.

Eating

There are more seafood **restaurants** in Rovinj than you can shake a stick at, some of which have an Istria-wide reputation for good food. Many of the harbourfront establishments are bland, overtouristed and worth avoiding, although one or two of them have inexpensive fish specials chalked up on boards outside, and you can munch your way through serviceable pizzas almost everywhere.

Picnic ingredients can be bought at the **supermarket** (Mon–Sat 7am–9pm, Sun 7am–noon) on Trg maršala Tita or in the open-air **market** on Trg Valdibora. The *Martin* **bakery** on Trg maršala Tita, or the *Brionka* opposite the bus station at Carducci 6, are the best places to pick up bread and cakes.

We have included the telephone numbers of those restaurants where it may be necessary to reserve a table.

Restaurants

Cantinon Obala Aldo Rismondo 18.The most reasonably priced restaurant on the harbourfront, serving fresh fish and boasting atmospheric interiors with super-high ceilings. Prices are extremely affordable unless you opt for the finest fish.

Giannino A. Ferri 38 ⓣ052/813-402. The best place in town for lobster, grilled shellfish and fish; *njoki* (gnocchi) and *fuži* dishes (pasta twists) are available, too. The cosy interior is filled with paintings and ceramics, while outdoors there are tables scattered across a cobbled street. Prices for the seafod specialities are above average but well worth the splash-out.

Monte Montalbano 75 ⓣ & ⓕ052/830-203. Right below St Euphemia's Church, this is the finest restaurant in town – with an extensive nouvelle cuisine menu and impressive wine list, it's the place where locals come to celebrate special occasions. A three-course meal with drinks will set you back 250–300Kn. Open Easter–Oct.

Toni Driovier 3. Cosy place with a growing gastronomic reputation, located down a narrow side street with tables crammed into a homely dining room. Good for shellfish served with freshly made pasta, and a knockout squid stew (*brudet od sipe*). Prices are moderate. Closed Wed.

Trattoria Dream Joakima Rakovca 18. If you tire of grilled fish and seafood then *Dream* might be just the ticket, with moderately priced pastas, risottos, healthy salads, and a range of desserts that go beyond the usual pancake and ice cream fare.

Veli Jože svetog Križa 1. The over-designed interior looks like a nautical junk shop, but the food is first class, with excellent fish dishes, steaks and pasta. Main courses are in the 100–150Kn range.

Ulika Vladimira Svalbe 34. More of an upmarket tavern serving wine and nibbles than a full-blown restaurant, *Ulika* is nevertheless an excellent place to sample local tipples, accompanied by cheese, anchovies, *pršut* and other indigenous deli-snacks. Try the *Istarska supa* (Istrian mulled wine with toasted bread dipped in it).

Drinking

For daytime drinking, the harbour area is full of places where you can sit outside and enjoy **coffee**, ice cream and cakes, although the two cafés patronized by locals on the main square – *Fontana* and *Viecia Batana* – serve stronger coffee and are more atmospheric.

In the evening, head for the knot of convivial **bars** on and around **Joakima Rakovca**, just behind the seafront, where stools and tables are stuffed into narrow pedestrian alleyways: rather than aiming for a specific destination here, it's really a question of seeing who's hanging out where and what kind of music is playing. There's a trio of trendy establishments on the south side of the old town peninsula: *Zanzi Bar*, on svetog Križa, serves up expensive cocktails in a loggia filled with comfy chairs; farther along, *Monte Carlo* has outdoor seating perched right above the shore; *Valentino*, farther still, is a rather pretentious wine and cocktail place which nevertheless benefits from its unique position right on the rocks. Trendiest of all is *Havana*, on Aldo Negri bb, with giant straw parasols, comfy bamboo chairs, pricey designer cocktails and Cuban cigars for sale. For indoor drinking, *Bethlehem* on Vodnjanska is a convivial place, crammed full of domestic and folksy trinkets – including a Christmas crib.

The Limski kanal and Vrsar

North of Rovinj, the main coastal route detours inland around the **Limski kanal**, a turquoise fjord lined with thick woods rising sheer on either side, which cuts a deep green wedge into the Istrian mainland. In Roman times this marked the boundary between the Poreč and Pula regions – "Lim" is derived from *limes*, a Latin word meaning "border" or "limit" – but it later became a favourite shelter of pirates, who used it as a base from which to attack the Venetians. An appealing local legend associates the *kanal* with pirate and adventurer **Captain Morgan**, who liked it so much he decided to settle down here with his crew, founding the village of **Mrgani** (which still exists 5km inland from the *kanal*) in the process.

Mussels and oysters are cultivated here – you can sample them, along with other fresh fish, in the *Viking* and *Fjord* **restaurants**, both expensive but highly rated by locals. If you've got a car, you can get down to the northern side of the water (and the two restaurants) via the side road which leaves the Rovinj–Poreč route near the village of **Kloštar**. The best way to see the inlet, however, is by **boat**. Numerous excursions, often including a fish picnic or a lunch stop en route, are advertised on the quaysides of Rovinj, Vrsar and Poreč; expect to pay around 200–250Kn for the trip.

Vrsar and around

Occupying high ground near the mouth of the Limski kanal is **VRSAR**, a picturesque hilltop village curled tightly around a campanile-topped summit. This beautifully preserved, tranquil place, a labyrinth of steep narrow alleyways, leafy patios and terraces, with blue-shuttered stone houses and sweeping hilltop views, has become a popular day-trip destination from Poreč. The (in)famous adventurer Giacomo Casanova visited twice in the late eighteenth century, mentioning the place fondly in his memoirs, and relatively little has changed since then. Crowning the hill is the nineteenth-century **Church of St Martin** (Crkva svetog Martina) with its recently added campanile (June–Sept daily 8.30am–7pm; 10Kn), an unimpressive white structure that you can climb for some wonderful vistas of the town and the sea beyond; the church hosts classical music concerts on Thursdays during the summer. The seafront below the village is far less interesting than the steep, mazey hillsides and somewhat spoilt by a marina and concrete-block hotels.

Twenty minutes' walk north of town, along the main road to Poreč, the grassy **Dušan Džamonija Sculpture Park** (Park skulptura; Tues–Sun 9–11am & 6–9pm; free) honours one of Croatia's greatest living sculptors with an extensive open-air display, right next to the summer house and studio where the artist still spends part of the year. Džamonija (born 1928) is an unabashed modernist, and the shiny aluminium eggs and enigmatic lumps of browned steel on display here will appeal to anyone whose tastes tend towards the abstract.

Practicalities

Buses from Poreč stop at the bottom of central Vrsar's hill, a short walk from the marina. The small **tourist office** uphill off the main square on Rade Končara 56 (June–Sept daily 8am–6pm; ⓣ052/441-187, ⓦwww.istra.com/vrsar) provides local information, while private accommodation (❶–❷) can be booked through Vrsar Tours on the seafront (ⓣ052/441-362). *Trošt* **restaurant**, located on the second floor of the marina reception on Obala maršala Tita 1A, serves some of the best seafood in the region on a terrace with (yacht-obstructed) sea views. On the hillside halfway between the waterfront and the old town centre, the laid-back *Baba* **bar** is a great place to snack on toasted sandwiches during the day and guzzle cocktails at night.

A kilometre south of town on the coast is one of the world's largest nudist colonies, **Koversada**. Established in 1960, this was the first of the Adriatic's naturist communities, and is nowadays a self-contained mini-city where up to fifteen thousand residents can dress as nature intended on a 24-hour basis. Stretching north of Vrsar there's a string of **campsites** on the coastal side of the main road to Poreč, beginning with *Autocamp Turist*, swiftly followed by the *Valkanela*, then *Camping Puntica*, which has a small bay to itself. Another couple of kilometres and you're in Plava Laguna, the first of Poreč's big package-hotel suburbs.

Poreč and around

How you react to **POREČ** (in Italian, Parenzo) may well depend on what time of year you arrive. From July to mid-September, Istria's largest tourist resort can seem positively engulfed by mass-market tourism; outside this

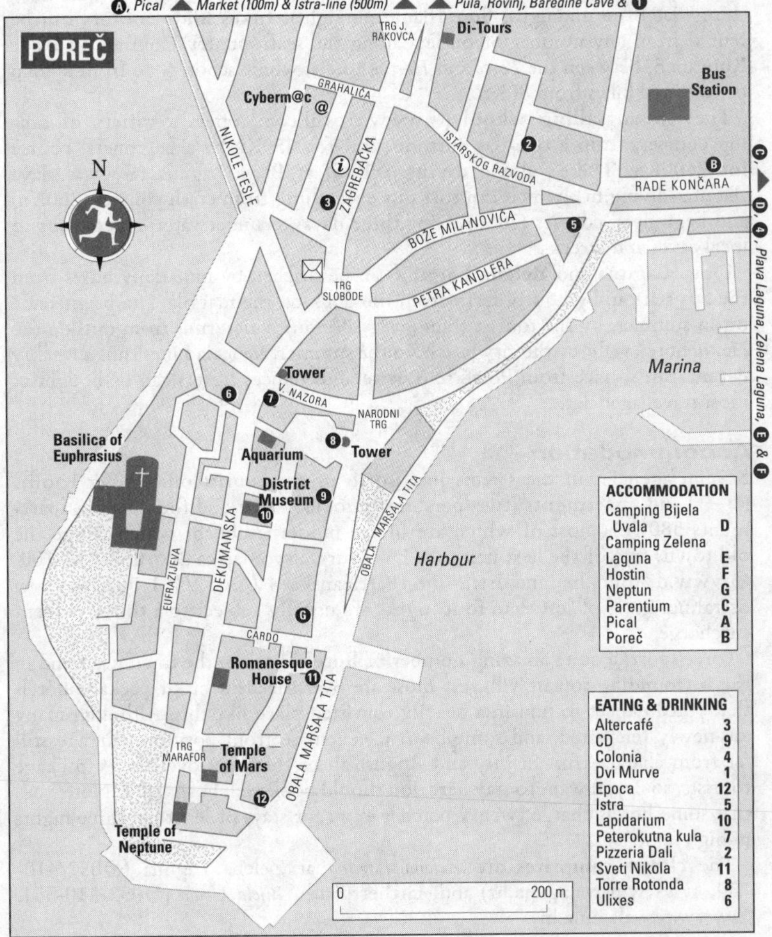

period it can be just as charming as any other well-kept former fishing port. Happily, Poreč's gargantuan hotel complexes are mainly concentrated outside the town, in vast tourist settlements like Plava Laguna and Zelena Laguna to the south, and Pical to the north, and the town's central core of stone houses and labyrinthine side streets – ice cream parlours and tacky souvenir shops notwithstanding – remain relatively unspoiled. Main points in Poreč's favour are the Romanesque **Basilica of Euphrasius**, Istria's one must-see ecclesiastical attraction, and the town's tourist facilities and transport links, which make it a convenient base from which to visit the rest of the Istrian peninsula.

Arrival and information

Poreč's **bus station** is just north of the town centre, behind the marina. From here, it's a five-minute walk to the **tourist office** at Zagrebačka 9 (summer Mon–Sat 8am–10pm, Sun 9am–1pm & 6–10pm; winter Mon–Fri 8am–3pm; ⓣ052/451-293, ⓦwww.istra.com/porec), where you'll probably receive a free map and brochures. You can **surf the net** at Cyberm@c, M. Grahalića 1 (Mon–Sat 8am–midnight, Sun 10am–midnight). **Bikes and scooters** can be rented from any number of outlets along the seafront; try Contigo on Rade Končara 5, between the *Poreč* and *Hostin* hotels, where scooters go from 200Kn per day and bikes from 80Kn.

The Crosail **sailing school** (ⓦwww.crosail.com) offers a variety of sailing courses, from a one-day introduction for 450Kn to a beginners' course for 2600Kn. There's also a **diving school** at Plava Laguna (ⓦwww.plava-laguna-diving.hr), which can sort out everything from crash courses (260Kn) and beginners' courses (2050Kn for three days) to underwater expeditions to local caves and wrecks.

Plava Laguna and **Zelena Laguna** can be reached by nine daily buses from the bus station, by hourly ferry from the dock on the maršala Tita promenade or, in summer, by the tourist train (every 30min) which runs from outside the *Hostin* hotel, right by the city beach. In the summer, Venezia Lines runs a weekly **catamaran** service from Poreč to Trieste and Venice; tickets can be bought at most travel agencies.

Accommodation

Several agencies in the streets just north of the tourist office offer **rooms** (❷–❸) and **apartments** (two-person studios ❹, three-and four-person apartments 580Kn), most of which are in the modern suburbs which fringe the old town; two of the best firms are Di-Tours, Prvomajska 2 (ⓣ052/432-100, ⓦwww.di-tours.hr) and Istra-line, Partizanska 4 (ⓣ052/451-067, ⓦwww.istraline. Stays of less than four nights are usually subject to a thirty percent surcharge.

Poreč sports a quite amazing number of **hotels**, both in the town itself and in the surrounding tourist villages; most are overpriced identikit package hotels that you'd expect to find in a heavily touristed place like this. Although many are newly renovated, and some boast excellent seafront positions, they're still far from characterful. In July and August all of them get overrun by package tourists, so if you want to stay here you should book well in advance. Note, too, that some hotels charge twenty percent extra for stays of less than three nights in high season.

The closest **campsites** are *Zelena Laguna* at Zelena Laguna (ⓣ052/410-700, ⓦwww.plavalaguna.hr) and, farther south, *Bijela Uvala* (ⓣ052/410-551, ⓦwww.plavalaguna.hr).

Hotels

Hostin Rade Končara 4 ⓣ052/408-800, ⓦwww.hostin.hr. By far the best hotel in town, right across from the city beach and surrounded by fragrant pine forest. The 41 spacious, modern en-suite rooms all have balconies (ask for a forest view, as some overlook a parking lot), a/c, dial-up connection and TV. The outdoor terrace is a great place for a leisurely breakfast, and there's a swimming pool with Jacuzzi, a sauna and a fitness centre. ❺

Neptun Obala maršala Tita ⓣ052/465-100, ⓦwww.riviera.hr. The most comfortable option in the centre, with a gloomy exterior but pleasantly refurbished rooms with bathrooms, TV and a/c; rooms with balconies are only slightly more expensive. ❺

Parentium 5km south of town in Zelena Laguna ⓣ052/411-500, ⓦwww.plavalaguna.hr. Unspectacular mega-hotel on a forested peninsula, with its own pebbly beach, a fitness centre with a pool and a slew of comfortable en-suite rooms. ❻

Pical 3km north of town centre, in Borik ⓣ052/465-100, ⓦwww.riviera.hr. Resort complex right on the beach and surrounded by pine forest, with two swimming pools and tennis courts nearby. En-suite rooms with bathtubs and TV are functional and have sea or forest views. ❻

Poreč just south of the bus station at Rade Končara 1 ⓣ052/451-811, ⓦwww.hotelporec.com. Newly renovated concrete-block hotel across from the harbour, offering poky but neat en suites with TV, a/c and balconies, plus a generous breakfast buffet. ❻

The Town and around

Poreč's star turn is the **Basilica of Euphrasius** (Eufrazijeva basilika; daily 7.30am–8pm; free), situated in the centre of the town just off Eufrazijeva. This sixth-century Byzantine basilica has incandescent mosaics that are comparable with the celebrated examples at Ravenna, and is actually the centre of a religious complex originally created by Bishop Euphrasius between 535 and 550, which includes a bishop's palace, atrium, baptistry and campanile. Entry is through the **atrium**, an arcaded courtyard whose walls incorporate ancient bits of masonry, although it was heavily restored in the last century.

The basilica was the last in a series of late-Roman and early-Byzantine churches built on this spot, the remains of which are still in evidence. Surviving stonework from the first, the **Oratory of St Maur** (named after the saint who

△ Mosaics in the Basilica of St Euphrasius, Poreč

is said to have lived in a house on the site), can be seen on the north side of the basilica. This was a secret place of worship when Christianity was still an underground religion, and fragments of mosaic show the sign of the fish, a clandestine Christian symbol of the time. Inside the basilica, the mosaic floor of a later, less secretive church has been carefully revealed through gaps in the existing floor. The present-day basilica is a rather bare structure: everything focuses on the apse, with its superb late thirteenth-century ciborium and, behind this, the **mosaics**, which have a Byzantine solemnity quite different from the geometric late Roman designs. They're studded with semi-precious gems, encrusted with mother-of-pearl and punctuated throughout by Euphrasius' personal monogram – he was, it's said, a notoriously vain man. The central part of the composition shows the Virgin enthroned with Child, flanked by St Maur, a worldly-looking Euphrasius holding a model of his church and, next to him, his brother. Underneath are scenes of the Annunciation and Visitation, the latter surprisingly realistic, with the imaginative addition of a doltish, eavesdropping servant.

On the far side of the atrium, roughly opposite the basilica's main entrance, the octagonal **Baptistry** (baptisterijum) is bare inside save for the entrance to the campanile, which you can ascend for views of Poreč's red-brown roof tiles (daily 10am–7pm; 10Kn). On the north side of the atrium is the **Bishop's Palace** (same times and price), a seventeenth-century building harbouring a fascinating selection of mosaic fragments which once adorned the basilica floor, and an exquisite collection of Baroque altarpieces. In summer, classical concerts are held weekly inside the atrium; tickets (30–40Kn) can be bought at most agencies in town.

The rest of town

After you've seen the basilica, the rest of Poreč can seem rather a let down, though it's a pleasant enough place to stroll around, with a handful of buildings to aim for, many of them spread along Dekumanska. Just off its northern end stands a **Venetian tower** from 1448, now used as a venue for art exhibitions. Just off Dekumanska at Glavinića 4, **Aquarium Poreč** (daily: June–Sept 9am–midnight; May & Oct 10am–11pm; Nov–April 10am–5pm; 25Kn) is billed as one of Istria's major attractions but is really rather modest, consisting of a short fish-tank-lined corridor leading to a gift shop. It's a colourful, relaxing place nevertheless, and gives you a chance to study living examples of the creatures you might be eating later in the evening.

Continuing south along Dekumanska, you come to the **District Museum** at no. 9 (Zavičajni muzej; May–Sept Mon–Sat 10am–1pm & 6–9pm, Sun 10am–1pm; Oct–April Mon–Fri 10am–1pm; 10Kn), housed in the handsome Baroque Sinčić palace. It displays archeological finds (mainly Greek and Roman) from the surrounding area, including various Roman tombstones, one of which depicts a patrician standing at the base of an olive tree – local olives were famed throughout Italy during antiquity. Upstairs, rooms are decorated with portraits of the family of Rinaldi Carli – Venetian ambassador to Constantinople in the late 1600s – dressed in Ottoman garb. Walk south towards the end of the peninsula and you'll find the distinctive thirteenth-century building with an unusual projecting wooden balcony known as the **Romanesque House** (Romanička kuća), which is now another venue for art shows (mid-June to mid-Sept daily 10am–noon & 8–10pm; free). Just beyond here, **Trg Marafor** occupies the site of the Roman forum and still contains remains of temples to Mars and Neptune – little is known about these, and they're now not much more than heaps of rubble.

The **beaches** around the old town, such as they are, are generally crowded and unpleasant, and it's better to take a boat from the harbour (every 15–30min; 15Kn) to the island of **Sveti Nikola**, though this too gets busy with sunbathers from its pricey *Fortuna* hotel. Alternatively, staying on the mainland, walk south beyond the marina, where pathways head along a rocky coastline shaded by gnarled pines to reach several rocky coves; you'll eventually end up at Zelena Laguna, where there are concreted bathing areas.

The Baredine Cave

One of the most popular excursions from Poreč is to the **Baredine Cave** (Jama Baredine; daily: July & Aug 9.30am–6pm; May, June & Sept 10am–5pm; April & Oct 10.30am–3.30pm; 45Kn; Ⓦ www.istra.com/baredine), a series of limestone caverns 7km northeast of town just off the road to **Višnjan** – it's well signed if you're driving. During a forty-minute tour, guides will lead you through five exquisite chambers of dangling stalactites and limestone curtains, and will also delight in telling you the legend of thirteenth-century lovers Gabriel and Milka, who got lost down here and died looking for each other. You'll probably also get to see a couple of captive specimens of the *Proteus anguineus*, a kind of salamander which is indigenous to the karst caves of Croatia and Slovenia, and looks like a pale-bodied worm with legs.

Eating

There's a decent sprinkling of places to **eat** in the old town, and for picnic ingredients or self-catering supplies you can head for the **market** just off Trg J. Rakovca. We have included the telephone numbers of those establishments where it may be necessary to book a table at weekends.

Altercafé Zagrebačka. Welcoming café which has a much bigger range of croissants, sandwiches and pastries than the other places in town. Good place for breakfast or a mid-sightseeing snack.

Dvi Murve Vranići, 3km north of the old town (150Kn in a taxi) ⓣ052/434-115, Ⓦ www.dvimurve.hr. One of the most acclaimed restaurants on this stretch of the coast. Deliciously prepared top-quality seafood is served on a spacious terrace; try the fish carpaccio, black risotto with scampi or salt-baked sea bass, and for dessert their *Dvi Murve crepes* are a must. Reservations essential.

Istra corner of Obala maršala Tita and Bože Milanovića ⓣ052/434-636. This ever-popular place is the best in town for traditional Istrian fare, offering top-of-the-range seafood, including the local speciality *jastog sa rezancima* (lobster with pasta noodles), with meaty alternatives such as *svinjski but* (roast pork in a rich sauce) and cheaper lunchtime favourites like *fuži* and *maneštra* (Istrian bean soup). It's a good idea to reserve on summer weekends.

Peterokutna kula Dekumanova 1 ⓣ052/451-378. The most atmospheric restaurant in town, serving elegantly presented seafood inside an ancient gate tower, with grotto-like seating areas and a wonderful rooftop terrace.

Pizzeria Dali just off Zagrebačka at Istarskog razvoda 11. Good-quality oven-baked pizza, salads and pasta dishes.

Sveti Nikola Obala maršala Tita 23 ⓣ052/423-018. Award-winning seafood restaurant serving up quality fillets of Adriatic fish in a range of innovative sauces, accompanied by the finest Croatian wines. For a formal dining experience with first-class service, you need look no further.

Ulixes Dekumanova 2 ⓣ052/451-132. Across the street from *Peterokutna Kula*, this place serves up excellent local food, either in a stone-clad interior stacked with rustic implements, or on an outdoor terrace in a walled garden. There are several imaginative variations on the usual fish and shellfish themes, and the service is welcoming and friendly.

Drinking

Despite Poreč's status as a package paradise, the **drinking** scene remains remarkably old-fashioned, with a visit to one of the innumerable *slastičarnice* for ice cream and coffee providing the main source of after-dinner entertainment.

There's less in the way of characterful cafés and bars, and the town can appear disastrously dead by the end of August, when the high-spending peak-season crowd is replaced by visitors of more modest means.

When the weather's good, the café-bars on **Obala maršala Tita** are currently the fashionable places to hang out: *CD*, at the northern end of Obala maršala Tita, resembles an upmarket furniture showroom, with sundry comfy chairs, and even a bed, strewn around a quirkily decorated interior; while *Epoca*, to the south, is a brash and lively drinking temple with cocktails on the menu and DJs serving up pop-techno beats. Tucked in behind the museum at Sv. Maura 10, *Lapidarium* (July & Aug only) has a pleasant courtyard lined with ancient tombstones and a regular programme of live jazz. Otherwise, try *Torre Rotonda*, housed in a medieval tower on Obala maršala Tita, an atmospheric place with snug seating inside the tower wall, and a panoramic terrace on top. The best place to drink late, dance, and catch occasional live bands is *Colonia*, an open-air disco-bar set among pine trees, 1km east of the centre on the path to Plava Laguna.

Novigrad

Eighteen kilometres north of Poreč, and reached by regular bus from Porec, **NOVIGRAD** (in Italian, Cittanova) is another pleasant peninsula-bound place with a Venetian-style campanile spearing skywards from its town centre, although it has lost most of its old buildings apart from a few toothy sections of town wall. There are a couple of privately run hotels here with more character than the accommodation in Poreč, and the atmosphere is more laid-back all-round – this is one place on the west coast where you can safely wander the streets without being mobbed by hordes of ice cream-wielding promenaders. At the tip of the peninsula, the parish **Church of St Pelagius** (Crkva svetog Pelagija) was the seat of a bishop until the mid-nineteenth century, and still boasts a few luxuriant Baroque furnishings – notably the balustraded altar supporting a parade of porky cherubs. The crypt in which the bones of St Pelagius are kept is usually locked, but a grilled window provides glimpses of a vaulted eleventh-century ceiling supported by a cluster of stout columns. Behind the church, the **Lapidarium** (Muzej lapidarium; June–Sept daily 9am–8pm; 10Kn), houses beautifully carved stone fragments from the town's Romanesque churches in a modern pavilion. On the eastern side of the town centre, behind the marina, the **Gallerion** at Mlinska 1 (Tues–Sun 7–11pm; 20Kn) celebrates Novigrad's maritime history with an entertaining display of model ships and Habsburg-era naval uniforms. For **bathing**, the stretch of rock-and-concrete beach on the south side of town is outshone by the wonderful stretch of coastline to the north, where the rocky reefs backed by woods are more attractive and less crowded.

Practicalities

Novigrad's **bus station** is 500m short of the town centre, where you'll find a helpful **tourist office** on the north side of the peninsula at Porporella 1 (mid-June to mid-Sept daily 8am–9pm; May to mid-June & mid-Sept to end Sept daily 8am–8pm; Oct–April Mon–Sat 8am–3pm; ⓣ & ⓕ052/757-075, ⓦwww.istra.com/novigrad). There are plenty of **private rooms** (❶) and apartments (two-person studios ❷–❸, three- to four-person apartments 380–480Kn) in and around the centre: two accommodation agencies worth trying are Montak, in the bus station building at Murvi bb (ⓣ & ⓕ052/757-603, ⓦwww.montakso.com), and Novigradski dom, between the bus station and the centre at Vladimira

Nazora 19 (Ⓣ052/757-042). *Torci 18*, at Torci 34 (Ⓣ052/757-799, Ⓦwww.torci18.hr, Ⓦwww.nautico.hr; ④), is a family-run **pension** situated at the end of the peninsula behind the sea wall, offering prim en-suite rooms with TV and air-conditioning grouped around a central courtyard with a restaurant. *Cittar*, beside the entrance to the old town at Venecijanski prolaz bb (Ⓣ052/757-739, Ⓦwww.cittar.hr; ⑤), was one of the first privately owned **hotels** established in Croatia: the rooms come with tasteful decor and wooden floors, TV, minibar, air conditioning and en-suite bath. *Rotonda*, at Rotonda 1 (Ⓣ052/757-110, Ⓕ052/758-140; ⑥), is in a renovated old building right on the seafront, and boasts spacious rooms with sea vistas and a rooftop terrace. There's a big area of packagey hotels just southeast of town, alongside a big woodland **campsite** right by the beach, the *Sirena* (Ⓣ052/757-159, Ⓦwww.laguna-novigrad.hr).

Eating in Novigrad is generally first-rate, but comes at a price. The restaurant of the *Torci 18* does a decent range of meat and fish dishes, although *Mandrač*, on the harbour, is better, with quality seafood including grilled scallops (*jakopove kapice*) and dishes with lobster (*jastog*). Hidden away in the backstreets at Zidine 5, *Damir i Ornela* (booking essential; Ⓣ052/758-134; closed Mon) is something of a cult place to eat hereabouts, serving up simple, excellently prepared fish dishes, including some unique, sushi-influenced raw-fish recipes. *Vitriol* café-bar on the seafront at Ribarnička 6 is the best place for sunset-watching, while the trendy *Cubano* bar opposite *Hotel Cittar* serves cocktails and sells Cuban cigars.

Inland Istria

You don't need to travel away from the sea for long before the hotels and flash apartments give way to rustic villages of heavy grey-brown stone, many of them perched high on hillsides, a legacy of the times when a settlement's defensive position was more important than its access to cultivable land. The landscape is varied, with fields and vineyards squeezed between pine forests, orchards of oranges and olive groves. It's especially attractive in autumn, when the hillsides turn a dappled green and auburn, and the hill villages appear to hover eerily above the early morning mists.

Istria's hilltop settlements owe their appearance to the region's borderland status. Occupied since Neolithic times, they were fortified and refortified by successive generations, serving as strongholds on the shifting frontier between Venice and Hungary, or Christendom and the Ottoman Turks. They suffered serious depopulation in the last century, first as local Italians emigrated in the 1940s and 1950s, then as the rush for jobs on the coast began in the 1960s. Empty houses in these half-abandoned towns have been offered to painters, sculptors and musicians in an attempt to keep life going on the hilltops and stimulate tourism at the same time – hence the reinvention of Motovun and Grožnjan in particular as cultural centres.

Istria's administrative capital, **Pazin**, is the hub of the bus network and, although it's the least attractive of the inland towns, it's the nearest base for visiting the fifteenth-century frescoes in the nearby village of **Beram**. Of the hill settlements, **Motovun** and **Buzet** are accessible by bus from Pazin or Pula, but you'll need your own transport to make side-trips to the likes of **Grožnjan** and **Oprtalj**. The train line from Pula to Divača in Slovenia (where you change for Ljubljana or Zagreb) can be useful, stopping at Pazin before passing close to **Hum**, **Roč** and **Buzet**, although a certain amount of walking is required to get to the last three. To explore the region properly, renting a car is almost imperative since bus and train schedules are erratic and unreliable.

The mass-tourist industry is much less evident here than on the coast: there are hotels in Motovun, Istarske Toplice and Buzet, and an increasing amount of the cosy farmhouse accommodation that the area seems to be made for. However, the relatively unspoiled nature of inland Istria has made it a magnet for aspirant **second-home owners** – cries of "Istria: the new Tuscany" are beginning to reverberate around Europe, and real-estate prices have gone through the roof as a result.

Pazin and Beram

Lying in a fertile bowl bang in the middle of the Istrian peninsula, unassuming **PAZIN** is an unlikely regional capital. A relatively unindustrialized provincial town, it was chosen following World War II by Yugoslavia's new rulers, who were eager to establish an Istrian administration far away from the Italianate coastal towns – the choice of Pazin was a deliberate slap in the face for cosmopolitan Pula. Although fairly bland compared to Istria's other inland towns, Pazin does boast a couple of attractions, most notably its medieval castle and the limestone gorge below, and it's also a useful base from which to visit the renowned frescoes in the nearby church at **Beram**.

Arriving at Pazin's **train** and **bus** stations, it's a straightforward downhill walk along the tree-lined Šetalište Pazinske Gimnazije to the inoffensive, largely low-rise centre, beyond which rears the **castle** (*kaštel*), a stern ninth-century structure, remodelled many times since, and one of the main reasons why Pazin never fell to the Venetians. Inside, the **Istrian Ethnographic Museum** (Etnografski muzej Istre; mid–June to mid–Sept Tues–Sun 10am–6pm; mid–Sept to mid–June Tues–Thurs 10am–3pm, Fri noon–5pm, Sat & Sun 11am–5pm; 15Kn; Ⓦwww.emi.hr) has a fine collection of traditional Istrian costumes housed in atmospheric medieval galleries, along with a wide-ranging display of rural handicrafts and a mock-up of a kitchen featuring the traditional Istrian *kamin* (hearth), a fire laid on an open brick platform around which the cooking pots were arranged.

The castle overhangs the gorge of the River Fojba below, where a huge abyss sucks water into an underground waterway which resurfaces towards the coast. This chasm was supposed to have prompted Dante's description of the gateway to Hell in his *Inferno*, and inspired Jules Verne to propel one of his characters – Matthias Sandorf from the eponymous book, published in 1885 – over the side of the castle and into the pit. In the book, Sandorf manages to swim along the subterranean river until he reaches the coast – a feat probably destined to remain forever in the realms of fiction. Verne himself never came to Pazin, contenting himself with the pictures of the castle posted to him by the mayor. Back in the town centre, the plain exterior of **St Nicholas's Church** (Crkva svetog Nikole) conceals a thirteenth-century core; the sanctuary vaulting is filled with late fifteenth-century frescoes, mostly showing Old Testament scenes, although there's a fine depiction of a sword-wielding St Michael in the central panel.

Pazin's **tourist office**, just short of the castle at Franine i Jurine 14 (June–Sept Mon–Fri 9am–7pm, Sat & Sun 10am–1pm; Oct–May Mon–Fri 9am–3pm, Sat 10am–1pm; Ⓣ052/622-460, Ⓦwww.tzpazin.hr), provides town plans, maps of biking and hiking trails and information on central Istria; they can also help you find accommodation in private **rooms** (➊) in Pazin and around. Otherwise,

accommodation in Pazin is limited to the *Motel Lovac*, Šime Kurelića 4 (Ⓣ & Ⓕ052/624-324; ❸), just off the main road to Poreč at the western end of town, but within easy walking distance of the centre; it boasts simple rooms with shared or private bath, and a restaurant. For **food**, the *Fontana*, a few doors up from the tourist office at Franine i Jurine 6, is an unspectacular but cheap source of pizzas, sandwiches and other snacks. *Pod Lipom*, Trg Pod Lipom 2a (five minutes east of St Nicholas's church, along Muntriljska and behind the town bowling court), is a traditional restaurant popular with locals, with cheap lunch dishes like *maneštra* and *fuži* chalked up on a board, and a regular menu of more substantial meaty fare.

Pazin's tourist office acts as the nerve centre of the town's **Jules Verne Club**, which publishes a newsletter and organizes various events, including the annual Jules Verne Days in late June. You can become a member by "donating a book or any other cultural material connected to Jules Verne for the club collection" (information from the tourist office).

Beram

Six kilometres west of Pazin, just off the road to Poreč and Motovun, **BERAM** is an unspoilt hilltop village with moss-covered stone walls and some of the finest sacred art in the region. One kilometre northeast of the village is the **Chapel of Our Lady on the Rocks** (Crkvica svete Marije na škriljinah), a diminutive Gothic church with a set of frescoes dating from 1475, signed by local artist Vincent of Kastav. The key (*ključ*) to the chapel is kept by the Gortan family in the village. You can call them ahead at Ⓣ052/622-088, or ask at the tourist office in Pazin to ensure that there's someone waiting in Beram for you. It's polite to give a small sum of money to the keyholder in lieu of an entrance fee.

Of the many well-executed New Testament scenes which cover the chapel interior, two large **frescoes** stand out. The marvellous, eight-metre-long equestrian pageant of the *Adoration of the Kings* reveals a wealth of fine detail – distant ships, mountains, churches and wildlife – strongly reminiscent of early Flemish painting, while on the west wall a *Dance of Death* is illustrated with macabre clarity against a blood-red background: skeletons clasp scythes and blow trumpets, weaving in and out of a Chaucerian procession of citizens led by the pope. A rich merchant brings up the rear, greedily clinging to his possessions while indicating the money with which he hopes to buy his freedom.

Dvigrad and Svetvinčenat

Southwest of Pazin, the main road and rail routes to Pula forge across a mixed landscape of woodland, cornfields and Mediterranean scrub. While you're unlikely to want to spend the night in any of the places along the way, a couple of them merit a brief stop-off.

Twenty kilometres out of Pazin, the frumpy town of **Kanfanar** was founded in the mid-seventeenth century by refugees from nearby **DVIGRAD**, a walled city suddenly abandoned by citizens demoralized by an outbreak of plague and raids by Uskok pirates. To reach Dvigrad, head west out of Kanfanar along the road to Rovinj and turn right onto a well-signed minor road leading downhill to the ruins. A cluster of moody grey ruins surrounded by farmland and forest, Dvigrad is an atmospheric place, with its huge crown of jagged battlements guarded by two massive towers. A path curls round one side of the battlements, passes through a ruined gate and leads into the ancient city, its rough paving stones now overgrown with weeds. At its northern end looms the shell of a twelfth-century basilica, the **Church of St Sofia** (Crkva svete Sofije). The road on the western side of the fortress zigzags up the hillside, affording impressive views back towards the dramatic ruins.

Five kilometres southeast of Kanfanar, the tiny town of **SVETVINČENAT** (known in local dialect as "Savičenta") lies just off the main Pula-bound road and rail routes, but is well worth a detour if you're a fan of well-proportioned Mediterranean town squares. Svetvinčenat's is certainly among the most attractive in Istria, watched over by the trefoil Renaissance facade of the **Church of the Assumption** (Crkva navještenja), which harbours several Mannerist altar paintings by sixteenth-century Venetians. Off to the left, the **castle** of the Grimani family, which dates back to the thirteenth century, sports a spacious courtyard (claimed to be the site of a witch burning in 1632, of a village woman who supposedly had a love affair with one of the Grimani family) where summer concerts are held, and a pair of grizzled-looking towers. An eighteenth-century town hall and loggia complete the ensemble.

Gračišće and around

Much quieter than the main road from Pazin, the road southeast towards **Labin** passes through rolling, vineyard-covered hills and a succession of quiet hill villages. The fortified settlement of **GRAČIŠĆE**, 6km out of Pazin, is the most interesting of these, its main gate leading through to a knot of atmospheric gravelly streets, crumbling grey houses and five churches. Just inside the gate is the porticoed **Church of St Mary-on-the-Square** (Crkva svete Marije na placu), whose fifteenth-century frescoes are usually visible through grilled windows even when the door is locked. The centrepiece is a stunning Adoration, in which mounted figures in medieval garb are greeted by a radiant Madonna and Child. The impressive Venetian-style building behind the church is the **Solomon Palace**, sporting a trio of Gothic windows; at one point, it used to be the summer palace of the bishops of Pićan, a now-insignificant village 3km down the road, which was an important ecclesiastical centre in the Middle Ages (quite why Pićan's bishops chose to spend their summer holidays here remains a mystery). On the other side of the village, the terrace behind the Baroque parish church provides terrific views of the surrounding countryside, with the western flanks of Mount Učka presiding over a landscape of sandy hills and mixed evergreen and deciduous forest. The **St Simeon's hiking trail** (10km), which starts just outside the town walls, takes you on a three-hour wander around the countryside, passing through quaint villages and fields of wild asparagus and strawberries.

Practicalities

The only **place to stay** in Gračišće is *Poli Luce*, a delightful **B&B** immediately as you enter through the town gate (Ⓣ052/687-081, Ⓦwww.konoba-marino-gracisce.hr; ❸). Set in a restored stone house with plenty of original detail, it has four comfortable en-suite rooms with tasteful rustic furniture. Next to it, *Konoba Marino* (closed Wed), owned by the same people, serves excellent home-made Istrian **food** including *maneštra* (chunky soup), homemade pasta, game dishes and tender chops of smoked pork loin.

If you don't want to stay in Gračišće itself, *Dol*, 15km east of the settlement at Gologorički Dol 6 (Ⓣ052/684-625; ❸), offers a series of cosy en-suite rooms, each with wooden floors and ceiling beams, and a balcony overlooking the farmyard. There's a restaurant serving up Istrian staples (most of what you eat here will come from the owner's farm), a mini-waterfall in the grounds, and the surrounding area is great for walks. Getting to **Gologorički Dol** can be a tricky business, however: either head southeast from Gračišće, turn left at **Zajci**, and head north for 5km; or double back to Pazin, make for Cerovlje, and head east through Gologorica.

Motovun

Fifteen kilometres northwest of Pazin is perhaps the most famous of the Istrian hill towns, **MOTOVUN** (in Italian, Montona), an unwieldy clump of houses straddling a green wooded hill, high above a patchwork of wheatfields and vineyards. The place has a genuine medieval charm, exuding a tranquil nobility unequalled in Istria. Like so many towns in Istria, Motovun was predominantly Italian-speaking until the 1940s (when racing driver Mario Andretti was born here), after which most of the inhabitants left for Italy. The problem of depopulation was partly solved by turning Motovun into an artists' colony – the godfather of Croatian naive art, Krsto Hegedušić, was one of the first painters to move here in the 1960s – and several studios and craft shops open their doors to tourists over the summer.

The Town

The main road from Pazin passes through **Kanal**, Motovun's modern valley-bottom suburb. From here a secondary road zigzags its way up towards the old town, eventually passing through two gates which breach the town's surviving walls. The first of the gates has a display of stone reliefs of Venetian lions inside the arch, while the second, 100m beyond, leads directly out onto a main square fronted by the Renaissance **St Stephen's Church** (Crkva svetog Stjepana), topped by a campanile whose crenellated top looks like a row of jagged teeth. Above the main altar, the eighteenth-century Venetian painting of the Last Supper is full of touching detail – note the dog under the table waiting for scraps. Motovun's water supply used to be kept in a vast tank beneath the square, hence the medieval well in front of the church bearing a relief of the town's skyline with its five towers. At the far end of the square, a path leads to a promenade around the town battlements made up of two concentric walls with a tiny moat (nowadays dry) in between. From here there are fantastic views over the Mirna valley and surrounding countryside, which produces some of the finest Istrian wines – Teran and Malvazija are among the better known.

The Motovun Film Festival

All accommodation in the entire region is likely to be booked solid during the **Motovun Film Festival** (ⓦwww.motovunfilmfestival.com), which usually straddles a long weekend at the end of July or beginning of August. Since its inception in 1999 the festival has established itself as Croatia's premier cinematic event, with feature films (European art-house movies for the most part) premiered on an open-air screen in the main town square. A healthy mixture of Croatian and international actors and directors attend, and awards in the shape of an aeroplane propeller are presented for the best films. Featuring a minimum of segregation between stars and public, the festival is also one of the key social events of the summer, with thousands of celebrants ascending Motovun's hill – most are here to enjoy the 24-hour party atmosphere rather than the films. Box offices at the entrance to the old town sell tickets to the screenings.

Practicalities

Buses to Motovun from Pazin and from Pula to Buzet pick up and drop off in Kanal, at the foot of Motovun's hill. There's a large car park in Kanal, and more limited parking facilities farther up towards the old town. Allow about 25 minutes to walk up to the old town from Kanal (slightly less on the way down). Montonatours, at Kanal 10 (Ⓣ052/681-970, Ⓦwww.montonatours.com), have **private rooms** (❶–❷) in and around Motovun, and can book you into B&B-style accommodation (❹) up in the old town. Also in the old town, the *Kaštel* **hotel** on the main square (Ⓣ052/681-735 or 681-607, Ⓦwww.hotel-kastel-motovun.hr; ❹) is housed in a building of medieval origins but offers thoroughly modernized en-suite rooms with TV and dial-up connection, and a generous buffet breakfast. For **eating**, one place not to miss is *Konoba Barbacan* (closed Mon & Tues), right outside the entrance to the old town. This tiny – and pricey – restaurant with a pleasant interior and an outdoor patio dishes up beautifully presented Istrian dishes with a nouvelle cuisine twist, with truffles served in all shapes and forms. *Pod Voltom* (closed Wed), inside the walls of the town gate below the hotel, is similarly truffle-minded, offering pasta, game dishes and steaks flavoured with the local fungus. Two kilometres north of town in the village of Livade, *Zigante* at Livade 7 (Ⓣ052/664-302, Ⓦwww.zigantetartufi.com) offers a plush, upmarket take on the whole truffle experience, with truffle-garnished steak, rabbit and duck dishes – accompanied by the best local wines – served up by smart and attentive waiting staff in a refined, starched-napkin environment. Back in Motovun, the best places to **drink** are *Antico*, which occupies a pleasant old-town courtyard just behind the parish church, and *Montona Gallery*, between the two main town gates, whose terrace comes with panoramic views of the surrounding hills.

Oprtalj

Immediately north of Motovun the road reaches the Mirna valley and a major crossroads: the right fork heads east towards Buzet; the left fork makes for Buje and the coast. Straight on, a minor road runs through the village of **Livade** before winding steeply and tortuously through thick forest to **OPRTALJ** (in Italian, Portole), which straddles a grassy ridge high above the plain. As with Motovun, this village was off the map for many years, half of its houses in ruins and tufts of grass growing from the walls of the rest. In recent years, however, it's had a new lease of life; old houses are being bought up by wealthy Europeans, new restaurants are opening and more and more visitors are finding out about the place. Both the fifteenth-century **St Mary's Church** (Crkva svete Marije) in the village centre, and the sixteenth-century **Chapel of St Rock** (Crkvica svetog Roka) at the entrance to town have some interesting fresco fragments you can glimpse through the windows; otherwise the nicest way to spend your time here is simply to wander, taking time out for a quiet drink in the *Café Volta* near the town gate – which also has a couple of pleasant **rooms** (Ⓣ052/644-216, Ⓕ052/664-010, Ⓔklaudio.ipsa@pu.t-com.hr; ❸) in a house nearby. For **eating**, *Konoba Oprtalj*, a few doors down from Café Volta, serves pasta dishes, sausages and pork chops in a folksy wood-beamed interior.

Grožnjan

Eight kilometres west of the Mirna valley crossroads, a side road darts up towards **GROŽNJAN** (Grisignana in Italian), another hill village which was given a new lease of life when many of its abandoned properties were offered to artists and musicians as studios. There's also a summer school for young musicians, the Jeunesses Musicales Croatia (Hrvatska glazbena mladež), many of whom take part in outdoor concerts organized as part of the **Grožnjan Musical Summer** (Grožnjansko glazbeno ljeto; Ⓦwww.hgm.hr), which takes place every August. Indeed high summer is the best time to come, when most of the artists are actually in residence and a smattering of galleries and gift shops open their doors. Outside this time, Grožnjan can be exceedingly quiet, but it's an undeniably attractive spot, with its jumble of shuttered houses made from rough-hewn, honey-brown stone, covered in creeping plants. Standing at the centre of the town is the **Church of St Vitus and St Modestus** (Crkva svetog Vida i Modesta), a largely unadorned eighteenth-century affair which harbours a much older pair of choir stalls, each carved with exuberant floral squiggles, and a lively modern altar painting of martyrs Vitus and Modestus being thrown to a collection of snarling felines. Slightly downhill from here, the graceful arches of a Renaissance **loggia** form one side of a tiny, gently sloping square, which looks out on what used to be the main town gate. Nearby battlements command superb views of the surrounding countryside, with Motovun perched on its hilltop to the southeast, and the ridge of Mount Učka dominating the horizon beyond it.

Practicalities

Unless you have your own **transport**, Grožnjan is difficult to get to: catching a Buzet–Buje bus as far as the hamlet of Bijele Zemlje, then walking uphill to Grožnjan via a signed minor road (3km), is your best bet. The seasonal **tourist office** inside the town hall at U. Gorjan 3 (May–Sept Mon 9am–12.30pm, Tues–Sun 9am–12.30pm & 4–7pm; Ⓣ052/776-131, Ⓦwww.groznjan-grisignana.hr) can help you find private accommodation. Should you wish to **stay** in the village, the Černac family, right in the centre at V. Gortan 5 (Ⓣ052/776-122; ❸), offers a clutch of rustically decorated rooms and apartments, and also sells homemade olive oil, wine and *rakija*. For **eating**, head to the chestnut-tree-shaded main square where you'll find two restaurants, the bustling upscale *Bastia* and the more down-to-earth *Pintur* (closed Mon), both serving traditional Istrian dishes. *Art Café*, just east of the church, is a chic place for a **drink**, its terrace offering expansive views down the valley.

Buje

Proceeding northwest from Grožnjan towards the Slovene border, you'll pass through the much larger town of **BUJE** (in Italian, Buie), its old quarter piled up on a hill with patches of newer development below. Buje was known as the "spy of Istria" for its hilltop site, and still commands an invigorating panorama, the cobbled streets looking out over fertile fields to the distant sea. The town ramparts, dating from the fifteenth to the seventeenth centuries, enclose a warren-like medieval centre which spreads uphill from the main road. Just down from the old town gate, the **Ethnographic Museum** (Etnografska zbirka; mid-June to mid-Sept Tues–Sun 9am–noon & 5–8pm; 5Kn) displays a musty collection of kitchen utensils, wine presses and hand-operated looms. Roughly opposite, the **Church of the Madonna of Mercy** (Crkva majke milosrđa) contains a fine collection of Baroque paintings, including a series of eight bible scenes by eighteenth-century Venetian painter Gasparo della Vecchia. From here, alleyways wind uphill to the parish **Church of St Servolo** (Crkva svetog Cervula), built in the sixteenth century on the site of a Roman temple – bits of salvaged Roman masonry can still be seen poking out of the church's unfinished facade.

Buje stands at the centre of an important vine-growing area, the harvest of which is celebrated during the **Grape Festival** (Praznik grožđa), when parades, open-air concerts and wine-guzzling span the third weekend in September.

Practicalities

Buses pick up and drop off at the main crossroads through town, a few steps away from the **tourist office** at Istarska 2 (mid-June to mid-Sept Mon–Sat 8am–9pm, Sun 8am–2pm; mid-Sept to mid-June Mon–Fri 8am–3pm; ⓣ052/773-353, ⓦwww.tzg-buje.hr). There's no **accommodation** in Buje itself, although *Volpia*, 3km northwest of town just off the road to Portorož (follow signs to Slovenia and take the turn-off for the village of Volpija; ⓣ052/777-425, ⓦwww.agriturizam-volpia.com; ❹), is one of the best rural hotels in the region. In a newly renovated stone house, it offers a supremely restful ambience, with sixteen rooms decorated in contemporary rustic style: spanking new wooden floors, chunky furniture and spacious bathrooms.

For **eating**, *Konoba Oliva*, just off Buje's main street on Via Giuseppe Verdi 9, is a good place to sample local pasta dishes and fresh seafood on a shaded terrace, but otherwise the best options are out of town. The restaurant at the *Volpia* prides itself on its traditional meat and fish recipes (you get a ten percent discount on meals if you stay here), while the village of **Brtonigla**, 5km southwest of Buje, boasts two outstanding restaurants: *Konoba Astarea*, at Ronkova 6 (open weekends only & closed July & Aug; ⓣ052/774-384), serves up some of the tastiest food in Istria, with meats prepared under a *peka* (a metal lid covered with embers); while the classy, upmarket *San Rocco*, Srednja ulica 2 (ⓣ052/725-000, ⓦwww.san-rocco.hr), offers impeccably prepared and served game, fish and truffle dishes. Prices in both places are higher than average, but well worth it.

Buzet, Roč, Hum and around

East of Motovun, the road to Buzet follows the course of the Mirna valley as it gradually narrows, running between wooded crags. Roughly midway between Motovun and Buzet, the small settlement of **ISTARSKE TOPLICE** is a spa centre of long standing, its sulphurous waters famous for alleviating back problems, rheumatism and skin complaints. The local **hotel**, the *Mirna* (ⓣ052/603-410, ⓦwww.istarske-toplice.hr; ❸), has smallish rooms with bath and TV, and an indoor swimming pool fed by the local springwater, that emerges ready warmed from the nearby cliffs at a temperature of 35°C.

Buzet

From Istarske Toplice it's only 10km northeast to **BUZET**, the second-largest town in the Istrian interior, whose original old hilltop settlement quietly decays on the heights above the Mirna River, while the bulk of the population lives in the new town below. Though it's not as pretty as Motovun or Grožnjan, Buzet has more **accommodation** and is a good base from which to explore the region. The town's importance as a truffle-hunting centre is celebrated by the **Buzetska Subotina** festival ("Buzet Saturday"; usually the second weekend of September), when an enormous truffle omelette is cooked on the main square and shared out among thousands of visitors, and local pop-rock bands play on a pair of outdoor stages in the town centre. The following day, locals dress up in traditional nineteenth-century clothes for a

Truffles: Istria's gold

The woods around Motovun and Buzet are one of Europe's prime hunting grounds for the **truffle** (*tartuf*), a subterranean fungus whose delicate taste – part nutty, part mushroomy, part sweaty sock – have made it a highly prized delicacy among the foodie fraternity. Truffles (which look like small tubers) tend to overpower whatever other ingredients they're mixed with, and so are used very sparingly in cooking – either grated over a freshly cooked dish, or used to give a defining flavour to a sauce.

The truffle-hunting season begins in late September and carries on through the autumn, with locals and their specially trained dogs heading off into the Istrian fog to sniff out the fungus. During this period most of the region's **restaurants** will have at least one truffle-based recipe on the menu, even if only a simple truffle-and-pasta dish or a truffle *fritaja* (omelette). Truffle dishes offered outside this period will most probably use preserved (rather than fresh) truffles – definitely worth trying, but not quite as mouthwatering as the just-unearthed variety.

To mark the start of the season, **Truffle Days** (Dani Tartufa) are organized in various places in the Motovun/Buzet region throughout September; these might involve truffle-tasting events, live music, or just lots of good-natured drinking. Best known of these fungus-fixated fiestas is the **Buzetska Subotina** ("Buzet Saturday"), when an enormous truffle omelette is fried up on the main square and then scoffed by an army of hungry celebrants (see oppostie). You can **buy truffles** and truffle-based products throughout the year in the specialist shops run by Zigante (wwww.zigantetartufi.com), who have outlets at J.B. Tita 12, Buje; Trg Fontana, Buzet; Livade 7, Livade; and Smareglina 7, Pula.

folkloric fiesta in the old town – the tourist office will have details. Another local speciality is *biska*, a mistletoe-flavoured brandy available in local hostelries; it can also be bought direct, along with other herbal firewaters, from Eliksir (Mon–Sat 11am–2pm, Sun 11am–1pm; ⓣ052/662-750), Vidaci 25, 3km out of town on the road to Cerovlje.

Old Buzet's cobbled streets and ruined buildings seem a world away from the largely concrete new quarter down on the valley floor. Standing on one of the old quarter's tiny squares, the **Town Museum** (Gradski muzej; Mon–Fri 12.30–3.30pm; 5Kn) has a small collection of Roman gravestones and a display of folk costumes; it's particularly strong on the functional wool and hemp garments worn by the hardy villagers of the **Ćićarija**, the ridge to the east which separates Istria from Slovenia. A plaque affixed to a nearby wall commemorates Stipan Konzul Istranin, a sixteenth-century Croatian writer active in the Reformation in Germany, and the first person to translate the New Testament into Croatian. An archway on the eastern side of the old town leads through to what remains of Buzet's medieval ramparts, from where there's an expansive view of the Mirna valley below, and east over lush green hills to the imposing grey ridge of the Ćićarija.

Practicalities

Buses arrive at the eastern end of the new town, while the train station can be found 2km uphill to the northeast. The **tourist office**, located on the new town's main square at Trg fontana 7/1 (Mon–Fri 8am–3pm, Sat 9am–2pm; ⓣ & ⓕ052/662-343, ⓦwww.buzet.hr), has information on private rooms (❶), most of which are in out-of-town farmhouses.

The *Fontana* **hotel**, Trg fontana 1 (ⓣ & ⓕ052/662-615, ⓔhotelfontana@pu.t-com.hr; ❸), is a plain but tolerable concrete place whose en-suite rooms come with worn furnishings and Croatian-only TV; the smaller *Sun Sport Motel* (Ⓣ052/663-140, Ⓕ662-138; ❸), on the corner of Sportska and Riječka, offers cosier, brighter, more modern en-suite rooms, although the ground-floor café can be noisy at weekends. Farther afield, *Volte*, 5km out of town on the Cerovlje road at Kozari bb (Ⓣ052/665-210 or 098 420 126, Ⓔbranko.golojka@ri.t-com.hr; ❸), offers a handful of homely rooms (three with en-suite facilities, two with shared) in a family house surrounded by wooded hills – there's an excellent restaurant on site.

For **eating**, most local foodies head up to the *Toklarija*, 5km south of town in **Sovinjsko polje** (see p.218). In Buzet, *Stara Oštarija*, in the old town at Petra Flega 5 (Ⓣ052/694-003; closed Tues), serves up local pasta dishes and steaks (most with the option of truffle-flavoured sauces) in a semi-formal ambience; an enclosed terrace gives good views of modern Buzet down below. More homely in style is *Paladin* (closed Sun), just northeast of the new town in the village suburb of Naselje Franječići, which serves up excellent pasta dishes garnished with seasonal goodies (such as asparagus, mushrooms and the ubiquitous truffle), alongside local sausages and pork chops. The liveliest place in town for a **drink** is *Club 190*, an unintentionally retro disco-bar boasting mirrored walls, mirrored ceilings, mirrored pillars and mirrored balls.

Roč

About 10km east of Buzet, framed against the backdrop of the limestone wall of the Ćićarija, the dainty village of **ROČ** sits snugly behind sixteenth-century walls so low that the place looks more like a child's sandcastle than an erstwhile medieval strongpoint. Roč has a strong **folk music** tradition, with performing skills passed down from one generation to the next, and almost the entire population is involved in some capacity or other with the local folk music society, **Istarski željezničar** ("Istrian railwayman"), which has a brass section, male and female choirs and an accordion band. Most members of the last are devoted exponents of the Trieština, an archaic form of accordion which features push-buttons instead of a keyboard, and is rarely found outside Istria and northeastern Italy. The best time to catch them is during the **international accordion festival** (Z armoniku v Roč), which takes place on the second weekend in May: the tourist office in Buzet will have details.

With their neat rows of sturdy stone farmhouses, the narrow lanes of Roč provide a wonderful environment in which to savour the rustic atmosphere of eastern Istria. There's a small display of **Roman tombstones** inside the arch of the main gate into town, and the Romanesque **St Barthol's Church** (Crkva svetog Bartula) in the centre, an ancient, barn-like structure lurking behind an enormous chestnut tree and sporting an unusually asymmetrical bell tower.

Practicalities

Buzet–Rijeka **buses** will drop you off at the Roč turn-off 500m from the village, while the **train** station (on the Pula–Buzet line) is about 1500m east of the village. If you fancy staying, *Drago Cerovac at* Roč 58 (Ⓣ052/666-481; ❷ including breakfast) has a handful of small, simply furnished rooms with WC and shower in the hallway – he also rents bikes (100Kn/day). *Marina Paladin*, Roč 30 (Ⓣ052/666-716; doubles ❶, triples 350Kn), has a couple of cramped rooms sleeping two or three, as well as a three-bedroom stone house that can be rented as a whole for 750Kn. Also in the centre of the village, *Boris Grželj* (Ⓣ052/662-112 or 091 517 7862) has a couple of swish self-catering apartments featuring a mixture of rustic and contemporary furnishings (four-person 500Kn, six-person

Croatian Cuisine

As you might expect from a country that touches on Mediterranean, central European and Balkan cultures, Croatian cuisine is a diverse mixture of mouth-watering culinary influences. The sinuous Adriatic coastline is justly famous for its seafood, and fish, shellfish, squid and octopus form the backbone of most restaurant menus. Locally sourced olive oil, fresh herbs, fruit and wine add to the authenticity of the eating-out experience. Inland, a solid central European diet of pork cutlets, poultry and cheesy strudels is the order of the day, while the grilled-meat snacks common to Balkan Europe retain a powerful presence in the street-food scene.

▲ Restaurant in Dubrovnik

▲ Split fish market

Seafood

The Adriatic sea offers up an endless variety of seafood, although cooking methods are kept simple. Fish is lightly seasoned and then slapped on the grill, before being delivered to the table with head, tail, skin and skeleton still intact. Peeling the white meat from the bones is all part of the ritual. The more ambitious restaurants will feature one or two boiled- or baked-fish recipes, often featuring traditional sauces of white wine or capers. Whatever kind of fish you order, it is invariably accompanied by *blitva*, a mineral-rich, spinach-like vegetable indigenous to the coast.

One Adriatic staple that you'll find almost everywhere is squid (*lignje*), delicious whether fried in breadcrumbs or grilled. The squid on offer are usually small, succulent beasties, although you shouldn't be perturbed if a single huge white rubbery thing with dangling tentacles is delivered to your table. One ubiquitous lunchtime dish is *crni rižot* or "black risotto", in which chewy chunks of squid come bathed in the creature's black ink.

Peka

One essential element of any traditional Adriatic kitchen is the *peka*, a bell-shaped lid of metal or clay which is covered in hot embers and then left on the hearth to slow-cook for several hours. It's a particularly favoured method of preparing succulent, flavoursome lamb, although octopus is the main ingredient on many of the offshore islands. Owing to the relatively long preparation time, *peka*-prepared dishes can rarely be ordered on spec. It's a good idea to reserve several hours in advance and, if possible, go as a group – it's impractical for restaurants to prepare *peka* dishes for one or two diners at a time.

▼ A peka dish

Istria

Jutting into the northern Adriatic, the Istrian peninsula is a cornucopia of culinary riches, with the seafood of the coast melding with the hearty meat-based fare of central Europe. Regional delicacies include oysters (*oštrige*) from the Limski kanal, cured ham (*pršut*), wild asparagus (*šparoga*) and truffles (*tartufi*) from the hills inland. Istrian meats, such as *kobasice* (big, spicy sausages) and *ombolo* (smoked pork loin), are often cooked on the *kamin* or open hearth. *Fuži* (pasta twists) and *njoki* (gnocchi) are very much local staples, and are often freshly made by hand in the more traditional country inns. One Istrian concoction you should definitely try at least once is *supa*, an earthenware jug of red wine mulled with sugar, olive oil and pepper, served with a slice of toast for dipping purposes.

Slavonia

The most distinctive culinary region of inland Croatia is the eastern province of Slavonia, where fiery red paprikas have been an essential ingredient in local recipes ever since the Ottoman Turks introduced them in the sixteenth century. As in neighbouring, goulash-saturated Hungary, meat and vegetables are cooked slowly in a big pot to produce a range of red-hued stews. The trademark dish of the Croatian southeast is *fish paprikaš*, for which catfish, pike-perch and carp are cut into big chunks and thrown into a paprika-flavoured broth. True connoisseurs of fiery food should try *fiš perkelt*, a thicker, spicier cousin of *paprikaš*, invariably eaten with noodles smothered in delicious cheese and bacon sauce.

Island oddities

Many of Croatia's islands have preserved traditional foodstuffs that you'd be hard put to find anywhere else. Krk, in the northern Adriatic, is famous for its *šurlice*, the homemade macaroni-like twists which, liberally smothered in lamb goulash, make you feel as if you're tasting pasta for the first time. Culinary capital of southern Dalmatia is the island of Vis, which quite apart from offering some of the best seafood restaurants in the region, is also home to delicious snack-food stand-bys such as the *pogača od srdele*, a savoury cake filled with anchovies, onions and tomato paste. It's also the birthplace of the *viški hib*, a succulent slab of pressed figs which, cut into wafer-thin slices, goes down a treat with the local *rakija*. Undisputed mecca for sweet-toothed travellers is a tiny sweet shop on the island of Korčula named Cukarin, a cult destination whose uniquely addictive croissant-shaped, citrus-flavoured biscuits are best enjoyed dipped in a glass of *prosecco* wine.

▼ Dolac market, Zagreb

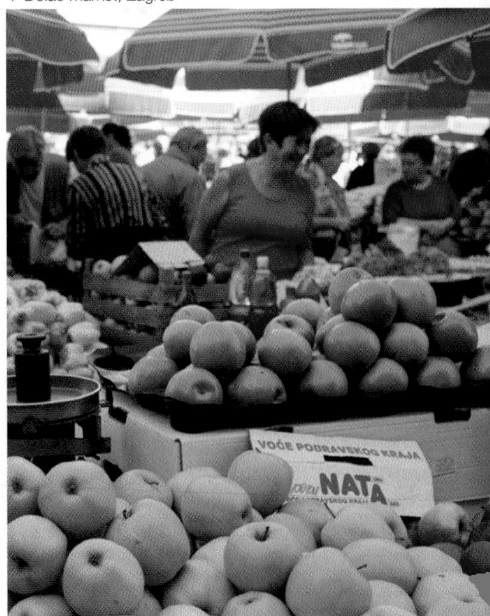

▲ Pršut

Pršut

Croatia's most celebrated hors d'oeuvre is *pršut*, home-cured ham served in thin, melt-in-the-mouth slices. *Pršut* is mainly produced in inland Istria and Dalmatia, where it's common for families to own a handful of pigs. The unlucky porkers are slaughtered in late autumn, and the hind legs from which *pršut* is made are laboriously washed, salted and flattened under rocks. They are then hung outside the house to be dried out by the *bura*, a cold, dry wind that sweeps down to the coast from inland Croatia. After that, the ham is hung indoors to mature, ready to be eaten the following summer. *Pršut* from Dalmatia is usually smoked at some stage during the maturing period, while that from Istria is left as it is, producing a significant difference in flavour between the two regions' produce.

1000Kn). For **food**, *Ročka konoba* (closed Mon) in the centre of the village is a good place for asparagus and truffles in season, as well as the regular repertoire of *ombolo*, *kobasice* and *fuži*.

If you've got your own transport, you can follow the road leading northwest out of Roč to get up onto the summit of the Ćićarija ridge (follow signs to the village of Nugla, pass through it, and keep going for about 3km). Crossing heathland covered in conifers and sub-alpine meadows, the road ends up at **Raspadalica**, a local beauty spot that serves as an ideal launch-pad for local hang-gliding enthusiasts, and offers fine views to everyone else – there's a superb panorama of the Mirna valley, with Buzet down below and the hill town of Motovun in the distance.

Hum

Just 7km east of Roč, a minor road leads south through rolling pastures towards the minuscule settlement of Hum. The road itself is known as the **Glagolitic Alley** (Aleja glagoljaša) after its series of open-air concrete sculptures by Želimir Janeš illustrating themes connected with Glagolitic (see box on p.226), an archaic form of Slavonic writing which was kept alive by priests in both Istria and the islands of the Kvarner Gulf before it finally succumbed to Latin script in the nineteenth century. Positioned by the roadside every kilometre or so, the sculptures mostly take the form of Glagolitic characters – seductively decorative forms that look like a cross between Cyrillic and Klingon.

Heaped up on a hill surrounded by grasslands and broken up by deciduous forest, **HUM** is the self-proclaimed "smallest town in the world", since it has preserved all the attributes – walls, gate, church, campanile – that a town is supposed to possess, despite its population having dwindled to a current total of just fourteen. Originally fortified by the Franks in the eleventh century, Hum was a relatively prosperous place under the Aquileian Patriarchs and the Venetians, and it still looks quite imposing as you pass through a town gate topped by a monumental, castellated bell tower. Beyond, the oversized, neo-Baroque **Church of the Blessed Virgin Mary** (Crkva blažene djevice Marije), built in 1802 as the last gasp of urban development in a shrinking town, lords it over a settlement which now amounts to two one-metre-wide streets paved with irregular, grassed-over cobbles and lined by chunky grey-brown farmhouses. One of the latter holds the **Aura Gallery-Museum** (Galerija-muzej Aura; April–Oct daily 11am–9pm; free), really just a gift-shop but an entertaining one nevertheless, offering Glagolitic characters modelled from clay or wood, and locally made honey, wine and *biska* brandy. Just outside the town walls, the Romanesque cemetery **Chapel of St Hieronymous** (Crkvica svetog Jeronima; get the key from *Humska Konoba*, see p.218) has a number of frescoes dating back to the late twelfth century, which display a melding of Romanesque and Byzantine styles typical of the northern Adriatic in the Middle Ages. As usual, the life of Jesus provides the subject matter: there's a fine *Annunciation* spanning the arch above the altar, together with a *Crucifixion*, *Pietà* and *Deposition* – the latter bordered by unusual rosettes and floral squiggles – on the walls. Most have been damaged by ancient, Glagolitic graffiti.

Practicalities

It's a bit awkward to reach Hum without your own transport. No buses venture this far, and Hum **train station** is 5km downhill just beyond the village of **Erkovčići**. The Grabar family at Hum 12 (Ⓣ052/660-004 or 091 575 7408, Ⓔdenis.grabar@inet.hr; ❶) have a couple of cosy doubles with shared facilities, and one self-catering apartment – the tourist office in Buzet (see p.215) will act as an intermediary if you can't get through to an English speaker. The small but charming *Humska Konoba* (May–Oct daily; Nov–April Sat & Sun only) serves good Istrian **food** on a cosy terrace with sweeping valley views; it gets crowded in summer.

Kotli

The half-abandoned hamlet of **KOTLI**, 2km northwest of Hum, has become something of a cult destination among summer bathers. It's here that the young River Mirna tumbles through a series of small depressions carved out of the smooth local limestone, creating a sequence of shallow, gurgling pools that some have compared to an open-air Jacuzzi – although low water levels often leave visitors wondering what all the fuss is about. Whether you're in swimming mood or not, it's a fine spot for a riverside ramble. On the far side of the river, Kotli itself is a moody clump of farmhouses and barns, half-hidden by runaway vegetation. One of the buildings has been refurbished and turned into a **café-restaurant**, *Kotlić* (open weekends only), which serves up excellent *maneštra* and other local staples on a shady terrace.

Reached by a minor road that leaves the Glagolitic Alley midway between Roč and Hum, Kotli can also be reached on foot from Buzet (2hr). The **footpath** starts on the south side of town, on the far side of the bridge over the River Mirna – the Buzet tourist office might give you a rough-and-ready hiking map for free.

Sovinjak, Sovinjsko Polje and Dragué

One of the most scenic routes heading out of Buzet is the one that climbs southwards to the hamlet of Svi Sveti (actually more of a road junction than a place), then follows a mountain ridge towards Cerovlje on the Pazin–Rijeka road. With the Mirna valley to the east and the Butoniga basin way down to the west, the ridge offers some of the best views of inland Istria's undulating landscape, with pudding-basin hills rising up above a patchwork of forests, vineyards, pumpkin patches and cornfields. To see this landscape at its best, consider a brief detour to the hilltop village of **SOVINJAK**, 6km west of Svi Sveti on a side road that loops back towards Istarske Toplice. There's not much there apart from a corral of ochre-and-brown houses drawn tightly around a dumpy-looking church, but it's an undeniably beautiful spot, its grassy ramparts looking out over the bottle-green woodland of the Buzet region, busy with truffle-hunters and their dogs during the autumn.

Two kilometres east of Sovinjak, the hamlet of **SOVINJSKO POLJE** is home to the *Toklarija* (reservations compulsory; ⓣ052/663-031; closed Tues), one of the nicest **restaurants** in Istria, if not the whole country. An atmospheric, intimate place housed in a venerable stone building with an oil press in the front room, it's famous for homemade pasta and seasonal local products – asparagus in spring, mushrooms and truffles in autumn – none of which comes cheap. A worthy alternative to the *Toklarija* is *Vrh* (ⓣ052/667-123; closed Mon), another 4km south in the village of **Vrh**, which serves up some of the best homemade *fuži* (fat scrolls of pasta stuffed with cheese, mushrooms and other goodies) anywhere in Istria, alongside plenty of pork and game dishes and some extraordinary herbal *rakijas* (*kopriva* – or nettle – being one particular favourite).

Returning to Svi Sveti and rejoining the southbound route to Cerovlje brings you after 10km to **DRAGUĆ**, a tiny village stranded among haystacks and cornfields on a thin finger of highland pointing west towards the lowlands of the Mirna basin. At the end of the finger, the fourteenth-century

Chapel of St Rock (Crkvica svetog Roka) contains frescoes similar to those in Beram, although slightly less well preserved – to get in, ask for the key (*ključ*) in the village square. There's a large *Journey of the Magi* on the left as you enter, with an *Annunciation* above it, and a *Martyrdom of St Sebastian* and *Flight into Egypt* on the right, all rendered in vivid greens and ruddy browns redolent of the surrounding countryside.

The east coast

Compared with the tourist complexes of the west, Istria's east coast is a quiet and undeveloped area with few obvious attractions. East of Pula, the main road to Rijeka heads inland, remaining at a discreet distance from the shoreline for the next 50km. Half an hour out of Pula the road passes through **BARBAN**, a grey, largely forgotten village overlooking Krapan Bay. Barban's only claim to fame is as the home of the annual **Tilting at the Ring** festival (Trka na prstenac; mid-Aug), which involves locals on horseback attempting to spear a ring on the end of a lance. A sporting contest which was widespread throughout the Mediterranean in the Middle Ages, it only survives in a few places – notably the Dalmatian town of Sinj.

From Barban, the road descends to cross the valley of Raška Draga before entering the village of **RAŠA**, formerly the southernmost outpost of the Labin coalfields before they were finally closed in 1999. Built by the Italians in 1937, Raša still has the feel of a model industrial settlement, with its rows of identical barrack-like houses softened by trailing vines. It also boasts a fine example of Mussolini-era architecture in **St Barbara's Church** (Crkva svete Barbare – Barbara being the patron saint of miners), an austere but graceful structure featuring a campanile in the shape of a pithead, and a curving facade representing an upturned coal barrow.

Labin

Five kilometres beyond Raša, **LABIN** is divided into two parts, with an original medieval town crowning the hill above, and a twentieth-century suburb, **Podlabin**, sprawling across the plain below. Labin was for many years Croatia's coal-mining capital, and earned itself a place in working-class history in 1921, when striking miners declared the "Labin Republic" before being pacified by the Italian authorities. There's precious little sign of mining heritage nowadays apart from the town museum and the one remaining pithead in Podlabin, the top of which still bears the word "Tito" proudly spelt out in wrought-iron letters. Subsidence caused by mining led to Labin's old town being partially abandoned in the 1970s and 1980s, although the subsequent decline of the coal industry, coupled with a thoroughgoing restoration programme, encouraged people to return. The offer of cheap studio space also encouraged artists to move to old Labin, and several ateliers and craft shops open their doors from April through to October. It's consequently one of the more attractive of Istria's hill towns – all the more so for its proximity to the beach at Rabac, only forty minutes' walk downhill.

The Town

Pula–Rijeka **buses** stop at the main bus station in Podlabin, from where you can pick up a local bus or walk uphill for twenty minutes to the main square of the

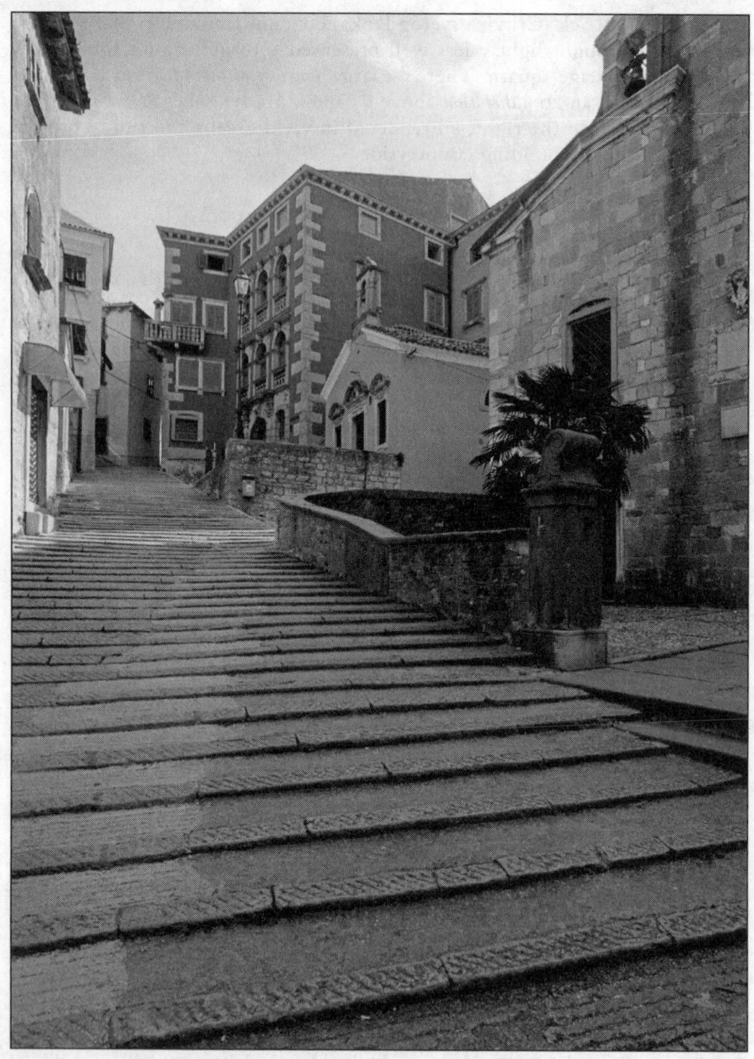

△ Labin

old town, **Titov trg**. From here, a rough cobbled path leads through the city gate into the heart of the old town, where steep alleys thread their way among a motley collection of town houses attractively decked out in ochres, oranges and pinks. Head up the old town's main street to find the **Church of the Birth of the Blessed Virgin Mary** (Crkva rođenja blažene djevice Marije); on its facade, a fourteenth-century rose window is upstaged by a seventeenth-century Venetian lion, and by a bust of patrician Antonio Bollari, who defended the town against Uskok pirates. The burgundy Batiala-Lazarini Palace next door now holds the **Town Museum** (Gradski muzej; June–Sept Mon–Fri 10am–1pm & 5–7pm, Sat

10am–1pm; Oct–May Mon–Fri 8am–2pm; 15Kn), with a small collection of Roman tombstones and a display of local costumes, including examples of the enormous woollen scarves which local women used to drape over their shoulders to cushion the load when carrying water or other heavy burdens. There's also a small but atmospheric re-creation of life inside a coal mine, which involves donning a (totally unnecessary) hard hat and embarking on a stooping walk between pit props. Directly opposite the museum, the **Municipal Art Gallery** (Gradska galerija; Mon–Fri 10am–3pm, Sat 10am–1pm; free) is the venue for interesting themed exhibitions during the summer.

From the gallery, continue up 1 Maja to reach the highest point of the hill, marking the western boundary of the old town. There's a viewing terrace here on the site of the (long demolished) medieval fortress, or **Fortica**, looking down towards Rabac on the coast, with the mountainous shape of Cres beyond. From here, you can descend the western flank of the old town's hill by walking down Guiseppine Martinuzzi, passing on the way the **Chapel of Our Lady of Carmel** (Crkvica Gospe od Karmene; mid-June to mid-Sept daily 10am–noon & 6–9pm; mid-Sept to mid-June Mon–Fri 10am–1pm), nowadays pressed into service as an art gallery hosting high-profile contemporary displays in the summer season. At the bottom of the street stands the eighteenth-century Franković Palace, which now holds the **Memorial Collection of Matthias Flacius Illyricus** (Spomen-zbirka M.F. Ilirika; same times as the Town Museum, but ask there first to check there will be someone in attendance; 10Kn), with books and manuscripts published by Matija Vlačić (1520–75), local Protestant and right-hand man to Martin Luther. One typical engraving of the time depicts the pope with the head of an ass, the torso of a woman and the legs of a dragon – the kind of image that would have pleased Vlačić's uncle and fellow reformist Baldo Lupetina, whose refusal to renounce his beliefs resulted in him being tied in a weighted sack and thrown into the Venetian lagoon.

Practicalities

Labin's **tourist office**, on Aldo Negri 20 (mid-May to mid-Oct Mon–Sat 8am–9pm, Sun 10am–1pm & 6–9pm; mid-Oct to mid-May Mon–Fri 7am–3pm; ⓣ052/855-560 or 852-399, ⓦwww.istra.com/rabac), can provide sundry brochures covering Labin and Rabac; there's also a seasonal information booth on Titov trg 10 in the old town. Veritas, down some steps from here at svete Katarine 8 (ⓣ052/885-007 or 855-974, ⓦwww.istra-veritas.hr), has **rooms** (❶) in and around the old town.

Of Labin's places to **eat**, *Velo Café*, Titov trg 10, fulfils the role of main-square café and prime lunching spot with considerable aplomb, and has a list of Istrian soups and pasta dishes chalked up on a board outside. *Kvarner*, just off the square below the town gate, offers a more tourist-oriented menu of grilled fish and steaks, although the outdoor terrace comes with good views towards the sea. The more expensive *Due Fratelli*, about 2km out of town on the road to Rabac at Montozi 6 (reservations advised at weekends; ⓣ052/853-577), offers top-notch fresh fish, which comes either grilled or oven-baked. For **drinking and nightlife**, there's a sprinkling of café-bars either on or just off Titov trg. Down in Podlabin, the buildings around the pithead have been transformed into the **Lamparna cultural centre**, which organizes gigs, raves, theatre and art exhibitions, and has a bar and Internet café. The Lamparna organizes the **Labin Art Republika festival** in July and August, when open-air performances, concerts and cultural events take place in the old town every Thursday and Friday evening.

Rabac

Buses run every two hours or so from the main bus station in Podlabin (passing through Titov trg in Labin) to the resort village of **RABAC**, squeezed into a narrow bay on the coast. You can also walk there in about forty minutes from Labin by heading along the Rabac road then taking the path which leads right into the woods just behind the Porta Tours tourist agency on the edge of town.

Initially developed by the Italians in the inter-war years as a workers' holiday settlement, Rabac nowadays has an almost totally modern appearance, its hillsides covered in apartment blocks and fringed by a line of hotels all run by the same company, Rabac Hotels (Ⓣ052/862-027, Ⓦwww.rabac-hotels.com). There's a reasonable shingle beach on the northern side of the bay, and the usual string of so-so bars and restaurants along the harbour, but all in all it's a bit too sanitized to compete with the west coast resorts. However, Rabac does get packed in early August with young hipsters who come down for the annual **Rabac Summer Festival** (Ⓦwww.rabacfestival.com), a weekend-long beach party with star DJs spinning techno and progressive house round the clock.

Should you want to **stay**, the four-star *Lanterna* hotel (Ⓣ052/862-220, Ⓔlanterna@rabac-hotels.com; ❼) is one of the best on this part of the coast. Somewhat cheaper **private rooms** (❶) are available from Veritas, back in Labin, or Kompas (June–Sept daily 8am–9pm; Ⓣ052/856-599, Ⓦwww.kompas-istra.com), on the southern side of the harbour. There's also the option of staying at the Oliva **campsite** (Ⓣ052/872-258, Ⓦwww.maslinicarabac.com), right on the beach and backed by attractive woodland.

Northeast of Labin

Northeast of Labin, the green edges of Istria drop steep and sheer into the sea, offering few viable places to build. Twelve kilometres out of Labin, the ancient and windswept hilltop settlement of **Plomin** is typical of the local villages – most of its inhabitants left for Italy in 1945, leaving the fishing port below to silt up; many of its old stone houses are now boarded up. Most Pula–Rijeka buses stop for a breather at the *Vidikovac* café 4km farther on, a popular viewpoint high above the rocky shore, with the grey outline of the island of **Cres** rising to the east. Cres is reachable by regular car ferry from the tiny port of **Brestova**, to which a side road descends a couple of kilometres farther on. Beyond Brestova, the road continues to twist and turn above the shore before descending towards Mošćenička Draga, the first in a string of resorts that make up the **Opatija Riviera**.

Travel details

Trains

Pazin to: Buzet (4 daily; 45min); Hum (8 daily; 20min); Pula (6 daily; 1hr); Roč (4 daily; 35min).
Pula to: Buzet (4 daily; 2hr); Hum (8 daily; 1hr 30min); Pazin (6 daily; 1hr); Rijeka (4 daily, bus connection from Lupoglav; 2hr); Roč (4 daily; 1hr 45min).

Buses

Buje to: Buzet (Mon–Sat 3 daily, Sun 2 daily; 1hr 30min); Novigrad (3 daily; 45min); Poreč (Mon–Sat 6 daily, Sun 2 daily; 1hr 30min); Pula (4 daily; 3hr); Rijeka (4 daily; 2hr 30min).
Buzet to: Buje (Mon–Sat 3 daily, Sun 2 daily; 1hr 30min); Motovun (Mon–Fri 1 daily; 45min); Pazin

(1 per week; 1hr 10min); Poreč (Mon–Fri 2 daily, Sat & Sun 1 daily; 2hr); Pula (Mon–Fri 2 daily, Sat & Sun 1 daily; 2hr 30min); Rijeka (Mon–Sat 7 daily, Sun 3 daily; 1hr 10min).
Novigrad to: Buje (3 daily; 45min); Buzet (2 daily; 2hr 15min); Poreč (7 daily; 30min); Pula (4 daily; 2hr 15min); Rijeka (4 daily; 4hr 30min); Rovinj (3 daily; 1hr 30min); Zagreb (4 daily; 5hr 30min).
Pazin to: Buzet (1 per week; 1hr 10min); Labin (1 daily; 1hr 10min); Motovun (July & Aug 1 daily, Sept–June 3 daily; 45min); Poreč (9 daily; 45min); Pula (Mon–Sat 8 daily, Sun 4 daily; 1hr); Rijeka (6 daily; 1hr); Rovinj (Mon–Fri 5 daily, Sat & Sun 1 daily; 40min); Zagreb (6 daily; 3hr 30min).
Poreč to: Buje (Mon–Sat 3 daily, Sun 2 daily; 1hr); Buzet (Mon–Fri 2 daily, Sat & Sun 1 daily; 1hr 30min); Lanterna (June–Sept; 5 daily; 30min); Novigrad (8 daily; 20min); Opatija (4 daily; 3hr 30min); Pazin (9 daily; 45min); Pula (12 daily; 1hr); Rijeka (12 daily; 2hr); Rovinj (8 daily; 1hr); Višnjan (9 daily; 15min); Vižinada (8 daily; 30min); Vrsar (12 daily; 15min); Zagreb (Mon–Fri 4 daily, Sat 1 daily; 5hr); Zelena Laguna (9 daily; 15min).
Pula to: Bale (hourly; 45min); Buje (5 daily; 2hr 40min); Buzet (Mon–Fri 2 daily; 2hr 30min); Dubrovnik (1 daily; 14hr); Fažana (Mon–Fri hourly, Sat 8 daily, Sun 6 daily; 30min); Istarske Toplice (2 daily; 2hr 15min); Karlovac (10 daily; 5hr); Labin (15 daily; 1hr); Novigrad (4 daily; 2hr 15min); Opatija (hourly; 2hr); Pazin (Mon–Sat 8 daily, Sun 4 daily; 1hr); Poreč (12 daily; 1hr 30min); Rijeka (hourly; 2hr 30min); Rovinj (hourly; 45min); Šibenik (4 daily; 9hr); Split (6 daily; 10hr); Svetvinčenat (5 daily; 45min); Varaždin (1 daily; 9hr); Vodnjan (hourly; 20min); Vrsar (1 daily; 1hr 30min); Zadar (3 daily; 6hr 30min); Zagreb (16 daily; 5hr 30min); Žminj (6 daily; 50min).
Rovinj to: Bale (Mon–Sat 12 daily, Sun 9 daily; 15min); Buje (2 daily; 1hr 30min); Buzet (1 daily; 2hr 15min); Dubrovnik (1 daily; 16hr); Kanfanar (Mon–Fri 8 daily, Sat & Sun 3 daily; 20min); Labin (5 daily; 2hr); Novigrad (3 daily; 1hr 30min); Pazin (Mon–Fri 5 daily, Sat 1 daily; 1hr); Poreč (Mon–Fri 4 daily, Sat 1 daily; 1hr); Pula (hourly; 45min); Rijeka (6 daily; 2–3hr); Split (1 daily; 11hr); Varaždin (1 daily; 7hr); Vrsar (4 daily; 30min); Zagreb (7 daily; 4–7hr).

Ferries

Brestova to: Porozina, Cres (hourly; 30min).
Pula to: Mali Lošinj (June–Sept 5 per week, Oct–May 1 per week; 3hr 20min); Silba (June–Sept 5 per week, Oct–May 1 per week; 5hr 20min); Zadar (June–Sept 5 per week, Oct–May 1 per week; 7hr 20min).

International catamarans

Pula to: Venice (mid-May to mid-Sept 1 per week; 3hr).
Poreč to: Trieste (mid-June to mid-Sept 1 per week; 1hr 15min); Venice (April 1 per week, May–June 3 per week, July & Aug 4 per week; 2hr 30min).
Rovinj to: Trieste (mid-June to mid-Sept 1 per week; 2hr 15min); Venice (April 1 per week, mid-May to mid-June 3 per week, mid-June to Aug 6 per week; 3hr 30min).

International trains

Pula to: Ljubljana (Mon–Fri 1 daily; 5hr 20min; change at Lupoglav; 1 daily direct train on Sat & Sun; 4hr 10min).

International buses

Buzet to: Koper (1 daily; 1hr 30min).
Novigrad to: Koper (1 daily; 2hr); Trieste (Mon–Sat 1 daily; 3hr).
Pazin to: Trieste (Mon–Sat 1 daily; 2hr 30min).
Poreč to: Koper (1 daily; 2hr 30min); Ljubljana (2 daily; 3hr); Munich (2 per week; 10hr); Piran (1 daily; 2hr); Portorož (1 daily; 1hr 50min); Trieste (4 daily; 2hr).
Pula to: Koper (1 daily; 3hr 30min); Milan (1 daily; 8hr 50min); Piran (1 daily; 3hr 30min); Portorož (1 daily; 3hr 20min); Trieste (4 daily; 3hr 30min); Venice (Mon–Sat 1 daily; 6hr).
Rovinj to: Koper (1 daily; 2hr 40min); Munich (1 per week; 11 hr); Padua (Mon–Sat 1 daily; 4hr 40min); Trieste (Mon–Sat 2 daily; 3hr); Venice (Mon–Sat 1 daily; 5hr).

The Kvarner Gulf

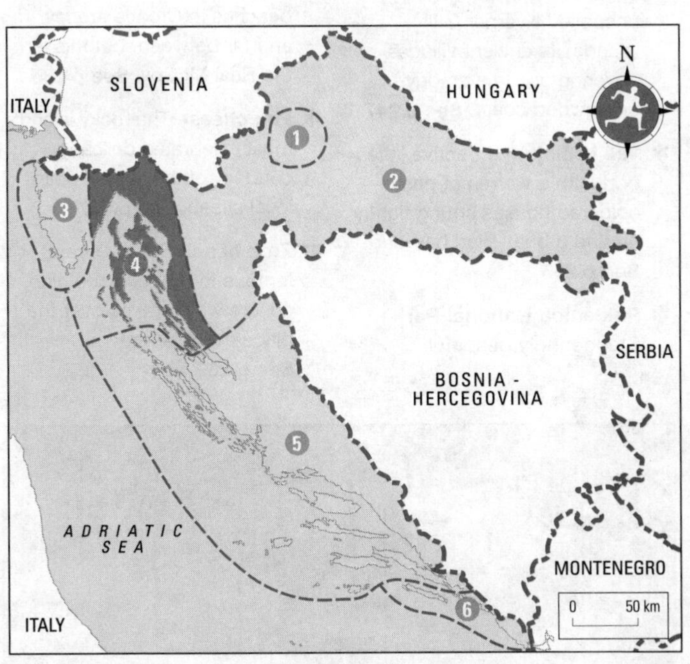

CHAPTER 4 Highlights

* **Eating in Opatija** This genteel seaside town boasts one of the finest collections of top-class seafood restaurants in the country. **See p.242**

* **Lovran** An Italianate, green-shuttered coastal town scattered with Habsburg-era villas. **See p.244**

* **Cres** One of the more unspoiled Kvarner Gulf islands, its ancient villages hovering above a craggy, uncrowded coast. **See p.247**

* **Veli Lošinj** An attractive little port with a warren of pastel-coloured houses strung tightly around a boat-filled harbour. **See p.255**

* **Paklenica National Park** Staggeringly beautiful mountain landscape offering an enticing mixture of karst wilderness, deciduous forests and fir-clad slopes. **See p.274**

* **Rab Town** Peninsula-hugging medieval town famous for its skyscraping church belfries. **See p.277**

* **San Marino** Truly sandy beaches in Croatia are few and far between, but this is the Real McCoy. **See p.285**

* **Pag cheese** The rocky island's most celebrated delicacy, courtesy of the sage-nibbling local sheep. **See p.287**

* **Zrće beach** Pebbly strand famous for the alfresco club culture which takes over the place every summer. **See p.289**

△ The Belle Epoque *Hotel Kvarner* in Opatija

4

The Kvarner Gulf

As the main road from Zagreb sweeps down to the Adriatic at Rijeka, the Kvarner Gulf – the large, deep bay which separates the Istrian peninsula to the north from Dalmatia to the south – is the first glimpse of Croatia's coastline for many visitors. It's a region which brings together many of the coast's most enticing features: grizzled coastal hills and mountains, an archipelago of ochre-grey islands, and fishing villages with narrow alleys and gardens groaning under the weight of subtropical plants.

Croatia's largest port and the area's economic and political centre, **Rijeka** is more of a transit point than a destination in itself, and most people push straight on to the **islands** that crowd the gulf to the south. Of these, **Krk** is the most accessible, connected to the mainland by a road bridge just half an hour's drive from Rijeka; the islands farther out – **Lošinj**, **Rab** and particularly **Cres** – feel more removed from the urban bustle. Each has its fair share of historic towns, whose shuttered, Italianate houses recall the long centuries of Venetian rule, along with some gorgeous coves and **beaches** – especially the sandy ones at Baška on Krk and Lopar on Rab. Although lush and green on their western flanks, the islands are hauntingly bare when seen from the mainland, the result of deforestation during the Venetian period, when local timber was used to feed the shipyards of Venice; the fierce northeasterly wind known as the **Bura** (see box on p.269) has prevented anything from growing there again. This denuded landscape is particularly evident on the most southerly of the Kvarner islands, **Pag**, with its bare, stony hills.

The coast of the mainland which flanks the gulf was traditionally known as the **Hrvatsko primorje** (literally, "Croatian littoral") to distinguish it from the Adriatic islands and Dalmatia – largely because it never fell under Venetian control. Because of its proximity to Habsburg central Europe this stretch of the Adriatic shoreline was the first to develop as a tourist destination, with **Opatija**, **Crikvenica** and **Novi Vinodolski** emerging in the late nineteenth century as swish winter health resorts patronized by the Viennese upper crust. They're fairly bland tourist centres nowadays, although Opatija and neighbouring **Lovran** preserve something of the spirit of the *belle époque*. The southern part of the Kvarner coastline is dominated by the stark and majestic **Velebit** mountains, which can be seen at their best in the **Paklenica National Park** at the southern end of the range.

Getting around the region is straightforward, with regular buses zooming up and down the Zagreb–Rijeka highway and the **Magistrala**, the main coastal road. Rijeka, very much the hub of the transport system, is the main departure point for buses and ferries to the islands.

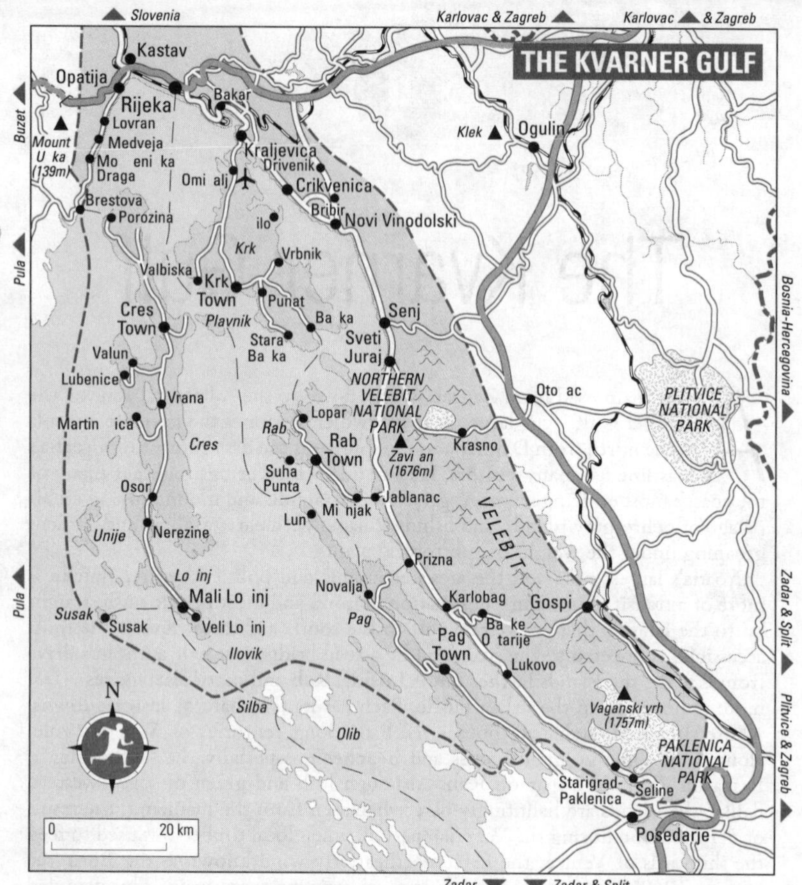

Rijeka

Rows of cumbrous cranes and rusty, sea-stained tankers front the soaring apartment blocks of Croatia's largest port, **RIJEKA** (pronounced "Ree-acre"), a down-to-earth industrial city which is the major ferry terminal along the Adriatic coast and an unavoidable transit point if you're travelling through the region by bus. Rijeka is far from beautiful, but it is the northern Adriatic's only true metropolis, harbouring a reasonable number of attractions and an appealing urban buzz; the hilltop suburb of **Trsat**, home to a famous pilgrimage church, is particularly attractive. Accommodation in town is limited to a handful of hotels, and if you want to **stay** in the area it may be better to aim for the Opatija Riviera to the west, an area amply served by Rijeka's municipal bus network.

Some history

Although Trsat is built on an ancient hilltop site which was occupied by both the Illyrians and the Romans, the port below didn't really begin to develop until the thirteenth century, when it was known – in the language of whichever power controlled it – as St Vitus-on-the-River, a name subsequently shortened to the rather blunt "River" – which is what Rijeka (and its Italian version, "Fiume") actually means. From 1466 the city was an Austrian possession, a prosperous port which remained under the direct control of Vienna until 1848, when Ban Jelačić brought it under Croatian administration. Rijeka became a bone of contention between Croatia and Hungary in the latter half of the nineteenth century, after the city was claimed by Budapest on the grounds that the Hungarian half of the Austro-Hungarian Empire should possess at least one outlet to the Adriatic. In 1868, an agreement between Croatia and Hungary – which was to have left the fate of Rijeka open to arbitration – was due to be signed by the Habsburg Emperor Franz Josef, but, in a notorious piece of trickery, an additional clause presenting the port to Hungary was literally pasted in at the last moment without the Croats' knowledge.

Rijeka under Hungarian rule was a booming industrial port with a multinational population – the centre was predominantly Italian-speaking, while the suburbs were increasingly Croat – and both Italians and Croatians laid claim to the city when it once again came up for grabs at the end of World War I. The 1915 **Treaty of London** had promised Dalmatia – but not Rijeka – to the Italians as a reward for joining the war on the Allied side, a promise that Britain and France were unwilling to keep come 1918. The Italians demanded Rijeka as the price for giving up their claim to territories farther south. In a plebiscite of October 1918, the city's inhabitants voted to join Italy (most of Rijeka's Croatian population actually lived outside the municipal boundary in the suburb of **Sušak,** and so were not represented), but the Allies remained firm, garrisoning the port with an Anglo-American and French force as a prelude to handing it over to the infant state of Yugoslavia. In September 1919, however, the Italian soldier-poet **Gabriele d'Annunzio** (see box on p.230) marched into Rijeka unopposed and occupied the city, establishing a proto-fascist regime which endured until January 1921. He was eventually forced to leave by an embarrassed Italian government, and the **Treaty of Rapallo** declared Rijeka a free city. Despite this, Rijeka was once again taken over by Italy following Mussolini's accession to power in 1922, an act which the Yugoslav government grudgingly accepted in the hope that it would deflect Italian territorial ambitions from the rest of the Adriatic.

Rijeka was returned to Yugoslavia after World War II, when most of the Italian population was induced to leave. In the years that followed, Rijeka's traditionally strong shipbuilding industry flourished anew, and the city acquired its high-rise suburbs. Rijeka's status as an economic powerhouse took a tumble in the immediate **post-independence** years, when the shipbuilding industry collapsed and the city's once-strong merchant fleet was sold off vessel by vessel. With traditional sources of employment drying up and a new post-communist business culture emerging to fill the gap, it's a surprise to discover that Rijeka is still a town with solid socialist leanings. In contrast to Adriatic cities like Zadar, Split and Dubrovnik, which tried to obliterate remnants of the socialist era by changing all the street names relating to that time, most of the street names in Rijeka have been the same since the break-up of Yugoslavia: there are squares and boulevards dedicated to Žrtava fašizma ("Victims of Facism") and President Tito, and even a Šetalište XIII divizije or "Promenade of the Thirteenth Partisan Division" – the idea of battle-hardened guerillas strolling along its dull grey length is delightfully absurd.

Gabriele d'Annunzio in Rijeka

Following World War I, Italy's failure to win Rijeka by diplomatic means was seen by many right-wing Italians as proof of the essential weakness of Italian democracy, provoking calls for an overthrow of parliamentary government in favour of some form of dictatorship. Disgruntled army officers calculated that an attack on Rijeka would be enormously popular with the Italian public, thereby preparing the ground for a coup within Italy itself. To lead the attack they chose the flamboyant poet, novelist and pilot **Gabriele d'Annunzio** (1863–1938). D'Annunzio was a compelling figure: a decadent aesthete who reinvented himself as a war hero, he volunteered for the Italian cavalry in 1915 and went on to serve with distinction in both the navy and air force, becoming a bombastic nationalist ideologue in the process.

D'Annunzio marched into Rijeka on September 12, 1919, at the head of 297 volunteers – whose numbers were soon swelled by regular soldiers tacitly lent to the enterprise by their commanding officers. He immediately declared Italy's annexation of Rijeka, a deed that the Italian government in Rome, suspicious of the radical d'Annunzio, disowned. By September 1920, d'Annunzio – who now styled himself "Il Commandante" – had established Rijeka as an independent state entitled the **Reggenza del Carnaro**, or "Regency of the Kvarner", which he hoped to use as a base from which to topple the Italian government and establish a dictatorship.

Under d'Annunzio, political life in Rijeka became an experiment in totalitarian theory from which fellow Italian nationalist Benito Mussolini was to borrow freely. D'Annunzio's main innovation was the establishment of a **corporate state**, ostensibly based on the Italian medieval guild system, in which electoral democracy was suspended and replaced by nine "corporations" – each corresponding to a different group of professions – by which the populace could be organized and controlled. The Regency was also a proving ground for fascism's love of spectacle, with d'Annunzio mounting bombastic parades of extravagantly uniformed followers, and mass meetings (often staged to make it appear as if the public had gathered spontaneously) featuring a call-and-response style of oratory which involved carefully scripted audience participation.

Successive Italian governments failed to take action against d'Annunzio, seeing him as a wild card with which to frighten the Allied powers still assembled at the Paris Peace Conference. Once Italian negotiators at the Conference had received what they thought was a reasonable chunk of Adriatic territory – Istria, Zadar and a couple of islands – they felt honour-bound to restore order to Rijeka, and Italian forces began a **bombardment of the city** on Christmas Eve 1920. D'Annunzio surrendered four days later, finally leaving town on January 18, thereby ending one of twentieth-century history's more bizarre episodes.

D'Annunzio's occupation of Rijeka demonstrated to Mussolini how easy it was to mount a show of force against disorganized political opponents, and provided him with the blueprint for his own successful coup, the **March on Rome** of October 1922. A theatrical personality in his own right, Mussolini was always rather jealous of the popularity enjoyed by the poet, and – despite rewarding him with a seat in the Italian senate – ensured that he was kept away from the political limelight.

Arrival, information and city transport

Rijeka's **train station** lies a few hundred metres west of the city centre on Krešimirova; **ferries** dock by the Riva, just south of the centre. The main **bus station**, handling all inter-city buses, is on the western fringe of the city centre at Trg Žabica. In addition, there are two smaller bus stations handling local services: buses to northern destinations (including Kastav, Opatija and Lovran) leave from Jelačićev trg on the east side of the city centre, while those heading south (to Bakar and Kraljevica) use a terminal a little way farther east on the Delta. Rijeka's **airport** is 25km south of town on the island of Krk; a taxi into the centre will set you back 300Kn. Bus transfer to and from Rab is available if booked in advance from Imperial (€25 return; ⓣ051/724-204 or 724-184, ⓦwww.imperial.hr).

The **tourist office** at Korzo 33 (mid-June to mid-Sept Mon–Sat 8am–8pm, Sun 8am–2pm; mid-Sept to mid-June Mon–Fri 8am–8pm, Sat 8am–2pm; ⓣ051/335-882, ⓦwww.tz-rijeka.hr) has town plans and a wealth of information on the Kvarner region, including the English-language *Kvarner Info*, with listings of cultural events. A livelier source of local listings information is the booklet-sized *Rijeka In Your Pocket* (ⓦwww.inyourpocket.com), given away free at the tourist office and in local hotels.

Municipal **bus tickets** can be bought from newspaper kiosks (valid for two journeys) or from the driver (valid for one). **Fares** are calculated according to a zonal system: most city destinations, including Sušak and Trsat, fall within zone 1 (8Kn from the driver; 11Kn from a kiosk); Opatija is in zone 3 (12Kn/18Kn), and Lovran lies in zone 4 (16Kn/22Kn).

Accommodation

There are very few private **rooms** in the town itself (the tourist office can provide you with a list of phone numbers), although there are plenty a short bus ride away along the Opatija Riviera. Rijeka's choice of **hotels** is also rather modest, although the city does boast one of Croatia's newest **youth hostels**.

The nearest **campsite** is *Preluk* (ⓣ051/621-913, ⓔtranzit@ri.t-com.hr), 8km north along the road to Opatija, on the cusp of the bay as the road wheels south towards Volosko; bus #32 (from Jelačićev trg or from opposite the train station) passes the entrance, but halts only on request – so remember to press the red button when you see the site approaching.

Hostels

Omladinski Hostel Rijeka Šetalište XIII divizije 23 ⓣ051/406-420, ⓦwww.hfhs.hr. Attractive inter-war villa converted into a youth hostel in 2006, featuring bright clean rooms with linoleum floors and pine beds. Rooms range in size from doubles to six-bed dorms; some come with en-suite WC and shower, others share facilities in the hallway. There's plenty of common-room space to hang out in, and the price includes breakfast in the ground-floor canteen. Dorm beds 130Kn, doubles 320kn.

Hotels

Bonavia Dolac 4 ⓣ051/357-100, ⓦwww.bonavia.hr. Fully renovated four-star hotel bang in the centre of town, with standards of service that you'd expect at this level. Rooms feature plush carpets, swish bathrooms, TV, minibar and a/c. ❻–❼

Continental Šetalište Andrije Kačića Miošića 1 ⓣ051/372-008, ⓦwww.jadran-hoteli.hr. Conveniently central two-star, but a bit old-fashioned and gloomy. The en-suite rooms with TV come with tired-looking brown furnishings but are otherwise habitable. ❹

Jadran Šetalište XIII divizije 46 ⓣ051/216-600, ⓦwww.jadran-hoteli.hr. On the shore 2km east of the centre, this minimalist grey box of a building is one of Rijeka's best examples of modernist architecture from the pre-World War I days. Recently refurbished rooms come with creamy colour schemes, Scandinavian-style furnishings, TV and a/c – some have bathtubs, but others only come with shower. The (more expensive) south-facing rooms have marvellous views across the water to the island of Cres. Bus #2 (direction Pećine) from the train station or from the Riva. ❺–❻

Neboder Strossmayerova 1 ⓣ051/373-538 or 373-541, ⓦwww.jadran-hoteli.hr. Just east of the centre, this eight-storey sliver of reinforced concrete known as the Neboder ("Skyscraper") was one of the most stunning buildings in Croatia when first thrown up in the 1930s, but is now an unspectacular hotel with a handful of renovated en suites on the upper floors. Rooms are simple and plain, but you get little balconies and fine views of town from the south-facing ones. ❹

The City

Much of Rijeka was rebuilt after World War II, though a fair number of nineteenth-century buildings remain, many of them in solid ranks along the **Riva**, a

△ Rijeka's main street

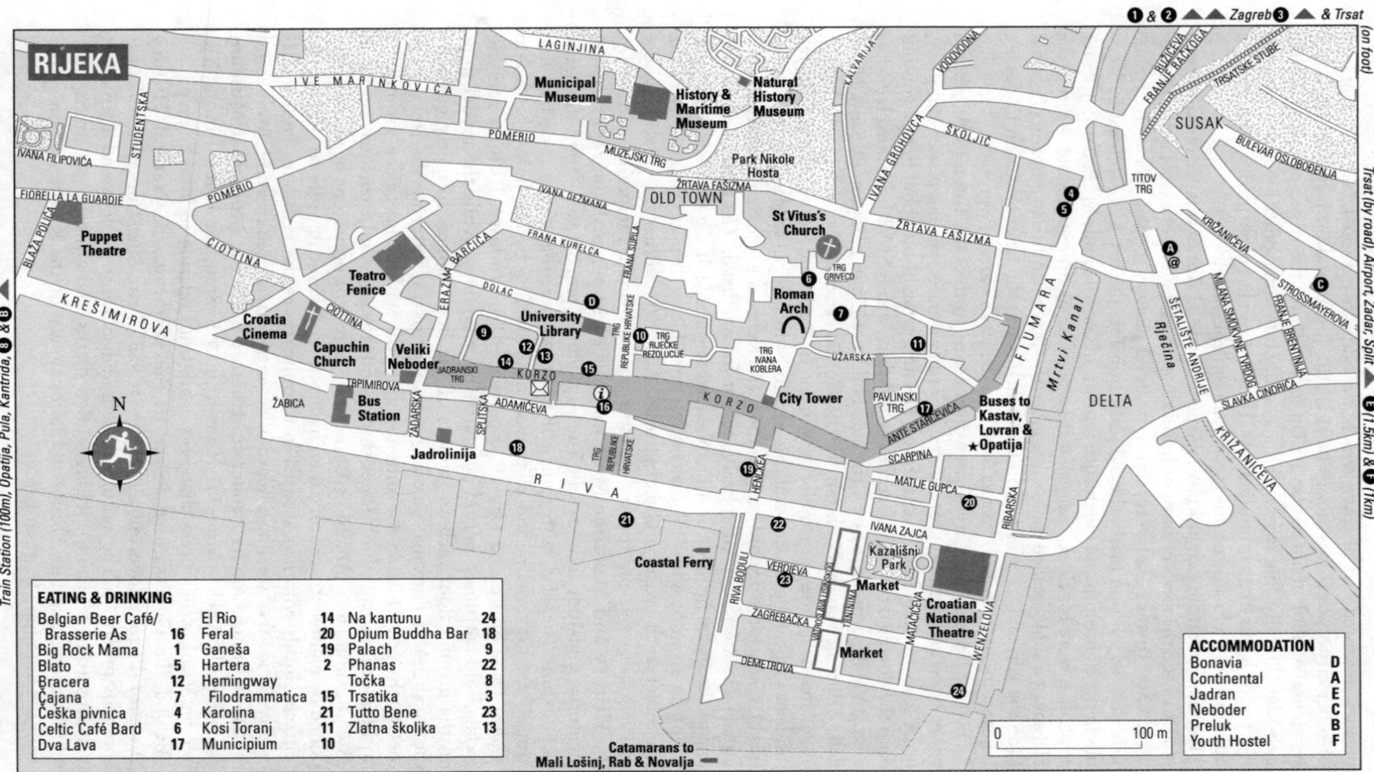
RIJEKA
1 & 2 Zagreb 3 & Trsat (on foot)
Trsat (by road), Airport, Zadar, Split E (1.5km) & F (1km)
Train Station (100m), Opatija, Pula, Kantrida, 8 & B
Municipal Museum
History & Maritime Museum
Natural History Museum
Park Nikole Hosta
OLD TOWN
St Vitus's Church
Roman Arch
City Tower
University Library
Teatro Fenice
Puppet Theatre
Croatia Cinema
Capuchin Church
Veliki Neboder
Bus Station
Jadrolinija
Coastal Ferry
Catamarans to Mali Lošinj, Rab & Novalja
Buses to Kastav, Lovran & Opatija
Kazališni Park
Market
Croatian National Theatre
Market
SUSAK
DELTA
Mrtvi Kanal
Rječina
LAGINJINA
IVE MARINKOVIĆA
STUDENTSKA
POMERIO
MUZEJSKI TRG
IVANA FILIPOVIĆA
FIORELLA LA GUARDIE
BLAŽA POLIĆA
CIOTTINA
KREŠIMIROVA
ŽRTAVA FAŠIZMA
IVANA DEŽMANA
FRANA KURELCA
FRANA SUPILA
ERAZMA BARČIĆA
DOLAC
TRG REPUBLIKE HRVATSKE
TRG RIJEČKE REZOLUCIJE
TRG IVANA KOBLERA
TRG GRIVICA
UŽARSKA
KORZO
JADRANSKI TRG
TRPIMIROVA
ŽABICA
ZADARSKA
SPLITSKA
ADAMIĆEVA
RIVA
I. HENCKEA
PAVLINSKI TRG
ANTE STARČEVIĆA
SCARPINA
MATIJE GUPCA
RIBARSKA
IVANA ZAJCA
VERDIEVA
RIVA BODULI
ZAGREBAČKA
DEMETROVA
VAROŠ VATROSLAVA LISINSKOG
TRININA
MATAČIĆEVA
WENZELOVA
FIUMARA
KALVARIJA
VODOVODNA
IVANA GROHOVCA
ŠKOLJIĆ
TITOV TRG
RUŽIĆEVA
FRANJE RAČKOGA
TRSATSKE STUBE
BULEVAR OSLOBOĐENJA
KRIŽANIĆEVA
MILANA SMOKVINE TVRDOG
FRANJE BRENTINIJA
STROSSMAYEROVA
ŠETALIŠTE ANDRIJE
SLAVKA CINDRIĆA
KRIŽANIĆEVA
N
0 100 m

EATING & DRINKING
Belgian Beer Café/ Brasserie As 16
Big Rock Mama 1
Blato 5
Bracera 12
Čajana 7
Češka pivnica 4
Celtic Café Bard 6
Dva Lava 17
El Rio 14
Feral 20
Ganeša 19
Hartera 2
Hemingway Filodrammatica 15
Karolina 21
Kosi Toranj 11
Municipium 10
Na kantunu 24
Opium Buddha Bar 18
Palach 9
Phanas 22
Točka 8
Trsatika 3
Tutto Bene 23
Zlatna školjka 13

ACCOMMODATION
Bonavia D
Continental A
Jadran E
Neboder C
Preluk B
Youth Hostel F

business-oriented part of town which, the odd café excepted, lacks the vibrancy of other city waterfronts along the Adriatic. Just inland on Jadranski trg is one surviving symbol of inter-war Italian architecture, the russet-coloured **Veliki neboder** (literally "big skyscraper"), a boldly functional office block whose grid-like facade looks like a monumental CD rack – and has unsurprisingly earned the building the nickname of *ormar-ladičnjak* or "chest of drawers".

Running east from Jadranski trg, the pedestrianized **Korzo** is Rijeka's main shopping area and the focus of most of its bustling streetlife. The one real landmark here is the **City Tower** (Gradski toranj), a medieval gateway topped by a later Baroque structure; its position marks the old seafront before the city was extended by landfills in the eighteenth and nineteenth centuries. Known locally as "Pod uriloj" (after the Italian word for clock, *orologio*), it has a relief on its street-facing side bearing the Habsburg double-headed eagle surmounted by busts of Austrian emperors Leopold I (on the left) and Charles VI (on the right). It was the latter's decision to declare Rijeka a free port in 1717 that kick-started the city's economic growth.

The gate beneath the City Tower gives access to the **Old Town** (Stari grad), a rather hopeful description for an area of scruffy squares, peeling plaster and shiny, black glass-fronted department stores. Heading straight on uphill brings you out onto the sloping Trg Grivica, at the top of which stands **St Vitus's Church** (Crkva svetog Vida), surmounted by a rotunda built in 1638 in imitation of Santa Maria della Salute in Venice. Look out for the Gothic **crucifix** above the high altar: in 1296, the story goes, a gambler was losing at cards outside the church and ran inside in a rage, flinging stones at this crucifix, which began to bleed. In response to this blasphemy, the ground beneath the man's feet is said to have promptly opened up and swallowed him completely, except for one hand. The faithful claim that one of the stones he threw is still embedded in the side of the wooden Christ.

Not far from St Vitus's – make a left turn along Žrtava fašizma – rises the late nineteenth-century Gubernatorial Palace (Guvernerova palača), whose marvellously over-the-top state rooms now provide a sumptuous setting for the **History and Maritime Museum** (Povijesni i pomorski muzej hrvatskog primorja; mid-June to mid-Sept Tues–Fri 9am–8pm, Sat 9am–1pm; mid-Sept to mid-June Tues–Fri 9am–1pm; 10Kn). It was here that d'Annunzio installed himself for his short period of power, until shelling by the Italian battleship *Andrea Doria* on Boxing Day 1920 persuaded him to leave. Its huge echoing rooms hold costumes, period portraits and weaponry, while the model ships on the ground floor include replicas of the huge tankers formerly made by the local 3 Maj shipyard, whose gates you'll pass if entering the town from the northwest. Outside the museum but still within the palace grounds, a **lapidarium** displays tombstones throughout the ages and a curious sculptural ensemble known as "Adamić 's Witnesses" – a row of ugly stone heads commissioned by eighteenth-century merchant Simon Adamić in order to ridicule the fourteen locals who had accused him (unjustly, as the Habsburg courts ultimately decided) of stealing a hoard of recently-discovered treasure. Just behind the lapidarium, a modern concrete structure holds the **Municipal Museum** (Muzej grada Rijeke; Mon–Fri 10am–1pm & 5–8pm, Sat 10am–1pm; 20Kn, free on Mon), which hosts changing exhibitions relating to local history.

Behind the Gubernatorial Palace to the northeast, the **Natural History Museum** (Prirodoslovni muzej; Mon–Sat 9am–7pm, Sun 9am–3pm; 10Kn) at Lorenzov prolaz 1 has beautifully presented displays on geology and marine life, including some ferocious-looking stuffed sharks, and a soothingly atmospheric subterranean aquarium. Shrubs and herbs typical of the Kvarner region sprout from the museum's fragrant garden.

From the University Library to the Capuchin Church

Returning downhill towards the Korzo along Frana Supila, you'll pass the **University Library** (Sveučilišna knjižnica; entrance round the corner on Dolac), which is home to the **Museum of Contemporary and Modern Art** (Muzej moderne i suvremene umjetnosti; Tues–Sun 10am–1pm & 5–8pm; ⓦwww.mmsu.hr; prices depend on what's on), which hosts exhibitions by leading contemporary artists from Croatia and abroad. In the same building, the **Glagolitic Exhibition** (Izložba glagoljice; Mon & Thurs 2–9pm, Tues, Wed & Fri 9am–2pm; for entry apply to the library information office on the floor above; 10Kn) tells the history of the archaic script which was common to the Kvarner region in the Middle Ages (see box on p.266). Despite the fact that most exhibits are copies rather than original manuscripts and inscriptions, it's a visually attractive display, marred only by the lack of English-language labelling. Marking the western end of Dolac at no. 13 is the **Teatro Fenice** cinema, built in 1913 in Futurist style but nowadays looking somewhat uncared for – appropriately enough, this was where Futurist ideologue F. T. Marinetti addressed meetings in support of d'Annunzio in 1919.

Finally, opposite the bus station on Trg Žabica rises the huge, striped neo-Gothic bulk of the **Capuchin Church** (Kapucinska crkva), built between 1904 and 1929 and fronted by a large double stairway.

Sušak and Trsat

East of the old centre, the thick, pea-soup-coloured River Rječina marks the edge of central Rijeka, beyond which lies the suburb of Sušak; between 1924 and 1941, walking between the city centre and here meant crossing from Italy into the Kingdom of Yugoslavia. On the north side of Titov trg, a Baroque gateway marks the start of the **Trsatske Stube**, a stairway of 538 steps, built in 1531 at the bidding of Uskok commander Petar Kružić. This leads up to the pilgrimage centre of **Trsat** (also reachable on bus #1 or #1a from Fiumara or the Riva), nowadays a suburb of Rijeka, occupying a bluff high above the modern centre. According to legend, Trsat is where the House of the Virgin Mary and Joseph rested for three years during its miraculous flight from the infidel in Nazareth to Loreto in Italy, where it was set down in December 1294. At the top, the **Church of Our Lady of Trsat** (Crkva gospe trsatske) supposedly marks the spot where the house rested. The church originally dates from the fifteenth century, but was almost completely rebuilt in 1824; it's now a place of almost exclusively female pilgrimage and worship – the more devout pilgrims sometimes scale Kružić's steps on their knees. The sanctuary features an altar with an icon of the Virgin, sent here by Pope Urban V in 1367, surrounded by necklaces and other trinkets hung there by grateful pilgrims, who are required to walk round the altar three times. At the side of the church is a **Franciscan monastery** whose chapel of votive gifts (*kapela zavjetnih darova*) is plastered with pictures and tapestries left by those whose prayers have been answered; the numerous enthusiastic paintings depicting events such as shipwrecks and car crashes in which the Virgin is supposed to have intervened are particularly striking.

Trsat Castle (Trsatska gradina; daily: April–June, Sept & Oct 9am–5pm; July & Aug 9am–8pm; Nov–March 9am–3pm; free, or 15Kn for a guided visit), across the road from the church, is an ivy-clad hotchpotch of turrets and towers, walkways and parapets that give views backwards up a huge grey tear in the mountains and forwards to Rijeka, under its dim yellowish haze of industrial smog. Beyond Rijeka is the island of Cres and, to the right, on the northwestern side of the Kvarner Gulf, the sheer mountain wall of Mount Učka. Parts of the castle date back to Roman times, when it was an important way-station on the trade routes linking the northern Adriatic with the Pannonian plain, but the fortress assumed its current shape primarily in the thirteenth century, when it became a stronghold of the Frankopans of Krk (see box on p.260). The castle was taken over in 1826 by vice-marshal Laval Nugent, the Irish-Austrian general who had commanded Habsburg forces during the Napoleonic wars. He made several Neoclassical additions to the place, including the family mausoleum in the shape of a Doric temple that dominates the central courtyard – the mausoleum occasionally serves as a gallery of contemporary art. The castle hosts open-air theatre, dance performances and concerts, and has a seasonal café.

Eating

Rijeka has less in the way of **restaurants** than a city of its size deserves, and most locals head for nearby Opatija if they want a slap-up meal. However, there's a handful of characterful eating places awaiting anyone prepared to venture beyond the main thoroughfares. There are also plenty of **snack** and sandwich joints along the Korzo, and a bustling fruit and veg **market** just beyond the eastern end of the Riva. We've included phone numbers for those restaurants where it's wise to book at weekends.

Restaurants

Belgian Beer Café/Brasserie As Trg republike Hrvatske 2. Multi-purpose eating, coffee-sipping and beer-guzzling venue, conveniently located midway between the port and the main shopping streets. An all-embracing menu includes vegetarian pasta dishes as well as steak-and-chips pub food. The wood-panelled interior generously sprinkled with Belgian flags helps to create a welcoming brasserie atmosphere, and the handful of bottled Belgian beers on offer just about justifies the name.

Blato Titov trg 8c. Unpretentious, cosy *konoba* with a simple menu of daily specials scratched on a blackboard, usually covering everything from mushroom omelettes to juicy steaks, with a lot of reasonably priced seafood thrown in. Good place to fill up on staples such as Dalmatian *pašticada* (beef stewed in prunes) or *pržene lignje* (fried squid).

Bracera Kružna 12. Located in an alleyway just off the Korzo, this is the best of the central pizzerias, with a range of well-presented thin-crust pies alongside pasta dishes and salads. Tends to fill up at lunchtimes, so arrive early or be prepared to wait.

Feral Matije Gupca 5b ⓣ051/212-274. Semi-formal seafood restaurant with high standards and higher-than-average prices – it's one of the best places in the region to eat *jakopske kapice* (scallops) and other shellfish. The brick-lined rooms have the feel of a cosy cellar. Closed Sun.

Ganeša Ignacia Henckea 1. Wholefood store that also serves as a vegetarian café, offering an enticing range of savoury pies, risottos, salads and sandwiches. With a handful of high stools and not much else, it's more of a quick-snack stop than a comfy sit-down venue. Open until 7pm (although the best stuff runs out a couple of hours beforehand).

Municipium Trg Riječke rezolucije 5. Smart city-centre establishment popular with the business crowd, and handy for downtown sightseeing. The standard Croatian repertoire of fish and meat dishes is augmented by a solid range of steaks. Closed Sun.

Na kantunu Demetrova 2. In a workaday grid of streets behind the market, this is a popular buffet serving up solid, satisfying and cheap seafood to an appreciative crowd of local port and office workers. Expect mackerel, sardines and other forms of *plava riba* (oily fish), as well as *oslić* (hake), shellfish and risottos. Closed Sun.

Trsatika Šetalište Joakima Rakovca 33. Right opposite Trsat's pilgrimage church, with a spacious outdoor terrace that offers excellent maritime vistas. The menu covers just about everything from inexpensive pizzas to lavish steaks and grilled fish, with some moderately priced pasta dishes (including *šurlice* from Krk;) in the middle. Closed Wed.

Tutto Bene Verdijeva 19. Simple fish, pasta and risotto-type dishes that you'd find in an old-fashioned inn, but served up in a stylish lounge-bar environment that seems to have fallen from the pages of an international lifestyle magazine. The perfect place for a combined fix of traditional food and urban cool.

Zlatna školjka Kružna 12a ⓣ051/213-782. Charming little seafood restaurant just off the Korzo, with an interior stuffed with nautical bric-a-brac. Plenty of shrimp and squid dishes (including an excellent and not too expensive *crni rižot* (inky squid risotto), as well as the full range of fish.

Drinking

For daytime drinking, the pavement **cafés** lining the Korzo or those girdling the church in Trsat are the places to hang out. The town also has a range of lively **drinking** venues to choose from at night.

Cafés and bars

Celtic Café Bard Trg Grivica 68, opposite St Vitus's Church. Cosy, laid back and intimate café-bar serving international beers to an older crowd.

Čajana A. Dalmatina 2/1. Quirky first-floor tearoom kitted out with distressed furniture and colourful objets d'art – the perfect place to relax over a pot of tea or tuck into toasted sandwiches and cakes. Closed Sun.

Češka pivnica Titov trg 6. Czech and other beers served up in a pair of narrow brick-lined chambers opposite the *Continental* hotel. Serves substantial soups and sausagey beer-snacks, too.

Dva Lava Ante Starčevića 8. A place to see and be seen, this hip bar with lots of glass and black-and-white designer furniture has music blasting until the wee hours at weekends. The two sidewalk terraces shaded by giant parasols are pleasant for a daytime drink.

El Rio Korzo, on the edge of Jadranski trg. Popular, latin-inspired hangout with colourful high-ceilinged interiors, pictures of Castro and other cigar-smoking Latin-American types, and loud music on Fri and Sat.

Hemingway Filodrammatica Korzo 28. One of the main city-centre coffee-sipping venues for more than a century, this favourite has recently re-emerged all trendified and decked out with minimalist decor and lounge-bar furnishings. During the day it's one of the best spots in Rijeka for people-watching; on weekend nights it transforms into a hip DJ bar.

Karolina Gat Karoline riječke bb. This glass box by the quayside comes into its own in the summer months, when café tables, DJ decks, and a crowd of fun-seeking locals explode out onto the surrounding flagstones.

Kosi Toranj Put Vele crikve 1. Loungey café-bar equipped with comfy sofas and floor-to-ceiling windows, catering for coffee-guzzling shoppers during the day and fans of DJ culture in the evening.

Opium Buddha Bar Riva 12a. Huge space offering a kitsch recreation of Orient-themed bars found elsewhere around the globe. Fills up at weekends with hedonistic, hormone-fuelled beautiful things – although at other times of the week it can resemble a social club for glum teenagers.

Palach Kružna 6. Hidden away in an alleyway which dives behind the Korzo just to the rear of the Erste bank, *Palach* has been the nerve centre of Rijeka's alternative scene since the late 1960s (when it was named, rather provocatively for the times, after the Czech anti-communist martyr Jan Palach). It comprises an art gallery, a roomy bar area scattered with distressed wooden tables, and a space for live gigs and club nights.

Phanas Ivana Zajca 9. A well stocked bar, two tiers of seating, and a young and stylish clientele make this one of the more popular places for a city-centre drinking session.

Nightlife and entertainment

Live rock, jazz and DJ-driven club nights take place at *Točka*, 2km west of the centre at Luki 19 (ⓦwww.club-tocka.hr), and *Big Rock Mama*, set amid old factories beside the Rječina river at Ružićeva bb – neither venue hosts events every night of the week, so it's best to check street posters before heading out. High-profile alternative gigs and rave parties occasionally take place at *Hartera*, an atmospheric former paper factory on the banks of the Riječina; otherwise large-scale rock and pop performances take place at the **Dvorana Mladost** in Trsat, a modern multipurpose auditorium located slightly uphill from Trsat church.

The **Croatian National Theatre** (Hrvatsko narodno kazalište; ⓣ051/337-114, ⓦwww.hnk-zajc.hr), on Ivana Zajca, is the place for opera, orchestral concerts and theatre. Gradsko kazalište lutaka, at B. Polića 6 (ⓣ051/325-688,

The Rijeka carnival

On the last Sunday before Shrove Tuesday, Rijeka plays host to the biggest **carnival** celebrations in Croatia, culminating in a spectacular parade. Much of the parade centres on carnival floats and fancy-dress costumes, although there is one authentic older element in the shape of the **zvončari**, young men clad in animal skins who ring enormous cow bells to drive away evil spirits. Many of the villages in the hills north of Rijeka have their own groups of *zvončari*, a tradition which has survived since pre-Christian times. The Rijeka parade, which normally culminates with a large party of *zvončari* strutting their stuff, usually kicks off at around 1pm and takes around five hours to complete. Afterwards, participants and spectators alike troop off to the Riva, where there's an enormous marquee, in which drinking and dancing continue into the early hours.

Ⓦwww.gkl-rijeka.hr), is the leading **puppet theatre** in this part of Croatia, with enchanting puppet shows for nursery- and primary-school age-groups taking place on Thursdays and Fridays at 6pm, Saturdays at 11am. Rijeka's two main **cinemas** are the Croatia, near the bus station at Krešimirova 2 (Ⓣ051/335-219), and the Teatro Fenice, at Dolac 13 (Ⓣ051/335-225).

The only spectator sport of note is **football**, with local team NK Rijeka (Ⓦwww.nk-rijeka.hr) playing at the all-seater Kantrida stadium, 6km west of the centre (bus #32 to Lovran passes by). Situated right by the sea, and with the imposing form of Mount Učka away to the west, it's a stirring arena in which to catch a game. Matches usually take place on Saturdays and tickets can be bought at the stadium on the day.

Listings

Airlines Croatia Airlines, Jelačićev trg 5 Ⓣ051/330-207, Ⓦwww.croatiaairlines.hr.

Books and newspapers Tisak, on the corner of the Korso and Trg 128 Brigade Hrvatske Vojske, is the place to find international newspapers and magazines. Nova (at Trpimirova 9) and VBZ (Korzo 32) both stock English-language paperbacks.

Bus station Trg Žabica. Information Ⓣ060 302 010.

Exchange Erste banka is at Jadranski trg 3a, with ATMs outside.

Ferry tickets Jadrolinija, Riva 16 (Mon, Wed, Fri & Sun 7am–8pm, Tues, Thurs & Sat 7am–6pm; Ⓣ051/666-100, Ⓦwww.jadrolinija.hr.

Hospital Krešimirova 42 (Ⓣ051/658-111), on the north side of the road, just west of the train station.

Internet access *Internet Club Cont*, ground floor of the *Continental* hotel (daily 7am–11pm); *Internet Café*, Ivana Zajca 24A, just off the Riva (Mon–Sat 7am–10pm).

Left luggage There's a *garderoba* at the bus station (daily 5.30am–10.30pm).

Pharmacy Jadranski trg 1 (24hr).

Post office The most central post office is halfway down the Korzo at no.13 (Mon–Fri 7am–9pm, Sat 7am–2pm); there's a 24hr branch beyond the train station at Krešimirova 7.

Taxi Both the train and bus stations have ranks outside; alternatively call Ⓣ051/335-138 or 332-893.

Travel agents GeneralTurist, Trg 128. Brigade Hrvatske vojske 8 Ⓣ051/214-590, Ⓦwww.generalturist.com; Ri Ak-Tours, Verdijeva 6 Ⓣ051/312-312, Ⓦwww.ri-ak-tours.hr; Maremonti, Korzo 40 Ⓣ051/212-911, Ⓕ051/215-091.

The Opatija Riviera

Just to the west of Rijeka, the **Opatija Riviera** (Opatijska rivijera) is a twenty-kilometre stretch of sedate seaside resorts lining the western side of the Kvarner Gulf. Protected from strong winds by the ridge of **Mount Učka**, this stretch of coast became the favoured retreat of tubercular Viennese fleeing the icy winter temperatures of central Europe. At the centre of the Riviera is the town of **Opatija**, whose success as a tourist resort in the latter half of the nineteenth century made it the Austro-Hungarian Empire's answer to the Côte d'Azur. The Habsburg ambience survives in some attractive *fin-de-siècle* architecture, the best of which is in the dainty town of **Lovran**, just southwest of Opatija. Beaches here tend to be of the concrete variety, unless you head for **Medveja**, just beyond Lovran, which has a much more enticing stretch of shingle. There's an abundance of good accommodation throughout the Riviera, although private rooms and pensions tend to be cheaper in Lovran than in Opatija.

The main Rijeka–Pula road cuts right through the Riviera. From Rijeka, bus #32 (daily 4.30am–10.30pm from Jelačićev trg; every 20–30min) travels via Opatija to terminate in either Lovran or **Mošćenička Draga**, the latter just south of Medveja. If you're approaching from Pula, most Rijeka-bound buses will drop you off in Lovran or Opatija.

Kastav

The best view of the Opatija Riviera is from the village of **KASTAV**, a worthwhile side-trip 10km northwest of Rijeka on the karst ridge which overlooks the gulf. A windswept knot of cobbled alleyways hemmed in by scraps of surviving fortification, Kastav is strong on atmosphere but short of real sights. Head first for **St Helena's Church** (Crkva svete Jelene), from whose terrace there's an expansive panorama of the waters below. On the other, landward side of the village is the **Crekvina**, the stark remains of an enormous church begun by the Jesuits but never finished. Given the village as a fief by the Habsburgs, the Jesuits proved unpopular masters, greedy for taxes. One of their civilian administrators, Frano Morelli, was drowned in a well on the main square in 1666 – a crime that was committed en masse by the villagers and therefore proved unpunishable.

Kastav is easily accessible from either Rijeka (bus #18) or Opatija (bus #37), but there may not be any information on return services when you get here, so check schedules before setting out if you can. There's a **tourist office** beside the old town gate at Kastav 47 (Mon–Fri 7am–3pm; ⓣ051/691-425, ⓦwww.tz-kastav.hr) and a couple of good places to **eat**. *Vidikovac*, on the sea-facing side of the village, has a large outdoor terrace where you can eat simple grilled meats, while the considerably more chic ★ *Kukuriku*, below the tourist office at Kastav 120 (ⓣ051/691-417; reservations a good idea at weekends), offers an upmarket take on Istrian-influenced cuisine, with a menu that changes every day – expect the best seafood, lamb and venison washed down by the finest local wines. Cultural events include the **Kastav Cultural Summer** (Kastafsko kulturno leto; consult ⓦwww.kkl.hr for the full schedule), a programme of open-air classical concerts and theatre held in July and August; and the **White Sunday and Monday** (Bela nedeja i beli pundejak) on the first Sunday and Monday in October, when new wine is tasted and there's folk dancing in the square.

Opatija

Fifteen kilometres out of Rijeka on the main coastal road to Pula lies **OPATIJA**, the longest established of the gulf's resorts. It's a town in the best tradition of seaside magnificence, pretty in an overpowering Austro-Hungarian sort of way, a monument both to genteel early twentieth-century tourism and to its subsequent decline. Opatija continues to be patronized by central Europeans of a certain age, and even in the height of summer there are times when you can stroll the length of the seafront without bumping into anyone under 40. At the weekend, however, Opatija's proximity to Rijeka (and, by extension, Zagreb) ensures a regular influx of day-trippers of all ages, when the shoreline promenade becomes jammed with strollers. Thanks to the big-spending habits of middle-class Croats, top-quality **seafood restaurants** have taken off in a big way in Opatija, turning the town into a major target for gastro-pilgrims.

Opatija was little more than a fishing village until the arrival in 1844 of Rijeka businessman **Iginio Scarpa**, who built the opulent Villa Angiolina as a holiday home for his family and aristocratic Habsburg friends, such as the Archduke Maximilian, future Emperor of Mexico, and Maria Anna, wife of Emperor Ferdinand I. In 1882 the villa was bought by **Friedrich Schüller**, head of Austria's Southern Railways; having supervised the completion of the line from Ljubljana to Rijeka, he decided to promote Opatija as a mass holiday destination and the town's first hotels (the *Kvarner*, *Krönprinzessin Stephanie* – today's *Imperial* – and *Palace-Bellevue*) soon followed. Owing to its mild climate, Opatija was originally a winter health-resort, with a season running from October to May. It soon developed a Europe-wide reputation: Franz Josef of Austria and Kaiser Wilhelm II of Germany held talks here in 1894, while playwright Anton Chekhov holidayed at the *Kvarner* in the same year. A decade later Isadora Duncan installed herself in a villa behind the *Krönprinzessin Stephanie* and was inspired by the palm tree outside her window to create one of her best-known dance movements – "that light fluttering of the arms, hands and fingers which has been so much abused by my imitators".

Arrival and information

Trains on the Ljubljana–Rijeka line stop at Matulji, 5km uphill from Opatija (regular local buses run from here down into town), though it's more convenient to arrive by **bus**; all buses stop at a central terminal on a small square facing onto the waterfront. Turn left from here and walk for five minutes up the main street, Maršala Tita, to reach the **tourist office** at no. 101 (mid-June to mid-Sept Mon–Sat 8am–8pm, Sun 6–10pm; mid-Sept to mid-June Mon–Fri 8am–3pm, Sat 8am–2pm; ⓣ051/271-310, ⓦwww.opatija-tourism.hr), which is well stocked with town maps and brochures; they also sell a map of hiking and biking trails on Mount Učka (20Kn). Taxi **boats** with erratic schedules shuttle people between Opatija and Lovran; they have stops right below the *Millennium* and *Admiral* hotels and can be booked on ⓣ051/279-181. Half-day boat tours of the Riviera (Opatija to Medveja and back; 100Kn) are advertised along the seafront. You can surf the **Internet** at La Habana, Maršala Tita 122 (daily 8am–midnight).

Accommodation

Accommodation in Opatija is expensive unless you opt for the private **rooms** (❶) and **apartments** (two-person studios ❷–❹, four-person apartments 500–650Kn) offered by numerous local agencies. The most helpful of these are easy to find along the central strip: head south of the bus station for DaRiva, Maršala Tita 170 (ⓣ051/272-990, ⓦwww.da-riva.hr), and north of the bus station for Katarina Line, Maršala Tita 75/1 (ⓣ051/272-110, ⓦwww.katarina-line.hr). The nearest **campsites** are *Preluk* (see p.231), 5km to the north, and *Autocamp Opatija*, 3km south at the small town of Ičići (ⓣ051/704-387, ⓕ704-046); the latter is a pleasant, wooded site on a terraced hillside about five minutes' walk above the main coastal road.

As for **hotels**, it's probably best to avoid the bland communist-era establishments which stretch a kilometre or so southwest of the centre, and opt instead for places strong on either *belle époque* atmosphere or twenty-first-century comfort. Bear in mind that peak-season rates (as expressed in the price codes in the reviews below) fall by as much as fifty percent between October and May, and that some hotels shut down out of season.

Hotels

Bristol Maršala Tita 108 ⓣ051/706-300, ⓦwww.hotel-bristol.hr. Gleaming lemon-yellow structure on the main street offering four-star comforts, *belle époque* elegance, and high-ceilinged rooms with all mod cons. ❼

Četiri Opatijska Cvijeta Maršala Tita 85 ⓣ051/295-000, ⓦwww.ugohoteli.hr. Four-star comforts in a huge, recently renovated hotel spread over four buildings. Rooms are decorated in warm cream, orange and burgundy shades, and there's a "wellness centre" offering a choice of beauty, massage and detox programmes. Some rooms have shower rather than bathtub, so be sure to ask if you mind about this. ❼

Galeb Maršala Tita 160 ⓣ051/271-177, ⓦwww.hotel-galeb.hr. Tastefully renovated nineteenth-century building in the centre, offering small, modernized rooms, all with TV, minibar, a/c and bathrooms. The more expensive rooms have sea views, and there are a couple of spacious suites. ❻

Ika Primorska 16, Ika, 3.5km south of Opatija on the road to Lovran ⓣ051/291-777, ⓦwww.hotel-ika.hr. Medium-sized, family-run hotel with plain but comfy rooms, all with en-suite shower, TV and a/c. Some of them are right beside Ika's pebbly beach; others, on the landward side, are cheaper. Bus #32 from Rijeka and Opatija passes right by. ❺

Kvarner-Amalia P. Tomašića 1–4 ⓣ051/271-233, ⓦwww.liburnia.hr. This is the grandest of the pre-1914 hotels – and it can't be beaten for atmosphere. Along with comfy rooms and old-world furnishings, it has a superb position right on the waterfront, with its own stretch of private beach, plus indoor and outdoor pools. The adjacent *Amalia* has slightly cheaper and simpler rooms. ❼

Millennium Maršala Tita 109 ⓣ051/202-000, ⓦwww.ugohoteli.hr. Rather swanky hotel bang in the centre, offering high standards of comfort and service. All rooms have sea views, and it sports a fitness centre with a sauna and Jacuzzi, plus a charming terrace café in the back. Calls itself a five-star but probably deserves four (some rooms have showers instead of bathtubs, for example). ❼

Miramar I. Kaline 11 ⓣ051/280-000, ⓦwww.hotel-miramar.info. Opulent, Austrian-run hotel occupying characterful nineteenth-century buildings, overlooking the seaside path midway between Opatija and Volosko. Also boasts a state-of-the-art spa, beauty and wellness centre; if you want to swan around like a latter-day Habsburg while having papaya mousse rubbed into your chest, then this is undoubtedly the place to do it. ❻

Palace-Bellevue Maršala Tita 144–146 ⓣ051/271-811, ⓦwww.liburnia.hr. Cheapest of the Habsburg-era places, whose lobby and bar areas still convey a whiff of *fin-de-siècle* opulence. The en-suite rooms have been recently renovated, but remain simple and affordable. ❺

Villa Ariston Maršala Tita 179 ⓣ051/271-379, ⓦwww.villa-ariston.hr. Small-scale hotel occupying an elegantly restored villa designed by Viennese architect Karl Seidl in Opatija's pre-World War I heyday. Most doubles are in the attic and come with atmospheric sloping roofs, as well as attached baths, TV, a/c and minibar. ❻

The Town

Modern Opatija is a long, straggling resort that has lost much of its original *fin-de-siècle* character. The town's main attraction is the **Šetalište Franza Josefa**, a splendid tree-shaded promenade which runs along the rocky seafront all the way to the old fishing village of Volosko (2km to the north) and the sedate resort of Lovran (6km to the south); it offers a far better way of exploring the town than the rather tatty and traffic-choked main street, **Maršala Tita**. Squeezed between the promenade and Maršala Tita, about 500m northeast of the bus station, lie the flowerbeds and lovingly clipped shrubs of the **Park Angiolina**, surrounding Scarpa's original **Villa Angiolina** (which sporadically opens for visitors; the tourist office should have details) and boasting rows of exotic palms. On the western edge of the park is the oldest and grandest of Opatija's hotels, the *Kvarner*, whose facade, complete with trumpet-blowing cherubs and bare-chested Titans, looks more like a provincial opera house than a hotel. Immediately west of the hotel, the **Juraj Šporer Art Pavilion**

(Umjetnički pavilion Juraj Šporer; times and prices depend what's on) hosts contemporary art exhibitions in an attractive colonnaded building that once served as a seafront patisserie. Opatija's **beach** – a cemented-over lido opposite the bus station – is the biggest let-down in the Adriatic; it's better to walk 3km south to the gravelly beach at **Ičići**, or catch a bus to **Medveja**, where there's a much bigger, shingly affair.

Offering a complete contrast to Opatija are the steep, narrow alleyways and shuttered houses of **Volosko**, once a separate village but now swallowed up by Opatija's suburban sprawl, an easy twenty minutes' walk northeast along the coastal promenade. Again, specific attractions are thin on the ground, but it's an atmospheric place for a short wander, with its whitewashed buildings arranged into a kasbah-like maze of streets, and a small fishing fleet in its tiny *mandrać* (inner harbour).

Eating and drinking

Provided you stay well away from the bland fare served up in hotel restaurants, Opatija is an excellent place in which to sample **Adriatic seafood** at its best – some of the town's restaurants are truly outstanding. Most of the **cafés** along Maršala Tita have had all trace of the *belle époque* ripped out of them, although the one beneath the *Palace-Bellevue* hotel has a good selection of cakes and a spacious terrace on which to see and be seen. There's no shortage of snack bars along the same road – *Pomodoro*, up an alleyway beside Maršala Tita 136, is the place to pick up pizza slices.

The harbour, 1km northeast of the bus station, is the prime evening **drinking** area, where a forest of chairs, tables and parasol stands spreads out from a cluster of flash cafés and cocktail bars. Of these, *Hemingway* is the only place that stands out, with its stylish brown-and-white colour scheme and long menu of designer cocktails. Back in the centre, the swish *Monokini* at Maršala Tita 96 attracts the hip crowd for its loungey atmosphere, DJs and monthly art shows. In **Volosko**, the *Kon-Tiki* is a chic and relaxing café right by the *mandrać*; while *Vološčica*, on the waterfront a little farther north, is a smaller, standing-room-only kind of place inside, although it too has an outdoor terrace. The best club on this stretch of coast is the *Colosseum*, right by Opatija's concrete lido.

Restaurants

We've included phone numbers for those restaurants where it's wise to reserve a table.

Amfora Črnikovica 4, Volosko ⓣ051/701-222, ⓦwww.restaurant-amfora.com. Succulent fresh fish in a pricey restaurant at the northern end of Volosko, its dining room overlooking a rocky, wave-battered cove. Try the fish platter (*riblji pladanj*), which usually features the grilled catch of the day garnished with the odd squid and shrimp.

Bevanda-Lido Zert 8 ⓣ051/712-772. Superior-quality seafood served up by attentive, liveried staff in a Neoclassical pavilion near Opatija's harbour. Good for fresh lobster, but there's also an extensive list of Croatian wines, plus the biggest choice of desserts in town.

Istranka Božidara Milanovića 2. Traditional tavern just uphill from Opatija's main street, with an interior hung with domestic knick-knacks and home-cured hams. Sometimes over-touristed in season, but nevertheless a reliable source of hearty soups, spicy sausages and fireside-grilled pork chops. Moderately priced, too.

Kaneta Nova cesta 64 ⓣ051/712-222. Cosy little pub-restaurant uphill from the centre, with pictures of old Opatija on the wall and very few tables. Good place for an inexpensive lunch of pasta or goulash, or a more substantial meaty meal – traditional dishes like *buncek* (smoked leg of pork) and *koljenica* (pork knuckle) are a speciality.

Le Mandrać Obala F. Supila 10, Volosko ⓣ051/701-357, ⓦwww.lemandrac.com. An upmarket place much favoured by local foodies, serving superb fish and shellfish dishes prepared with a modern European slant. Chic interior, and an outdoor terrace overlooking Volosko's *mandrać* (inner harbour).

Madonnina Pava Tomašića 3 (signposted just off Maršala Tita near the tourist office). Best place in

Hiking on Mount Učka

Dominating the skyline above Opatija and Lovran is the long, forest-covered ridge of the **Učka massif**, which divides the Kvarner region from central Istria and is protected as a Nature Park (®www.pp-ucka.hr). A tunnel under Učka's northern branch provides a fast road link between Rijeka and the Istrian hinterland, but there's an older, more scenic route which climbs from Rijeka via the village of Veprinac over the northern shoulder of the mountain, passing a turn-off to the 1396-metre summit of **Vojak** before zigzagging down to join the newer main road on the other side. Rather than driving all the way to Vojak, however, the best way to enjoy Učka's wooded slopes is to walk. Paths are well marked, and the *Učka* **map** (25Kn), available from the tourist offices in Opatija and Lovran, is an invaluable guide. For avid hikers, the more elaborate mountaineering guide to Učka, also available from the tourist office, is a good buy at 55Kn.

Lovran is the starting point for the most direct **hiking route** up the mountain – the ascent takes around three and a half hours. A flight of rough-hewn steps begins immediately behind Lovran's old centre, leading to the small Romanesque Chapel of St Rock on the edge of the village of **Liganj**. Join the road into Liganj for a couple of hundred metres, before heading uphill to the right through the hamlets of **Dindići** and **Ivulići** – semi-abandoned clusters of farmhouses and moss-covered dry-stone walls. From Ivulići it's a steady two-hour ascent through oak and beech forest before you emerge onto a grassy saddle where an expansive panorama of inland Istria suddenly opens up, revealing the knobbly green and brown forms of the peninsula's central hills; the peak of Vojak is another twenty minutes' walk to the right. At the top, there's an observation tower, TV mast and splendid views of Rijeka and the spindly form of Cres beyond. An **alternative ascent**, which takes about fifty minutes longer, starts just behind the **Medveja campsite** (see p.246) and ascends to the village of **Lovranska Draga** before climbing steeply up a wooded ravine to join the main path from Lovran.

From Vojak, a path descends north to **Poklon** (1hr), where you meet up with the old Rijeka–Istria road. There's a terrace offering another view of the Kvarner Gulf here, and a mountain hut and restaurant, though they're only open sporadically. Follow the road 1km west from Poklon to reach the *Dopolavoro* **restaurant**, invariably packed out with day-tripping Rijeka folk at weekends (when you might have to reserve; ⓣ051/299-641) who come to sample its top-notch Istrian cuisine and game dishes such as venison, pheasant and boar. On Sundays, **bus #34** from Opatija climbs as far as Poklon once a day, making this a good starting point from which to tackle Vojak if time is short. From Poklon, you can work your way southeast back to Lovran (roughly a 2hr walk) by a downhill path which ultimately joins the main route you came up on.

town for a filling, cheap feed, serving up pizzas, pasta and salads in a bustling, convivial interior – there's also an outdoor terrace facing the *Kvarner* hotel.

Mali Raj Maršala Tita 191. The name of the restaurant means "little heaven", which is not a bad description of this clifftop terrace on the promenade between Opatija and Ičići. Splash out on lobster, grilled fish and shellfish, or tuck into the more moderately priced grilled meats.

Plavi Podrum Obala F. Supila 12, Volosko ⓣ051/701-223. Smart establishment right on Volosko's harbour, renowned for its expertly prepared seafood. You can opt for simple, tasty meals like *fritaja* (omelette) sprinkled with a range of seasonal goodies, or linger over more substantial fish and lobster dishes while splashing out on the extensive wine list.

Villa Ariston Maršala Tita 179 (can also be entered from the seafront promenade) ⓣ051/271-379. Top-of-the-range seafood, plus pork and chicken in rich sauces, and a long wine list. You can sit either inside, in what looks like a nineteenth-century French drawing room, or outside in the palm-packed garden.

Lovran and around

It's an easy hour's walk south along the coastal promenade from Opatija to **LOVRAN**, following a rocky shore punctuated by two pebbly coves at Ičići and Ika. On arrival you'll find an Italianate, green-shuttered little town with a small harbour, fringed by palatial *belle époque* villas whose curly wrought-iron

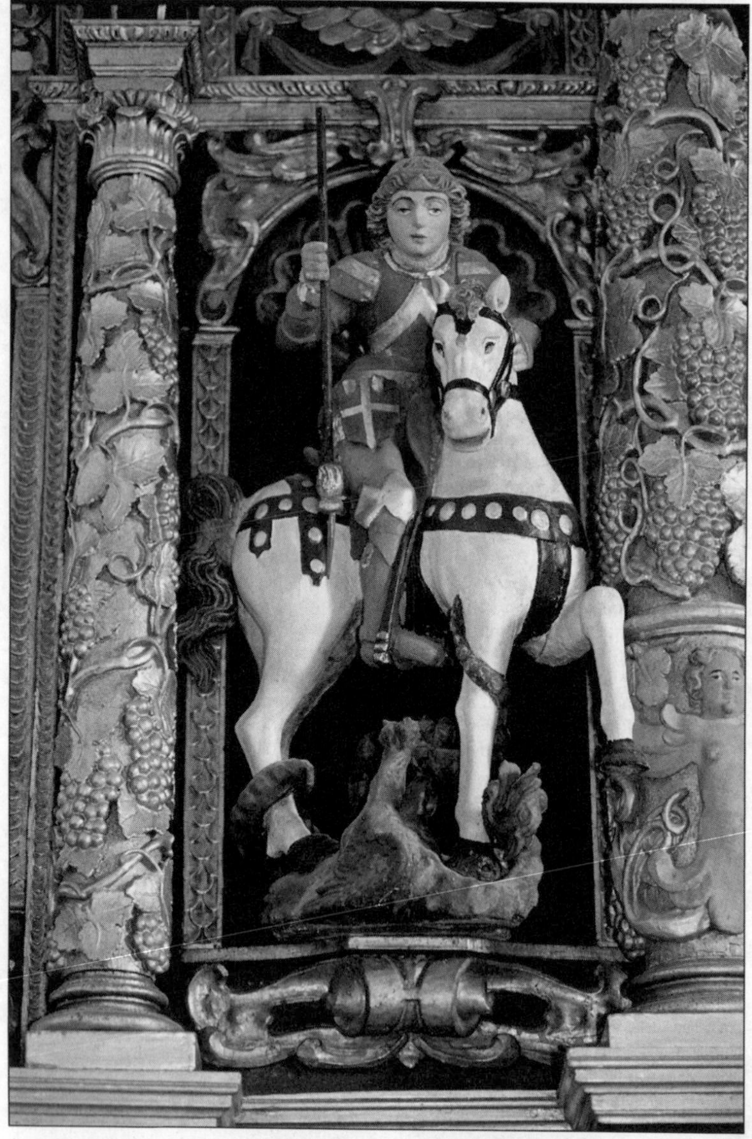

△ Relief of St George slaying the dragon in Lovran

balustrades are covered in green espaliers. Behind the main street, **Maršala Tita**, a small old quarter climbs the hill. Vine-shaded cobbled alleys converge on the fourteenth-century **St George's Church** (Crkva svetog Jurja); the frescoes behind the main altar, which date from 1479, are reminiscent in style of the wall paintings at Beram and other Istrian churches. Opposite the church, the **House of St George** bears an eighteenth-century relief of the saint slaying a dragon above the doorway; it's become something of a town trademark.

Habsburg-era villas are scattered all over Lovran. Many were taken over by the state and turned into flats after World War II; sadly, none are open to the public. Some of the best are concentrated northeast of the centre along Maršala Tita, where you can hardly miss the Secessionist **Villa Gianna** at no. 23, a mauve-pink confection built in 1904 by local architect Attilio Maguolo. It's embellished with ornate Corinthian columns and winged dragons clutching shields inscribed with the initials IP, a reference to the original owner, Iginio Persich. Farther on, beyond the *Excelsior* hotel, another group of villas lurks in shady seaside gardens. The most famous of these is the **Villa Frappart** on Viktora Cara Emina, another Secession-inspired work built for Viennese lawyer Michel Ruault Frappart by Karl Seidl in 1890. An eclectic Byzantine-Gothic building, whose colonnaded entrance gives it palatial pretensions, it now houses an elite music school.

Practicalities

Buses pick up and drop off on Lovran's main street, where most of what you need is located. There's a helpful **tourist office** (June–Sept Mon–Sat 8am–2pm & 5–8pm, Sun 8am–noon; Oct–May Mon–Sat 8am–3pm; ⓣ051/291-740, ⓦwww.tz-lovran.hr) which dispenses free town plans and brochures just off Maršala Tita, down a side alley behind the harbour.

Accommodation

Plentiful private **rooms** (❶) and **apartments** (studios ❷, four-person apartments from 450Kn) are available from three agencies (usually open June–Sept 8am–8pm, Oct–May Mon–Fri 9am–3pm): Stanger, Maršala Tita 128 (ⓣ & ⓕ051/293-266, ⓔtourist-agency-stanger@ri.t-com.hr); Hill, Trg slobode 15 (ⓣ051/293-700); and dmc Lovrana 1873, Stari Grad 1 (ⓣ051/294-910, ⓔlovrana@lovranske-vile.com). Fully equipped apartments in some of Lovran's more expensively restored turn-of-the-century **villas** can be arranged through Lovranske Vile, Poljanska 27, Ičići (ⓣ & ⓕ051/704-276, ⓦwww.lovranske-vile.com), although they don't come cheap and there's a minimum two-night stay; rates start at about 900Kn per night for a two-person studio and go up to 1800Kn per night for a four-bed apartment.

Hotels

Bristol Maršala Tita 27 ⓣ051/291-022, ⓦwww.liburnia.hr. Recently renovated, sporting a private beach and a charming array of creaky-floored rooms with reproduction nineteenth-century furniture. Inland-facing rooms come with en-suite shower and TV, while the more expensive sea-facing rooms have baths and balconies. ❺–❻

Excelsior Maršala Tita 15 ⓣ051/292-233, ⓦwww.liburnia.hr. Concrete tourist palace built in the 1970s, offering spacious rooms – most have balconies – with TV, minibar, and dowdy-brown colour schemes. Also has seawater-fed indoor and outdoor pools, a sauna and tennis courts. ❻

Lovran Maršala Tita 19 ⓣ051/291-222, ⓦwww.hotel-lovran.hr. Nineteenth-century building overlooking the coastal path, with high-ceilinged en suites boasting TV and nondescript contemporary furnishings. Inland-facing rooms are a bit dark and stuffy; those on the seafront side are bright and pleasant. The hotel has its own tennis courts. ❺

Park Maršala Tita 60 ⓣ051/706-200, ⓦwww.hotel-park-lovran.hr. Renovated Hasbsburg-era building offering modern stylish rooms with TV, a/c and sea views – although they're not exactly spacious and most come with shower cubicle rather than bathtub. There's also a sauna and gym. ❻

Stanger 26. Divizije 2 ⓣ051/291-403, ⓕ294-345, ⓔdragan.stanger@hep.hr. Cosy bed and breakfast in a modern, three-storey house a stone's throw from the centre uphill from Maršala Tita. Rooms are en suite with tiny balconies. The owners speak Italian and German. ❷

Villa Astra Victora Cara Emina 11 ⓣ051/704-276, ⓦwww.lovranske-vile.com. Lovran's most exclusive hotel, this beautifully restored four-star villa, surrounded by lush subtropical plants, sports six tastefully decorated en-suite rooms, a gourmet restaurant and a lovely outdoor terrace with a heated pool. High-season rates from 1820Kn. ❾

Villa Eugenia Maršala Tita 34 ⓣ051/294-800, ⓦwww.eto.hr. Primarily catering to a business clientele, this modern hotel boasts fifteen en-suite rooms with sleek minimalist design, private balconies, high-speed Internet connection, TV and minibar. ❼

Eating

Knezgrad Trg slobode 12. Quality meat and fish dishes at moderate prices; there are often cheap lunchtime menus chalked up on a board outside.

Kvarner Maršala Tita 65. Excellent fresh seafood, slightly pricier than at *Knezgrad*, overlooking the harbour.

Najade Maršala Tita 69 ⓣ051/291-866. The best place to eat in town, with a big outdoor terrace, attentive service and freshly caught fish – the *punjene lignje* (squid stuffed with *pršut* and cheese) is exceptional. Expect to pay 250–350Kn per person for a three-course meal with drinks.

Oaza Maršala Tita 37. Probably the town's cheapest place to eat, serving a range of pizza and pasta dishes.

Pod Voltun Stari Grad 23, just off Maršala Tita. A good place for a quick bite, with burgers, hot dogs and sandwiches served from a small window stand.

Drinking and entertainment

There are plenty of places offering **coffee** and ice cream along Maršala Tita; best for night-time **drinking** is *Lovranski Pub* at no. 41, a cosy subterranean hideaway with a secluded outdoor terrace.

The Lovran area is famous for its chestnut trees, which were originally imported from Japan in the seventeenth century. They are harvested in mid-autumn, an event celebrated by the **Marunada Chestnut Festival** (call the tourist office for details) which takes place over three weekends in October: the first two weekends see festivities in hill villages above town, while the final weekend takes place in Lovran itself. The festival is used as an excuse for making a wide variety of cakes flavoured with chestnut purée, which are sold in all the local cafés.

Around Lovran: Medveja and Mošćenička Draga

Three kilometres beyond Lovran, the small village of **MEDVEJA** has the area's best **beach** – a long crescent of shingle which can get crowded on summer weekends. Immediately behind the beach there's a small **tourist office** (June–Sept Mon–Fri 8am–3pm & 4–7pm, Sat 8am–noon & 4–7pm, Sun 10am–1pm & 4–7pm; ⓣ051/291-296, ⓔtzm.medveja@ri.htnet.hr), which can help you find local **rooms** (❶) or apartments (studios ❸, four-person apartments from 450Kn). There's also a well-appointed and spacious **campsite** (ⓣ051/291-191, ⓦwww.liburnia.hr), attractively tucked into a steep-sided valley, with a supermarket and grill restaurant on site. Four kilometres farther on lies **MOŠĆENIČKA DRAGA**, the Riviera's last settlement, unattractively squeezed around the monster-sized *Marina* hotel. Here there's another popular stretch of pebbly beach, and a **tourist office** on Aleja Slatina bb (mid-June to mid-Sept daily 7am–9pm; ⓣ051/739-166, ⓦwww.tz-moscenicka-draga.hr). The AnnaLinea agency, which has offices by the main road and near the beach (Ⓣ & Ⓕ 051/737-207, Ⓦ www.annalinea.hr), rents out private **rooms** (❶–❷) and apartments (studios ❸, four-person apartments 480–550Kn).

Cres and Lošinj

The westernmost of the Kvarner islands, **CRES** and **LOŠINJ** (really a single island divided by a narrow artificial channel), together make up a narrow sliver of land which begins just south of the Istrian coast and extends most of the way across the Kvarner Gulf. Allegedly the place where Jason and the Argonauts fled with the Golden Fleece, the islands were originally known as the "Absyrtides"; according to locals, Medea killed her brother Absyrtus here as he pursued her and threw his remains into the sea, where two of his limbs became Cres and Lošinj.

Cres (pronounced "tsress") is the second largest of the Adriatic islands, only beaten in size by neighbouring Krk. It marks the transition between the lush green vegetation of northern Croatia and the bare karst of the Adriatic, with the deciduous forest and overgrown hedgerows of northern Cres – the so-called **Tramuntana** – giving way to the increasingly barren sheep-pastures of the southern part of the island. Sheep apart, there's not much agriculture on the island, and the only other economic activities are fishing and tourism. Despite its proximity to the mainland, Cres is by far the wilder and more unspoiled of the two islands, boasting a couple of attractively weatherbeaten old settlements in **Osor** and **Cres Town**, as well as numerous villages and coves in which modern-day mass tourism has yet to make an impact.

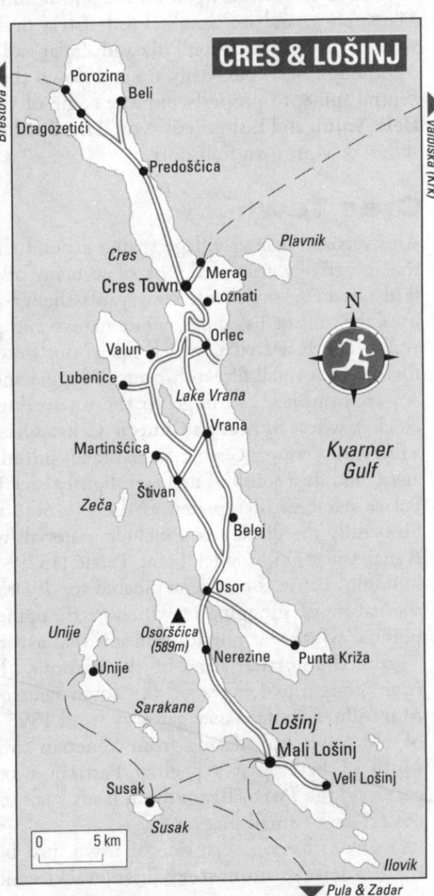

Lošinj (pronounced "losheen") is smaller and more touristed than Cres, with a thick, woolly tree cover that comes as a relief after the obdurate grey-greenness of southern Cres. Long overshadowed by its neighbour, Lošinj developed a thriving maritime trade after the demise of the Venetian Republic, with a large fleet and several shipyards, and later emerged as a holiday destination – like Opatija on the mainland, it started out in the late nineteenth century as a winter health-resort for sickly Viennese. Nowadays the island's main town, **Mali Lošinj**, is a magnet for holidaymakers from central Europe, though even here you'll find a characterful old town and port relatively unsullied by concrete mega-developments. Its near-neighbour **Veli Lošinj**, which lies within walking distance, is smaller and offers more in terms of fishing-village charm – although it too can get crowded in August.

Access to the islands

Getting to the islands is relatively straightforward. **Ferries** run hourly from **Brestova** (see p.222), just south down the Istrian coast from Opatija, to **Porozina** in northern Cres, and once every ninety minutes from **Valbiska** on Krk to **Merag** on Cres. Most **buses** plying the Rijeka–Cres–Lošinj route use the Brestova ferry crossing, although at least one bus daily goes via Valbiska. If you're driving, bear in mind that both ferries attract lengthy queues on summer weekends – so it's best to arrive early or bring a good book. There's also a daily catamaran service between Rijeka and Mali Lošinj, stopping in Cres Town and Martinšćica, and on Susak. From Istria or Dalmatia, each of the two ferries weekly that run between Pula and Zadar call at Mali Lošinj.

Although buses run daily up and down the main road along the island's hilly central spine, to properly explore some of the smaller places on Cres – such as **Beli**, **Valun** and **Lubenice** – you'll need either plenty of time and good walking shoes, or your own transport.

Cres Town

An oversized fishing village strung around a small harbour, **CRES TOWN** has the attractively crumpled look of so many of the towns on this coast: tiny alleys lead nowhere, minuscule courtyards shelter an abundance of greenery spilling over the rails of balconies, while mauve and pink flowers sprout from cracks in walls. **Trg F. Petrića**, which opens out onto the harbour, is the town centre, flanked by a small fifteenth-century loggia and a sixteenth-century clock tower. An archway leads through to the square known as **Pod urom** ("Beneath the clock"), where **St Mary's Church** (Crkva svete Marije; daily 9am–6.30pm) boasts a fifteenth-century Gothic–Renaissance portal featuring a fine relief of the Virgin and Child. Just south of here, set slightly back from the harbour, the Gothic Petris Palace has been designated as the site of a yet-to-be-opened **town museum**. Hopefully the display will include materials relating to Cres's most famous son, Renaissance philosopher Frane Petrić (1529–1597), who was born in this very building. Petrić is best remembered for *Il Delfino* ("The Dolphin"), a treatise on the nature of snogging in which Petrić opines, "the moment of the kiss is the point at which our physical and spiritual natures meet and become one".

From the northern end of the harbour, the main street, **Creskog statuta**, runs along the fringes of the town centre before ending up at the **Porta Marcella**, a Renaissance gateway from 1595 that stands at one end of a stretch of old town wall dating from Venetian times. A couple of hundred metres south of here, past a peeling Partisan war memorial, another Renaissance gateway, the **Porta Bragadina**, leads back into the mazy centre of town via a collection of small piazzas.

Over on the southern side of town, just behind a rather ugly shipyard area, the **Franciscan monastery** (Franjevački samostan; open for Sun Mass) holds a shaded cloister and a small **museum** (by appointment, ⓣ051/571-217; 5Kn), in which flaky portraits of Franciscan theologians are outshone by Andrea de Murano's *Virgin and Child* of 1475, a warm depiction of a fat and mischievous Jesus with dove in hand.

Swimming in Cres takes place along the concreted Lungomare promenade, which stretches west of town as far as the campsite some 1500m away in the suburb of Melin; there's a naturist section on the far side.

Practicalities

Buses stop near the petrol station just off the harbour area, where a narrow alleyway leads to the **tourist office** at Cons 10 (June–Sept Mon–Sat 8am–8pm, Sun 9am–1pm; Oct–May Mon–Fri 8am–3pm; ⓣ051/571-535, ⓦwww.tzg-cres.hr), which has a respectable stock of English-language brochures and can tell you just about everything you need to know about the island. Bikes (80Kn/day) and scooters (200Kn/day) can be rented from the Šumice kiosk in front of the *Hotel Kimen* (see below). Diving Cres (aka Padi Diving) in the Kovačine campsite (April–Oct; ⓣ051/571-706, ⓦwww.divingcres.de), offers half-day trial dives for beginners from 260Kn, and takes experienced divers on excursions to undersea cliffs and submerged rock formations in the seas around Cres.

Rooms (❶–❷) and apartments (studios ❷–❸, four-person apartments 420–550Kn) in the old town and in the suburb of **Melin**, 1km to the west, are available either from the Croatia travel agency next door to the tourist office (daily 8am–8pm; ⓣ051/573-053, ⓦwww.cres-travel.com), which also has an Internet terminal (1Kn/min), or the Cresanka Turist Biro round the corner on the harbour (daily 8am–8pm; ⓣ051/571-161, ⓦwww.cresanka.hr). Also in Melin is the *Kimen* **hotel**, an unseemly concrete structure set back from the Lungomare (ⓣ051/571-161, ⓦwww.hotel-kimen.com; ❺), with box-like but acceptable en-suite rooms, an excursion desk and an Internet corner (30Kn/hr). Swisher and more expensive en-suite rooms with modern furnishings, TV and air-conditioning are available another 500m west along the Lungomare at the thirteen-room *Kuća Kovačine* (ⓣ051/573-150, ⓦwww.camp-kovacine.com; ❺), which lies inside the Kovačine **campsite**. The site itself occupies a terraced seaside area shaded by olives and other trees, is home to a popular diving school (introductory dives start at 290Kn), and has a large naturist section on the far side.

There are plenty of **eating** opportunities around Cres harbour: *Slastičarnica Baccio* has good pastries and excellent ice cream; and *Konoba Kopac* on Osorska, a narrow alley just inland from the harbour, serves up succulent grilled fish in a stone interior lit from lampshades made out of wicker baskets. Marginally classier *Riva* has a prime waterside position, and is the best place to try top-quality fish such as *orada* (gilthead) and *škrpina* (groper). Slightly farther afield, *Gostionica Belona*, opposite the Partisan war memorial on Šetalište XX travnja, has a similar range of meat and seafood, and does a good *lignje nažaru* (grilled squid). Cres is famous for its **lamb** (*janjetina*), and one of the best places to try it is *Bukaleta*, just 5km outside Cres Town in the village of Loznati; to find it, follow the main road to Lošinj and take the signed turn-off leading you right to the restaurant. Open seasonally (April–Oct) and usually packed in August (reserve on ⓣ051/571-606), this restaurant has been dishing out top-quality lamb dishes for the last 25 years – try the lamb soup, fried lamb steak or lamb *al forno*, served with delicious oven-baked bread, potatoes and salads, and then top it off with the homemade honey biscuits.

There's no shortage of **cafés** along the seafront, although they can sometimes get a bit blustery – in which case head for the more sheltered *Café Kadena* beside the church on Pod urom.

Beli

North of Cres Town, the island narrows into a long, high ridge, descending steeply towards the sea on either side. The road dives from one side of the ridge to the other, swapping views of the Istrian peninsula to the west and the mainland from Rijeka to Velebit to the east. Thirteen kilometres north of Cres Town a minor road forks right off the main road, passing through half-deserted hamlets and oak and chestnut forests en route to the village of **BELI**. Huddled atop a knobbly hill high above the channel dividing Cres from Krk, Beli is an impressive agglomeration of ancient stone houses, many of them now left uninhabited as locals move away in search of work. It's gloriously rustic and peaceful, and there's a small shingle cove below the village at the end of a steep road.

Beli is also home to the **Caput Insulae Ecology Centre** (Eko-centar Caput Insulae; daily 9am–7pm; 20Kn; ⓦwww.caput-insulae.com), established in the mid-1980s to monitor and protect the community of **griffon vultures** (see box opposite) indigenous to Cres. Located at the end of a stony road to the left as you enter the village, the centre has an exhibition on the vultures, with photographs and English-language text, and a small aviary in the back garden where sick vultures are often kept before being returned to the wild. They can also provide directions for the centre's **ecology paths** (*eko-staze*), three circular hiking trails which start here and lead through the forest, passing through a mixed area of pasture, forest, abandoned villages and *gradine* (the small, walled-off areas of cultivable land typical to Croatia's limestone areas) on the way. The most interesting of the trails is the 7km red path that takes you past twenty

The griffon vultures of Cres

The white-headed **griffon vulture** (*bijeloglavi sup*) formerly lived all over the Kvarner region, coexisting with a local sheep-farming economy that guaranteed the carrion-eating birds a constant supply of food. With the decline of sheep-rearing in the twentieth century, vulture numbers fell dramatically and communities of the birds are nowadays only found on the northeast coast of Cres and in a few isolated spots on Krk and the mainland. When conservationists first came to the area in the mid-1980s there were 24 pairs of vultures on the island; that number has now risen to about seventy, not least because locals have been educated to leave dead animals for the vultures to clear up rather than removing them from the fields themselves.

Fully grown griffon vultures have a wingspan of 2.5m, can weigh 8–10kg, live for up to 60 years, and can spot a sheep or donkey carcass from a distance of 6km. Their nesting area in the rocky cliffs on the eastern side of the island between Beli and Merag is now protected by law: it's forbidden to sail within 50m of the cliffs, as frightened young birds may fall out of their nests if disturbed. The vultures nest in December and produce one egg per pair, the young bird staying with its parents until August, when it begins a five-year roving period – which could take it to other vulture colonies in the Balkans or Near East – before returning to the island to breed. The main **threats** to the vultures are telephone wires, electricity power lines and contact with man-made poisons, such as the bait left out for vermin; the vulture population of Plavnik, an uninhabited island off the east coast of Cres, disappeared completely after the food chain had become contaminated in this way.

open-air sculptures by Ljubo de Karina, inscribed with Glagolitic script and poems by local poet Andro Vid Mihičić. The vultures themselves regularly scour the sparsely inhabited northern extremities of Cres in search of food – there's quite a good chance of spotting one, but don't count on it.

There are two daily **buses** from Cres to Beli on weekdays; in addition, the daily Cres–Porozina–Rijeka bus stops 7km away on the main road. *Pansion Tramontana* (Ⓣ051/840-519 or 091 544-4807, Ⓔpansion-tramontana@ri.t-com.hr; ❸) offers comfortable B&B accommodation, although it's difficult to get a place here in summer unless you book well in advance. The only **campsite** is the *Brajdi* (Ⓣ051/840-532, Ⓕ840-522), below the village near the beach, where there's also a small **grill-restaurant**. Back in the village, the *Gostionica Beli*, a cosy place decorated with farm tools, has a wider range of fish and meat dishes – including local roast lamb – and is also a good place for a drink. Beli is a good base for scuba-diving, with Diving Base Beli, based at *Pansion Tramontana* (March–Nov; Ⓣ051/840-519, Ⓦwww.diving-beli.com), offering introductory dives and week-long courses.

Valun, Lubenice and Martinišćica

About eight buses a day leave Cres Town for Mali Lošinj, a spectacular journey at times as the road hugs the island's central ridge before descending towards the sea at Osor. Eight kilometres south of Cres Town a minor road heads right towards the sparsely populated western side of the island. After 5km a side road descends to **VALUN**, a tiny fishing village with colourful houses crowding round its harbour, a quiet shingle beach and ultra-clear waters – it's very popular with weekending Italians, but remains more or less free from development. Three buses a week on the Cres Town–Mali Lošinj route stop in Valun, but only two go directly back to Cres Town, so you need to plan ahead and get timetable information in Cres Town before you set out, or rent a car. Cresanka **tourist agency** just behind the harbour (June–Sept daily 8am–9pm; Ⓣ051/525-050, Ⓦwww.cresanka.hr) has **rooms** (❶), and there's the very attractive small *Zdovice* **campsite** 100m east of the harbour, right on the beach (Ⓣ051/525-050, Ⓦwww.cresanka.hr). For **eating**, *Konoba Toš Juna* has a terrace on the harbourfront and is a good place to try the local *škampi* (shrimps) and *creška janjetina* (Cres lamb).

From Valun a narrow road leads 5km southwest to **LUBENICE**, a windswept village occupying a ridge high above the shore. Almost medieval in appearance, it's like a more extreme version of Beli – a depopulated cluster of half-ruined stone houses and a dwindling permanent population of around twenty. The square at the entrance to the village boasts an invigorating view of the rugged western coast, with a pair of idyllic, secluded pebbly coves far below; they're only accessible by boat or via a very steep and tiring path. The village hosts alfresco **classical music** concerts on the main square as part of **Lubenice Music Nights** (Lubeničke glazbene večeri) every Friday evening in July and August; tickets can be bought from the Autotrans agency (Ⓣ051/572-050, Ⓦwww.autotrans.hr) back in Cres Town (40Kn, with transportation). There are only five weekly buses (at the time of writing, two on Mondays & Wednesdays and one on Fridays) from Cres Town to Lubenice, so you'll need a car to explore thoroughly.

Back on the main road to Lošinj, you'll see **Lake Vrana** appear below and to the west, an emerald-green ellipse of fresh water that supplies both Cres and Lošinj – but for this lake, both islands would be utterly dry, and you can't swim here due to its importance as a source of drinking water. Shortly after you pass the lake, there's a turn-off to the right (west) running 9km down to the small village of **MARTINIŠĆICA**, which has a long shingle beach. Modern and lacklustre in comparison to Valun or Lubenice, it nevertheless boasts a well-organized if over-large **campsite**, just west of the village on the Slatina peninsula (Ⓣ051/574-127, Ⓦwww.slatina-camping.de), with pitches set close to the shore between shrubs and pines.

Osor

Set beside the narrow strait which divides Cres from Lošinj, **OSOR** is an erstwhile cathedral town which has shrunk to the size of a hamlet. It's the oldest settlement on either island, a prosperous Roman city which some historians believe once had a population of fifteen thousand, although a couple of thousand seems more realistic. Osor's regional importance survived into the medieval era, thanks in part to the reputation of eleventh-century holy man (and later saint) Gaudentius, who established the now ruined monastery of St Peter here and turned Osor into a centre of Glagolitic manuscript production. Driven out by local nobles, Gaudentius died in exile in Rome – from where his remains miraculously returned to Osor in a sea-borne wooden chest; they're now kept on the high altar of Osor's cathedral. Under Venetian rule, Osor was a typical casualty of the decline in Mediterranean trade which followed the discovery of America and the opening up of the transatlantic economy. Visiting in 1771, the Italian traveller Abbé Fortis described it as a "corpse of a town, in which there are more houses than inhabitants".

The Town

Osor nowadays is a small village with a permanent population of around seventy, its streets exuding a peace that, on a hot summer's day, it seems nothing will ever disturb. The cobbled kernel of the village stands just above the **Kavuada**, the narrow channel – just 11m wide – which divides Cres and Lošinj. Dug either by the Romans or their Illyrian predecessors, it's now spanned by a swing bridge that opens at 9am and 5pm every day to let boats through. Presiding over a funnel-shaped main square is the **Church** (originally Cathedral) **of the Assumption** (Crkva Uznesenja), completed in 1497 and boasting an elegant trefoil facade in smooth, pale stone. The small **Archeological Museum** (Arheološki muzej; May to mid-June Mon–Fri 10am–noon; mid-June to mid-Sept daily 10am–noon & 7–9pm; 10Kn) in the Venetian town hall opposite has Roman relics and a model of medieval Osor enclosed by extensive town walls, stretches of which survive in much reduced form.

On the other side of the square, a narrow street runs past the fifteenth-century **Bishop's Palace**, now a sporadically open lapidarium harbouring bits of masonry from Osor's many churches, several of which are covered with the *plutej*, a plait-like design characteristic of Croatian medieval art. The most imposing item on display is the **bishop's throne**, a composite work made from Romanesque stone fragments taken from the graveyard of St Mary's Church – the backrest is embellished with a fine carving of two birds hovering above a lion-like beast. Ten minutes north of the square, past the graveyard, lies Bijar Bay, where a small beach is overlooked by the ruins of the thirteenth-century **Franciscan monastery**, another important centre of Glagolitic culture in its day.

Practicalities

Osor's limited number of **rooms** (❶) can be booked through the sporadically open kiosk at the entrance to *Preko Mosta* campsite (Ⓣ051/237-350, Ⓔbookings@jazon.hr, Ⓦwww.jazon.hr), across the bridge on the Lošinj side of town. Vacancies are rare in high season, and you're best advised to email in advance if your heart is set on staying here. In addition to *Preko Mosta*, there's another campsite, the beautifully situated *Bijar* (Ⓣ051/237-027, Ⓦwww.jazon.hr), which has a shady seafront position on the northern side of town. For **eating**, *Konoba Livio* serves up decent pizza in a pleasant courtyard, while ✱ *Konoba Bonifačić* has a wider range of local seafood, Cres specialities like *janjeći žgvacet* (lamb stew) and a beautiful garden setting.

The **Osor Evenings** (Osorske večeri), a festival of chamber music, has been staging performances in the Church of the Assumption in July and August for the last thirty years – the tourist office in Mali Lošinj (see below) will have schedules and details.

Mali Lošinj

Straggling along either side of a deep sheltered bay, **MALI LOŠINJ** is a fast-growing resort whose outer layers of apartment and bungalow developments have failed to destroy the charm of its elegant core, where slender cypresses and spiky green palms poke up between tiers of peach and orange houses, covered in purple bougainvillea. Most of the hotels have been kept well out of the way on the Čikat peninsula just west of town, together with an enormous campsite and the island's most crowded beaches.

Arrival and information

Ferries from Pula and Zadar, and **buses** from Rijeka and Cres, stop at the northern end of Mali Lošinj's harbour, near the **tourist office** at Riva lošinjskih kapetana 29 (mid-June to mid-Sept Mon–Sat 8am–9pm, Sun 9am–1pm; mid-Sept to mid-June Mon–Fri 8am–3pm; Ⓣ & Ⓕ051/231-547, Ⓦwww.tz-malilosinj.hr). Staff here have bundles of free brochures and local maps, including one of the town and another covering foot- and bike-paths all over the island.

Jadrolinija, Riva lošinjskih kapetana 20 (Ⓣ051/231-765, Ⓦwww.jadrolinija.hr), and Lošinjska Plovidba, Riva lošinjskih kapetana 8 (Ⓣ051/231-077, Ⓦwww.losinjplov.hr), sell **ferry tickets** for the nearby islands of Susak, Ilovik and Unije as well as for Pula, Zadar, Rijeka and Novalja. Private boats moored in Mali Lošinj harbour offer half-day excursions to Susak (100Kn and upwards) or panoramic **island tours** (160–200Kn, with lunch included). **Mountain bikes** and **windsurf boards** can be rented (both about 70Kn per hour) on the seafront promenade in Čikat, in front of the *Bellevue* hotel. The near by **scuba-diving** centre (Ⓣ051/233-900, Ⓦwww.diver.hr) rents out gear and offers crash courses from 375Kn.

Accommodation

There's a wealth of accommodation in town. Numerous agencies offer private **rooms** (❶–❷) and apartments (two-person studios ❷, four-person apartments 520Kn): most helpful is the ✱ Cappelli agency, on the main road at the northern entrance to town at Kadin bb (Ⓣ051/231-582, Ⓦwww.cappelli-tourist.hr). Also worth trying are Lošinjska Plovidba (see above) and Manora, on the opposite side of harbour at Priko 29 (Ⓣ051/520-100, Ⓦwww.manora-losinj.hr). At the northwestern end of Čikat, a thirty-minute walk from the town centre, the vast *Autocamp Čikat* **campsite** occupies a wooded site with good access to the beaches (Ⓣ051/232-125, Ⓦwww.camps-cres-losinj.hr).

Of the **hotels**, there are a couple of four-star options, a rare occurrence in small coastal towns of Croatia, as well as a few family-run places. Note that some establishments close their doors out of season. Most of the package hotels on the Čikat peninsula are run by Jadranka (central booking on Ⓣ051/661-101, Ⓦwww.jadranka.hr) and are all much of a muchness.

Hotels

Alhambra Čikat bb Ⓣ051/232-022, Ⓕ232-042. This Jadranka property, housed in an attractive pastel-pink nineteenth-century villa surrounded by palms, offers slightly-dowdy rooms (although some have recently undergone minor renovation). ❹

Apoksiomen Riva lošinjskih kapetana 1 Ⓣ051/520-820, Ⓦwww.apoksiomen.com. The most stylish place in town, with a prime location right on the Riva, swish four-star rooms with marble-tiled bathrooms, wonderful sea vistas and original artwork on display. There's also a pleasant café on the ground floor. Open April–Oct. ❻

Bellevue Čikat bay Ⓣ051/231-222, Ⓕ231-268. The best of Jadranka's hotels, within walking distance of the town centre, this enormous rectangle of a hotel sports an indoor pool, sauna, beach bar and Internet corner. ❺

Villa Anna Velopin 31 Ⓣ051/233-223, Ⓦwww.vila-ana.hr. Smart rooms with modern furnishings, TV, attached bathroom and a small outdoor pool. The ground-floor nightclub ensures that this is no longer the quiet hideaway it used to be. ❺

Villa Favorita Sunčana Uvala Ⓣ051/520-640, Ⓦwww.villafavorita.hr. A short walk from the *Aurora*, in a renovated Habsburg-era mansion surrounded by nicely landscaped gardens. The hotel has an outdoor pool, a sauna and massage room, and offers eight spacious en suites with a/c, TV, minibar, and dial-up connection. ❼

Villa Margarita Bočac 64 Ⓣ051/233-838, Ⓦwww.vud.hr. Medium-sized place in the winding alleyways above the harbour, boasting nice en-suite rooms with TV and a/c, as well as nifty apartments (from 960Kn) and a decent restaurant. Open Easter–October only. ❺

The Town

Most life in Mali Lošinj revolves around the quayside **Riva lošinjskih kapetana**, where rows of potted cacti and subtropical plants line a harbourfront overrun in summer with souvenir stalls and café tables. The Riva's southern end opens out into the triangular open space of Trg Republike Hrvatske, from where **Braće Vidulića**, the main street, runs inland through the oldest part of town. Once you've clambered around the stepped alleys and winding streets, there's not much to see save the **Art Collections** (Umjetničke zbirke; June–Sept daily 10am–noon & 7–9pm; Oct–May call Ⓣ051/231-173 and they'll open it for you; 20Kn), displayed in the former House of Culture just behind the harbourfront at Vladimira Gortana 35. Inside lie the combined hoards of two private collectors, beginning with that of art critic and poet Andro Vid Mihičić, which concentrates on Croatian twentieth-century works, notably the mottled cityscapes of Paris-trained Emanuel Vidović. The second collection, that of Giuseppe Piperata – a Lošinj doctor who emigrated to Italy in 1945 but was prevented from taking his most valuable paintings with him – inclines more towards the Baroque. Highlights include Francesco Solimena's busy and agitated *Meeting with Rebecca*, and Il Guercino's more contemplative *Allegorical Landscape with Female Figures*, a pastoral scene of washerwomen beside a duck-filled pond.

The best place to swim is around **Čikat Bay**, 3km west of town, where a coastal path runs past a succession of concreted bathing areas, rocky beaches and a couple of stretches of pebble. It's a laid-back area, good for strolling whatever the season, with Habsburg holiday villas sheltering among wind-bent tamarisks and pines, and cafés and shacks renting out snorkelling gear and surfboards along the more popular stretches.

Eating, drinking and entertainment

For **snacks**, there are plentiful bakeries around town that sell bread, pastries and *burek*. There's a (not particularly cheap) fruit and veg **market** just uphill from the harbourfront on Braće Vidulića, and a fish market (Mon–Sat mornings only) on Trg Republike Hrvatske. **Drinking** and nightlife are centred on the cafés along the Riva, a few bars on Braće Vidulića, and tame Euro-discos in the hotels.

Restaurants

Artatore Artatore 132 ⓣ051/232-932. Fine dining 7km north of town, just off the road to Cres, in an establishment renowned for its fresh seafood, home-baked bread, and baked lamb – ring in advance if you want to order the latter. Elegant furnishings, and a lengthy list of top Croatian wines.

Barracuda Priko 31. Long-standing tourist favourite on the opposite side of the harbour to the Riva, offering attractive views of the yacht-lined quayside from its palm-fronted terrace. Expect excellent seafood risottos, good fresh fish, and a handful of recipes that depart from the traditional tourist-restaurant repertoire, such as shark in white-wine sauce and grilled fillet of tuna.

Konoba Corrado Sv. Marije 1 ⓣ051/232-487. Walled garden shaded by vine-trellises, just off the eastern end of Braće Vidulića. Smallish menu of fresh fish (both grilled and baked), as well as fresh scallops (*jakopove kapice*) and other shellfish. House specialities, including octopus or lamb baked *ispod peke* (under a charcoal-covered bell), should be ordered at least a day in advance. Extensive list of Istrian and Dalmatian wines.

Lanterna Sveti Martin bay, fifteen minutes' walk east of the town centre. Romantically situated on a small harbour beside a ruined boathouse, this is a good place to admire the sunset and tuck into excellent, not-too-pricey Adriatic food. There's a good mix of fish, shellfish, risottos and grilled cuts of meat. Roast Cres lamb is also on the menu, but has to be ordered 24 hours in advance.

Silvana Lošinjskih pomoraca 2 ⓣ052/232-591, ⓦwww.silvana.hr. In suburban streets east of the town centre this restaurant doesn't offer that much in the way of a view, but the food is first class. Fish and shellfish are among the best in town, while traditional meat dishes like roast lamb (*pečena janjetina*) and lamb stew (*janjeći žgvacet*) add variety to the menu. Impeccable service, and an interesting list of Croatian wines.

Valentin Trg žrtava fašizma 2. There are no outstanding pizzerias in central Lošinj, but this harbourside joint is the best of a rather ordinary bunch.

Bars

Mini Marina del Conte 1. In an alleyway just off the harbour, this is a wonderfully rustic-looking bar with bare stone interior and a couple of wooden benches (the rest is standing room only). Live rock and jazz at the weekends – although goodness knows how they manage to squeeze the musicians onto the tiny stage.

Zanzibar Riva Lošinjskih kapetana bb. This feels like two different bars depending on whether you choose to sit inside or out: the cramped and cosy interior, decorated with exotic wood-carvings, is just round the corner from the seafront, while the big alfresco terrace with loungey furniture is on the quayside.

Veli Lošinj

Despite the name (*veli* means "big", *mali* "little"), **VELI LOŠINJ** is actually a smaller, quieter version of Mali Lošinj, a warren of pastel-coloured houses strung tightly around a tiny natural harbour. It's a forty-minute walk from the centre of Mali Lošinj – follow Braće Vidulića uphill, head straight over the crossroads, and take the path downhill to the right to Baldarka Bay. From here you can pick up a wonderfully scenic shoreline path, which winds past a sequence of rocky bays before arriving at the *Punta* hotel, with Veli Lošinj's harbour just beyond. The main road from Mali to Veli Lošinj is quite scenic too, shaded by thick pine forest and with azure bays and rocky beaches just below.

Once you arrive, you can't miss the hangar-like Baroque **St Anthony's Church** (Crkva svetog Antuna), which contains a fine tempera-on-wood *Madonna with Saints* (above a side door on the left as you enter) painted by Bartolomeo Vivarini in 1475.

Originally commissioned by the Venetian senate, the painting was paraded around Venice every year on the anniversary of the Battle of Lepanto to celebrate the famous naval victory over the Ottomans, until being bought by a Lošinj family shortly after the fall of the Venetian Republic. On the opposite side of the harbour from the church, the **Lošinj Marine Education Center**, Kaštel 24 (daily: June–Sept 9am–noon & 5–10pm; April, May & Oct 9am–2pm; Nov–March 10am–noon; Ⓦwww.blue-world.org; free) has a small but very informative and entertaining display on Adriatic marine life, the main focus being the group of 120 or so bottlenose dolphins that frequent the waters around Lošinj and Cres. There's a thirty-minute documentary film with English subtitles, touch-screen computer info – and a kiddies' corner complete with instructions on how to annoy your parents by honking like a sea-turtle. You can also pick up information on how to support local conservation initiatives, most notably by adopting one of the dolphins for €20 a year – see Ⓦwww.plavi-svijet.org for more details.

Just behind the harbour, a narrow alleyway leads to a crenellated **Venetian tower**, built in 1455 to discourage raids by the Uskoks of Senj (see p.272). It now houses a small **museum** (daily: Easter to mid-Sept 10am–noon & 7–9pm; mid-Oct to mid-Nov 10am–noon; 8Kn), which tells the story of the island through an attractively displayed assemblage of nautical trinkets and paintings of old ships. The star exhibit is a replica of the Apoxymenos (which translates literally as the "man scraping himself off"), a Roman statue of a sporty youth conducting his ablutions with the aid of a dirt-removing body knife. The original, found off the coast of Lošinj in 1999, is currently in storage at the archeological museum in Zagreb, but may well be displayed in Mali Lošinj in the near future.

The best place to **swim** is by the rocks which lie next to the path from Mali Lošinj; there are also a few concreted areas near the packagey *Punta* hotel on Veli Lošinj's northwestern fringes. In front of the hotel, the **Lošinj Diving Center** (Ⓣ051/232-155, Ⓦwww.losinj-diving.com) rents out gear and offers a crash course for about 800Kn.

Practicalities

Rooms (❶) and **apartments** (studios ❸, four-person apartments from 520Kn) are available from Val, Obala Maršala Tita 34 (Ⓣ & Ⓕ051/236-352, Ⓦwww.losinj-val.com); Palma, slightly inland from the port at Vladimira Nazora 22 (Ⓣ051/236-179, Ⓦwww.losinj.com); or ASL Turist, Obala Maršala Tita 17 (Ⓣ & Ⓕ051/236-256, Ⓦwww.island-losinj.com). **Hostel** *Zlatokrila*, Kaciol 26 (May–Sept; Ⓣ051/236-312; 120Kn per person), occupying a pair of houses just inland from the harbour, offers sixty beds in a variety of dorms, and a nice palm-shaded terrace. The *Punta* **hotel**, Šestavina bb (Ⓣ051/662-000, Ⓦwww.jadranka.hr; ❺), offers comfortable en-suite rooms, most of which come with sea-facing balconies. It also has a wellness centre offering spa and beauty treatments, and thirteen tennis courts at its disposal. Cosier **pension**-style accommodation is available at the *Saturn* (Ⓣ051/236-102, Ⓦwww.losinj-val.com; ❸), which has neat, bright but cramped rooms right on the harbour above a trendy little café, and the charming *Vila San*, just above the harbour at Garina bb (Ⓣ & Ⓕ051/236-527, Ⓦwww.vila-san.hr; ❸); surrounded by lovely terraced gardens, it offers roomy en suites with TV and nice views of the harbour below. *Pjacal*, at Kaštel 3 (Ⓣ051/236-244, Ⓦwww.pjacal.com; ❸), a back street behind the harbour, is a B&B run by a Croatian-German couple offering neat little en-suite rooms decked out in whites and blues, and a buffet breakfast in the back garden.

The *Vila San* has a good **restaurant**; otherwise head for the Rovenska harbour at the eastern end of town, where there's a trio of excellent grilled fish restaurants by the waterside. The best is *Bora Bar*, Rovenska 3, which offers delicious risottos and homemade pastas, fresh fish (either grilled or oven-baked), and a quality choice of Istrian wines. Next-door *Sirius* at Rovenska 4 is more staid in style, but can always be counted on for excellent fresh seafood and outstanding lobster.

Susak

About 9km west of Lošinj, **SUSAK** is one of the most interesting of the smaller Kvarner islands. Its clay and sand composition gives it an appearance quite different from the rocky terrain of the other Adriatic islands, with ochre-coloured cliffs covered in clumps of bamboo-like reeds. Susak's isolation has produced a distinctive way of life: islanders still speak their own dialect and have retained many traditions and customs, including an unusual method of singing directly from the throat and a local costume which consists of gaudy green-and-yellow skirts worn with even brighter pink tights. Postcards and guidebooks would have you believe you'll see this all the time, although hardly anyone ever wears it nowadays. The island's industry, fish-canning, has long since died out, and many islanders emigrated to the Americas in the early twentieth century (hence the sizeable Susak community in Hoboken, New Jersey). The remaining population relies on money sent back by relatives to supplement income from sales of, among other things, Susak's **wines** – the red *pleskunac*, and *trojišćina*, an intriguing, dry rosé.

Susak village, the island's only settlement, sits on a wonderfully shallow bay filled with mud-brown sand. There's another, similarly sandy bay a short walk round the headland to the east. Narrow streets climb up from the seafront to the oldest part of the village, which grew up around an eleventh-century Benedictine monastery. The only surviving part of the monastery is **St Nicholas's Church** (Crkva svetog Nikole), inside which there's a large wooden twelfth-century crucifix known by the locals as *Veli Buoh* – the "Great God".

Susak gets its fair share of **day-trippers**; a Jadrolinija ferry does the rounds of the local islands three times daily in July and August (less often during the rest of the year), departing from Mali Lošinj early in the morning and returning later in the day. There are also excursions to Susak in smaller boats (from around 100Kn per person), leaving from Mali Lošinj's Riva. There's a limited number of private **rooms** (❶) on Susak but they're usually reserved months in advance – the tourist office in Mali Lošinj can give you a list of telephone numbers (they're also posted on the Ⓦwww.tz-malilosinj.hr website), but won't make bookings on your behalf. You can tuck into grilled squid and freshly caught fish at a small *konoba* in an alleyway behind St Nicholas's Church.

Susak celebrates its annual feast-day on July 30, when hundreds of émigrés return to the island for a day of folk music, eating and drinking – don't expect to find any accommodation on or around the island on this date.

Krk

The largest of the Adriatic islands, **KRK** (pronounced "Kirk", with a strongly rolled *r*) is also one of the most developed, a result of its proximity to Rijeka,

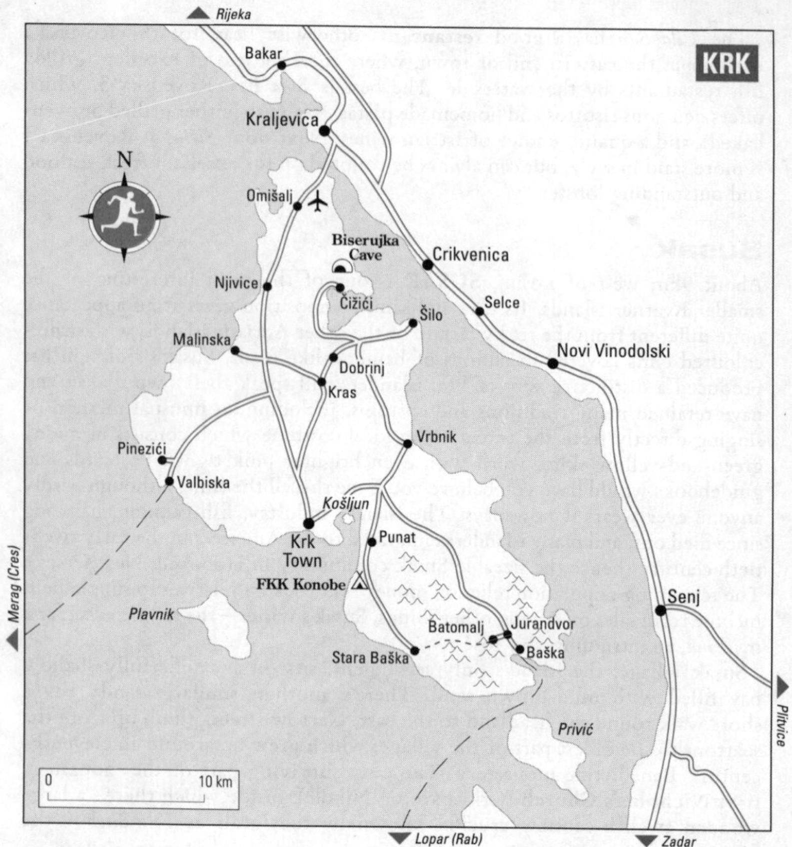

whose airport is situated on the island. Much of the north is taken up by package-oriented mega-developments like those at **Omišalj** and **Malinska**; the south and east, by contrast, offer grey, furrowed mountain peaks, lustrous vineyards, olive plantations and sun-bleached villages. The main settlements are **Krk Town**, in the middle of the island, a historic little place with scraps of city wall surrounding a compact old centre, and **Baška** in the far south, a quirky fishing village with a spectacular sandy beach.

Krk was originally a Roman base called Curictum; Caesar is supposed to have had an encampment on the island, and was defeated by Pompey in a naval battle just offshore in 49 BC. Later, Krk fell under the sway of the Venetians, who in 1118 gave control of the island to the Dukes of Krk, subsequently known as the **Frankopans** (see box on p.260), one of the region's most powerful feudal families. Krk returned to the Venetian fold in 1480, after which it shared in the fortunes of the rest of the Adriatic: a long, slow decline, followed by a sudden economic upsurge in the late twentieth century thanks to the tourist industry. In addition, the construction of the **bridge** linking Krk to the mainland enabled many locals to take jobs in Rijeka or elsewhere without having to move away from the island, thereby saving Krk from the rural depopulation which has afflicted other parts of the region.

Its proximity to the big city hasn't stopped Krk from preserving a few peculiarities of its own. Enduring **specialities** found only on the island include *šurlice*, long, thin tubes of **pasta** dough, traditionally eaten *sa gulašom* (with goulash) or *sa žgvacetom* (with lamb stew), and Vrbnička Žlahtina, an excellent white **wine** from Vrbnik on Krk's east coast. The island also preserves an archaic **musical tradition** in the form of the *mijeh*, a bagpipe made out of a goat's stomach, whose shrill, atonal squalls of noise form the backdrop to the dances performed at the **Krk Folklore Festival** (Smotra folklora otoka Krka; usually July or August), which is hosted by a different town on the island each year. The equally strident *sopila* (a screechy oboe-type instrument indigenous to Istria and Krk) is celebrated at the annual **Meeting of Sopila**

△ Olives growing on Krk

The Frankopans

The story of the Frankopans on Krk begins with the shadowy **Dujmo I**, who was given control of the island by the Venetians in the twelfth century. His successors managed to turn the island into a hereditary fiefdom which came to be known as the *državina* ("statelet"), an autonomous territory only nominally under Venetian control. As the **Dukes of Krk**, Dujmo's descendants used the island as a base from which to extend their power to the mainland, grabbing a coastal strip stretching from Bakar to Novi Vinodolski in 1225, expanding northeast into continental Croatia, and establishing footholds in Ogulin and Ozalj to create an arc of family estates.

The name of **Frankopan** was officially adopted in 1430, when Duke Nikola received papal support for his claim to be descended from the ancient Roman patrician family of Frangepan – a move which, it was hoped, would accord the dynasty the prestige needed to compete with the other great houses of Europe. Frankopan power on Krk, however, was on the wane, and the defeat of **Duke Ivan VII** by the Hungarians in 1480 was used by the Venetians as an excuse to finally take back control of the island. On the mainland, branches of the Frankopan clan remained powerful well into the seventeenth century, when in 1671 **Fran Krsto Frankopan**, the head of the family, was executed alongside his brother-in-law Petar Zrinski (see box on p.134) after leading an anti-Habsburg rebellion.

Players (Susret sopaca; first weekend in July) in the village of **Pinezići**, 8km northwest of Krk Town – the tourist office in Krk town will have details of both events.

There are occasional **flights** to Krk from Zagreb, and regular **buses** from Rijeka to Krk Town, a journey of about ninety minutes. Alternatively, passenger **ferries** run in summer from Lopar on Rab to Baška (July & Aug 5 daily; rest of the year 1–2 daily), and from Merag on Cres to Valbiska (9 daily).

Krk Town

The island's main centre, and in the full throes of rapid expansion, modern **KRK TOWN** meanders over a series of hills in formless abandon, though at its heart there's still a small, partly walled city criss-crossed by narrow cobbled streets. The main fulcrum of the town is **Trg bana Jelačića**, a large open space just outside the town walls to the west, looking out onto a busy little harbour.

Arrival and information

Buses from Rijeka arrive at the **bus station** on the harbourfront, two minutes' walk west of Trg bana Jelačića. There's no public transport to and from Rijeka **airport**, 20km away at the northern end of Krk island; a taxi into Krk Town will cost 150–180Kn. The **tourist office**, up some steps in the northwest corner of Vela placa (June–Sept Mon–Fri 8am–3pm, Sat 8am–1pm, Sun 8am–noon; Oct–May Mon–Fri 8am–3pm; Ⓣ & Ⓕ051/221-414, Ⓦwww.tz-krk.hr), has free town plans, a map of hiking paths on the Prniba peninsula just east of town, and information on cultural events. You can use the **Internet** at Krk Sistemi, on the second floor of the bus terminal (daily 9am–2pm & 4–10pm; 30Kn/hr).

Accommodation

Private **rooms** (❶–❷) and **apartments** (studios ❸–❹, four-person apartments 530–630Kn) are available from innumerable agencies around town, with only tiny variations in price from one to the next: most convenient are Autotrans (Mon–Sat 8am–9pm, Sun 9am–1.30pm; Ⓣ051/222-661, Ⓦwww.autotrans.hr), in the bus station building 500m west of Trg bana Jelačića, on the other side of the harbour; and Aurea, at the northern entrance to town at Vršanska 26L (you'll see it on the right as you enter Krk from the Rijeka direction; May–Sept daily 8am–8pm; Oct–April Mon–Fri 8am–3pm, Sat 8am–1pm; Ⓣ051/221-777, Ⓦwww.aurea-krk.hr).

There's an HI-affiliated **hostel** in the town centre, and a brace of **campsites**. Krk's popularity with guests from northern Europe ensures that its **hotels** are overpriced for what they offer. Apart from *Marina*, all the others hog the water's edge to the east of town and most get taken over by package tourists in July and August, so be sure to book ahead.

Hostels and campsites

Camping Ježevac Ⓣ051/221-081, Ⓔjezevac@zlatni-otok.hr. A large site set among coastal woodland ten minutes' walk south of the bus station.

Camping Politin Ⓣ051/221-351, Ⓔpolitin@zlatni-otok.hr. An exclusively naturist site on the eastern side of town just beyond the *Koralj* hotel.

Hostel Krk D. Vitezića 32 Ⓣ & Ⓕ051/220-212, Ⓦwww.hfhs.hr. Perfectly situated in a quiet

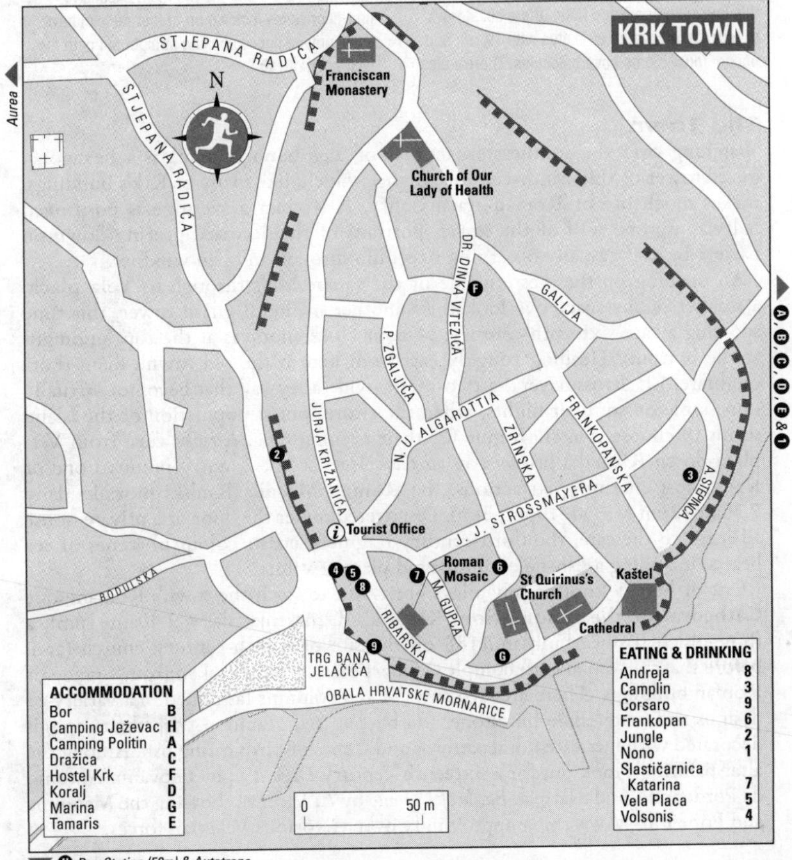

corner of the old town, occupying the restored building of the island's first-ever hotel. The shaded patio hosts a restaurant serving some unusual dishes such as ostrich goulash as well as good-quality mainstays; the rooms (five doubles, three triples, seven quads and two six-beds) are neat and tidy, and guests can use a washing machine and rent bikes for 75Kn per day. Beds 140Kn per person with breakfast, 180Kn half-board (thirty-percent surcharge for stays of less than three days).

Hotels

Bor Šetalište Dražica 5 ⓣ & ⓕ051/220-200, ⓦwww.hotelbor.hr. Right next to the *Dražica* hotel complex, this small private hotel is the best value in Krk, offering eighteen spacious en-suite doubles with TV; sea-facing rooms are only slightly more expensive. ⑤

Dražica Ružmarinska 6 ⓣ051/655-755, ⓦwww.hotelikrk.hr. A ten-minute walk east of town, this unexciting package hotel offers six storeys of recently renovated en suites with TV, a/c and phone; most rooms have balconies. There's also an outdoor swimming pool and a terrace bar-restaurant. ⑤

Koralj Vlade Tomašića bb ⓣ051/655-400, ⓦwww.krkonline.com. A little uphill from *Dražica*, this modern concrete three-star has a nice position among pine woods and offers neat, bright en-suite rooms, a fitness centre with sauna and solarium, and a decent restaurant. There's also an excursion desk at the reception. ⑤

Marina Obala hrvatske mornarice bb ⓣ051/221-128, ⓦwww.hotelikrk.hr. Although a little run-down and due for renovation, this hotel can't be beaten for convenience – it's slap-bang on the seafront and all eighteen rooms have sea views. Open May–Oct. ⑤

Tamaris Ružmarinska 6 ⓣ051/655-755, ⓦwww.hotelikrk.hr. Part of the *Dražica* complex, this two-storey, three-star affair is the most personable of the three, with recently spruced-up rooms now sporting a/c and TV. The more expensive first-floor suites (holding up to four people) have small private patios opening straight out onto the seafront path. ⑥

The Town

Watching over the southeastern corner of **Trg bana Jelačića** is a hexagonal guard tower of thirteenth-century vintage which, like many of Krk's buildings, makes much use of Roman-era masonry. A Roman gravestone is positioned halfway up one wall of the tower, portraits of the deceased peering down on passers-by as if casually observing street life through an open window.

An opening on the western side of the square leads through to **Vela placa**, a smaller public space overlooked by another medieval guard tower, this time sporting a rare sixteenth-century 24-hour clock (noon is at the top, midnight at the bottom). Heading roughly east from here is the old town's main thoroughfare, J.J. Strossmayera, a two-metre-wide alleyway that becomes virtually impassable on summer nights, when the entire tourist population of the island seems to choose it as the venue for their evening *corso*. A right turn from Vela placa down Ribarska brings you to *Café Mate* at no. 7, entry point to one of Krk's most charming attractions, the **Roman Mosaic** (Rimski mozaik; daily 7.30am–2pm & 5.30–10pm; 5kn). Discovered under the floor of a private house adjacent to the café, the third-century fragment boasts colourful scenes of sea beasts, including a fish-tailed humanoid playing a flute.

East of here, a knot of tiny alleys opens out towards the town's Romanesque **Cathedral of the Assumption** (Katedrala Uznesenja; daily 9.30am–1pm), a three-aisled basilica built in 1188 on the site of a fifth-century church (and, before that, a Roman bath complex) incorporating pillars taken from a range of Roman buildings. There are two rows of ten columns fashioned in a variety of designs and materials – limestone, marble and red granite – with their capitals decorated with intricate floral patterns and scenes of birds eating fish. Among the altar paintings, look out for a sixteenth-century *Deposition* by Giovanni Antonio da Pordenone, and a largish *Battle of Lepanto* by A. Vicenti, showing the Madonna and Pope Pius V watching approvingly over victorious Venetian forces.

Built alongside the cathedral, from which it is separated by a narrow passageway, is another Romanesque structure, **St Quirinus's Church** (Crkva svetog Kvirina), whose campanile sports an onion dome topped by a trumpet-blowing angel. The campanile's lower storey is now a **Treasury** (Riznica; April to mid-Oct daily 9.30am–1pm; 10Kn) housing numerous artworks amassed by the bishops of Krk, most famously the *Madonna in Glory*, a silver-plated altarpiece made in 1477 by Venetian workshops for the last Duke of Krk, Ivan VII. It's a – literally – dazzling piece of craftsmanship, with central panels showing reliefs of the coronation of the Virgin and side panels depicting various saints. Behind the cathedral, a surviving stretch of wall and a stout cylindrical tower is what remains of Krk's **Kaštel**, medieval residence of the Frankopans. The courtyard is sometimes used as a concert venue in summer.

On the northern side of Strossmayera, steep cobbled streets seem to tunnel their way through a largely residential part of the old town which, largely devoid of cafés, shops and streetlighting, has the feel of a half-abandoned rural village. Standing at the northern apex of this maze, the **Church of Our Lady of Health** (Crkva majke božje od zdravlja) is worth a quick look if it's open – the nave is framed by two graceful lines of Romanesque arches, each held aloft by salvaged Roman columns. Diagonally opposite is the much larger church of the **Franciscan monastery** (Franjevački samostan), which rarely opens its doors outside mass times.

Krk's main **bathing** area lies to the east of town, where a sequence of small rocky coves provide a variety of atmospheric perches. There's a naturist beach about twenty minutes' walk east, by the *Politin* campsite.

Eating

Picnic supplies can be bought from the **supermarket** (daily 7am–9pm) opposite the bus station. *Slastičarnica Katarina*, Matije Gupca 2, is the best place for **ice cream**, while *Vela Placa* on Vela placa 7 has a lovely terrace and a good selection of cakes; there are also a couple of busy **cafés** on the waterfront. For fresh fish, head to one of the **restaurants** on the waterfront, where a number of decent establishments on either side of the *Corsaro* restaurant all fill up fast on summer evenings.

Restaurants

Andreja Vela placa 6. In summer this cosy little place gets a bit too touristy, but year-round this is one of the best places to sample local favourites such as *šurlice sa gulašem* (homemade pasta with goulash).

Camplin A. Stepinca bb. Pizza and pasta dishes, with lovely sea vistas from its sidewalk terrace.

Corsaro Obala Hrvatske mornarice 1. A good waterfront venue for shellfish, squid risotto and seafood pasta.

Frankopan Trg svetog Kvirina 1. Just inland from the waterfront restaurants, *Frankopan* serves up shellfish and seafood in a slightly more formal atmosphere, with a restful terrace facing the cathedral.

Nono Krčkih iseljenika 8, just east of the old town. The best place for authentic Krk recipes, augmenting the customary seafood with roast lamb, *šurlice* and other regional favourites – although the mock-rustic interior comes across as trashy rather than traditional.

Nightlife and entertainment

Trendiest of the **bars** in Krk is *Jungle*, just up from Trg bana Jelačića on Stjepana Radića, which turns into a mainstream disco after 11pm. *Volsonis* cocktail bar and gallery on Vela placa, the square opposite the tourist office, is the most atmospheric place for a drink – it's set in an underground vault and boasts a small collection of archeological finds.

There's a busy programme of cultural happenings in July and August, with folk, pop and classical **concerts** taking place in the Kaštel, or on Trg Kamplin just in front of it – the tourist office will provide a calendar of events.

Punat and around

Seven kilometres east of Krk Town, the village of **PUNAT** is set on the tranquil, enclosed bay of Puntarska draga. It's not the most evocative town on the island – a largely modern place made up of souvenir stalls, apartment blocks and a massive marina just to the north of town. However, there's a promising sequence of gravel **beaches** to the south, which quickly fade into quieter, rockier stretches of coast.

The main reason to come here is to take a taxi boat (boat owners tout for custom along the harbourfront; 15Kn return) across the bay to the islet of **Košljun**, about 800m offshore, where there is a **Franciscan monastery** (Franjevački samostan; Mon–Sat 9.30am–6pm, Sun 10.30am–12.30pm; 15Kn) founded by monks settled here by the Frankopans in 1447. From Košljun's jetty, a path leads up to the monastery church, which has a lofty, wooden-beamed interior. Look out for the 1532 polyptych by Girolamo da Santacroce on the high altar, showing scenes from the life of the Virgin. Stretching across the arch above the altar is a large and dignified *Last Judgement*, executed in 1654 by E. Ughetto, whose swirling panoramas of heaven, hell and purgatory provide a contrast with the simpler but no less harrowing *Stations of the Cross* by the twentieth-century Expressionist Ivo Dulčić. A side gallery holds pen-and-ink drawings by the naive painter Ivan Lacković-Croata, and there are some rather more off-the-wall exhibits in the cloister outside, like a one-eyed sheep in a glass case and a two-headed lamb in a bottle. The adjoining **museum** has an interesting mishmash of stuff, including some ancient typewriters and gramophones and a display of local costumes. Outside, a confusing array of paths leads through the wilderness of the monastery gardens, although Košljun is so small that it's difficult to get really lost. In the summer, classical concerts are held here on Wednesday nights; the tourist office in Punat should have details.

Practicalities

Krk–Baška **buses** pick up and drop off in a car park on the southeastern side of Punat. It's a short walk north along the seafront from here to the **tourist office**, housed in the same building as the post office (mid-June to mid-Sept Mon–Sat 8am–8pm, Sun 8am–noon; mid-Sept to mid-June Mon–Fri 8am–3pm; ⓣ051/854-970, ⓦwww.punat.com), where you can collect a free town plan and the *Pastirske staze* map of local hiking routes in the green hills above town.

Nearby Marina Tours, on the seafront at Obala 81 (ⓣ051/854-375, ⓦwww.marina-tours.hr), and Punat Tours at Obala 94 (ⓣ051/854-104, ⓦwww.hoteli-punat.hr) are the places to enquire about **rooms** (❶) and **apartments** (studios ❷–❸, four-person apartments 490–620Kn). There's a **youth hostel** (ⓣ & ⓕ051/854-037, ⓦwww.hostel-punat.com; 105Kn per person with breakfast; April–Oct) in a bright-yellow and blue building in the centre, two blocks behind the seafront at Novi put 8; it has thirty reasonably clean rooms, only two of which are doubles. The *Park* **hotel** (ⓣ051/854-024, ⓦwww.hoteli-punat.hr; ❺ B&B, ❻ all-inclusive), right on the seafront in the centre of the village, sports a blue and white nautical decor throughout and boasts roomy en suites, some of which have recently been renovated. The spacious *Pila* **campsite** south of town has its own concrete beach (ⓣ051/854-122, ⓦwww.hoteli-punat.hr), while four kilometres south of town on the road to Stara Baška, a side road descends to the *FKK Konobe* naturist campsite (ⓣ051/854-036, ⓦwww.hoteli-punat.hr), a self-contained resort with its own restaurants and shops.

Stara Baška

A minor road heads south out of Punat towards **STARA BAŠKA**, 12km distant, a tiny place clinging to a narrow coastal strip at the base of the sage-covered slopes of the 482-metre Veli Hlam – this would be the most beautiful spot on the island if it weren't for the unsightly holiday homes. There are several small stretches of shingle **beach**, the best of which is in Oprna Bay 2km north of the village, visible from the road as you descend from the direction of Punat.

There are only two weekly buses from Punat to Stara Baška, so you might be better off renting a car to get here – unless you want to walk over the hills from Batomalj (see below), near Baška. The Zala agency in the centre of the village (Ⓣ & Ⓕ 051/844-605 and 844-755, Ⓔ zala@ri.t-com.hr) has **rooms** (❶), and there's a **campsite**, the *Škrila*, on the shoreline at Stara Baška's northern end (Ⓣ 051/844-678 or 844-725, Ⓔ skrila@ri.t-com.hr). The *Nadia* **restaurant** is the best place to eat – fresh local fish like *škarpina* (groper) and *kovač* (John Dory) are pricey but worth it – and also has rooms (Ⓣ 051/844-686 or 844-663, Ⓔ novica-mladenovic@ri.t-com.hr; ❸).

Baška and around

Lying at the island's southern end, and connected by frequent bus to Krk Town, **BAŠKA** is set in a wide bay ringed by stark mountains. At the heart of a rapidly modernizing town lies the kind of fishing village that wouldn't look out of place in Brittany or Cornwall, a tangle of crooked alleyways and colourful houses perched on a steep slope facing the sea. Baška's star attraction, however, is its two-kilometre stretch of **beach**, a mixture of sand and fine shingle that from a distance looks like a long crescent of demerara sugar – not that you'll be able to appreciate this in July and August, however, when its entire surface is covered with parasols, beach towels, and pink-hued north Europeans contentedly roasting themselves in the sun. Despite the crowds, it's undoubtedly one of the best beaches in the Adriatic, and the view – embracing the bare offshore island of Prvić and the Velebit mountains in the background – is dramatic whatever the time of year. In season, taxi boats shuttle bathers to and from the shingle coves of Prvić, or to the succession of bays east of Baška – of which long, shallow **Vela Luka** is the most alluring.

Twenty minutes' walk inland from Baška (back along the main road to Krk), **St Lucy's Church** (Crkva svete Lucije; daily 10am–3pm & 5–9pm; 10Kn) in the village of **JURANDVOR** is the site of one of Croatian archeology's most important discoveries: the inscription known as the **Baška tablet** (Bašćanska ploča). Recording a gift to the church from the eleventh-century King Zvonimir, the tablet is the first mention of a Croatian king in the Croatian language and the oldest surviving text in the Glagolitic script (see box on p.266). The original tablet is now in the Croatian Academy of Arts and Sciences in Zagreb, but there's a replica inside the church, and most places on the island seem to have sprouted copies.

As you head west from Jurandvor, a minor road leads to the hillside village of **BATOMALJ**, 1km away, the starting point for the path across the mountains to Stara Baška. The walk takes about three hours, rising steeply before skirting the 482-metre peak of Veli Hlam – it's well maintained and marked in either direction, although the going can be very tough in wind, rain or hot sun.

Practicalities

Buses terminate at a gravelly car park, from where it's a five-minute walk downhill to the town's main T-junction. Turn right here to find Baška's **tourist office** at Kralja Zvonimira 114 (July & Aug Mon–Sat 7am–9pm, Sun 8am–noon;

The Glagolitic script

The origins of Glagolitic go back to ninth-century monks **Cyril and Methodius**, chosen by the Byzantine emperor to convert the Slavs to Christianity. In order to translate the Gospels into the Slav tongue, Cyril and Methodius developed a new alphabet better suited to its sounds than either Latin or Greek. They began their missionary work with a trip to Moravia in 863, enjoying great success before the arrival of competing missions from Western Europe, and although their alphabet never caught on in Moravia, followers of Cyril and Methodius brought it to the Adriatic seaboard, where Croatian priests adopted it.

The script, which came to be known as **Glagolitic** (because so many manuscripts began with the words "*U ono vrijeme glagolja Isus...*" or "And then Jesus said..."), is an extremely decorative 38-letter alphabet which borrowed some shapes from Greek, Armenian and Georgian, but which also contained much that was original. Other disciples of Cyril and Methodius made their way to Bulgaria, where they produced a modified version of the script, called **Cyrillic** in recognition of one of their mentors, versions of which are still used today in Russia, Ukraine, Bulgaria, Serbia and Macedonia.

Glagolitic took root in the areas of Croatia where Byzantine influence was at its strongest; even given the Roman Church's growth in power, and Rome's use of Latin in church services, Croatian clerics stuck with the Glagolitic script and the Slav liturgy.

A succession of popes opted to tolerate Glagolitic rather than risk alienating the Adriatic clergy and driving them back into the embrace of Byzantium, and Glagolitic proved surprisingly enduring. Glagolitic prayer books were produced by clerics in Senj using the new printing technology from the 1490s onwards, and the script was still in use come the Reformation.

Ottoman advances finally brought an end to book production at Senj, and Adriatic Croatia's masters – whether Austrian or Venetian – increasingly regarded the use of Glagolitic as a sign of Slav resistance. Abbé Fortis, travelling round the Kvarner Gulf in the 1770s, noted that the Bishop of Rab was sending out Italian-speaking priests to counter the influence of local Glagolitic-using clergy. In inland Istria the script remained in use rather longer, but the Austrians prohibited its use in public documents in 1818. The growth of Croatian nationalism occasioned a Glagolitic revival in the late nineteenth century, but the universal dissemination of the Roman alphabet through secular education had by this stage condemned Glagolitic to obscurity in linguistic terms.

There is, however, currently something of a **Glagolitic revival** going on in coastal Croatia, although this is less to do with its everyday usefulness than its visual appeal – the character looks great on souvenir mugs and T-shirts. Aesthetic considerations aside, the number of Croats who could write their name in Glagolitic remains very small indeed.

Sept–June Mon–Fri 8am–3pm; ⓣ051/856-544, ⓦwww.tz-baska.hr), which has a generous supply of brochures and town maps, and also provides an invaluable hiking map – drawn up by Czech tour guides who cleared and marked local goat-tracks to provide their own tourists with more in the way of outdoor activities. Squatina Diving, at the far end of the beach at Zarok 88a (April–Oct; ⓣ051/856-034, ⓦwww.squatinadiving.com), offers a one-day introductory course to **scuba-diving** (65Kn) and plenty of two- and four-day courses.

Private **rooms** (❶) and **apartments** (studios ❷–❸, four-person apartments 400–550Kn) are available from two agencies right beside the town's main T-junction: Primaturist, Kralja Zvonimira 98 (July & Aug daily 8am–10pm;

Ⓣ051/856-132, Ⓦwww.primaturist.hr), and next-door Guliver, also at Kralja Zvonimira 98 (July & Aug daily 9am–10pm; Ⓣ051/856-004, Ⓦwww.pdm-guliver.hr).

Most characterful of the **hotels** is the *Tamaris*, Emila Geistlicha bb (Ⓣ051/864-200, Ⓦwww.baska-tamaris.com; double rooms ❻; studio apartments ❻), a medium-sized place occupying a fine position on the southwestern shoulder of Baška's beach. All Baška's other accommodation falls under the aegis of a single company (Ⓦwww.hotelibaska.hr): the four-star *Zvonimir*, Emila Geistlicha 34 (Ⓣ051/656-810; ❼), has a beach-front position and comfortable recently renovated rooms; while the three-star *Corinthia I*, *II* and *III*, just behind the *Zvonimir* (all Ⓣ051/656-111; ❻), are more impersonal in style. *Camping Zablaće* (Ⓣ051/856-909, Ⓦwww.hotelibaska.hr) is an enormous, largely shadeless **campsite** which runs for about 1km along the southern end of the beach. At the eastern side of Baška, *Bunculuka* is a naturist site with its own stretch of beach in the next bay along (Ⓣ051/856-806, Ⓦwww.hotelibaska.hr).

The best place **to eat** is *Cicibela*, on the seafront below the tourist office at Emila Geistlicha bb, offering excellently prepared seafood and a respectable range of steaks. *Ribar*, right on the seafront at Palada bb, serves big portions of well-prepared seafood and has nice views of the harbour.

Eastern Krk

There are no major resorts on the **eastern side of Krk**, but a succession of attractive small settlements and the Biserujka cave provide reason enough to make a brief foray into the region. You'll need your own transport in order to explore: towns in this part of the island are connected by infrequent buses to Krk Town, but not with each other, meaning that you can only visit one of them in the course of a day-trip.

Vrbnik

East of Krk Town, a minor turning branches off the main road to Baška and climbs over a low ridge towards the fertile plain of the **Vrbničko polje**, where lush vineyards supply the wineries of **VRBNIK**, a small town perched on a fifty-metre-high sea cliff. The highly regarded local tipple, the dry white Vrbnička Žlahtina, is served in numerous local wine cellars, and the town itself – a network of narrow cobbled alleys which occasionally part to reveal views of Crikvenica and Novi Vinodolski across the water – is worth a quick amble.

There are four daily buses (Mon–Fri only) from Krk Town to Vrbnik – you'll have to catch the early morning service if you want to return the same day, as the last bus usually returns in the early afternoon. The **tourist office** (Easter–Oct daily 8am–8pm; Ⓣ051/857-479, Ⓦwww.vrbnik.net/tz) on Placa vrbničkog statuta 4 gives out local information and brochures, while the Salvia agency on Retec 2 (Ⓣ051/857-471, Ⓦwww.vrbnik.net/salvia) can book private **rooms** (❶) and **apartments** (studios ❷, four-person apartments 480Kn). There's also a small **hotel**, the *Argentum*, in the eastern part of town at Supec 68 (Ⓣ051/857-370, Ⓕ857-352; ; May to mid-Sept), offering ten neat en-suite rooms with sea-facing balconies and TV. *Nada*, at the sea-facing tip of the town at Glavača 22, has a good seafood **restaurant** upstairs and an evocatively fusty cellar hung with hams downstairs, where you can try the family's wine accompanied by local cheese and *pršut*. A couple of hundred metres east of the main square at Frankopanska 1, *Gospoja* is a larger, more modern cellar with equally excellent wines and nibbles.

Šilo

Thirteen kilometres north of Vrbnik on the eastern side of Krk is **ŠILO**, a largely modern village which nevertheless boasts some wonderful stretches of fine shingle beach and fine views of the mountainous mainland. The **tourist office** on the seafront at Stara cesta bb (mid-June to mid-Sept daily 8am–3pm; mid-Sept to mid-June Mon–Fri 8am–3pm; Ⓣ & Ⓕ051/852-107, Ⓦwww.tzo-dobrinj.hr) gives out a few brochures, while the Šiloturist agency at Na Vodici 2 (Ⓣ & Ⓕ051/852-203, Ⓦwww.siloturist.com) handles **rooms** (❶–❷) and apartments (studios ❷–❸, four-person apartments 550–650Kn) here and in Dobrinj. There's a big beachside **campsite**, the *Tiha*, on the peninsula on the eastern side of the bay (Ⓣ051/852-120, Ⓦwww.hotelmalin.hr).

Dobrinj

Five kilometres west from Šilo, **DOBRINJ** is an inland version of Vrbnik, a hilltop village from whose church there's an expansive view north towards the sprawl of Rijeka and Mount Učka, with the resorts of Lovran and Opatija lurking at its feet. Rather like the hill towns of nearby Istria, Dobrinj seems to be reinventing itself as a cultural centre, and there's plenty to see if you're here in summer, when everything's open. On the tiny main square, the former St Anthony's Church (Crkva svetog Antuna) now houses a **gallery** which hosts varied art shows in summer, while an impossible-to-miss creamy-pink town house round the corner hosts seasonal exhibitions of contemporary painting and sculpture. Between the two, a one-room **Religious Art Collection** (Sakralna muzejska zbirka; mid-June to mid-Sept daily 10am–noon & 7–9pm; free) boasts, among other trinkets, a fifteenth-century reliquary containing the head of St Ursula, and a fourteenth-century altar cloth decorated with a Coronation of the Virgin sewn with gold thread. Just off the main square, the **Ethnological Collection** (Etnografska zbirka; mid-June to mid-Sept daily 10am–noon & 7–9pm; free) contains three floors of agricultural tools, ceramics and costumes.

It's feasible to visit Dobrinj on a day-trip from Krk Town by public transport, as there's a single **bus** from Krk Town to Dobrinj on weekdays and a couple of buses that return to Krk – check exact times at the Autotrans desk at Krk Town's bus station before setting out. The homely *Zora* **restaurant** on Dobrinj's main square is one of the best places on the island to eat *šurlice*.

The Biserujka Cave

North of Dobrinj, it's 4km to the village of Čižići on the muddy Soline bay, from where a well-signed road heads north to the **Biserujka Cave** (Špilja Biserujka; daily: April, May & Oct 10am–3pm; June & Sept 10am–5pm; July & Aug 10am–7pm; 30Kn), another 3km beyond on a coastal heath. The cavern is only about 150m long, but is well worth visiting – the stalagmite and stalactite formations are impressive, and you may also be lucky enough to catch sight of the cave's bat population. There is no public transport to the cave.

Rijeka to Senj

Heading southeast from Rijeka, it's a while before you're finally free of the city's industrial sprawl, which stretches way down the coast as far as the bridge to Krk.

About 10km out of the city, nestling around the northern end of Bakar Bay, **Bakar** is a case in point, a once pretty place nowadays dominated by a vast oil refinery. It preserves its narrow streets, a derelict castle and a handful of crumbling town houses built by local mariners, but as a whole the place doesn't invite much more than a quick wander.

Ten kilometres farther on, at the far end of Bakar Bay, **Kraljevica** is another example of an old coastal town almost entirely swallowed up by the industry of the Rijeka hinterland. It began life as the seventeenth-century stronghold of Croatia's leading aristocratic families of the time, the Frankopans and the Zrinskis – the latter built two fortified palaces here, the Stari and Novi Grad, although they've since been much rebuilt and aren't open to the public.

Crikvenica

CRIKVENICA has been a tourist resort since the 1890s, when Archduke Josef, brother of Emperor Franz Josef, earmarked it for development in a deliberate challenge to the pre-eminence of Opatija. He went so far as to name Crikvenica's first hotels – the *Erzherzog Josef* (now the *Therapia Palace*) and the *Erzherzogin Clothilde* – after himself and his wife. Following World War I, Crikvenica went on to prosper for a time as one of Yugoslavia's more modish playgrounds, though nowadays whatever charm it once possessed has been lost with the construction of the modern hotels and apartment blocks which straggle along its seafront. There really isn't anything to do but loll around on the succession of gravelly **beaches** which stretch northwest from the centre. **Strossmayerovo Šetalište** is the town's liveliest artery, leading along the waterfront from the main Trg Nikole Cara via a tangle of hotels, restaurants and tourist shops.

Practicalities

Crikvenica is easily reached by hourly **bus** from Rijeka. The **tourist office** is at Trg Stjepana Radića 1c (July & Aug daily 8am–10pm; rest of the year Mon–Fri 8am–2pm; ⓣ051/241-051, ⓦwww.tzg-crikvenice.com), a block north of the bus station. They share the space with Crikvenica Tourist agency (June–Sept daily 8am–10pm; Oct–May Mon–Fri 8am–3pm; ⓣ051/241-249, ⓦwww.crikvenica-tourist.net), which books **rooms** (❶) and **apartments** (two-person studios from ❷, four-person apartments from 500Kn); you can also try Autotrans in the bus terminal (June–Sept Mon–Sat 8am–8pm, Sun 9am–noon & 6–9pm; ⓣ051/243-800, ⓦwww.autotrans.hr). **Hotels** in Crikvenica are plentiful and mostly cater to package tourists. The privately run *Crikvenica* has the best position, right in the centre of town at Strossmeyerovo Šetalište 8, with small

The Bura

One of Kvarner's most famous natural phenomena is the **Bura**. A cold, dry north-easterly, it blows across the central European plain and gets bottled up behind the Adriatic mountains, escaping through the passes at places like Senj, where it is claimed to be at its worst. It's said that you can tell the Bura is coming when a streak of white cloud forms atop the Velebit, the mountain ridge which stretches down the coast. At its strongest, it can overturn cars and capsize boats. When it's blowing, ferry crossings between the mainland and the islands are often suspended, and the road bridge to Krk as well as the road to Starigrad–Paklenica will either be off limits to high-sided vehicles, or closed altogether.

slightly gloomy en-suite rooms, some with sea-facing balconies (ⓣ051/241-199, ⓦwww.hotelcrikvenica.hr; ❹).

Novi Vinodolski

Nine kilometres south of Crikvenica, the resort town of **NOVI VINODOLSKI** ("Novi" for short) straggles along the main road for a couple of kilometres. It's actually of far greater historical significance than its rather suburban appearance might suggest; it was here that the so-called **Vinodol Statute** (Vinodolski zakon), the oldest extant document in Croatian, was signed in 1288, recognizing the rule of the Frankopans over the surrounding district and the rights of the local citizens. Modern Novi is a dull sort of place, its waterfront lined with large hotels leading up to a scrappy harbour. Up above the main road there's a small old quarter piled up on the hill, where you can view the austere, sole remaining tower of the thirteenth-century Frankopan **castle** in a central square. Also on the square is a small **Town Museum** (Gradski muzej; July & Aug Mon–Sat 9am–noon & 7–9pm, Sun 9am–noon; Sept–June Mon–Fri 9am–noon; 12Kn), with a rather perfunctory display relating to the statute, as well as folk costumes from the surrounding area. There's not much beach to speak of here, merely a string of concreted platforms near the hotels.

Practicalities

There's an enthusiastic **tourist office** on the main road, 200m south of the bus stop (mid-May to Sept daily 8am–8pm; Oct to mid-May Mon–Sat 7am–3pm; ⓣ & ⓕ051/244-306, ⓦwww.tz-novi-vinodolski.hr); Novi Turist agency, next door at Kralja Tomislava 8 (ⓣ051/792-210, ⓦwww.novi-turist.hr), has **rooms** (❶). Several shoreline **campsites** lie along the string of attractive bays south of Novi, all of them pleasant, isolated spots to stay, though you'll need your own transport to get to them. The first, *Punta Povile* (ⓣ051/793-083), is 3km south of Novi on the northern flanks of the Teplo inlet; 12km farther on is *Sibinj* (ⓣ051/796-905), followed after another 3km by *Bunica V* (ⓣ053/616-718). There are several **hotels** in Novi, the best of which is the recently opened *Tamaris* (ⓣ051/792-280, ⓦwww.hoteltamaris.hr; ❺), a modern four-star affair offering ten spacious, well-decorated rooms with TV, fast Internet connection, minibar, air-conditioning and balconies; it also sports a lovely terrace with a whirlpool, surrounded by fragrant pine woods. *Konoba Lucija*, Vinodolska 6 (ⓣ051/245-755), is the place to go for fresh seafood and homemade pasta, while *Konoba Studec*, set among vineyards 3km northwest of town (well signed off the road to Bribir) serves a tasty range of nibbles alongside locally-made Zlahtina (a medium-dry white) and Simfonija (a red dessert wine not unlike port).

Vinodol and around

Stretching for some 20km inland from Novi Vinodolski to the northwest, **VINODOL** (literally "vineyard vale") is one of the most beautiful valleys in this part of Croatia. A trough of lush greenery and fruit trees bordered by rugged limestone escarpments, Vinodol was a major wine-producing area until the phylloxera epidemics of the nineteenth century virtually wiped out the entire crop – large-scale vine-growing has only recently been reintroduced. There's a lot of private accommodation in the straggling villages lining the valley, and for those who have their own transport, the area is a more rustic and characterful place to stay than overdeveloped Crikvenica and Novi Vinodolski.

The largest of the Vinodol villages is **BRIBIR**, 8km uphill from Novi Vinodolski and served by six Novi–Bribir–Crikvenica buses daily. A sleepy place grouped around the single surviving tower of a twelfth-century Frankopan castle, it's the starting point for several hiking trails up the steep, scrub-covered slope that forms the eastern side of the valley. You can get a hiking map from the Vinodol tourist office on Bribir's main square (Mon–Fri 8am–2pm; ⓣ051/248-730, ⓦwww.tz-vinodol.hr). They'll also fix you up with rooms (❶) and apartments (studios ❷, four-person apartments 450–500Kn) in the valley: you could do worse than plump for Eda Čor, Gradac 51, Bribir (ⓣ051/248-145), who has a family-sized apartment with two double bedrooms and kitchen-diner; or the Gašparini family, Kričina 25a, Bribir (ⓣ051/248-051), who offer a self-catering apartment with a beautiful garden and tiny pool. For eating, *Konoba Lucija* at the southern end of the village has a full range of seafood and steaks, as well as succulent twirls of homemade pasta known as *bribirski makaruni*. A cult place to eat hereabouts is *Vagabundina koliba*, Kičeri 31a, Lukovo (ⓣ051/248-708 or 098 943-2885; closed Mon), a mountain hut located 15km above Bribir at the end of a challenging mountain road – dishes based on locally harvested goodies include *polpetice od koprive* (nettle fritters) and wild asparagus, when in season.

Twelve kilometres farther up the valley from Bribir, the village of **DRIVENIK** is the site of one of the most attractive remaining Frankopan castles, built in the fourteenth-century to control the then-busy trade routes leading from Vinodol to inland Croatia. The castle is empty and overgrown inside, although the stout cylindrical towers and well-preserved outer walls are impressive enough to merit a visit. The nearby cemetery has great views down the valley.

Senj

"May God preserve us from the hands of Senj." So ran a popular Venetian saying, inspired by the warrior community known as the **Uskoks** (see box on p.272), who in 1537 made **SENJ** their home and used it as a base from which to attack Adriatic shipping. Locals proudly claim the Uskoks as Croatian freedom fighters who helped slow the Ottoman advance, although their penchant for piracy earned the enmity of Venice and Dubrovnik.

Modern Senj is a rather gloomy little town of mazy alleyways, but worth a very brief stop-off to visit its **fortress** and **museums**. It stands at the beginning of the road which heads inland over the Vratnik pass towards the Plitvice lakes and Karlovac – although there's little public transport on this route and it's much easier to reach the lakes from Split or Zadar.

The only surviving reminder of the Uskoks in Senj nowadays is the **Nehaj Fortress** (daily: May–June & Sept–Oct 10am–6pm; July & Aug 10am–9pm; 15Kn), which looks over the town from a rubble-covered peak to the left of the harbour – "Nehaj" means "fear not" or "heedless". It was constructed in 1558 under the auspices of Uskok commander Ivan Lenković, who obtained building materials by demolishing all the churches and monasteries which lay outside the town walls and so couldn't be defended against the Turks. Inside are three floors of exhibits illustrating the history of the Uskoks, featuring weaponry, costumes, and excellent English-language commentary. The view from the battlements justifies the climb, with the convoluted street plan of central Senj spread out immediately below, and the pale, parched flanks of Krk across the water.

The main focus of the town below is a scruffy harbourfront square, dotted with café tables, behind which lies a warren of alleyways and smaller piazzas. If you face inland and go left off the square, you'll come to the **Town**

The Uskoks

One result of the Ottoman Empire's steady advance into Bosnia and Croatia in the early sixteenth century was the creation of a mass of refugees who, forced from their lands in the Balkan interior, gravitated towards the Adriatic coast and began to organize themselves into military groups in order to repel further Ottoman encroachment. These anti-Turkish fighters were collectively known as **Uskoks**, although the name subsequently came to be applied to one particular group from Hercegovina, who took control of the fortress of Klis and defended it against Turkish forces until it finally fell in 1537.

The Uskoks subsequently withdrew to Senj, from where they mounted further resistance. Senj was under **Austrian rule** at the time, and the Uskoks were regarded as a useful component in the empire's defences. However, the Uskoks were consistently – perhaps deliberately – underpaid, forcing them to turn to piracy in order to survive. Harassing Adriatic shipping from their fifteen-metre-long rowing boats, they considered anything Turkish a legitimate target, which in practice meant attacking the (usually Venetian) ships on which Turkish goods were transported. The Austrians turned a blind eye, regarding Uskok piracy as a convenient way of challenging Venetian dominance of the Adriatic. The Uskoks also had few qualms about attacking Christian subjects of the Ottoman sultan, especially if they were Orthodox. The Rab-born churchman Markantun Dominis (see box on p.282), who briefly served as Bishop of Senj, even suggested that the Uskoks would abandon piracy if they were allowed to take the Orthodox Serbs and Vlachs of the Turkish-controlled interior and sell them off as slaves.

Uskok commanders were often regarded as heroes fighting for the Catholic cause, but the lack of security for Adriatic shipping ultimately proved too much for the Venetians, who began a propaganda campaign accusing the Uskoks of eating the raw hearts of their enemies and dipping bread in their blood. In 1615 the Venetians provoked the so-called **Uskok War** with Austria in an attempt to bring an end to the problem. The Uskoks gave a good account of themselves until their Austrian protectors, eager for an accommodation with Venice, withdrew their support. According to the terms of the 1617 Treaty of Madrid, the Austrians agreed to destroy the Uskok fleet and resettle the Uskoks inland. Senj was occupied by the Austrian navy, and the Uskoks left for new homes in Otočac, just to the southeast, or in the Žumberak hills north of Karlovac.

Museum (Gradski muzej; mid-June to mid-Sept Mon–Fri 7am–3pm & 6–8pm, Sat 10am–noon & 6–8pm, Sun 10am–noon; rest of year Mon–Fri 7am–3pm; 15Kn), housed in the fifteenth-century Vukasović mansion. It's a lacklustre display of archeological fragments and engravings illustrating the many literary figures to have come out of Senj over the centuries – foremost among them Pavao Ritter Vitezović (1652–1713), the poet and politician whose extravagantly titled *Kronika aliti spomen vsega i svieta vikov* ("Chronicle and Remembrance of Everything and the World from the Beginning") was one of the first history books to try to place the story of the Croats in a global framework. Just east of here, below a much-rebuilt cathedral of Romanesque origins, the rich **Religious Art Collection** (Sakralna baština; mid-June to Aug Mon–Sat 9am–noon & 6–9pm; rest of year Mon–Fri 7am–3pm; 5Kn) recalls the time when Senj was both the seat of a powerful bishopric and a major printing centre for Croatian-language religious texts. Among the Glagolitic missals, episcopal robes, paintings and silverware lie two exquisitely wrought fourteenth-century processional crosses, the biggest of which features a central relief of the Lamb of God surrounded by winged beasts symbolizing the evangelists – the lion for Mark, the bull for Luke, the eagle for John, and an angel for Matthew.

Practicalities

Buses plying the Rijeka–Zadar–Split coastal route pull up on the waterfront close to the main square. The **tourist office**, about 400m north along the seafront at Stara cesta 2 (July & Aug daily 7am–8pm; rest of year Mon–Fri 7am–2pm; ⓣ053/881-068, ⓦwww.tz-senj.hr), will help out with basic information and might have a free town map.

The best **food** in Senj can be found at the *Martina*, which offers a range of grilled meat, fish and shellfish on an outdoor terrace looking towards the sandy-coloured eastern shores of Krk. *Lavlji Dvor*, in the tangle of streets just east of the museums at Petra Preradovića 2 is another good lunch option; there are also several pavement **cafés** on the main seafront square, as well as numerous tiny **bars** largely catering to the locals, in the narrow streets that wind away from here.

Senj to the Paklenica National Park

Continuing south from Senj, the Magistrala picks its way beneath the rocky slopes of the **Velebit**, the mountain chain which follows the coast for some 100km. A stark, grey, unbroken wall, it's initially a forbidding sight, although there are patches of green pasture and forest just below its string of summits. Two areas, **Paklenica** and **Northern Velebit**, have been designated as protected national parks. Some of the best views of the Velebit are to be had from the eastern coasts of Rab and Pag, from where the range towers over the coast like the waves of a frozen sea.

There are few coastal settlements of any size along this stretch of the Adriatic – understandably, given the steep and rocky terrain, which leaves precious little space for houses, agriculture or tourist resorts. It's also one of the trickiest stretches of the Magistrala to drive, with the road twisting its way around a seemingly endless sequence of deeply indented bays and rocky spurs. The scenery, however, is magnificent, and there are some nice coves into which **campsites** have been attractively squeezed – *Rača* (ⓣ053/883-209), on the southern side of Sveti Juraj, and *Žrnovica*, 5km farther south, are two of the most pleasant.

About 20km south of Sveti Juraj a side road descends to the port of **Jablanac**, from where regular ferries cross the narrow Velebit channel to Mišnjak on the island of Rab. Most coastal buses don't make the detour to Jablanac, dropping off on the main highway 4km away instead, so if you're heading for Rab it's best to catch a direct Rijeka–Senj–Rab Town bus. Jablanac itself is small, unspectacular and not the kind of place you would want to get stuck in, although it does offer the chance to take a peek at the picturesquely rocky bay of **Zavratnica**, thirty minutes' walk southeast along the coast. Jablanac is also the departure point for hikes around Northern Velebit National Park (see box overleaf). **Prizna**, 13km to the south, is similar: hourly ferries leave for Žigljen on Pag from its small harbour, just off the Magistrala.

The larger but equally unrewarding town of **Karlobag**, another 13km south, is the starting point for a minor road which winds inland over the mountains, struggling up through the rugged terrain before arriving at **Gospić**, the main town of the **Lika** region. This is another potential route up towards the Plitvice lakes, although there's little to stop for en route other than the sheer barrenness

Hiking in Northern Velebit National Park

Northern Velebit National Park, an area comprising 109 square kilometres and protected since 1999, has fast been gaining popularity as a hiking destination, with a number of marked trails, some magnificent geomorphic attractions and a number of comfortable, well-maintained mountain huts along the way.

The most impressive natural feature is **Hajdučki i Rožanski kukovi**, two impressive rock formations that spread over 1220 acres of massive limestone peaks separated by a deep funnel and hiding more than 150 pits underneath. Of these, **Luka's Cave** (Lukina jama) is the deepest at 1392m. The best way to reach Rožanski kukovi is along the **Premužić trail**, an easily hikeable 57-kilometre path built between 1930 and 1933 which leads from **Zavižan** (1676m), the principal peak of the northern Velebit, to Baške Oštarije in the central part of the mountain range. Zavižan can be reached by car from Senj: follow the main road to Karlobag, pass through the village of Jurjevo, then take the signed road to the left of the Magistrala leading to the villages of Oltari and **Krasno** (where you'll find the national park office; see below). From here, take the dirt road up to **Zavižan mountain lodge**, which sits at 1594m and doubles as the highest meteorological station in Croatia. An easy fifteen-minute walk leads to a botanical garden of plants and flowers indigenous to the Velebit mountain range; you could also follow a 2hr 30min ascent along the Premužić trail to Rossijeva koliba mountain shelter in **Rožanski kukovi**.

Another popular trail leads from the coastal access point of **Jablanac** to **Veliki Alan** mountain pass. The marked path starts at the Dr Miroslav Hirtz mountain hut in Jablanac, and leads through the hamlet of **Donji Baričevići** all the way to Alan mountain hut (1305m). From here, you can enjoy splendid views of the sea below with the islands of Rab and Pag in the distance. If you've come up this way, you can then walk another ten minutes up from the hut to meet the Premužić trail at 1379m; it is at this point the trail crosses from northern to central Velebit.

Note that northern Velebit's **weather** is very unpredictable – it may seem sunny on the coast below, but a storm might be raging up on the mountain once you reach a certain altitude. Make sure you don't hike alone, and talk to the **national park office** in Krasno (Ⓣ053/851-113 or 884-551, Ⓦwww.np-sjeverni-velebit.hr), who might be able to provide you with a map, advice on which routes to take and contact information for mountain lodges and shelters – you need to announce your arrival at most of these in advance.

of the landscape, which can be oddly riveting. Travelling through the area in the 1870s, the future archeologist Arthur Evans (then Balkan correspondent for the *Manchester Guardian*) described the area as a "Croatian Siberia" – "a strange, wild land ... with its scattered oases of fertility, its chaotic rocks, underground rivers, and mysterious caverns; a country – as everywhere else in Illyria – presenting the most startling contrasts of nakedness and cultivation."

The Paklenica National Park

The coast south from Karlobag is similarly sparse on attractions until you reach the village of **STARIGRAD-PAKLENICA**. A straggling line of modern seaside houses and apartments, it constitutes the handiest base for the **PAKLENICA NATIONAL PARK** (Ⓦwww.paklenica.hr), the Velebit's last great flourish before the ridge trails inland to meet the Dinaric range on Croatia's border with Bosnia-Hercegovina. The park, designated as such in 1949, is the most accessible area for hiking in the Velebit and contains some of the country's finest karst landscapes, featuring gorges, grizzled mountains and caves. It also contains three quite different climate zones – coastal, continental and sub-alpine – which makes its weather unpredictable and, at times, extreme.

The park comprises two limestone gorges, Velika Paklenica and, 5km to the south, Mala Paklenica (literally, Big Paklenica and Small Paklenica), which run down towards the sea, towered over by four-hundred-metre-high cliffs. **Mala Paklenica** has deliberately been left undeveloped in order to protect its status as a (relatively) untouched wilderness – paths are not maintained or marked with the same thoroughness as in Velika Paklenica, and you'll need good maps (available from local shops and the national park office in Starigrad) if you want to explore.

Into the park

The entrance to the **Velika Paklenica** gorge is about 2km inland from Starigrad, reached by a road which heads east just south of the *Hotel Alan*; there's no public transport along this route. After you pass through the half-abandoned, stone village of Marasovići; there's a ticket booth where you pay an entrance fee (30Kn or 40Kn including entry to the Manita Peć cave) and receive a basic free map, if you haven't already picked one up from the national park office in Starigrad (see overleaf). You can park here, or at a second car park 2km farther on inside the park.

Just beyond the ticket booth, the roadside Paklenica Mill (Paklenički mlin; mid-June to mid-Sept daily 8am–7pm) contains a small ethnographic display and, if there's enough water in the local stream, a working demonstration of how these water-driven corn-grinding mills actually worked. Beyond the mill, the gorge begins to narrow in earnest, with dramatic rock outcrops towering above a boulder-strewn riverbed. After about twenty minutes of moderate ascent, the path passes a sequence of **underground tunnels** (*bunkeri*) built by the former Yugoslav Army to serve as a high-security bomb shelter for state officials. They're currently being renovated and should soon hold a display devoted to the flora and fauna of the park.

Another 45 minutes' walk up the main trail, a well-signposted side-path heads right to **Anića kuk**, a craggy peak lying a steep climb to the south. Beyond here, the main path levels out for a while, passing through elm and beech forest – surprisingly lush after the arid Mediterranean scrub of the coast below. After another fifteen minutes, a second side-path ascends steeply to the left. A strenuous forty-minute walk up here will bring you to **Manita peć** (July–Sept daily 10am–1pm; June & Oct Mon, Wed & Sat 10am–1pm; May Wed & Sat 10am–1pm; April Sat 10am–1pm), a complex of stalactite-packed caverns about 500m long. From here you can either turn back the way you came, or head on for another hour and a half (the path leads from the left of the cave as you emerge) up some fairly steep and none-too-easy slopes to **Vidakov kuk**, an eight-hundred-metre-high peak that gives fine views over the coast and islands.

Back on the main path, it's about twenty minutes to the Lugarnica hut, where you can get food and drink (June–Sept daily 10.30am–4.30pm; April, May & Oct weekends only), and a further thirty minutes to the Paklenica mountain hut, the starting point for assaults on the major peaks above. The most prominent of these is **Vaganski vrh**, which at 1757m above sea level is the southern Velebit's highest peak. The views from the top are spectacular, but you'll need to be reasonably fit, have a good map and make an early start if you're going to attempt the hike up.

A circular walk, taking in the **Mala Paklenica** branches off the main trail some ten minutes after the turn-off for Anića kuk. Climbing steeply across the Jurasova glava ridge, this heads south to the neck of the Mala Paklenica gorge, which leads down towards **Seline** on the coast. The canyon is beautifully rugged, the trail not too difficult to follow, and there are some impressive rock formations en route. The whole hike takes about seven hours from entrance to exit, and you can do it in reverse from Seline if you prefer.

Don't forget Paklenica's potential as a **beach** resort: the best spot for sunbathing is the shoreline stretching south of the *Hotel Alan*, where a narrow band of shingle backed by olive and fig trees culminates in a broad cape overlooked by a ruined medieval tower. The water is beautifully clear, with good views of the tawny hills to the south and west, and even on August weekends it doesn't get too crowded.

Practicalities

Most coastal buses plying the Rijeka–Zadar route run through Starigrad, stopping near the *Hotel Alan* (handiest for the national park) or at the northern end of the village, where there's a small harbour. The latter stop is convenient for the **tourist office**, on the landward side of the road at Trg Tome Marašovića 1 (July & Aug daily 8am–9pm; Sept–June Mon–Sat 8am–noon; ⓣ023/369-255, ⓦwww.rivijera-paklenica.hr), where you can pick up leaflets about the park and advice on what to see. The **national park office**, 500m south along the main highway (Mon–Fri 8am–3pm, Sat & Sun 8am–noon & 5–8pm; ⓣ023/369-202, ⓦwww.paklenica.hr), is also useful if you're planning trips into the mountains – they sell detailed hiking maps, can advise on weather conditions and book rooms in the Paklenica mountain hut in Velika Paklenica. One popular local excursion is the boat trip up the **Zrmanja River** (see p.303). The tourist office and all the hotels will put you in touch with agencies organizing these – expect to pay around 250Kn per person including lunch.

Koma Maras, in the shopping mall in front of *Hotel Alan* at F. Tuđmana 14 (daily 9am–1.30 & 5.30–9pm; ⓣ023/359-206, ⓦwww.koma-maras.hr), will find rooms or apartments in Starigrad or Seline. Camping isn't allowed in the park itself, but there's an abundance of **campsites** in Starigrad, including a large, well-tended site occupying a pleasantly shingly stretch of beach next to the national park office (ⓣ023/369-202), and several smaller ones tucked neatly into private gardens on the access road to the entrance to Velika Paklenica. All the hotels listed below have good **restaurants** offering the usual repertoire of seafood risottos and fresh fish; there's also a string of inexpensive grills along the main road through Starigrad, and stores in which to stock up on provisions.

Starigrad hotels

Alan Franje Tuđmana 14 ⓣ023/209-073, ⓦwww.bluesunhotels.com. High-rise, 330-bed package hotel offering plush en-suite rooms with TV, a/c and minibar. Convenient for the park entrance, and a short walk from the best bits of beach. Also boasts a set of rather swanky tennis courts, an outdoor swimming pool, whirlpool baths and a sauna, and beauty treatments are also available on site. March to early Nov. ❼

Rajna Franje Tuđmana 105 ⓣ023/359-121, ⓦwww.hotel-rajna.com. Medium-sized place on the main highway, sporting ten standard en-suite rooms with TV and a/c in the main building, and rustic-style accommodation in restored stone cottages slightly inland. The nearest hotel to the park entrance, thus popular with trekkers. The owner organizes 4WD trips into the Velebit mountains. ❸

Vicko Jose Dokoze 20 ⓣ023/369-304, ⓦwww.hotel-vicko.hr. Swanky, intimate family hotel on the main highway, just up from the tourist office and about 1500m north of the main park entrance. Neat rooms with TV and a/c in the three-star main building, and brighter, plusher rooms in the nearby four-star seafront villa. The quality of the hotel restaurant means that it's worth paying an extra 80–90Kn for half-board. Main building ④, villa ⑤

Seline hotels

Croatia put Jaza bb ☎023/369-190, ⓦwww.pansion-croatia.com. Small, family-run hotel at the northern end of Seline, on a nice stretch of beach, offering a couple of cosy en-suite doubles and several two- or four-person apartments. ③

Kiko Ante Starčevića bb ☎023/369-784, ⓦwww.pansion.kiko.com. Another small waterside hotel, offering rooms with TV and attached bathroom, and five apartments with a/c. Staff are helpful and knowledgeable, and there's a restaurant with a nice leafy patio. ③

Rab

South of Krk and east of Cres, mainland-hugging **RAB** is the smallest but arguably the most beautiful of the main Kvarner Gulf islands. Its eastern side is rocky and harsh, rising to a stony grey spine that supports little more than a few goats, but the western side is lush and green, with a sharply indented coast and some beautiful – if crowded – coves. Medieval **Rab Town** is the island's highlight, while the **Lopar peninsula** at the northern end of the island possesses some of the sandiest beaches in the country. The place can get crowded, especially in July and August, but not disastrously so.

Rab's main link with the rest of Croatia is the **car ferry** which connects Jablanac on the mainland with **Mišnjak** on the island's southern tip. The two daily (three in summer) Rijeka–Rab **buses** use this ferry, finishing up in Rab Town. If you miss the bus, you'll have to take the ferry as a foot passenger and walk or hitch from the Magistrala to Jablanac harbour (4km) and from Mišnjak to Rab Town (8km). You can also hop over to Rab by ferry from Baška on Krk to Lopar, though bear in mind that this leaves you a good 10km from Rab Town and buses don't always connect with the ferry arrivals, so you may have a wait on your hands. Between June and September, there's also a daily **catamaran** service from Rijeka via Rab to Novalja on Pag.

Rab Town

Rab's main attraction is **RAB TOWN**, a perfectly preserved late-medieval Adriatic settlement squeezed onto a slender peninsula, along which are dotted the city's trademark sequence of Romanesque campaniles. It's a genuinely lovely place: a tiny grey-and-ochre city, enlivened with splashes of green palm, huddles of leaning junipers and sprigs of olive-coloured cacti which push their way up between balconied palaces. The population today is only a third of what it was in Rab's fourteenth-century heyday, although it's swelled significantly by the influx of

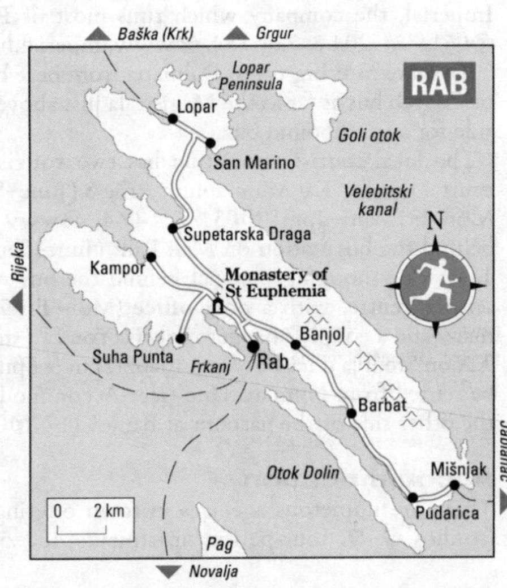

summer visitors, who create a lively holiday atmosphere without overly compromising the town's medieval character.

Starting out as a base for Roman and then Byzantine fleets, Rab Town (Arbe in Italian) grew into a prosperous, self-governing commune until its incorporation into the Venetian state in 1409. Following this, the town's privileges were gradually eroded, trade was redirected towards the mother city and, after two outbreaks of plague in the mid-1400s, urban life went into a steep decline. Things did not improve until the late nineteenth century, when Rab began to benefit from central European society's growing interest in Adriatic rest cures. In 1889, Austrian professors Leopold Schrötter and Johann Frischauf launched a strategy to develop Rab as a tourist destination, and 1897 saw the formation of the Società d'abellimento di Veglia (Society for the Beautification of Rab), a kind of embryonic tourist board. Thanks to the efforts of Austrian and Italian naturists, Rab – or, more accurately, the Frkanj peninsula just west of town – was one of the first **naturist resorts** in Europe, a status popularized further by the visit of English **King Edward VIII** (accompanied by future wife Wallis Simpson) in the summer of 1936. Whether Edward actually got his tackle out or not remains the subject of much conjecture, but his stay on Rab provided the inspiration for a recent Croatian musical, *Kralj je gol* (literally "The King is Naked", although in colloquial Croatian it means much the same thing as the expression "Emperor's New Clothes"). After visiting Rab, Edward and Wallis continued down the Adriatic aboard a luxury yacht packed with sundry toffs and royal hangers-on. Pursued by Europe's press, the trip turned into the celebrity media-fest of its day, with thousands of locals lining the streets to ogle the couple when they came ashore at Šibenik, Split and Dubrovnik. The only journalists who failed to follow the cruise were the British – the idea that their monarch was romancing an American divorcee was too mind-bogglingly scandalous to report.

Arrival and information

Rab's **bus station** is in the modern shopping centre just northeast of the Old Town, a five-minute walk from Trg svetog Kristofora. **Catamarans** operating the Rijeka–Rab–Novalja route dock at the eastern tip of the Old Town. Minibus transfer from and to Rijeka airport is available if booked in advance from Imperial, the company which runs most of Rab Town's hotels (€25 return; ⓣ051/724-204 & 724-184, ⓦwww.imperial.hr).

If you're **moving on** to Dalmatia from here by public transport, take a Rijeka or Zagreb bus as far as the Magistrala just above Jablanac, then wait by the roadside for a southbound bus.

The local tourist association has two **tourist offices**, the main one on the central square, Trg Municipium Arbe 8 (June–Sept daily 8am–10pm; Oct–May Mon–Fri 8am–3pm; ⓣ051/724-064, ⓦwww.tzg-rab.hr), and a seasonal one behind the bus station on Mali Palit (June–Sept daily 8am–10pm; ⓣ051/771-111). The shopping precinct behind the bus station serves as the town's main service centre, with a **post office** (Mon–Fri 7am–8pm, Sat 7am–2pm), pharmacy and a couple of supermarkets. You can surf the **Internet** at *Internet Digital XX* on Srednja ulica bb (daily 10am–2pm & 6pm–midnight; 30Kn/hr). Bikes can be rented from Numero Uno (see "Accommodation", p.280), or from Lero, on the other side of the harbour at Banjol 117 (ⓣ051/725-533).

Accommodation

There are numerous agencies in town offering **rooms** (❶–❷) and apartments (studios ❷–❸, four-person apartments 420–550Kn), either in the old town

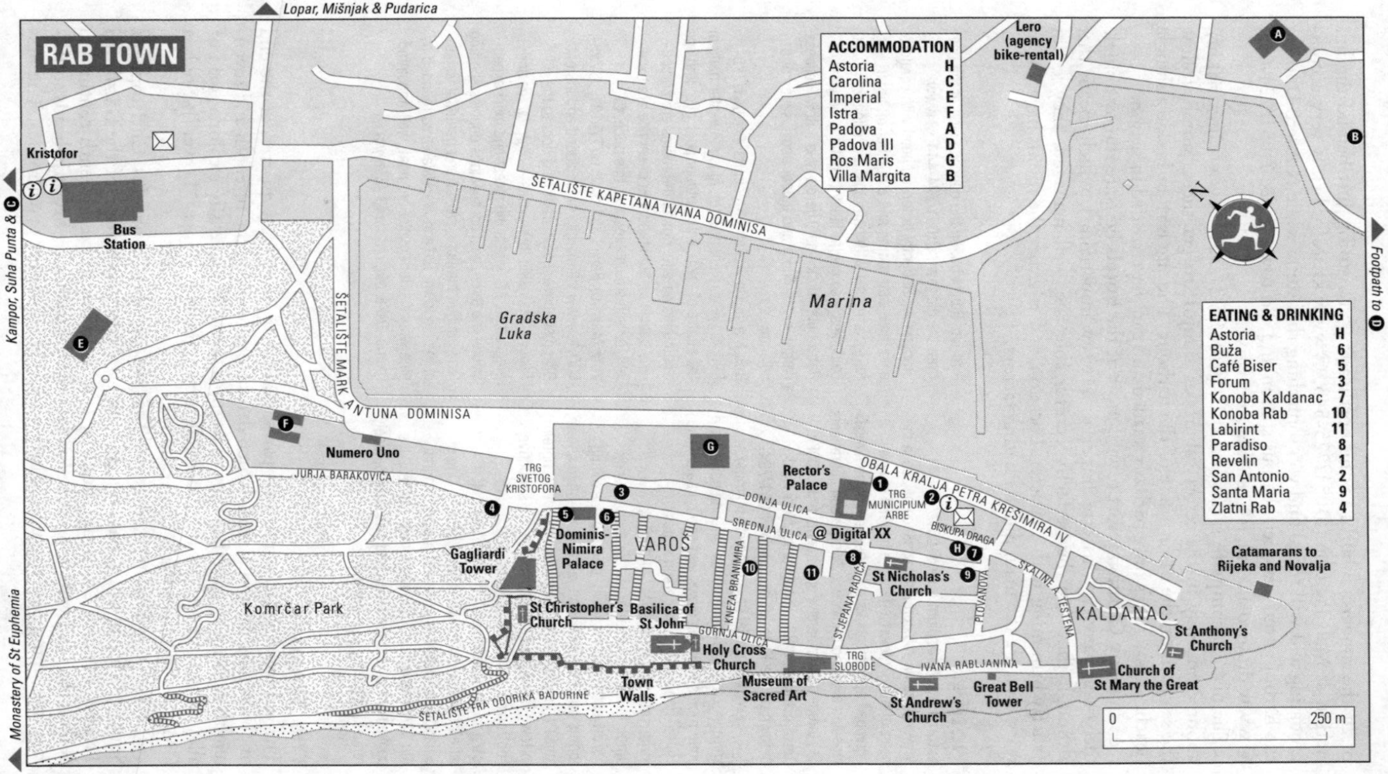

RAB TOWN
ACCOMMODATION
Astoria H
Carolina C
Imperial E
Istra F
Padova A
Padova III D
Ros Maris G
Villa Margita B
EATING & DRINKING
Astoria H
Buža 6
Café Biser 5
Forum 3
Konoba Kaldanac 7
Konoba Rab 10
Labirint 11
Paradiso 8
Revelin 1
San Antonio 2
Santa Maria 9
Zlatni Rab 4
Lopar, Mišnjak & Pudarica
Kampor, Suha Punta & C
Monastery of St Euphemia
Footpath to D
Lero (agency bike-rental)
Kristofor
Bus Station
ŠETALIŠTE KAPETANA IVANA DOMINISA
ŠETALIŠTE MARK ANTUNA DOMINISA
Gradska Luka
Marina
Numero Uno
JURJA BARAKOVIĆA
TRG SVETOG KRISTOFORA
OBALA KRALJA PETRA KREŠIMIRA IV
Rector's Palace
TRG MUNICIPIUM ARBE
DONJA ULICA
SREDNJA ULICA
@ Digital XX
BISKUPA DRAGA
Gagliardi Tower
Dominis-Nimira Palace
VAROŠ
KNEZA BRANIMIRA
STJEPANA RADIĆA
St Nicholas's Church
PLOVANOVA
SKALINE A. TEŠTENA
Catamarans to Rijeka and Novalja
Komrčar Park
St Christopher's Church
Basilica of St John
GORNJA ULICA
Holy Cross Church
TRG SLOBODE
IVANA RABLJANINA
KALDANAC
St Anthony's Church
Church of St Mary the Great
Town Walls
Museum of Sacred Art
St Andrew's Church
Great Bell Tower
ŠETALIŠTE FRA ODORIKA BADURINE
0 250 m
N

or in the modern suburbs to the northeast: Kristofor, just behind the bus station at Mali Palit bb (ⓣ051/725-543, ⓦwww.kristofor.hr), is very accommodating and will try to find you something that suits; while Numero Uno, on the harbourfront between the bus station and old town (ⓣ & ⓕ051/724-688, ⓦwww.dmmedia.com), is a reliable alternative.

The nearest **campsite** is the *Padova III* (ⓣ051/724-355, ⓦwww.imperial.hr), about 2km away in the resort suburb of **Banjol**; to get there, simply follow the sea path on the eastern side of the harbour. The site is right beside a shingle beach, although it's only partially shaded and can get crowded in season.

As in many Croatian resort towns, most of the **hotels** here are run by a single mega-company (in this case Imperial; ⓦwww.imperial.hr), which means that although they may be perfectly comfortable and well managed, they're not exactly brimming with character. Location, and whether the rooms have TV or sea views, are the main differentiating factors.

Hotels

Astoria Trg Municipium Arbe ⓣ051/774-844, ⓦwww.astoria-rab.com. Renaissance palace in the heart of the old town, offering a handful of well-equipped apartments with kitchenette, plush furnishings and exposed brickwork. Two-person apartments ❹, three- or four-person apartments from 800Kn.

Carolina Kampor bb, Suha Punta, 5km west of town on the Kalifront peninsula ⓣ051/724-133, ⓦwww.imperial.hr. A concrete mammoth surrounded by pleasant woods, offering comfy en-suite rooms with sea views and several balconied suites. Rooms ❻, two-person suites ❽

Imperial Palit bb ⓣ051/724-522, ⓦwww.imperial.hr. Sizeable three-star a short walk northwest of the old town, offering unexciting rooms due for renovation, all with en-suite shower and TV. Its main advantage over the other hotels in town is that it's surrounded by the seductive subtropical lushness of Komrčar Park. ❻

Istra M. de Dominisa bb ⓣ051/724-134, ⓔhotel-istra@hi.t-com.hr, ⓦwww.hotel-istra.hr. One of a handful of hotels in town not run by Imperial, the *Istra* has a more intimate family-run feel. It's convenient for the old town, and has simple, nicely renovated rooms with en-suite shower. ❺

Padova Banjol bb, on the opposite side of the bay from the old town ⓣ051/724-444, ⓦwww.imperial.hr. Recently tarted-up hotel with comfortable three-star rooms and a number of larger four-star rooms with bathtubs, a/c, minibar, TV and balconies – so you're likely to get a good view of Rab's belfried skyline. There's also a new wellness centre with outdoor and indoor pools, sauna and solarium. ❻

Ros Maris Obala Petra Krešimira 4 ⓣ051/778-899, ⓦwww.rosmaris.com. Plush four-star bang in the centre of town, with outdoor pool, gym and spa treatments on-site. Not all the rooms are particularly spacious, but standards of service are excellent, as you would expect at this price. ❽

Villa Margita Banjol 323 ⓣ051/777-181, ⓕ725-930, ⓦwww.vilamargita.hr. Secluded and intimate B&B just above the seafront next door to the *Padova*, set inside three villas – *Margita, Rio* and *Magdalena. Margita* is the nicest and most expensive of the three, with six spacious doubles sporting faux-antique furniture, a/c, TV and beautiful vistas of the old town. *Rio* and *Magdalena*, surrounded by pine woods, offer smaller but neat, well-appointed rooms. *Rio* & *Magdalena* ❺, *Margita* ❻

The Town

The old town divides into two parts: **Kaldanac**, the oldest quarter, at the end of the peninsula, and **Varoš**, which dates from between the fifteenth and seventeenth centuries. Together they make up a compact and easily explored grid of alleyways traversed by three parallel thoroughfares: Donja ("Lower"), Srednja ("Middle") and Gornja ("Upper") ulica.

The old town is entered from **Trg svetog Kristofora** (St Christopher's Square), a broad open space overlooked by the jutting bastion of the **Gagliardi Tower** (Tvrđava Galijarda), built by the Venetians in the fifteenth century to defend the landward approaches to the town. From here, **Srednja** heads southeast, squeezing past rows of tightly packed three-storey townhouses. The first

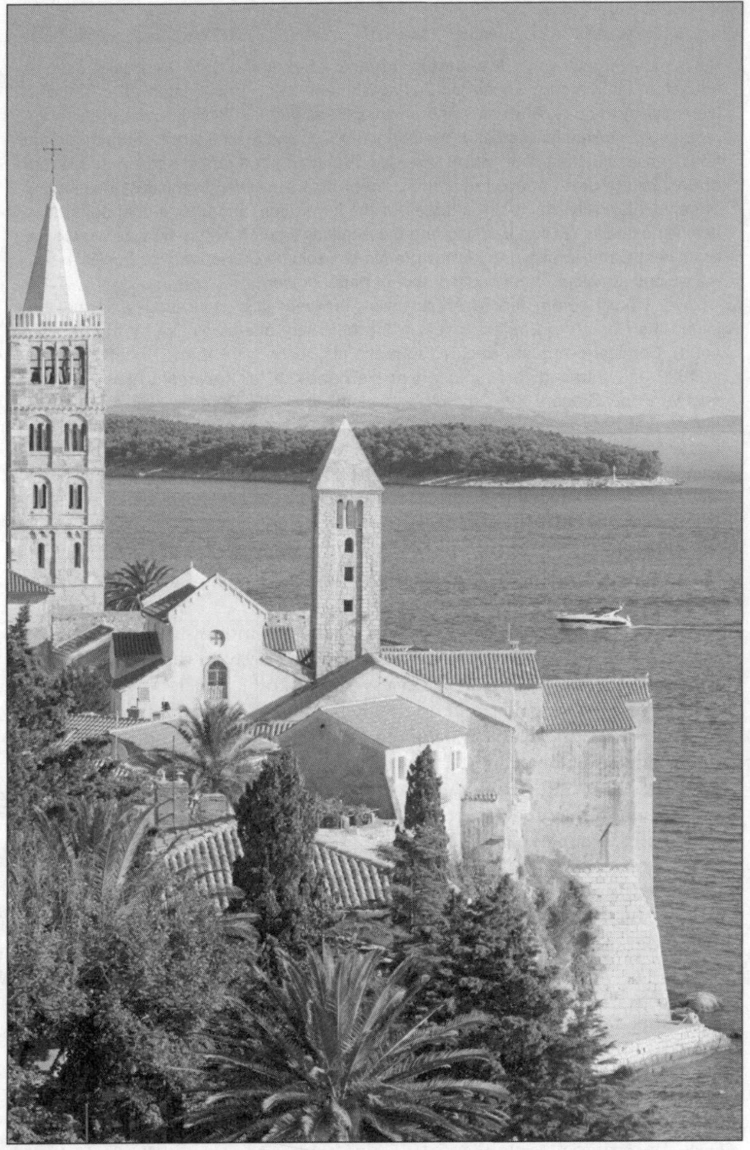

△ Rab Town

of these is the Renaissance **Dominis-Nimira Palace**, where the scholar, priest and sometime archbishop of Split, Markantun Dominis (see box overleaf), was born. The building is relatively plain save for some Gothic window frames, although a rather fine carving of the Nimira family crest, flanked by a small boy and rampant lion, adorns a doorway just down an alleyway to the left.

Markantun Dominis (1560–1624)

Rab's most famous son is **Markantun Dominis** (Mark Anthony de Dominis), a Jesuit-educated churchman whose anti-establishment rhetoric infuriated the Catholic hierarchy of the day. After studying philosophy at Padua, Dominis quickly gained a reputation in scientific circles for his work on optics and the influence of the moon on tides, while simultaneously rising speedily through church ranks, serving as bishop of Senj before being appointed archbishop of Split. However, Dominis's questioning of papal infallibility made him a target for the Inquisition, and after a brief sojourn in Venice he fled in 1614 to England and the Anglican Church, where he was feted as a prominent Catholic dissident and wrote his ten-volume *De Repubblica Ecclesiastica* – a vicious attack on the worldly nature of papal power.

Never wholly committed to Anglicanism, however (it's been suggested that he joined the Church of England because of the salary offered to him by the English court), Dominis eventually decided to make his peace with Rome. He left England in 1622 and returned to Rome, where his hopes of fair treatment rested on his relative Pope Gregory XV. On Gregory's death in 1623, Dominis was accused of heresy and imprisoned, living out the rest of his days in a windowless cell in the Castel Sant'Angelo from where, he declared to visitors, "I can best contemplate the kingdom of heaven." Dominis died before he could be brought to trial, and his body was burnt posthumously on Rome's Campo dei Fiori – an ignominious end for a man whose scientific and philosophical work was later to influence figures as diverse as Descartes and Newton.

After about five minutes' walk, Srednja opens out into a small piazza mostly taken up by a dinky Venetian loggia and, tucked away in the corner, the tiny Gothic **St Nicholas's Church** (Crkva svetog Nikole), which nowadays hosts a sporadically open art gallery. Left from here lies Trg Municipium Arbe, where the Venetian Gothic **Rector's Palace** (Knežev dvor) now houses the town council offices. The balcony facing the square is supported by three sculpted lions' heads sporting (from right to left) closed, half-open, and wide-open jaws – although they look more like overweight household pets than fearsome beasts of the savanna.

The churches of St Mary and St Anthony

Southeast of Trg Municipium Arbe lies the older part of town, **Kaldanac**, built on the site of the original Illyrian-Roman settlement of Arba. Kaldanac was largely abandoned after the plagues of the fifteenth century, and some of its older buildings still feature the bricked-up windows and doors which it was hoped would prevent the spread of disease. Occupying the highest part of Rab is the Romanesque **Church of St Mary the Great** (Crkva svete Marije Velike; still known locally as the Katedrala even though the bishopric was taken away from Rab in 1828). The west front is striped pale grey and pink, with a series of blind arches cut by a Renaissance doorway that supports a harrowing Pietà of 1414. Inside are crumbling, brown walls flecked with agate-coloured marble and a set of almost gaudily carved chestnut choirstalls, dominated by the main altar and its delicate ciborium of grey marble. A few steps away from the cathedral at the head of the peninsula, **St Anthony's Church** (Crkva svetog Antuna) preserves its original rib-vaulted apse and an imposing wooden sculpture of St Anthony (said to be twelfth century), flanked by fifteenth-century pictures of St Christopher and St Tudor – the latter clad in Roman armour.

Along Ivana Rabljanina and Gornja ulica

Walk northwest along the ridge-top Ivana Rabljanina from the Church of St Mary and you pass the largest and most beautiful of Rab's campaniles, the perfectly symmetrical twelfth-century **Great Bell Tower** (Veli zvonik; mid-June to mid-Sept daily 10am–1pm & 7.30–9.30pm; 5Kn). Topped by a balustraded pyramid, the 25-metre-high tower employs a simple architectural device: the windows on the lower storey have one arch, the windows on the second storey have two, those on the third have three, and so on. The tone of the tower's bell was mellowed – legend tells – by gold and silver dropped into the casting pot by Rab's wealthier citizens.

Rab's other three campaniles are spaced along Ivana Rabljanina and its continuation, **Gornja ulica**. The first, a utilitarian piece of relatively unadorned masonry from the late twelfth century, is attached to **St Andrew's Church** (Crkva svetog Andrije). The second – capped by a bulbous spire reminiscent of a bishop's mitre – is a seventeenth-century affair belonging to St Justine's Church (Crkva svete Justine), a small Renaissance structure that's now the **Museum of Sacred Art** (Muzej sakralne umjetnosti; currently closed for restoration; ask at the tourist office). Inside there's an assortment of manuscripts, stonework and robes, and a mid-fourteenth-century polyptych by Paolo Veneziano showing a Crucifixion flanked by saints – St Christopher is on the right, standing beside St Thecla, shown wearing a glamorous green outfit despite the fact that she actually spent most of her life living in a cave. Pride of place goes to the reliquary holding the **skull of St Christopher**, a gold-plated casket made by a Zadar craftsman at the end of the twelfth century. Various scenes round the sides of the box depict the events surrounding the saint's martyrdom: he was beheaded by the Romans after an attempt to have him shot failed, the hand of God having turned the arrows back on his assailants. It's said that the head was brought to Rab by a local bishop in the eleventh century when the town was under attack from the Saracens – St Christopher kindly obliged, saving the town by hurling rocks back at the besiegers.

The final campanile, a simple thirteenth-century structure similar to the one belonging to St Andrew's, stands beside the ruined **Basilica of St John the Evangelist** (Bazilika svetog Ivana Evanđeliste), which probably dates from the sixth or seventh century. The church was abandoned in the 1830s and much of its masonry taken away to mend the town's other sacred buildings, although the graceful curve of its apse can still be seen. At the top end of Gornja ulica, steps lead up to St Christopher's Church on the right, which has a small **lapidarium** (July & Aug daily 10am–1pm & 7.30–9pm; ask at the tourist office at other times; 5Kn suggested donation) containing tombstones and other masonry. From here, more steps scale a short fifty-metre stretch of Rab's medieval town **walls**, giving fine views back over the roofs and towers. A gate through the wall leads into the fragrant **Komrčar Park**, a shady place set on the ridge from where you can walk down to the concreted bathing spots on the west side of the peninsula.

The Monastery of St Euphemia

Thirty minutes' walk northwest of town along the seaside path is the Franciscan **Monastery of St Euphemia** (Samostan svete Eufemije; June & Sept Mon–Sat 9am–noon & 3–5pm; July & Aug daily 10am–noon & 4–6pm; 5Kn). Built in 1446, it has a delicate cloister and a museum in the library above, containing illuminated manuscripts, a headless Roman figure of Diana and a fifteenth-century wooden image of St Francis. The monastery has two churches: one dedicated to St Euphemia, and the larger church of St Bernardin, which has a gory late-Gothic crucifix, a seventeenth-century wooden ceiling decorated with scenes from the life of St Francis, and a polyptych painted by the Vivarini brothers in 1458, showing a Madonna and Child flanked by two tiers of saints.

Beaches and coves

Šetalište Fra Odorika Badurine, the waterside walkway on the west side of town (reached via steps from Komrčar Park), is actually one of the best urban beaches in Croatia – it doesn't amount to much save for a concrete strand, but the water is super-clear, and there are plenty of trees to provide shade if you're not in the mood to be grilled senseless. There are also some attractive shingle beaches east of town beyond the *Padova* hotel, but far more popular is the **Frkanj peninsula**, 1km west of the town as the crow flies. The peninsula boasts numerous rocky coves backed by deep green forest, and there's a large naturist area on the far side. You can reach the peninsula from the harbour by taxi boat or by walking the 3km from **Suha Punta**, a tourist complex at Rab Town's western end housing the *Carolina* hotel, accessible by a side road which leaves the Rab–Kampor route just beyond the Monastery of St Euphemia. Beyond here lies a further sequence of bays and coves, slightly less busy than those of Frkanj and reachable by following tracks through the coastal forest.

Pudarica beach, 8km away from Rab Town in the direction of Barbat, towards the Mišnjak ferry landing, is popular with a young crowd. It has a 24-hour party atmosphere similar to that in Novalja (see p.289), watersports galore, and swimming pool with a Jacuzzi; eight buses daily leave Rab Town for Barbat, and there's a free bus shuttling party people back and forth nightly between 10pm and 4am.

Eating and drinking

There are plenty of good seafood **restaurants** in the old town, and although some are quite stylish they remain affordable – no one wants to price themselves out of a very competitive market. *Kiflić*, Srednja 26, is the best source of fresh bread, pastries and muffins, and also sells local speciality *rapska torta* – a deliciously sweet cake consisting of crushed almonds wrapped in sugary pastry.

Of Rab Town's **cafés**, *Zlatni Rab*, Jurja Barakovića 1, and *Café Biser*, on the corner of Trg svetog Kristofora and Srednja ulica, have the best cakes and desserts, while the latter is also an eternally popular daytime spot for coffee-sipping. At night, the main Trg Municipium Arbe becomes a huge outdoor bar, with cafés such as *San Antonio* and *Revelin* covering the flagstoned expanse with their tables. The nearby Donja ulica is another venue for late-night supping, while *Forum* is a lively, if not downright raucous, place to spend a summer weekend.

Restaurants

Astoria Trg Municipium Arbe 7 ☎051/774-844. Top-notch restaurant next door to the tourist office on the main square, serving good-quality seafood dishes on a lovely terrace. The fish comes grilled, baked, or cooked in traditional sauces – try the monkfish (*grdobina*) in white-wine sauce. There's an impressive list of classy Croatian wines, and the moussy concoctions on the dessert menu make a nice change from the pancakes and ice cream on offer elsewhere. A little on the pricey side. Reserve at weekends.

Buža Ugalje bb. Sit-down snack bar in a narrow alley just off Trg svetog Kristofora, with excellent toasted sandwiches, soups, and a decent menu of cocktails come the evening.

Konoba Kaldanac Biskupa Draga bb. Features wooden benches stuffed into a narrow alleyway just off the main square. A good place to try some cheaper fish dishes, and also serves simple risottos and seafood pasta. Fills up quickly.

Konoba Rab Kneza Branimira 3. Cosy split-level place with folksy touches – with fishing nets and dried herbs hanging from the thick stone walls, it looks like a cross between a boathouse and granny's cottage. A good range of seafood and traditional meat dishes such as *teleća koljenica* (calf knuckle). Local speciality *janjetina pod peku* (pieces of lamb cooked in an ember-covered pot) has to be ordered a day in advance.

Labirint Srednja ulica 9. Delicious seafood and friendly service in a split-level collection of dining rooms. The scampi, squid, and grilled and baked fish dishes are also served on an open terrace with whitewashed walls. You could do worse than try the "fish in the style of a Rab housewife", which is catch of the day pan-fried with white wine, garlic and herbs. Good service and an extensive choice of Croatian wines.

Paradiso Stjepana Radića. Café, vinotheque, and restaurant-pizzeria in a pleasant courtyard.

Santa Maria D. Dokule 6. Swish place in an atmospheric courtyard setting. Sumptuous range of seafood and a handsome selection of classic meat dishes (everything from *wiener schnitzel* to *filet mignon*), none of which will break the bank.

Entertainment

Two annual **festivities** of interest in Rab Town are the **Rab Knights Tournament**, celebrated for the last ten years with crossbow contests and other medieval-style events (May 9, June 25, July 27 and August 15), and the **Rapska fjera festival**, when the town literally reverts to the Middle Ages – three hundred amateur actors are hired to recreate the olden times with games, dances, traditional cooking and other cultural events spread over four days in late July.

Kampor and the Lopar peninsula

Six kilometres northwest of Rab Town – and connected to it by seven buses daily – **KAMPOR** is a small, scattered village with a deep swath of shallow sandy beach. It doesn't get too crowded even in high season, and there are a couple of small **campsites** behind the beach, as well as private **rooms** (❶) available through agencies in Rab Town or by asking around. About 1km inland from Kampor, back along the road to Rab, lies the **Graveyard of the Victims of Fascism** (Groblje žrtava fašizma), a site commemorating the concentration camp established here by the Italian occupiers in 1942. It's referred to locally as the "Slovene Cemetery" owing to the large numbers of Slovenes who were imprisoned and died here, although it housed a wide range of Partisans, Jews and political undesirables, rounded up in the Italian-controlled portions of Slovenia and Croatia. Most of the internees were crowded together in flimsy tents – some five thousand died in the winter of 1942–43 alone, starved of food and drink by Italian officials. After the collapse of Italy in September 1943, most of the able-bodied survivors joined Tito's Partisans, who were briefly in control of the island before the arrival of a German garrison. The site is a dignified and restful place, with long lines of graves – one for every four people who died – surrounded by well-tended lawns, trees and shrubs.

The Lopar peninsula

Another road climbs out of Rab to the north, making its way down the island's broad central valley. After passing the sprawling settlement of Supetarska Draga, the main road reaches a T-junction at the neck of the Lopar peninsula. The left turn leads to the village of **LOPAR**, a handful of houses spread around a muddy bay from where the ferry leaves for Krk. The sandy beach here isn't particularly picturesque, but is usually empty. The right turn leads to **SAN MARINO**, 1km south, a largely modern village which nevertheless lays claim to being the birthplace of St Marin, a fourth-century stonemason who fled persecution by crossing the seas to Italy, founding the town that subsequently became the republic of San Marino. Today's settlement stretches around a vast expanse of sand known as **Veli mel** (*mel* being an archaic word for "beach", although it's also referred to hereabouts

The Adriatic gulag: Grgur and Goli otok

While lounging around on the beaches of the Lopar peninsula you're sure to catch sight of the island of **Grgur**, little more than a kilometre offshore, site of a women's prison until the 1960s and once decorated with a giant "Tito" and *petokraka* (the five-pointed communist star), both carved painstakingly out of bare rock. Immediately to the south-east is the notorious **Goli otok** ("Bare Island"), an obstinate hummock of mottled rock that was used as an island jail for communists who remained loyal to the Soviet Union after Stalin's break with Tito in 1948. Over a period of five years in the late 1940s and early 1950s, a total of fifteen thousand *informburovci* (supporters of the Informburo, the Moscow-based organization which co-ordinated the work of communist parties world-wide) were "re-educated" on Goli otok through forced labour in the island's quarry. Few of the inmates were guilty of seriously plotting against the regime; the majority were minor figures who had simply spoken out against Tito in private and been betrayed by a colleague or friend. On arrival, prisoners were forced to pass through a chicken-run of lined-up guards bearing sticks, before submitting to a regime of beatings and torture; recalcitrant prisoners had their heads immersed in buckets of human excrement, while those who confessed their ideological errors were recruited to torture the others.

As ideological tensions lessened in the mid-1950s, Goli was used to incarcerate all manner of non-political prisoners, and the prison regime became more bearable. Sent here as an army deserter, Romany singing legend Šaban Bajramović played in goal for the prison football team and performed in the prison orchestra, going on to become a pan-Yugoslav musical superstar after his release. Despite being common knowledge, the existence of Goli otok was not officially admitted until the 1980s, by which time Tito – on whose personal initiative the camp had been established – was already dead.

as Rajska plaža – "Paradise Beach" – or simply "Copacabana"), backed by cafés and restaurants and packed with families in July and August. The bay on which Veli mel is situated is unusually shallow, and you can paddle almost all the way to an islet about 1km offshore. There's a sequence of smaller, progressively less crowded sandy beaches beyond the headlands to the north, beginning with Livačina Bay, followed by the predominantly naturist Kaštelina Bay slightly farther up.

Even more secluded sandy bays are to be found at the northern end of the Lopar peninsula. They can be reached either by taxi boat (30–40Kn return) from the tourist port at the northeastern corner of Veli mel, or by following the tracks that lead out of San Marino to the north, crossing a sandy heath covered by prickly evergreens before dropping down into a series of picturesque coves – two of which (Stolac and Sahara) are reserved for naturists.

There are nine **buses** daily from Rab to Lopar, all of which pass the beach at San Marino. All services pass the **tourist office** (June–Sept daily 7.30am–9pm; Ⓣ051/775-508, Ⓦwww.lopar.com) at the T-junction between Lopar and San Marino. The Numero Uno office on the beach at San Marino (Ⓣ051/775-073) is the place to enquire after private **rooms** (❶) and **apartments** (studios ❷, four-person apartments 400–500Kn). There's a large **campsite**, the *San Marino* (Ⓣ051/775-133, Ⓕ775-290), just behind the Veli mel beach.

Pag

Seen from the mainland, **PAG** is a stark and desolate pumice-stone of an island that looks as if it could barely support any form of life. Around eight thousand people live here, looking after three times as many sheep, who scour the stony slopes in search of the odd blade of grass. Hot afternoons, when neither man nor beast stirs, always seem hotter here than anywhere else. On the arid eastern side of the island, seemingly nothing grows except for a grey-green carpet of sage. The two main settlements are **Pag Town**, with its attractive historic centre, and **Novalja**, a bland modern settlement whose beach-based nightlife is fast earning it the title "the Croatian Ibiza".

Pag's main claim to fame is a hard, piquant sheep's **cheese** (*paški sir*), which has a taste somewhere between mature cheddar and parmesan; you'll find it in supermarkets all over the country. The distinctive taste is due to the method of preparation – the cheeses are rubbed with a mixture of olive oil and ash before being left to mature – and the diet of the sheep, which includes many wild herbs (notably the ubiquitous sage) flavoured by salt picked up from the sea by the wind and deposited on vegetation across the island. Indeed, Pag is a salty kind of place all round: the precious stuff is the island's main industry, with saltpans stretching out along the island's central valley – even the tap water here tastes slightly brackish. Pag's other traditional industry is **lace-making**, a craft that for the moment remains refreshingly uncommercialized. Small pieces are sold from doorways by the lacemakers themselves, often wearing the dark, full-skirted local costume that seems to have endured here more than anywhere else on the Adriatic.

Approaching Pag from the north, there's an hourly **ferry** from Prizna, on the mainland 3km below the Magistrala, to **Žigljen**, 5km north of Novalja. The island's southern end is connected to the mainland via the **Pag Bridge** (Paški most), about 26km north of **Posedarje** on the Magistrala. The only public transport on the island is provided by the buses that ply the route between Rijeka and towns in Dalmatia (about eight daily), which pass through Novalja and Pag Town.

Pag Town

PAG TOWN originally lay about 3km south of its present site – the Pag salt industry was an attractive target for predatory neighbours and the inhabitants of Pag were able to play one aggressor off against another until the town was sacked by forces from Zadar in 1395 and many of its leading citizens killed. The Venetians, who had taken control of the area by the 1420s, hired the architect Juraj Dalmatinac (see p.334) to build a new island capital from scratch, creating the present town with its tight grid of narrow streets along one side of a deep bay. Venetian traveller Abbé Fortis, visiting in the late eighteenth century, called it a dismal place, adding that "I found not a single man of good sense in all that town; everybody is interested in the salt pits, and whoever talks not of salt is not regarded." Pag Town today is a neat little place, with a couple of well-preserved churches and a pleasant seafront promenade.

Arrival, information and accommodation

Buses stop at a car park on the northern edge of town, a short walk from the **tourist office** by the bridge across the Lokunjica (May 8am–3pm & 6–9pm; June–Sept daily 8am–10pm; Oct–April Mon–Fri 8am–3pm; ⓣ & ⓕ023/611-286 or 611-301, ⓦwww.pag-tourism.hr), which gives out a wealth of brochures and a map of hiking and biking trails around the island.

Rooms (❶) and **apartments** (studios ❷, four-person apartments 450–550Kn) are available from Perla, on the main road into town at bana Jelačića 21 (ⓣ023/600-003, ⓦwww.perla-pag.hr); Mediteran (ⓣ & ⓕ023/611-238, ⓦwww.mediteran-pag.com), behind the bus stop; or from Meridian 15

(Ⓣ023/600-030, Ⓦwww.meridijan15.hr), opposite the bus stop next to the *Pagus* hotel.

The nearest **campsite** is *Šimuni* (Ⓣ & Ⓕ023/697-441, Ⓦwww.kamp-simuni.hr), on the island's western shore, 8km away on the road to Novalja. It's a large site incorporating shops, restaurants, a windsurfing school and a handsome stretch of shingle beach; Pag–Novalja buses will drop you near the site's access road.

Hotels

Biser A.G. Matoša 7 Ⓣ023/611-333, Ⓦwww.hotel-biser.com. Medium-sized concrete building on the opposite side of the bay to the town centre, offering decent en suites with a/c and TV, some with sea views. ④

Pagus Ante Starčevića 1 Ⓣ023/611-310. Large three-star right on the seafront with spacious en-suite rooms and its own stretch of pebble beach. Underwent complete renovation in 2006–7. ⑥

Plaža M. Marulića 14 Ⓣ023/600-855, Ⓦwww.plaza-croatia.com. Newish four-star across the bay from Pag's old town, with stylish balconied en-suite rooms, a swimming pool, fitness centre, and a cocktail bar on the terrace below. ⑥

Tamaris Križevačka bb Ⓣ023/612-277. Small family-run hotel just uphill from the town centre, offering neat en-suite rooms with TV, and quality food in the downstairs restaurant. Open mid-April to Sept. ⑤

Tony Dubrovačka 39 Ⓣ023/611-370, Ⓦwww.hotel-tony.com. Medium-sized, family-run hotel 2km west of town on the northern side of Pag's bay. The en-suite rooms are simply decorated, but the location is relaxing, and there's a secluded stretch of pebble beach at the bottom of the garden. Food in the restaurant is excellent so it's well worth paying an extra 30–40Kn for half-board. ④

The Town

Flanking the town's central square, Trg kralja Petra Krešimira IV, are two of architect Juraj Dalmatinac's original buildings: the **Rector's Palace** (Knežev dvor), now a café and supermarket, and the **Parish Church** (Župna crkva), on the other side of the square; the rose window on the church facade echoes the patterns found in Pag lace. A relief above the main door shows the Virgin sheltering the townspeople (some wearing traditional Pag skirts) beneath her cloak, while inside the church, lean stone columns sport capitals bearing a variety of carved beasts, including griffins, and dolphins drinking from cups. Zvonimirova heads west from the main square towards the one surviving bastion of Pag's (largely dismantled) fortifications, topped by the curious-looking lookout tower known as the Skrivanat, which has an asymmetrical gate-like arch cut through the middle.

A causeway-like strip of land connects central Pag with its suburbs on the western side of Pag bay, where you'll also find the town's main pebble **beach**. Behind it lies the Lokunjica, a muddy lagoon, and the saltpans, which stretch south for 6km. Walking along the west bank of the saltpans for 3km brings you to **Stari grad** (Old Town), the original town which was abandoned in the 1440s. There are a few ruined buildings here, including the cloister of a Franciscan monastery, and a church dating from 1392 with a fine Gothic relief of the Virgin above the portal – it served as the model for the relief adorning the parish church in the new town. A statue of the Virgin inside the old town church is taken in procession to the new parish church on August 15 (Assumption) each year, where it's kept until September 8 (Birth of the Virgin).

Eating, drinking and entertainment

Good places for traditional **food** are *Konoba Bile*, up from the parish church on Jurja Dalmatinca, which dispenses local wine from barrels and serves up an accompanying array of cheeses, smoked hams and anchovies; and *Konoba Bodulo*, just northwest on Vangrada, which serves fresh fish and shellfish in a vine-shaded courtyard with wooden benches and stone walls. The best restaurant in town is undoubtedly *Na Tale*, at the end of the seafront on S. Radića 2, where you can dine on mussels, squid and fish (including succulent white fish in wine-and-herb sauces), in a relaxing tree-shaded courtyard. There are numerous **café-bars** on the main square and along the waterfront, and two **discos**: *Peti magazin*, in one of the old salt warehouses over the bridge from the tourist office, and *Vanga*, right next door to the tourist office.

Pag is the venue of two **carnivals**: the first an authentic local event immediately before Lent, the second on the last Saturday in July, a re-enactment of the first for the benefit of tourists. Both feature parades and a good deal of folk music and traditional dancing, and the pre-Lenten carnival culminates with the burning of the effigy known as Marko, whose ritual death is claimed to rid the community of all the bad things which have happened over the previous year. Both carnivals traditionally featured performances of *Paška robinja* (*Slave Girl of Pag*), a play of Renaissance origins concerning a captive of the Turks who is purchased and freed by a good Christian knight. Made up of rhyming couplets delivered in a monotone, it's nowadays considered too boring for the average audience, and is no longer performed every year.

Novalja and around

Twenty kilometres north of Pag Town, **NOVALJA** is the island's main resort, much more developed and crowded than Pag Town, and famous as *the* 24-hour party destination for young Croatians. Originally a Roman settlement dating from around the first century AD, it preserves a few ancient remains, including an underground **water conduit** (*vodovod*; also known by locals as the "Italian Hole"). This can be entered from the basement of the **town museum** (gradski muzej; mid-June to mid-Sept daily 9am–1pm & 6–10pm; 10Kn), housed in a modern building on Kralja Zvonimira and clearly signposted just north of the seafront. The museum features a small ethnological display, paintings by local artists, traditional wine-making equipment and, the star exhibit, a bunch of encrusted amphorae from a shipwrecked Roman merchant ship dating back to the first century BC. The wreck, discovered in 2004 in the nearby Vlaška Mala bay, has since been protected as an archeological sight. There's a curving gravel beach at the south side of town, from where a stony path leads south to the much larger, pebbly **Straško beach**. Two kilometres south of town on the road to Pag Town, a side road descends to the east-facing **Zrće beach**, a vast, gravelly expanse with a view of the pale ochre hills of eastern Pag and the greenish Velebit mountains beyond. There's a sandier beach in the next bay to the north, about ten minutes' walk away, although it's more exposed to the wind.

In summer, a string of alfresco **DJ bars** set themselves up on Zrće beach, turning the area into a dance-till-dawn paradise for clubbers. Zagreb-based establishments like *Papaya* and *Aquarius* decamp here for the holiday season, although it's local outfit *Kalypso* that has been on the beach the longest – and has developed a cult following in the process. All three organize live concerts and DJ-driven party nights from late June through to early September. Food and drink is served round the clock, so you can just about spend 24 hours partying and chilling on the beach if you want to. Minivans shuttle party-goers back and forth between Zrće and Novalja's seafront; they stop right outside the popular *Cocomo* cocktail-bar in Novalja and run every hour until midnight.

Practicalities

Buses stop at the entrance to town, from where it's a short walk down Slatinska to Novalja's car-free seafront. The rather swanky **tourist office** is right there at Šetalište hrvatskih mornara 1 (May, June & Sept daily 8am–1pm & 4–6pm; July & Aug daily 7am–10pm; Oct–April Mon–Fri 8am–3pm; ⓣ & ⓕ053/661-404, ⓦwww.tz-novalja.hr). **Rooms** (❶) and **apartments** (two-person studios ❷, four-person apartments 480–520Kn) are available from Sunturist, near the bus stop at Kranjčevićeva bb (ⓣ053/661-211, ⓦwww.sunturist.com). Aurora Travel, a few steps east at Slatinska bb (ⓣ053/663-493, ⓦwww.aurora-travel.hr), offers more of the same, as well as B&B accommodation in local pensions (❷). The **campsite** at Straško beach (ⓣ053/661-226, ⓦwww.turno.hr) is like a small town in its own right, with shops, bars and spaces for four thousand campers – a third of which are reserved for naturists.

As for Novalja's **hotels**, there are just two in town and both are overpriced: *Loža* at Trg Loža 1 (ⓣ053/661-326, ⓦwww.turno.hr; ❺) has a lovely position right on the seafront and adequate en-suite rooms with TV and sea-facing balconies or French windows, while the concrete-block *Liburnija* on the opposite end of the seafront at Šetalište hrvatskih mornara bb (ⓣ053/661-328, ⓦwww.turno.hr; ❺) offers more basic en suites. The best hotel on the island (and on this stretch of the coast), *Hotel Boskinac* (ⓣ053/663 500, ⓦwww.boskinac.com; ❻; closed Jan), lies 1km north of town in Stara Novalja. This delightful four-star, surrounded by pine forests, vineyards and olive groves, offers eight spacious rooms and three suites, each with a separate seating area, bathroom and exquisite Mediterranean-inspired decor. The **restaurant** (open to non-guests, but you must reserve) dishes out top-notch island specialities prepared with homegrown ingredients, and there's a wine cellar with an impressive selection of Croatian and imported wines.

Back in town, there are plenty of places along Novalja's waterfront serving up inexpensive if undistinguished food. *Steffani*, in the centre at Petra Krešimira IV 28, is definitely worth the extra expense, cooking up a superlative range of fish, shellfish, Pag lamb either stewed or roasted, and local snails.

Travel details

Trains

Rijeka to: Zagreb (3 daily; 4hr).

Buses

Cres Town to: Beli (Mon–Fri 2 daily, Sat 1 daily; 30min); Lubenice (5 weekly; 40min); Mali Lošinj (Mon–Fri 6 daily, Sat & Sun 4 daily; 1hr 45min); Veli Lošinj (Mon–Fri 6 daily, Sat & Sun 4 daily; 2hr); Osor (Mon–Fri 6 daily, Sat & Sun 4 daily; 45min); Rijeka (4 daily; 2hr 30min); Valun (5 weekly; 20min); Zagreb (2 daily; 5hr 30min).
Krk Town to: Baška (9 daily; 50min); Dobrinj (Mon–Fri 1 daily; 45min); Punat (9 daily; 15min); Rijeka (hourly; 1hr 30min); Vrbnik (Mon–Fri 2 daily; 30min); Zagreb (2 daily; 5hr).
Lovran to: Liganj (11 daily; 15min); Lovranska Draga (11 daily; 20min); Rijeka (every 30min; 45min).
Mali Lošinj to: Cres Town (Mon–Fri 6 daily, Sat & Sun 4 daily; 1hr 45min); Osor (Mon–Fri 6 daily, Sat & Sun 4 daily; 45min); Rijeka (4 daily; 3hr 30min–4hr); Zagreb (2 daily; 6hr 30min).
Novalja to: Pag Town (Mon–Sat 7 daily, Sun 2 daily; 35min); Rijeka (Mon–Sat 2 daily, Sun 1 daily; 3hr); Split (1 daily; 4hr 30min); Zadar (3 daily; 1hr 30min); Zagreb (7 daily; 5hr).
Opatija to: Kastav (Mon–Fri 9 daily, Sat 5 daily, Sun 2 daily; 20min); Lovran (every 30min; 15min); Rijeka (every 30min; 30min).
Pag Town to: Novalja (Mon–Sat 7 daily, Sun 2 daily; 35min); Rijeka (Mon–Sat 2 daily, Sun 1 daily; 3hr 45min); Split (1 daily; 4hr); Zadar (Mon–Sat 4 daily, Sun 2 daily; 1hr); Zagreb (8 daily; 5hr 30min).
Rab Town to: Kampor (Mon–Sat 7 daily, Sun 1 daily; 15min); Lopar (Mon–Sat 11 daily, Sun 9 daily; 30min); Rijeka (July & Aug 3 daily; Sept–June 2 daily; 3hr); Senj (July & Aug 3 daily; Sept–June 2

daily; 2hr); Zagreb (July & Aug 4 daily; Sept–June 3 daily; 6hr).
Rijeka to: Cres (4 daily; 2hr 30min); Crikvenica (hourly; 45min); Dubrovnik (Mon–Sat 4 daily, Sun 3 daily; 12–13hr); Kastav (every 30min; 30min); Krk Town (hourly; 1hr 30min); Lovran (every 30min; 45min); Mali Lošinj (4 daily; 3hr 30min–4hr); Novi Vinodolski (hourly; 1hr); Opatija (every 30min; 30min); Pag (Mon–Sat 2 daily, Sun 1 daily; 3hr 45min); Rab Town (July & Aug 3 daily; Sept–June 2 daily; 3hr); Senj (12 daily; 1hr 30min); Šibenik (12 daily; 6hr); Split (12 daily; 8–9hr); Starigrad-Paklenica (12 daily; 3hr 35min); Zadar (12 daily; 4hr 40min–5hr); Zagreb (hourly; 2hr 30min–4hr).
Starigrad Paklenica to: Rijeka (12 daily; 3hr 30min); Split (12 daily; 4hr 15min–5hr); Zadar (hourly; 1hr–1hr 20min).

Ferries

Baška to: Lopar (May, June & Sept 2 daily; July & Aug 5 daily; 50min).
Jablanac to: Mišnjak (July–Aug: every 30min; Sept–June: 14 daily; 30min).
Mali Lošinj to: Pula (mid-June to mid-Sept 2 per week; Oct–May 1 per week; 3hr 35min); Susak (1 daily; 1hr); Zadar (mid-June to mid-Sept 2 per week; 7hr).
Porozina to: Brestova (hourly; 30min).
Prizna to: Žigljen (hourly; 20min).
Rijeka to: Dubrovnik (June–Sept 4 per week; Oct–May 2 per week; 20hr); Hvar (June–Sept daily; Oct–May 2 per week; 12–14hr); Korčula (June–Sept daily; Oct–May 2 per week; 18hr); Split (June–Sept daily; Oct–May 2 per week; 10–12hr); Zadar (June–Sept daily; Oct–May 2 per week; 6hr).
Valbiska to: Merag (every 90min; 30min).

Catamarans

Cres to: Mali Lošinj (1 daily; 2hr–2hr 30min); Rijeka (1 daily; 1hr 20min); Susak (6 per week; 1hr 30min–1hr 50min).
Mali Lošinj to: Cres (1 daily; 2hr–2hr 30min); Rijeka (1 daily; 3hr 20min–3hr 50min); Susak (6 per week; 1hr 10min); Zadar (July & Aug 2 per week; 3hr 15min).
Novalja to: Rab (1 daily; 45min); Rijeka (1 daily; 2hr 30min).
Rab to: Novalja (1 daily; 45min); Rijeka (1 daily; 1hr 45min).
Rijeka to: Cres (1 daily; 1hr 20min); Mali Lošinj (1 daily; 3hr 20min–3hr 50min); Novalja (1 daily; 2hr 30min); Rab (1 daily; 1hr 45min); Susak (6 per week; 2hr 40min–3hr 10min).

Domestic flights

Rijeka to: Zagreb (3 per week; 35min).

International trains

Rijeka to: Ljubljana (2 daily; 2hr 30min).

International buses

Rijeka to: Berlin (2 per week; 11hr 45min); Ljubljana (2 daily; 2hr 30min); Međjugorje (1 daily; 14hr); Munich (1 daily; 8hr 30min); Prague (2 per week; 12hr); Sarajevo (5 per week; 16hr); Trieste (6 daily; 2hr 30min).

International ferries

Rijeka to: Bari (June & Sept 1 per week; July & Aug 2 per week; 26–32hr).

5

Dalmatia

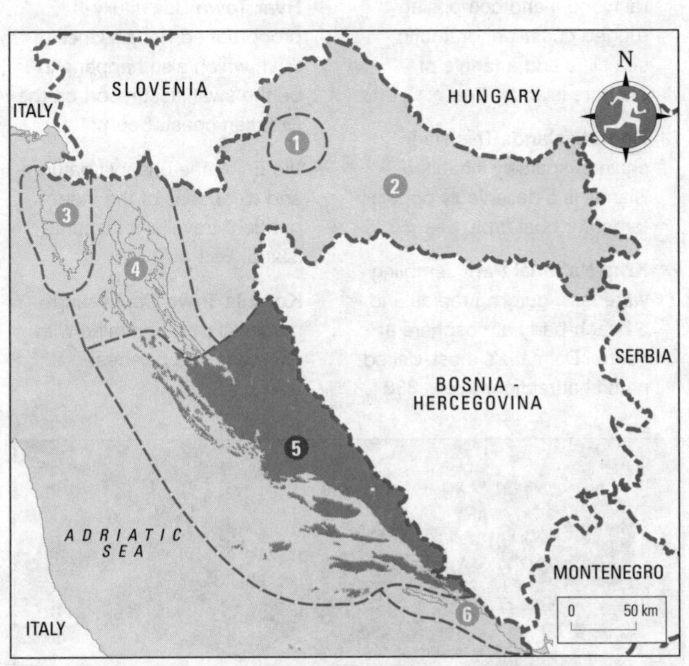

5 DALMATIA

CHAPTER 5

Highlights

* **Zadar** Bustling port city whose narrow pedestrianized alleys are bursting with café life. See p.306

* **Dugi otok** The most unspoilt island in the Zadar archipelago, with a stunning coastline and a string of picturesque villages. See p.323

* **Telašćica Bay** Compact natural wonderland comprising rugged coastline, dramatic sea cliffs and a tangle of offshore islands. See p.324

* **Kornati islands** This stark chain of sparsely inhabited islands is a deservedly popular target for boat trips. See p.328

* **Krka National Park** Tumbling waterfalls, gurgling rapids and a beach-party atmosphere at central Dalmatia's most-visited natural attraction. See p.338

* **Trogir** A warren of stone-paved streets presided over by a stunning Romanesque cathedral. See p.343

* **Split** With their unique tangle of Roman and medieval remains, the streets of the Dalmatian capital are a living textbook of Mediterranean history. See p.352

* **Hvar Town** Beautifully proportioned Renaissance town which also happens to be the swankiest resort on the Croatian coast. See p.400

* **Vis** Enjoy the unspoilt nature and clear seas of the independent traveller's favourite island. See p.411

* **Korčula Town** Captivating medieval port brimming with churches and palaces. See p.419

△ Hvar town, main square

5

Dalmatia

Stretching from Zadar in the north to the Bay of Kotor (now part of Montenegro) in the south, **Dalmatia** possesses one of Europe's most dramatic shorelines, as the stark, grey wall of the coastal mountains sweeps down towards a lush seaboard ribbon dotted with palm trees and olive plantations. Along the coast are beautifully preserved, Venetian-influenced medieval towns that wouldn't look out of place on the other side of the Adriatic, poised above some of the clearest waters in Europe, while offshore are myriad islands adorned with ancient stone villages and enticing coves. The tourist industry boomed in the 1970s and 1980s before collapsing during the 1991–95 war and, though visitor numbers have risen rapidly since the return of peace, the crowds are rarely difficult to avoid: the Adriatic islands can swallow up any number of sightseers, while tourist settlements on the mainland have been kept well away from the main towns.

The contrast between the arid maquis of Dalmatia's stony interior and the fertile seaboard is reflected in the region's **dual personality**: the towns on the coast and islands have long enjoyed a thriving Mediterranean civilization, while their unsettled hinterland has been much more prone to the political uncertainties and population movements of the Balkan interior. People on the coast have traditionally been able to make a living through fishing, olive-growing, wine-making or trade, whereas life in the interior – the more arid parts of which are often called *kamenjar* ("stone-field") in Croatian – has always been much harsher.

Dalmatia's long history of Roman, Venetian and Italian cultural penetration has left its mark on a region where children still call adult males *barba* ("beard" – Italian slang for "uncle") and respected gents go under the name of *šjor* (the local version of *signore*), but modern Dalmatia's identity is difficult to pin down. People from northern Croatia will tell you that life is lived at a much slower pace in Dalmatia, whose inhabitants are joshingly referred to as *tovari* ("donkeys") by their compatriots, though the briefest of visits to bustling regional centres like Zadar will be enough to persuade you that these clichés are somewhat wide of the mark. What is true is that Dalmatia is slightly poorer than the north: local industries took a battering in the war and recession of the 1990s, and tourism – the mainstay of the local economy – is only now beginning to regain its pre-1991 levels. A recent boost to the region's economic fortunes was provided by the completion of the **Zagreb–Split motorway** (Autocesta Zagreb–Split) in 2004, dramatically reducing journey times and making the coast even more accessible to visitors from the rest of Europe.

Although Dalmatia is culturally and historically a unified region, we've divided the following account into two halves, recognition in part of the

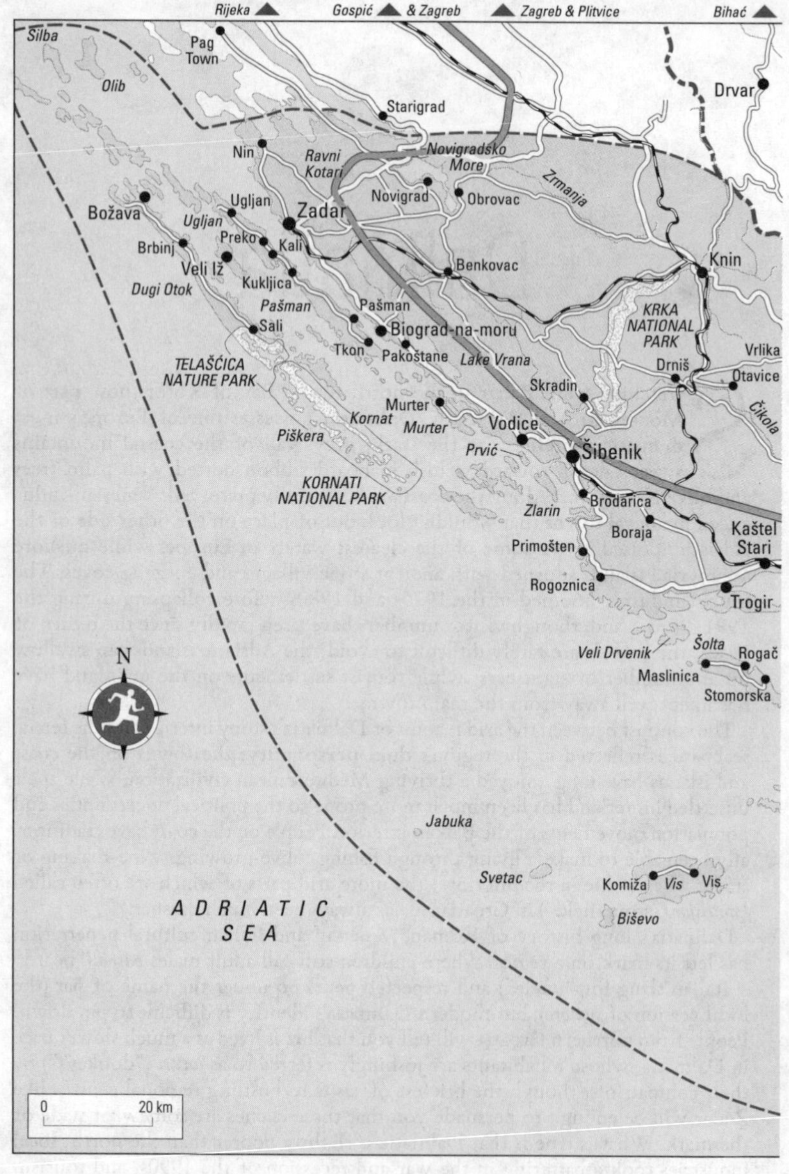

regional roles played by the province's two great cities, **Zadar** and **Split**. Almost everything in **northern Dalmatia** revolves around the busy port of Zadar, from which ferries depart for the islands of the **Zadar archipelago**, many of them blissfully unspoilt. From Zadar many visitors head south to the cathedral city of **Šibenik**, a useful gateway to the natural splendours of the **Kornati islands** and **Krka National Park**. **Southern**

DALMATIA

Dalmatia's major centre is Split, a teeming, chaotic but ultimately addictive city which controls ferry access to the tourist-deluged islands of **Hvar**, **Brač** and **Korčula**, as well as relatively off-the-beaten-track places like **Vis** and **Lastovo**. Road traffic pours out of Split and onwards along the coast, passing through the pebble-beach resorts of the **Makarska Riviera** before arriving in Dubrovnik (which forms the subject of chapter 6).

Getting around Dalmatia is quite straightforward. There's one main road, the Jadranska Magistrala, or Adriatic Highway; frequent **buses** run up and down it every day of the week, connecting all the major centres – you can travel from Zadar to Dubrovnik in around seven hours – though be aware that picking up buses in smaller centres often involves waiting by the side of the Magistrala until something turns up. For visitors with their own transport, the **Zagreb–Split motorway** not only provides the quickest way of getting to the region from northern Croatia, but also provides a nifty means of travelling between Zadar, Šibenik and Split, running a few kilometres inland from the coastal Magistrala. Just about every inhabited island is connected by some kind of regular local **ferry** or catamaran, and there's also a coastal service which cruises up and down from Rijeka to Dubrovnik five times weekly throughout the summer (twice a week in winter), calling at most of the major ports and islands en route and continuing to Bari in Italy at least once a week in summer. Ferries also ply the Zadar–Ancona route in summer.

Some history

Although initially colonized by the **Greeks**, who established themselves on the islands of Vis (Greek Issa) and Hvar (Pharos) at the start of the fourth century BC, the area was first called Dalmatia by the **Romans**, who may have based the name on the Illyrian word *delmat*, meaning a proud, brave man. With the imposition of Roman rule over local Illyrian tribes in the first century BC, power drifted away from the old Greek towns to new centres of imperial power on the mainland like **Jadera** (Zadar) and **Salona** (Solin, near Split). The Latinate urban culture which grew up here was largely unaffected by the fall of the Roman Empire and the brief period of Ostrogoth rule that followed, and was soon reorganized into the Byzantine Province of Dalmatia. The Avar-Slav invasion of 614 did considerable damage to town life, however, weakening Zadar and completely destroying Salona (although a new settlement founded by the fleeing Roman-Illyrian citizenry would eventually become Dalmatia's largest city, Split). The Byzantines soon re-established nominal control of the region, but increasingly left the hinterland to the **Croats**, who arrived here soon after the Avars.

By the eleventh century, the Croatian state – and later its successor, the Hungaro-Croatian kingdom – was successfully challenging both Byzantium and newly emergent Venice for control of the coast. Increasing numbers of Croats moved into the towns, and Croatian entrenched itself as the popular language, even if Latin was still used in writing. When Ladislas of Naples, during his brief stint as King of Hungary-Croatia, sold his rights to Dalmatia to Venice in 1409, most Dalmatian towns were given a choice – accept Venetian rule peacefully and retain a degree of autonomy, or submit by force. Contrary to Dalmatian expectations, however, the Venetians kept the towns on a short leash, muzzling traditions of municipal government by imposing on each of the cities an all-powerful rector (*knez*) responsible directly to the doge, and redirecting all import and export trade through Venice. Class divisions within Dalmatian society prevented any concerted opposition to Venetian rule, however, and rebellions were few and far between – the commoners' revolt launched by **Matija Ivanić** (see p.399) on Hvar in 1510, for instance, was as much against the local oligarchy as the occupying power.

Under the Venetians, Dalmatia was integrated into the wider Mediterranean world more than at any time since the days of the Roman Empire, opening up its cities to Renaissance culture and Italianate architecture. But however many fine loggias and campaniles the Venetians built, it would be a mistake to think that the locals had turned into good Venetians – the urban elite of fifteenth-century Dalmatia clearly saw themselves as Croats, and were keen to develop the local language as a medium fit for their patriotic aspirations. Prime movers were **Marko Marulić** of Split, whose *Judita* (Judith) of 1521 was the first ever epic tale "composed in Croatian verse", as its own title page proclaimed; and **Petar Zoranić** of Zadar, whose novel *Planine* (Mountains) of 1569 contains a scene in which the nymph Hrvatica (literally "Croatian girl") bemoans the lack of Dalmatians who show pride in their own language.

Venetian political control went largely unchallenged, however, because of the growing threat of the **Ottoman Turks**. The Venetians did their best to live in peace with the Turks in order to ensure the smooth functioning of trade, although major conflicts – notably the **Cyprus War** (1570–71) and the **Candia War** (1645–69) – occasionally brought roving armies to the Dalmatian hinterland. The Ottoman **defeat** outside Vienna in 1683 finally provided Venice with the opportunity to push the Turks back into Bosnia, but by this stage decades of conflict had changed the make-up of the Dalmatian population, as Croats from the interior had fled to the coast. Much of the hinterland itself had been devastated and repopulated with migrants from the Balkan interior, most of whom were classified as **Vlachs** (*vlah* or *vlaj* in Croatian) – a name which was sometimes applied to the nomadic tribes descended from the original Roman-Illyrian population, at others to all migrant stockbreeders from the interior. More important than the niceties of ethnic distinction, however, was the fact that the majority of Vlachs belonged to the Orthodox faith and, largely because they came under the jurisdiction of the Serbian Orthodox Church, came increasingly to regard themselves as Serbs.

Questions of ethnic identity are further complicated by the fact that the Venetians referred to all inlanders, regardless of who they were, as **Morlachs** (*morlacchi*), a term thought to originate in the combination of the name Vlach with the Greek word *mavro*, meaning "black" or "dark". The Morlach label came to be applied to all the inhabitants of Dalmatia who lived outside the cultured world of the coastal towns and islands and, although the hard life of the Morlachs was romanticized by foreign travellers (see box overleaf), they were shunned by the urban population on the coast, who were rarely aware of their existence except at fairs and markets. Until the twentieth century even educated Croats knew little about the hinterlanders, referring to them all as *morlaci*, *zagorci* (highlanders) or *vlaji* (a term still used as a put-down in Split, where anyone who can't see the sea from their house is a *vlaj*; see box on p.353), regardless of where they came from or what religion – Catholic or Orthodox – they professed.

For more than 350 years Venice gave the Dalmatian towns peace, security and – ultimately – economic and political stagnation. The fall of the Republic in 1797 was followed by a brief Austrian interregnum until, in 1808, **Napoleon** incorporated Dalmatia into his **Illyrian Provinces**, an artificial amalgam of Adriatic and west Slovene territories with its capital at Ljubljana. The reforming French played an important role in pulling Dalmatia out of its torpor, building roads, promoting trade and opening up the region to modern scientific and educational ideas. There's little evidence that the French were popular, however: their decision to close down the monasteries deeply offended local Catholic feeling, and they also dragged Dalmatia into wars with the Austrians and the British, who occupied Vis in 1811 and shelled Zadar in 1813.

Hopes that Dalmatia would be unified with the rest of the Croatian lands after its incorporation into **Austria** in 1815 were soon dashed. Instead, Dalma-

Images of Dalmatia: Alberto Fortis and the Morlachs

Western images of Dalmatia owe much to the writings of eighteenth-century Venetian **Alberto Fortis**, a lapsed priest, natural scientist and tireless traveller who contributed more to the outside world's knowledge of the eastern Adriatic than anyone before or since. Fortis was particularly taken by the **Morlachs** (see p.299), the inhabitants of inland Dalmatia who had never been assimilated into the coast's urban Mediterranean culture. Although the Morlachs were well known to the Venetian administrators who controlled the coast, Fortis was the first outsider to visit Morlach villages and write about them with any sympathy. He described the Morlachs' often abysmal living conditions, noting the tiny houses in which families slept alongside their cattle, adding that in households which actually possessed a bed, the husband slept on it while the wife was relegated to the floor. He admired their capacity for honesty, hospitality and lifelong friendship, as well as their code of honour – which allowed plenty of room for blood feuds and vengeance. He was particularly taken by the **epic poems** which Morlach bards recited to the accompaniment of the *gusla* (a hideously droning bowed instrument). For Fortis, the Morlachs weren't just living examples of the noble savages he had read about in Jean-Jacques Rousseau, they were the nearest thing that Europe still had to the heroic ideals of Homeric Greece.

Fortis was travelling at a time when epic poems were all the rage in Western Europe. His journeys were partly financed by Scottish laird, the Earl of Bute, whose interest in **heroic folk tales** had been fired after reading *Ossian*, an epic poem thought to be the work of third-century Celtic bards (although it was subsequently revealed to be a forgery). Both Bute and Fortis reckoned that the study of oral literature in inland Dalmatia would prove that all the valiant hero-nations of Europe had somehow been shaped by their epic poetry, and their enthusiasm soon caught on. Fortis's *Travels into Dalmatia* (1774) was an international sensation, provoking a craze for all things Morlach which lasted well into the next century. His translation of the epic poem *Hasanaginica* – a tale of conflict on the Croatian–Ottoman border – was rendered into German by Goethe, and into English by Sir Walter Scott. Romantic novelist Prosper

tia became a separate province of the Habsburg Empire, Italian was made the official language, and German- and Italian-speaking bureaucrats were brought in to run the administration. By mid-century Dalmatia had just over 400,000 inhabitants, of whom 340,000 were Slavs and only 16,000 were Italians, and yet the first Croatian language schools didn't open until the 1860s. Many Croats living in the coastal towns still saw fluency in Italian as a mark of social and cultural superiority, and felt that they had little in common with those from inland. Things began to change in 1848, when the newly formed Croatian **Sabor** (Parliament) in Zagreb renewed calls for the reunification of Dalmatia with the rest of Croatia. The Viennese court quashed the idea, but could no longer prevent the growth of Croatian national consciousness in the Adriatic towns.

The creation of a Dalmatian Assembly in 1861 opened up a political arena which was dominated by the **Narodnjaci** (Nationalists), who wanted the reunion of Dalmatia with the historic heartlands of continental Croatia, and the **Autonomaši** (Autonomists), who regarded Dalmatia as a unique cultural entity populated by "Slavo-Dalmatians" rather than Croats. The Autonomaši tended to be supported by Italians or italianized Croats who looked to Italy – which had emerged as a unified kingdom in 1861 – rather than Austria, although the Austrian defeat of an Italian navy off the island of Vis in 1866 put paid to any immediate likelihood that Dalmatia was about to be swallowed up

Merimée included *Hasanaginica* – alongside numerous purportedly Morlach poems which he simply made up himself – in his collection *La guzla ou choix de poésies illyriques recueillies dans la Dalmatie, la Bosnie, la Croatia et l'Hercegovinie* (The Gusla, or a Selection of Illyrian Poetry from Dalmatia, Bosnia, Croatia and Hercegovina; 1827). As great a figure as Pushkin was taken in by Merimée's book, reprinting some of the Frenchman's fraudulent epics in his *Poems of the Western Slavs*.

Nineteenth-century travel writers tended to use Fortis's work as a guidebook, uncritically repeating his comments on the Morlachs. Even Balthasar Hacquet, whose *L'Illyrie et la Dalmatie* (Illyria and Dalmatia; 1815) was in many ways better informed than Fortis about the South Slavs, still managed to include a fair share of Arabian Nights-style nonsense about the Morlachs, such as the assertion that "When local gendarmes capture a *haiduk* [bandit], there is no need to tie them up: it suffices to cut the waist cord of his ample trousers, which fall around his ankles and prevent him from taking flight."

What none of these travellers got to grips with was the question of who the Morlachs actually were, though the term itself became increasingly redundant as the Morlachs began to identify themselves as Serbs and Croats rather than submitting to the labels applied to them by others. Dalmatia could still be a place of dramatic contrasts, however. The sight of men in embroidered jackets and with pistols stuck in their belts made a big impression on Maude Holbach, whose tellingly entitled *Dalmatia: the Land Where East meets West* (1908) gushingly informed readers that "the Dalmatians look more like stage brigands than peaceful subjects of the Austrian Empire". The Fortis effect probably reached its high-water mark, however, with *Black Lamb and Grey Falcon* (1937) by **Rebecca West**, whose prose was always more enthusiastic when she was writing about the macho types of the Balkan hinterland rather than the civilized urbanites of the Adriatic coast. This type of response to Dalmatia is less popular now than it was, not least because the events of 1991–95 suddenly made traditional Western views of southeastern Europe appear naive and over-romanticized.

by the new state across the Adriatic. The importance of the Battle of Vis was not lost on the local Croats, who began to celebrate its anniversary with much pomp in order to annoy their Italian neighbours. The Narodnjaci won control of the Dalmatian Assembly in 1870, and Croatian became the official language in the Assembly in 1883, though it wasn't introduced into the civil service or the law courts until 1912.

Despite Italian claims, the whole of Dalmatia except Zadar and Lastovo fell to the Kingdom of Serbs, Croats and Slovenes (subsequently Yugoslavia) in 1918. However, the threat of **Italian irredentism** remained strong, especially after Mussolini came to power in 1922. The Italian occupation of Dalmatia between 1941 and 1943 only served to worsen relations between the two communities, and at the war's end most remaining Italians fled.

The advent of socialism in 1945 failed to staunch major **emigration** to the New World and Australasia. After World War II, the traditional olive-growing and fishing economy of the Adriatic islands and villages was neglected in favour of heavy industry, producing a degree of rural depopulation which has only partly been ameliorated by the growth of tourism. The arrival of package tourists in the 1960s brought Dalmatia hitherto unimagined prosperity (although much of the money earned from tourism went to the big Yugoslav travel companies based in Belgrade), while urban-dwellers from inland cities like Zagreb and Belgrade increasingly aspired to **vikendice** ("weekend houses") on the coast, changing the profile of the village population and turning the Adriatic into a vast recreation area serving the whole of Yugoslavia.

Many of the holiday homes owned by Serbs ended up being abandoned, sold or blown up by right-wing thugs after the **break-up of Yugoslavia**, in which Dalmatia suffered as much as anywhere else in Croatia. After securing control of the hinterland areas around Knin and Benkovac, Serbian forces never quite reached the sea – despite attempts to subdue Zadar. Coastal hotels soon filled with refugees, however, and the tourist industry wound down owing to lack of custom. With the resumption of peace, Slovene, Italian and German tourists were quick to return to their former stomping grounds, and by the turn of the century they had been joined by Hungarians, Poles, Czechs and Brits – making Dalmatia one of the most cosmopolitan summer playgrounds in the whole of Europe.

Northern Dalmatia

The main urban centre of northern Dalmatia is **Zadar**, an animated jumble of Roman, Venetian and modern styles that presents as good an introduction as any to Dalmatia's mixed-up history. It's within day-trip distance of the medieval Croatian centre of **Nin**, and is also the main ferry port for the unassuming northern Dalmatian islands of **Silba**, **Ugljan**, **Pašman** and **Dugi otok**, where you'll find peaceful villages, laid-back and fairly empty beaches, and relatively few package hotels.

The next major town south of Zadar is **Šibenik**, with a quiet historic centre and a spectacular fifteenth-century cathedral, and the most convenient base from which to visit the tumbling waterfalls of the **Krka National Park**. The main natural attraction in this part of Dalmatia is the **Kornati archipelago**, a collection of captivatingly bare and uninhabited islands accessed from the village of **Murter**. Further down the coast, ancient **Trogir** is one of the loveliest towns on the entire seaboard, an almost perfectly preserved example of a Veneto-Dalmatian town of the late Middle Ages.

Along the coast to Nin

Approaching from the north, your first sight of Dalmatia is the lofty concrete span of the **Maslenica Bridge** (Maslenički most) as it sweeps across the **Maslenica Gorge**. The original bridge was destroyed by Serb forces in autumn 1991 in an attempt to sever Dalmatia's communications with the rest of the country, and it wasn't until January 1993 that the Croatian army regained control of Maslenica (breaking a UN-brokered ceasefire in the process). The new Maslenica Bridge, opened in 1996, is notoriously susceptible to strong winds – if the Bura is blowing it's often closed to high-sided vehicles, bikes and trailers, and in bad storms it's shut altogether.

Novigrad

To the south of the Maslenica Bridge is the **Novigradsko more** ("Novigrad Sea"), a large, sheltered lagoon bordered by grey-brown hills. Just beyond the bridge, past the village of Posedarje, there's a southbound turning for the little town of **NOVIGRAD**, tucked away on the west side of the lagoon beneath a ruin-crowned hill. Novigrad has something of a history of being a frontline town: it was an important point in Venice's line of defences against the Turks, and held out successfully except for a short period in 1646–47, when Ibrahim Pasha seized the fortress. More recently it was occupied by the Serbs until it was won back in the Maslenica Bridge operation of 1993, although it remained so close to the front line that the locals couldn't return to their houses for another two years.

Nowadays Novigrad is a sleepy little place, consisting of S-bend of solid stone houses set on a quay lined with small fishing craft, and narrow streets winding uphill. The otherwise unremarkable **parish church** (*župna crkva*) contains a Gothic statue of the Pietà which is paraded around town on the third Sunday of September. Just uphill, a **town museum** (Mon–Fri 9am–noon; 10Kn) occupies the shell of another late-medieval church, its main hall scattered with fragments of medieval church carvings, a seventeenth-century bell presented to Novigrad by the islanders of Pag and other sundry items. On the other side of the parish church you can pick up paths to the hilltop **castle** (*fortica*), where Elizabeth Kotromanić, Queen of Hungary, was murdered in 1386. The castle is now in ruins, but the climb is worth it for the views north over the Novigradsko more to the ridge of the Velebit mountains.

Practicalities

The main coastal buses don't make the detour to Novigrad, so if you're dependent on public transport you'll have to make for Zadar first and pick up local services from there. These pull up on Novigrad's Riva, where the **tourist office**, occupying the maroon-coloured former town hall (Mon–Sat 8–11am & 4–9.30pm, Sun 8–11am; ⓣ023/375-051, ⓔtz-novigrad@zd.htnet.hr), has information on local **rooms** (❶) and apartments. The *Osam ferala* **pension**, on the right as you enter town (ⓣ023/375-114; ❷) has simply furnished en-suite rooms above a small restaurant. At the opposite end of the Riva at Elizabete Kotromanić bb, *Apart-hotel Agava* (May–Oct; ⓣ023/375-255, ⓦwww.gastrocom.hr; studios ❹, four-person apartments 620Kn) offers swish self-catering units with ceramic floors and pine furnishings. Just beyond the *Agava*, the *AdriaSol* campsite (ⓣ023/375-111, ⓦwww.adriasol.com) is a neat, Austrian-run establishment which sits on a pleasant stretch of pebbly **beach** – it's a bit exposed to the Bura, but the views of the Velebit mountains are superb. Back in the centre of Novigrad, *Konoba Mika*, with a terrace above the Riva, grills freshly caught fish on an open hearth.

Zrmanja Gorge

On the eastern side of the Novigradsko more, huge rock portals announce the entrance to the narrow canyon of the **Zrmanja Gorge**, one of the most remarkable karst formations in the country, its sheer sides rising as high as 200m. The best way to see the gorge is by **boat**: departures are usually advertised on Novigrad's harbourfront, or, with 24 hours' notice, the tourist office will arrange for a local boatman to take you. It's also possible to take a **raft trip** down the upper stretches of the Zrmanja, with excursions beginning at

Kaštel Žegarski, 25km upriver from Novigrad, and finishing at Muškovci a further 10km downstream. In season, both Flash Touring and Contra set up stalls on Novigrad's Riva offering such trips; you can also enquire at the tourist office, or at hotel receptions in Starigrad-Paklenica or Zadar – expect to pay 250–300Kn per person.

Nin

To the west of the Maslenica Bridge, the Magistrala forges across the **Ravni kotari** (literally "flat districts"), a fertile expanse of farmland and one of the few places in Dalmatia where you'll see cows, sheep and pumpkins alongside more commonplace Mediterranean features such as vineyards, olive groves and maquis. About 15km beyond Posedarje, another side turning leads north to **NIN**, erstwhile ecclesiastical capital of Croatia and now a sleepy, beach-fringed town, set on a broad bay facing the southwestern extremities of the island of Pag. Initially settled by the Liburnians followed by the Romans, Nin later became a royal residence of the early Croatian kings and a major see of their bishops from 879. Like everywhere else along the coast it fell under Venetian rule in the fifteenth century, and was soon threatened by Ottoman advances, until in 1646 the Venetians evacuated the town and then shelled it from the sea, after which it slipped quietly into decay. By the time T.G. Jackson got here in 1887 Nin was no more than a large village whose inhabitants were so wan and malaria-stricken that his guides wouldn't let him stay there overnight.

The malaria has gone, but apart from that Nin can't have changed much since Jackson's visit, preserving a scattering of Roman ruins, crumbling walls and a clutch of quaint old churches testifying to the town's former importance. Nin also boasts some decent **beaches**, with alluring sandy stretches north and east of town and a more pebbly affair at the tourist settlement of Zaton to the west.

The Town

The town is built on a small island connected to the mainland by two bridges: Gornji most and Donji most ("upper bridge" and "lower bridge"). Donji most is your most likely starting point, across which lies the main street; this leads past the plain-looking **St Aselus's Church** (Crkva svetog Azela), an eighteenth-century structure built on the site of Nin's former cathedral and dedicated to a first-century martyr held by local tradition to be the town's first bishop. Inside, a small chapel to the right of the main altar holds a fifteenth-century statue of the Madonna of Zečevo, which commemorates an apparition of the Virgin on a nearby island. A copy of the statue (the original is too fragile) is borne in a procession of boats to Zečevo on May 5, the anniversary of the vision. Next door, the **treasury** (*riznica*; summer only; Mon–Sat 9am–noon & 6–9pm; 10Kn) houses an extraordinary collection of gold- and silver-plated reliquaries, beginning with a ninth-century chest of Carolingian origin containing the shoulder blade of St Aselus, and decorated with reliefs of SS Marcela, Ambrozius and (on the extreme left with hands raised) Aselus himself. Fourteenth-century Zadar goldsmiths produced the nearby reliquary for Aselus's arm, as well as skull reliquaries for Aselus and Marcela – their lids embossed with angels and griffins. The treasury's collection of St Aselus's body parts is rounded off by a dainty casket in the shape of a foot.

A little farther up the main street and just off to the right, the small cruciform **Church of the Holy Cross** (Crkva svetog Križa) is the oldest church in the country, with an inscription on the lintel referring to Župan (Count) Godezav dated 800 AD. A simple whitewashed structure with high, Romanesque windows and a solid dome, it's sometimes open in summer, though it's bare inside apart from the simple stone slab which serves as an altar – ask at the tourist office or at the **Archeological Museum** at the top of the main street (Arheološki muzej; Mon–Sat: June–Aug 9am–10pm; Sept–May 9am–1pm; 10Kn). This small but excellently presented museum kicks off with an ancient Liburnian *peka* (a cooking pot on top of which embers are piled), which looks identical to those still in use in Dalmatian kitchens today. The imported ceramics dredged up from Liburnian wrecks in Zaton harbour include a wealth of north Italian tableware and a dog-faced ornamental jug from Asia Minor. One room is devoted to two eleventh-century Croatian ships (one of which has been fully reconstructed) rescued by marine archeologists from shallow waters nearby. Possibly sunk in front of Nin port in order to prevent attack, these were easily manoeuvrable, eight-metre-long vessels that could be used either for fishing or fighting, and could easily be pulled up onto land or hidden in small bays. A collection of early medieval stonework culminates with a large stone font sporting a clumsily engraved inscription honouring Višeslav, one of the first Christian rulers of the embryonic Croatian state. There's also a model of the Roman temple whose scrappy remains lie round the corner from the museum. Beyond the temple ruins lie a surviving stretch of town wall and the Gornji most, over which the austere, barn-like thirteenth-century **St Ambrose's Church** (Crkva svetog Ambroza) stands silent guard.

Entering Nin on the main road from Zadar, you'll notice another tiny church, **St Nicholas's** (Crkva svetog Nikole), an eleventh-century structure. Surrounded by slender Scots pines, it was built on an ancient burial mound and later fortified by the Turks – the resulting crenellations give it the appearance of an oversized chesspiece. The interior is almost always locked, but it's an impressive site nevertheless, with a fine view over the blustery lowlands to the worn shape of Nin and the faint, silver-grey ridge of the Velebit mountains in the distance.

Nin's superb **beach** is an easy three-kilometre walk from town – head north from the landward side of Donji most, passing a small boat harbour before ascending to meet a small crossroads, where you carry straight on. After a while you'll pass *Camping Ninska Laguna* (see overleaf), then branch off on a path which leads through a purply-green, heather-like carpet of grasses and reeds before emerging onto a duney shore. The beach is genuinely sandy and wonderfully uncommercialized – save for a stretch at the extreme northwestern end which boasts the inevitable straw-parasolled beach bar. Whichever part of the beach you end up on, there's a spectacular view of the Velebit mountains across the water. Don't be alarmed if you catch sight of fellow bathers smearing themselves in sludge: the reedy area behind the beach is rich in **medicinal mud**, particularly effective in easing rheumatic and muscular complaints.

Practicalities

The only way to reach Nin by public transport is from Zadar, with local **buses** (approximately every hour) dropping passengers at an unmarked road junction at the western, mainland side of town. There's unlikely to be any timetable information here, although the helpful **tourist office** (June–Aug Mon–Fri 8am–8pm, Sun 8am–1pm; Sept–May Mon–Fri 8am–3pm; ⓣ & ⓕ023/265-247, ⓦwww.nin.hr), beside Donji most at Trg braće Radića 3, can advise on return services to Zadar. The Lotos agency diagonally opposite (ⓣ023/265-555, ⓦwww.lotos-nin.com) is the best place to enquire about private **rooms** (❶) and **apartments** (two-person apartments ❷, four-person apartments from 460Kn). *Perin Dvor* is a cosy **pension** on the old town's main street beside Donji most

(Ⓣ023/264-307; ④), offering four nicely furnished en-suite rooms with air conditioning and TV, and a pleasant terrace restaurant outside. *Camping Ninska Laguna* (Ⓣ023/264-265, Ⓦwww.ninskalaguna.hr), on the way to the beach, is an orderly little place with a reasonable amount of shade, although it tends to get cramped in season. For **food**, the *Perin Dvor* has good home cooking in a nice garden. *Konoba Dalmacija*, between the old town and the bus stop, offers the best in the grilled fish line.

Zadar

The ancient capital of Dalmatia, **ZADAR** is a bustling town of around 80,000 people, but it preserves a relatively small-town feel, with a compact historic centre crowded onto a tapered thumb of land jutting northwest into the Adriatic. Pretty comprehensively destroyed in the last war by the Allies – it was bombed no fewer than 72 times – it lacks the perfectly preserved, museum-like quality of so many of the towns on this coast, displaying instead a pleasant muddle of architectural styles, where lone Corinthian columns stand alongside rectangular 1950s blocks, and Romanesque churches compete for space with glass-fronted café-bars. Zadar is a major ferry port, so you'll pass through here if travelling on to the islands of the Zadar archipelago – Ugljan, Pašman, Dugi otok and a host of smaller islets. As the major urban centre between Rijeka and Split, Zadar boasts a university, established by Dominican monks in 1396 and claimed to be the oldest in Croatia, a smattering of cultural distractions and numerous leafy patios. The presence of big hotels on the outskirts of town ensures that the central streets are swarming with life in July and August; outside that time, Zadar's relaxing café culture is left very much to the locals and students.

Long held by the Venetians (who called it Zara), Zadar was for centuries an **Italian-speaking** city, and you'll find the Latin influence still strong – Italian is widely understood, particularly by older people, and the place has much of the vibrancy of an Italian coastal town. It was ceded to Italy in 1921 under the terms of the Treaty of Rapallo, before becoming part of Tito's Yugoslavia in 1947, when many Italian families opted to leave.

Postwar reconstruction resulted in the current patchwork of old and new architectural styles, although further damage was meted out in 1991, when a combination of Serbian irregulars and JNA (Yugoslav People's Army) forces came dangerously close to capturing the city. As the country slid towards all-out war in early autumn 1991, JNA artillery units quickly took control of the low hills around Zemunik airport east of the city, leaving Zadar open to bombardment. JNA-Serb forces reached the high-rise suburbs but never pressed on towards the centre, possibly fearing the heavy losses that would be incurred in hand-to-hand street fighting. Despite the UN-sponsored ceasefires of 1992, Zadar remained exposed to Serbian artillery attack right up until 1995, when the Croatian Oluja offensive finally drove them back.

After some years spent in the economic doldrums, today Zadar has a more dynamic feel than some of the other Dalmatian towns and has become one of Croatia's major sailing destinations, with a number of regattas and sailing events throughout the year. Other main money-earners are tuna fishing, with most of the catch exported directly to Japan, and the almost totally refurbished German-run Borik hotel development – built in the 1980s, this was given a wide berth by

CENTRAL ZADAR

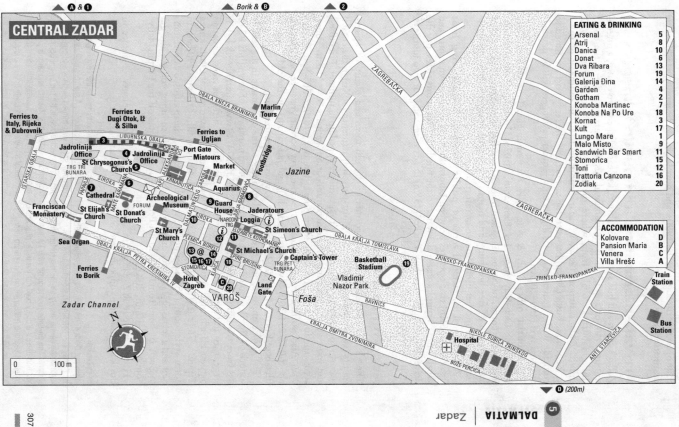

EATING & DRINKING	
Arsenal	5
Atrij	8
Danica	10
Donat	6
Dva Ribara	13
Forum	19
Galerija Đina	14
Garden	4
Gotham	2
Konoba Martinac	7
Konoba Na Po Ure	18
Kornat	3
Kult	17
Lungo Mare	1
Malo Misto	9
Sandwich Bar Smart	11
Stomorica	15
Toni	12
Trattoria Canzona	16
Zodiak	20

ACCOMMODATION	
Kolovare	D
Pansion Maria	B
Venera	C
Villa Hrešć	A

A & 1
Borik & B
2
D (200m)

Ferries to Italy, Rijeka & Dubrovnik
Ferries to Dugi Otok, Iž & Silba
Ferries to Ugljan
Ferries to Borik
Jadrolinija Office
Jadrolinija Office
Port Gate
Miatours
Market
Marlin Tours
Footbridge
Jazine
St Chrysogonus's Church
Cathedral
Archeological Museum
Guard House
Aquarius
Jaderatours
Loggia
St Simeon's Church
Franciscan Monastery
St Elijah's Church
St Donat's Church
St Mary's Church
St Michael's Church
Captain's Tower
Sea Organ
Hotel Zagreb
Land Gate
Varoš
Foša
Basketball Stadium
Vladimir Nazor Park
Hospital
Train Station
Bus Station
Zadar Channel
Liburnska Obala
Istarska Obala
Obala Kneza Branimira
Obala Kralja Petra Krešimira IV
Obala Kralja Tomislava
Zagrebačka
Zrinsko-Frankopanska
Kralja Dmitra Zvonimira
Nikole Šubića Zrinskog
Ante Starčevića
Bože Perčića
Ravnice
Trg Tri Bunara
Trg Pet Bunara
Narodni Trg
Forum
Široka
Papavije
Mate Karamana
Pape Aleksandra
Krnarutića
Dalmatinskog Sabora
Jurja Barakovića
Elizabete Kotromanić
Plemića Borelli
Spire Brusine
Stomorica
Klaića
0 100 m

tour operators throughout the 1990s, and now looks like becoming a fashionable destination once again.

Arrival, information and public transport

Zadar's **train** and **bus stations** lie about 1km east of the town centre, a fifteen-minute walk or a quick hop on municipal bus #5. **Ferries** arrive at the quays lining Liburnska obala, from where the town centre is a five-minute walk uphill. Zadar's **airport** (ⓦwww.zadar-airport.hr) is 12km southeast of town at Zemunik; buses (30Kn) between the airport and the ferry port are timed to coincide with Croatian Airlines flights only – other passengers will be dependent on a taxi (150–200Kn).

The **tourist office** (July & Aug daily 8am–midnight; June & Sept daily 8am–8pm; Oct–May Mon–Fri 8am–3pm; ⓣ023/316-166, ⓦwww.tzzadar.hr), on the corner of Narodni trg and Mihe Klaića, has helpful multilingual staff and a wealth of free brochures and maps. The tourist board's website, ⓦwww.zadar.hr, is another useful source of information.

Zadar's most characterful form of **public transport** is the **rowing boat** (barkarijol; 5Kn) that operates between Liburnska obala in the town centre and Obala kneza Trpimira across the water to the north. For **local bus rides**, pay the driver (8Kn flat fare) or buy a ticket (13Kn) in advance, valid for two journeys, from newspaper and tobacco kiosks.

Accommodation

There's a smattering of private **rooms** in the old town and plenty of **apartments** (two-person apartments ❸, four-person apartments 450Kn) in the coastal suburbs to the west, although they're speedily snapped up in summer. Friendliest and most accommodating of the accommodation agencies is Marlin Tours, across the footbridge from the ferry port at Jeretova 3 (ⓣ023/305-920, ⓕ305-919). Also worth a try are Miatours, near the ferry port at Vrata svetog Krševana bb (ⓣ023/254-300, ⓦwww.miatours.hr), and Jaderatours, in the old town on Elizabete Kotromanić (ⓣ023/250-350, ⓦwww.jaderatours.hr).

The *Borik* **campsite**, next to the hotel complex of the same name in the seaside suburb of **Borik** (also known as Puntamika), 4km northwest of town (bus #5 or #8 from the train and bus stations; ⓣ023/332-074, ⓦwww.hoteliborik.hr), is large, tidy and shaded by a variety of deciduous and coniferous trees. Croatia's biggest HI-affiliated **youth hostel** lies nearby on the waterfront at Obala kneza Trpimira 76 (bus #5 or #8; ⓣ023/331-145, ⓦwww.hfhs.hr), with 290 beds in dorm-style rooms (95Kn per person with breakfast), a cheap alfresco café-restaurant and a relaxing, laid-back atmosphere. Note that in summer, you can also get to Borik by boat from Obala kralja Petra Krešimira IV just off the Forum (daily; hourly 8am–10pm; 20Kn).

Hotels in central Zadar are in short supply, but there's plenty of choice in Borik. See the maps opposite and on p.307 for locations.

Hotels

Albin put Dikla 47 ⓣ023/331-137, ⓦwww.albin.hr. Family-run hotel in a residential area 3km north of the centre, handy for the beach facilities at Borik. The en-suite rooms come with TV and a/c, and there's a dinky pool out the back, plus an excellent seafood restaurant on the ground floor. Bus #5 or #8 from the bus/train stations. ❹

Borik Borik, 4km northwest of the centre ⓦwww.media.falkensteiner.com. A seafront holiday complex set in well-tended gardens and boasting a long pebble beach. It's run by the German Falkensteiner Hotels & Resorts and targets package-holidaying families, leaving little room for individual travellers, especially in July and August, when it is block-booked by travel agencies. The

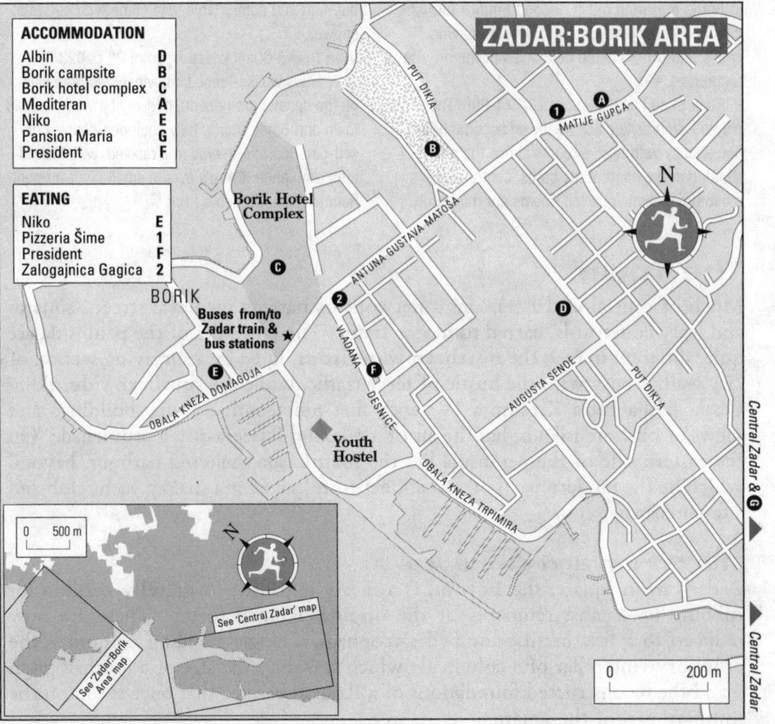

Funimation (ⓣ023/206-100) is the swankiest, but there's a one-week minimum stay. *Adriana Select* (ⓣ023/206-300) is a chic, stylish four-star affair with all junior suites; *Puntamika* (ⓣ023/206-400), an adequate three-star, is your best bet for stays of fewer than three nights; *Donat* (ⓣ023/206-500) is an acceptable block of a hotel with antiseptic interior. Get there on bus #5 or #8 from the train and bus stations, or hourly boat from Obala kralja Petra Krešimira. March–Oct. *Funimation* 6 (all-inclusive), *Adriana Select* 6 (half-board), *Puntamika* 6, *Donat* 5

Kolovare Bož e Peričića 14 ⓣ023/203-200, ⓔprodaja@hotel-kolovare.t-com.hr. Five minutes south of the bus and train stations, this is currently the only mid-range/business-class hotel within convenient walking distance of the centre. Renovated en-suite rooms have a/c and TV, and there's a swimming pool. 5

Mediteran Matije Gupca 19 ⓣ023/337-500, ⓦwww.hotelmediteran-zd.hr. Small private hotel northeast of the beach at Borik. All rooms come with balcony, en-suite shower and TV; some of the more expensive ones have a/c and minibar. Take the boat, or hop on bus #5 or #8 to *Camping Borik* and walk five minutes uphill. 5

Niko Obala kneza Domagoja 9 ⓣ023/337-880, ⓦwww.hotel-niko.hr. Small, swish, private hotel across the seafront just west of Borik, above the restaurant of the same name. Spacious rooms have plush furnishings, a/c, TV and minibar, and many sport balconies providing lovely vistas of Zadar's old town. There are plans to add a swimming pool, and the restaurant is top-notch. 6

Pansion Maria Put Petrića 24 ⓣ023/334-245, ⓦwww.pansion-maria.com. Family-run B&B in a suburban street midway between the centre and Puntamika. Doubles and triples are smallish but comfortable, with en-suite WC/shower and (in some cases) TV and a tiny balcony. Some rooms come with bright white colour schemes, others are stuffed with old-fashioned furniture and china ornaments. Breakfast is in a covered patio in the garden. German, Italian or English spoken depending on which member of the family you manage to get hold of. 4

President Vladana Desnice 16 ⓣ023/333-696, ⓦwww.hotel-president.hr. Intimate luxury hotel in Borik, featuring plush Second Empire furnishings and conscientious staff. Dine on caviar, snails and other choice delicacies in the on-site restaurant. 8

Venera Šime Ljubića 4a ⓣ023/214-098. The only *pension*-style place (really an accommodation agency with twelve rooms above the office) situated in the heart of the Varoš, central Zadar's most atmospheric quarter. Rooms are minuscule but neat and comfortable, and come with en-suite shower. 3

Villa Hrešć Obala kneza Trpimira 28 ⓣ023/337-570, ⓦwww.villa-hresc.hr. Lovingly restored villa on the coastal promenade, midway between the old town and Borik. Bright, fully equipped doubles or self-catering apartments in a relaxed, well-looked-after ambience. There's even a small open-air pool. Rooms 5, apartments from 6

The Town

Much of central Zadar remains a network of narrow medieval streets, squares and leafy courtyards, barred to motor traffic. The two sides of the peninsula are quite different in feel: the **northern waterfront**, lined by a surviving section of city wall, is busy with the hustle of ferry traffic, while the **southern side**, along Obala kralja Petra Krešimira IV, with fine nineteenth-century buildings and views of offshore islands, has the air of a relaxing Riviera-town promenade. On the eastern side of the peninsula lies the **Jazine**, the sheltered harbour, beyond which lie the modern parts of town, uneventful save for a snazzy yacht club and a few marinas.

The Forum and cathedral

Zadar's main square, the **Forum**, is a messy expanse – a gravelly parking lot rubbing up against remnants of the original Roman forum. These are now reduced to a few hastily dumped sarcophagi, a single standing column – the only surviving pillar of a colonnade which was once the size of a football pitch – and the reconstructed foundations of a Roman basilica that once stood on the southern part of the square.

Much of the original stone from the Forum found its way into the adjacent ninth-century **St Donat's Church** (Crkva svetog Donata; summer only: daily 9am–10pm; 6Kn, plus 3Kn for a small leaflet guide), a hulking cylinder of stone built – according to tradition – by St Donat himself, an Irishman who was bishop here for a time. It's an impressive example of Byzantine church architecture, resembling from the outside San Vitale in Ravenna and Charlemagne's Palatinate Chapel in Aachen. The cavernous, bare interior has a pleasing simplicity: a high-ceilinged circular space with a gallery held up by six chunky supports and two Corinthian columns. It was deconsecrated in 1797, subsequently serving as a shop, military store and museum, but for the moment it lies empty, used only for concerts held in July and August as part of the annual **St Donat Music Evenings** (Glazbene večeri u svetog Donatu).

The modern, concrete **Archeological Museum** opposite (Arheološki muzej; Mon–Sat 9am–1pm; in summer also Mon–Sat 5–7pm; 10Kn) has a neatly displayed collection, setting off with the Neolithic period on the top floor and moving on through Liburnian, Roman and medieval Croatian periods as you descend. There are several examples of the characteristic Liburnian gravestone or *cipus*, a tapering bollard-like affair crowned with carved leaf shapes, rather like a fat stalk of asparagus (there are a few more stacked up in the yard at the back). The medieval Croatian stonework also catches the eye, particularly the fancifully rendered griffins; these flank the depiction of Christ and his angels on the eleventh-century carved doorway which once adorned the portals of the (long since demolished) St Lawrence's Church.

St Mary's Church and the Church Art Exhibition

On the same side of the square as the museum, **St Mary's Church** (Crkva svete Marije) dates from 1066 and includes some salvaged Roman and medieval pillars in the nave, though its trefoil Renaissance frontage was added in the sixteenth century, and the interior was given a thorough refurbishment in the eighteenth, when the rippling stucco balconies of the gallery were added. The Romanesque bell tower next door is the oldest in Dalmatia, having been built in 1105.

The adjacent **convent** is of more interest, having recently been converted to house a **Permanent Exhibition of Church Art**, more commonly referred to as Gold and Silver of Zadar (Stalna izložba crkvene umjetnosti, or Zlato i srebro Zadra; Mon–Sat 10am–1pm; in summer also Mon–Sat 6–8pm, Sun 10am–1pm; 20Kn), a storehouse of Zadar's finest church treasures and very much the pride of the city. The first floor has numerous reliquaries, including a richly ornamented twelfth-century casket containing the arm of St Isidore and a thirteenth-century reliquary for the shoulder blade of St Mark, which resembles a small grand piano mounted on three clawed legs. Some very diverse iconic representations of the Madonna and Child include a Paolo Veneziano work from the 1350s, in which the rigidity of sacred painting is softened with a touch of naturalistic portraiture, with the eyes of the Virgin fixing the viewer. On the second floor there's a large fifteenth-century gang of apostles carved in wood by the Venetian Matej Moronzon in 1426, and an early six-part polyptych by Vittore Carpaccio, one panel of which features a much-reproduced picture of a youthful, tousle-haired St Martin of Tours lending his cloak to a beggar. Altogether, it's a fabulous museum, subtly arranged, beautifully lit and just small enough to be manageable in a single visit.

The cathedral

On the northwestern side of the Forum, the twelfth- and thirteenth-century **Cathedral of St Anastasia** (Katedrala svete Stošije; daily Mass at 7pm) is a perfect example of the late Romanesque style, with an arcaded west front reminiscent of the churches of Pisa and Tuscany. Around the door frame stretches a frieze of twisting acanthus leaves, from which various beasts emerge – look for the rodent and bird fighting over a bunch of grapes – while to either side hang figures of four apostles, engagingly primitive pieces of stonework which were probably taken from the facade of an earlier church on this site. You can climb up the cathedral's 56-metre **campanile** (April–Oct daily 9.30am–1pm & 5–8pm; 10Kn) for sweeping vistas of Zadar's rooftops and the islands in the distance. The campanile was only finished in the 1890s by the English writer and architect T.G. Jackson; if you've been to Rab you may find it familiar – he modelled it on the cathedral bell tower there.

The cathedral's **interior** is high and capacious, with a nave greedily out of proportion to the narrow aisles hidden away on each side. The lofty arcade is pretty enough, with pillars picked out in red marble, but it can't help but look a little lost in the broad expanses of flat, grey stone. At the eastern end, the Gothic ciborium of 1332 sports a series of deftly chiselled columns, each with a different geometric design, enclosing a ninth-century altar engraved with fat crosses and palms. The side altar at the end of the left-hand aisle is surmounted by a plain marble casket holding the bones of St Anastasia, made – as the workmanlike inscription records – in the time of Bishop Donat in the ninth century. Details concerning Anastasia herself are impossible to pin down: according to one legend she was a fourth-century martyr put to death in Sirmium (now Sremska Mitrovica in Serbia), although her cult probably came to Zadar from Aquileia

△ Zadar cathedral

in northern Italy, where she was honoured as a saintly Roman woman who performed many miracles.

West of the forum

Hidden away behind the cathedral lurks the **Orthodox Church of St Elijah** (Crkva svetog Ilije), which originally ministered to the needs of the Greek sailors in the Venetian navy before being handed over to the Serbian Church in the mid-eighteenth century, when the campanile – now with tufts of grass growing between its heavy blocks of stone – was added. Following Široka (subsequently J. Bjankinija) west from here, you'll soon arrive at **Trg tri bunara**, given its name by the three wells (*tri bunara*) dating from the eighteenth century on its northern side.

Turn left down A. Papavije and bear left again at the end to find the **Franciscan monastery** (Franjevački samostan), said to have been founded by St Francis himself when he visited Zadar in 1219, and purportedly the oldest Gothic church in Dalmatia. Its real claim to fame is the fact that the Zadar Peace Accord of 1358, which freed Dalmatia of Venetian rule, was signed in its sacristy. Today it is a fairly dull renovation with a flat eighteenth-century roof and a pleasing courtyard lined with the graves of Zadar nobles. The working well at the centre served as one of Zadar's only sources of drinking water during the recent Croat–Serb conflict.

The Seafront and the Sea Organ

West of the Fransiscan Monastery, alleys emerge out onto the seafront boulevard of Obala kralja Petra Krešimira IV, where there's a fine view across the water to the hilly island of Ugljan. The palm-lined seafront path attracts a steady stream of strollers, most of whom ultimately gravitate towards the so-called Sea Organ (Morske orgulje) near the peninsula's northeastern tip. Designed by local architect Nikola Bašić and completed in 2005, Zadar's newest tourist attraction consists of a stone stairway descending towards the sea. Wave action pushes air through a series of underwater pipes and up through niches cut into the steps, producing a selection of mellow musical notes. The organ is at its best when the sea is choppy, but even during calm periods the tranquil tones of the organ will be sufficient to lull you into a meditative state. Plans are afoot to build another of Bašić's innovative set-pieces as a companion to the Sea Organ. Provisionally entitled Greeting to the Sun (Pozdrav suncu), it will consist of a huge light-sensitive disk which accumulates solar power during the daytime and radiates a hypnotic glow at night.

Around the Port Gate

Returning to Trg tri bunara and heading north brings you to the ferry dock and a length of **city wall**, one of the few surviving stretches of a defensive system completed in 1570, just in time to save Zadar from a two-year Turkish siege. You can follow these fragments of wall southeast towards the **Port Gate** (Lučka vrata), a Roman triumphal arch, later topped with a relief of St Chrysogonus, the city's protector, on horseback.

Slightly uphill from the gate is **St Chrysogonus's Church** (Crkva svetog Krševana), a more impressive building outside than in, with a west front similar to the cathedral's and a superb colonnaded east end. To one side stands a squat, unfinished tower which never rose above the height of the church's facade, and an angular, musclebound modern statue of the Zadar-born writer **Petar Zoranić** (1508–c.1560), whose Arcadian romance *Planine* (Mountains) is often credited with being the first novel written in Croatian. On the other side of the street, the interior of the **Zagrebačka banka** incorporates elements of the medieval St Thomas's Church (Crkva svetog Tome), which once stood on this spot, with stubby remains of columns running along the floor and gravestones mounted on one of the walls.

Cut southeast along Krnarutića to reach the **market** (mornings only), which fills a small square hard up against the walls. Here you'll find all manner of fruit and vegetables brought in daily from the surrounding countryside, while traders in an adjacent hall sell freshly caught fish. It's a colourful scene, though no longer as exotic as it was when Maude Holbach travelled through Dalmatia in the early 1900s, remarking on the peasants who, "seated on the ground in the fashion of the East, offered their eggs and vegetables for sale in the strangest tongue that ever assailed my ears. At first glance they seemed to me more like North American Indians than any European race."

Narodni trg and St Simeon's Church

Just beyond the market, another gate leads through to the pedestrian bridge which crosses the Jazine and gives access to modern Zadar. In the other direction from the footbridge, Jurja Barakovića heads up to **Narodni trg**, which took over from the Forum as the main focus of civic activity in the Middle Ages. It's overlooked by the sixteenth-century **Guard House** (Gradska straža), a low, single-storey building with a soaring square clock tower, built in 1562. The niche to the left of the main entrance houses a fine bust of the Venetian governor G.G. Zane from 1608, sporting stylized furrowed brows and a veritable carpet of a beard. Immediately opposite, the **Town Loggia** (Gradska loža; Mon–Fri 9am–noon & 6–9pm, Sat 9am–1pm; 5Kn) has been enclosed in plate glass and transformed into an art gallery.

Southeast of Narodni trg, on Trg Petra Zoranića, the Baroque **St Simeon's Church** (Crkva svetog Šimuna) was rebuilt in the seventeenth century to act as a fitting shrine for the bones of St Simeon, one of Zadar's patron saints, who is supposed to have held the Christ child in the Temple. The body was originally stored in the Church of St Mary the Great until its demolition to make way for the city walls in 1570.

St Simeon's silver-gilt **reliquary** now forms the main feature of the high altar, where it's held aloft by two Baroque angels cast in bronze from captured Turkish cannons. An extravagant work of art, ordered by Queen Elizabeth of Hungary in 1377, the reliquary was fashioned from 250 kilos of silver by a team of local artisans working under the supervision of a Milanese silversmith. The story goes that Elizabeth so wanted a piece of the saint's body that she broke off a finger and hid it in her bosom, where it immediately began to decompose and fill with maggots – a process only reversed when she returned the finger to its rightful place. The creation of the reliquary was her way of atoning for the theft, though it also had a political dimension: her patronage of the cult of St Simeon increased the local popularity of her husband, King Louis of Anjou, who was at that time engaged in keeping Zadar free from the clutches of Venice. The lid of the reliquary shows the bearded saint in high relief; on the front, two panels dramatize the discovery of St Simeon's body in a monastery on the outskirts of Zadar and Louis of Anjou's triumphant entry into the city after relieving Zadar from an eighteen-month Venetian siege. The centre panel is a rough copy of Giotto's fresco of the *Presentation in the Temple* in Padua. The reliquary is opened every year on the feast of St Simeon (Oct 8).

Trg pet bunara and the Varoš quarter

Beyond St Simeon's Church a low flight of steps leads to the five wells that give **Trg pet bunara** its name and which were the city's main source of drinking water until the late nineteenth century. Completely repaved in 1998, the square is now used as a summer venue for open-air concerts and theatre peformances but still has an antiseptic aspect that seems out of keeping with the grizzled pentagonal **Captain's Tower** (Kapetanova kula; Mon–Fri 10am–1pm & 5–8pm,

Sat 10am–1pm; 10Kn) at its north end. The tower now doubles as a four-level gallery with changing exhibits of works by contemporary Croatian artists and can be climbed for some nice views from the top. Immediately southeast of here lies the entrance to the somewhat neglected but peaceful **city park** conceived in 1832 by Austrian Governor Welden, laid out on a jutting, arrow-shaped bastion which once formed the landward side of Zadar's defences.

Southwest from Trg pet bunara is the **Land Gate** (Kopnena vrata), a triumphal arch topped by a row of eight cattle skulls – thought to be a death symbol intended to ward off would-be invaders – and a monumental winged lion of St Mark; tellingly, this symbol of Venetian power dwarfs the civic emblem – another relief of St Chrysogonus on horseback – immediately below it. On the far side of the gate lies the **Foša**, a narrow channel which once fed Zadar's moat and is now a small harbour crowded with pleasure boats. Follow this around and you're back on Zadar's southern waterfront, Obala kralja Petra Krešimira IV.

Alternatively, heading northwest from the Land Gate along Špire Brušine (subsequently Plemića Borelli, then Madijevaca) leads you back into the city centre through the charming **Varoš quarter**, whose atmospheric narrow alleys are packed with little boutiques and cafés. On the corner of Špire Brušine and M. Klaića, the main portal of **St Michael's Church** (Crkva svetog Mihovila) is topped by an animated fourteenth-century relief of St Michael spearing a demon, flanked by Zadar's ubiquitous patrons, Anastasia and Chrysogonus. Peering out from the facade higher up are three fish-eyed male heads, the remains of a crudely carved late Roman gravestone. Continuing along Borelli and Madijevaca, passing the yellow brick Austrian courthouse (Sudska palača), you'll eventually emerge beside St Mary's Church on the corner of the Forum.

Eating and drinking

While **central Zadar** would never feature in any gourmet's grand tour, there are plenty of unpretentious sit-down places serving up simple grills and fish dishes. The swankier seafood restaurants are mostly located in the city's north-western suburbs.

△ Zadar cafés

For **snacks** and **picnics**, the daily market just inside the old town walls off Jurja Barakovića is the place to get fruit, veg, local cheeses and home-cured hams. There's a **supermarket**, Konzum (daily 6.30am–9pm), on the corner of Široka and Dalmatinskog sabora, and a larger branch just across the footbridge over the Jazine on Josipa Jurja Strossmayera. The *Sandwich Bar Smart*, M. Klaića, is the place to get a sandwich filled with local *pršut* or Slavonian *kulen* sausage.

For **drinking**, the central strip from Narodni trg to the Forum is well supplied with terrace cafés and ice-cream parlours. However, many of the more atmospheric café-bars are in the **Varoš** quarter: from Narodni trg, head down Klaića and its continuation, Varoška, before bearing right into Stomorica – en route you'll pass a string of tiny establishments with outdoor seating crammed into narrow alleys. On warm summer evenings most customers end up either perching precariously on benches or standing in the street.

Be sure to try a shot of *maraschino*, a cherry dessert liqueur that's been produced in Zadar since the sixteenth century; it can be found in most bars and cafés, and is also sold as a souvenir in hand-woven bottles.

Cafés and bars

Arsenal Poljana Natka Nodila. Housed in the former Venetian navy's storehouse, this huge galleried space is filled with lounge-bar furniture, and also has clothes boutiques and gallery spaces off to either side. A great place for drinks and cocktails on any night of the week, it also serves as Zadar's main venue for live rock and jazz.

Atrij Jurja Barakovića 6. Popular daytime coffee-sipping venue on the way to the footbridge from the old town, featuring a relaxing inner courtyard, a pavement terrace outside, good coffee and delicious French-style pastries.

Danica Široka bb. Café and cake shop opposite the theatre, with the biggest range of sweets and pastries in the city.

Donat Trg sv Stošje. The best of Zadar's ice cream parlours, with outdoor seating right by the cathedral and a full range of non-alcoholic drinks. Both this and the café next door (*Lloyds*) are popular vantage points from which to observe the ebb and flow of the evening *korzo*.

Galerija Đina Varoška. Chic and comfy café in one of the tightest-packed alleyways of the Varoš quarter – savour the unique Zadar experience of listening to music simultaneously pumped out by three or four cafés.

Garden Bedemi zadarskih pobuna. Open-air garden bar occupying a stretch of the city walls, founded by UB40's drummer and tour manager in 2004 and already something of a Zadar institution. You can relax in sofas, sprawl on mattresses looking out to port, or perch beside the central water feature. Slightly more expensive than elsewhere in town, but not punishingly so. DJ-driven club nights at weekends, when there may be an entrance charge.

Kult Stomorica. An eternally popular hangout in the Varoš quarter, with lots of outdoor seating in an attractively tatty residental courtyard. Additional attractions include an al-fresco cocktail bar, and occasional live gigs are laid on in high summer.

Toni M. Klaića. Tiny but enduringly popular café-bar occupying a key junction on the route into the Varoš quarter, attracting a slightly older crowd than *Galerija Đina* or *Kult*.

Zodiak Šimuna Ljubavca 2. Another long-standing Varoš favourite, with poky but cosy interior and outdoor wooden-bench seating. The eclectic range of non-pop music on the CD system attracts everyone from old rockers to dreadlock-wearing alternative types.

Restaurants: central Zadar

Dva Ribara Borelli 7. Conveniently placed city-centre eatery with minimalist interior full of matt-black furnishings and straight lines. There's a wide-ranging meat and fish menu, but *Dva Ribara* is particularly known for its pizzas, which keep the locals coming in droves.

Konoba Martinac A. Paravije 7. Cosy little tavern in the alleyway leading to the Franciscan monastery, dishing up fresh fish, excellent squid and scampi on a small garden terrace. The house speciality is veal in shredded tuna sauce – possibly a bit rich for some palates, but well worth trying if you're in the mood for a flavour clash.

Konoba Na Po Ure Špire Brusine 8. Trendy spot with stylish stone interiors, folksy decor, a few wooden benches out front and a more secluded small patio out the back. Given it offers some of the tastiest and cheapest fish dishes in town, a great *pašticada* and a decent wine list, too, it's not difficult to see why this place is popular with the locals.

Kornat Liburnska obala 6 ⓣ023/254-501. Harbourside restaurant at the quiet end of Zadar's main ferry dock, offering superior seafood in a moderately formal atmosphere (the wait staff wear ties, but this doesn't mean that you have to). The grilled fresh fish is first-class and the breadth of recipes quite impressive (check out the sea bass in scampi sauce, or monkfish cooked in white wine). There's a generous selection of quality Croatian wines.

Lungo Mare Obala kneza Trpimira 23. On the seafront promenade midway between the old town and Borik, this is a popular choice with Zadar folk who are after decent food in a relaxed setting. Seating is on a large terrace shaded by trees and there's a large selection of fresh fish and shellfish and a decent list of Croatian wines.

Malo Misto Jurja Dalmatinca 3. Neighbourhood bar-restaurant that keeps the locals happy with inexpensive staples like *grah* and *girice* during the winter, and opens up a terrace serving moderately priced grilled meats in the summer.

Stomorica Stomorica 12. A basic but well-executed repertoire of grilled fish and grilled squid served up in a tiny interior, with outdoor tables in the neighbouring alleys.

Trattoria Canzona Stomorica 8. The pizzas, pastas and salads on offer here are reasonably competent, but the real attraction of this Italian-themed place is the setting, with a snug confusion of wooden tables indoors and outdoor seating in one of the old town's most animated backstreets.

Restaurants: Borik and around

Niko Obala Kneza Domagoja 9 ⓣ023/337-888. Upmarket seafood restaurant hidden away in an anonymous street just off the seafront west of Borik. They serve superbly prepared fish and shellfish and a wonderful tiramisu – it's the kind of place where Zadar people go for a special meal.

Pizzeria Šime Matije Gupca 15. Monster-sized terrace restaurant uphill from Borik, known for its filling, inexpensive and reasonably authentic thin-crust pies. Can get packed out in July and Aug.

Zalogajnica Gagica Antuna Gustava Matoša bb. Cult Zadar snack bar opposite the entrance to the Borik complex, doling out *burek* and cheap grills such as *čevapi* and *pljeskavice*. At night the terrace attracts a lively cross section of Zadar folk and is a good place for a drink.

Nightlife and entertainment

Popular **clubs** include *Forum*, a youth-oriented disco on three floors, right by the basketball stadium on Obala kralja Tomislava; and *Gotham*, 2km northeast of the old town at Marka Oreškovića 1, a futuristically themed complex with a cinema, DJ nights and live gigs (anything from Croatian pop to jazz) on the terrace in summer. The Croatian Playhouse (Hrvatska kazališna kuća; ⓣ023/314-586, ⓦwww.kuz.hr), on the corner of Široka and Dalmatinskog sabora, is the main venue for serious **drama** and **classical music**; the churches of St Donat and St Chrysogonus are also used as chamber music venues from early July to mid-August. Zadar's **Puppet Theatre** (Kazalište lutaka), Sokolska 1 (ⓣ023/311-122), is among the best in the country.

Although Zadar has a first division football team, most locals (like all good Dalmatians) support Hajduk Split in preference to their underachieving home-town side. However the local **basketball** team, Zadar, is one of the major forces in the Croatian game, and a source of local pride. Look out for posters advertising games, usually played on Saturdays from September to April at the Košarkaško igralište, on the eastern fringes of the old town just off Obala kralja Tomislava.

Festivals

The most internationally prestigious of Zadar's summer arts festivals is the **St Donat's Musical Evenings** (Glazbene večeri u sv. Donatu; ⓦwww.donat-festival.com; early July to early August), featuring solo and chamber-music performers from around the world making the most of the excellent acoustics at St Donat's church. Running more or less concurrently is the **Zadar Theatrical Summer** (Zadarsko kazališno ljeto; late June to early Aug), with theatre and dance groups from all over the country – imaginative use of the city's historic spaces (venues include the Church of St Dominic and various courtyards) makes for some striking visual entertainment. More accessible for non-Croatian audiences is **Zadar Dreams** (Zadar snova; July or Aug), a festival of alternative theatre, performance art and music held in old town churches and squares.

Listings

Airlines Croatia Airlines, Natka Nodila 7 ⓣ023/250-101.
Airport 12km southeast of town at Zemunik ⓣ023/313-311, ⓦwww.zadar-airport.hr.
Banks Nova Banka, Trg sv Stošije 3 (Mon–Fri 8am–8pm, Sat 8am–noon).
Car rental Budget, Obala kneza Branimira 1 ⓣ023/313-681; Dollar/Thrifty, Bože Peričića 14 ⓣ023/315-733.
Ferry tickets Jadrolinija, Liburnska obala 7 (ⓣ023/254-800, ⓦwww.jadrolinija.hr); Jadroagent, Natka Nodila bb (ⓣ023/251-447, ⓔjadroagent-zadar@zd.htnet.hr); MiaTours, Vrata sv. Krševana (ⓣ023/254-300, ⓦwww.miatours.hr).
Hospital Just east of the centre, opposite the *Kolovare* hotel, at Bože Peričića 5 ⓣ023/315-677.
Internet access *HG spot*, Stomorica 8 (daily 7am–midnight).
Left luggage At the bus station (Mon–Sat 9am–10pm, Sun 5–10pm) and opposite Jadrolinija office (daily 6.30am–10pm).
Pharmacy Donat, just off Široka at Braće Vranjana 14, and Centar, at Jurja Barakovića 6, both have 24hr counters. For emergencies, call ⓣ023/302-929.
Post office/telephones The main branch is at Kralja S Držislava 1 (Mon–Sat 7am–9pm).
Taxis Try the ranks on Liburnska obala (ⓣ023/251-400); or the rank at Ante Starčevića 2.
Travel agents Atlas, Obala kneza Branimira 12 (ⓣ023/235-850, ⓦwww.atlas-croatia.hr); Croatia Express, Široka 14 (ⓣ023/250-502, ⓦwww.croatiaexpress.hr); Generalturist, Obala kneza Branimira 1 (ⓣ023/318-997, ⓦwww.generalturist.hr); and Oxygenium, Špire Brusine 10/2 (ⓣ023/300-160, ⓦwww.oxygenium.hr), sells plane tickets and organizes local excursions – including trips to the Kornati islands; Zara Adventure, D. Farlattija 7 (ⓣ023/342-368, ⓦwww.zra-adventure.hr), organizes trekking trips in the Paklenica gorge and the northern Velebit mountains.

The Zadar archipelago

The small, often bare islands of northern Dalmatia – sometimes called the **Zadar archipelago** – see much less in the way of mass tourism than those in the south, and their unspoilt, largely rural nature provides them with bags of off-the-beaten-track allure. The northern end of the archipelago is full of semi-abandoned islands boasting beautiful bays and lush inland scenery, although few other than **Silba** possess significant tourist facilities. Unsurprisingly, considering its proximity to Zadar, **Ugljan** is the most urbanized island of the group, although it's still a soothingly laid-back kind of place, as is its neighbour **Pašman**, to which it is connected by road bridge. Hidden away on the far side of Ugljan, little **Iž** provides the perfect venue for a bout of pure relaxation. Farther out, the long and barren island of **Dugi otok** shelters the rest of the archipelago from the open sea, and offers most in the way of stunning scenery, including the beautiful **Telašćica Bay** – the archipelago's most celebrated natural beauty spot.

The northern archipelago: from Zadar to Silba

There are several Jadrolinija-operated catamaran and ferry routes from Zadar into the northern islands of the archipelago. The first route calls in at the barren islets of Rivanj, Sestrunj and Zverinac before arriving at the larger and slightly more touristed islands of **Molat** and **Ist** – the latter, with its main settlement squatting on a beautiful shallow bay, is particularly worthy of a day-trip; it can also be reached by a catamaran service via Molat, Brgulje and Zapuntel. Another catamaran heads via **Olib** for the green island of **Silba**, which has a reasonable amount of private accommodation and is the one place in this part of the Adriatic you're likely to want to stay for a couple of days. You can also get to Silba and Ist via the Zadar–Mali Lošinj car ferry run by Jadrolinija (5 weekly in summer; 3 weekly in winter) or the Lošinjska Plovidba ferry that departs five times weekly from Zadar towards Pula, stopping in Silba and Mali Lošinj.

Silba

Eight kilometres in length and only 1km wide at its narrowest point, **Silba** probably gets its name from the Latin word *silva* (wood) and is still covered with trees (notably *crnika* or Mediterranean black oak), giving it an atmosphere quite different from that of its largely scrub-covered neighbours. The island's one settlement, **SILBA TOWN**, has an air of relaxed luxury, its palm-shaded stone houses and their walled gardens serving as reminders of the island's erstwhile commercial wealth, when sailing ships from Silba dominated the carrying trade between Dalmatia and Venice – only to be put out of business by the steam-powered ships of the nineteenth century. Nowadays a permanent population of about three hundred is swelled tenfold in summer, when weekenders from Zadar and independent travellers from all over Croatia come to enjoy the island's uniquely relaxing rural atmosphere.

Silba Town straddles the island's narrowest point, its narrow car-free streets sloping down towards two bays. The one on the western side of town contains the ferry dock and has some splendid sections of pebble beach – great places from which to observe the sun setting over the open sea. The bay to the east is home to a yachting marina and a broad, shallow beach with a sandy sea floor. Although there's no official naturist beach on the island, Uvala Mavrova, fifty minutes' walk south of the village, is the place to let it all hang out.

Practicalities

Silba's **tourist office**, in the village school, a few steps north of the church (July & Aug Mon–Sat 7am–noon, Sun 8–11am; ⓣ023/370-010, ⓦwww.silba.net), posts a list of private **rooms** (❶) and **apartments** (two-person apartments ❷, four-person apartments from 420Kn) on their website and may help you make contact with the owners if you can't find an English-speaker. The season is short on Silba and many private-room hosts may not be in residence outside the peak July–August period. For **eating**, *Konoba Žalić*, just uphill from the dock, succeeds in being all restaurants to all men, with cheap pizzas, moderate grills and fish of the day – specialities of the house are octopus or lamb baked *ispod peke*. *Konoba Mul*, by the marina, serves up succulent grilled fish on a terrace decorated with fishing nets and other nautical knick-knacks.

Ugljan and Pašman

Just 5km west of Zadar, long, thin **Ugljan** is the most densely populated of all the Adriatic islands, yet remains somewhat rural in feel. Despite the presence of small colonies of package tourists, the bulk of the tourist industry here revolves around independent travellers, and there's plenty of private accommodation, ideal for a spot of relaxation after the urban bustle of Zadar. Much of the island luxuriates under a green covering of olive plantations, which produce some of Croatia's best olive oil (the name Ugljan comes from the Croatian word for oil, *ulje*), although you're unlikely to find it on sale in the local shops – most of the island's farmers produce only a small surplus, and the whole business is surprisingly uncommercialized. Immediately south of Ugljan, and linked to it by a road bridge, the island of **Pašman** is even sleepier than its neighbour, with local activity confined to a few low-key fishing villages strung out at the base of a green central ridge.

Beaches on both islands are modest – most no more than concreted quays with short stretches of shingle – but they have one major advantage over those on the mainland: once you get in the water, the feel of the sea bed beneath your feet is distinctly sandy rather than rocky.

The fifteen daily **ferries** from Zadar to Ugljan drop you at the town of Preko, from where there are buses (usually coordinated to meet incoming ferries) running north to Ugljan village and Muline on the tip of Ugljan island, and south to the resort of Kukljica and to Pašman island.

Preko and Kali

Standing opposite Zadar, **PREKO** (literally "on the other side") is Ugljan's largest village, and feels very much like a dormitory suburb of Zadar – a quiet, unspectacular settlement, comprising a few residential streets and a small harbour. Locals swim at **Jaz**, a wide shallow bay 1km north of the harbour with a sandy sea floor, or the rocky coast of **Galevac** (also known as Školjić, or "little island"; accessible by taxi boat in season from the quayside in Preko), an islet 80m from the shore, where there's also a Franciscan monastery set in its own park. It was once the site of a Croatian-language printing press, moved here from Zadar in 1925 to escape italianization; there's little to see now, although an exhibition of monastic treasures is under construction. The pleasant surrounding subtropical vegetation is like a little piece of Eden gone to seed. Overlooking the town to the west (and looking deceptively close) is the **Fortress of St Michael** (Tvrđava svetog Mihovila), an hour or so's walk along the road that heads uphill from the main island road on the western fringes of Preko. The fortress, which dates from 1203, was already largely ruined by the time the JNA – fearing it might be used as an observation post – shelled it in 1991. The views east to Zadar and west to the long, rippling form of Dugi otok – and, on a clear day, Ancona and the Italian coast – are marvellous.

As you head south, Preko runs gently into **KALI**, spread around a small hillock a kilometre or two down the coast. More immediately picturesque than Preko, Kali is also firmly committed to the local fishing industry, with trawlers crammed into the two harbours either side of its peninsula. There's little to do beyond wandering the pinched, sloping streets, although the sight of Kali's fishing boats setting sail into the evening twilight is an evocative one – something that you won't see in the more touristy islands further south.

Practicalities

The Zadar **ferry** docks midway between Preko and Kali – turn left and walk along the seafront for ten minutes to get to Preko's main harbourside square. At the far end of the square, set back slightly from the waterfront, the **tourist office** (July & Aug daily 8am–2pm & 3–9pm; June & Sept Mon–Sat 8am–1pm & 6–8pm; Oct–May Mon–Fri 8am–2pm; Ⓣ & Ⓕ023/286-108, Ⓔtz-preko@zd.htnet.hr) is friendly, informative and will point you in the direction of **rooms** (❶) and **apartments** (two-person apartments ❷, four-person apartments from 430Kn) in Ugljan. If you want a **hotel**, the somewhat run-down *Preko*, up some steps from the harbour (mid-April to mid-Oct; ⓣ023/286-041, ⓦwww.coning.hr; ④), has simple, sparsely furnished en-suite rooms, some with good sea views.

Konoba Barbara, which you'll pass when walking from the ferry dock to the village centre, is a good place to **eat** fish, and there are numerous harbourside **cafés** from which to admire the twinkling lights of Zadar across the water. **Bikes** and small **boats** can be rented from ad hoc operators on the harbourfront during the season.

Around Ugljan island

Ten kilometres north of Preko, and served by nine daily buses from the ferry dock, **UGLJAN VILLAGE** is smaller and much more rustic, and its broad pebbly bay is an attractive spot for swimming. The **tourist office** (summer only: Mon–Sat 8am–9pm, Sun 8am–noon & 6–9pm; ⓣ023/288-011, ⓦwww.ugljan.hr) is right off the seafront next to the *Ugljan* hotel and gives out heaps of brochures, leaflets and maps of biking and hiking trails around the island. The *Ugljan* (ⓣ023/288-024, ⓔhotel-ugljan@zd.t-com.hr; ③) is a fairly standard concrete box, but has a lovely position on the harbour and offers basic but bright en-suite rooms, some with sea-facing balconies; you can rent bikes and boats here, too. There are also – at the last count – about nine **campsites,** mostly small affairs hidden away in private gardens. The fifteenth-century **Convent of St Hieronymus** at the end of the village by the sandy Mostir beach is worth a look for its serene atmosphere, a Gothic church (currently closed for renovation) and tranquil olive- and pine tree-shaded gardens; ring the bell at the entranceway before noon or after 5pm and one of the nuns will let you in. Also accessible from Preko by bus, the village of **MULINE**, 4km beyond Ugljan at the northern tip of the island, has three more campsites about a kilometre's walk from the bus stop, set side by side amid picturesque woodland, together with an attractive bay with a quiet beach.

Five kilometres south of Preko on the road to Pašman lies **KUKLJICA**, a small fishing hamlet on a wide green bay. In season it's normally full of central European tourists, who block-book the bungalow complex on the pine-covered eastern side of the bay, but even so things rarely get too busy. A well-signed path leads from the southern end of Kukljica's harbour to **Sabušica Bay** on the western edge of the island, where there's a quieter, concreted bathing area with naturist sections on its fringes. The **tourist office** (daily 8am–9pm; ⓣ023/373-276, ⓦwww.kukljica.hr), located at the time of writing just behind the harbourside market, is set to move to the old olive mill on the seafront by *Zelena Punta*; staff give out brochures and can help you find private **rooms** (①) and **apartments** (two-person apartments ①, four-person apartments from 400Kn). Most package tourists stay at the past-its-heyday *Zelena Punta* complex (ⓣ023/373-337, ⓦwww.zelenapunta.com) on the eastern side of the bay, which has cubicle-like **bungalows** with balconies (④ half-board) and swisher kitchen-equipped **apartments** (④) sheltering under pines and surrounded by concrete and stone beach areas. **Eating** in Kukljica is limited to a few restaurants and pizzerias on the harbour, the best of which are *Barba Tome* and *Stari Mlin*.

Kukljica is famous for the festivities marking **Our Lady of the Snows** (Gospa od sniga) on August 5, which celebrate a "miraculous" summer fall of snow here some four hundred years ago. Every year a statue of the Madonna is carried in a procession of small boats from Kukljica to a seaside chapel lurking behind the headland to the south – a regatta in which the entire village takes part. Quite why the August snowfall should have been adopted as a Catholic miracle is unclear, beside its usefulness in providing the excuse for another feast day dedicated to the Virgin.

Pašman

About nine buses a day make the journey from Preko to **PAŠMAN VILLAGE**, 15km south of the Ždrelac strait, the first real settlement on tranquil **Pašman island**. A faded little place, the village has a pleasant shallow bay, Lučina, on its northern side. The **tourist office**, on the dusty road that passes for a seafront (July & Aug 8am–8pm, irregular hours rest of the year; Ⓣ & Ⓕ023/260-155) will give you a wealth of brochures about biking and hiking routes around the island and can also direct you towards private **rooms** (❶) and **apartments** (two-person apartments ❷, four-person apartments from 375Kn). There's a pleasant family-run **pension** right next to the tourist office with five bright en-suite rooms and a generous breakfast buffet (Ⓣ023/260-111; ❸), as well as two **campsites** on Lucina Bay, the *Lučina* and *Kod Jakova*. Just around the corner from the tourist office, *Lanterna* (Ⓣ023/260-179, Ⓕ260-200; ❸) sports swish rooms and apartments, most with sea vistas. On the ground floor is the *Lanterna* **restaurant**, whose terrace is a bit too exposed to southerly winds, so it's best to dine instead in the basement, where food, including all the local fish specialities, is cooked over a stone hearth.

Just beyond the next hamlet, **Ugrinći**, a lane to the right winds up onto Ćokovac Hill, site of the **Monastery of SS Cosmas and Damian** (Kuzma and Damjan; Mon–Sat 4–6pm). Initially a twelfth-century Venetian fortress, it was taken over by Benedictines fleeing Biograd-na-moru in 1125, when that town was razed by the Venetians. In 1346, the monastery itself was destroyed by Venetians but reconstructed in Gothic style a few years later. An important centre of Glagolitic culture until it was closed down by the French in 1808, the monastery was reoccupied in the 1930s and is currently the only permanently occupied Benedictine establishment in Croatia (though Benedictine nunneries, for some reason, are more widespread). The main reasons to visit are to see the late fourteenth-century crucifix above the altar, and to take in the view of modern Biograd-na-moru (see p.325) on the mainland.

The bus terminates in **TKON**, Pašman island's main centre, which is directly connected to Biograd-na-moru by ten ferries daily. Tkon is less developed than Biograd, and is a much better place to stay if you don't like package resorts: the **tourist office** on Tkon's main street (Mon–Sat 8am–1pm & 5–8pm, Sun 8am–noon; Ⓣ023/285-213, Ⓦwww.tkon.hr) will help you find a **room** (❶). For **eating**, the best place in town is *Trta-Mrta*, in a narrow alleyway just behind the tourist office, dishing out tasty fish specialities on a pleasant patio with a giant fish tank. For a place **to swim**, follow the road south out of Tkon to find a string of sandy coves; if you push on for 2km you'll come to the Sovinje naturist camp, which has a splendid sandy beach.

Iž

Engulfed by maquis and untended olive trees, the little island of **Iž** is easily reached from Zadar, although the daily car ferry leaves you stranded at **Bršanj** (a bay rather than a village in its own right) at the south end of the island, and it's preferable to catch one of the two weekly ferries (currently Friday and Sunday) to the settlement of **Veli Iž** 7km further north. Friday's ferry only gives you an hour or so in Veli before heading back to Zadar, while the Sunday service allows you to spend at least a couple of hours on the island. It's a scenic sea voyage, with the boat squeezing through the channel that divides Ugljan from Pašman before working its way round the sheer western side of Ugljan.

A delightfully uneventful agglomeration of ruddy-brown fishermen's houses strung around a deep bay, **VELI IŽ** itself sees a modicum of low-key tourism in July and August, falling back into a deep sleep the rest of the year. There's a small marina popular with the Italian yachting contingent at one end of the bay, and a couple of cafés and restaurants strung along the harbourfront. Private **rooms** (❶) can be booked at the **tourist office** in the Dom Kulture (House of Culture) on the harbour, although it's only sporadically open in July and August. Simple en-suite rooms, along with yoga and meditation programmes and a health-food restaurant, are available at the **Hotel Korinjak** (Ⓣ023/277-064, Ⓦwww.korinjak.hr; ❺ full board; June–Sept only), a standard four-storey concrete block on a small peninsula north of the ferry dock. Activities on Iž boil down to exploring the paths leading up onto the wooded hillsides behind the village, or indulging in a swim – you can splash around in the shallow water in front of the hotel, or walk north past the next bay to find a long stretch of rocks, where the coastline – and the people – get barer the further you go.

Dugi otok

Dugi otok ("Long Island") is the largest and probably the most beautiful of the Zadar archipelago islands, 43km long and at no point more than 4.5km wide. Fewer than 2000 people live here, and parts of the island are very remote – some settlements are accessible only by sea, and fresh water supply can be limited. It boasts a wilder and more dramatic landscape than either Ugljan or Pašman, with sheer cliffs on its western side and a rugged, indented coastline that is justifiably popular with the yachting fraternity. Dugi otok's main attraction is **Telašćica Bay**, which is best approached from the island's main settlement, **Sali**, although the quiet villages and headlands of the northern part of the island are also worth a visit. It's also a possible base from which to visit the Kornati archipelago, with boat captains in Sali offering trips, though the archipelago is more usually approached from Murter (see p.327).

There are a couple of **ferries** daily during summer, as well as several catamarans per week; note that outside summer the schedule is less regular and making this a day-trip might be a challenge. Sali, **Božava** and **Brbinj** are the main entry points, but there are few buses linking one to the other, so you'll need a car if you want to explore the island's single north–south road, with its spectacular views of the rest of the Zadar archipelago to the east. In addition to the regular Zadar–Sali and Zadar–Brbinj services, weekly Ancona–Božava ferries operate in summer.

There are no campsites on the island, but private **rooms** and **apartments** aplenty. If you're driving, note that the island's only petrol station is just north of Sali in Zaglav.

Northern Dugi otok

Despite **BRBINJ**'s importance as a ferry port there's nothing much here apart from a tiny seasonal **tourist office** (Mon–Sat 8am–1pm & 4–9pm). Hop straight onto one of the buses which head north to **BOŽAVA**, a small fishing village of 150 inhabitants, with an attractive harbour and a path leading east round the headland to a rocky coast overlooked by swooning trees. The **tourist office** (July & Aug daily 8am–9pm, in theory; Ⓣ023/377-607, Ⓦwww.dugi-otok.hr), at the northern end of the harbour, can help you locate private **rooms** (❶) and **apartments** (two-person apartments ❷, four-person apartments from 400Kn), while the *Božava* **hotel** complex (late April to end Oct; Ⓣ023/291-291, Ⓦhttp://bozava.zadar.net), set among fragrant pines west of the harbour and with its own rocky beach, sports three sections: the tastefully refurbished three-star *Agava* (❻) offers apartments with balconies, air conditioning and TV; the three-star *Lavanda* (❺) has pleasant en-suite rooms with the best sea views and an outside swimming pool; while the four-star *Maximi* (❻) has thicker carpets, flat-screen TVs and swish modern bathrooms. There isn't much choice when it comes to **eating**; the best of the three restaurants on the seafront is *Oleandar*, which serves unspectacular but decent seafood.

Driving northwest out of Božava on the road to the village of Soline, you get a good view of the north of the island as it finishes in a flourish of bays and peninsulas. To get to one of the island's best beaches, follow the road up the westernmost of these peninsulas, **Veli rat**, then take a left turn onto an unmarked gravel track about 3km out of Božava and proceed about 1km through fragrant forest (drivers will have to park about halfway down). At the end of the path you'll come to **Sakarun**, a 500-metre-long bar of pebbles (and sadly some garbage, washed onshore by the numerous sail boats), which commands a shallow bay. As you carry on up Veli rat, the road terminates beside a stumpy, ochre lighthouse, built in 1849 by the Austrians, who painted it with egg whites. It is now a popular spot for bathing, with an attractively rocky coastline stretching away on both sides.

Southern Dugi otok

The island's largest village and the centre of a prosperous fishing industry, **SALI** is a quiet place, though the smattering of cafés round the harbour provide the requisite air of Mediterranean vivacity on warm summer nights. The **tourist office**, on the western side of the harbour (July & Aug daily 8am–9pm; Sept–May Mon–Fri 8am–3pm; Ⓣ & Ⓕ023/377-094), is well supplied with local info, while the Kartolina agency on the opposite side of the harbour (Ⓣ023/377-191, Ⓔkartolina@email.t-com.hr) books **rooms** (❶) and **apartments** (two-person apartments ❷, four-person apartments from 420Kn). There's also a **hotel**, the *Sali* (Ⓣ023/377-049, Ⓦwww.hotel-sali.hr; ❹), over the hill from the harbour in the next bay to the north, Saščica. It boasts a magnificent position right above an azure pine tree-shaded bay and four pavilions offering pleasant en-suite rooms with balconies, air conditioning and TV, as well as a diving centre and bike rental (100Kn per day). Five kilometres northwest of Sali, the lovely bay-hugging hamlet of Zaglav is home to *Pansion Roko*, Zaglav 28 (Ⓣ023/377-182 & 098 627 133, Ⓦwww.pansion-roko.hr; ❷), offering small but neat en-suite rooms with lam floors, TV and teeny balconies. It's well worth paying the extra 100Kn or so for half board: the fresh fish and shellfish in the downstairs **restaurant** are among the best on the island.

The best time to be in Sali is the first weekend in August, when the Saljske užance **festival** takes place, with outdoor concerts, drinking and feasting, and performances of *tovareća muzika* ("donkey music" – so called because it's a tuneless racket that sounds like braying), which features the locals raucously blowing horns.

Telašćica

It's about 3km from Sali to the northern edge of **Telašćica Bay**, a seven-kilometre channel overlooked by smooth hills interspersed with numerous smaller bays which run down to the tangle of islands at the northern end of the Kornati archipelago. The flora along the shoreline marks the transition from the green vegetation of the Zadar archipelago to the bare wilderness of the Kornati – banks of deep forest slope down towards the western shore of the bay, where maquis-covered offshore islands rise like grey-brown cones from the water – and the whole place has been designated a **nature park** (Ⓦ www.telascica.hr).

Telašćica can't quite compete with the Kornati in terms of stark beauty, but it's much more accessible. To get there, take the signposted minor road (you pay the 30Kn entrance fee here) which heads west from the Sali–Božava route about 1500m out of town. The road terminates at one of Telašćica's numerous small bays, from where a path leads south to the appropriately named **Uvala mira** ("Bay of Peace") about 4km beyond and a short distance from the park's main attractions. There's a bar and **restaurant** here, and a path that leads, after five minutes' walk up a wooded hillside, to a stretch of ruddy clifftop looking out towards the open sea. Five minutes south of the restaurant lies **Jezero mira**, a saltwater lake cut off from the sea by a narrow barrier of rock at the lake's southernmost end. The rock is a favourite with naturists, while the lake itself, a few degrees warmer than the sea and apparently possessing therapeutic qualities, is popular swimming territory. Note that it's full of shrimp, which nibble your legs if you stand still long enough – not as unpleasant an experience as it sounds.

There's a smattering of private **accommodation** options in the nature park itself, as well Robinson Crusoe-style huts in some of the secluded bays around the island, mostly with no water or electricity. Val Tours agency in Biograd-na-Moru (see below) books such stays, and you can also enquire at the tourist office in Sali.

Zadar to Šibenik

About 20km southeast of Zadar, **BIOGRAD-NA-MORU** was one of the towns developed by Croatia's medieval kings to challenge the pre-eminence of Zadar and Split. Petar Krešimir IV moved the archiepiscopate of Split here in the mid-eleventh century, and it was in Biograd that the Hungarian kings were crowned monarchs of Croatia after 1102. Biograd's period of greatness came to an end on Good Friday 1125, when the Venetians razed the town to its foundations, a catastrophe from which it never really recovered.

Modern Biograd is one of the major package resorts on this part of the coast, with uninspiring beaches that tend to get crowded in season. There's little of an old town left, and save for the interesting archeological collection at the two-floor **town museum** on the seafront (mid-May to Oct Mon–Sat 9am–noon & 7–9pm; Nov to mid-May Mon–Fri 8am–2pm; 10Kn), which includes cargo from a sixteenth-century sunken merchant ship and some medieval sculptures, there's not much to keep you here more than a day or two. It's mainly of interest as a base for visiting Lake Vrana (see p.326) or the Kornati islands (p.327), and for its ferry connections with Tkon on the island of Pašman (see p.322).

Biograd practicalities

The **tourist office** is hidden in a courtyard just off Trg hrvatskih velikana 2 (summer Mon–Sat 8am–9pm, Sun 8am–2pm; rest of the year Mon–Fri 8am–4pm; Ⓣ 023/383-123, Ⓦ www.tzg-biograd.hr), where buses pull in. From here it's a short walk to Val Tours (daily 8am–8pm; Ⓣ 023/386-479,

ⓦwww.val-tours.hr) at Trg hrvatskih velikana bb, which can sort you out with **rooms** (❶) or bed-and-breakfast arrangements (❷). The Ilirija agency on the seafront (daily 8am–8pm; ⓣ023/383-121, ⓦwww.turistbiro.com) is another good source of rooms (❶) and **apartments** (two-person apartments ❸, four-person apartments from 450Kn). The *Ilirija* (ⓣ023/383-165, ⓦwww.ilirijabiograd.com; ❺; closed mid-Oct to Easter), right on the seafront, is the most central **hotel**, with its own stretch of beach and three annexes; *Ilirija* is the best, offering newly refurbished en-suite rooms with air conditioning and TV. Another good option, 1km out of town on Ivana Meštrovića 1, is *Bolero* (ⓣ023/386-888, ⓦwww.hotel-bolero.hr; ❺), with spacious balconied en-suite rooms.

The *Aquarium* **restaurant** on the Riva is a good place for a slap-up seafood feast, while *Konoba Vapor* next door to the museum offers grilled fish and schnitzels in a stone-clad, fisherman's-cottage-type setting; there are also numerous cheaper grill houses and pizzerias in the streets behind the seafront. *In Vino Veritas* (5–11pm), in an alleyway beside the parish church, is a wonderfully atmospheric place dishing out *pršut*, *srdele* and local wine to an appreciative cross-section of tourists and locals. **Nightlife** revolves around the many café and cocktail-bars along the Riva; the best is the loungey *Lavender Bed Bar* next to *Ilirija* hotel, which has comfy sofas on a pine tree-shaded terrace facing the beach and hosts frequent DJ nights. *CarpyMore Dalmatian Pub*, in an alleyway between the seafront and the bus station, has a huge ground-floor bar area with plenty of cosy corners packed with domestic knick-knacks, and an upstairs room with pool tables.

Most of the travel agencies on Biograd's Riva offer **boat trips to the Kornati islands**, although it's worth noting that many of these "Kornati" trips actually aim for Telašćica Bay on Dugi otok (see p.324) – a beautiful and worthwhile destination in its own right, but not, strictly speaking, part of the Kornati archipelago. Ask to be shown on a map precisely where the trip is going in order to avoid disappointment. Val Tours runs regular trips to the (real) Kornati from 250Kn per person and books rustic accommodation on Ugljan and Pašman.

Pakoštane and Lake Vrana

Five kilometres south of Biograd and a short hop by local bus, **PAKOŠTANE** is an inoffensive little resort with a few stretches of pebbly beach next to its small harbour. There's a well-appointed *Club Mediterranée* resort on the northern outskirts, but little else to get excited about save for the presence of **Lake Vrana** (Vransko Jezero), the largest natural lake in Croatia, just 1km inland. This thirteen-kilometre-long, reed-shrouded stretch of water is especially popular with wading birds such as herons and ibises, alongside bullfinches, terns and (in winter) large numbers of ducks and coots. Now a nature reserve (Park prirode Vransko Jezero; ⓦwww.vransko-jezero.hr), the lake and its shores still support human activities such as farming, tourism and fishing, except for one area near the northwestern corner of the lake specifically designated as a strict ornithological reserve, owing to the presence of a colony of purple herons.

The most accessible parts of the lake are on the northwestern shore, on either side of the strict reserve: here numerous farm tracks branch off the road from Pakoštane, passing through dense reed beds towards the shore. The village of **Vrana**, straggling along the northern shoulder of the lake about 3km out from Pakoštane, was occupied by the Serbs in 1991–95 and still presents a disconcerting picture of ruin and reconstruction. In the sixteenth century it was one of the westernmost outposts of Ottoman power in the Adriatic, evidence of which exists in the shape of a derelict **caravanserai**, built in 1644 by order of local-born Jusuf Mošković, and reputedly the largest in Europe at the time.

Practicalities

There are only a couple of daily **buses** (one on Sunday) from Biograd to the northwestern end of the lake and Vrana village, although you could just as easily hike there in twenty minutes from Pakoštane, which is served by much more frequent buses from Biograd and Zadar. **Cycling** is also an option: a map of biking routes round the lake is available from the **tourist office** (summer daily 8am–8pm; ⓣ023/381-892, ⓦwww.pakostane.hr), inside the town hall building at the main entrance to town, and bikes can be rented for about 80Kn per day from the Ilirija agency in Biograd (see opposite) or from Cat, next to the bus stop in Pakoštane (ⓣ023/381-401, ⓔcat-centar-tours@zd.t-com.hr). Both Cat and Dalmaturist, on Trg Kraljice Jelene beside the church (ⓣ023/381-990, ⓔdalma-turist-pakostane@zd.t-com.hr), can sort out **private rooms** (❶) and **apartments** (two-person apartments ❸, four-person apartments from 450Kn) in Pakoštane. There are also two **campsites**, the *Crkvine* (ⓣ023/381-433), on the northern shore of the lake, complete with café-restaurant and a small stretch of beach, and *Kozarica* (ⓣ023/381-070), next to *Club Med*.

Murter and the Kornati archipelago

Around 25km south of Biograd, a side road heads west towards the small island of **Murter**, linked to the mainland by bridge. The main settlement, **MURTER TOWN**, at the northern end of the island, is a frumpy little place that soon gets choked by visitors and their cars in July and August – largely as a result of the town's status as the main gateway to the Kornati archipelago. Day-trips to the latter are organized by most of Murter's travel agencies, but once you've been on one of these there's little in town to justify a longer stay. Murter's waterfront is not exactly designed for leisurely strolling: most of it is just a grubby car park. There's a hideous concrete **beach** at the western end of town, and an infinitely more attractive pebble affair at **Slanica Bay**, fifteen minutes' walk farther west – there's rarely enough room to swing a bikini here on summer weekends, but it's an enchanting place from which to watch the sun set over the Kornati once the crowds have thinned.

Murter practicalities

There are nine **buses** a day from Šibenik to Murter (only seven on weekends), passing through **Vodice** (the place to change if you're approaching from the north) en route before pulling into Murter's main square, Trg Rudina. There's a small **tourist office** on the square (mid-May to June daily 8am–2pm & 6–9pm; July & Aug daily 8am–10pm; Sept to mid-May Mon–Fri 8am–3pm; ⓣ022/434-995 or 434-950, ⓦwww.tzo-murter.hr), which doles out free town plans, sells a National-Park-approved map of the Kornati, and advises on which agents are offering the best trips to the islands. The official **Kornati National Park office** is just off the square at Butina 2, second floor (Mon–Fri 8am–3pm; ⓣ022/435-740, ⓦwww.kornati.hr); they give out park information, and sell maps and diving and fishing permits.

Rooms (❶) and **apartments** (two-person apartments ❸, four-person apartments 450–550Kn) are available from the Coronata bureau on Trg Rudina

(June & Sept daily 8am–10pm; July & Aug 7.30am–11pm; ⓣ022/435-933, ⓦwww.coronata.hr) and KornatTurist on the same square (ⓣ022/435-855, ⓦwww.kornatturist.hr). Marina Hramina, ten minutes' walk to the east, has a small **hotel**, the *Stomorin* (ⓣ022/434-411, ⓦwww.marina-hramina.hr; ❺), where the simple, cosy en-suite rooms with air conditioning overlook the yachts; alternatively, the four-storey, box-like *Colentum* offers comfortable, smart rooms, most of them with balconies facing the beach at Slanica (ⓣ022/431-111, ⓦwww.hotel-colentum.hr; ❻; mid-April to mid-Oct). There's a small **campsite** at Slanica and a string of larger ones south of town: the *Plitka Vala* (3km away; ⓣ022/435-268, ⓦwww.btp.hr), *Kosirina* (4km away on a lovely rocky bay; same contact numbers as the Plitka Vala) and *Jezera* (5km away; ⓣ022/439-600, ⓦwww.jezera-kornati.hr) – Šibenik–Murter buses pick up and drop off at each of them.

There are a few **places to eat** in the town centre. The stylish *Zameo ih vjetar* at Hrvatskih vladara 5 offers good pizza and pasta dishes, as well as some interesting salads, soups and appetizers in a minimalist Japanese-inspired interior and on the pleasant terrace in the back. *Tic Tac* on Hrokešina 5, a narrow alleyway leading to the harbour, is an established place dishing up good-quality seafood and grilled meat staples; it's popular with both locals and tourists, so you'll need to reserve on ⓣ022/435-230. *Mate*, on the corner of Luke and Kornatska, offers excellent, moderately priced seafood pasta and risotto dishes, alongside expertly grilled (and more expensive) fresh white fish. *Čigrađa*, 3km southwest of town, enjoys a magnificent pine-shaded beach setting – perfect for watching the sun set – and serves the usual array of (rather pricey) seafood specialities. Back in town, *Slastičarna Zelena*, Trg Rudina, is the place to pick up doughnuts and pastries at breakfast time, as well as cakes and ice cream throughout the day.

Both Trg Rudina and Matije Gupca, an alleyway immediately east of it, have their fair share of café-bars, although the best place for late-night **drinking** is *Lantana*, a beach bar a few metres away from the *Čigrađa* restaurant; they put on frequent gigs and DJ nights. Eseker, just east of Trg Rudina on the marina side of town (ⓦwww.esekertours.hr), is the place to rent small **boats** (from 230Kn/day), **scooters** (230Kn/day upwards) and **bikes** (60Kn/day).

The Kornati archipelago

Scattered like pebbles to the south of Dugi otok lie the ninety or so islands of the **Kornati archipelago**, grouped around the 35-kilometre-long island of Kornat. A national park since 1980, the Kornati archipelago comprises a distinctively harsh and bare environment, almost devoid of life. The islands range in colour from stony white to pale ochre or green, sometimes mottled with patches of low shrub and hardy sage. They were once covered in forest until it was burned down to make pasture for sheep, who proceeded to eat everything in sight. The dry-stone walls used to pen them in are still visible, although the sheep themselves – save for a few wild descendants – are no more.

The islands were originally owned by the nobles of Zadar, who allowed the peasants of Murter to raise flocks and grow olives on the islands in return for a share in the cheese and oil thus produced. When the Zadar nobility fell on hard times in the nineteenth century, the islands were sold to the Murterians – and their descendants (the Kurnatari) remain the owners of most of the land on the Kornati to this day. Despite the number of stone cottages scattered over the islands (**Vruje**, on Kornat, is the biggest single settlement with fifty houses), most Kurnatari actually live in Murter nowadays – returning to the islands for a few months in the summer, when they come to relax, fish, or take advantage of the growing opportunities offered by tourism. The popularity of the Kornati with the international yachting fraternity is having a profound impact on the archipelago's development, with shoreline restaurants serving top-quality seafood springing up in every available cove. There's a fully equipped yachting marina on the island of Piškera, on the western side of the archipelago, and an even bigger one on the island of Žut, which lies just outside the park boundaries to the east.

Unless you have access to a boat, the easiest way of seeing the Kornati is to go on one of the **day-trips** arranged by one of the travel agents in Murter; Atlas, Coronata and KornatTurist are among the most reliable. Travel agencies in Biograd-na-moru (see p.326), Sali (p.324) and Zadar (p.318) also offer similar trips. Wherever you start, excursions are likely to set off around 8 or 9am and return at 5 or 6pm, weaving in and out of the islands on the western side of the archipelago, stopping a couple of times so that you can stretch your legs, swim and consume some of the local food and drink. Prices start at around 200Kn per person if you're travelling from Murter, 250Kn if you're approaching from Biograd, Sali or Zadar, and include the national park entrance fee, and probably lunch with wine too. If you're approaching the islands independently, look out for the rubber dinghies operated by national park wardens, which cruise the area selling entrance tickets (50Kn). If you need more information, the **Kornati** National Park **office** is just off Murter's main square (see p.327).

Staying in one of the island's **stone cottages** is popular with visitors who want a period of complete peace and quiet, local agencies call it "Robinson turizam" in order to lend it the requisite desert-island-like appeal. You'll have to arrange accommodation through KornatTurist in Murter (see opposite) well in advance, however, and commit yourself to a reasonably lengthy stay because of the logistics involved (stays of seven days or more are preferred). Prices are around 3500–3900Kn per week for a two-person apartment, or 5000–5700Kn per week for a four-person apartment, including return boat transfer. Once you're there provisions will be delivered to you by boat twice a week; if you've chosen one of the islands with a marina or restaurant you'll also be able to eat out. Small boats can be rented through the agencies for about 700Kn per week. Some of the growing number of UK-based travel agencies offering stays in Kornati cottages are listed on pp.34–35.

Vodice

The rapidly expanding town of **VODICE**, 9km south of the Murter turn-off, is, unaccountably, central Dalmatia's most successful package-holiday destination, and also one of its least atmospheric – there's not much of an old town and most of the beaches are concrete. It has good bus connections with Murter and a convenient ferry link with the alluring islands of Zlarin and Prvić, but is otherwise an unwieldy behemoth of a resort which may not prove to be the characterful Dalmatian getaway you were looking for.

Practicalities

Most coastal buses call in at Vodice's **bus station**, at the eastern end of the waterfront; the **tourist office** is on the seafront at Obala Vladimira Nazora 2 (summer Mon–Sat 8am–10pm, Sun 9am–7pm; spring & autumn Mon–Sat 8am–8pm; winter Mon–Sat 8am–4pm; ⓣ022/443-888, ⓦwww.vodice.hr). Private **rooms** (❶) and **apartments** (two-person apartments ❸, four-person apartments 460–560Kn) can be booked through Nik, Ante Poljička 2 (ⓣ & ⓕ022/441-730,

Ⓦwww.nik.hr). If you want **hotel** comforts and are prepared to pay for them, the high-rise three-star *Punta* (Ⓣ022/451-451, Ⓦwww.hotelivodice.hr; ❻) is a good choice, offering smart en-suite rooms on a pine-covered peninsula, as well as cheaper, more basic rooms in its three annexes (❺); the recently renovated *Olympia* (❻) on the other side of the bay at Ljudevita Gaja 2 has similar balconied en suites. For **eating**, you'll find innumerable cafés and pizzerias along the harbour, together with several restaurants offering German-language menus and slightly higher than average prices. Of the seafront restaurants, *Arausa* does the best seafood, especially seashell dishes; *Adria* has the biggest menu of mainstays; *Porat* is the best choice for grilled meat and fish; while *Gušter*, in a narrow alleyway leading off from the Riva, has the most ambience. The most unusual restaurant in town is *Santa Marija*, a little up from the seafront on Pamuković Kamila, serving up a mix of tasty Cro-Mex food in a colourful interior and on the fig tree-shaded patio across the street. The open-air *Hacienda* **club** (summer only), on the main road to Šibenik, attracts clubbers from all over the coast for its star DJ guests and themed nights.

Šibenik and around

ŠIBENIK is one of the few towns on the Adriatic not to have a Greco-Roman heritage. Originally founded around an eleventh-century Croat fortress, it fell firmly under the control of the Venetians in the fifteenth century, becoming an important strongpoint in their struggles against the Ottomans. As the main town of middle Dalmatia, Šibenik was a thriving industrial port until the 1990s, when war and recession conspired to close down the aluminium and chrome factories, and the city entered the new century as one of Dalmatia's most economically depressed areas. It's not a resort, and there's little point in stopping if you're looking for somewhere quiet with a beach, though the maze-like medieval centre is good for idle wandering and the cathedral is one of the finest architectural monuments on the coast. As a transport hub, Šibenik isn't as important as Zadar or Split, but there are ferries to a handful of offshore islands, and buses inland to the waterfalls of the **Krka National Park** and the medieval castle at **Knin**.

Arrival, information and transport

Šibenik's **bus station** is just southeast of the city centre on Obala Hrvatske mornarice, with a left luggage office in the ticket hall (daily 7am–10pm). The **train station**, for what it's worth (trains run from here only to the inland town of Knin, where there are infrequent connections to Split or Zagreb), is ten minutes' walk further south. The **tourist office**, on the seafront at Obala Franje Tuđmana 5 (May to mid-Sept daily 8am–8pm; late Sept to April Mon–Fri 8am–2pm; Ⓣ022/214-411, Ⓕ214-266; Ⓦwww.sibenik-tourism.hr), is a relatively helpful source of information on the whole Šibenik area, and gives out brochures and a free city map.

Travel agents offering **excursions** from Šibenik include Atlas, Trg Republike Hrvatske 2 (Ⓣ022/330-232, Ⓦwww.atlassibenik.com); Ivante, Prvićka 12 (Ⓣ022/200-433, Ⓦwww.ivante.hr); and Mag Tours, next door at Obala Franje Tuđmana 2a (Ⓣ022/201-150, Ⓦwww.magtours.com); all of which organize day-trips to the Kornati islands (250Kn–300Kn) and the Krka National Park (220Kn). Slaptours, near the train station at Fra Jerolima Milete 7 (Ⓣ022/311-460, Ⓦwww.slaptours.hr), specializes in rafting trips on the

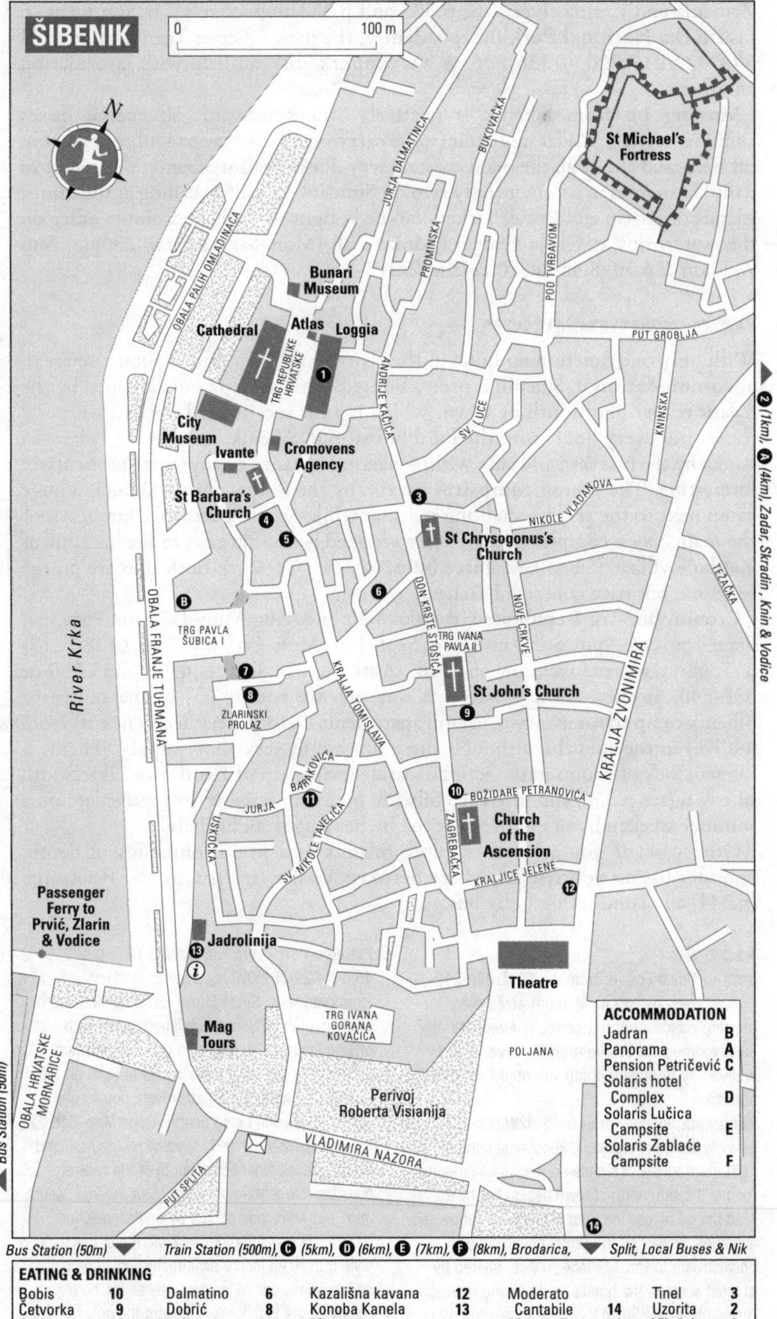

EATING & DRINKING

Bobis	10	Dalmatino	6	Kazališna kavana	12	Moderato Cantabile	14	Tinel	3
Četvorka	9	Dobrić	8	Konoba Kanela	13	Pizzeria Toni	7	Uzorita	2
Cohiba	4	Indigo	11	Maestro	5			Vijećnica	1

Zrmanja and Cetina rivers (see p.303 and p.381 respectively). If you want to visit **Krka National Park** independently, the park office at Trg Ivana Pavla II 5 (Ⓣ022/217-720, Ⓕ336-836, Ⓦwww.npkrka.hr) can help with information and maps.

Moving on from Šibenik is relatively straightforward: all coastal **buses** running between Zadar and Split (some carry on all the way to Dubrovnik) stop off here, and although the main coastal **ferry** doesn't call at Šibenik, there are five daily departures in summer (only two on Sunday) to Vodice, calling at the minor islands of Zlarin and Prvić. Tickets can be bought from the Jadrolinija office on the waterfront at Obala Franje Tuđmana bb (Mon–Sat 4.45am–8.30pm, Sun 7–11am & 6.30–8.45pm; Ⓣ & Ⓕ022/213-468).

Accommodation

With only one functioning hotel in the centre, and a handful in suburban areas, **accommodation** in Šibenik is pretty limited. Things aren't much helped by the *Solaris* **resort** 6km south of town, which is a bit too isolated for its own good (buses run every hour from the local bus stop in Šibenik, next to the Jadranska banka by the market), and isn't within walking distance of anywhere particularly interesting. The nearest **campsites** are run by the resort: *Solaris-Lučica* is a huge camp next to the resort's yachting marina; while *Solaris-Zablaće* is 2km north of the main *Solaris* complex, situated in a wooded peninsula next to the harbour of **Zablaće** village (Šibenik–Zablaće buses run every 1–2hr). Both sites are on the seashore, but have concrete beaches.

Cromovens, Trg Republike Hrvatske 4 (July & Aug Mon–Fri 9am–9pm, Sat 9am–1pm & 6–9pm, Sun 9am–1pm; Sept–June Mon–Fri 9am–2pm; Ⓣ022/212-515, Ⓦwww.cromovens.hr) and Nik, Ante Šupuka 5 (Ⓣ & Ⓕ022/338-550 or 338-540, Ⓦwww.nik.hr), will sort out **private rooms** (❶) in the centre of Šibenik or **apartments** (two-person apartments ❸, four-person apartments from 440Kn) in the suburbs, although these too are in very short supply. There's a bigger stock of rooms in the scruffy seaside settlement of **Brodarica**, 7km south of town (see p.336) and linked to Šibenik by urban bus – if you arrive late on a summer weekend you might save time by heading straight there.

Otherwise, if you want to explore Šibenik and its surroundings in depth, consider basing yourself anywhere between Vodice (see p.329) and Primošten (p.341) and commuting in by bus.

Hotels

Jadran Obala Franje Tuđmana 52 Ⓣ022/212-644, Ⓦwww.rivijera.hr. Medium-sized place offering nondescript but perfectly adequate en-suite rooms with TV. Right on the Riva, a 5min walk away from everything you might want to see. ❺

Panorama Šibenski most bb Ⓣ022/213-397, Ⓦwww.hotel-panorama.hr. Functional cube of 1970s vintage, with simple no-nonsense en-suite rooms. It's 4km north of town beside the main road bridge across the Krka estuary – a renowned local beauty spot offering truly magical views downstream towards Šibenik, a vista shared by at least some of the hotel's south-facing rooms. Buses plying the Šibenik–Vodice route stop off in the adjacent car park. ❺

Pension Petričević Podsolarsko 78 Ⓣ022/350-494, Ⓕ022/351-071, Ⓦwww.infoadriatic.com/petricevic. Small family-run B&B 5km south of town, offering simply furnished rooms with private facilities, as well as a good ground-floor pizzeria. It's just off the main road to Split, on the approach road to the *Solaris* resort; you'll need a car as buses don't stop nearby. Open May–Oct. ❷

Solaris Ⓣ022/361-007, Ⓦwww.solaris.hr. Bland holiday development 6km south of the centre, boasting five three-star hotels (*Ivan*, *Andrija*, *Jakov*, *Jure* and *Niko*), and girdled by undistinguished beaches consisting of either concrete or car-park-style gravel. An indoor swimming-pool complex and wellness centre is shared by all the hotels. Hourly buses to Šibenik represent the only form of escape. ❻

The City

Clinging to the side of a hill, Šibenik's ancient centre is a steep tangle of alleys, steps and arches bisected by two main arteries, **Zagrebačka** and **Kralja Tomislava** (the latter popularly known as Kalelarga), which run between Trg Republike Hrvatske, the core of the city, and the modern square known as Poljana maršala Tita. Entering the old town along Zagrebačka from Poljana, it's not long before you emerge into the first of Šibenik's tiny medieval squares, Božidara Petranovića, overlooked by the **Church of the Ascension** (Crkva Uspenja Bogomatere). The main feature of this Baroque building is the belfry built onto the facade, a curious but elegant structure resembling a pair of bay windows. The church is now the seat of a Serbian Orthodox bishop, whose see extends inland to cover the traditionally Serb-inhabited area around Knin. A few steps further on lies **St John's Church** (Crkva svetog Ivana), with a balustraded outside staircase said to be the work of sculptor Nikola Firentinac (who also worked on the cathedral) linking the ground floor to a gallery. The church's four-storey bell tower holds Šibenik's first mechanical clock, a contraption dating from 1648. Beyond here, Zagrebačka becomes Don Krste Stošića, a stepped street which leads up to the small, plain **St Chrysogonus's Church** (Crkva svetog Krševana), now home to seasonal art exhibitions.

Heading down one of the alleys leading off to the left brings you out onto Kralja Tomislava, where a sharp right delivers you to **St Barbara's Church** (Crkva svete Barbare), site of a modest **Collection of Church Art** (Zbirka crkvene umjetnosti; summer Mon–Fri 9.30am–noon & 5.30–8pm, Sat 9.30am–1pm; 5Kn). Its star exhibit is a small fifteenth-century polyptych of the Madonna and Child flanked by saints, painted by Blaž Jurjev of Trogir, the leading Dalmatian artist of his day, who is credited with introducing Italian Renaissance styles to the eastern Adriatic. Down an alley beside the church, the fifteenth-century **Rector's Palace** (Kneževa palača) is nowadays home to the **City Museum** (Muzej grada Šibenika; summer daily 10am–1pm & 7–10pm; rest of the year Mon–Fri 10am–1pm; free), which hosts prestigious seasonal exhibitions.

The cathedral and around

Immediately to the north of the City Museum lies Trg Republike Hrvatske and the Gothic Renaissance **St James's Cathedral** (Katedrala svetog Jakova; daily 9am–7.30pm), the product of a long-running saga that stirred the imaginations and emptied the pockets of the townspeople here during the fifteenth century. Plans for a new cathedral were originally drawn up in 1402, but war, lack of funds and disputes over the site delayed the start of work until 1431, when a group of Italian architects oversaw the erection of the Gothic lower storey of the present building. In 1441, dissatisfaction with the old-fashioned Gothic design led to the appointment of a new architect, **Juraj Dalmatinac** (see box overleaf), who presided over three decades of intermittent progress, interrupted by perennial cash shortages, two plagues and one catastrophic fire. The cathedral was just below roof height when he died in 1473 and his Italian apprentice **Nikola Firentinac** ("Nicholas of Florence" – he is thought to have been a pupil of Donatello) took over, completing the roof and the octagonal cupola, although both may have been designed by Dalmatinac. The resulting edifice is an intriguing mixture, with Venetian Gothic portals and windows at ground level and a Florentine Renaissance dome at the top.

Entry to the cathedral is by the north door, framed by arches braided with the leaves, fruit and swirling arabesques which led to Dalmatinac's style being dubbed "floral Gothic". Two lions roar companionably at each other, supporting remorseful and rather crudely carved figures of Adam and Eve. Inside, the church is a harmonious blend of Gothic and Renaissance forms; the sheer space and light of the east end draw the eye towards the soft grey Dalmatian stone of the raised sanctuary. Follow the stairs down from the southern apse to the **Baptistry**, Dalmatinac's masterpiece. It's an astonishing piece of work, a cubbyhole of Gothic carving, with four scallop-shell niches rising from each side to form a vaulted roof, beneath which cherubim scamper playfully.

Back outside the cathedral, around the exterior of the three apses, Dalmatinac carved a unique **frieze** of 71 stone heads, apparently portraits of those who refused to contribute to the cost of the cathedral and a vivid cross section of sixteenth-century society. On the north apse, beneath two angels with a scroll, he inscribed his claim to the work with the words *hoc opus cuvarum fecit magister Georgius Mathei Dalmaticus* – "these apses have been made by Juraj Dalmatinac, son of Mate." Given the narrowness of Šibenik's central streets, it's difficult to get a reasonable view of the cathedral's barrel roof, made from a line of enormous stone slabs and considered a marvel of construction at the time, though you should be able to catch sight of the statue high up on the southeast corner – a boyish, curly-haired Archangel Michael jauntily spearing a demon.

Trg Republike Hrvatske itself is lined with historic buildings including, directly opposite the cathedral, the town hall with its sixteenth-century **loggia**, much restored after World War II bombing, part of which now houses a café. On the north side of the square is the small **Bunari Museum** (summer months daily 10am–11pm; 30Kn) inside a restored vault with a couple of fifteenth-century wells. Here Šibenik's history is portrayed through interactive multimedia (and multilingual) displays primarily geared towards children; there's also a pleasant museum café downstairs where you can browse magazines. Climb the alleyways

Juraj Dalmatinac

Juraj Dalmatinac (George the Dalmatian; c.1400–73) was the most prolific stonemason of the Dalmatian Renaissance, but little is known of the man save for the works he left behind. Born in Zadar some time around 1400, he learnt his trade in Venice, setting up a workshop there which made his reputation as a mason. The Šibenik town authorities engaged him to supervise completion of the cathedral in 1441, paying him 150 golden ducats a year as well as covering his family's moving expenses and providing free housing.

Work on the cathedral frequently stalled owing to lack of cash, and Dalmatinac filled in his time by working on commissions elsewhere, notably in Split, where he sculpted the **sarcophagus of St Anastasius** in the cathedral (see p.362), and at Ancona, where he completed the facade of the cathedral. In 1464 he replaced Michelozzo Michelozzi as the overseer of fortification work in Dubrovnik, where he finished the finest of the system's many bastions, the **Minčeta Fortress** (p.450). Following working visits to Urbino and possibly Siena, he returned to Šibenik, where he died in 1473, the cathedral still unfinished.

Dalmatinac's great skill was to blend the intricate stoneworking techniques of the Gothic period with the realism and humanism of Renaissance sculpture. His stylistic innovations were carried over to the next generation by his pupils **Andrija Aleši** and **Nikola Firentinac**, who were involved in the completion of Šibenik cathedral before going on to produce their own masterpieces in Trogir. A bronze statue of Dalmatinac by the famous Croatian sculptor Ivan Meštrović now stands at the entrance to St James's Cathedral, opposite the main portal.

leading up to the northeast from the square and you'll eventually emerge at **St Michael's Fortress** (Kaštel svetog Mihovila) on the top of the hill. The nearest and most accessible of the system of fortifications constructed by the Venetians to keep Šibenik safe from the Ottomans, the fortress was built on the ruins of the earlier Croatian citadel. Nowadays there's not much inside except for rubble, although the ramparts afford a panorama of the old town (including a clear view of the cathedral's roof), Šibenik bay beyond, and the endless green ripple of offshore islands in the background. From the fortress, what remains of Šibenik's **city walls** plunge downhill to meet the sea, forming the old town's northern boundary.

Eating and drinking

There's a growing number of reasonable **restaurants** in and around the tourist-trodden old town, although most local foodies head for out-of-town establishments such as *Zlatna Ribica* in Brodarica (see overleaf). Plentiful pastries, cakes and ice cream can be picked up from *Bobis*, on the corner of Zagrebačka and Petranovićeva, or *Maestro* on Kralja Tomislava. If you want to buy fresh fruit and veg, there's a **market** just uphill from the bus station. For **drinking**, there's a stretch of youth-oriented café-bars on the seafront just north of the *Jadran* hotel, and a handful of more characterful places in and around the old town.

Cafés and bars

Cohiba Stube Petra Kaera bb ⓦwww.cohiba.hr. In the heart of Šibenik's old town, *Cohiba* boasts a swanky outdoor terrace café at street level and a raucous disco-bar down below. DJ-driven party nights at weekends – look out for posters or check the website.

Dobrić Dobrić 1. Enjoyable old-town drinking den with irregular wedge-shaped interior, matt-black walls and loud alternative sounds on the CD player. A tempting range of affordable cocktails, too.

Indigo Jurja Barakovića 5. Lounge bar on three levels, squeezed into a tall, narrow house of medieval vintage, with an inviting array of comfy sofas and couches strewn across the terrace.

Kazališna kavana Kralja Zvonimira bb. Small, chic place with coffee-and-cream colour scheme and a small outdoor terrace. The name means "theatre café" – appropriately enough, it's just behind the municipal theatre (where ER heart-throb Goran Višnjić first trod the boards).

Moderato Cantabile Stjepana Radića 1. Popular daytime coffee-drinking and newspaper-reading venue with big, bright interior and large outdoor terrace. Named after a popular song penned by Šibenik-born crooner (and Croatian national treasure) Arsen Dedić.

Restaurants

Četvorka Trg Dinka Zavorovića 4. Chic little place with a cosy café-bar on one level, and a small dining area on the floor above. Good steaks, and outdoor seating on a terrace overlooking a tiny Baroque square.

Dalmatino Fra Nikole Ružića 1. With antique furniture and archaic agricultural implements strewn around the place, this is an atmospheric spot in which to sample fresh fish. It's also a wine shop with a good range of local tipples.

Konoba Kanela Obala Franje Tuđmana. The only decent place on the seafront, although overpriced, serving fresh seafood on a pleasant terrace with wooden tables.

Tinel Trg pučkih kapetana ⓣ022/331-815. Occupying a dainty tree-shaded terrace opposite the Church of St Chrysogonus, this restaurant serves up simple lunches like *fažol sa kobasicom* (beans with sausage), mid-priced staples like wine goulash and *pašticada*, and more expensive steaks and fish.

Pizzeria Toni Zlarinski Prolaz 1. In a passageway next to Trg Pavla Šubića, this place has a lovely outdoor terrace by an ancient church and dishes up cheap tasty pizza, pasta, sandwiches and *palačinke* (crêpes). It doubles as a popular beer hall at night.

Uzorita bana Jelačića 58. Characterful establishment featuring dining rooms hung with hams and cooking pots, specializing in seafood specialities such as baked octopus, and shellfish from the nearby Krka estuary. A little out of the way (it's 1km uphill from the centre near the NK Šibenik football ground), but well worth the trip.

Vijećnica Trg republike Hrvatske. Smart and stylish restaurant occupying the arcaded front of the former town hall, and with excellent views of the cathedral. Good pastas and salads, and lavish main courses utilizing the best of the local seafood.

South of Šibenik: Brodarica and Krapanj

South of Šibenik along the Magistrala, the first place you come to is **BRODARICA**, an undistinguished village which stretches along the road for some 3km. Unlike Šibenik, however, Brodarica can boast a huge stock of private accommodation – and with Šibenik–Brodarica buses shuttling back and forth every hour from the local bus stop opposite the Jadranska banka by the market, and Šibenik–Split services trundling through roughly every hour, it makes a handy if rather functional base from which to tour the region.

The modest **tourist office** at the southern end of the village, beside the Magistrala at Krapinjskih Spužvara 1 (June to mid-Sept 9am–9pm; ⓣ022/350-612, ⓦwww.tz-brodarica.hr), can provide bus times and details of the ferry to Krapanj (see below). Tudić agency, situated in a roadside kiosk at the northern entrance to Brodarica (July & Aug daily 9am–8pm, at other times call to check; ⓣ022/350-695) arranges **rooms** (❶) and **apartments** (two-person apartments ❸, four-person apartments 450–580Kn); if you're coming from Šibenik, get off at the first bus stop in the village; coming from Split, get off at the third. The same firm runs the *Pansion Zlatna Ribica*, down beyond the tourist office at Krapanjskih Spužvara 46 (ⓣ022/350-695, ⓦwww.zlatna-ribica.hr; ❸), which offers cosy air-conditioned rooms with TV and a top-notch **restaurant** famous for its superbly grilled fish – it's probably the best place to eat seafood in the whole Šibenik region and not over-expensive, so advance reservations are recommended (ⓣ022/350-300).

Krapanj

Brodarica is largely populated by families from **Krapanj**, a few hundred metres across the water, which has the minor distinction of being the smallest inhabited island in the Adriatic. Boats cross from Brodarica hourly (but none on Sunday), arriving at a sleepy harbour backed by an enjoyable warren of grey-brown houses. The one bona fide attraction is the fifteenth-century **Franciscan monastery** (Franjevački samostan) ten minutes' walk north of the harbour, where a **museum** (June–Sept Mon–Sat 9am–noon & 5–7pm; 15Kn) contains a couple of Renaissance paintings and a collection of sponges. Diving for sponges used to be the main occupation on Krapanj, although there's not much evidence of this now, save for a couple of shops on the harbour selling spongy souvenirs. Krapanj fills up with Croatian weekenders in July and August, when there's a fair number of sunbathers sprawled out on either side of the quay – the rest of the time women clad in traditional black widows' weeds outnumber other residents four to one.

Zlarin and Prvić

Neither Šibenik nor Brodarica offers much in the way of beaches, and unless you fancy squeezing onto the horrendously overcrowded strands at nearby Vodice (see p.329), your best bet is to head for the nearby islands of **Zlarin** and **Prvić**, where you stand a good chance of finding a secluded bit of rocky shoreline and crystal-clear water. There's no mass tourism on the islands, and no cars – merely a succession of orderly and neat little villages kept alive by a trickle of independent tourists and weekending Croatians. The islands are served by the five daily Šibenik–Vodice passenger ferries (though only two on Sundays), which call in at Zlarin before proceeding to Prvić Luka on the southeastern side of Prvić, and Šepurine on the island's northwestern shore. From either Šibenik or Vodice, you could feasibly fit all three villages into a single day's sightseeing, although most visitors favour a more relaxing approach. If you're planning **to stay** on the islands, note that private rooms on Prvić can be booked in advance through most travel agencies in Vodice (see p.329).

The ferry trip from Šibenik is a treat in itself, with the boat ploughing its way through **St Anthony's Channel** (Kanal svetog Ante), a narrow, cliff-lined waterway which leads from the bay of Šibenik out into the open sea. At the far end of the channel lies the sixteenth-century **St Nicholas's Fortress** (Tvrđava svetog Nikole), a monumental triangular gun battery placed here by Venetian engineers to keep enemy shipping away from Šibenik's port. Classical music concerts and rave parties are sometimes hosted here in summer, with concertgoers ferried to the venue by a flotilla of small boats; tickets to these events can be bought through Cromovens agency in Šibenik (see p.332).

Zlarin

Thirty minutes out from Šibenik, the boat docks at the village of **ZLARIN**, an attractive huddle of houses at the apex of a broad bay. There's a tourist office on the harbour (July & Aug daily 9am–noon & 6.30–9pm; ⓣ022/553-557), which can organize private **rooms** (❶), and there's a brace of shops selling souvenirs fashioned from coral, which existed in some abundance off the shores of Zlarin until being over-harvested in the early twentieth century. There's a lone **hotel** on the island, *Koralj* (ⓣ022/553-621, ⓔfour.lion@hi.t-com.hr; ❹), above the seafront restaurant, a short walk from the ferry landing, with simple en-suite rooms and a spacious garden in the back. Paths on the western side of the bay will take you to an abundance of rocky bathing areas backed by pines. Zlarin's rarely open **parish church** is famous for housing the body of fourth-century Roman martyr St Fortunatus, a relic obtained for the island by a resourceful local priest in 1781. Every fifty years the remains are paraded through the village on April 23 – the next celebration is due in 2050, so there's no need to pack your bags just yet.

Prvić

A fifteen-minute ferry journey away, the main settlement of Prvić, **PRVIĆ LUKA**, is another unassuming, bay-hugging village with a charmingly soporific atmosphere. The only sight of note is the **parish church** just up from the harbour, which boasts an extrovert collection of Baroque altarpieces as well as the tomb of Šibenik-born humanist and all-round brainbox Faust Vrančić (see box overleaf). Private **rooms** (❶) and **apartments** (two-person apartments ❸, four-person apartments from 500Kn) can be located through the **tourist office** (summer only Mon–Sat 11am–1pm & 6–9pm, Sun 9am–noon; ⓣ022/448-083), just beyond the church on the main road to Šepurine; while the nearby *Art Pension* (ⓣ022/448-220 & 091 548 5849; ❷, or ❹ half-board), run by a charming Polish-Croatian couple, has a small stock of cosy en suites. One of the most stylish small **hotels** on this stretch of coast, the *Hotel Maestral* (April to mid-November; ⓣ022/448-300, ⓦwww.hotelmaestral.com; ❺), can be found in the beautifully restored school building smack in the centre of the village. It offers twelve tastefully furnished air-conditioned en-suite rooms with original details, including cool stone interiors and wooden shutters. It also has the excellent *Val* restaurant on the ground floor (with an impressive wine list), a lovely breakfast terrace on the side of the building, a fitness room and a sauna. You can **bathe** on the rocks on either side of the bay.

A single road leads northwest out of Prvić Luka, passing olive groves and offering some great vistas before arriving after fifteen minutes in **ŠEPURINE** (which

Faust Vrančić (1551–1617)

Renaissance Šibenik produced many learned minds, most famously **Faust Vrančić** (Faustus Verantius), the author of *Machinae novae* (1615) – a book of machines and contraptions whose inventiveness rivalled the mechanical fantasies of Leonardo da Vinci. The album of 49 copper engravings included pontoon bridges, suspension bridges, wind-powered flour mills with rotating roofs and, most famously, **Homo volans** – a picture of a man jumping from a tower with a primitive parachute. Equipped with a square of sail-canvas, Vrančić opined in the accompanying text, "a man can easily descend securely and without any kind of danger from a tower or any other high place". It is not known whether Vrančić ever tried this at home.

Machinae novae was written towards the end of a busy intellectual life. The young Faust studied in Bratislava and Padua before becoming administrator of the Hungarian city of Veszprém, and in 1581 was appointed secretary to the court of **Emperor Rudolf II** in Prague – a renowned meeting place for humanists from all over Europe. He subsequently retired to become a Pauline monk in Rome, where he probably became acquainted with Leonardo's drawings, and was moved to compile his *Machinae*. Vrančić's other major (and, in terms of Croatian culture, far greater) work was his *Dictionarium quinque nobilissimarum Europae linguarum* (Dictionary of the five most noble languages of Europe, 1595), a lexicon including Latin, Greek, German, Hungarian and "Dalmatian" (Croatian). It was the first real Croatian dictionary, setting a standard which all future language reformers would be obliged to follow.

is also the next stop for the Vodice-bound ferry; note that tickets must be bought at the Jadrolinija kiosk in the harbour), an attractive and beautifully preserved fishing village spread beneath a mushroom-topped church tower. Šepurine has the best **beach** in the area, a wonderful S-bend of shingle stretching away south of the ferry dock. The sporadically open **tourist office** (Mon–Sat 9am–11am), 200m south of the landing stage and housed in the local primary school, will put you in touch with local landladies offering **rooms** (❶). The nearby *Ribarski dvor* **restaurant** offers some of the best grilled fish and shellfish in the region, and has prices to match.

Krka National Park

Šibenik stands at the mouth of the River Krka, which rises just outside Knin and flows through a sequence of gorges, lakes and rapids before meeting the sea. Although the whole stretch of the **Krka valley** between the towns of Knin and Skradin has national park status, it's the section of the park just east of **Skradin**, only 12km out from Šibenik, that most visitors gravitate towards. Here the river descends via a sequence of mini-waterfalls at Skradinski buk (Skradin Falls) before flowing through a small but picturesque canyon to the town of Skradin itself. The upper reaches of the river are much less swamped by crowds, although there's a good deal worth seeing here, including two historic monasteries and another stretch of falls – all of which are accessible by national park-operated excursion boats.

Visiting the park

There are two main entrance points to the national park: the town of **Skradin** itself, 4km north of Skradinski buk, from where national park boats ferry visitors to the falls, and **Lozovac**, on the hill just above Skradinski buk, from where a bus shuttle service leads down to the river. There are several **buses** daily from Šibenik to Skradin (only two on weekends), passing through Lozovac on the way, making it possible to visit as a day-trip from the city – although there's little information on return services once you arrive, so it's a good idea to check the relevant times at Šibenik bus station before setting out. An early start is advised if you want to explore more than just the area around Skradinski buk – boat timings mean that a full day is required if you want to venture into the upriver sections of the park. The **entrance fee** (July & Aug 70Kn; March–June, Sept & Oct 50Kn; Nov–Feb 20Kn), payable at pavilions sited on the main approaches to Skradinski buk, includes travel on the shuttle boats and buses, but lengthier boat excursions to the upper stretches of the river cost extra. The **Krka National Park office** in Šibenik at Trg Ivana Pavla II 5 (Ⓣ022/217-720, Ⓕ336-836, Ⓦwww.npkrka.hr) has some free maps and brochures.

Skradin

The classic approach to the park is via **SKRADIN**, a pleasing, one-street town of stone houses with a marina squeezed into one of the river's small inlets. It's the only place with any **accommodation** in the environs of the park: the **tourist office**, on the waterfront at Obala bana Šubića 1 (mid-May to mid-Sept daily 8am–8pm; rest of the year Mon–Fri 9am–4pm; Ⓣ022/771-306, Ⓦwww.skradin.hr), has information on **private rooms** (❶). The *Skradinski buk* **hotel**, bang in the centre of the village at Burinovac bb (Ⓣ022/771-771, Ⓦwww.skradinskibuk.hr; ❹), is much swankier than similarly priced places back in Šibenik, its small en-suite rooms equipped with cool Scandinavian-style furnishings, TV and air conditioning. There's a string of **cafés** along the waterfront, and a superb seafood **restaurant** in the shape of the *Bonaca*, which serves up local fish and shellfish on an outdoor terrace slightly uphill from the marina.

Into the park

Krka National Park boats leave Skradin's harbourfront hourly for the trip up to **Skradinski buk**, a twenty-minute journey; should you miss the boats, you can walk by following the road from Skradin along the river's right bank, taking you between steep, scrub-covered hills (50min). Skradinski buk itself is a bit like a smaller Plitvice – a five-hundred-metre sequence of seventeen mini-cascades spilling over barriers of travertine (limestone sediment), behind which lie pools surrounded by reeds and semi-submerged forest. One of the more dramatic sequences is just up from the boat landing, with several tiers of waterfall tumbling into a broad, shallow pool – it's the only part of the park where swimming is permitted, and is full of holidaymakers on warm summer days. From here the main path crosses over to the eastern side of Skradinski buk, climbing past a collection of poky stone watermills positioned directly above the rushing Krka. There's also a network of short wooden walkways which break off from the main path, leading you above the gurgling waters and through the thick riverine vegetation. It's a beautiful location, and you could spend an entire day here, lolling around on the rocks beside the tumbling water.

After climbing past the cataracts for 1km or so the path levels out, arriving at the bus stop used by the national park's shuttle services to Lozovac. A kiosk here handles information and tickets for the boat excursions to the northern stretches of the river (a fairly obvious path descends from the kiosk to the quay from which these boats depart). The most popular northbound trip (reckon on 2hr for the journey there and back; 70Kn; April–Oct) takes you to the islet of **Visovac** just upstream from Skradinski buk, where you can visit a Franciscan monastery nestling among a thick cluster of cypresses. The monastery has a small collection of seventeenth-century paintings and, in its valuable library, some incunabula and a beautifully illustrated fifteenth-century *Aesop's Fables*, one of only three such in the world. From here another boat continues 10km further upstream to **Roški slap** (2hr return; 100Kn for the Skradinski Buk–Visovac–Roški slap excursion; March–Oct), a set of falls only slightly less dramatic than those at Skradinski buk. Finally, another boat takes you from Roški slap through a rugged canyon-scape to the the **Krka monastery** (2hr return; 60Kn; March–Oct), a Serbian Orthodox foundation nestling in a lovely rustic setting on the western bank of the river, with a church rich in incense and icons. If you want to fit the entire Skradinski buk–Visovac–Roški slap–Krka monastery itinerary into one day, it's advisable to contact the national park office (see p.339), which can help with planning.

Drniš and Knin

Thirty-four kilometres inland from Šibenik, the small market town of **DRNIŠ** has little to recommend it. It was occupied by Ottoman forces during the sixteenth century, when it was known as "little Sarajevo", though most of the relics of the Turkish period were obliterated when they were driven out, and the only surviving reminder is a sixteenth-century mosque, since incorporated into St John's Church (Crkva svetog Ivana). There's also a ruined tower picturesquely located above the River Čikola, and an irregularly open **Town Museum** (10Kn), which has a rather limited collection of works by local sculptor Ivan Meštrović (see box on p.369); some pieces disappeared during the Serbian occupation in 1991.

Meštrović hailed from the village of **OTAVICE**, 10km east, where he is buried in the hilltop **Meštrović Mausoleum**, a simple cube topped by a dome designed by Meštrović himself. He began the work in 1926, intending it as a family mausoleum, and was buried here after his death in the USA in 1962. Inside, an Art Nouveau-inspired sculpture of the Crucifixion is watched over by a pale, Buddha-like face, hinting at the religious syncretism towards which Meštrović leaned throughout his life. During the Serbian occupation, the bronze doors (bearing touching portraits of the Meštrović family) were stolen, reliefs were damaged, and the tombs desecrated; restoration is in progress.

Drniš is the centre of a large area devoted to the making of *pršut* (home-cured ham), and most local families keep a few pigs. Late November's *svinokolja* or **pig slaughter** is the key event of the local agricultural year, when up to ten thousand of the beasts meet their deaths.

Knin

Some 20km inland from Drniš is the rather plain town of **KNIN**, which became notorious as the epicentre of the Serbian rebellion of 1990–95, when it was the capital of the Serbian-controlled parts of Croatia, the so-called **Republic of the Serbian Krajina** (Republika srpske krajine, or RSK). Something like ninety percent of Knin's population was Serbian by the early 1990s, making it the obvious focus for Serbian discontent in the Dalmatian hinterlands. Control of Knin was always important to Serbian military planners: the town stands on the rail line between Zagreb and Split, and to remove the town from Zagreb's control

– it was argued – would seriously weaken Croatia's bargaining power should Yugoslavia ever fall apart.

Many of the key players in the ensuing Serb-Croat conflict came from Knin: Milan Babić, the RSK's first leader; Milan Martić, the Knin police chief who built up the Krajina's first armed forces; and Colonel Ratko Mladić, commander of the Knin military garrison, who practised ethnic cleansing here, forcibly ejecting Croat families from nearby villages, before becoming head of the Bosnian Serb army in 1992. The Serbian irregulars based in Knin during 1991–95 – who called themselves the *knindža*, in imitation of ninja-style comic strip heroes – melted away when the Croatian army launched the Oluja ("Storm") offensive in August 1995, and Knin's recapture on the morning of August 5, 1995, brought the war in Croatia to a rapid conclusion: Serbian resistance elsewhere in the country collapsed within two days, and pictures of President Franjo Tuđman kissing an enormous Croatian tricolour flying from **Knin fortress** were seen on TV across the world. Most Serb civilians fled in the wake of their defeated army in August 1995 and, though many have returned, the present population is still only a fraction of what it was. The castle is worth visiting if you're passing through, and the arid, wind-blasted appearance of the local scenery exerts a certain fascination.

Knin's **train** and **bus stations** are next to one another on the main street, and it's easy to pick a route up to the fortress on the hill above. There's been a castle here since at least the tenth century, and it was the seat of the medieval Croatian state's last effective king, Zvonimir, towards the end of the eleventh century. The castle's fall to the Turks in 1522 hastened a change in the demographic profile of the area, with fleeing Catholics being replaced by a predominantly Orthodox population from the Balkan interior. The fortress has been impressively restored, with a central keep surrounded by concentric rings of walls, and outlying towers squatting on outcrops of rock. The battlements offer an extensive panorama of the surrounding countryside, with a view of Knin below in its bowl of brownish hills and the grey ridge of the Dinaric mountains to the northeast on the border with Bosnia-Hercegovina – the best place to enjoy it is from the terrace of the **café-restaurant** inside the fortress.

The best option for an overnight **stay** is *Hotel Mihovil*, 3km north of town on the road to Bosansko Grahovo (Ⓣ022/664-444, Ⓦwww.zivkovic.hr; ④), with unfussy en-suites with TV. The on-site restaurant serves mouth-watering steaks.

From Šibenik to Trogir

Heading south from Šibenik, most traffic follows the coastal Magistrala, although there's an inland route which cuts through the arid mountains before rejoining the main road at Trogir. It's worth taking if you like spit-roast **lamb** – a couple of roadside restaurants in the village of **Boraja**, 15km outside Šibenik, are famous for it.

Primošten

The small town of **PRIMOŠTEN**, 20km south of Šibenik, is the best place on this part of the coast to rest up and do nothing for a while. Heaped up on an island that's joined to the mainland by a short causeway, it's enchanting when seen from a distance, although on closer inspection most of the houses date from the twentieth century, and there's nothing of specific interest to do apart from strolling the coastal path, Lungomare, that circles the island and offers glimpses of beautiful villas and sweeping sea views. Extensive pebble and rock **beaches**

△ Primošten

lapped by ultra-clear water fringe the wooded promontory to the north of the town, where there are also a number of hotels.

Practicalities

Primošten's small **bus station** is uphill on the landward side of the causeway. From here it's a short walk to the **tourist office**, on the small square that marks the entrance to the old town (June, Sept & Oct daily 8am–9pm; July & Aug daily 8am–10pm; Nov–May Mon–Fri 8am–2pm; ⓣ022/571-111, ⓦwww.summernet.hr/primosten). Private **rooms** (❶–❷) and **apartments** (two-person apartments ❸–❹, four-person apartments 520–710Kn), available from Nik agency at Raduča 2 (daily 8am–10pm; ⓣ022/571-200, ⓦwww.nik.hr) and Dalmatinka Turist Buro on Zagrebačka 8 (ⓣ022/570-323, ⓦwww.dalmatinka.biz) are probably a better deal than the package-style *Zora* **hotel** (ⓣ022/581-022, ⓦwww.azalea-hotels.com; ❽ all inclusive), a typical 1960s seaside establishment on the wooded promontory north of town, which has functional en-suite rooms with balconies, air conditioning and TV. A cosy alternative is *Villa Koša*, right on the seashore just east of town at Bana Jelačića 4 (ⓣ022/570-365, ⓦwww.villa-kosa.htnet.hr; ❸), offering bright modern rooms with pine flooring and private bathroom, as well as a handful of swanky apartments (❹–❺). The *Adriatik* **campsite** (ⓣ022/571-223, ⓦwww.camp-adriatic.hr), about 3km north of town on the main coastal road, has good tree cover and an attractive rocky beach.

For **food**, the *Buffet Aligator*, in a nameless alley just uphill from the tourist office, is good for cheap fried squid snacks; the nearby *Gostiona Dalmacija* has a more extensive range of seafood risottos, grilled scampi and fish; *Babilon* on top of the hill has the nicest setting, on a lovely terrace with splendid vistas; and the tiny atmospheric *Konoba Papec* on Uvala Mala Raduča does excellent Dalmatian snacks. Best of the lot however is *Konoba Torkul*, on the mainland side of the causeway at Grgur Ninskog bb (ⓣ020/570-670), serving up excellent grilled fish and shellfish in an old stone house – the two-person seafood platter (*riblji pladanj*) is a gastronomic showcase well worth trying. Wherever you eat, be sure to try the local Primošten **wine**, Babić – a smooth, dry red.

Aurora, 2km from the town centre (follow the Magistrala in the Split direction and then head uphill), is one of the best **clubs** in central Dalmatia, with a string of European techno and house DJs guesting here over the summer – look out for posters in Primošten, Split and Šibenik or check Ⓦwww.auroraclub.hr.

Trogir and around

Thirty kilometres east of Primošten and about 20km west of Split, **TROGIR** is one of the most seductive towns on the Dalmatian coast, a compact brown-beige welter of palaces, jutting belfries and shambling streets fanning out from an antique central square. Founded by Greeks from Vis in the third century BC, Trogir can compare with any of the towns on the coast in terms of historic sights, and its **cathedral** is one of the finest in the Adriatic. It's also a good base for further exploration: the swarming city of Split is a short ride away on the #37 bus, and between the two lies a string of time-worn fishing villages known collectively as **Kaštela**, after the little "castles" built here by Trogir nobles to serve as country retreats.

Arrival and information

Trogir's **old town** is built on an oval-shaped island squeezed between the mainland and the larger island of **Čiovo**, while modern Trogir has spread onto the

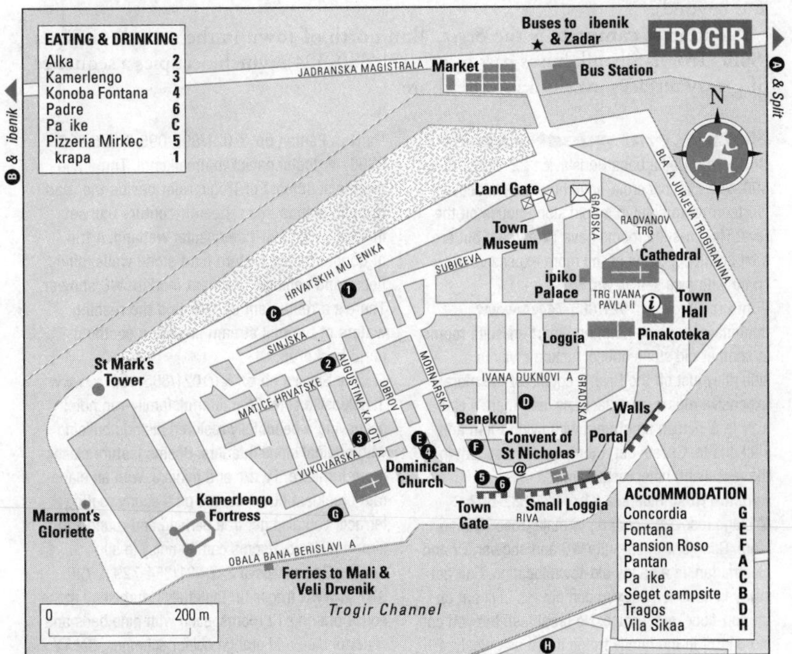

mainland, stretching along the coast for several kilometres. Inter-city **buses** pick up and drop off on the main street in the new town, just opposite the bridge which leads over to the old town. Also on the mainland side of the bridge is a small bus station (left luggage daily 6am–9pm), where the #37 bus from Split, along with the summer shuttle bus between Šibenik and the ferry landing in Split (every 30min), terminate. Head over the bridge and straight through the town centre to find the **tourist office** on the main square, Ivana Pavla II (daily: June–Sept 8am–9pm; rest of the year 8am–2pm; ⓣ & ⓕ 021/881-412, ⓦ www.dalmacija.net/trogir.htm*)*, which has basic town maps and brochures. You can surf the net at Benekom, Ribarska 2 (Mon–Sat 9am–10pm, Sun 2–10pm).

Ferries to the nearby islands of Mali and Veli Drvenik (see p.349) depart daily from the eastern end of Trogir's Riva (Obala bana Berislavića); tickets can be purchased on board.

Accommodation

There's a generous handful of small **hotels** in or around Trogir's old town, although prices are slightly higher here than in the rest of central Dalmatia. **Rooms** (❷) and **apartments** (two-person studios ❸, four-person apartments from 540Kn) are available from a handful of agencies in town – if you want anything in or near the old town, be sure to ring ahead. Staff at Čipiko, in the Čipiko Palace opposite the cathedral at Gradska 41 (summer daily 8am–9pm; winter Mon–Sat 8am–1pm; ⓣ & ⓕ 021/881-554, ⓔ pacipiko@inet.hr), tend to be a bit laid-back about precise arrangements but will do their best to ensure you get a roof over your head. Portal, Obala bana Berislavića 3 (ⓣ 021/885-016, ⓦ www.portal-trogir.com), has a bigger range of better-quality rooms and apartments, and also covers a wider geographical area (Trogir, Čiovo, Drvenik and beyond).

The nearest **campsite** is the *Seget*, 4km north of town in the suburb of Seget (Split-Trogir-Šibenik buses pass by; ⓣ 021/880-394), which occupies a sequence of grassy terraces overlooking the shore.

Hotels and guesthouses

Concordia Obala bana Berislavića 22 ⓣ 021/885-400, ⓦ www.concordia-hotel.htnet.hr. Attractive fourteen-room hotel in an old stone house on the Riva. The en-suite rooms have TV and a/c but are a bit cramped. Some of the more expensive ones come with nice sea views. ❺

Fontana Obrov 1 ⓣ 021/885-744, ⓦ www.fontana-commerce.htnet.hr. Smart en-suite rooms in another old stone house, tucked away in a side alley just off the Riva. A couple of the more expensive rooms have Jacuzzis, and there's also a 2- to 3-person apartment with living room and kitchenette. Guests get a ten percent discount in the (excellent) hotel restaurant. ❺

Pansion Roso Ribarska 21 ⓣ 021/882-602, ⓔ blago.roso@st.t-com.hr, ⓔ maja_roso@yahoo.com. Rooms with en-suite WC and shower, TV and electric fan, in a handy old-town location. Can get stuffy in summer, but you can always chill out on the top-floor roof terrace. No breakfast, but you can store stuff in the family fridge if you ask nicely. ❷

Pantan Pantan bb ⓣ 021/895-095 & 095 905 6890, ⓔ doctor.pavic@hotmail.com. Three kilometres southeast of Trogir, right beside the road to Split, stands this sixteenth-century mill set in reedy, wildfowl-rich coastal wetland. A trio of double rooms feature bare stone walls, pine floors and ceilings, and neat modern WC/shower. There's a restaurant on site, and the rushing waters of the mill stream provide a soothing aural backdrop. ❹

Pašike Sinjska bb ⓣ & ⓕ 021/885-185, ⓦ www.hotelpasike.com. Characterful, family-run hotel occupying a beautifully restored historic building with original stone interiors. Rooms feature classy repro furniture, TV, a/c and minibar, with an elaborate breakfast buffet served on a sunny rooftop terrace; you also get free parking and round-trip airport pick-up. Rooms can be noisy in summer. ❺

Tragos Budislavićeva 3 ⓣ 021/884-729 & 796-970, ⓦ www.tragos.hr. Tastefully refurbished stone house offering 12 rooms, each with pine beds and cheerful blue and orange colour schemes, Sat TV and modern WC and bathroom (half come with shower cabinets, the others have tubs). 6

Vila Sikaa Obala kralja Zvonimira 13 ⓣ021/881-223, ⓦwww.vila-sikaa-r.com. Bed-and-breakfast in a waterfront building directly opposite the old town, offering snug en-suite rooms with TV and a/c, many with excellent views of the old town. 5

The Town

Across the bridge from the mainland, the old town is entered via the seventeenth-century **Land Gate** (Kopnena vrata), a simple arch topped with a statue of the town's protector, St John of Trogir (Sveti Ivan Trogirski), a miracle-working twelfth-century bishop. Straight ahead, the outwardly unassuming Garagnin palace now houses the **Town Museum** (Gradski muzej; June to mid-Sept daily 9am–1pm & 4–9pm; rest of the year opens for exhibits only; 10Kn), a largely disappointing collection of pictures and documents which boasts one stand-out exhibit, a serene fifteenth-century relief of Virgin and Child rendered in milky white marble by local sculptor Ivan Duknović. The museum's lapidarium, accessed by a separate entrance round the corner, boasts Roman tombstones, sundry chunks of early Christian masonry, and Renaissance family crests which once hung above the portals of patrician houses.

The cathedral

Immediately east of the museum lies Trogir's main street, Gradska, which leads straight down to **Trg Ivana Pavla II**, a creamy-white square flanked by some of the town's most historic buildings. Dominating them all is **St Lawrence's Cathedral** (Katedrala svetog Lovrijenca; Mon–Sat 9am–7pm, Sun at Mass time), a squat Romanesque structure begun in 1213 and only finished with the addition of a soaring Venetian Gothic campanile some three centuries later. A previous church on this site had been damaged by Saracen raiders in the twelfth century, but the town's control of lucrative trade routes with the Balkan interior helped pay for the construction of a new one.

△ Trogir

The cathedral's most distinctive feature is its **west portal**, an astonishing piece of work carved in 1240 by the Slav master-mason **Radovan**. Radovan laid claim to his work in an immodest inscription above the door, calling himself "Most excellent in his art" – a justifiable claim given the doorway's intricate mix of Orthodox iconography with scenes from ordinary life and legend, showing figures of apostles and saints, centaurs and sirens, woodcutters and leather-workers jostling for position in a chaos of twisting decoration. Roughly speaking, there is a gradual movement upwards from Old Testament figures at the bottom to New Testament scenes on the arches and lunette. Adam and Eve frame the door and stand with anxious modesty on a pair of lions. On either side, a series of receding pillars sit upon the bent backs of the undesirables of the time – Jews and Turks – while above is a weird menagerie of creatures in writhing, bucking confusion, laced together with tendrilled carvings symbolizing the months and seasons. The sequence begins with March (the year started with the Annunciation as far as the Church was concerned), symbolized by a man pruning vines, and a wild-haired youth blowing a horn (a reference to the March winds). Further on, a man killing a pig represents the autumn (pig-slaughtering and sausage-making still form an important part of the Croatian calendar), while another character in clogs cooks what look like sausages. The lunette above comprises two scenes fringed by curtains, in imitation of the two-level stages on which medieval miracle plays were often presented. The Nativity is portrayed on the upper level, and the Bathing of Christ below, with shepherds and magi crowding the wings. Above the lunette, the uppermost arch is decorated with scenes from the life of Christ.

Left of the portal, small circular windows are framed by a serpent tearing apart a half-naked libertine. Farther over to the left lies the fifteenth-century **Baptistry**, a fine piece of Renaissance stonework executed by **Andrija Aleši** of Dürres, thought to have been an Albanian noble who fled the Turks and had to learn a trade in order to earn a living. He was apprenticed to Juraj Dalmatinac (see box on p.334) at Šibenik, and was in many ways his stylistic successor. The portal, topped by a relief of the Baptism of Christ, gives way to a coffer-ceilinged interior, where a frieze of cherubs carrying a garland leads round the walls, overlooked by a relief of St Hieronymous in the cave in smooth milky stone.

The **interior** of the cathedral is atmospherically gloomy, its pillars hung with paintings illustrating scenes from the life of St John of Trogir. At the head of the nave stand a Romanesque octagonal pulpit, its capitals decorated with griffins and writhing snakes, and a Baroque high altar canopied by an ornate thirteenth-century ciborium; the beautiful set of mid-fifteenth-century choirstalls were carved in Venetian Gothic style by local artist Ivan Budislavić. The north aisle of the cathedral opens up to reveal **St John of Trogir's Chapel** (Kapela svetog Ivana Trogirskog), another spectacular example of Renaissance work, mostly carried out by Juraj Dalmatinac's other pupil Nikola Firentinac, together with the Trogir sculptor Ivan Duknović. God the Creator is pictured at the centre of a barrel-vaulted ceiling, from which a hundred angels gaze down. The space below is ringed by life-size statues of saints, each of which occupies a niche framed by cavorting cherubs. Firentinac's statues of St John of Trogir and St Paul, both portrayed as bearded sages pouring over their prayer books, are masterpieces of sensitive portraiture. Duknović's equally impressive statue of St John the Evangelist, here depicted as a curly-haired clean-shaven youth, is thought to bear a deliberate resemblance to a favourite son of Trogir-based aristocrat Koriolan

Čipiko, who may well have had a hand in commissioning the sculptures for the chapel. At floor level there are more cherubs, this time peeping cheekily from behind half-open doors – which here symbolize the passage from life to death.

Finally, further along the north aisle from St John's Chapel lies the sacristy, which houses the **treasury** (*riznica*; summer Mon–Sat 9am–8pm, Sun 4–7pm; 10Kn), a mundane collection of ecclesiastical bric-a-brac. The best exhibits are the fine inlaid storage cabinets carved by Grgur Vidov in 1458, a fourteenth-century Gothic jug, scaled and moulded into snake-like form, and a silver-plated reliquary of St John of Trogir which is paraded around town on his feast day.

The rest of the old town

Opposite the cathedral entrance is the **Čipiko Palace**, a well-worn fifteenth-century Venetian Gothic mansion whose balustraded triple window – with Venetian Gothic arches held aloft by florid Corinthian capitals – is said to be the work of Andrija Aleši. There's nothing inside except the Čipiko tourist agency, though it's noteworthy for being the erstwhile home of the Čipikos, Renaissance Trogir's leading noble family. Their best-remembered representatives are the aforementioned Koriolan Čipiko (1425–93), Venetian admiral and author of *De bello asiatico*, an account of his wartime experiences with the fleet, and Alviz Čipiko, who commanded a galley from Trogir at the Battle of Lepanto in 1571. It was in the Čipiko family library that the first known manuscript of "Trimalchio's Feast", a hitherto undiscovered fragment of Petronius' *Satyricon*, was discovered in 1653, sending a frisson of excitement through literary circles all over Europe.

On the other side of the square, the **Town Loggia** (Gradska loža), with its handsome clock tower and classical columns, dates from the fifteenth century, though its pristine appearance is explained by a late nineteenth-century restoration. The large relief on the east wall of the loggia, showing Justice flanked by St John of Trogir and St Lawrence (the last holding the grill on which he was roasted alive), is another work by Firentinac, identifiable by the presence of his personal "signature", the flower-covered pillars on either side. The relief was damaged in 1932, when a Venetian lion occupying the (now blank) space beneath the figure of Justice was dynamited – an act carried out by locals keen to erase Italian symbols from a town which was still coveted by Italian nationalists. Mussolini, eager to resurrect territorial claims in Dalmatia, raged against "Yugoslav barbarism" and forced the Yugoslav government into a grovelling apology. The loggia's south wall has been disfigured by a surprisingly lifeless Meštrović relief of Petar Berislavić, sixteenth-century Bishop of Zagreb and Ban of Croatia, who fought a losing battle against the advance of Ottoman power.

Next to the loggia, the former bishop's palace provides a fine setting for the **Pinakoteka** (July & Aug daily 9am–7pm; 20Kn), a display of sacred art culled from Trogir's churches. Among a number of painted crucifixes and altarpieces is Blaž Jurjev's fifteenth-century polyptych showing a Madonna and Child flanked by six saints, in which the Virgin proffers a pear-shaped breast to the infant. There are also full-length, life-size portraits of John the Baptist and St Jerome, painted to decorate the cathedral organ shutters by Gentile Bellini in 1489.

South of Trg Ivana Pavla II, the ever-narrowing Gradska leads on to the **Convent of St Nicholas** (Samostan svetog Nikole; June to mid-Sept 10am–noon & 4–6pm; rest of the year on request at the tourist office; 10Kn), whose treasury is famous for an outstanding third-century Greek relief of Kairos, discovered in 1928. Sculpted out of orange marble, it's a dynamic fragment representing the Greek god of opportunity – once passed he's impossible to seize hold of, and the back of his head is shaved just to make it even more difficult. The rest of the collection focuses on Byzantine-influenced sacred paintings from the sixteenth century, and the painted chests in which girls new to the convent brought their "dowries" (gifts to the convent in the form of rich textiles and ornaments) in anticipation of their wedding to Christ.

Along the Riva

Gradska makes a sudden dog-leg to the right before emerging through the **Town Gate** (Gradska vrata) onto the Riva, a seafront promenade facing the island of Čiovo. Hard up against the gate stands the so-called **Small Loggia** (Mala loža), nowadays occupied by souvenir sellers. On either side of the gate are a few stretches of what remain of the medieval **town walls**, large chunks of which were demolished by the Napoleonic French, who hoped the fresh sea breezes would help blow away the town's endemic malaria. To the right, past a gaggle of cafés, is the campanile of the **Dominican Church** (Crkva svetog Dominika), a light, high building with a charming relief in the lunette above the main door; it shows a Madonna and Child flanked by Mary Magdalene, clad in nothing but her own tresses, and Augustin Kažtotić (1260–1323), Bishop of Trogir and subsequently Zagreb. A small praying figure next to Kažotić represents his sister Bitkula, who commissioned the work. The main feature inside is the tomb of Šimun and Ivan Sobota, which bears a Firentinac relief of the Pietà surrounded by mourners. The coffin below is decorated with more of Firentinac's trademark flowery, pinapple-topped pillars.

Farther along, the fifteenth-century **Kamerlengo Fortress** (summer months daily 9am–7pm; 10Kn) was named after the Venetian official – the *kamerling* – who ran the town's finances. An irregular quadrilateral dominated by a stout octagonal tower, it's a wonderfully atmospheric venue for a quick stroll on the battlements and hosts concerts and theatre and dance performances in summer months. Beyond lies the town's football pitch, on the opposite side of which looms the tapering cylinder of **St Mark's Tower** (Kula svetog Marka), a sandcastle-style bastion built at the same time as the Kamerlengo. Despite selling the kind of kitschy Dalmatian pop-folk albums you wouldn't want to be seen dead with, the House of Music CD shop inside St Mark's tower boasts a truly fascinating display of ancient musical instruments and costumes.

Finally, at the far end of the island is **Marmont's Gloriette**, a graffiti-covered, six-pillared gazebo which looks out onto Čiovo's rusting shipyard. It was built for Marshal Marmont, the French governor of Napoleon's Illyrian Provinces; just and progressive, Marmont was probably the best colonial ruler the city ever had, and the Gloriette serves as some sort of modest tribute.

Eating, drinking and entertainment

Eating out in Trogir is a joy, with dozens of restaurants tucked away in the courtyards of the centre. There's also a hugely enjoyable **market** opposite the bus station, where you'll find fruit, veg, cheeses, hams and homemade wines and spirits offered by local farmers, haphazardly bottled into all kinds of containers. As far as **drinking** is concerned, all the old town's squares are stuffed with café tables in summer, and it's simply a question of picking a space that suits. In the evening, head for Radvanov trg behind the cathedral, which soon fills up with drinkers drawn by the trio of stylish café-bars around its edges. *Padre*, occupying a roofless ruined building next to the town gate, is a cool place for cocktails.

The **Trogir Cultural Summer** (Trogirsko kulturno ljeto; early July to late Aug) features pop music, classical concerts and folklore events on various outdoor stages in the town centre and inside palaces and churches.

Restaurants

Alka Augustina Kažotića 15. Don't be fooled by the touristy signs pointing the way, this is one of the longest-established and best restaurants in Trogir, serving up suberb grilled fish and shellfish, and a mean *pašticada*. Pleasant courtyard seating down an alley opposite the restaurant entrance.

Kamerlengo Vukovarska 2. Top-class fish and scampi cooked on an outdoor charcoal grill in an L-shaped courtyard.

Konoba Fontana Obrov 1. With an outdoor terrace right on the Riva, this is one of the classiest places in town, offering the widest range of meat and fish dishes, all excellently prepared and presented.

Pašike Obala hrvatskih mučenika. On the main thoroughfare in front of *Pašike* hotel, this place has a 26-year-old tradition of dishing up well-prepared traditional specialities like black risotto and anchovies, *Kaštelanski makaruni* (homemade pasta in meat sauce), and grilled fish and shellfish. Live folk music and wait staff clad in traditional dress are part of the experience.

Pizzeria Mirkec Riva. Popular pizza joint right on the seafront offering good pizza and pasta, as well as other Dalmatian mainstays.

Škrapa Augustina Kažotića. Cheap and cheerful feeding station serving up seafood risottos, *lignje na žaru* (grilled squid) and other standards, with wooden bench seating on the street outside. Fills up early.

Mali Drvenik and Veli Drvenik

There's little in the way of decent beaches around Trogir, and it's well worth considering a ferry trip to **Mali Drvenik** or **Veli Drvenik** if a lazy day by the sea is what you're after. Lying some 12km west of town, these small, sparsely populated islands are increasingly popular with yachtspeople, but are little visited by other travellers, making them perfect for a quiet getaway. Boats sail from Trogir twice a day – although occasionally the return times may make it impossible to visit the islands on a day-trip, more often than not you will be able to spend a day on one of the islands and be back in town by nightfall. There are precious few roads on the islands (wheelbarrows and mini-tractors provide the only forms of transport), but they're criss-crossed by farm tracks, making them perfect for relaxed rambling. You'll find accommodation, food and drink on Veli Drvenik should you wish **to stay**.

Veli Drvenik

Fifty minutes' sailing time from Trogir, **VELI DRVENIK** is the livelier of the two islands, with its eponymous main village sprawling attractively on either side of a deep bay. The village itself is popular with second-home owners from the mainland, while its harbour frequently fills with touring yachts – all of which helps to keep the village shop and a couple of cafés in business. The water in the bay is clean enough to swim in, and there are several attractive coves elsewhere on the island – **Krknjaši bay**, a forty-five-minute walk to the east, has a partly pebbly beach and views southeast towards the island of Šolta. Konoba Krknjaši, immediately behind the beach, serves up freshly caught fish in a garden filled with rosemary, lavender and other fragrant shrubs. The interior of the island, covered in prickly bushes, abandoned olive plantations and fig trees, is a great place for walks – there's little real tree cover, however, so it's best to bring a hat.

There's no tourist office on the island, but private **rooms** (❶) can be arranged in advance through the Portal agency in Trogir (see p.344) – the Trogir tourist office (see p.344) will also have a list of Drvenik addresses, but might not ring up hosts on your behalf. There's also an excellent family-run **pension** in the shape of *Mia*, overlooking Veli Drvenik's harbour at Bobovišće 5 (T021/893-038, W www.free-st.t-com.hr/mia; contact Portal travel agency in Trogir if the owner's English isn't up to making a reservation; ❷ with breakfast, ❸ half board), which offers a range of cosy rooms and two- to four-person apartments, all with TV, air conditioning and fridge. Sumptuous home cooking makes it well worth paying a few extra kuna for half board. The owner is an expert on local herbs, and makes invigorating *rakija*, marmalade and massage oils from the grasses he's collected round the island. He will also drive you round the island on his tractor buggy for a small extra fee. A couple of harbourside **restaurants** serve up fresh fish, although they tend to open only when yachts appear in the bay. The coolest place to hang out in the village is *Atelje* (evenings only), an art gallery just below the *Mia* pension run by a Finnish–Croatian couple, which also serves wine in the garden courtyard.

Mali Drvenik

Lying a few kilometres off Veli Drvenik's western shore, maquis-covered **MALI DRVENIK** has a much wilder, untouristed air. The main port is a grubby little place with few amenities, and is little more than a staging post on the way to **Vela Rina**, a broad bay twenty minutes' walk away on the other side of the island. There's not much here apart from bare rocks and a view of the open sea, but it's an undeniably beautiful spot – you could easily while away several hours here if you come well prepared (there's precious little shade and certainly no cafés).

Kaštela

East of Trogir the coastline swings around towards Split in a wide, curving bay, sheltered from the open sea by the island of Čiovo and Split's jutting peninsula. During the fifteenth and sixteenth centuries, local nobles lined this fertile sweep of coast with country houses, fortified against pirate raids to give them the appearance of castles – the settlements which have grown up in their wake go under the collective name of **KAŠTELA**. The castles were built to protect the agricultural lands to which the nobles owed their wealth, but they were also rural retreats where their owners spent the summer months and received guests. Koriolan Čipiko was the first of the Trogir worthies to move out here, in 1481; his house subsequently earned the epithet Kaštel stari ("Old Castle") in order to differentiate it from those which followed, and seven summer houses survived to become the nuclei of the fishing villages that exist here now. Most of these castles were converted into flats years ago and can't be visited, but the villages look endearingly time-worn and have accessible places **to swim** if you're staying in Trogir. The villages are only separated from each other by a kilometre or two, and strolling from one to another makes for a wonderful seaside walk whatever the time of year. The #37 Trogir–Split bus links them all – the best thing to do is to hop off at, say, Kaštel Štafilić, head for the waterfront and proceed eastwards along the coastal path; you can return to the main road to pick up a bus when you've had enough.

The road from Trogir passes Split airport before arriving at the first of the villages, **KAŠTEL ŠTAFILIĆ**. There's a pleasant shingle **beach** on Štafilić's western fringes, although the castle around which the village grew is now crumbling and derelict. **KAŠTEL NOVI**, immediately beyond, is perhaps most typical of the villages – an agreeable if unremarkable huddle of ancient houses with a simple, fortified tower at its centre, and not much else to speak of – save for the attractive octagonal tower of the church of St Rock (Crkva svetog Roka). **KAŠTEL STARI**, a short walk away, has a decent stretch of stony **beach**, and a reasonable two-star **hotel** in the shape of the *Palace*, Obala kralja Tomislava 82 (Ⓣ021/206-270, Ⓦwww.kastelanska-rivijera.com; ❹), a venerable pre-World War I establishment with a modern accommodation block tacked on the side. **KAŠTEL LUKŠIĆ**, just beyond, is marginally livelier, with several cafés scattered along its seafront. The castle itself, a chunky brown cube built by Trogir's Vitturi family in the 1560s, has been tastefully restored, serving both as a seasonally open **art gallery** and the **tourist office** (June–Sept Mon–Sat 8am–1pm & 6–10pm; Oct–May Mon–Fri 8am–3pm; Ⓣ021/228-355, Ⓦwww.dalmacija.net/kastela.htm), which has information on the whole Kaštela region. The Ostrog Tourist Agency (Mon–Fri 8am–noon & 5–8pm; Ⓣ021/227-594, Ⓦwww.ostrog.hr), 100m farther along the shore, can organize **rooms** (❶) in the village. Kaštel Lukšić runs imperceptibly into **KAŠTEL KAMBELOVAC**, where you'll find the *Baletna Škola* **restaurant** near the harbour; serving up cheap lunchtime soups and stews as well as the best fresh seafood, this has something to suit most tastes and pockets. A kilometre beyond, **KAŠTEL GOMILICA** is the most picturesque of the villages, its fortress squatting impressively on a small islet joined to the mainland by a bridge. It's probably not worth covering the remaining 3km to the last outpost of Kaštela, **KAŠTEL SUĆURAC**, which is just 10km short of Split and within alarming proximity of the city's industrial installations.

Southern Dalmatia

The hub around which everything in **Southern Dalmatia** revolves is **Split**, Croatia's second city and the most vibrant centre on the coast. It grew out of the Roman palace of Dalmatian-born Emperor Diocletian, and successive layers of ancient, medieval and modern architecture have given the centre a unique – albeit chaotic – urban character. Inland from the city, the ruins of the Roman city of **Salona**, and the medieval Croatian stronghold of **Klis**, are the main draws.

The coast south of Split is probably mainland Dalmatia's most enchanting stretch, with the mountains glowering over a string of long pebble beaches, although a sequence of modern tourist resorts is beginning to put the squeeze on the fishing villages. The crowded resorts of the **Makarska Riviera** are justifiably popular family holiday centres, but it's the southern **islands** which are the real highlight of any trip to Dalmatia. Easiest to reach from Split is **Brač**, boasting some nice beaches at **Supetar** and a truly wonderful one at **Bol**, while lying off the southern coast of Brač is the long thin island of **Hvar**, whose capital, **Hvar Town**, rivals Dubrovnik and Trogir for the number of venerable stone buildings lining its ancient alleys. It's also a fashionable hangout for urbane Croats: chic bars rub shoulders with Gothic palaces and chapels, and water taxis convey bathers to idyllic offshore islets. Much the same can be said of the island of **Korčula**, south of Hvar, whose fascinating medieval capital, **Korčula Town**, offers a mixture of urban tourism and lazy beachcombing.

Farther out, but still only a few hours by boat from Split, the islands of **Vis** and **Lastovo** were only opened up to foreign tourists in 1989, after previously serving as naval bases. Wilder and less visited, both are obligatory destinations for travellers who want a piece of the Adriatic to themselves. You can rejoin the mainland from Korčula by a short ferry-ride to the **Pelješac peninsula** – virtually an island itself – which is joined to the coast by a slim neck of land at **Ston**, whose magnificent town walls were built to defend the northernmost frontiers of the Dubrovnik Republic.

As in northern Dalmatia, most public transport in the region is provided by the frequent inter-city **buses** which plough along the coastal highway, the Magistrala. In addition, Split has good bus links with all the large towns of inland Croatia, and is also the main **ferry** port for all the islands in this section. Hopping from one island to the next is feasible up to a point: Hvar is a good base for onward travel to Korčula and Lastovo; moving on from Brač and Vis usually involves heading back to Split first.

Split

SPLIT is one of the Adriatic's most vibrant cities: an exuberant and hectic place full of shouting stall-owners and travellers on the move. At the heart of the city, hemmed in by sprawling estates and a modern harbour, lies the crumbling old town, which grew out of the former **palace** of the Roman Emperor Diocletian. The palace remains the central ingredient in the city's urban fabric – lived in almost continuously since Roman times, it's gradually been transformed into a warren of houses, tenements, churches and chapels by the various peoples who came to live here after Diocletian's successors had departed.

Modern Split is a city of some 220,000 inhabitants, swollen by post-World War II economic migrants and post-1991 refugees – a chaotic sprawl of hastily planned suburbs, where factories and high-rise blocks jangle together out of an undergrowth of discarded building material. As Croatia's second city it's a hotbed of regional pride, and disparagement of Zagreb-dwellers is a frequent, if usually harmless, component of local banter. The city's two big industries – shipbuilding and tourism – suffered immeasurably as a result of war, and the economic slump which followed the collapse of communism and municipal belt-tightening has led to a decline in subsidies for the city's traditionally rich cultural scene. This is more than made up for by the vivacious outdoor life that takes over the streets in all but the coldest and wettest months: as long as the sun is shining, the swish cafés of the waterfront Riva are never short of custom.

Not surprisingly, Split is home to one of the more authentic **carnival seasons** in Croatia – a tradition which has only recently been revived – when masked revellers take over the streets and squares of the old town on the night of Shrove Tuesday and during the weekend before it. Split's other big day is May 7, when the **Feast of St Domnius** (Sveti Dujam or, more colloquially, Sveti Duje), the city's protector, is celebrated with processions, masses and general festivity. Domnius is also the patron saint of woodwork, and you'll see craftsmen selling chairs, tables, barrels and carvings in Split market on the days surrounding the feast.

Fetivi, boduli and vlaji

Although the inhabitants of Split – **Splićani** – may appear to be a homogenous body, they traditionally belong to three distinct groups. The old urban families – the **fetivi** – cultivate the art of talking fast with minimal lip movement. Another, more pejorative, term for a born-and-bred Splićanin is *mandril* (a mandrill, the baboon native to West Africa): it's best not to call someone a *pravi splitski mandril* (a "real Split monkey") unless you know them well enough to get away with it.

The *fetivi* are augmented by the **boduli**, immigrants from the Adriatic islands who – according to local stereotypes – have a reputation for parsimony and keeping themselves to themselves, although they're also admired for their *bodulska furbarija*, or "islanders' cunning". In recent decades the two groups have been joined by the **vlaji** ("Vlachs"; see p.299), who migrated to the city from the Dalmatian hinterland and now throng the high-rise suburbs that stretch away from the centre. Local jokes have always condemned the *vlaji* to playing the role of rural unsophisticates, although it's often conceded that it was their hard work in the construction and shipbuilding industries that made modern-day Split what it is. The *vlaji* are born survivors – passing through the *vlaški fakultet* ("Vlach faculty") means something akin to studying at the university of life. Nowadays the distinctions between the above groups are fast dying out, and the only real demarcation lines in Split society are between those well established in the city and the more recent arrivals from Hercegovina, who descended on Split in increasing numbers in the 1990s – either to make a fast buck or to escape the troubles in their own country.

Some history

According to conventional wisdom, Split didn't exist at all until the emperor Diocletian (see box overleaf) decided to build his retirement home here, although recent archeological finds suggest that a Roman settlement of sorts was founded here before Diocletian's builders arrived. **Diocletian's Palace** was begun in 295 AD and finished ten years later, when the emperor came back to his native Illyria to escape the cares of empire, cure his rheumatism and grow cabbages. But this was no simple retirement, and the palace no ordinary retirement home. Diocletian maintained an elaborate court here in a building that mixed luxurious palatial apartments with the infrastructure of a Roman garrison: the northern half of the palace was occupied by servants and the garrison; to the south lay the imperial suites and public buildings. The palace as a whole measured some 200m by 240m, with walls 2m thick and almost 25m high, while at each corner there was a fortified keep, and four towers along each of the land walls.

The palace was home to a succession of regional despots after Diocletian's death, although by the sixth century it had fallen into disuse. In 614, it was suddenly repopulated by refugees fleeing nearby Salona, which had just been sacked by the Avars and Slavs. The newcomers salvaged living quarters out of Diocletian's neglected buildings, improvising a home in what must have been one of the most grandiose squats of all time. They built fortifications, walled in arches, boarded up windows and repelled attacks from the mainland, accepting Byzantine sovereignty in return for being allowed to preserve a measure of autonomy. The resulting city developed cultural and trading links with the embryonic Croatian state inland, and was absorbed by the Hungaro-Croatian kingdom in the eleventh century.

By the fourteenth century, Split had grown beyond the confines of the palace, with today's Narodni trg becoming the new centre of a walled city that stretched as far west as the street now known as Marmontova. **Venetian rule**, established in 1420, occasioned an upsurge in the city's economic fortunes, as the city's port was developed as an entrepôt for Ottoman goods. Turkish power was to be an ever-constant threat, however: Ottoman armies attacked Split on numerous occasions, coming nearest to capturing it in 1657, when they occupied Marjan hill before being driven off by reinforcements hastily shipped in from Venice, Trogir and Hvar.

During the nineteenth century, **Austrian rule** brought industrialization and a railway to the city. Austrian stimulation of Adriatic shipping also helped speed the development of Split's port facilities, while the Italian seizure of Rijeka in 1919 (see box on p.230) encouraged the Yugoslav government to develop Split as an alternative centre of maritime trade. Split's biggest period of growth occurred after World War II, when the development of heavy industry attracted growing numbers of economic migrants from all over the country. Many of these newcomers came from the Zagora, the rural uplands stretching from the central Dalmatian coast to the Hercegovinian border, and ended up working in the enormous shipyards – colloquially known as the Škver – on Split's northwestern edge, providing the city with a new working-class layer. It was always said that productivity at the Škver was directly related to the on-the-pitch fortunes of **Hajduk Split** (see box on p.367), the football team which more than anything else in Split served to bind traditional inhabitants of the city with recent arrivals. Beginning with the big televised music festivals of the 1960s, Split also became the nation's unofficial **pop music** capital, promoted as a kind of Croatian San Remo. Since then generations of balladeering medallion men have emerged from the city to regale the nation with their songs of mandolin-playing fishermen and dark-eyed girls in the moonlight.

Diocletian (245–312)

Born the son of slaves, **Diocletian** was a native of Dalmatia – and possibly grew up in Salona, next door to Split. Despite his humble origins he proved himself quickly in the Roman military, becoming emperor in 284 at the age of 39. For 21 years he attempted to provide stability and direction to an empire under pressure – goals he achieved with some measure of success, even organizing the last triumph imperial Rome was ever to see. In the belief that the job of running the empire was too big for one man, Diocletian divided the role into four, the **Tetrarchy**, carefully parcelling out responsibility among his partners – a decision which some historians believe led directly to disintegration and civil war. Diocletian was also renowned for his persecution of Christians: those martyred during his reign included the patron saints of Split, Domnius and Anastasius, along with many other leading religious figures, Sebastian, George, Theodore and Vitus among them.

The motives for Diocletian's early **retirement** have been the subject of much speculation. It was obviously planned well in advance by a man who feared his health was no longer up to the rigours of government. As a highly innovative emperor, Diocletian obviously saw the very concept of retirement – a total novelty among Roman rulers – as a logical adjunct to his other reforms. However the power-sharing system he left behind soon disintegrated once he was no longer at the helm. The Tetrarchy had been welded together by inter-family marriage: after her father's retirement, Diocletian's own daughter, Valeria, stayed in Rome as the wife of Galerius, one of the Tetrarchs. On Galerius's death she received a proposal of marriage from his nephew Maximinus Daza, but was banished to Syria when she refused. When Diocletian tried to intercede on her behalf, he was cold-shouldered by his heirs – and the embittered ex-emperor appears to have poisoned himself in despair. Licinius, the new strongman in the eastern half of the Empire, arranged the murder of both Valeria and Diocletian's wife Priscia in 314.

The city was briefly **shelled** by the Yugoslav Navy in 1991 but was otherwise largely untouched by Serb–Croat hostilities, although refugees have added to the city's housing problems. None of this has damaged the spirit of the Splićani themselves, who remain famous for their self-deprecating humour, best exemplified by the writings of **Miljenko Smoje** (1923–95), a native of the inner-city district of Veli Varoš. Smoje's books, written in Dalmatian dialect, document the lives of an imaginary group of local archetypes and brought the wit of the Splićani to a nationwide audience. An adaptation of his works, *Naše malo misto* (Our Little Town), was the most popular comedy programme in Croatian – and probably Yugoslav – television history. The city's tradition of irreverence lives on in the weekly newspaper and national institution **Feral Tribune**, a mixture of investigative reporting and scathing political satire which has been a thorn in the side of successive recent administrations.

Arrival, information and city transport

Both the **train** and **inter-city bus stations** are five minutes' walk southeast of the centre on the main harbourfront road, Obala kneza Domagoja, along which are ranged all the **ferry** and **hydrofoil** berths. Split's **airport** is around 20km northwest of town between Kaštela and Trogir. Croatia Airlines buses (30Kn) connect with all of that airline's incoming flights, dropping passengers on the waterfront Riva, near the Croatia Airlines office. Alternatively, the #37 Trogir–Split bus (every 20–30min; 15.50Kn) passes along the main road some 200m in front of the airport – an unlit metal shed on the far side of the road marks the stop – and terminates at the suburban bus station on Domovinskog rata, twenty minutes' north of the centre. A taxi from the airport will cost 160–200Kn.

The city's **tourist office** is located right in the heart of the old town, in the Chapel of St Rock on the Peristyle (June–Sept Mon–Fri 8am–8pm, Sat

Moving on from Split

Split is an excellent base for onward travel, with **buses** to every conceivable destination in Croatia, as well as daily services to Mostar, Međugorje and Sarajevo in Bosnia-Hercegovina, and Belgrade in Serbia. There are two daily **trains** to Zagreb, calling at Knin and Karlovac on the way.

Split is the Dalmatian coast's main Jadrolinija terminal, with regular **local ferries** to the islands of Brač, Vis, Lastovo, Hvar and Korčula; it's also a major stop on the summer **coastal ferry** service, which connects Split with Rijeka, Rab, Zadar and Dubrovnik. In summer, the coastal ferry carries on to Bari in Italy (1 or 2 weekly) and Igoumenitsa in Greece (1 weekly), while from June to September there are ferries roughly every day to Ancona in Italy. For the main coastal ferry, pre-booking is recommended. Tickets and reservations for all the above ferry services can be made through Jadrolinija, which runs a couple of ticket kiosks along Obala kneza Domagoja, and a larger sales counter in the main passenger terminal at the end of Obala kneza Domagoja (Ⓣ021/355-399, Ⓦwww.jadrolinija.hr). An alternative Ancona service is run by Adriatica Navigazione: reservations are handled by Jadroagent (Ⓣ021/338-335, Ⓦwww.jadroagent.com) in the main passenger terminal.

In addition, Split Tours runs daily **hydrofoils** (slightly faster than regular ferries) to Brač, Hvar, Korčula, Šolta and Vis (mid-May to mid-Sept), and the Italian port of Ancona (Jan to late Oct); tickets can be bought from the Split Tours counter in the main ferry terminal (Ⓣ021/338-219, Ⓦwww.splittours.hr); or from their office at Obala Lazareta 3 (Ⓣ021/346-100).

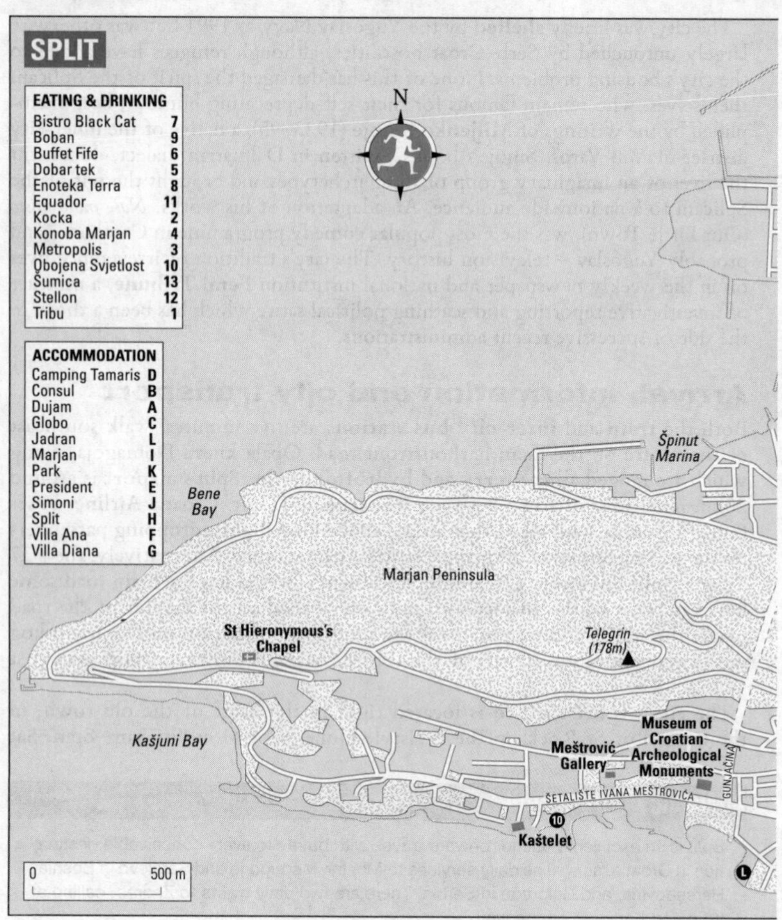

8am–7pm; Sun 9am–1pm; Oct–May Mon–Fri 9am–5pm; ⓣ021/345-606, ⓦwww.visitsplit.com). The staff can provide a free map and a list of museums and their opening times, as well as giving out general advice. However, the privately run **Turist Biro** on the Riva (see "Accommodation" opposite) is usually much better informed about accommodation options in the city.

As for **city transport**, it's generally easiest to walk, though for journeys out to the Marjan peninsula and some of Split's museums you may need to take one of the city's **buses**. These are frequent and operate between 5am and midnight; tickets can be bought from the driver or conductor (9Kn) or from newspaper and tobacco kiosks (9Kn, valid for two journeys) and should be punched when you board. Tickets for Kaštela and Trogir are priced according to a zonal system – most of Kaštela is in zone 3 (15.50Kn one-way from the conductor or 22.50Kn return from a kiosk); Trogir is in zone 4 (18.50Kn one-way from the conductor or 29Kn return from a kiosk). The principal nodal points for the municipal bus network are Trg republike, at the western end of the Riva (for the Marjan

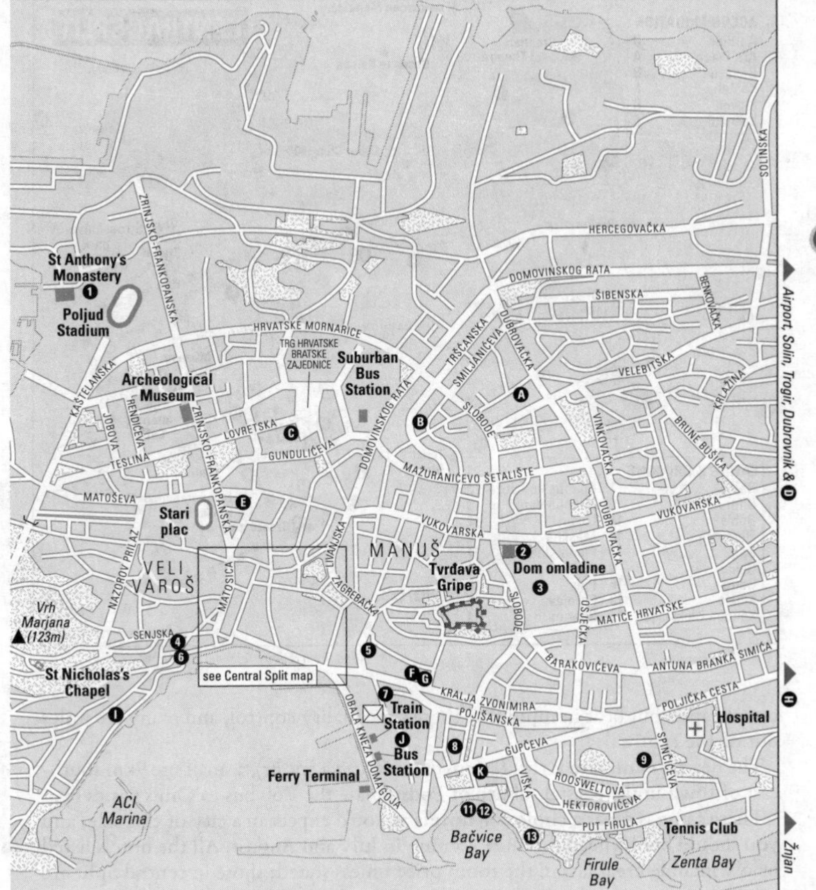

peninsula and Solin/Salona); Zagrebačka, opposite the market on the eastern side of the old town; and the suburban bus station on Domovinskog rata (for Kaštela and Trogir). There are **taxi** ranks outside the train and bus stations, and at both the eastern and western ends of the Riva.

Accommodation

There are plenty of private **rooms** (❶–❷) in Split, and it's easy to find one even in high season providing that you arrive early in the day – contact the Turist Biro on the waterfront at Riva 12 (Mon–Fri 8am–8pm, Sat 8am–7pm, Sun 9am–1pm; Ⓣ & Ⓕ021/342-544 or 342-142, Ⓔturist-biro-split@st.htnet.hr). There are very few rooms in the old town, though the nearby residential districts of Manuš and Veli Varoš can be equally atmospheric. Single travellers usually have to pay for a double room, or be prepared to team up with a stranger. The unregistered rooms offered by touts at the bus station may work

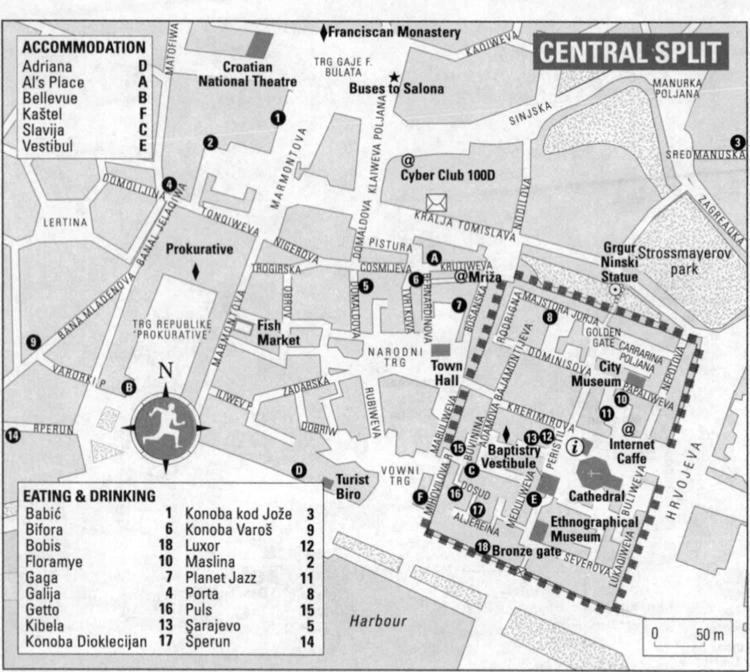

out cheaper, but bear in mind that there's no quality control, and many are miles out of the centre.

The nearest **campsite** is the *Tamaris* (Ⓔ nmaric@acmt.hr), a small site 9km south-east of town in the coastal suburb of Podstrana – the #60 bus to Omiš passes by.

There's not as great a choice of **hotels** as you'd expect in a city of this size, and you should book ahead if you're coming in July and August. All the hotels listed below include breakfast in the room price unless stated; those in central Split are marked on the map above.

Hostel

Al's Place Kružićeva 10. Old-town hostel run by an expat Brit who's a mine of local information. Located in an old stone house on two floors, each with a six-bed dorm and a communal shower/WC. There are also tea and coffee-making facilities and a shared fridge. There's an Internet terminal (10Kn/30min) and you can get your washing done for an extra 30Kn. Fills up quickly in summer, but Al will do his best to find you a place somewhere. Open April–Oct. Beds 120Kn.

Hotels

In and around the old town

Adriana Riva 8 Ⓣ021/340-000, Ⓦwww.hotel-adriana.hr. Superbly situated small hotel offering modern doubles and swanky apartments, located above the seafront café-pizzeria of the same name. Complete with deep carpets, minibars and a/c, the rooms are plush enough to satisfy both comfort-conscious tourists and business travellers – but demand is high, so book early. ❻

Bellevue Bana Jelačića 2 Ⓣ021/345-644 or 347-499, Ⓕ362-383, Ⓦwww.hotel-bellevue-split.hr. A once-elegant nineteenth-century pile superbly situated at the western end of the Riva. Rooms come with TV and WC/shower, but are dowdily furnished – those overlooking the flagstoned expanse of Trg republike have a certain charm; others can be gloomy and depressing. ❺

Kaštel Mihovilova širina 5 Ⓣ091 120 0348 & 091 574 2267, Ⓦwww.kastelsplit.com. Historic stone building in a bustling location inside the palace walls, offering a mixture of doubles, triples and apartments. Rooms come with lam floors, peachy-coloured decor, and smallish wc/shower. No breakfast. ❹

Slavija Buvinina 3 ⓣ021/323-840, ⓦwww.hotelslavija.com. Fully renovated old town hotel featuring smallish, comfortable doubles (plus some triples and quads) with modern furnishings, en-suite shower, a/c and TV. Rooms on the fourth floor have fantastic roof-level views from their terraces. Some rooms are subject to noise from nearby cafés, but providing you stay out until closing time this is unlikely to be a problem. ❺

Vestibul Iza vestibula 4 ⓣ021/329-329, ⓦwww.vestibulpalace.com. Swanky designer hotel occupying a Renaissance town house in an atmospheric old-town location. Rooms are modest in size, but feature exposed brickwork, matt-black textiles, moody lighting and modern bathrooms. You can take breakfast in a plant-filled atrium, or outside in a courtyard where the central hall of Diocletian's palace once stood. ❼

Outside the old town

Consul Trščanska 34 ⓣ021/340-130, ⓦwww.hotel-consul.net. Mid-sized place in a quiet residential street 1.5km northeast of the old town, close to the suburban bus station. Rooms in muted greens come with shower, TV and a/c. Nothing special, but worth bearing in mind if more centrally located hotels are full. ❻

Dujam Velebitska 27 ⓣ021/538-025, ⓦwww.hoteldujam.com. Simple, cheery two-star located 2km northeast of the old town in a converted former student hall of residence. Rooms are small and minimally furnished but come with en-suite shower and TV. A 30 min walk from the centre or bus #9 from Lazareti. ❺

Globo Lovretska 18 ⓣ021/481-111, ⓦwww.hotelglobo.com. Smart, comfortable four-star offering plush en suites in tasteful greens and yellows. Only a 10min walk from the old town, but uninspiringly situated amid greying office blocks and half-abandoned pedestrian zones. ❻

Jadran Sustjepanski put 23 ⓣ021/398-622, ⓦwww.hoteljadran.com. Smallish hotel, a 15min walk southwest of the old town, with smart rooms, all with TV. ❺

Marjan Obala kneza Branimira 8 ⓣ021/399-211, ⓦwww.hotel-marjan.com. Dowdy 1960s high-rise which is much nicer inside than out. Functional but comfortable rooms with TV, bath and balcony, some with views back towards the old town (a 5–10min walk away). ❻

Park Hatzeov perivoj 3 ⓣ021/406-400, ⓕ406-401. Recently renovated hotel 500m southeast of the centre, directly above Bačvice beach. Smart rooms and chic reception areas give the place a somewhat more exclusive air than the rest. Formerly known as the *Imperial*, it was Split's top hotel in the 1920s and 30s, and the place where Italian forces formally surrendered Split to the Partisans in 1943. The refined hotel restaurant serves quality international food. ❼

President Starčevića 1 ⓣ021/305-222, ⓦwww.hotelpresident.hr. Newish four-star located five minutes' walk north of the old town, offering plush rooms decked out in warm colours, each with a/c, minibar and shower. Regular doubles are on the small side and only have showers – so if you want to swing a cat and then relax in the tub, you'll have to shell out on a "superior" room. ❻

Simoni Na toć 4 ⓣ021/488-479, ⓦwww.sobesimoni.com. Family-run, seven-room guesthouse with cramped but clean doubles, each with tiny wc/shower. Can get stuffy in high summer, but superbly situated on the far side of the railway station from the centre. No breakfast. ❷

Split Put Trstenika 19 ⓣ021/303-111, ⓦwww.hotelsplit.hr. Concrete three-star 3km east of the centre, on a bluff overlooking the shore. Rooms come with TV, minibar, bath and disconcertingly bright blue-and-white 1980s decor. All have small balconies, some looking across the water to the island of Brač, and there's a small open-air pool. Bus #17, or a 30min walk along the coastal path. ❻

Villa Ana Vrh Lučac 16 ⓣ021/482-715, ⓦwww.villaana-split.hr. Refurbished stone house in the atmospheric Radunica district, just east of the old town and ideally situated for the port and stations. Rooms are bright, spacious, pine-floored affairs with en-suite shower, TV and minibar – but there are only five of them, so ring in advance. ❺

Villa Diana Kuzmanića 3 ⓣ021/482-451, ⓦwww.villadiana.hr. Virtually next-door to the *Villa Ana* and occupying a similarly tastefully restored old house, the *Villa Diana* offers small but neat doubles with parquet floors, exposed stonework, warm colours and flat-screen TVs. Only four doubles and one three-person apartment, so book ahead. ❺

The City

Split may be the largest town in Dalmatia, but nearly everything worth seeing is concentrated in the compact **old town** behind the waterfront Riva, made up in part of the various remains and conversions of Diocletian's Palace itself, and the medieval additions to the west of it. You can walk across this area in about ten minutes, although it would take a lifetime to explore all its nooks and crannies. On either side the old town fades into low-rise suburbs of utilitarian stone houses grouped tightly around narrow alleys – **Veli Varoš**, west of the old town, and **Manuš**, to the east, are the most unspoiled – and, although there are no specific sights, worth a brief wander. West of the city centre, the wooded **Marjan peninsula** commands fine views over the coast and islands from its heights. The best of the beaches are on the north side of Marjan, or east of the ferry dock at **Bačvice**.

The palace

Despite its importance, don't expect **Diocletian's Palace** to be an archeological "site": the shape and style of the palace have to be extrapolated from what remains, which itself is obscured by centuries of addition and alteration – the map opposite gives an idea of the palace's original ground plan, but doesn't show contemporary features. The palace occupies the eastern half of the old town, though apart from certain set-piece buildings – notably the cathedral (originally Diocletian's mausoleum) and the baptistry (once a temple) – it has been built upon so much by successive generations that it is no longer recognizable as an ancient Roman structure. Little remains of the imperial apartments, although the medieval tenements, shops and offices which have taken their place were built in large part using stones and columns salvaged from Diocletian's original buildings. Despite its architectural pedigree, the palace area hasn't always been the most desirable part of the city in which to live. During the inter-war period it was dubbed the *get* ("ghetto") and – abandoned to the urban poor, down-at-heel White Russian émigrés and red-light bars – became synonymous with loose morals and shady dealings. Nowadays the palace area is once more the centre of urban life, hosting a daily melee of tourists and shoppers.

Robert Adam and Diocletian's Palace

Our knowledge of Diocletian's Palace owes much to the eighteenth-century Scottish architect **Robert Adam**, who set out to provide a visual record of what remained of the palace, believing that contemporary European builders had much to learn from Roman construction techniques. Adam arrived in Split in 1757 with a team of draughtsmen; they spent five weeks in the city despite the hostility of the Venetian governor, who almost had them arrested as spies. This didn't prevent Adam from enjoying the trip: "the people are vastly polite, everything vastly cheap; a most wholesome air and glorious situation" was how he summed the town up. The resulting book of engravings of the palace caused a sensation, offering inspiration to Neoclassical architects all over Britain and Europe. Mindful of Adam's success, Austrian Emperor Josef II commissioned Frenchman **L.F. Cassas** to supply a wider-ranging set of engravings of Dalmatia's ancient buildings, which was also published to great acclaim. A sign that attitudes towards Dalmatia were beginning to be coloured by imperial rivalries in the region came in the French edition of Cassas's book, the accompanying text accusing Adam of having travelled "like an Englishman, that is to say with that national egoism which counts England for everything and the rest of the world for nothing". "When the English travel", it went on, "the desire to appropriate precedes the desire to instruct." Whatever its original motive, Adam's work was seminal in the development of the Georgian style in England, and large chunks of London, Bath and Bristol may be claimed to owe something of their space, symmetry and grace to Diocletian's buildings in Split.

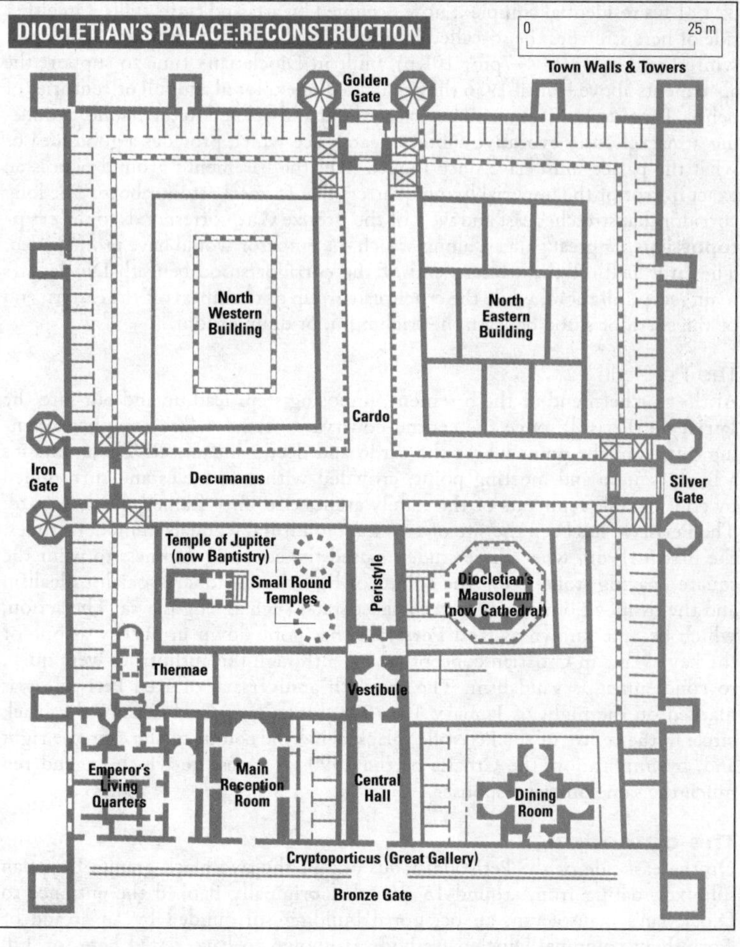

The best place to start exploring is on the seaward side, at Split's broad and lively waterfront, the **Riva** (officially the Obala hrvatskog naradnog preporoda, or Quay of the Croatian National Revival, although hardly anyone ever calls it that). Running along the palace's southern facade, into which shops, cafés and a warren of tiny flats have been built, the Riva is where a large part of the city's population congregates day and night to meet friends, catch up on gossip or idle away an hour or two in a café. It's also the obvious venue for mass gatherings and celebrations, most notably on July 10, 2001, when tens of thousands flocked here to welcome home native Splićanin and Wimbledon tennis champion **Goran Ivanišević**.

The main approach to the palace from the Riva is through the **Bronze Gate** (Mjedena vrata), an anonymous and functional gateway that originally gave access to the sea, which once came right up to the palace. Inside is a vaulted space which once formed the basement of Diocletian's central hall, the middle part of his residential complex, now occupied by arts and crafts stalls. On either side of here stretches the so-called **basement** (*podrum*; daily: summer 8am–8pm; winter 8am–noon & 4–7pm; 10Kn), built in Diocletian's time to support the apartments above – until 1956 they remained unexplored and full of centuries of debris. Large tracts have now been cleared out and opened to the public, producing a marvellously evocative subterranean space which provides a good idea of what the palace must have once looked like; the basement's ground plan is an exact mirror of the imperial living quarters that formerly stood above. The long corridor that stretches east and west of the Bronze Gate corresponds to the **cryptoporticus**, or great gallery, along which the emperor would have promenaded. The large hall off the western end of the corridor stood beneath Diocletian's main reception room, while the cruciform group of chambers off the eastern end of the corridor stood beneath the triclinium, or dining room.

The Peristyle

At the northern end of the basement, imposing steps lead up and out into the **Peristyle** (Peristil), once the central courtyard of the palace complex, opening out from the point where the cardo and decumanus meet. These days it's a lively square and meeting point, crowded with café tables and surrounded by considerable remnants of the stately arches that once framed the courtyard. The Peristyle has been the site of two major cultural scandals in modern times, the first in 1968, when three students used the cover of darkness to paint the square's paving stones red – the colour of both revolutionary socialist idealism and the ossified political elites in socialist states such as Yugoslavia. The action, which became known as **Red Peristyle**, has gone down in history as one of the key events in Croatian conceptual art, although the authorities were quick to condemn it as vandalism. The thirtieth anniversary of Red Peristyle was marked on the night of January 10, 1998, when Igor Grubić painted a black circle in the centre of the Peristyle (black being the colour of the extreme right and, by implication, the Croatia of the 1990s) – a gesture which engendered much the same official response.

The cathedral

On the east side of the Peristyle stands one of the two black granite Egyptian sphinxes, dating from around 15 BC, that originally flanked the entrance to Diocletian's mausoleum, an octagonal building surrounded by an arcade of Corinthian columns. Diocletian's body is known to have rested here for 170 years until it mysteriously disappeared – no one knows where. The building was later converted into the **Cathedral of St Domnius** (Katedrala svetog Dujma; Mon–Sat 7am–noon & 5–7pm; 10Kn) and a choir added.

The cathedral porch is entered through an arch guarded by two Romanesque lions with a motley collection of human figures riding on their backs, including Greek-born Maria Lascaris, wife of Hungarian King Bela IV, who briefly took refuge from the Tatars in the nearby stronghold of Klis. The walnut and oak main **doors** – carved in 1214 by local artist Andrija Buvina with an inspired comic-strip-style sequence showing 28 scenes from the life of Christ – are scuffed and scraped at the bottom, but in fine condition further up. On the right looms the six-storey **campanile** (same times as cathedral; 5Kn), begun in the thirteenth century but not finished until 1908 – the climb up is worth the effort for the panoramic view over the city and beyond.

Inside, the **dome** is ringed by two levels of Corinthian columns dating from the first century BC, while a frieze depicting racing chariots, hunting scenes and, in one corner, portraits of Diocletian and his wife Priscia, runs around the base. The rest of the constricted interior is stuffed with miscellaneous artworks. Immediately to the left of the entrance, the **pulpit** is a beautifully proportioned example of Romanesque art, sitting on capitals tangled with foliage, snakes and strange beasts. As you move clockwise round the church, the next feature you come to is the **Altar of St Domnius**, honouring the first bishop of Salona's underground Christian community, who was beheaded in 304. Built by Giovanni Morlaiter in 1767, the altar features a pair of angels holding a reliquary on which a group of celestial cherubs cavort – a symbol of man's journey to the afterlife.

Farther around lies the church's finest feature, the **Altar of St Anastasius** (Staš), which preserves the bones of a Christian contemporary of Domnius who, on Diocletian's orders, was thrown in a river with a stone tied to him. Sheltering under an extravagant canopy, the saint's sarcophagus bears Juraj Dalmatinac's cruelly realistic relief, the *Flagellation of Christ* of 1448, showing Jesus pawed and brutalized by some peculiarly oafish persecutors, while just above is a figure of St Anastasius with a millstone round his neck. The Baroque **high altar**, occupying the arch which leads through to the choir, features a pair of delicate, gilded angels supporting what looks like a cherub-encrusted carriage clock bearing paintings on each of its faces; an ornate coffered ceiling with ten paintings on Old Testament themes by Matej Ponzoni-Pončun fills the arch above. Farther around is Bonino of Milan's fifteenth-century **Altar of St Domnius**, where the saint's bones were once kept. Sheltered beneath a flowery Gothic ciborium, this uses an ancient Roman sarcophagus bearing a relief of a man with hunting dogs as a base, on which rests a larger sarcophagus etched with a reclining figure of the bishop.

Behind the high altar, the **choir** was tacked onto the mausoleum in the seventeenth century, and still feels a very different part of the church. It's worth peering closely at the latticed choir stalls, which include some particularly delicate wood-carving – the oldest in Dalmatia, dated to about 1200. To the right, a flight of steps leads up to the **treasury** (*riznica*; 10kn), which holds a melange of chalices, handwritten missals, thirteenth-century Madonnas and reliquary busts of the city's three great martyrs – Domnius, Anastasius and Arnerius (Arnir), a bishop of Split who was stoned to death in 1180.

Leaving the cathedral and heading round the side brings you to the entrance to the early medieval **crypt** (*kripta*; same times as cathedral; 5kn), where a tomb-like passageway emerges into a circular, domed space surrounded by pointy-arched niches. There are no exhibits down here, but the architectural simplicity of the place exerts a wonderful chill-out effect.

The baptistry

Opposite the cathedral, a narrow alley runs from a gap in the arched arcade down to the attractive **baptistry** (*krstionica*; same times as cathedral; 5Kn), a temple built in Diocletian's time and variously attributed to the cults of Janus or Jupiter, with an elaborate coffered ceiling and well-preserved figures of Hercules and Apollo on the eastern portal. Later Christian additions include a skinny statue of John the Baptist by Meštrović (a late work of 1954) and, more famously, an eleventh-century baptismal font with a relief showing a Croatian ruler receiving homage from a man prostrate at his feet – most probably a priest being ritually inducted into the service of both God and king. Above the two figures runs a swirling pleated pattern known as *plutej*, a design typical of the Croatian Romanesque which has subsequently been adopted as a national symbol – you'll also see it around the bands of policemen's caps.

The vestibule and beyond

At the southern end of the Peristyle, steps lead up to a cone-shaped, roofless chamber which once served as the palace **vestibule**, in which visitors would wait before being summoned into the presence of the ex-emperor. On the far side of the vestibule, a venerable stone house on Severova accommodates Split's **Ethnographic Museum** (Mon–Fri 9am–9pm, Sat 9am–1pm; 10Kn), where a suite of superbly restored medieval rooms provide the perfect background to a display of Dalmatian folk costumes.

Beyond here, the area once occupied by Diocletian's private apartments is nowadays one of the poorest parts of the city, where medieval tenement buildings brush up against the sea-facing walls of the palace. The sequence of interlocking small squares have a desolate, half-forgotten air which seems miles away from the tourist-tramped areas nearby. The area used to be the favoured meeting-place of Split's prostitutes and drug addicts, and is still fondly referred to by locals as the *kenjara* ("shit-hole"). At the south end of this area, along Severova, windows in the palace wall provide an excellent vantage point from which to spy on goings-on down on the Riva while, to the west, Alješijeva threads its way through one of the most abandoned and mysterious parts of the palace, eventually bringing you out at Mihovilova širina (see opposite).

North of the Peristyle

North of the Peristyle, Dioklecijanova follows the line of the former *cardo* past rows of tottering medieval houses. A right turn down Papalićeva leads to the Juraj Dalmatinac-designed **Papalić Palace**, a typical example of the sturdy Gothic town houses built by Split's fifteenth-century aristocracy. An unobtrusive gateway leads through to a secluded, ivy-covered courtyard centred on a well adorned with the star and feathers symbol of the Papalić family, with a delicate loggia at ground level and an outdoor stone stairway leading to the first-floor apartments. It now houses the **City Museum** (Gradski muzej; Tues–Fri 9am–9pm, Sat & Sun 9am–4pm; 10Kn), with well-laid-out displays of medieval weaponry, figureheads from eighteenth-century galleys and sculptural fragments – including a serene Pietà by Nikola Fiorentinac. A first-floor reception room with a restored wooden-beam ceiling contains pictures and manuscripts relating to Marko Marulić (1450–1524), frequent guest of the Papalić family and author of the biblically inspired epic *Judita*, one of the first poems to be written in the Croatian language.

Continuing north along Dioklecijanova soon brings you to the grandest and best preserved of the palace gates, the **Golden Gate** (Zlatna vrata). This was the landward – and therefore most important – entrance to the palace, and the beginning of the main road to Salona. The arched niches (now empty) originally contained statues, and the four plinths on top of the gate once supported likenesses of Diocletian and the three other tetrarchs.

Just outside the gate there's another Meštrović work, the gigantic statue of the tenth-century Bishop **Grgur Ninski**. It was completed in 1929 to mark the 1000th anniversary of the Synod of Split, at which Grgur, Bishop of Nin, fought for the right of his people to use their own language in the liturgy instead of Latin. Catching the bishop in stiff mid-gesture, it's more successful as a patriotic statement than as a piece of sculpture. This bronze mammoth used to stand in the Peristyle before it was moved during World War II, when the Italian occupiers attempted to cleanse the town centre of anything resembling a Croatian national symbol.

Narodni trg to Marmontova

Returning to the Peristyle and heading west along the ancient *decumanus*, now Krešimirova – a shop-lined alley which, despite its narrowness, is the old town's main thoroughfare – takes you out through the Iron Gate (Željezna vrata) into **Narodni trg** ("People's Square", usually known as "Pjaca", the local version of the Italian word *piazza*). This replaced the Peristyle as the city's main square in the fourteenth century, and is overlooked to the east by a Romanesque clock tower with the remains of a medieval sundial, behind which looms a taller, older belfry. The north side of the square is dominated by the fifteenth-century **Town Hall** (Gradska vijećnica), with a ground-floor loggia of three large pointed arches supported by stumpy pillars – it frequently plays host to major art or history exhibitions in the summer.

West of the square lie the bustling narrow streets and passages of the medieval town. To the south, Marulićeva leads down towards **Mihovilova širina**, a small square whose café-bars get packed on warm summer evenings, and the adjoining Trg braće Radića, more popularly known as **Voćni trg** (Fruit Square) because of the market that used to be held here. There's a large statue of Marko Marulić, supplied by the industrious Meštrović, in the middle, and an octagonal tower that once formed part of the fifteenth-century Venetian castle, or *kaštel* – most of which has now either disappeared or been incorporated into residential buildings. A passageway to the left of the tower brings you back out onto the Riva.

Amble west along the Riva to reach the foot of **Marmontova** – the pedestrianized thoroughfare which marks the western boundary of the medieval town. Near the southern end of Marmontova is **Trg republike**, an elongated square set back from the water and surrounded on three sides by the grandiose neo-Renaissance city council buildings known as the **Prokurative** – it's put to good use as a venue for outdoor concerts in summer. From here, Marmontova heads north, passing the animated **fish market** on Kraj svete Marije – the scene of shopping frenzy most mornings, especially Fridays – and a few remaining bastions of the star-shaped seventeenth-century fortifications which once surrounded the town, before arriving at Trg Gaje Bulata. This broad open space is overlooked by the **Croatian National Theatre** (Hrvatsko narodno kazalište, or HNK), a plain brown construction much rebuilt after a fire in 1971 and unadorned save for a group of statues on the third floor representing the arts.

On the northern side of the square, the church of the **Franciscan monastery** (Franjevački samostan) is worth a peek for the large fresco behind the high altar, a flamboyantly expressionistic work by contemporary Dubrovnik artist Ivan Dulčić. A central figure of Jesus hovers above the Adriatic coastline, offering salvation to the matchstick forms below, most of which are dressed in colourful Dalmatian costumes. On his left are Cyril and Methodius, inventors of Glagolitic, the script used by the medieval Croatian church, while floating in the sky are a bull, lion and eagle – symbolizing SS Luke, Mark and John the Evangelist respectively.

North of the old town

Immediately to the west of the theatre is another modern square, Ujevićeva poljana, from which Zrinsko-Frankopanska spears north towards the city's modern residential districts. Appearing almost immediately on your left is the **Stari plac**, a scruffy sports ground that was home to football team Hajduk Split until 1979, when they moved to a brand new stadium up the road (see p.367). Despite its nondescript appearance, the Stari plac has an almost religious significance to locals, and many of the cafés around the ground retain a strong sporting theme, their walls covered with Hajduk memorabilia and TVs permanently tuned to sporting channels. The Stari plac now serves as the ground of Split rugby club – it's only in Split and nearby Makarska that the sport seems to be played with any seriousness in Croatia.

The Archeological Museum

Continue up Frankopanska for ten minutes to reach the **Archeological Museum** at no. 25 (Arheološki muzej; Tues–Fri 9am–1pm & 5–8pm, Sat & Sun 9am–1pm; 10Kn), with a stylish display of Illyrian, Greek, medieval and – particularly – Roman artefacts, mostly plucked from the rich excavation sites at nearby Salona. Exhibits include delicate votive figurines, amulets and – in a section entitled "domestic life" – an oil lamp embellished with a tiny peep-show of lewd love-making. Outside, the arcaded courtyard is crammed with a wonderful array

△ Roman sarcophagus

of Greek, Roman and early Christian stelae, sarcophagi and decorative sculpture. There are three key exhibits. Two of these, to the left of the entrance, are **Salonan sarcophagi** from the third century AD: one depicts the Hippolytus and Phaedra legend and is in superb condition – the marble still glistens – while the other is of a Calydonian boar hunt, which in Robert Adam's pictures stood outside Split's baptistry. The third, a sarcophagus away to the right of the entrance, is much later, dating from the fourth century. Known as the **"Good Shepherd"**, it has been the subject of much speculation on account of its mixing up of the Christian motif of the shepherd with pagan symbols of Eros and Hades on its end panels.

Poljud Stadium and St Anthony's Monastery

Carry on up the road for another five minutes and you'll catch sight of the **Poljud Stadium** over the brow of the hill. Built for the 1979 Mediterranean

Hajduk Split

Few football teams are as closely associated with their home city as **Hajduk Split**. Formed in February 1911 by Croatian students returning from Prague – who had witnessed the fervour created by Czech teams Sparta and Slavia – the club is named after the Robin Hood-like brigands who opposed both Ottoman and Venetian authority from the Middle Ages onwards. Hajduk was an explicitly Croatian team at a time when Split was still part of the Austro-Hungarian Empire and, later, towards the end of World War II, the entire squad was shipped to Italy by the Partisans in order to play demonstration matches as an explicitly anti-fascist team. They were also the first team in Yugoslavia to play with a *petokraka* (Communist five-pointed star) on their jerseys, and the first team to remove it when it became clear that Yugoslavia's days were numbered.

A large part of the Hajduk mystique comes from their success on the pitch: they were Yugoslav champions twice in the 1920s, three times in the 1950s, four times in the 1970s, and went on to become champions of Croatia in 1992, 1994 and 1995. They're also famous for their loyal fans, known as the **torcida** (after the Brazilian fans that Hajduk supporters had seen footage of during the 1950 World Cup). Split's version of the *torcida* launched itself in October 1950, providing the team with maximum, Rio-style support for the title-decider against Red Star Belgrade – the first time that torches, banners and massed chanting had been seen on the terraces in this part of Europe. Hajduk won the match, but football purists were shocked by the levels of popular frenzy displayed. The Yugoslav regime, which had since 1945 condescendingly regarded Hajduk as "their" club, was horrified by the idea that football supporters could organize themselves without the leadership of the Party. *Torcida* founder Vjenceslav Žuvela was given a three-year prison sentence and the captain of the team was expelled from the Communist Party. Today, Hajduk and the *torcida* remain an unavoidable part of the urban landscape, and victories over traditional enemies like Dinamo Zagreb are still celebrated with city-wide rejoicing. Some would argue that the team has become all-important to the local population as other symbols of Dalmatian identity are gradually eroded and the act of supporting Hajduk becomes one of the few communal experiences left.

Tickets for matches (20–50Kn) are sold from kiosks at the southern end of the ground. Most of the *torcida* congregate in the northern stand (*tribina sjever*), while the poshest seats are in the west stand (*tribina zapad*). Beer and popcorn are available inside, and there are numerous snack bars offering drinks and grills immediately outside. Remember to bring a sheet of newspaper to sit on: the seats are filthy. Neither the official club website (Ⓦwww.hnkhajduk.com), nor the *torcida* site (Ⓦwww.torcida.org) are likely to have much information in English.

Games and now home to Hajduk Split football team (see box, p.367), it's a strikingly organic structure, the curving roofs of its stands suggesting the sides of a fishing boat's hull or a gargantuan seashell.

Tucked away on the seaward side of the stadium, the cloister of **St Anthony's Monastery** (Samostan svetog Ante) boasts a handsome collection of medieval tombstones – most notably that of fifteenth-century Archbishop of Split Thomas Niger, pictured here with an alarmingly squid-like face that has to be seen to be believed.

The Marjan peninsula

Criss-crossed by footpaths and minor roads, the wooded heights of the **Marjan peninsula** offer the easiest escape from the bustle of central Split. From the old town it's an easy ten-minute walk up Senjska, which ascends westwards through the district of Veli Varoš, arriving after about ten minutes at the *Vidilica* **café** on Marjan's eastern shoulder. There's a small Jewish graveyard round the back of the café, and a terrace out front offering fantastic views of Split, the offshore islands and the mainland mountain chains to the south and east – in summer, arrive here at about 6pm to see the whole landscape bathed in evening sunshine. To the right of the café a stepped path climbs towards **Vrh Marjana**, where there's a wider view of the coast and islands, although there's an even better panorama from the peninsula's highest point, 175-metre-high **Telegrin**, about 1km farther west.

Keeping to the left of the *Vidilica* brings you to a path which heads round the south side of the hill, arriving after about five minutes at the thirteenth-century **St Nicholas's Chapel** (Sveti Nikola), a simple structure with a sloping belfry tacked on to one side like a buttress. From here, the path continues for 2km, with wooded hillside to the right and the seaside suburbs of Marjan's south coast on the left, before arriving at **St Hieronymous's Chapel** (Sveti Jere), a simple shed-like structure pressed hard against a cliff – medieval hermits used to live in the caves which are still visible in the rock above. From here you can descend towards the road which leads round the base of the peninsula, or cross its rocky spine to reach Marjan's fragrant, pine-covered northern side. Paths emerge at sea level near **Bene** bay, where you'll find a combination of rocky and concreted bathing areas and a couple of cafés. You can also get to Bene by taking bus #12 from Trg republike (every 30min).

The Museum of Croatian Archeological Monuments

Marjan's main cultural attractions are on its southern side, in the suburbs of Zvončac and Meje, about twenty minutes' walk from the centre or a short ride on bus #12 from Trg republike. Heading west along Šetalište Ivana Meštrovića brings you first to the **Museum of Croatian Archeological Monuments** (Muzej hrvatskih arheoloških spomenika; Mon–Fri 9.30am–4pm, Sat 9.30am–1pm; 20Kn), housed in an oversized concrete edifice with huge open-plan halls and piped-in organ muzak. The museum makes a concerted attempt to remind people of Split's medieval Croatian heritage, a phase of local history that's often forgotten in the enthusiasm for all things connected with Diocletian. Displays include a motley collection of jewellery, weapons and fragmentary reconstructions of chancel screens and ciboria (the canopies built over a church's main altar) from ninth- and tenth-century Croatian churches.

The Meštrović Gallery and the Kaštelet

A couple of minutes farther along Šetalište Ivana Meštrovića at no. 39, the **Ivan Meštrović Gallery** (Galerija Ivana Meštrovića; Tues–Sat 9am–9pm; Sun noon–9pm; 20Kn) is housed in the ostentatiously palatial building that the country's

Ivan Meštrović (1883–1962)

Ivan Meštrović was born in Slavonia to a family of itinerant agricultural labourers, but his parents soon moved back to their native Dalmatia, settling in Otavice near Drniš. Meštrović was too busy tending sheep on Mount Svilaja to attend school, and had to teach himself to read and write. At the age of 16 he displayed some drawings in a local inn, prompting locals – including the mayor of Drniš – to apply to art schools on his behalf. He was turned down, but managed to land a job with a Split stonemason, thus beginning his training as a sculptor.

Awarded a place at the **Viennese Acadamy** in 1901 (quite a feat considering his background), he was soon exhibiting with the Art Nouveau-influenced Secession group. At the age of 22, Meštrović was already receiving big public commissions – like the Secession-influenced *Well of Life* (1905) which still stands outside the Croatian National Theatre in Zagreb. By the time he moved to Paris in 1907 a distinctive Meštrović style was beginning to emerge, blending the earthy Romanticism of Rodin with the grace of Classical sculpture and the folk motifs of southeastern Europe. This **eclecticism** may help explain why Meštrović – considered too daring by traditionalists but not daring enough by the moderns – never enjoyed the reputation abroad which he did at home. Like many men of his generation, Meštrović was convinced that the Austro-Hungarian state could not survive, and that the expanding Kingdom of Serbia would provide the basis of a future Yugoslav state in which all South Slavs could live as equals – he had grown up in an area of mixed Serb–Croat settlement and was familiar with the folk culture of both communities. When the Austrian government invited Meštrović to represent them at the Rome International Exhibition of 1911, he chose to exhibit in the Serbian pavilion instead (of the 23 artists in the Serbian pavilion, incidentally, 14 were Croat). On the outbreak of World War I Meštrović moved to Italy, until Italian designs on Dalmatia led to him moving to London, where his involvement with the Yugoslavist cause helped land him a one-man show at the Victoria and Albert Museum in 1915. The exhibition was an enormous success – Britain and Serbia were allies at the time, and attendance at the show was seen as a sign of support for the war effort. In 1918 Meštrović hailed the creation of Yugoslavia as the "greatest accomplishment that our people have hitherto performed", although his enthusiasm would subsequently wane. He was made Rector of the Academy of Fine Arts in Zagreb in 1923, and was in constant demand as an artist over the next two decades, working on monumental public projects such as the *Grgur Ninski* sculpture in Split (1928) and two vast, muscular Indians on horseback for Grant Park in Chicago (1928). His **architectural work** was in many ways more innovative than his sculptural, developing a cool, sepulchral style which found expression in the Račić mausoleum in Cavtat (1923), the Meštrović family mausoleum in Otavice (1927–31) and the Art Pavilion in Zagreb (1939).

In 1941, Meštrović was **imprisoned** by the Ustaše because of his history of pro-Yugoslav activity, but after four months Ante Pavelić summoned the sculptor to his office, apologized and told him he was free to emigrate. Meštrović eventually made his way to America, where he became Professor of Sculpture at the University of Notre Dame, Indiana. Much of his **later work** was religious, although he'd been tackling sacred subjects on and off ever since 1916, when the cycle of reliefs displayed in Split's Kaštelet was begun.

most famous modern sculptor (see box above) planned as his home and studio. Fronted by a veranda supported by Ionic columns, the house was completed in 1939 – Meštrović lived in it for just two years before fleeing to Zagreb to escape the Italian occupation in 1941.

Even if you're not mad about Meštrović, this is still an impressive collection, although the emphasis is on smooth female nudes and tender Madonnas rather than the ideological and historical subjects with which he made his reputation. Some of the religious pieces have considerable emotional depth (look out for a particularly tortured Job from 1946), although his other work can sometimes appear facile – such as the slightly daft *Joyful Youth* or the giant and ungainly *Adam and Eve*. Portraits of members of his immediate family in the ground-floor drawing room are refreshingly direct, especially the honest and sensitive *My Mother* from 1909.

Meštrović's best work can be seen in the so-called **Kaštelet** ("little castle"; in theory Tues–Sun 10am–5pm, but check at the Meštrović Gallery first; admission with gallery ticket) about 200m further up the road. Built in the sixteenth century as the fortified residence of the Capogrosso family, but long used for other purposes (it was at various times a tannery and a hospital), the Kaštelet was virtually a ruin when Meštrović bought it in 1939 to house his **Life of Christ** cycle, a series of reliefs in wood that he'd been working on since 1916. Presided over by a mannered but moving *Crucifixion*, the cycle spreads like a frieze across all four walls of the church, borrowing stylistically from Assyrian bas-reliefs, Egyptian tomb paintings and Archaic Greek art. The result is an immensely powerful piece of religious sculpture, with rows of rigidly posed, hypnotically stylized figures in which the sum of Meštrović's eclecticism is for once greater than its parts. It's said that Meštrović began the cycle in response to the horrors of World War I, which may go some way to explaining its spiritual punch.

East of the centre

There's not much of interest east of the old town save for the main city beach of **Bačvice**, a few minutes' walk south past the railway station. This simple crescent of sand and shingle can't compare with the beaches farther south, but it remains a popular – and crowded – destination for Splićani of all ages. Bačvice is also the spiritual home of *picigin*, a game only played in and around Split, which works rather like a netless version of volleyball in the sea, involving a lot of acrobatic leaping around as players try to prevent a small ball from hitting the water. The front has recently been given a facelift thanks to the chic modern three-tier pavilion, resembling a cross between an Art Deco seaside building and a hi-tech metal tent, that curves gracefully round the beach. There are several cafés and a couple of swanky eating places inside (see p.372). A coastal path leads east from Bačvice past a couple of smaller bays, passing the tennis club where Goran Ivanišević honed his skills. There are several more cafés along the way, and the whole stretch is a popular strolling area all year round.

Tvrđava Gripe and the Croatian Maritime Museum

Northeast from the Old Town, the narrow streets and old stone houses of the Manuš quarter stand between the palace and **Tvrđava Gripe** (Gripe Fortress), an imposing seventeenth-century bastion built by the Venetians to keep Ottoman armies at bay. A gateway on the western side of the fortress leads through to a large courtyard-like expanse lined with former barrack buildings. One of these now holds the **Croatian Maritime Museum** (Hrvatski pomorski muzej; Mon–Fri 9am–2pm & 6–9pm, Sat 10am–1pm; 10Kn), an entertaining collection of nautical knick-knacks ranged over several halls. The display opens with a huge Roman storage vessel unearthed by marine archeologists – it was probably used to store a catch of fish, although it looks big enough to accommodate an average-sized family of humans. Elsewhere there's a fantastic array of model ships through the ages, and an impressive display of nineteenth-century torpedoes, built for the Austro-Hungarian navy in Rijeka by pioneering Croatian engineer Ivan Blaž Lupis and his English colleague Robert Whitehead.

Eating

Surprisingly, good sit-down **restaurants** are in short supply along the well-worn tourist trail of the old town, although there are several nice places a short walk away. Restaurants tend to stay open until 11pm or midnight; some have a separate menu of *marende* (cheap brunches), which is often chalked up on a board outside.

For self-catering and snacks, the daily **market** at the eastern edge of the old town is an excellent place to shop for fruit, veg and local hams and cheeses, while there's a handily placed Gavrilović **supermarket** (daily 7am–11pm) at the ferry terminal on Obala kneza Domagoja. The 24-hour Dobar tek **bakery** directly opposite the market on Zagrebačka offers a dizzying array of fresh buns, cakes and strudels. *Babić*, next to a certain American hamburger joint at Marmontova 7, is a good place to pick up takeaway pizza slices, *pršut* sandwiches and pastries. The best **cakes** and sweets are from *Bobis*, which has a large café on the Riva and a smaller outlet on Marmontova.

Restaurants

Central Split

Floramye Grgura Ninskog. Old-town tourist favourite offering reliable if unspectacular food, breezy service and reasonable prices – the main selling point is the outdoor seating in a medieval square. Traditional standards like stuffed peppers and *pašticada* sit alongside seafood pastas and fresh fish.

Galija Kamila Tončića 12, on the corner with Matošića. The city's best pizzeria – a small, unpretentious and cheap place with breezy service and wooden-bench seating on the western fringes of the old town. No outdoor terrace, though.

Kibela Kraj svetog Ivana 5. Functional *konoba* in the alleyway opposite the cathedral, doling out cheap Dalmatian staples to the locals for much of the year, and offering a tourist-oriented menu of seafood and schnitzels over the summer. Look out for dishes of the day chalked up on a board outside.

Konoba Dioklecijan Dosud. Also known as *tri volte* ("The Three Arches"), this unpretentious wine bar-cum eatery is a cult location among Split bohemians, partly owing to its atmospherically gloomy interior and an outdoor terrace built into the walls of Diocletian's palace. Turns into a laid-back restaurant in summer, when there's a limited but well-chosen menu of cheap local seafood standards. The *pršut* is among the best in town and makes for an excellent nibble-snack.

Konoba kod Jože Sredmanuška 4. A 10min walk northeast of the old town in a back alley (head north along Zagrebačka and turn right into Sredmanuška after you've passed Strossmayerov park), this is one of Split's best seafood restaurants – with a homely, intimate atmosphere and fishing nets hung from the walls – and not too expensive. Choose between quick and cheap meals like *crni rižot* (squid risotto) or opt for the best fresh fish and lobster.

Konoba Marjan Šperun. Family-run joint just west of the old town, with tasty, reasonably priced dishes in the squid, shrimp and fresh fish line. Only a few tables, so be prepared to wait.

Konoba Varoš Ban Mladenova 7 ⓣ021/396-138. Handily situated just west of Trg republike – it's up an alley behind the *Hotel Bellevue* – this is a good place for reasonably priced *marende* (lunches) as well as expensive slap-up evening meals featuring excellent fresh fish. Much patronized by locals, it soon fills up.

Maslina off Marmonova. Tucked into an unlikely corner, with sixteenth-century fortifications on one side and a medieval wall on the other, this airy, conservatory-like pavilion serves absolutely everything from pizzas through shellfish to steaks. You can expect reliable quality and reasonable prices.

Sarajevo Domaldova 6. In the heart of the old town, this rather old-fashioned restaurant (complete with plush seating and bow-tied wait staff) is way past its best, but still offers a reasonably reliable range of moderately expensive Dalmatian fish and meat dishes, including an excellent *pašticada*.

Šperun Šperun. Friendly and popular place offering the customary range of grilled fish and seafood – the pan-fried sea-bass (*lubin*) is well worth a try. Checked tablecloths, kooky paintings and exposed stonework give the interior a welcoming feel, and there's a small street-side terrace, too.

Out from the centre

Bistro Black Cat corner of Petrova and Šegvića. If you fancy a change from the Dalmatian risottos and seafood dishes on offer elsewhere, then head for this friendly place midway between the old town and Bačvice beach. Soups, quiches, chilliconcarnes, salads and a host of other international café-restaurant dishes, served up in a bar-like interior or on the street-corner terrace.

Boban Hektorovićeva 49 ⓣ021/543-300. Smart and rather formal restaurant, in a residential street some 2km east of the old town, with a long tradition of serving top-notch seafood. Superb fish dishes, elegantly presented, and an extensive wine list.

Buffet Fife Trumbićeva obala 11. Unpretentious, characterful feeding station just west of the old town, with a tightly packed wooden-benched interior and a glass-enclosed porch. Renowned for its inexpensive home cooking – usually served up in enormous portions – with cheap standards such as *ribice* (small fish, deep-fried) and *fažol*, augmented by daily seafood specials. The house wine is unsophisticated but potent.

Enoteka Terra Prilaz brace Kaliterna 6. Upmarket wine cellar in stone-clad surrounds, offering an intoxicating array of top-quality Croatian wines (available by the glass as well as by the bottle), and a small but delicious choice of seafood – the marinated fish carpaccio makes for a deluxe dainty nibble-snack, and there are plenty of grilled or baked fish main courses, too.

Stellon Bačvice. Chic but not overpriced pizza and pasta restaurant in the pavilion above Bačvice beach. A safe bet for vegetarians, with some satisfying main courses (try the penne with broccoli) and good salads.

Šumica Put Firula 6 ⓣ021/389-897. Long-established rendezvous for the smart set, just east of Bačvice beach, with a big outdoor terrace and a formal, starched-napkin interior. They serve excellent seafood and a full range of shellfish, as well as succulent schnitzel-style meals typical of inland Croatia. Prices are higher than average, but deservedly so.

Drinking

There are plenty of **pavement cafés** along the waterfront and around the Peristyle for daytime and evening drinking. The Riva is the classic venue for hanging out and people-watching; there's not much to choose between the numerous cafés along it, although those at its western end are slightly more posey and expensive than those to the east. From the Riva, evening crowds flow into the old town, where crumbling palaces and squares provide the perfect ambience for late-night supping. Most café-bars in the old town stay open until 11pm or midnight; longer hours are observed by the establishments in the pavilion at Bačvice beach, and in the next two bays along the coastal path to the east.

Cafés and bars

Equador Bačvice. Snazzy latin-themed bar in the pavilion above Bačvice beach, with deep, comfy chairs and a range of cocktails, nibbles and salads.

Gaga Iza Loža 5. One of a trio of enjoyable café-bars in the small square behind the town hall, its loungey outdoor seating attracting coffee-thirsty shoppers during the daytime, hedonistic youth at night.

Getto Dosud 10. Arty bar occupying an ancient building in the palace area, with a quirkily decorated suite of rooms inside, and a marvellous, partly shaded garden courtyard with plenty of places to sit or perch.

Luxor Peristil. Legendary Split café opposite the cathedral, recently the subject of a controversial makeover. The beautifully restored medieval stonework rubs shoulders with unsettlingly garish modern frescoes. Luckily, you can enjoy your coffee or cocktails on the steps outside.

Planet Jazz Grgura Ninskog. Tightly packed L-shaped bar with outdoor seating in a time-weathered courtyard, immediately northeast of the Peristyle, attracting a youngish cross section of Split society.

Porta Majstora Jurja. Cosy, convivial café-bar with poppy music, decent cocktails, and outdoor seating crammed into an atmospheric old-town alleyway. If it's full, try the equally welcoming *Teak* on the opposite side of the street.

Puls Mihovilova Širina. This bar in an atmospheric corner of the old town is one of those places that almost everyone passes through at least once in the course of their Friday-night wanderings. Post-industrial interior, and one of the most popular terraces (consisting of tiny tables and chairs jammed onto a stone stairway) in the whole of Split.

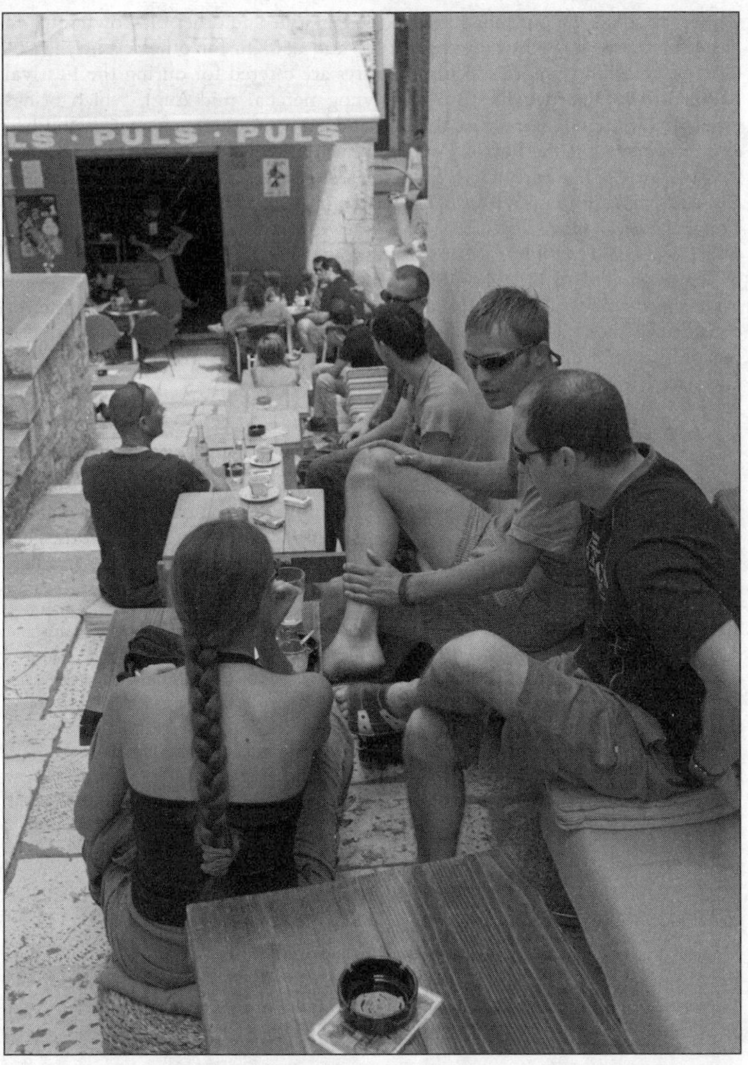

△ Split street café

Entertainment and festivals

Top-class **drama**, **classical music**, **opera** and **ballet** are staged at the prestigious Croatian National Theatre (Hrvatsko narodno kazalište, or HNK), Trg Gaje Bulata 1 (ⓣ021/363-014, ⓦwww.hnk-split.hr; box office Mon–Fri 9am–2pm & 4–8.30pm, Sat 9am–noon & 5–8.30pm, Sun 6–8.30pm). The **Split Summer Festival** (Splitsko ljeto; mid-July to mid-Aug; ⓦwww.splitsko-ljeto.hr; tickets from the HNK box office) hosts a spate of cultural events – including top-quality theatre, a lot of classical music and at least one opera – many performances of which take place on outdoor stages in the Peristyle and other old-town squares. Seats for the operas cost between 100Kn and 250Kn, for other events significantly less. Slightly more subcultural tastes are catered for during the **Festival of Creative Disorder** (Festival kreativnog nereda; mid-Aug), which brings together various counter-cultural events and happenings. One longer-established alternative event is the **Festival of New Film and Video** (Festival novog filma i videa; late Sept to early Oct), featuring independent short films from Croatia and full-length foreign releases. The prime **cinema** for this is Kinoteka Zlatna Vrata, Dioklecijanova 7 (Ⓣ021/361-524), which also has a regular programme of art house and cult films. Mainstream movies are shown at the Marjan cinema on Trg republike (Ⓣ021/347-838).

The best way to find out **what's on** is to keep an eye out for posters or consult the back pages of local newspaper *Slobodna Dalmacija* – good for serious culture and cinema listings, though not so well informed about pop or alternative happenings.

Live music and clubbing

There's a modest but varied range of **nightlife** venues in Split – street posters are the best source of information on what's going on where. Numerous open-air pop concerts are held in summer, when both the Prokurative and the inner courtyard of Tvrđava Gripe are pressed into service as venues. Note that the club scene may quieten down a bit during July and August, when many local revellers leave town for the islands.

Kocka Savska bb Ⓦwww.kocka.hr. Alternative club in the basement of the concrete Dom Omladine youth centre, 15min northeast of the old town just off Slobode. Weekly menu of live gigs, DJ nights and film evenings.

Metropolis Matice Hrvatske 1. Located in the Koteks shopping centre northeast of the old town, this is a mainstream disco venue of many years' standing, with occasional international DJ appearances. Fri & Sat only.

Obojena Svjetlost Šetalište Ivana Meštrovića bb. On the beach on the southern side of the Marjan peninsula, this open-air disco-bar stays open until the early hours in summer, and often stages live Croatian rock-pop gigs. To find it, head down the steps opposite the Mestrović museum.

Tribu Osmih Mediteranskih igara 3. Top DJs, cocktails, and a swimming pool. North of the centre near the Poljud stadium, this is the best place to catch Split's beautiful young things at play.

Shopping

Most of Split's high-street shops, including a growing number of classy boutiques and souvenir shops, are squeezed into the narrow alleys and tiny squares of the old town. Opening times are generally Mon–Fri 9am–8pm, Saturday 9am to 1 or 2pm.

Biseri zemlje Julija Nepota 6 Ⓦwww.biserizemlje.hr. This upmarket deli is a treasure trove of natural homegrown goodies, including wines, *rakija*, biscuits, jams, honeys and more.

Cro Fan Shop Dioklecijanova 5 Ⓦwww.cro-fan-shop.com. Official outlet for Hajduk Split kit – more expensive (but better quality) than the fake shirts sold in the nearby market.

Dallas Narodni trg. CDs of Croatian rock, pop and folk.

Knjižara Tin Ujević Morpurgova poljana. Bookshop with a good selection of English-language paperbacks, international art and design books, and guidebooks.

Studio Naranča Majstora Jurja 5. Graphic art, cool postcards and other well-designed arty gifts.

Uje Marulićeva 1 Ⓦwww.uje.hr. *Uje* is local dialect for olive oil and this shop sells innumerable local varieties of the stuff – alongside herbal soaps, domestic sweets and other natural products.

Utopia Dosud. Comic books and second-hand vinyl LPs in the courtyard of the *Getto* café-bar (see p.372).

Listings

Airlines Air Dalmatia, Obala kneza Domagoja bb ⓣ021/338-447, ⓦwww.airdalmatia.hr; Croatia Airlines, Riva 9 ⓣ021/362-997, ⓦwww.croatia airlines.hr; ČSA, Dominisova 10 ⓣ021/343-422.

Airport enquiries ⓣ021/203-555, ⓦwww .split-airport.hr.

Banks Dubrovačka Banka, Obala kneza Domagoja 4 (Mon–Fri 8am–7pm, Sat 8am–noon); Hypo Banka, Peristil (Mon–Fri 8am–8pm, Sat 8am–noon); Splitska banka, Sinjska 2 (Mon–Fri 8am–7.30pm, Sat 9am–noon); Zagrebačka Banka, Riva 10 (Mon–Fri 7.30am–7pm, Sat 8am–noon). All the above have ATMs outside.

Bookshops A small selection of English-language paperbacks can be found at Algoritam, Bajamontijeva, or at Morpurgo, Narodni trg.

Car rental Avis-Sub Rosa, *Hotel Marjan* ⓣ021/399-000, ⓦwww.subrosa.hr; Budget, *Hotel Marjan* ⓣ021/399-214; Hertz, Tomića stine 9 ⓣ021/360-455, ⓦwww.hertz.hr.

Consulates UK, Riva 10, 3rd floor ⓣ021/346-007.

Ferry terminal enquiries ⓣ021/338-333.

Hospital Firule, Spinčićieva 1 ⓣ021/556-111.

Internet access *Cyber Club 100D*, Sinjska 2/4 (Mon–Sat 9.30am–10pm, Sun 5–10pm); *Internet Caffe*, Grgura Ninskog 9 (Mon–Sat 10am–10pm); *Mriža*, Kružićeva 3 (Mon–Sat 9am–9pm, Sun 9am–2pm).

Launderette Modrulj, Šperun (daily 8am–8pm).

Left luggage At the bus station (daily 6am–10pm) and the train station (daily 6–10.30am, 11am–5pm, 5.30–11pm).

Pharmacy Dobri, Gundulićeva 52, just south of the suburban bus station, is open 24hr.

Police Trg hrvatske bratske zajednice 9 (ⓣ021/307-111), west of the suburban bus station.

Post office Northwest of Diocletian's Palace at Kralja Tomislava 7 (Mon–Sat 7am–9pm) and southeast of the palace at Obala kneza Domagoja 3 (Mon–Sat 7am–9pm).

Taxis There are taxi ranks at the eastern and western ends of the Riva, or ring ⓣ970.

Travel agencies Atlas, Nepotova 4 (ⓣ021/355-833, ⓦwww.atlas.hr), east of the Golden Gate, organizes yacht charter, rafting on the River Cetina, and trips to Međugorje, as well as handling international airline tickets. Maestral, Kaleta 2 shopping centre, R. Boškovića 13/15 (ⓣ021/470-944, ⓦwww.travel-maestral .hr), organizes private accommodation on the Dalmatian islands; Split Tours, Obala Lazareta 3 (ⓣ021/346-100), at the eastern end of the Riva, offers canyoning trips on the Cetina alongside other local excursions.

Telephones At the post office.

Inland from Split

Inland from Split lies the **Zagora**, a highland area that stretches from the mountain ridge just behind the coast to the Hercegovinian border farther east. A rocky, scrub-covered plateau, scattered with villages eking a living from thin and unproductive soil, the Zagora is economically poorer than the coastal strip, and many of its inhabitants (the "Vlaji" of Split lore – see box on p.353) have decamped to seek work in the big city nearby.

Most people breeze through the area en route for northern Croatia, although there's a smattering of worthwhile sights. The Roman city of **Salona** and the medieval fortress of **Klis** are only a few kilometres outside Split, and easily reached on local buses while, slightly farther afield, the Marian pilgrimage centre of **Sinj** can also be visited on hourly buses from the city.

Salona

Five kilometres inland from Split, at the foot of the mountains that divide the coastal plain from the Zagora, is the sprawling dormitory suburb of **Solin**, a characterless modern town which has grown up beside the ruins of **SALONA**, erstwhile capital of Roman Dalmatia and probable birthplace of Diocletian. The town once boasted a population of around 60,000 and was an important centre of Christianity long before Constantine legalized the religion throughout the empire – prominent leaders of the faith (future saints Domnius and Anastasius among them) were famously put to death here by Diocletian in 304. It was later the seat of a powerful Byzantine bishopric until 614, when the town was comprehensively sacked by a combined force of Slavs and Avars, and the local population moved off to settle in what would subsequently become Split.

Located on the northwestern fringe of Solin, the **ruins of Salona** (June–Sept Mon–Fri 9am–7pm, Sat 10am–7pm, Sun 4–7pm; Oct–May Mon–Fri 8am–3pm; 20Kn) stretch across a hillside just above the main road to Kaštela and Trogir. Bus #1 (Mon–Sat every 25–35min, Sun hourly) from central Split – pick it up from the square in front of the Croatian National Theatre – passes the main entrance to the ruins. En route you'll see stretches of the **aqueduct** built by Diocletian to bring fresh water to his palace from the hills to the north – numerous refurbishments later, it's still very much in use. Salona itself was extensively excavated at the end of the nineteenth century, and although most movable remains were packed off to museums years ago there's still a great deal to see. With ancient ruins scattered among meadows, olive groves and vineyards, the location is a peaceful and evocative one, giving views to the hazy industrial suburbs across the bay.

The part of the site closest to the entrance is **Manastirine**, an early necropolis for Christian martyrs piled high with sarcophagi around the impressive ruins of a fifth-century basilica. Within its walls are the graves of Domnius and his nephew Primus, Salona's first bishop. Nearby, the former summer villa of Don Frane Bulić (the doyen of Croatian archeology, who spent the first half of the twentieth century digging here) incorporates various Roman fragments, including gravestones, in its walls. Below Manastirine, the path leads along a stretch of old city wall as it zigzags above the fields, providing a superb view of a spectacular stretch of ruined basilicas – most complete of which is Salona's fifth-century **cathedral**. Downhill to the south, the arched form of the first-century **Porta Caesarea** is easily identified, marking the boundary between the oldest quarters of Salona (to the west) and the so-called Urbs Nova ("New Town") to the east. What was once Salona's main east–west street heads through the gate, soon disappearing into the private gardens and orchards of modern-day Solin. Sticking instead to the wall-top westward path takes you past another early Christian basilica before arriving at the second-century **amphitheatre**. A reasonably well-preserved structure, it originally seated around 18,000 spectators and is probably the most extensive relic on the site. From here you can descend to the busy Split–Zadar highway and catch a bus back to town (there's a stop served by the #37 Split–Trogir service 100m to the right and through the pedestrian underpass), or return the way you came.

Klis

The town of **KLIS** grew up around a strategic mountain pass on the trade routes linking the coast with the hinterland of the Zagora. The steep rock pinnacle around which the modern town huddles was first fortified by the Romans before being taken over by the expanding medieval kingdom of the Croats; kings Mislav (835–45) and Trpimir (845–64) both based their courts here. Klis remained in Hungaro-Croatian hands until the sixteenth century, when the Turks, already in command of Bosnia, began pushing towards the coast. Commanded by Captain **Petar Kružić**, who paid for the Trsat staircase in Rijeka (see p.235), Klis withstood sieges in 1526 and 1536, but finally succumbed to Ottoman attack in 1537, when attempts to relieve the citadel ended in farce. Badly drilled reinforcements sent by the Habsburgs fled in fear from the

Turks, and their attempts to re-board their boats in Solin bay caused many vessels to sink. Kružić himself – who had left the fortress to make contact with the hapless reinforcements – was captured and executed: the sight of his head on a stick was too much for Klis's remaining defenders, who gave up the fortress in return for safe passage north, where they resumed the struggle from the security of Senj (see box on p.272).

△ Klis

The present-day town straggles up the hillside beneath the fortress and is divided into three parts: **Klis-Varoš**, on the main road below the fortress; **Klis-Grlo**, at the top of the hill where the Drniš and Sinj roads part company; and **Klis-Megdan**, off to one side, where you'll find the main gate to the site (Tues–Sun: June–Sept 9am–7pm; Oct–May 10am–4pm; 10Kn). The **fortress** (*tvrđava*) is a remarkably complete structure, with three long, rectangular defensive lines surrounding a central strongpoint, the Položaj maggiore ("Grand Position", a mixed Croatian–Italian term dating from the time when Leonardo Foscolo captured the fortress for the Venetians in 1648), at its eastern end. There's no real museum display and very little labelling, but the fortress interior is immediately impressive, with cobbled walkways zigzagging their way up through a succession of towered gateways. You can peek inside several dusty storehouses, barrack blocks and – near the fortress's highest point – an ancient stone chapel that briefly served as a mosque during the Ottoman occupation. The views from the walls are truly breathtaking, with the marching tower blocks and busy arterial roads of suburban Split sprawling across the plain below, and the islands of Šolta and Brač in the distance.

Practicalities

Driving to Klis, take the old road which heads inland from Solin (rather than the new dual carriageway which skirts Klis to the east), go through the tunnel that separates Klis-Varoš from Klis-Grlo, and turn left when you see the sign for the *tvrđava*. **Bus** #34 goes from Split to Klis-Megdan, but it's relatively infrequent, so it may be better to catch a Split-Sinj bus (most, but not all, go through Klis), get off opposite the *Castel* **café** in Klis-Varoš, and walk up the steps just uphill from the café, subsequently bearing left to follow the road that winds its way up and round the hill (15min).

There's an enthusiastic **tourist office** (Ⓣ021/240-578) behind the *Belfast* **café**, on the square just below the fortress entrance, but staff shortages ensure that it's only sporadically open in summer. Klis is famous for the three spit-roast lamb (*janjetina na ražnju*) **restaurants** by the road junction in Klis-Grlo, each of which advertises its wares by having a carcass or two slowly revolving over open fires by the roadside. Portions are priced by the kilogram and are invariably served with spring onion (*kapulica*).

North to Sinj

From Klis, the road forges across the stony uplands of the Dalmatinska Zagora towards Sinj, 20km farther on. It's a route traversed by frequent buses from Split, although you'll need your own transport to make the worthwhile side-trip to the **Vranjača Cave** (Špilja Vranjača; Easter–Oct daily 9am–5pm; ask at the nearby post office if there's no caretaker at the entrance; 30Kn), along a side road to the east. To get there turn right about 3km beyond Klis and head through the village of **Dugopolje** ("Long Field", so named because it's in a typical *polje*, or fertile depression, common to karstic areas) towards a group of hamlets known collectively as Kotlenice. In the first of these, **VLADOVIĆI**, there's a small car park from which a gravel track leads to the cave. Discovered by the grandfather of the cave's current caretaker and guide, the cave is explored via a steep stairway which descends some 100m down into a chamber about 150m long, filled with honey-brown stalactites and stalagmites. The 65-million-year-old formations grow at a rate of 1mm every thirty-five years and include fluted limestone curtains and forms resembling the bunched heads of cauliflowers.

Sinj and beyond

Back on the Split–Sinj route, the road crosses infertile heath before descending into **SINJ**, a provincial market centre laid out in a bowl between the hills. It's famous locally for the **Sinjska gospa** (Our Lady of Sinj), a supposedly miraculous image of the Virgin dating from around 1500 which hangs in the local parish church (on the last altar on the left-hand side as you enter). It's claimed that prayers to the Sinjska gospa saved the town on Ascension Day 1715, when the locals drove away a superior force of Ottoman Turks – the image still draws pilgrims from all over Dalmatia, and is paraded through the town every year on August 15.

Victory over the Turks is also celebrated annually by the **Sinjska alka** (usually the first weekend of August) – a sort of medieval joust in which contestants, clad in eighteenth-century cavalry costume, gallop down a steeply sloping street at the southern end of town, and attempt to thread their lances through a ring dangled from a rope. First recorded in 1715, the Alka is one of the few remaining examples of the equine contests which once took place in all the Adriatic towns and cities, and its survival in Sinj is seen as a powerful symbol of regional identity by the locals. Membership of the Alkarsko Društvo, the association of riders allowed to take part in the Alka, is still seen as a badge of knightly prowess in a part of the country where traditional patriarchal values still rule. It remains an authentic expression of living folklore, a riotous, boozy business involving all the surrounding villages and taking up the whole day in a blaze of colour, costume and procession. Tickets for the main spectator stand are hard to get hold of (costing from 70Kn to 150Kn, they usually go on sale in travel agents in Split and Makarska a few weeks before the contest), but the atmosphere is worth savouring whether you get a grandstand view or not. More details can be had from the small **tourist office** (Mon–Fri 9am–3pm; ⓣ021/826-352) next to the modern and central *Alkar* **hotel** (ⓣ021/824-474, ⓕ824-505, ⓦwww.hotel-alkar.hr; ❸), which has neat, recently refurbished en-suite rooms.

Beyond Sinj, the main road heads northwest towards Knin, while an alternative route heads southeast towards the small town of Trilj, a useful base for exploring the landscapes around the River Cetina (p.380).

The Southern Dalmatian coast

The coast **south of Split** is perhaps the most dramatic in the country, with some of the Adriatic's best beaches sheltering beneath the papier-mâché heights of the karst mountains, all easily accessible on the frequent coastal bus service. Most of the beaches are pebble or shingle, and all are served by at least one campsite and (usually) a stock of private rooms.

Immediately south of Split, however, lies an uninspiring twenty-kilometre stretch of modern apartments and weekend houses culminating in one of south Dalmatia's most prominent industrial white elephants, the derelict ferro-chrome plant at **Dugi rat**. Once beyond here things improve markedly, with the historical town of **Omiš** marking the entrance to the rugged **Cetina gorge**, and a useful base from which to visit the strange and wonderful lakes at **Imotski** inland. South of Omiš stretch the celebrated beaches of the **Makarska Riviera** – which runs from Brela to Gradac – dramatically perched at the base of the **Biokovo mountains**. **Ploče**, the one other big town between Makarska and Dubrovnik, is an industrial port rather than a resort, and the rest of southern Dalmatia is relatively low on attractions until you get to Dubrovnik itself, covered in chapter 6.

Plentiful **buses** zoom up and down the Magistrala between Dubrovnik and Split, though Makarska and Ploče are the only places along this stretch of coast which have proper bus stations with timetable information. Elsewhere, you'll just have to wait by the roadside until something turns up (during the day, it's unlikely you'll have to wait more than an hour). Makarska and Ploče are also useful **ferry** hubs: the former has links with Sumartin on Brač, the latter has regular services to Trpanj on the Pelješac peninsula. Note that travelling between Makarska and Dubrovnik entails passing through a small chunk of **Bosnia-Hercegovina** – visas aren't required for this, but be prepared for passport checks.

Omiš

The first town of any size south of Split is **OMIŠ**, at the end of the Cetina gorge, a defile furrowed out of the bone-grey karst by the River Cetina. For centuries, Omiš was an impregnable pirate stronghold – repeated efforts to winkle them out, including one expedition in 1221 led by the pope himself, all failed. These days the town is rather dominated by the Magistrala, which passes just south of the old quarter, a huddle of cramped alleys spread out along a pleasant central street, Knezova Kačića. Remnants of the old city walls survive, and two semi-ruined Venetian fortresses cling to the bare rocks above. The lowest of these is the **Mirabela**, reached by a zigzagging path that begins behind Omiš parish church. A steep scramble up staircases affords access to the roof of its tower (June–Sept daily 8am–noon & 4.30–8.30pm; 10Kn), which offers a good view of the offshore island of Brač. Perched more precariously on a pinnacle of rock higher up is a slightly more ruined stronghold, the **Fortica**. It can be reached from the southeastern end of town, just behind the harbour, via a steeply ascending road, then a goat track, in about ninety minutes – you'll be rewarded with a stunning panorama of the offshore islands. The new town lies to the south, a featureless stretch of post-World War II buildings behind the main town **beach**, composed of hard and uninviting sand – you're better off heading for the long shingle beaches of **Duće**, about 2km back along the Magistrala, or for the nice shingle beach at the village of **Nemira**, 3km southeast.

Practicalities

As well as the inter-city **buses** plying the Magistrala, Omiš is also served by local bus from Split (#60, from the Lazareti bus stop at the eastern end of the Riva). The **tourist office**, just off the Magistrala on Trg kneza Miroslava (mid-June to mid-Sept Mon–Fri 8am–8pm, Sat 8am–noon; mid-Sept to mid-June Mon–Fri 8am–3pm; Ⓣ & Ⓕ 021/861-350, Ⓔ tz-omis@st.tel.hr), has details of local excursions up the Cetina Gorge (see opposite).

Perched on a hilltop on the opposite side of the river to the town centre, the *Villa Dvor* **hotel** (Ⓣ 021/863-444, Ⓦ www.villadvor.hr; ❻) is an intimate, medium-sized place with bright en-suite rooms, each equipped with air conditioning, flat-screen TV and Internet connection – many have sweeping views of either the coast or the canyon inland. Private **rooms** (❶) and apartments can be booked through Active Holidays, Knezova Kačića bb (Ⓣ 021/861-829, Ⓦ www.activeholidays-croatia.com), and Slap, Trg Poljički bb (Ⓣ 021/871-108 or 757-336, Ⓔ slap@st.hinet.hr), are the places to make enquiries. There are two **campsites**: *Galeb* (Ⓣ 021/862-130), just north of town and handy for the beaches of Duće; and Lisičina, just inland from Omiš's central bridge (Ⓣ 021/861-332), is small, reasonably well shaded, and has the cliffscapes of the Cetina gorge as a backdrop. There are plenty of places **to eat** on Knezova Kačića. The atmospheric *Konoba u našeg Marina* serves up local wines accompanied by *pršut*, local cheeses or anchovies; while the nearby *Milo* has a wider range of meaty grills and seafood. *Pod odrnom* is good for shellfish and scampi, *Maharadža*, 1km out of the centre on the road to Split, for tasty Indian food. The **cafés** of Trg Stjepana Radića, at the eastern end of Knezova Kačića, are lovely places to sit outside in the summer.

Omiš is famous for its festival of local **klape** – the traditional male-voice choirs of Dalmatia – which takes place on weekends throughout July, usually culminating on the last weekend of the month with open-air performances in the old town. *Klape* are an important feature of Dalmatian life, and almost every town or village has at least one of them. Songs deal with typical Dalmatian preoccupations such as love, the sea and fishing, and are usually sung in local dialect. The festival is well worth a trip from Split; the Omiš tourist office will have details.

Inland from Omiš: the Cetina gorge and Imotski

The River Cetina rises just east of Knin (see p.340) and flows down to meet the sea at Omiš, carving its way through the karst of the Zagora to produce some spectacular **rock formations** on the way. The most eye-catching portions are those just outside Omiš, and 23km upstream near Zadvarje, although there's no public transport along the valley so you'll need a car to see all the interesting bits. Over the summer, boat trips are advertised on Omiš's quayside (20Kn per person; they depart when full), but they only go about 5km upstream before stopping at the *Radvanove Mlinice* restaurant. In addition, a tractor-pulled "tourist train" makes the same journey a couple of times a day in season – the timetable will be pinned up at numerous points around town. You can also **raft** down the upper stretches of the gorge (see "Rafting down the River Cetina", opposite).

Rafting down the Cetina

Rafting down the River Cetina is fast becoming the premier activity-holiday attraction in southern Dalmatia, with a growing number of local travel agents offering the trip. Excursions usually start at Penšići, 16km upstream from Omiš, and end up at Radmanove Mlinice 10km farther down. The river only gets wild after strong rains, so most trips involve a gentle descent rather than a white-knuckle, whitewater ride – giving you plenty of time to admire the dense riverine vegetation and rugged cliffs on either side. Rafting excursions can be arranged in Omiš through Active Holidays or Slap (see opposite), or Adria Tourist, Trg kralja Tomislava 4 (Ⓦwww.rafting-pinta.com). If you're based in Split, Trogir or Makarska, local branches of Atlas will organize the trip. Expect to pay 200–250Kn per person.

Out of Omiš, the first few kilometres of the **Cetina gorge** are truly dramatic, with the mountains pressing in on a narrow winding valley. Farther up, the valley floor widens, making room for some swampy stretches of half-sunken deciduous forest. There's a string of good waterside **restaurants** along this part of the gorge: *Kaštil Slanica*, 4km out of Omiš, specializes in freshwater fish as well as *žablji kraci* (frogs' legs) and the tasty *brudet od jegulje* (spicy eel soup), while the larger *Radmanove Mlinice* (boat trips from Omiš often end up here), about 1500m farther on, is known for its trout, as well as lamb baked *ispod peke*.

Soon after the *Radmanove Mlinice* the road turns inland, twisting its way up onto a plateau surrounded by dry hills streaked with scrub. The village of **ZADVARJE**, at the top of a steep sequence of hairpins, offers views of the most impressive stretch of the gorge. Follow a sign marked *Vodopad* (Waterfall) in the centre of the village to a scruffy car park on the edge of a cliff, from where there's a view northeast towards a canyon suspended halfway up a rock face, with the river plunging down via two waterfalls to a gorge deep below. The cliffs lining the canyon sprout several more minor waterfalls whenever the local hills fill up with rain.

From Zadvarje, you can either head south to rejoin the Magistrala, or carry on northwards through **Šestanovac** to a major T-junction 7km beyond at **Cista Provo**, where you're faced with a choice of routes – eastwards to the lakes of Imotski (see below), or westwards to **TRILJ**. This otherwise unassuming rural town offers some of the best **accommodation** in the area in the shape of the *Sveti Mihovil* hotel, Bana Jelačića 8 (Ⓣ021/831-790, Ⓦwww.avanturist-club.com; ❺), which offers smart rooms with private bathroom and TV, and excellent dining in the attached *Čaporice* **restaurant**, with Zagora specialities such as *arambašići* (stuffed cabbage leaves) and the ubiquitous *žablji kraci*. The hotel is an excellent base for adventure tourism, arranging rafting and kayaking on the Cetina, horse-riding in the hills, and mountain bike rental (100Kn/day). Beyond Trilj you can continue northwest towards Sinj, or head east along the road to Livno in Bosnia-Hercegovina.

Imotski

Many of the buses that pass through Omiš from Split are bound for **IMOTSKI**, a provincial town set amid stony hills hard up against the Hercegovinian border. Unfortunately these buses don't follow the Cetina gorge route, but it's a highly scenic ride nevertheless, climbing over scrub-covered mountains south of Omiš before ploughing through fertile valleys thick with vineyards. Buses drop you at the eastern end of town, from where it's a short walk downhill to a main square hemmed in by green-shuttered stone houses. Most visitors come to Imotski to gawp at the two lakes on the outskirts of town, reached by following Ante Starčevića westwards from the square. A ten-minute walk brings you to the first of these, the so-called **Modro Jezero** or Blue Lake, which occupies a monstrous hole in the karst formed by the collapse of underground caverns. The depression is 290m deep, and fissures near the bottom keep the lake fed with water whenever the local rock is saturated with rainfall. In dry summer weather the water level drops dramatically, revealing a deep basin with sheer cliffs on one side and steep scree-covered slopes on most others. A path switchbacks its way down into this veritable moon-crater of a place, offering several vantage points en route before arriving at the water's edge. The going is rough and gravelly, so don sensible footware (and try and ignore the locals nonchalantly traipsing down in their flip-flops). Fifteen minutes' walk along the main road west out of town, the **Crveno Jezero** ("Red Lake") is if anything an even more astonishing sight than its Blue counterpart, owing its name to the russet hues of the surrounding cliffs. The lake stands at the bottom of a pit some 300m wide and 500m deep – water usually fills the lower 250–300m. You can't get down to the water's edge, but you get a marvellous view of this awesome hole in the ground from the roadside viewing point, which is right on the rim of the depression.

Once you've seen the lakes there's no compelling reason to stay, although the attractive string of **cafés** along Šetalište Stjepana Radića will ensure that you're well watered before you leave.

The Makarska Riviera

South of Omiš the road twists round the headlands of the Biokovo mountains into the section of coast known as the **MAKARSKA RIVIERA**, a string of resorts boasting long pebble beaches ranging from the over-exploited to the relatively unknown. Most of the villages here were originally based a kilometre or two inland until the growth of tourism, when families abandoned their old homes and built new houses down on the coast. The town of **Makarska**, roughly in the middle of the region, has the best nightlife and is a good base from which to tackle the ascent of the **Biokovo range**, while **Brela**, just to the north, has managed to preserve something of its chic, coastal-village-made-good atmosphere. Many of the other coastal settlements are quite bland in comparison, although archaic hill villages above Makarska and **Tučepi**, and a quirky monastery at **Zaostrog**, provide the area with plenty of character.

Brela

Surrounded by aromatic pine groves, the northernmost settlement of the Makarska Riviera, **BRELA**, sports a fine strand of beach next to a steep warren of alleyways, where a mixture of old stone houses and modern holiday homes pokes out from a blanket of subtropical vegetation. The beach, backed by a clutch of hotels, stretches for a couple of kilometres to the north of the town centre before being broken up by little rocky headlands.

The **tourist office** lies just behind a parade of shops midway along the seafront (irregular opening times; ⓣ & ⓕ021/618-455, ⓦwww.brela.hr). Nearby tourist agencies Adria-service (ⓣ021/618-393, ⓦwww.as-adria.hr) and Bonavia (ⓣ021/619-019, ⓦwww.bonavia-agency.hr) have a plentiful supply of **rooms** (❶–❷) and **apartments** (two-person apartments ❸–❹, four-person apartments 520–690Kn). The best of Brela's **hotels** (ⓦwww.brelahotels.com) are the three-star *Maestral* (ⓣ021/603-671, ⓦwww.bluesunhotels.com; ❻) and the ziggurat-like four-star *Soline* (Ⓣ021/608-891, Ⓦwww.bluesunhotels.com; ❻), both of which are large and comfortable package-oriented complexes 500m north of the centre along the coastal path, with good beach access. The *Konoba Feral* **restaurant**, beside Brela's tiny port on Obala kneza Domagoja, is the place to go for scampi, lobster and fresh fish.

Baška Voda

BAŠKA VODA, 3km southeast along the Magistrala (though you can just as easily walk along the coastal path), is modern, less charming and more commercialized than Brela, although it has plenty of decent accommodation and makes as good a base as any for exploring this part of the coast. The **Archeological Collection** (Arheološka zbirka; Mon–Sat 7–9pm; 5Kn) just off the Riva has a small but imaginatively presented selection of finds from Gradina, the hillock immediately west of the centre, which was the site of a settlement from the Bronze Age to late Roman times. There's a re-creation of a late Roman hearth, and some simply decorated storage vessels and glassware.

Some Split–Makarska buses pass right along Baška Voda's waterfront, although most coastal services pick up and drop off high above the centre on the Magistrala, from where it's a fifteen-minute walk down Put kapelice to the seafront. Here you'll find a helpful **tourist office** at Obala svetog Nikole 31 (daily 8am–9pm; Ⓣ & Ⓕ021/620-713, Ⓦwww.baskavoda.hr) and a string of agencies – Duga, Obala svetog Nikole 9 (Ⓣ021/620-405, Ⓦwww.duga-baskavoda.hr); As, Podluka 21 (Ⓣ021/620-704, Ⓦwww.as-adria.hr); and Mariva, Obaa svetog Nikole 29 (Ⓣ021/620-463, Ⓦwww.marivaturist.hr), to name but three – offering **rooms** (❶) and **apartments** (two-person apartments ❷, four-person apartments from 530Kn). Of the **hotels**, the *Horizont* (Ⓣ021/604-555, Ⓦwww.hoteli-baskavoda.hr; ❻), a few steps south, is one of the best hotels on the Dalmatian coast and earns its four-star rating, with spongy carpets, gleaming bathrooms and air conditioning. There's a **campsite**, the *Baško Polje* (Ⓣ021/612-329, Ⓔkamp.baskopolje@club.adriatic.hr), at the southern end of town near the exit off the Magistrala – if approaching by bus, get off at the Baško Polje stop (rather than the central Baška Voda one) and walk downhill.

For some of the best **food** in the area, catch a taxi to *Konoba Biston*, 5km uphill from Baška Voda in the hillside village of **Bast**, where you can dine on succulent *pršut*, tasty homemade bread and an excellent *pašticada*.

Makarska

MAKARSKA, 10km south of Baška Voda, is a lively seaside town ranged round a broad bay, framed by the Biokovo massif behind and two stumpy pine-covered peninsulas on either side. A leading package holiday centre since the 1960s, Makarska offers some of the liveliest nightlife on the coast, and is exceedingly popular with the youth of Croatia and Bosnia-Hercegovina as a result. Makarska's seafront can be frenetic with activity in July and August, but the place can be soothingly quiet in May, June and September, when it makes the perfect base for exploring the arid, rocky landscapes of Mount Biokovo (see box, p.386).

Despite being the home town of Hajduk, Lazio and Middlesbrough footballer Alen Bokšić, Makarska is more famous for its **rugby** than its soccer. The popularity of the oval ball here is largely due to the efforts of New Zealanders and Australians of Croatian stock, who came home in search of their roots and decided to form a team. Makarska consistently finish the season as Croatian rugby champions – although, to be honest, they've only got about six other teams in the country to play against.

Arrival, information and accommodation

The town **bus station** is on the Magistrala, a five-minute walk from the seafront, where you'll find the **tourist office** at Obala kralja Tomislava bb (June–Sept daily 7am–9pm; Oct–May Mon–Fri 9am–3pm; Ⓣ & Ⓕ021/612-002, Ⓦwww.makarska.com). It's a well-organized outfit whose output includes a free town map, advice on hiking Mount Biokovo and a leaflet detailing local mountain bike trails. You can surf the **net** at *Internet club m@ster*, just off the Riva at Jadranska 1 (daily 9am–midnight). **Bikes** and scooters can be rented from numerous outlets in town, including Rent-a-fun just off the Riva at Jadranska 2.

Rooms (❶) and **apartments** (two-person apartments ❷, four-person apartments from 530Kn) are on offer from innumerable agencies around town; most are open mornings and evenings with a long siesta break in the afternoon. Grouped on or near the seafront are Makarios, Kralja Zvonimira 14 (Ⓣ021/611-077, Ⓦwww.adriatours-croatia.com); Mariva, Kralja Tomislava 15a (Ⓣ021/616-010, Ⓦwww.marivaturist.hr); and Turist Biro, Obala kralja Tomislava 2 (Ⓣ021/611-688, Ⓦwww.touristbiro-makarska.com); while Eurotours is 100m west of the bus station at Ante Starćevića 48 (Ⓣ021/611-062, Ⓔeurotours-makarska@st.htnet.hr).

The nearest **campsite** is the *Baško Polje* on the southeastern outskirts of Baška Voda (see overleaf). The town's **hotels** are mostly package-oriented establishments dating from the 1970s and 80s, all of which have undergone various levels of refurbishment in recent years. Each of the hotels listed below may be full to the rafters in July and August, so don't bank on getting a room if you're just turning up on spec. They're open all year unless otherwise stated.

Hotels

Biokovka Put Cvitačke 9 Ⓣ021/602-200, Ⓔbiokovka@st.t-com.hr. Sizeable three-star 2km west of the centre, offering plain en-suite rooms, an indoor pool, and a health-spa treatment centre. Rooms on the north side have dull landward views. ❹

Biokovo Obala kralja Tomislava bb Ⓣ021/615-244, Ⓕ615-081, Ⓦwww.hotel-biokovo.hr. Hogging a waterside position right on the Riva, this is the handiest hotel for the town centre, although its popularity with tour groups ensures that it fills up fast. The rooms are tastefully decorated and en suite, with shower. ❻

Dalmacija Kralja Petra Krešimira IV bb Ⓣ021/615-777, Ⓕ612-211, Ⓦwww.hoteli-makarska.hr. Plain high-rise 1km west of the centre, much improved inside after recent renovations, offering neat rooms with attached bathroom (most with shower). April–Oct. ❺

Makarska Potok 17 Ⓣ021/616-622, Ⓦwww.makarska-hotel.com. Medium-sized, well-looked-after place about 5min uphill from the Riva, with simple en-suite rooms, some of which are rather frumpily furnished. May–Oct. ❹

Meteor Kralja Petra Krešimira IV bb Ⓣ021/602-600, Ⓕ611-419, Ⓦwww.hoteli-makarska.hr. Pale concrete ziggurat 1km west of the centre, offering modernized four-star rooms with en-suite bathtubs, minibar and a/c. There's also an outdoor pool and a sauna on site. Prices vary greatly according to room position and size of balcony. ❺–❻

Porin Marineta 2 Ⓣ021/613-744, Ⓦwww.hotel-porin.hr. Medium-sized hotel bang in the centre of town, in a nineteenth-century waterfront villa that once served as the municipal library – although recent renovations have left few of the original features intact. Compact en suites with TV, some of which are subject to noise from nearby cafés. ❺

The Town

Despite two hundred years of Turkish occupation, little of Ottoman vintage survives in Makarska, and the Venetian and Habsburg-era buildings on the seafront Riva coexist with modern apartment blocks thrown up after the tourism boom. All that survives of the old town is one central square, **Kačićev trg**, which slants up just behind the waterfront to the Baroque **St Mark's Church** (Crkva sveti Marko). Outside is Ivan Rendić's statue of **Andrija Kačić-Miošić** (1704–60), the Franciscan friar whose *Razgovor ugodni* *naroda slovinskoga* ("A Pleasant Conversation of the Slav People") was the most widely read book in the Croatian language until the twentieth century, after which its archaic style fell out of fashion. Kačić's work, a history of the Croats written in verse, and containing material taken from folk poems recounting Slav heroism in the face of the Ottoman Turks, was a landmark in the creation of a modern Croatian consciousness.

There's a rather pedestrian **Town Museum** (Gradski muzej; Mon–Fri 9am–1pm & 5/6pm–7/9pm, Sat 9am–noon; 10Kn) on the Riva, featuring old nautical relics and photographs. The **Franciscan monastery** (Franjevački samostan), just east of the centre, is worth visiting for the enormous contemporary mosaic in the apse of its church. Completed by Josip Biffel in 1999, it's rich in greens and turquoises, with Christ the Pantokrator presiding over an array of colourful sea creatures. The **Seashell Museum** (Malakološki muzej; Mon–Sat 11am–noon & 5–7pm, Sun 11am–noon; 10Kn) in the monastery courtyard is more engrossing than you might expect, its colourful exhibits shown to maximum advantage in a stylish and well-planned display.

Beaches and villages

The main **beach** is west of town, where a seafront path backed by the main package hotels stretches for some 2km. Far more attractive is naturist-friendly **Nugal**, an enticing stretch of pebble squeezed between red-streaked cliffs 3km southeast of town – to get there, head to the eastern end of Makarska's Riva and pick up the marked trails leading up into the woods.

Behind Makarska lies a verdant zone of olive groves and orchards peppered with ancient stone-built **villages**, all set on a steep slope that rises to meet the sheer rock wall of the Biokovo ridge. Providing your calf muscles are up to the gradients, the area is easily accessed by following Put Makara north from Makarska's main square and simply heading straight on; once you get above the town there's any number of gravel-track itineraries you can follow. Assuming you're not scaling Biokovo itself (see box overleaf), the most obvious destination to aim for is the so-called **Biokovo Botanical Garden** (Biokovski

△ Makarska

Mount Biokovo

The long grey streak of the **Biokovo** ridge hovers over the Makarska Riviera for some 50km, and its highest point – 1762m **Sveti Jure** just above Makarska – is the highest point in Croatia. Much of it falls within the boundaries of the **Biokovo Nature Park** (Park prirode Biokovo; ⓦwww.biokovo.com), formed in order to preserve the area's unique combination of lush pine forests, Mediterranean scrub and arid, almost desert-like fields of stone. It takes five to six hours to climb Sveti Jure from Makarska: head uphill from St Mark's Church, cross the Magistrala and continue to the village of Makar, from where a marked path leads to the 1422-metre-high subsidiary peak of **Vošac** (3–4hr). It's a steep climb, but there's a stunning panorama of Makarska and its beaches at the top. Unless you fancy breaking your journey at the Vošac mountain hut (weekends only; ⓣ021/615-422), it's another two hours' hike to Sveti Jure itself, where you'll be rewarded with a beautiful view of the Dalmatian islands.

Be warned, however, that Biokovo is not suitable for occasional hikers, and ill-prepared tourists are more likely to come to grief on its slopes than anywhere else in Croatia. The ascent is strenuous, slippery and prone to swift weather changes, so you'll need proper footwear, waterproofs, plenty to drink and an accurate weather forecast from the tourist office in Makarska. Another essential item of equipment is the 1:25000 map of Biokovo published by SMAND and available from Makarska tourist office free of charge (some kiosks and travel agents in town sell it).

You can **drive** to the top in summer by taking the road to Vrgorac and Mostar just south of Makarska, then turning left after 7km up a steeply ascending track which works its way up to the summit from the southeast – although you'll require nerves of steel to negotiate the hairpins. Biokovo Active Holidays, Gundulićeva 4, Makarska (ⓣ021/679-655, ⓦwww.biokovo.net), organizes **guided walks** up Sveti Jure and early morning **jeep trips** to watch the sunrise.

botanički vrt), a well-signed seventy-minute walk northeast of town just above the attractively weathered hamlet of Kotišina. Established in the inter-war years by local priest Jure Radić, the garden occupies a part scree-covered slope directly below the grey cliffs of Biokovo. Seeded with plants indigenous to the rocky, arid regions of central Dalmatia, the garden has lost much of its orderly layout since Radić's time, and nowadays doesn't look any different from the surrounding maquis. It's a beautiful spot nevertheless, and the walk here is accompanied by great views back across Makarska with the islands of Brač and Hvar in the background.

Eating

The town centre has scores of **restaurants** along the Riva, although in many of these establishments price and quality tend to vary from one season to the next: standards are reasonably reliable in those we've listed below.

Restaurants

Decima Trg Tina Ujevića. Unpretentious *konoba* just behind the Riva, which seems to keep both tourists and locals satisfied with a filling and not-too-pricey range of Croatian standards such as *grah*, *girice* and grilled fish.

Jež Kralja Petra Krešimira IV 90. Formal restaurant tucked away behind the *Dalmacija* and *Meteor* hotels, offering supremely good fish and shellfish. A seafood starter here will set you back as much as a main course elsewhere, but will probably justify the price tag.

Peškera Šetalište dr. Franje Tuđmana bb. Pretty much unrivalled for the choice and quality of its seafood, and nicely situated midway between the town centre and the package hotels.

Riva Obala kralja Tomislava 6. Classy restaurant with plush interior decorated with nautical bric-a-brac, and a large outdoor terrace shaded by ancient twisting trees. Fresh fish and seafood are very good indeed: the meat dishes, by comparison, are rather ordinary. The wine list rounds up most top Croatian labels, and a few French ones too.

Stari Mlin Prvosvibanjska 43. Traditional Dalmatian fish dishes, with the welcome addition of funky decor and informal service.

Family-run but imaginative with it; Thai and other global recipes sometimes appear on the menu.

Susvid Kačićev trg. Good-quality, moderately priced meat and fish on a central square-side terrace. Owned by the same people as the *Peškera* and with much the same menu.

Drinking, nightlife and entertainment

Simply cruise the Riva to find a place to **drink**: the terrace of the *Biokovo* hotel is as good a place as any to start, with good coffee and a respectable selection of cakes. East of here, a nightly *korzo* flows past the string of lively café-bars crowded into the Lištun, the narrow pedestrian street which connects Kačićev trg with the far end of the Riva. Most of the bars are indistinguishable from each other save for the music they're blaring out – and it can get so crowded here at weekends that the main priority is simply to grab a table wherever you can. For a change of style try *Rockatansky*, round the corner from the Lištun on Fra Filipa Grabovca, an animated and welcoming hole decorated with rock album covers and regularly featuring live rock, blues and jazz gigs on an impossibly tiny stage; or *Art Café*, just above Kačićev trg at Don M. Pavlinovića 1, which offers more soothing sounds in a tranquil garden, and occasional live music or DJ nights in a club-like space inside. *Tempet*, midway along the Riva at Obala kralja Tomislava 11, and *Ivma*, at the eastern end of the Riva at Marineta 3, are the best places for ice cream.

Deep, on the Osejava peninsula just beyond the Riva's eastern end, is a café-bar and nightclub in a cave; *Grota* enjoys an equally exotic location, occupying a sea cave just west of the Riva at Šetalište svetog Petra bb.

Running throughout July and August, the **Makarska Cultural Summer** (Makarsko kulturno ljeto) features concerts and theatre performances in town squares, chamber music in the town church, and carnival-style events on the Riva – pick up a schedule from the tourist office.

Tučepi and Podgora

While Makarsksa preserves something of its historic character, its near-neighbour to the southeast, **TUČEPI**, is almost wholly modern, with off-white concrete hotels and holiday villas lining a neatly manicured seafront. However there's a great deal of character in the villages just uphill from the shore, most notably **GORNJE TUČEPI** ("Upper Tučepi"), a knot of stone houses that can be reached by car via the main Makarska-Vrgorac road or on foot by heading uphill from Tučepi itself (45min). There's a lot to enjoy up here, with a network of minor roads and farm tracks leading past vineyards and olive groves towards a succession of half-abandoned hamlets, all cowering under the shadow of the Biokovo massif.

You can **walk** to Tučepi from Makarska in under an hour by following paths which climb up onto the wooded plateau just east of Maskarska's Riva; otherwise, all southbound **buses** stop off on the Magistrala, just uphill from Tučepi's seafront. Tučepi's **tourist office**, just behind the seafront at Kraj 46 (ⓣ021/623-100, ⓦwww.tucepi.com), can provide a rudimentary map of the town and the hillside settlements. The hotels along the seafront are booked solid by package tourists in season, and independent travellers are thus dependent on the **rooms** (❶) and **apartments** (two-person apartments ❷–❸, four-person apartments 480–560Kn) rented out by Ratours, just downhill from the Magistrala at Donji Ratac 24 (ⓣ021/623-200, ⓦwww.ratours.com) – there are plenty in town and a few in the hillside villages above. There are two excellent **restaurants** right next to each other in Gornje Tučepi: both *Jeny* and *Konoba Opačak* serve up the best in local cuisine washed down with the help of robust red wines.

Podgora

Four kilometres south of Tučepi, **PODGORA** is also predominantly contemporary in feel, with a small harbour at its northwestern end and a string of package hotels to the southeast. What makes it slightly different from its Makarska neighbours is that it retains a still-functioning fleet of trawlers (fishing on an industrial scale has disappeared almost everywhere else in southern Dalmatia), many of which turn themselves into tourist excursion boats in summer. There's a **tourist office** on the seafront at Branimirova 87 (ⓣ021/625-560, ⓦwww.podgora.hr); you can rent **rooms** (❶) and apartments (two-person apartments ❸, four-person apartments from 560Kn) from the nearby Puntatours, Branimirova 83 (ⓣ021/625-404, ⓦwww.puntatours.com). The *Sutikla* (ⓣ021/625-377), set among trees on the Sveta Tekla peninsula just beyond the hotels, is a reasonable **campsite**.

The southern Makarska Riviera

After a cluster of unremarkable resorts around Igrane and Živogošće, the next point of interest beyond Podgora is **Drvenik**, 20km to the southeast. It's really two settlements separated by a small headland – Donja Vala to the north, and Gornja Vala to the south – each of which has a soothing pebble beach backed by palms. There's a small **tourist office** in Donja Vala, run by the tourist association in nearby Gradac (Mon–Sat 8am–noon & 5–7pm, Sun 8am–noon; ⓣ021/697-511, ⓦwww.gradac.hr), which has details of **rooms** (❶). Four kilometres further on is the quiet and charming village of **ZAOSTROG**, built around a sixteenth-century **Franciscan monastery** (Franjevački samostan), with a simple, plant-filled cloister and a small **museum** (daily 4.30–7.30pm; 10Kn), displaying church silver and traditional agricultural implements. There's a long **beach** in front of the monastery, and the path leading north out of Zaostrog back towards Drvenik leads past some attractive rocky coves. Zaostrog has two **campsites**, the slightly scruffy *Viter* at the centre of the village, and the more attractive *Uvala Borova*, which occupies pine-shaded terraces about 1500m to the south. The Makarska Riviera peters out at **Gradac**, 8km beyond Zaostrog, a frumpy but inoffensive little town with a shingle beach on each side of the central church-topped peninsula.

Ploče to Dubrovnik

Eleven kilometres farther south of Gradac, the industrial port of **PLOČE** (which, for a brief period in the 1980s, was named Kardeljevo in honour of the bespectacled Slovene ideologist and Tito sidekick Edvard Kardelj) is one of the few genuine eyesores on the Adriatic coast. Developed to provide the cities of the Balkan interior with an outlet to the sea, Ploče lost its *raison d'être* with the break-up of Yugoslavia, and the town's ill-planned ensemble of tower blocks and dockside cranes slid into stagnation. It's still of marginal importance as a transport hub, however: **rail** services to the Bosnian capital Sarajevo have been re-established (currently summer only, but check for the latest information locally), and there are also a few daily **ferries** to Trpanj on the Pelješac peninsula, where you can pick up buses to Orebić (see p.431). Ploče's bus and train stations are next to each other just off the seafront, about two minutes' walk from the ferry dock.

From Ploče, the Magistrala cuts inland to Opužen, where the main road to Mostar and Sarajevo in Bosnia-Hercegovina (see box below) breaks off to the east, passing through the small town of Metković before arriving at the border. Meanwhile, the Magistrala ploughs on across the broad, green delta of the **Neretva River**, once an expanse of marsh and malarial swamp but now – after reclamation – some of the most fertile land in the country. Despite intensive cultivation, significant patches of reedy wetland still survive, providing the perfect habitat for nesting marsh harriers, crakes and bitterns. The area is criss-crossed by streams and irrigation channels, and it's possible to take a **boat trip** through the waterways, although these have to be booked in advance through one of the travel agencies on the coast (notably Atlas, which has offices in Makarska, see p.383; and Dubrovnik, see its Listings section on p.466) – a day-long trip including lunch will set you back upwards of 330Kn.

South of the delta, the Magistrala rejoins the coastline at **Klek**, a delightful village squatting beside a wonderful crescent of shingle beach. If you fancy a quick swim before resuming your journey southwards, this is the place to take it. Immediately beyond Klek, the road enters the nine-kilometre stretch of coast which is actually part of **Bosnia-Hercegovina** (keep passports handy). This corridor was awarded to the Republic after 1945 in order to give it access to the sea, although it has no strategic or economic value at present – Bosnia-Hercegovina's trade, such as it is, still goes through Ploče. The corridor's only real settlement is the ghastly holiday village of **Neum**. Food and cigarettes here are slightly cheaper than on the Croatian side of the border, and most Croatian intercity buses make a pit-stop here so that passengers can do a spot of shopping. Farther south, the lumpy mountains of the Pelješac peninsula close in against the coast until the turn-off for Ston (see p.434), where the mountains join the mainland and the dividing strip of water peters out in a chain of aquamarine salt flats.

Travelling on to Bosnia-Hercegovina

Bosnia-Hercegovina, or **BiH** (pronounced "bey-ha"), as it is colloquially known, is in theory a unified state comprising two "entities" – the so-called **Serbian Republic** (Republika srpska; RS), which roughly covers the east and northwest of BiH, and the **Muslim-Croat Federation**, which covers the rest. Within the Muslim–Croat entity, Croatian-dominated Hercegovina is virtually a state within a state, paying little heed to the government in Sarajevo. Despite the political differences between them, travel between the entities is unrestricted. Most of what you are likely to want to see – dramatic, still-beautiful Sarajevo, Ottoman-influenced Mostar, and the Catholic pilgrimage centre of Međugorje – are all in the Muslim-Croat Federation.

Citizens of the EU, USA, Canada, Australia and New Zealand do not need a **visa** to enter Bosnia-Hercegovina; nationals of other countries should check current regulations with the Bosnian consulate in their home country before setting out.

Public transport from Croatia to the Muslim-Croat Federation is relatively straightforward. The Ploče–Mostar–Sarajevo **rail** line was reopened in 1999, and there are numerous **buses**, with at least one departure a day from Zagreb, Split and Dubrovnik to destinations like Sarajevo, Mostar and Međugorje. The official **currency** of Bosnia-Hercegovina is the convertible mark (konvertabilna marka; KM), although you'll find that in Croatian-dominated Hercegovina, euros and Croatian kuna are more readily accepted.

Large tracts of Bosnia-Hercegovina are still heavily **mined**. Stick to roads and pavements, and never go wandering off across waste ground or into the countryside.

č

…rd-largest of Croatia's Adriatic islands, **BRAČ** is the nearest of the major …o Split, and is correspondingly busy in season. The south coast fishing village of **Bol**, with its spectacular beach, is the main attraction, although the beaches at **Supetar** (where ferries from Split arrive) on the north coast are no mean substitute. Away from the coast, the island's starkly beautiful interior has undoubted allure, its scrub-covered karst uplands dotted with fertile depressions containing vines, olives and orange trees, or by the great man-made piles of limestone that characterize the Dalmatian islands, built up over centuries by smallholders clearing a place in which to grow crops.

Brač was, until the development of the tourist trade, dependent on the export of its **stone** – a milky-white mix of marble and limestone – which was used in structures such as Berlin's Reichstag, the high altar of Liverpool's Catholic cathedral, the White House in Washington and, of course, Diocletian's Palace in Split. The island's other major source of wealth was the grape harvest, though the *phylloxera*

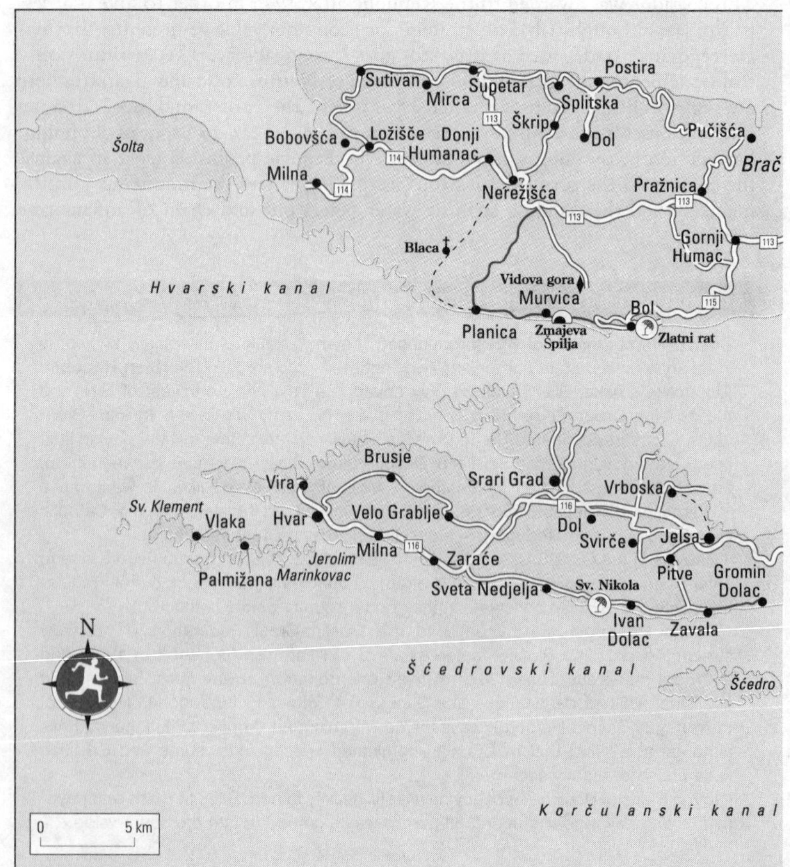

(vine lice) epidemics of the late nineteenth and early twentieth centuries forced many winemakers to emigrate. Even today, the signs of this depopulation are all around in the tumbledown houses and overgrown fields of the interior.

Getting to the island

Bol is served by **flights** from Zagreb between April and September inclusive. There are several **ferries** a day from Split to Supetar, plus **catamarans** from Split to Bol and to Milna, on the western side of the island, daily between mid-June and mid-September; there's also a ferry from Makarska on the mainland to Sumartin on the eastern tip of Brač, although there are only two or three connecting buses from here to Supetar daily. Supetar is the main hub of the island **bus** network, with frequent departures southwest to Milna, east to Pučišća, and south to Bol. If you're travelling on to **Hvar**, note that some excursion operators in Bol offer trips there (they'll be chalked up on signboards in the harbour), which may be more convenient than going all the way back to Split to pick up a regular ferry.

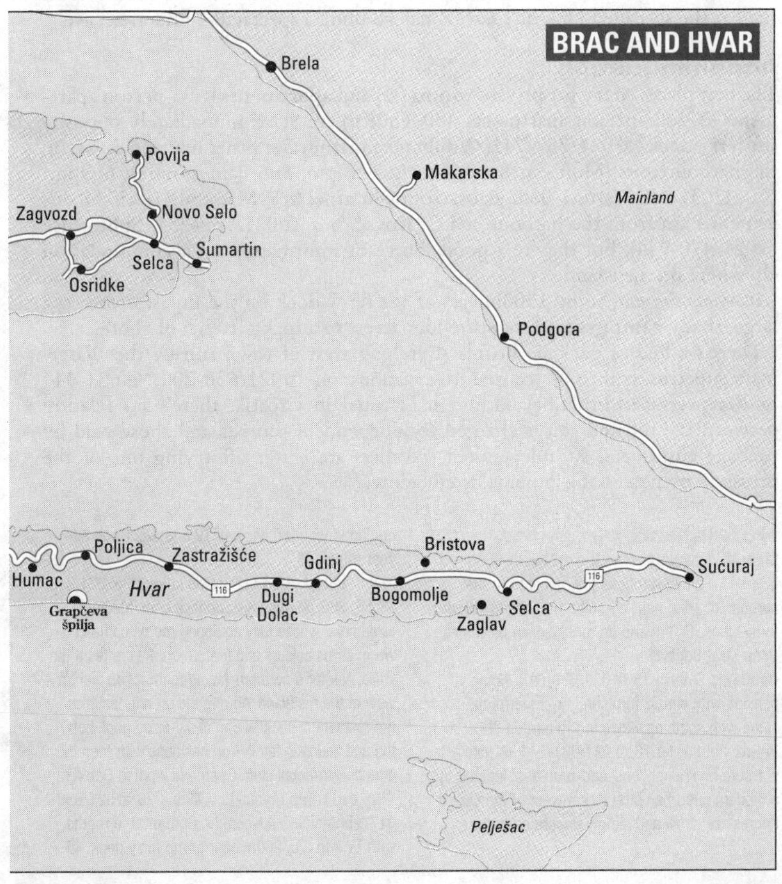

Supetar

Despite being the largest town on the island, **SUPETAR** is a sleepy place onto which package tourism has been painlessly grafted. With a decent beach, a clutch of good restaurants and not too much noise, it's a relaxing, family-oriented resort and a good base from which to explore the rest of the island.

Arrival and information

Ferries from Split arrive at the modern quay just off Supetar's old harbour, roughly opposite the **bus station**. In between lies the **tourist office** at Porat 1 (June & Sept daily 9am–4pm; July & Aug daily 8am–10pm; Oct–May Mon–Fri 9am–1pm; ⓣ & ⓕ021/630-551, ⓦwww.supetar.hr), which is well supplied with tourist bumph. Several places rent out **bikes**, including M&B just outside the bus station. You can check your emails at the *Parangal* **Internet café**, west of the centre along Put Vele Luke.

The clear waters around Supetar are perfect for **diving**. The Dive Center Abyss (ⓣ & ⓕ021/630-421, ⓦwww.divecenter-abyss.com) in the *Kaktus Hotel* complex, west of town, rents out gear and arranges crash courses (from around 220Kn), and runs excursions for experienced divers to underwater beauty spots such as the so-called Dragon's Ear (Zmajevo uho), a spectacular undersea cave.

Accommodation

The best places to try for private **rooms** (❶) and **apartments** (two-person apartments ❸, four-person apartments 480–650Kn) are Start, immediately opposite the ferry dock (ⓣ021/757-741, ⓔdubravka.matulic@st.htnet.hr); and Atlas, on the harbourfront (Mon–Sat 8am–2pm & 3–10pm, Sun 8am–noon & 6–9pm; ⓣ021/631-105, ⓕ631-088, ⓔbractour@hi.htnet.hr). Maestral, is an inconvenient 2km from the harbour at I.G. Kovačića 3 (ⓣ021/757-234, Split office ⓣ021/470-944), but they're a good source of information on accommodation elsewhere on the island.

Autocamp Supetar, some 1500m east of the ferry dock on the Pučišća road, is a large, shady **campground** that provides access to a rocky stretch of shore.

There's a line of package **hotels** stretching west of town run by the Waterman/Supetrus company (central reservations on ⓣ021/630-200, ⓕ631-344 or ⓔsvpetrvs@st.htnet.hr), although as usual in Croatia, there's no relation between the inflated prices charged to independent tourists and those paid by package customers, so independent travellers are better off trying one of the privately owned establishments listed below.

Hotels and pensions

Mandić Vladimira Nazora 9 ⓣ021/630-966 or 630-911. Family-run hotel just uphill from the harbour, offering neat en-suite rooms with modern furnishings, TV, a/c and (in most cases) balconies. Open May–Sept. ❺

Opačak 1 Svibnja 15 ⓣ021/630-018. Homely pension with simply furnished en-suite rooms, some with soothing views of the garden. ❸

Palute Put pašike 16 ⓣ021/631-541, ⓔpalute@st.t-com.hr. Friendly bed-and-breakfast located in a modern suburban street 1km west of the centre. Rooms are small and simply decorated but are equipped with WC/shower, TV and a/c. Open all-year round. ❸

Villa Adriatica Put Vele Luke 31 ⓣ021/343-806, ⓦwww.villaadriatica.com. Medium-sized hotel whose fully equipped rooms come in warm citrus colours and feature quirky crafts on the walls. Ask for a northern-facing room if you want a view of the mainland. Among the on-site facilities are restaurant, cocktail bar, dinky-sized pool, hot tub and sauna. A family-run business with friendly, attention-to-detail staff. Open mid-April to Oct. ❻

Villa Britanida Hrvatskih velikana 26 ⓣ021/630-017, ebritanida@st.t-com.hr. Comfortable rooms with TV and a/c, 200m east of the ferry dock. ❺

The Town

Much of Supetar has the appearance of an affluent suburb, with rows of neat villas nestling amid lush, well-kept gardens. Something of an old town survives, however, its mottled, rust-brown stone houses grouped around a horseshoe-shaped harbour, from where a shoreline road heads west towards a line of modern hotels. The small **town museum** (Gradski muzej; daily 10am–noon & 8–11pm; 10Kn), next to the Baroque parish church, is a mundane affair, and you'd do best to head out to the **beaches** west of town, long stretches of pebble around a shallow bay perfect for paddling and snorkelling.

Standing on a peninsula screened by dark cypresses just beyond the beaches, the **town cemetery** is as much a sculpture park as a burial site, thanks in large part to **Ivan Rendić** (1849–1932), whose eclectic amalgam of Egyptian, Classical and Byzantine styles can be seen on many of the family tombs here. Rendić was one of the leading Croatian sculptors at the turn of the twentieth century and, as a native of Supetar, was repeatedly commissioned by wealthy families to design funerary monuments here, giving the cemetery a uniquely unified sculptural style. The first tomb, belonging to the Čulić family, is immediately inside the gate – a dome supported by four squat pillars and bursting with eccentric knobbly accretions which seems almost Aztec in inspiration. More tombs lie east of here in the lower part of the cemetery, where the cupola-crowned Rendić family mausoleum raises a sarcophagus to the skies on solid pillars in a manner reminiscent of Lycian tombs in southern Turkey.

Ironically, Rendić was passed over when the cemetery's grandest sepulchural monument, the **Petrinović Mausoleum**, was commissioned by the Supetar-born, Chile-based shipping magnate, Francisco Petrinović. Ivan Meštrović turned down the job in protest at the way in which Rendić had been snubbed, and the task eventually fell to Meštrović's contemporary **Toma Rosandić**. The resulting structure is a beautiful piece of sepulchral art: a neo-Byzantine dome pokes above the trees, topped by a kneeling angel, his long wings spearing skywards. The four external pillars carry reliefs of mourners, some playing musical instruments, others bearing flowers. Behind the mausoleum is a well-head, also by Rosandić, bearing a relief of bare-backed strongmen gripping rams by their horns.

Eating and drinking

The best of the **places to eat** in the centre begin with *Palute*, Porat 4 (owned by the same family as the *Palute* bed and breakfast), which has a good choice of fresh grilled fish, reasonable prices, and seating right on the harbourfront. The slightly more stylish *Vinotoka*, just inland from the harbour at Dobova 6, has a wider menu including meat dishes and an extensive choice of local wine. *Bistro Punta*, on the shore some 200m beyond the town cemetery, offers a well-balanced and reasonably priced menu of schnitzel fare and local fish on an attractive outdoor terrace. *Jastog*, amid residential streets west of the town centre at bana Jelačića 7, has an attractive terrace shaded by kiwi plants. It's a great place for shellfish, fresh white fish and lobster, and lighter meals (such as the seafood risottos) are superb. Try to leave room for pudding – the *rožata* (Dalmatian baked custard) is hard to resist.

As far as **drinking** is concerned, *Barbara*, on the eastern side of the harbour near the tourist office, is the coffee-supping venue of choice for locals and visitors alike, while *Ben Quick*, west of the harbour on Put Vele Luke, attracts a wide range of night-time tipplers with its relaxing outdoor terrace and list of cocktails. Follow Put Vele Luke farther uphill to find a brace of bars belting out loud music to a youngish crowd.

West from Supetar

Five kilometres west of Supetar, the village of **SUTIVAN** straggles along the shore behind its rocky beach. Almost all the buildings here are made out of the local marble and, although there are no specific features of interest, it's a pretty enough little settlement of narrow alleys and ancient houses, and there's a pleasant coastal foot- and cycle-path leading back towards Supetar. The **tourist office** (July–Sept 7am–10pm; ⓣ021/638-357, ⓦwww.sutivan.hr), in the centre of the village right by the bus stop, shares a building with the Likva tourist agency (ⓣ021/638-476, ⓦwww.likva.hr), which can fix you up with accommodation in private **rooms** (❶) and **apartments** (studios ❸, four-person apartments from 480Kn).

The road to the southwest of Sutivan heads inland through **Ložišća**, a picturesque settlement spread across a steep ravine, with narrow, cobbled alleys hugging the hillside. Thrusting up from the valley floor is a parish church bell tower, built in 1920 and sporting a fanciful, onion-domed belfry by Rendić.

Milna

Beyond Ložišća, the road crosses the island's empty uplands before twisting down towards the nicest of Brač's harbourside towns, **MILNA**. The capital of a short-lived Russian protectorate over Brač during the Napoleonic wars, Milna is a delightful, picture-postcard port that curves round one of the island's many deep bays. The old village climbs uphill from the shore, a pleasant enough ensemble of narrow lanes and stone houses on either side of an eighteenth-century parish church and an adjacent nineteenth-century loggia. Behind the loggia looms an ancient crumbling house that's curiously known as *Anglešćina* after a local myth connecting its construction with an English crusader. All in all it's a relaxing little place.

The **tourist office** (June & Sept Mon–Sat 8am–1pm & 3–8pm, Sun 8am–noon & 4–8pm; July & Aug daily 8am–10pm; ⓣ021/636-233, ⓔtzo-milna@st.tel.hr) is in the main square. Private **rooms** (❶) and **apartments** (two-person apartments ❸, four-person apartments from 460Kn) are available from Dupin, at the northern end of the Riva (May–Sept ⓣ021/636-082; Oct–April ⓣ021/489-024, ⓦwww.dupin-tours.hr). Best of the **hotels** is the *Illyrian Resort* (ⓣ021/636-566, ⓦwww.illyrian-resort.hr; ❺), an ensemble of modern blocks on the forested northern cusp of the bay, offering swish self-catering apartments. More modest is the *M Milna* (ⓣ021/636-116, ⓕ636-550; ❹), a three-storey off-white structure on the south side of the bay with unassuming, grey-brown en suites. The *Fontana* **restaurant**, on the harbourfront, offers a satisfying repertoire of fish, shellfish and steaks. There's a sprinkling of **cafés** along the harbourfront, of which *Fjaka* is the most pleasant and is worth a stop-off by virtue of its name alone – it's Dalmatian dialect for "slobbing around in the afternoon".

East from Supetar

Three buses daily make the short detour inland from Supetar to the village of **ŠKRIP**, the oldest continually inhabited settlement on Brač. Founded by the Illyrians, it's now a sleepy nest of stone houses with heavy stone roof tiles that seem in permanent danger of slipping off, while its hilltop position affords views towards the terraced ridges of the Mosor massif on the mainland. The eastern end of the village is the oldest bit, with a ruined sixteenth-century castle overlooking a smaller fortified stone residence which now serves as the **Museum of Brač** (Brački muzej; daily 10am–6pm in theory, if not always in practice;

10Kn), displaying a well-preserved Roman relief of Hercules discovered locally, and sundry nineteenth-century agricultural tools. Outside the museum lie the remains of Iron Age walls and a Roman mausoleum, which local legend says contains a wife or daughter of Diocletian.

Škrip is a restful, rustic place **to stay**: the *Konoba Herkules* hotel (Ⓣ091 223 3417, Ⓦwww.herkules.hr; ④) offers simple but bright rooms in a modern three-storey house built in traditional Brač marble, and also has a **café-restaurant** with a cypress-shaded terrace and a delicious menu of fresh seafood and Brač lamb. The sea is a thirty-minute downhill walk from here – either by road to Splitska or by track to Postira, both of which have a few stretches of rocky strand. A better place to swim if you have your own transport is **Lovrečina Bay**, some 7km east of the Škrip turn-off (it's 4km beyond the next settlement along the coast, Postira), where there's a fine shingle beach overlooked by the remains of an early Christian basilica.

Bol and around

Brač's second town, **BOL** is the most celebrated beach resort on the island, largely because of its proximity to the beautiful Zlatni rat (Golden Cape), a 400-metre-long pebbly promotory which stretches into the sea just west of town. Before the advent of modern tourism Bol was very much an isolated community, stranded on the far side of the Vidova gora, the mountain ridge which overlooks this stretch of coast. In the seventh century, its isolation attracted Romans fleeing the Croat invasion, but over the following centuries Bol was attacked repeatedly by pirates, Saracens, Turks and just about anybody else who happened to be passing. Nowadays there's no denying the beauty of Bol's setting, or the charm of its old stone houses, although it soon fills up with visitors during high season.

Arrival and information

Buses from Supetar stop just west of Bol's harbour, at the far end of which stands the **tourist office** (June–Aug daily 8.30am–10pm; June & Sept daily 8.30am–3pm & 5–9pm; Oct–May Mon–Fri 8.30am–3pm; Ⓣ021/635-638, Ⓕ635-972, Ⓦwww.bol.hr), which has free leaflets, and maps of the island (useful if you're walking to Blaca; see p.398). You can surf the net at *Interactiv*, Rudina 8 (9.30am–3pm & 4.30–10.30pm).

There are a couple of **windsurfing centres** on the shore west of town, on the way to Zlatni rat, offering board rental (about 250Kn per day) and a range of courses (about 600Kn for eight hours). Reputable outfits include Big Blue, in front of the *Hotel Borak* (Ⓦwww.big-blue-sport.hr), and Orca, a little farther west on the way to Zlatni rat (Ⓣ021/635-650, Ⓦwww.orca-sport.com). Next to Orca, Diving Centre Bol (Ⓣ021/635-367, Ⓦwww.nautic-center.bol.com) organizes scuba-diving courses from around 2000Kn, and rents out gear. Boltours (see below) and Big Blue also rent out mountain bikes (from 100Kn/day) and there are plenty of smaller outfits on the path to Zlatni rat renting out cheaper bicycles (from 70Kn a day) and scooters (360Kn a day).

Accommodation

Private **rooms** (②) and **apartments** (two-person studios from ③, four-person apartments from 630Kn) can be obtained from Boltours, 100m west of the bus stop at Vladimira Nazora 18 (mid-April to mid-Oct daily 8am–10pm with possible afternoon break; Ⓣ021/635-693 or 635-694, Ⓕ635-695,

Ⓦwww.boltours.com), or from Adria, 100m farther west at Vladimira Nazora 28 (daily 8am–9pm; Ⓣ021/635-966, Ⓦwww.adria-bol.hr).

The best of the **hotels** is the *Kaštil*, housed in a historic building right on the waterfront at Frane Radića 1 (Ⓣ021/635-995, Ⓦwww.kastil.hr; ❻; March–Oct), and featuring tastefully modernized en-suite rooms with TV and air conditioning – all rooms come with a sea view. The *Villa Giardino*, just uphill from the centre at Novi Put 2 (Ⓣ021/635-900 or 635-286, Ⓔvilla.giardino@st.htnet.hr; ❺; Easter–Oct), offers bright, homely rooms with air conditioning and en-suite facilities, a lovely breakfast terrace and relaxing garden – it's booked up well in advance during July and August and doesn't take credit cards.

There's a trio of package hotels nestling among the pines on the way to Zlatni rat, all run by the Bluesun group (Ⓣ021/635-210, Ⓦwww.bluesunhotels.com) and expensive for individual travellers who haven't booked as part of a package. Running from east to west, these are the four-star *Riu Borak* (❼), four-star *Elaphusa* (❻) and the all-inclusive three-star *Bonaca* (❽), all recently refurbished and offering good access to the beach.

Several **campsites** lie in the new part of town uphill from the centre: both *Ranč* (Ⓣ021/635-635) and the adjacent *Meteor* (Ⓣ021/635-630) are pleasantly situated in olive groves on Hrvatskih domobrana, well signed from the main road into town.

The Town

Bol town itself is a reassuringly low-rise affair, with a couple of rows of old stone houses set above an attractive harbour packed with small boats and pleasurecraft. The main attraction along the seafront is the **Branislav Dešković Gallery**, housed in a former Renaissance town house, which contains a good selection of twentieth-century Croatian art. Most big names get a look in – sculptor Ivan Meštrović, Dubrovnik expressionist Ivan Dulčić and contemporary painter Edo Murtić among them. Farther east lies the late fifteenth-century **Dominican monastery** (Dominikanski samostan; daily 10am–noon & 5–8pm; 10Kn), dramatically located high on the promontory just beyond Bol's centre. Its museum holds crumbling amphorae, ancient Greek coins from Hvar and Vis, Cretan icons and an imposing Tintoretto *Madonna with Child* from 1563 among its small collection. An archway leads through the accommodation block to the superbly maintained monastery gardens overlooking the sea.

However, Bol's principal draw remains **Zlatni rat**, located a pleasant twenty-minute walk west of the centre along an attractive tree-lined promenade. Composed of fine shingle and backed by pines, the cape juts out into the sea like an extended finger, changing shape slightly from one year to the next according to the action of seasonal winds. With a series of large hotels positioned behind the promenade, the cape can get crowded during summer, but the presence of extra beach space on the approach to the cape, and rockier coves beyond it, ensures that there's enough room for everyone. Naturism is tolerated on the far side of the cape, and in the coves beyond.

Eating, drinking and nightlife

Given that so many guests have half-board arrangements in their hotels, it's not surprising that central Bol has a relatively meagre roster of places **to eat**.

For drinking, there are several **cafés** and ice cream parlours along the front. If you don't fancy the easy-listening crooners who seem to be on permanent duty in Bol's hotels, the best **nightlife** on offer is at *Faces* **disco**, a semicircular

△ Bol harbour

concrete structure uphill from the northern entrance to the town – Croatian pop stars perform here over the summer.

Cafés and bars

Loža Mandrać bb. At the eastern end of Bol's Riva, near the tourist office, this café would be a nondescript coffee-and-ice-cream joint were it not for its fantastic port-side position, with seating built into the curving harbour wall.

Marinero Rudina. In side streets up above Bol's bus stop, this animated café-bar is by-passed by many tourists and has a refreshingly local feel as a result. Outdoor seating in a triangular, tree-covered park.

Pivnica Moby Dick Porat bolskih pomoraca bb. A late-opening bar directly above the Loža (see above), with a welcoming pub-like interior and a terrace packed with easy chairs overlooking the harbour. Also serves pizzas.

Varadero Frane Radića bb. Outdoor lounge-bar set around an ancient harbour-side tree, with wicker sofas, grass parasols and a suitably decadent list of cocktails.

Restaurants

Dva Ferala Frane Radića. Traditional seafood dishes, fusion food (Adriatic fish with exotic sauces), pastas and risottos served up on a large patio shaded by trees, bushy herbs and a laurel hedge. Transforms itself into a cocktail bar as the night wears on. Open from 5pm.

Konoba Gušt Frane Radića 14. Characterful place with agricultural implements and old photographs hanging on the wall, with an extensive menu of traditional Dalmatian dishes, with a wide range of fresh fish and a satisfying *pašticada*.

Mlin A Rabadana. Midway between the harbour and the Dominican monastery, *Mlin* is another rustically decorated place, but this time with a big olive-shaded terrace overlooking the sea – tasty eats include seafood risottos, grilled mussels, *brudet*, and (if you order in advance) lamb roasted *ispod peke* style. Opens at 5pm.

Ribarska kućica Ante Starčevića bb. Seaside pavilion right beside a rocky stretch of beach, serving seafood risottos and a broad range of fish dishes – including *gregada* (fish in a white wine-based broth).

Taverna Riva Frane Radića 5. Fine dining on a terrace right above the Riva, with formal wait staff, superbly prepared grilled fish, and an extensive list of Croatian wines. Opens at 6pm.

Around Bol

Looming over Zlatni rat to the north is the 778-metre peak of **Vidova gora**, the highest point on any Adriatic island. It's accessible via an asphalt road which leaves the Supetar–Bol road just south of the village of Nerežišća, and there's also a marked walking trail (2hr each way) from the centre of Bol, which heads uphill immediately beyond the *Faces* discotheque. A small tavern at the summit sometimes serves roast lamb during summer, but most people come simply to savour the view, encompassing Zlatni rat and Bol down to the left, with the islands of Vis and Hvar visible farther out.

Tucked away at the head of a valley on the western flanks of the Vidova gora is the **Hermitage of Blaca** (Pustinja Blaca; Tues–Sun 8am–5pm, though check in the tourist office at Bol or Supetar as times can vary; 20Kn), about 12km out of Bol. You can walk there by following the road (which later degenerates into a track) west from Zlatni rat, passing the village of Murvica before heading inland at Blaca bay. The route is easy to follow and takes about three hours each way – a worthwhile but unshaded walk along a rugged hillside with the sea far below. You can cut out some of the effort by taking a boat trip (advertised in Bol harbour in high season) to Blaca bay and continuing from there. If you're driving, take the turn-off for Vidova gora midway between Supetar and Bol, then turn right after about 2km onto the signed gravel track for Blaca (just about passable for cars, but rough on the suspension). From the end of the track, walk along the path which heads downhill past deserted hamlets before arriving at the monastery after about forty minutes.

The hermitage was founded in 1588 by monks fleeing the Turks; the last resident – Niko Miličević, an enthusiastic astronomer who left all sorts of bits and bobs, including an assortment of old clocks and a stock of lithographs by Poussin – occupied the hermitage in the 1930s. You can also look around the ascetic living quarters and the kitchen, with its forest of blackened iron utensils surrounding an open hearth. But the principal attraction is the setting, with the simple buildings hugging the sides of a narrow, scrub-covered ravine. Islanders from all over Brač attend the **pilgrimage** to Blaca on the first weekend after Assumption (August 15).

Back on the Bol–Supetar road it's worth making a brief northbound detour to take a peek at the village of **Nerežišće**, where a small pine tree can be seen growing out of the roof of the tiny parish church. It seeded a century ago and was somehow allowed to grow unmolested, adopting a stunted, bonsai-like appearance in the process.

Hvar

HVAR has long been one of the most popular Croatian islands. People talk of its verdant colour, fragrant air and mild climate, and at one time local hoteliers even had enough faith in the weather to offer a money-back guarantee if the temperature ever dropped below zero. And Hvar is undeniably beautiful – a slim, green slice of land punctured by jagged inlets and a steep central ridge streaked with the long grey lines of limestone spoil heaps built up over the centuries by farmers attempting to carve out patches of cultivable land. The island's main crop is **lavender**, which was introduced in the 1930s and covers the island in a spongy grey-blue cloak every spring before finding its way onto souvenir stalls across the island.

Intensively but tastefully developed as a tourist resort, the island's capital, **Hvar Town**, is one of the Adriatic's most bewitching – and best preserved – historic towns, and is a good base from which to explore the rest of the island, which is fairly low-key in comparison. Buses out of Hvar Town either take the old road across the central ridge, or speed through the recently built tunnel to reach the northern side of the island, where **Stari Grad** and **Vrboska** boast some good beaches, old stone houses and an unhurried, village feel. **Jelsa**, farther east, can't quite compete with its two neighbours in terms of rustic charm, but has more accommodation than Vrboska, which is only a forty-minute walk away. East of Jelsa, the island narrows to a long, thin mountainous strip of land that extends all the way to isolated **Sućuraj**, which is linked to the mainland by regular ferries, although there's virtually no public transport between here and the rest of the island.

Some history

Around 385 BC, the Greeks of Paros in Asia Minor established a colony on Hvar, naming it **Pharos** (present-day Stari Grad). After a period of Roman then Byzantine control, the island was thoroughly slavicized in the eighth century, when it was overrun by the **Narentani**, a Croatian tribe from the Neretva delta. The new arrivals couldn't pronounce the name Pharos, so the place became **Hvar** instead. The settlement nowadays known as Hvar Town began life as a haven for medieval pirates. The Venetians drove them out in 1240, and encouraged the citizens of Stari Grad to relocate to Hvar Town, which henceforth became the administative capital of the island.

For the next two centuries the island was a self-governing commune which swore fealty to Venetian, Hungarian and Bosnian rulers at different times. The Venetians returned to stay in 1420 and ushered in a period of urban and cultural efflorescence. The aristocracy's wealth still came from the agricultural estates located on the fertile plain just east of Stari Grad, but the ascendancy of Hvar Town was confirmed by a rule stipulating that nobles had to spend at least six months of the year there in order to qualify for seats on the island's governing council.

As in most other Dalmatian towns, the nobles of Hvar had succeeded in excluding the commoners from municipal government by the fifteenth century. The most serious challenge to this oligarchical state of affairs came with the **revolt of 1510** led by **Matija Ivanić**, a representative of the non-noble shipowners and merchants who felt that real wealth and power had been denied to them. The revolt got off to a bad start when a priest in Hvar Town claimed that the crucifix on which the plotters had sworn an oath had begun to sweat blood in a divine warning of the violence to come. The townsfolk lost their enthusiasm for the revolt but it took off elsewhere on the island, especially around Vrbanj, Vrboska and Jelsa. Ivanić himself led a raid on Hvar Town, sacking the houses of the nobles and killing many of the occupants, and Hvar's surviving aristocrats fled to the mainland and awaited Venetian intervention.

Venetian emissary Sebastiano Giustignan initially failed to quell the rising. His troops (mostly Croats from the mainland) were an unruly lot, and looted Vrboska before being driven out of the town in August 1512. In control of the bulk of the island for two years, Ivanić led another attack on Hvar Town in August 1514, massacring those noble families who had returned. Fearful that the revolt might spread to other Dalmatian cities, the Venetians this time reacted with swift effectiveness, defeating the rebels and hanging their leaders from the masts of their galleys. Ivanić himself escaped, dying in exile in Rome.

Despite all this, sixteenth-century Hvar went on to become one of the key centres of the Croatian Renaissance, with poets like **Hanibal Lucić** and **Petar Hektorović** (see box on p.408) cultivating intellectual links with Dubrovnik and penning works which were to have a profound influence on future generations. This golden age was interrupted in 1571, when the notorious corsair **Uluz Ali** (see box on p.403) sacked Hvar Town on behalf of the Turks and reduced it to smouldering rubble. Rebuilt from scratch, the town soon reassumed its importance as an entrepôt on the east–west trade routes. Later, the arrival of long-haul steamships becalmed Hvar Town, which drifted into quiet obscurity until the tourists arrived in the late nineteenth century – largely due to the efforts of the Hvar Hygienic Society, founded in 1868 by locals eager to promote the island as a health retreat. The first ever guidebook to the town, published in Vienna in 1903, promoted it as "Austria's Madeira", and it has been one of Dalmatia's most stylish resorts ever since.

Getting to Hvar

As an important stop off on the Split-Vela Luka-Lastovo route, Hvar Town is served by at least one daily ferry and at least one catamaran throughout the year. There's also a once-a-week connection (currently Tues) with Vis. However, only foot passengers can get on and off in Hvar Town, so if you're bringing a vehicle to the island you'll have to approach via the island's other main port, Stari Grad, instead. This is served by regular ferries from Split (three daily in winter; six in summer). The main **coastal ferry** (daily in summer) also stops at Stari Grad, connecting the island with Split and points to Rijeka in the north, Korčula and Dubrovnik to the south. During summer there are also ferries from **Ancona** in Italy to Stari Grad. Foot passengers arriving at Stari Grad's port can catch local buses from the quay to the centre of Stari Grad, Hvar Town or Jelsa. You can also reach the island on one of several daily ferries from Drvenik (see p.388) on the mainland to Sućuraj – though the poor bus connections mean that this approach is only really of use if you're travelling by car. Lastly, throughout the season there's a daily **catamaran** service from Jelsa to Split via Bol on Brač.

Travelling on from the island, you'll find that queues for car ferries build up fast in summer, so arrive early. Advance reservations can be made at the Jadrolinija office on the quayside in Hvar Town.

Hvar Town

The best view of **HVAR TOWN** is from the sea, with its grainy-white and brown scatter of buildings following the contours of the bay, and the green splashes of palms and pines pushing into every crack and cranny. Once you're on terra firma, central Hvar reveals itself as a medieval town full of pedestrianized alleys overlooked by ancient stone houses, providing an elegant backdrop to the main leisure activity: lounging around in cafés and watching the crowds as they shuffle round the yacht-filled harbour. After Dubrovnik, Hvar is probably the most fashionable of the Adriatic resorts among the Croats themselves, and there's something of the south of France in the chic *korzo* that engulfs the town at dusk.

Arrival and information

Ferries dock on the eastern side of Hvar Town's bay on Obala oslobođenja. From here, it's a couple of hundred metres to the **tourist office**, on the corner of the main square, Trg svetog Stjepana (June & Sept Mon–Sat 8am–1pm & 4–9pm, Sun 10am–noon & 6–8pm; July & Aug daily 8am–2pm & 3–10pm; Oct–May Mon–Sat 8am–1pm; Ⓣ & Ⓕ021/741-059, Ⓦwww.hvar.hr). The **bus station** is a few steps east of the main square on Trg M. Miličića, and the **Jadrolinija** office (daily 7am–1pm & 2–9pm) is on the ferry dock, with an ATM just outside. You can check your emails at *Internet Access* (May–Oct daily 9am–midnight) on Ivana Vucetića, one of the narrow stepped streets leading uphill from Obala Oslobođenja.

Luka Rent, Dolac (Ⓣ021/742-946, Ⓦwww.lukarent.com) rents out bikes (70Kn/day), boats (300Kn/day) and scooters (300Kn/day). The Jurgovan Diving Centre in front of the *Hotel Delfin* rents out gear, organizes courses for beginners and also rents out boats and bikes (Ⓣ021/742-490, Ⓦwww.jurgovan.com).

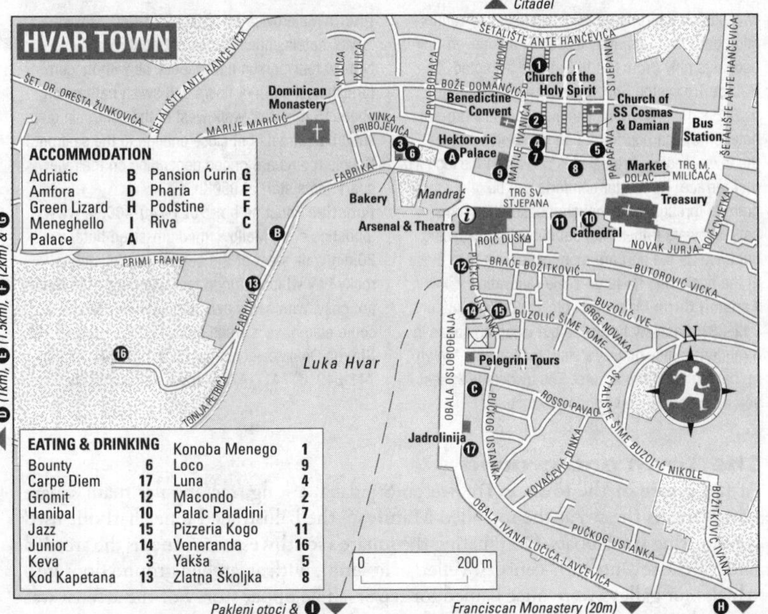

Accommodation

Private **rooms** (❶–❷) and **apartments** (two-person studios ❸, four-person apartments 400–750Kn) are available from Pelegrini Tours, near the ferry dock on the Riva (Mon–Sat 8am–10pm, Sun 6–8pm; ⓣ021/742-743 or 742-250, ⓦwww.pelegrini-hvar.hr).

Hvar Town is oversupplied with soulless package **hotels**, most of which belong to the Sunčani Hvar conglomerate – a long-term plan to modernize all of them means that partial closure and refurbishment will be ongoing over the next five years. There are a couple of characterful, independently run choices outside the centre or on nearby islets. None of Hvar's hotels is particularly cheap unless you travel out of season, and they all fill up quickly in July and August – when you might be forced to consider staying in Stari Grad or Jelsa instead. The hotels listed below are open all year round unless stated otherwise.

Hostel

Green Lizard Lučica bb ⓣ021/742-560, ⓦwww.greenlizard.hr. Plainly decorated but clean and comfy house just uphill from the Franciscan monastery, offering a mixture of dorms, doubles and triples – mostly bright, white-walled affairs with tiled floors. Some rooms have en-suite shower/WC, others share facilities in the hallway. Breakfast isn't included, but you can use the kitchen. Open Easter–Oct. Dorms 130Kn per person, rooms ❸–❹.

Hotels

Adriatic Fabrika bb ⓣ021/741-024, ⓕ742-866, wwww.suncanihvar.hr. Plain but perfectly habitable en-suite rooms on the western side of the harbour. Prone to noise from nearby clubs, but the top-floor swimming pool is a major plus. ❻

Amfora Tonija Petrića bb ⓣ021/741-202, ⓕ741-711, ⓦwww.suncanihvar.hr. Monstrously proportioned, seven-hundred-bed lump of concrete, west of town on the Veneranda headland. Rooms are swish and comfortable, however, and there's an indoor pool, gym and casino. ❻

Meneghello Palmižana ⓣ091/478-3110, ⓕ021/741-427, ⓦwww.palmizana.hr. Luxury villa settlement on the island of Sveti Kliment, 5km west of Hvar, connected to town by regular boat shuttle. Most of the accommodation comes in the form of attractive stone-clad self-catering bungalows sleeping three or four, although there are also some two-person apartments, all surrounded by cactus-filled gardens. From May to September seven-day bookings only (from Sat to Sat) are accepted. ❻

Palace Trg svetog Stjepana bb ⓣ021/741-906, ⓕ742-420, ⓦwww.suncanihvar.hr. Habsburg-era hotel on the harbourfront, part of which occupies the town loggia – breakfast is served on the loggia's roof terrace. Three-star comforts can be taken for granted throughout, although most of the rooms have showers rather than bathtubs. Rooms facing out towards the port are more expensive than those at the back. Due for large-scale renovation. ❻

Pansion Ćurin Majerovića bb ⓣ021/741-989 or 742-281. Sparsely furnished but clean en suites in a modern family house, a short walk west of town up behind the Amfora hotel. The owners will meet you at the port if you ring in advance. ❹

Pharia Majerovica bb ⓣ021/778-080, ⓦwww.orvas-hotels.com. A range of bright rooms and two- to four-person apartments, all with modern furnishings, parquet floors and swish bathrooms, about 15 minutes' walk west of the centre. In quiet suburban streets but close enough to the seafront. Double rooms are priced depending on their view; apartments start at 950Kn. ❺

Podstine Podstine bb ⓣ021/740-400, ⓦwww.podstine.com. Mellow, medium-sized hotel a 20min walk west of the centre, overlooking a rocky bay which is good for swimming. The rooms are cosy, with sea views and satellite TV, and some also have a small balcony. May–Oct. ❻–❼

Slavija Obala oslobođenja bb ⓣ021/741-820 or 741-840, ⓕ741-147, ⓦwww.suncanihvar.hr.

The Town and around

At the centre of the town is Trg svetog Stjepana, a long, rectangular main square which meets the sea at the so-called **Mandrać**, the balustraded inner harbour used for mooring small boats. Dominating the square's southwestern corner is the arcaded bulk of the seventeenth-century Venetian **arsenal**, with an arched ground floor into which war galleys were once hauled for repairs. The upper storey of the arsenal was adapted in 1612 to house the town **theatre** (*kazalište*; daily: summer 9am–1pm & 5–11pm; winter 11am–noon; 20Kn), the oldest in Croatia and one of the first in Europe. It was built by Venetian governor Pietro Semitecolo to assuage the distrust between nobles and commoners which had continued since the Ivanić rebellion, since the theatre was a civic amenity that all classes could enjoy together. The gaily painted interior, complete with two tiers of boxes, dates from the early 1800s, when locals revived and renovated the theatre after a period of neglect. The auditorium is entered through a small picture gallery (same times), which has a modest collection of twentieth-century Croatian work. The terrace outside the theatre is the perfect place from which to observe the milling crowds on the square below.

The cathedral and treasury

Towering over the eastern end of the square is the trefoil facade of **St Stephen's Cathedral** (Katedrala sveti Stjepan; no fixed opening hours – try mornings), a sixteenth-century construction whose spindly four-storey campanile employs the typical Venetian device of having one window on the first floor, two windows on the second, and so on up to the top. The interior is fairly unremarkable save for two notable artworks: a Venetian *Madonna and Child* (on the fourth altar on the right), a Byzantine-influenced, icon-like image painted in around 1220, which exudes a spiritual calm quite different from the tortured Baroque altarpieces nearby; and a touching fifteenth-century Pietà by Spanish artist Juan Boschetus (in the opposite – south – aisle), although its power is somewhat lessened by being framed within a larger and later work.

Immediately next door to the cathedral, the **Bishop's Treasury** (*riznica*; daily: summer 9am–noon & 5–7pm; winter 10am–noon; 10Kn) houses a small but fine selection of chalices, reliquaries and embroidery. Look out for a nicely worked sixteenth-century bishop's crozier, carved into the shape of a serpent encrusted with saints and embossed with a figure of the Virgin, attended by Moses and an archangel.

Uluz Ali and the raid on Hvar

As one of the archetypal bad guys of Dalmatian history, the corsair **Uluz Ali** gets a passing mention in most of the local museums – and yet few make an effort to explain who he actually was. Born Luca Galeni in Calabria in 1508, he was captured by the Ottoman Turks off Naples and became a galley slave, until conversion to Islam won him his freedom. He made his name as a corsair, raiding Mediterranean shipping from the safety of Ottoman-controlled North Africa, was appointed *bey* (viceroy) of Algiers in 1568 and captured the city of Tunis from the Spanish the following year. In 1571, with the maritime forces of the **Holy League** (Austria, Venice and Spain) massing to take on the Ottoman navy in the eastern Mediterranean, Uluz Ali assembled a fleet of eighty ships to mount a diversionary attack on Venetian possessions in the Adriatic. After an unsuccessful raid on Korčula he arrived off Hvar Town on August 17. The population fled to the safety of their hilltop citadel and could only watch helplessly as Ali's men torched their dwellings below. The raiders meted out similar punishment to Stari Grad, Jelsa and Vrboska before withdrawing to rejoin the rest of the Ottoman fleet.

In an important postscript to the raid, the ships of the Holy League eventually caught up with the Ottomans at **Lepanto**, near Corfu, on October 7. The Turkish fleet was scattered, but it was something of a Pyrrhic victory for the Western powers. The Holy League began to fragment and the Venetians, weakened by their losses, had to give up Cyprus to the Turks in order to secure peace.

North to the citadel

The rest of the old town backs up the hillside north from the square with a grid of narrow lanes and alleys hiding a series of understated architectural gems. Just uphill from the cathedral, the diminutive **Church of the Holy Spirit** (Crkva svetog Duha) has a small but striking Romanesque relief of God the Creator above the portal, while just down the steps from here the **Church of SS Cosmas and Damian** (Crkva svetog Kozme i Damjana) sports a fine barrel-vaulted roof. West of here lies the main "street" in this quarter of town – actually more a flight of steps – the steep Matije Ivanića. The striking roofless **palace** at its southern end – a grey shell punctuated by delicately carved Gothic windows – is popularly ascribed to the Hektorović family, but was more likely commissioned by another noble family, the Užičić, in 1463, and never finished. Behind it, the **Leporini Palace** is identifiable by a carving of a rabbit – the family emblem – halfway up the wall, to the left of the awning belonging to the *Leporini* restaurant. Further up Ivanića lies the **Benedictine convent** (Benediktinski samostan; Mon–Sat 10am–noon & 5–7pm; 10Kn), founded by the daughter-in-law of the sixteenth-century Hvar poet Hanibal Lucić, which occupies the poet's former town house. Inside there's a small display of devotional paintings, and lace made by the nuns.

Head to the top of Ivanića to find the path which zigzags its way up an agave-covered hillside to the **Citadel** (Fortica; June–Sept 8am–midnight; Oct–May 9am–dusk; 10Kn), built by the Venetians in the 1550s with the help of Spanish engineers – the structure is still known colloquially as *Španjola* by the locals. There's a marine archeology collection in one of the halls, with an attractively presented display of amphorae and other sediment-encrusted Greco-Roman drinking vessels, although the real attraction is the view from the citadel's ramparts. Largely intact stretches of defensive wall plunge down the hillside towards the terracotta roofs of Hvar Town below, while beyond stretch the deep green humps of the Pakleni islands just offshore and the bulky grey form of Vis farther out to the southwest.

△ Hvar, seen from the citadel

The Dominican monastery

A couple of hundred metres west of Trg svetog Stjepana, slightly set back from the shoreline, are the remains of a **Dominican monastery** (you can see its surviving bell tower from the citadel), an important centre of religious and political life until it was expropriated by French administrators in 1811 and allowed to fall into ruin. It was here in 1525 that Friar Vinko Pribojević famously addressed the Hvar nobility with his paper *De origine successibisque slavorum* (Of the Origin and History of the Slavs), a landmark text in the development of Croatian national self-consciousness. Pribojević floated the not unreasonable idea that all Slavs were ethnically related, but added the improbable hypothesis that they had their origins in Dalmatia, from where the Croatian brothers Čeh, Leh and Rus set out to found the Czech, Polish and Russian nations respectively. The tale of the three brothers is a common theme in Slavic folklore: it crops up in Poland and Russia as well as in the Croatian Zagorje town of Krapina.

The surviving apse of the monastery church now holds a small **archeology collection** (*arheološka zbirka*; May–Oct: daily 10am–noon & 8.30–10.30pm; 10Kn), with exhibits from prehistoric through to Roman times. Besides flint arrows and axe-heads from two of the island's caves – the Grapčeva and Markova – where the island's first Neolithic inhabitants holed up, there are ceramics from the late Neolithic Hvar Culture, including an anthropomorphic four-legged brazier, the most arresting item in an unassuming collection.

The Franciscan monastery

Occupying a headland just southeast of Hvar Town's ferry dock is the **Franciscan monastery** (Franjevački samostan; May–Oct Mon–Fri 10am–noon & 5–7pm; 20Kn), founded in 1461 by a Venetian sea captain in thanks for deliverance from shipwreck. There's a small collection of paintings in the former refectory, most famously a dramatic, near life-size seventeenth-century *Last Supper* by Matteo Ingoli of Ravenna, which covers almost the entire back wall. Smaller-scale devotional works in the neighbouring room include a tranquil *Mystical Wedding of St Catherine* painted in around 1430 by a follower of Blaž Jurjev of Trogir.

Next door is the pleasingly simple monastic **church**, with beautifully carved choir stalls and a fanciful partition of 1583. Built to separate the commoners from the nobility, the latter is decorated with six animated scenes of the Passion by Martin Benetović, a local seventeenth-century painter, and a brace of less expressive polyptychs by Francesco da Santacroce. Look out for the extravagant dragon candle-holders that push out above the panel detail below. The floor is paved with gravestones, including that of poet and playwright Hanibal Lucić by the altar, identifiable by the fleur-de-lys and dove's wing of the family crest. In the small side chapel, there's a moving *Christ on the Cross* by Leandro Bassano.

The Pakleni otoci

There are 3km of rock and concrete **beaches** east of Hvar Town in front of the big hotels, although if you want to swim it's better to head for the **Pakleni otoci** (which get their name from either *pakao* ["hell"] or *paklina* ["resin"] depending on which of the locals you talk to), a chain of eleven wooded islands just to the west of town, three of which – Sveti Jerolim, Marinkovac and Sveti Klement – are easily reached by water taxi from Hvar's harbour (30–60Kn return). Sveti Klement has a pair of decent restaurants, and there are rudimentary café-snack bar facilities on the other two.

Nearest to the coast, **SVETI JEROLIM** is a purely naturist island which has a beach popular with same-sex couples on its far side. Immediately west, the slightly larger **MARINKOVAC** boasts two popular beaches, the sandy Ždrilca on the northern side and U Stipanska on the south. West of Marinkovac, **SVETI KLEMENT** is the largest of the Pakleni and has a correspondingly wider range of facilities. Boats disgorge their passengers at Palmižana yachting marina on the island's northern side, from where it's a short walk over the island's wooded spine to **Palmižana** proper, a small hillside hamlet boasting a hotel (the *Meneghello*; see p.401) and a couple of café-restaurants. At the bottom of the hill lies an attractive bay with a tiny crescent of sandy beach, a smooth sandy seabed for paddling on, and plenty of rocky bathing perches on either side. A marked path leads west from Palmižana along the island's central ridge (follow the signs to Konoba Dioniz), passing through maquis rich in wild rosemary before arriving at the village of **Vloka**, a kasbah-like huddle of houses surrounded by groves of enormous cacti. Dioniz itself, on the southern side itself, is a great place to sample freshly caught fish, seasonal vegetables and local wine.

Eating, drinking and nightlife

There are dozens of places to eat in Hvar Town, none of them too expensive. For a daytime **snack**, the **bakery** on the harbour, near the Mandrać, is the best place for *burek*, pizza slices and pastries. Among the **restaurants**, expect to see plenty of seafood pasta, seafood risotto, and expertly grilled fish – you can make a good meal out of one of the first two even if your budget doesn't stretch to the latter. One speciality particular to Hvar is *gregada*, a stew of fish cooked in white wine – few restaurants bother to serve it in single portions, however, so you'll have to order it for two or more people to make it worthwhile. Note that many restaurants are only open from April to October.

For **drinking**, the cafés and bars around the main square and along the harbour are packed from mid-morning onwards. Trade thins out for a few hours during the hottest part of the day, until the crowds return for the evening *korzo*. Some bars stay open until 2am or later in July and August – but all close up much earlier outside this period.

Restaurants

Bounty Fabrika bb. Heavily touristed but reasonably priced place serving up simple grilled fish, grilled meat and seafood risottos. The main attraction is the location, with outdoor tables arranged right on the inner harbour.

Hanibal Trg svetog Stjepana. Reliable standards of food and service in this long-established main-square venue. Pretty much everything in the Croatian culinary repertoire gets a look in.

Junior Pučkog ustanka 4. Informal, easy-going place offering the usual seafood dishes, none of which is too expensive, including a mean shrimp pasta (*špageti sa kozicama*). Tables are scattered across a narrow medieval street.

Kod Kapetana Fabrika bb. Homely family-run establishment boasting a big port-facing terrace. The fish, shellfish and steaks on offer are always good quality.

Luna alleyway off Matije Ivanića. Familiar seafood recipes, including excellent grilled fish, lobster and *gregada*, in a modern, white-walled interior with contemporary arty touches.

Macondo Groda. This place has got style and quality, yet remains informal, and for a slap-up seafood feast there are few better places: fresh white fish is always of good quality, and the *škampi buzara* (unpeeled prawns in wine sauce) is excellent. It's tucked away in a backstreet uphill from the main square (head up Matije Ivanića and take the second right).

Palac Paladini Groda, in an alleyway off Matije Ivanića. Good range of medium to expensive seafood and Croatian standards, with outdoor seating in a high-walled garden courtyard stuffed with plants.

Pizzeria Kogo Trg svetog Stjepana. The most dependable of the town's pizzerias; also offers decent pasta dishes and hearty steaks too. Usually open all year round and remains popular with locals as well as tourists.

Yakša Groda, in an alleyway off Matije Ivanića. A recently renovated sixteenth-century palace filled with minimalist designer furnishings, offering upmarket food with friendly informal service. Imaginative fish recipes, a large selection of wines from Hvar and elsewhere, and some delicious desserts.

Zlatna Školjka Groda, in an alleyway off Matije Ivanića. Intimate covered-patio atmosphere, attentive service and great food in an upscale restaurant offering an imaginative take on local cuisine. Choose between traditional seafood dishes like *gregada* or unusual meat dishes such as rabbit in fig sauce.

Cafés, bars and clubs

Carpe Diem Obala oslobođenja. Prime meeting place for Croatia's beautiful people, with relaxing wicker chairs and cushions outside, and a brash and often crowded bar inside. Cocktail quality can be unpredictable and service veers from courteous to contemptuous, but this is still the place to see and be seen.

Gromit Obala oslobođenja. Day- and night-time café-bar on the Riva, a popular vantage point from which to admire the expensive yachts moored in the harbour. A decent choice of pastries and cakes makes this the ideal stop-off either for breakfast or afternoon snacking.

Jazz Burak bb. Laid-back, intimate bar in the tangle of streets leading south of the main square. Jungle-themed decor, a decent list of cocktails, and a playlist that features more than just top-forty sounds.

Keva in an alleway behind Fabrika. Raucously enjoyable black hole of a place just off the port-side path. Can be a tight squeeze on summer weekends.

Konoba Menego Matije Ivanića. Cosy tavern with wooden barrels for tables, on the steep street leading uphill from the main square. Wines (from Vloka, on the island of Sveti Klement; see overleaf) are served by the glass or by the carafe, and there's a snack menu comprising anchovies, cheese and homemade sausage.

Loco Trg svetog Stjepana. The best of a long line of stylish youth-oriented bars, running from the main square in the east to the *Hotel Adriatic* in the west. Relaxing, quirky and chic.

Veneranda on the hillside on the western side of the harbour. Occupying the surviving fortifications of a Venetian fortress, this outdoor club comes into its own at the weekends, when international DJs are shipped in to entertain the crowds until dawn. Different styles of music on different nights – so look out for posters.

Stari Grad

Twenty kilometres east across the mountains, straggling along the side of a deep bay, **STARI GRAD** is a popular and busy resort, though more laid-back than Hvar Town. The narrow streets of central Stari Grad are as atmospheric as anywhere in the Adriatic: a warren of low stone houses bedecked with window-boxes, and narrow alleyways suddenly opening out onto small squares.

Arrival, information and accommodation

Stari Grad's **harbour**, 3km west of town, is the island's main terminal for car ferries from the mainland. Buses on the Hvar-Stari Grad route call in at the terminal before proceeding to Stari Grad's **bus station**, a simple plastic shelter on the edge of the centre, a short walk from the Riva. You'll find the **tourist office** in the harbourside market at Nova Riva 2 (July & Aug daily 8am–2pm & 5–9pm; Sept–June Mon–Fri 8am–2pm, Sat 10am–noon; ⓣ021/765-763 & 021/766-231, ⓦwww.stari-grad-faros.hr).

The Mistral agency (Mon–Sat 9am–12.30pm & 6.30–8.30pm, Sun 7–9pm; ⓣ021/765-281) and Hvar-Touristik (daily 9am–1pm & 6–8pm; ⓣ021/717-580, ⓔinfo@hvat-touristik.de), both on the Riva, can arrange accommodation in private **rooms** (❶) and **apartments** (two-person studios from ❷, four-person apartments 450Kn). Stari Grad's concrete **hotels** (all April–Oct), grouped around the north side of the bay, are a pretty characterless bunch all round: the two-star *Helios* (ⓣ021/765-865, ⓦwww.heliosfaros.hr; ❹) is plain but adequate, while the three-star *Arkada* (ⓣ021/765-555, ⓦwww.heliosfaros.hr; ❺) and *Lavanda* (ⓣ021/306-330, ⓦwww.heliosfaros.hr; ❺, all-inclusive ❻) are slightly plusher. On the south side of town, *Autocamp Jurjevac* (ⓣ021/765-843, ⓦwww.heliosfaros.hr) occupies a partly shaded site in what used to be the town park, and rents out en-suite four-person **bungalows** for 500Kn.

The Town

The old part of Stari Grad has been pleasantly renovated, and backs onto the main street as it twists its way along the waterside. Just back from the water is Stari Grad's most famous sight, the **Tvrdalj** (daily: June & Sept 10am–1pm; July & Aug 10am–1pm & 5–8pm; 10Kn), the summer house and walled garden of the sixteenth-century poet and aristocrat Petar Hektorović (see box overleaf). Those expecting a stately home might be disappointed: the original crenellated structure disappeared behind the present plain facade in the nineteenth century, and Hektorović's extensive gardens – which once featured clipped rows of box and medicinal herbs, as well as cypresses and oleanders sent by fellow poet Mavro Vetranović of Dubrovnik – have now been largely divided up into allotments, although a portion has been tidied up and returned to its former glories. It's still a remarkably restful location, however, built around a central cloister with a turquoise pond fed with sea water and packed with mullet. Hektorović littered the place with inscriptions (carved round the pond and on the walls of the house in Latin, Italian and Croatian) to encourage contemplation: "Neither riches nor fame, beauty nor age can save you from Death" is one characteristically cheerful effusion.

The lane to the right of the Tvrdalj as you face it leads up to the **Bianchini Palace** (Palača Biankini; June–Sept daily 10am–noon & 7–9pm; 10Kn), an impressively restored Renaissance pile which boasts a dramatic display of Roman amphorae – rescued by marine archeologists from a fourth-century shipwreck – in the ground-floor lobby. Upstairs are finds from ancient Greek Pharos, including pottery fragments, clay figurines and a *louterion* – a stone basin used for washing before a ceremony or sacrifice.

To the left of the Tvrdalj a lane leads up to the **Dominican monastery**, a fifteenth-century foundation half-heartedly fortified with the addition of a single sturdy turret after Uluz Ali's attack of 1571. Rooms off the cloister house a **museum** (June–Sept Mon–Fri 10am–noon & 5.30–7.30pm; 10Kn), which contains an absorbing collection of Greek gravestones from Pharos, Creto-Venetian icons and a *Deposition* by Tintoretto. According to local tradition, the

Petar Hektorović and the Tvrdalj

Renaissance poet and Hvar noble **Petar Hektorović** (1487–1572) is primarily remembered for his *Ribanje i ribarsko prigovaranje* ("Fishing and Fishermen's Conversations"), the first work of autobiographical realism in Croatian literature. Written in 1556, when he was already an old man, the 1680-line poem was inspired by a three-day boat trip to Brač and Šolta in the company of two local fishermen, Paskoje and Nikola, who despite being commoners are accorded a dignity which was rare for the literature of the period. Hektorović had lived through the Ivanić rebellion of the early sixteenth century, and perhaps intended *Ribanje* as a message to his fellow aristocrats – treat the lower orders with a bit of humanity, and the bonds of society will hold.

This sense of *noblesse oblige* also underpinned Hektorović's plans for the **Tvrdalj**, which he began in 1514 and carried on building for the rest of his life. As well as a place of repose for himself, it was intended to be a fortified refuge for the locals in time of attack – a self-sufficient ark which would provide food from its garden and fresh fish from the mullet pond. Hektorović's typically Renaissance fondness for order and balance was reflected in the symbolic inclusion of a pigeon loft in the main tower, to emphasize the point that the Tvrdalj was a refuge for creatures of the sky as well as the sea and earth. The house was built in simple unadorned style, both because Hektorović had a taste for rusticity and because he didn't want to provoke the locals with a display of lordly luxury. Local Venetian commanders actually sanctioned the diversion of manpower resources from Hvar Town to assist Hektorović in its construction, since it freed them from the responsibility of defending the people of Stari Grad from pirates.

The Tvrdalj never fulfilled its intended purpose: it was damaged during Uluz Ali's raid of 1571, and Hektorović died the following year before finishing the thing off, though it was renovated and preserved by his descendants until the nineteenth century, when new owners arrived and its shape was radically changed. Ironically, the one thing which most people find so memorable about the Tvrdalj – the restful arched cloister surrounding the fishpond – wasn't part of Hektorović's original plan, added instead by the Niseteo family in 1834.

figures of Joseph of Arimathea, Mary Magdalene and the young man leaning over Christ's body in the picture are portraits of Hektorović, his granddaughter Julija and her husband Antun Lucić – although more sober analysts have pointed out that many of the stock figures in the artist's paintings possess similar faces. There's also a small display of Hektorović's effects, including a 1532 edition of Petrarch's *Sonnets* and a copy of Polybius's *Histories*.

In the fields immediately south of the monastery, the Chapel of St Nicholas (Crkvica sveti Nikole) was the scene of an extraordinary demonstration of religiosity in 1554, when the hermit **Lukrecija of Brač** chose to be walled into a small side-room, where she lived on bread and water until her death 35 years later. Heading east from the monastery and then turning left back towards the town centre brings you past **St John's Church** (Crkva svetog Ivana), a twelfth-century Romanesque church with some sixth-century mosaics inside, and **St Stephen's Church** (Crkva svetog Stjepana), a plain, weatherbeaten example of Dalmatian Baroque with a fine Venetian campanile. Embedded in a wall opposite the church is a Roman-era gravestone relief of Winged Eros leaning nonchalantly on an upside-down torch – a classic symbol of death.

From here, the narrow streets leading back through the centre towards the Tvrdalj boast an atmospheric line-up of simple medieval stone houses. One of them, at Vagonj 1, now accommodates the **Moria art gallery** (Ⓦwww.moria.hr), scene of some of the best contemporary exhibitions on this part of

Croatia's **Islands**

It's on Croatia's islands that the country's laid-back Mediterranean character reveals itself to the full: here you'll find the pace of life more relaxed, the countryside more unspoilt and the cicadas more vociferous. Many of the bigger islands boast modern hotels and a fully developed tourist industry, although the package-oriented culture fades the farther from the coast you go. Some of the islands easily accessible from the mainland are also quieter: Vis, Lastovo, Silba and Veli Drvenik exude a half-abandoned, end-of-the-world appeal. For true connoisseurs of desert-island idylls, the middle-of-nowhere cottages available for rent on the Kornati islands offer the perfect getaway – although you'll have to book well in advance.

▲ Nugal beach, Makarska Riviera

▲ Rab, Kvarner Gulf

Island landscapes

Despite their proximity to the mainland, Croatia's islands have a very different character to that of the urbanized coast. Many of them were vibrant trading or vine-growing centres until changes in the nineteenth century economy provoked a mass wave of emigration, lending them a semi-abandoned, rustic feel, only partially overlaid by the annual influx of tourists. On southern Adriatic islands like Brač and Hvar, evidence of once-intensive agricultural activity is provided by the mysterious-looking stone walls which straggle across miles of terraced hillside. The walls are the remains of spoil-heaps left centuries ago by farmers compelled to clear their land of rocks in order to create pockets of cultivable space.

In the northern Adriatic, the islands of Pag, Rab and Krk are lushly forested on their western flanks, but appear startlingly bare when approached from the east. Stripped of trees by timber-hungry Venetians, they possess the hypnotically alien quality of the surface of the moon.

Beaches and swimming

On Croatia's islands pretty much every stretch of seashore qualifies as a "beach" (*plaža*) in Croatian, although they frequently turn out to be rocky outcrops rather than the perfect crescents of shingle or sand that you might have been dreaming of. Almost everywhere, however, the sea is unbelievably clear and swimming is safe; stony sea bottoms are the only hazard, so be sure to pack a pair of plastic sandals. Nude bathing has been an acceptable feature of the Croatian Riviera ever since being popularized by early twentieth-century aristocrats, and many beach areas have a designated section for naturists. If not, simply head for a secluded section of coast and let it all hang out.

Gorgeous stretches of sand do exist, and are often made all the more special for the extra effort required in getting to them. The Lopar peninsula on the island of Rab (see p.277) is particularly noted for its sandy coves, and you will find sandcastle-building opportunities aplenty on Korčula (p.418), Vis (p.411) and Lopud (p.472).

Off-shore hideways

Croatia's islands are dotted with the erstwhile holiday homes of the rich and powerful. The nobles of Renaissance Dubrovnik built palatial summer-houses on the islands of Šipan and Lopud, the ruins of which are still visible. Nineteenth-century Archduke Maximilian of Habsburg turned Lokrum, just off Dubrovnik, into his own private island, laying out a cactus-filled botanical garden which draws visitors to this day.

The greatest island getaway of them all was the Brijuni archipelago in the northern Adriatic, developed as an exclusive resort by the Kupelweiser family in the 1890s, and adopted as an official residence by Yugoslavia's communist ruler Josip Broz Tito after 1945. Tito and his guests – who included crème-de-la-crème celebrities like Richard Burton, Elizabeth Taylor and Sofia Loren – stayed in luxury seaside villas, surrounded by a private hunting reserve and a safari park stocked with the exotic beasts presented to Tito by world leaders. With the safari park now open to the public, Brijuni makes for a great excursion.

Wildlife

Having to rise at dawn to catch the early-morning ferry back to the mainland is one of the few drawbacks of holidaying on Croatia's islands. However, it presents the best chance you have of spotting the Adriatic's dolphin population, who seem to prefer the pre-breakfast hours as the best time to indulge in playful leaping. A 120-strong community of bottlenose dolphins can be found off the shores of Lošinj, where the quaint fishing port of Veli Lošinj is home to a marine education centre detailing local conservation efforts. The neighbouring island of Cres is one of the few remaining parts of Mediterranean Europe where griffon vultures can still be found, happily gorging themselves on the carcasses of local sheep and goats. An ecology centre at Beli has a display devoted to the creatures, groups of which can frequently be sighted circling the island in search of carrion.

A more incongruous sight are the mongooses of the island of Mljet: imported in the nineteenth century to rid the island of snakes, they can still bee seen scuttling around the undergrowth of the island's National Park.

▼ Bottlenose dolphin off the shores of Lošinj

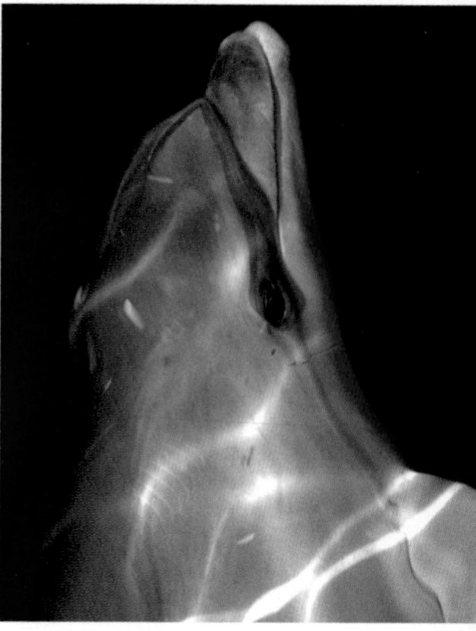

▲ The *moreška*, Korčula

Island festivals

The natural insularity of Croatia's offshore communities has led to the preservation of numerous festival traditions which have all but died out on the mainland. Most famous of these are the sword dances of Korčula (variously called the *moreška*, *kumpanjija* or *moštra*), where each town and village performs a ritual dance in the form of a mock battle, usually on the name-day of the community's patron saint. On the face of it, these dances appear to be a celebration of sixteenth-century military victories against the Ottoman Turks, although they probably date back to age-old pagan fertility rites. The *moreška* of Korčula town has become a major tourist attraction, with performances taking place once or twice a week during the holiday season.

Celebration of the pre-Lenten carnival is common throughout Croatia, but is rarely marked with so much attention to archaic ritual as on Lastovo, where the annual *Poklad* involves dressing a puppet in a red military uniform, dragging it through the streets, suspending it above the town on ropes and pulleys, and finally having it burnt to much rejoicing. The destruction of the puppet symbolizes the cleansing of the village of everything bad that has happened during the course of the previous year, and ensures fertility and prosperity in the coming one.

Croatia's top ten island beaches

Susak island (see p.257)
Lopar peninsula Rab (see p.277)
Sakarun Dugi otok (see p.324)
Zlatni rat Brač (see p.396)
Lumbarda Korčula (see p.426)
Šunj Lopud (see p.473)
Palmižana Hvar (see p.405)
Stiniva Bay, **Vis** (see p.411)
Lokrum island (see p.459)
Krknjaši Veli Drvenik (see p.349)

▲ Šunj beach, Lopud

the coast – there's also a large, well-preserved fragment of Roman mosaic in the basement.

There are rock and concrete **beaches** on the northern side of the bay in front of the hotels, from where a path carries on beyond the *Arkada* mega-hotel to a much less sanitized area of rocks backed by pines. Much better is the bay favoured by locals on the other (southern) side of the bay – simply walk along the Riva to the end of town and you'll find a shallow rocky bay perfect for snorkelling.

Eating, drinking and entertainment

Eating in Stari Grad is rarely a problem: the backstreets of the old town offer a generous sprinkling of *konobe*, most of which are friendlier and cheaper than the affluence-attuned establishments back in Hvar Town. The town's **drinking** scene revolves around the laid-back cafés lining the harbourfront.

Star Grad's most important annual event is the **Feast of St Rock** on 16 August, when an effigy of the saint is paraded around town and outdoor concerts last throughout the evening. The summer season also sees chamber concerts in the Dominican Monastery (contact the tourist office for details) and a mid-August international literature festival organized by the Moria Art Gallery (see opposite).

Restaurants

Buffet Zrin northern side of the harbour. On the coastal path leading towards the package hotels, this homely restaurant in an ancient building serves up tasty pizzas and other inexpensive dishes. Garden seating facing towards a pebbly beach.

Eremitaž northern side of the harbour. Occupying one half of the same stone structure as the *Zrin* (see above), this is one of the best places in town for grilled fish and seafood. Shaded terrace out front.

Konoba Galerija Ljubić Srinjo kola. In the warren of narrow streets behind the harbour, this wine tavern-restaurant serves up simple home cooking and tasty snacks, and also stages concerts and quirky art events.

Jurin Podrum Duolnja kolja. Traditional *konoba* in the narrow streets east of the Tvrdalj, offering a tasty range of home-cooked seafood dishes washed down with local wines.

Restorančić Antika Duolnja kolja. Old-town parlour strewn with antique furniture and bric-a-brac, and serving local specialities like *pašticada*, baked octopus and other seafood, with a few international dishes thrown in. A touch more expensive than the others, but still affordable.

Jelsa

The tiny port and fishing village of **JELSA** sits prettily by a wooded bay 10km east of Stari Grad. Tucked away behind a nineteenth-century waterfront, the old quarter, a maze of ancient alleys and lanes, climbs up the hill; the two big hotels on either side of the bay, fronted by concrete bathing platforms, seem oddly out of place. Just off the quayside is the charming octagonal sixteenth-century **Chapel of St John** (Crkva svetog Ivana), squeezed into one of the old squares and overhung by the balconies of the surrounding Renaissance buildings. Up from here is the town's fortified **parish church**, which managed to resist Uluz Ali's attack of 1571, though it's hard to make out the original design as the facade and bell tower were added in the nineteenth century. Opening times are unpredictable – if you do manage to get in, look out for the wooden Gothic statue of the Madonna (brought here from the mainland in 1539 to keep it safe from the Ottomans) on the high altar. You can avoid the crowded **beaches** by taking a taxi boat to the Glavica peninsula near Vrboska (see overleaf).

Practicalities

Buses stop about 300m inland from the harbour, where you'll find a **tourist office** on the western side (June & Sept Mon–Sat 8.30am–12.30pm & 6.30–8.30pm,

Sun 9am–noon; July & Aug Mon–Sat 9am–10pm, Sun 9.30am–12.30pm & 6.30–9.30pm; Oct–May Mon–Fri 9am–noon; Ⓣ021/761-017, Ⓦwww.tzjelsa.hr). Private **rooms** (❶) and **apartments** (two-person studios from ❸, four-person apartments from 480Kn) are available from Globus, in between the bus station and the harbour (daily 8am–noon & 4–9pm, Ⓣ021/761-955, Ⓦwww.globus-tours.hr); and Atlas (Ⓣ021/761-605), on the harbour beside the tourist office. Among the most characterful places to stay is the family-run *Pansion Murvica* (Ⓣ021/761-405, Ⓦwww.geocities.com/gurdulic2001; ❸), located in a residential street behind the bus station, which offers nifty studio apartments with TV and kitchenette. Best of the packagey hotels is the *Mina* on the south side of the bay (Ⓣ021/761-122, Ⓦwww.hoteli-jelsa.hr; ❺), a concrete eyesore of 1980s vintage that just about deserves two and a half stars – but not the three advertised. In front of the hotel is a **campsite**, also called *Mina* (Ⓣ021/761-210, Ⓕ761-227), occupying a pine-shaded promontory overlooking the sea and with good access to a pebbly beach.

Pansion Murvica serves up decent **food**; otherwise the best of the restaurants for local fish and shellfish are *Konoba Frina*, occupying a walled garden in the narrow streets beyond the octagonal chapel; and *Konoba Nono*, a signed five-minute walk inland from the village centre, which offers delicious traditional dishes in a rustic interior. *Arsenal*, on the north side of the harbour, offers a more varied range of French-influenced international cuisine, and charges slightly higher prices. *Dgigibaoo*, east of the centre on the way to the *Mina* hotel and campsite, is a lively **café-bar** with a respectable range of pizzas and cakes. *Tabu*, over on the north side of the harbour, with soft furnishings and lounge-bar DJs, is the perfect place for an evening chill-out.

Vrboska

The sleepy little village of **VRBOSKA** is strung along the side of another of the island's deep bays, about 4km from Jelsa, and is easily reached by bus or water taxi, or by following the coastal path which begins on the north side of Jelsa harbour.

The two sides of Vrboska, on either side of the inlet, are joined by three small and picturesque bridges. Perched above the quayside is the unusual, fortified **St Mary's Church** (Crkva svete Marije; Mon–Sat 10am–noon & 6–7pm), dating from 1580, which was extensively fortified to resist attacks from pirates and the Turks. The result is a high, unadorned edifice with a crenellated tower on the southeast corner, and a hefty bastion on the northwest – a protruding, angular structure that looks like the prow of a beached dreadnought. The interior is partly paved with grave slabs and from the sacristy you can get onto the roof for a view of the town below. A couple of minutes away, the Baroque **St Lawrence's Church** (Crkva svetog Lovre; Mon–Sat 10am–noon & 6–7pm) has a small art collection, including a stagey-looking polyptych depicting St Lawrence flanked by John the Baptist and St Nicholas on the high altar, nowadays attributed to Paolo Veronese, although local tradition ascribes it to Titian. To the right, there's a *Madonna of the Rosary* by Leandro Bassano.

There's a series of **beaches**, including a couple of naturist ones, on the Glavica peninsula 2km northeast of town. You can find quieter spots by walking north from Vrboska, straight over Kaštilac hill (where there's a ruined tower), to the isolated bays of Hvar's north coast. From here there's a great view of the southern flanks of Brač and, away in the distance, the stark ridge of Mount Biokovo on the mainland.

Practicalities

Buses from Hvar Town and Stari Grad stop in the centre of the village on the north side of the inlet, a couple of doors down from the **tourist office** (July & Aug Mon–Sat 8am–noon & 6–9pm, Sun 10.30am–noon & 6.30–8pm; Sept–June Mon–Fri 8am–2pm; ⓣ021/744-137). Across the bridge from here and along the harbourfront, Spes tours (ⓦwww.spes-tours-vrboska.hr) will sort you out with rooms pure-and-simple (❶), rooms with breakfast (❷), or apartments (two-person studios from ❷, four-person apartments from 530Kn). The *Gardelin* **restaurant**, just east of the village on the path to Jelsa, is the place to go for *gregada*, *brudet* and other fishy specialities; *Bufet Skojić*, on the harbourfront, offers a more straightforward line in pizzas and seafood risottos.

Vis

A compact hump rearing dramatically out of the sea, **VIS** is situated farther offshore than any of Croatia's other inhabited Adriatic islands. Closed to foreigners for military reasons until 1989, the island has never been overrun by tourists, and with only two or three package-oriented hotels on the whole island, this is definitely one place in Croatia where the independent traveller rules the roost. Croatian holiday-makers have fallen in love with the place over the last decade, drawn by its wild mountainous scenery, some interesting historical relics and two good-looking small towns – **Vis Town** and **Komiža**. The latter is the obvious base for trips to the islet of **Biševo**, site of one of Croatia's most famous natural wonders, the **Blue Cave**.

Ferries run year round between Split and Vis Town (1 or 2 daily; 2hr 30min; once a week these call in at Hvar on the way), though in winter the trip can get mighty rough. From mid-July to late August there are also two weekly ferries from Ancona in Italy.

Some history

Vis's history has been shaped by its strategic position on the sea approaches to central Dalmatia. The **Greeks** settled here in the fourth century BC, choosing the island as a base because of its convenience as a stepping stone between the eastern and western shores of the Adriatic, and founding **Issa** on the site of

Food and drink on Vis

The waters off the island of Vis represent one of the richest fisheries in the Adriatic, and it's no wonder that the local restaurants offer some of the freshest seafood in Dalmatia. However, the island's principal culinary trademark is the **pogača od srdele** (anchovy pasty), also called *viška pogača* or *komiška pogača* depending on which town you're staying in. Traditionally, the *komiška pogača* includes a richer combination of ingredients (including tomatoes), and it's this version which is sold by most local bakeries and cafés.

The island's other claim to gastronomic fame is the delicious **Viški hib**, a deliciously sweet slab of compressed figs and herbs, which is served in tiny thin slices and goes down a treat with the local *rakija*.

Vis is also famous for a brace of fine local **wines** – the white *Vugava* which thrives in the stony soil in the southeast of the island, and the red *Viški plavac* which prefers the sandy terrain farther west.

present-day Vis Town. Hvar took over as the major mid-Adriatic port in the late middle ages, and Vis became a rural retreat for Hvar nobles. When the fall of Venice in 1797 opened up the Adriatic to the competing navies of the European great powers, Vis initially fell to the **British**, who fortified the harbour and fought off Napoleon's navy in 1811. The **Austrians** took over in 1815, famously brushing aside Italian maritime ambitions in another big sea battle here in 1866. Vis's position was once more exploited during World War II (see box on p.417), when Josip Broz **Tito**'s Partisan movement was briefly based here. After the war, the island was heavily garrisoned and used for military training, a situation which, along with the decline of traditional industries like fishing and fish canning, encouraged successive waves of **emigration**. The island had 10,000 inhabitants before World War II; it now has fewer than 3000. According to local estimates, there are ten times more Komiža families living in San Pedro, California, than in the town itself.

Vis Town

VIS TOWN's sedate arc of grey-brown houses stretches around a deeply indented bay, above which looms a steep escarpment covered with the remains of abandoned agricultural terraces. There's not much of the ancient Greek settlement of Issa to be seen, apart from a few chunks of unadorned masonry – most of which have been absorbed into the dry-stone walls of local gardeners – on the hills above town.

Arrival and information

Just to the right of the ferry dock as you step off the boat, Vis's **tourist office** (summer Mon–Sat 9am–1pm & 6–9pm; winter Mon–Fri 9am–1pm; Ⓣ & Ⓕ021/717-017, Ⓦwww.tz-vis.hr) is a mine of local information and can help with directions to out-of-town beaches, which might be quieter than the ones here or in Komiža. The Ionios agency, on the Riva, 200m left of the ferry dock (daily 8am–10pm; Ⓣ021/711-531, Ⓔionios@st.hinet.hr), rents out bikes (70Kn/day) and scooters (260Kn/day). Bikes can also be rented outside the *Hotel Issa* (60Kn/day). Diving Center Vis, operating out of a hut by the Franciscan monastery (Ⓣ021/711-367, Ⓦwww.anma.hr), rents out scuba-diving gear and offers courses. You can **surf the net** at *Biblia*, just behind the harbourfront on ulica Žrtava fašizma.

Accommodation

The most reliable sources of **rooms** (❶–❷) and **apartments** (two-person studios ❸, four-person apartments 450Kn) are the Ionios agency (see above) and Navigator, right opposite the ferry dock at Šetalište stare Isse 1 (Ⓣ021/717-786, Ⓦwww.navigator.hr). One source of private accommodation with friendly hosts is *Teni & Joško Tomić*, Zagrebački 3 (Ⓣ021/711-871), who have a handful of two- to four-person apartments in a modern family house slightly uphill from the seafront, most with views overlooking the town.

Of the **hotels**, the best is the *Paula*, Petra Hektorovića 2 (Ⓣ021/711-362, Ⓔhotel-paula@st.htnet.hr; ❺), set amid the picturesque alleyways of the eastern suburb of **Kut**. It's a family-run affair, offering smart modern rooms with TV, as well as some three- and four-person apartments. In town, a worthy alternative is the stately, Habsburg-era *Tamaris*, on the waterfront at Obala sv. Jurja, east of the ferry dock (Ⓣ021/711-350, Ⓔtamaris@st.htnet.hr; ❺), which has cosy en-suite rooms with TV, air conditioning and squeaky parquet floors, as well as a

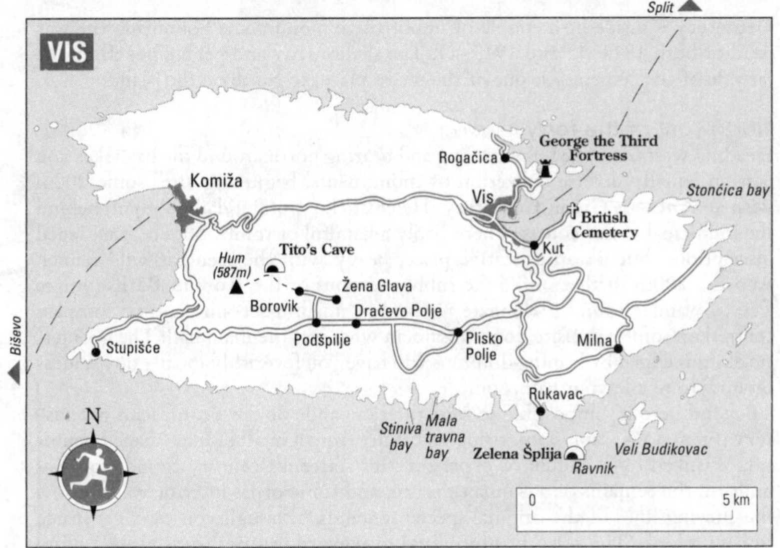

handful of attic apartments costing 950Kn for two or three people. About 800m west of the ferry dock at Apolonija Zanelle 5, the modern *Issa* (May–Sept only; Ⓣ & Ⓕ021/711-124, Ⓔissa@st.t-com.hr; ❺) is owned by the same firm as the *Tamaris* and costs just as much, but hasn't received the same amount of investment: the en-suite rooms are adequate but slightly tatty and don't all come with air conditioning and TV.

The Town

The most attractive parts of town are east of the ferry landing (to the left as you get off the boat). A five-minute walk along the front brings you to the venerable **Church of Our Lady** (Gospa od Spilica), a squat sixteenth-century structure harbouring a *Madonna and Saints* by Girolamo da Santacroce, just beyond which is the Austrian defensive bastion known as **Gospina baterija** (Our Lady's Battery). A barrack block at the rear of the bastion has been transformed into the **Town Museum** (Gradski muzej; June–Sept Tues–Sun 10am–1pm & 5–9pm; 20Kn), a small but well-organized collection mixing Greco-Roman finds with nineteenth-century wine presses and domestic furniture. The star exhibit is the bronze head of a Greek goddess, possibly Aphrodite, from the fourth century BC, which is claimed to be by a student of Praxiteles, although only a replica is on display – the original is locked up in the town vaults.

Another 500m east along the seafront lies the suburb of **Kut** (literally "quiet corner" or "hideaway"), a largely sixteenth-century tangle of narrow cobbled streets overlooked by the summer houses built by the nobility of Hvar – the stone balconies and staircases give the place an undeniably aristocratic air. Kut's **St Cyprian's Church** (Crkva svetog Ciprijana) squats beneath a campanile adorned with unusual sun and rose motifs. There's a fine wooden ceiling inside, although it's difficult to gain access outside Mass times.

Continuing round the bay from Kut for another fifteen minutes brings you to a small wooded peninsula, and a tiny walled garden containing a **British**

Cemetery – inside lie a couple of unobtrusive monuments honouring the war dead of both 1811–15 and 1943–44. The shallow bay and pebble **beach** on the far side of the cemetery is one of the nicest places to bathe on the island.

Northwest of the ferry landing

Heading west from the ferry landing and bearing north around the bay takes you past an equally diverse collection of monuments, beginning after some 200m with an **Ancient Greek Cemetery** (Helenističko groblje; daily 4–8pm) behind the municipal tennis courts. There's only a handful of tombstones bearing faded inscriptions, but it's an evocative place, heavy with the scent of wild fennel. Another 200m further on lie the rubbly remains of the **Roman Baths** (you're free to wander round if the gate is open), a smallish second-century complex centred on some exquisite floor mosaics in what was the main hall. The geometric designs edged by leaping dolphins will have you feverishly jotting down ideas on how to re-tile your bathroom.

Beyond here it's impossible to miss the campanile of the **Franciscan monastery** (Franjevački samostan), rising gracefully from a small kidney-shaped peninsula. Flanked by a huddle of cypresses, this sixteenth-century foundation was built on the remains of a Roman theatre, and some of its interior walls follow the curving lines of the original spectator stands, although you can't get inside to have a look. The adjacent **municipal graveyard** features some elegant nineteenth-century funerary sculpture, and a lion-topped memorial to those who died in 1866's **Battle of Vis**, when Austrian battleships under Admiral Tegethoff scattered the Italian fleet.

Beyond the monastery, the road continues along the shoreline past the *Hotel Issa*. After twenty minutes, a track breaks off to the right and brings you in ten minutes to the **George the Third** fortress, built by the British in 1813 to guard the entrance to Vis harbour. At the time of writing visitors can wander at will through this remarkably well-preserved complex (although access may become more difficult once the authorities decide what to do with it), entering the main courtyard through a doorway topped by a crude carving of the Union Jack. A passage leads through the sturdily built barrack blocks, emerging onto a sea-facing gun terrace shaded by palms and agaves.

Returning to the road and heading northeastwards uphill takes you past **Fort Wellington** (accessible in five minutes via goat-track), a ruined white tower constructed by the British after 1811, which crowns a blustery ridge providing fine views back towards Vis Town to the south, or out towards the island of Hvar over to the northwest. Beyond here, the road drops down into Rogačica bay, where a concrete-lined tunnel on the far side of the inlet was once home to one of the Yugoslav navy's top-secret **submarine pens**.

Eating and drinking

Vis's harbour is a popular overnight stop-off for yachtspeople, which helps to explain why the standard of **restaurants** in town is so high. For **snacks**, *Pekarna Kolđeraj* on Obala sv. Jurja offers all you need in the fresh bread and pastries line, and is the place you're most likely to find Vis's famous *pogača od srdele*.

Restaurants

Kaliopa Vladimira Nazora 32. If you're after a unique ambience then you can't do any better than *Kaliopa*, with chairs and tables buried amid the palms and shrubs of a walled garden. The seafood here is as excellent as you would expect, but be prepared to splash out.

Kantun Biskupa Mihe Pušića 17. Fresh fish grilled over an open hearth in an interior that mixes centuries-old stone walls with abstract artworks. There's also an outdoor terrace facing the yacht-lined quay. Meat-eaters can content themselves with an excellent Dalmatian *pašticada*. Local wines and excellent herbal *rakijas* round out the picture.

Karijola Šetalište viškog boja 4. Perched on a terrace midway between the town centre and Kut, this is the best place for a quality thin-crust pizza. Settle your stomach with *Karijola*'s range of irresistible *rakijas* – the *rakija od mirte* (grappa flavoured with misletoe) has aphrodisiac qualities, we have been led to believe.

Peronostora Blues Trg 30-og svibnja 1. Despite being named after a vine-rotting disease, this is one of the best places to sample (expensive but excellent) local wines, accompanied by fishy nibbles (such as smoked tuna) or rather off-beat main courses – try the mackerel in white wine sauce, or tuna chunks shish-kebabbed on a skewer with vegetables. You can choose between the distressed interior with vinyl record player (and a big pile of real vinyl records), or the Riva-facing terrace with palm-tree canopy.

Pojoda Don Cvijetka Marasovića 8, Kut. More excellent fresh fish, grilled or baked, served on a terrace shaded by orange, lemon and lime trees. Look out, too, for old-fashioned peasant dishes such as *orbiko* (barley, peas and shrimps), and *pojorski bronzinić* (a broth of barley, lentils and squid) – both are listed as starters but are filling enough to serve as mains. Whatever you order, a bottle of local Vugava serves as the ideal accompaniment.

Val Kut. Quality seafood on a palm-shaded terrace just back from the quay. Alongside the customary grilled fish and shellfish, dishes of the house include *pasta fažol na brodet* (pasta with a thick soup full of beans, shellfish and other goodies) and *caponata* (a kind of aubergine-based ratatouille). Minor quibbles – like paying 10Kn for a nonexistent cover – can be overlooked.

Bars

Bejbi Šetalište stare Isse. Pronounced "baby", this is the most laid-back drinking hangout in town, with a funkily decorated café indoors, and bamboo-shaded bar in the yard.

Lambik Kut. A respectable list of cocktails, to be enjoyed while sprawled across the loungey furnishings strewn across the adjoining square, or the distressed armchairs in the beautiful arcaded courtyard at the back.

Komiža

Buses leave Vis harbour five times daily for the 25-minute trip to the pleasant town of **KOMIŽA**, the island's main fishing port. Compact and intimate, Komiža's curved harbourfront is lined with palm trees and fringed by sixteenth- and seventeenth-century Venetian-style houses with intricate wrought-iron balconies. Dominating the southern end of the harbour is the **Kaštel**, a stubby sixteenth-century fortress whose appearance is slightly unbalanced by the slender clock tower which was built onto one of its corners at the end of the nineteenth century. It now holds a **Fishing Museum** (Ribarski muzej; June–Sept Mon–Sat 10am–noon & 7–9pm, Sun 7–9pm; 10Kn), whose worthy displays of nets and knots are enlivened by the presence of a reconstructed *falkuša*, one of the traditional fishing boats with triangular sails which were common hereabouts until the early twentieth century. At the other end of the harbour, on a tiny square known as the **Škor** (local dialect for *škver*, the part of the harbourfront onto which fishing boats were pulled up for repairs), the mid-sixteenth-century **Palača Zanetova** is a stately but dilapidated building which was once a ducal mansion – look out for the carved Virgin and Child high up on the front wall.

Among the town's churches, the most notable is the sixteenth-century **Gospa Gusarica**, whose name loosely translates as "Our Lady of the Pirates" – it's said that a painting of the Virgin was stolen from the church by pirates, but floated back into port when they were shipwrecked. The church is set amid trees on a little beach at the northern end of town near the Biševo hotel, and has an eight-sided well adorned with reliefs of St Nicholas, protector of fishermen and patron of Komiža.

About a kilometre southeast of the town on a vineyard-cloaked hillock is the seventeenth-century **Benedictine monastery** (known as *mušter*, the local dialect word for monastery), fortified in the 1760s to provide the townsfolk with a refuge in case of attack by pirates. Surrounded by defensive bastions, it's a good vantage point from which to survey the bay of Komiža below. Most of the island's population congregate beneath the monastery every year on St Nicholas's Day (Sveti Nikola; Dec 6), when an old fishing boat is hauled here by hand and then set alight – the idea of sacrificing a boat to the patron saint of seafarers reveals just how much pre-Christian practice is preserved in Mediterranean Catholicism.

The best of the **beaches** are south of town: head past the Kaštel, follow the coastal road for ten minutes, then head round the back of the disused Neptun fish canning factory, and you'll find yourself on a coastal path that leads past a sequence of attractive coves.

Practicalities

Buses from Vis Town terminate about 100m behind the harbour, from where it's a short walk south to the **tourist office** (summer Mon–Fri 8am–1pm & 6.30–8pm, Sat & Sun 6.30–8pm; winter Mon–Fri 8am–1pm; ⓣ021/713-455, ⓔtzg-komize@st.htnet.hr), on the Riva just beyond the Kaštel. Staff here can point you in the direction of agencies offering excursions to the Blue Cave on Biševo (see p.418). Adventure specialists Alternatura, between the bus station and the harbour at Hrvatskih mučenika 2 (ⓣ021/717-239, ⓦwww.alternatura.hr), are the people to ask about scuba-diving, pony-trekking, and hang-gliding from nearby Mount Hum.

The town's only **hotel** is the *Biševo* (ⓣ021/713-144, ⓕ713-098, ⓔmodra.spilja@st.t-com.hr; ❺), a simple but comfortable package-tour-oriented place about five minutes' walk from the centre at the northern end of the bay. **Rooms** (❷) and **apartments** (studios ❸, four-person apartments 460–600Kn) are available from a number of agencies in the centre, most reliably Alternatura (see above); Darlić & Darlić, on the harbourfront (daily 10am–noon & 5–7pm; ⓣ021/717-205, ⓦwww.darlic-travel.hr), and Srebrna, a little way back from the harbour on Ribarska (daily 8am–noon & 4–9pm; ⓣ021/713-668, ⓦwww.srebrnatours.hr).

For **food**, the *Kolđeraj* **bakery**, right on the Riva at Trg kralja Tomislava 1, will sort you out with a freshly baked *Komiška pogača*, as well as other sweet or savoury pastries. The tourist-trap **restaurants** on the harbourfront will sort you out with a serviceable pizza but don't represent value for money as far as seafood and steaks are concerned. Far better to head for *Konoba Bako* just off Ribarska, which has a vine-shaded terrace right on the beach and some wonderful fish dishes; or the next-door *Jastožarna*, serving up succulent lobster and grilled fish in attractive stone-clad surroundings. For **drinkers**, the day begins and ends on the central Škor, which is ringed by lively and friendly café-bars.

Mount Hum and the south coast

Rearing up above Komiža to the southeast is **Mount Hum**, which at 587m is Vis's highest point. The summit is best accessed by following the old Komiža–Vis Town route (not the new one traversed by buses), which works its way round the southern side of the island. About 6km out of Komiža, take a left to the hamlet of Žena Glava followed by a second left to Borovik, from where a deteriorating asphalt road heads uphill to the summit. There's a small chapel at the top, and a panorama of the Adriatic that reveals just why Vis was so strategically important: you can pick out the pale grey stripe of the Italian coastline far away to the west, and the mountains of the Croatian mainland to the east. Also visible are many of the uninhabited islands of the mid-Adriatic: the hump of Svetac immediately to the west, the unearthly volcanic pyramid of Jabuka beyond it and, to the southeast, Croatia's farthest-flung Adriatic possession, **Palagruža** – according to legend, the last resting place of Diomedes, King of Argos and leading participant in the siege of Troy.

Nearing Hum's summit by road, you'll pass an overgrown concrete stairway leading to **Tito's Cave** (Titova špilja), a group of caverns from which the Marshal directed the war effort during 1944. Once a popular attraction, the caves fell into disuse after 1991, and there's nothing here now – save for a vague whiff of history.

Vis in World War II

The collapse of Italy in the autumn of 1943 led to a power vacuum in the Adriatic, with both the Germans and Tito's Partisans racing each other to take control of the region's major ports and islands. Eager to support the Partisan effort, the British occupied Vis in early 1944, and in June of that year Vis was chosen as the temporary headquarters of the Partisan high command, headed by Tito himself. Having narrowly escaped a German attack on his previous stronghold, Drvar in western Bosnia, Tito was evacuated to Italy by the Allies at the end of May. He sailed for Vis on board the HMS *Blackmore* on June 7, entertaining the officers' mess, it is said, with a near-perfect rendition of "The Owl and the Pussycat".

Tito immediately took up residence in a cave on the southern flanks of Mount Hum, while his staff meetings took place in another cave next door. British officers who had never met Tito before entertained all kinds of wild ideas about who this shadowy guerilla leader really was. Novelist **Evelyn Waugh** (then a British liaison officer) was obsessed with the idea that Tito was a lesbian in disguise, and continued to spread this rumour for reasons of personal amusement even after meeting the Partisan supremo in person – it's said that Tito upbraided Waugh about this during a trip to the beach, the Marshal's skimpy trunks leaving no room for further doubt about his gender.

Vis soon became a vast **armed camp**, hosting 10,000 Partisans and 700 British and American commandos. The island was an excellent base from which to harry German positions on nearby islands, although commando raids on rugged Brač (where the Scottish Highlanders indulged in a *Guns of Navarone*-style attempt to capture Vidova Gora) were extremely costly in terms of Allied lives. Despite the need for constant vigilance against German attacks, the daily existence of those stationed on Vis was made more than bearable by the the endless opportunities for swimming, sunbathing and drinking the local wine. For the local population, things were not quite so jolly: all men between the ages of 15 and 50 were called up by the Partisans, while women, children and the elderly were evacuated to a tent-camp in British-controlled Egypt, where many died in the stifling heat.

Vis was the site of the first meeting between Tito and the head of the royalist Yugoslav government in exile, Ivan Šubašić, who arrived there on June 16. After concluding the Tito–Šubašić Agreement, which provided de-facto recognition of Tito's primacy in Yugoslavia, the signatories went on a motor-boat excursion to the Blue Cave on Biševo, where they indulged in skinny dipping, followed by a lunch of lobster and wine. Fitzroy Maclean, Winston Churchill's personal envoy at Partisan HQ, noted that the sea was choppy on the way back and that "several of the party were sick".

Ultimately Tito feared that he would lose his political independence if he accepted British protection on Vis for too much longer, and chose to reassert himself with a show of disobedience. On September 18 he abandoned Vis in the dead of night, flying to join the Soviet Red Army in Romania in a Russian plane. Vis's brief period in the political limelight was over.

Returning to the road along the south of the island, another 5km from the Žena Glava turn-off is the village of **PLISKO POLJE**, where the British constructed a speedily improvised airstrip in 1944 by linking together innumerable metal plates. It was long ago pulled up and replaced by vineyards, the fruits of which can be sampled at *Konoba Roki* (☎021/714-004 and 098 303 483) in the village – a great place to sit in a shady courtyard trying out the local *rakija* (flavoured with *rogač*, carob) and red and white wines, accompanied by *pršut*, homemade cheese, and fishy main courses. Roki's speciality is octopus or lamb baked *ispod peke* (beneath a lid covered with hot embers), although for these dishes advance reservations are advised.

Biševo and the Blue Cave

Each morning small boats leave Komiža harbour for the short crossing to **Biševo**, a tiny islet just to the southwest of Vis. There's a seasonally inhabited hamlet just up from Biševo's small harbour, and a couple of attractive coves, but the main attraction here is the **Blue Cave** (Modra špilja; 30Kn) on the island's east coast, a modestly sized but entrancing grotto which can only be reached by sea. It's been a tourist attraction since the 1880s, when a minor Viennese painter Eugen von Ransonnet-Villet dynamited the entrance to the cave to widen it for boat access, and the Lloyd steamer company began advertising it as the "Austrian Capri". It probably deserves the hype: when the sun is at its height, water-filtered light shines in through a submerged side entrance to the cave to bathe everything in the cavern in an eerie shimmering blueness. Owing to the narrowness of the entrance, the cave can't be entered when the sea is choppy, which can happen on all but the calmest of summer days; ask the tourist office in either Komiža or Vis Town about conditions.

There are two ways to **visit the cave**; the easiest is to take an excursion from either Komiža or Vis Town (all the private room agencies offer tours, costing 100–120Kn including the cave entrance fee), although it's also possible to take a taxi boat from Komiža harbour to the island, from where you can walk to a spot near the cave entrance. Either way, you'll be transferred to a small boat and ferried into the cave. You can take a dip in the cave if you want – although be warned that the volume of tourist traffic often means that you won't be able to spend as long there as you might wish.

Korčula

Like so many islands along the coast, **KORČULA** was first settled by the Greeks, who gave it the name Korkyra Melaina, or Black Corfu, for its dark and densely wooded appearance. Even now it's one of the greenest of the Adriatic islands, and one of the most popular, thanks largely to the charms of its main settlement, **Korčula Town**, whose surviving fortifications jut decorously out to sea like the bastions of an overgrown sandcastle. There are good beaches at the village of **Lumbarda** 7km away, and an attractive port town in the shape of **Vela Luka** at the island's northwestern tip.

The main Rijeka–Dubrovnik **ferry** drops you right at the harbour at Korčula Town. In addition, local ferries travel daily between Split and Vela Luka at the western end of Korčula island, from where there's a connecting bus service to Korčula Town. There's also a daily **bus** service from Dubrovnik, which crosses the narrow stretch of water dividing the island from the mainland via car ferry

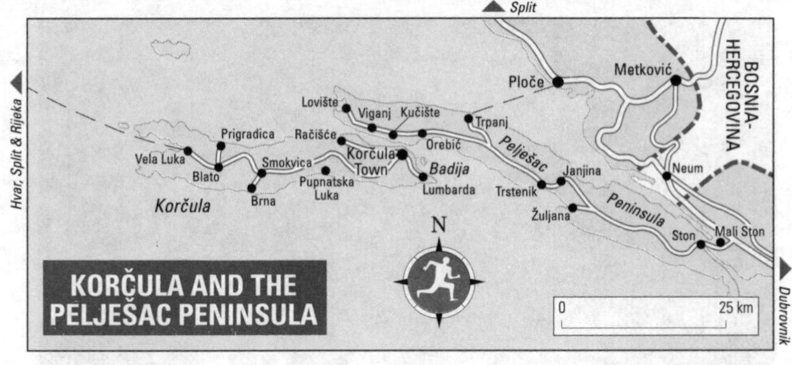

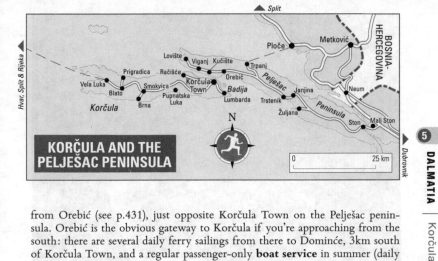

from Orebić (see p.431), just opposite Korčula Town on the Pelješac peninsula. Orebić is the obvious gateway to Korčula if you're approaching from the south: there are several daily ferry sailings from there to Domince, 3km south of Korčula Town, and a regular passenger-only **boat service** in summer (daily 6am–8pm) that brings you to the centre of town. If you arrive at Domince on one of the ferries from Orebić, you can avoid the thirty-minute walk into town by waiting for one of the Lumbarda–Korčula buses, which call in at the Inkobrod shipyard just uphill from the harbour.

Korčula Town

KORČULA TOWN sits on an oval hump of land, a medieval walled city ribbed with a series of narrow streets that branch off the main thoroughfare like the veins of a leaf – a plan designed to reduce the effects of wind and sun. Controlling access to the two-kilometre-wide channel which divides the island from the Pelješac peninsula, the town was one of the first Adriatic strongpoints to fall to the Venetians – who arrived here in the tenth century and stayed, on and off, for more than eight centuries, leaving their distinctive mark on the culture and architecture of the town. Korčula's golden age lasted from the thirteenth to the fifteenth centuries, when the town acquired its present form and most of its main buildings were constructed, but a catastrophic outbreak of plague in 1529 brought an end to Korčula's expansion. Further disaster was narrowly averted in 1571 when, in the run-up to the Battle of Lepanto, Uluz Ali (see box on p.417) turned up outside the town. The Venetian garrison withdrew without a fight, leaving the locals to defend themselves under the command of local priest Antun Rožanović – they managed to repulse Ali, who went off to destroy Hvar Town instead.

With the decline of Mediterranean trade that followed the discovery of America, Korčula slipped into obscurity. The twentieth century saw the development of shipyards east of town, and the emergence of tourism. The first guests arrived in the 1920s, although it wasn't until the 1970s that mass tourism changed the face of the town, bequeathing it new hotels, cafés and a yachting marina.

Korčula's most famous event is the performance of the **Moreška** sword dance (see box on p.423), which traditionally falls on St Theodore's Day (July 29) – although these days it's re-enacted weekly throughout the summer for the benefit of visitors. Another good time to be in town is **Easter Week**, when the religious brotherhoods (charitable associations formed in medieval times) parade

△ Korčula Town

through the town with their banners – individually on the days preceding Good Friday, then all together on Good Friday itself. A comparatively recent event – but planned to become an annual feature if funds permit – is the seaborne re-enactment of the 1298 **Battle of Korčula** (Sept 7 or nearest convenient date), when the Genoese under Admiral Lamba Doria defeated a numerically superior Venetian fleet, capturing Marco Polo in the process.

Arrival and information

Korčula's **bus station** is 200m southeast of the old town. The **tourist office** (June–Sept Mon–Sat 8am–8pm, Sun 8am–3pm; Oct–May Mon–Sat 8am–noon & 5–8pm, Sun 8am–noon; ⓣ020/715-701, ⓕ715-866, ⓦwww.visitkorcula.com), over on the western side of the peninsula, can tell you almost everything that there is to know about the island.

Bikes can be rented from outside the *Park* hotel (30Kn/hour, 90Kn/day). If you're moving on from Korčula by boat, book **ferry tickets** through the Jadrolinija office on Plokata 19 travnja (Mon–Fri 7.30am–8pm, Sat 7.30am–2pm, Sun 8am–1pm). You can check your email at Media Optima, Trg svete Justine bb, just off Plokata 19. travnja.

Accommodation

There are numerous agencies dealing in private **rooms** (❷) and **apartments** (two-person studios ❹, four-person apartments from 620Kn), of which the

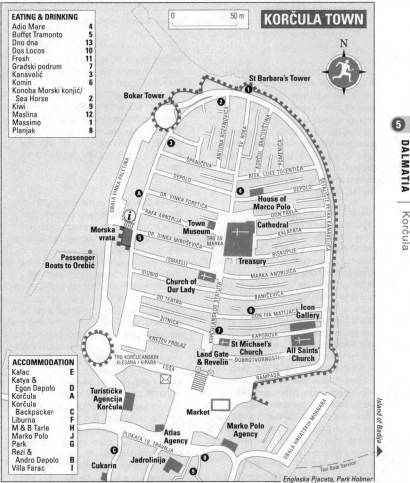

KORČULA TOWN

EATING & DRINKING

Adio Mare	4
Buffet Tramonto	5
Dno dna	13
Dos Locos	10
Fresh	11
Gradski podrum	7
Kanavelić	3
Komin	6
Konoba Morski konjić/ Sea Horse	2
Kiwi	9
Maslina	12
Massimo	1
Planjak	8

ACCOMMODATION

Kalac	E
Katya & Egon Depolo	D
Korčula	A
Korčula Backpacker	C
Liburna	F
M & B Tarle	H
Marko Polo	J
Park	G
Rezi & Andro Depolo	B
Villa Farac	I

Tinocomputers (50m) & D (50m) ▼ Bus Station (100m), E (2km), F, G, ▼ H, I, J, 10, 11, 12, 13 & St Anthony's Hill

◀ B, Maksimilijan Vanka Gallery (500m) & Fort Wellington

Island of Badija ▶

longest-standing are the Marko Polo agency at Biline 5 (ⓣ020/715-400, ⓕ715-800, ⓔmarko-polo-tours@du.tel.hr); and Turistička Agencija Korčula, just off Plokata 19. travnja (ⓣ020/711-067, ⓕ711-710, ⓔhtp-korcula@du.tel.hr). Many private hosts post details of their accommodation online at ⓦwww.ikorcula.net and ⓦwww.korculanet.net.

The nearest **campsite** is the *Kalac* (ⓣ020/711-182, ⓕ711-746, ⓔkalac@htp-korcula.hr), next to the *Bon Repos* hotel. Pitches are situated in tiny clearings between trees, guaranteeing a degree of privacy – though the site can be noisy in season. There are smaller, quieter alternatives, none of which has more than about thirty places each, in the small bays west of town on the road to the village of Račišće. Four kilometres out is the *Palma* (ⓣ020/711-272), tucked away in a private garden; another 2km brings you to the *Vrbovica*, at the northern end of village of Luka Banja on the lovely Vrbovica bay (ⓣ020/721-311); and 2km farther on is the *Oskorušica*, idyllically situated among olive trees (ⓣ020/710-747). Korčula–Račišće buses pass all three campsites.

Hostel

Korčula Backpacker – One Love Hostel ⓣ020/716-755 or 098 997 6353, ⓦwww.korculabackpacker.com. Enjoyable if occasionally cramped private hostel with friendly hosts. Its 65 beds are arranged in four- and six-bed dorms crammed into a three-storey nineteenth-century house, with a WC and shower on each floor. The cellar bar, with vaguely Middle Eastern couches and cushions, is a great place to unwind and make contacts after a day spent exploring the island. Beds 120Kn per person.

Guesthouses and apartments

Katya & Egon Depolo ul. Hrvatske bratske zajednice 62 ⓣ020/721-172, 098 357 582 or 099 682 9536. Modern apartments on the top two floors of a historic stone house midway between the bus station and the old town. They can be rented out as four- to six-person apartments or as smaller two-person units. English or Italian spoken depending on which member of the family you get hold of. Two-person apartments ❹

Rezi & Andro Depolo ul. Svetog Nikole bb ⓣ020/711-621, ⓔtereza.depolo@du.t-com.hr, ⓔviladepolo@hotmail.com. Friendly family house just west of the old town with four rooms, each with hardwood floors, TV, ensuite shower/WC, electric kettle and – in three of the rooms – great views of the old town. Breakfast is available on request, and there's a nice big outdoor terrace to eat it on. Open all year; three-day minimum stay preferred in summer. ❷

M & B Tarle Šetalište Frana Kršinića bb ⓣ020/711-712. Roomy family house 1km east of the old town, offering a mixture of simply furnished en-suite doubles and family-sized apartments with kitchen. The top-floor rooms with attic ceilings are the most popular. Big back garden. Breakfast is available on request. Open March–Dec. Rooms ❷, four-person apartments 580Kn.

Villa Farac Šetalište Frana Kršinića 106 ⓣ020/711-825 or 091 542 9040. Pair of apartments, each with kitchenette: one is a simple studio with great views of the Pelješac peninsula, the other is a groovy split-level affair with spiral staircase, a/c and kitchenette. Mid-May to mid-Oct. ❹

Hotels

Korčula Obala Vinka Paletina bb ⓣ020/711-078, ⓕ711-746, ⓔmarketing@etp-korcula.hr. The oldest and best of the town's hotels, occupying the Austrian-built former town hall right in the old town, and boasting an elegant waterfront terrace. Former guests include Rebecca West and World War I stormtrooper-novelist Ernst Jünger. ❻

Liburna Obala Hrvatskih Mornara bb ⓣ020/726-006, ⓕ711-746, ⓔmarketing@etp-korcula.hr. Occupying a promontory 1500m east of the old town, this was the leading hotel on the island when first built in 1985, but now looks a bit like a socialist-era period piece. However, the en-suite rooms are comfy and come with TV, and some have superb views of the old town. ❺

Marko Polo Šetalište Frana Kršninića bb ⓣ020/726-131, ⓕ726-300, ⓔmarketing@etp-korcula.hr. On high ground east of town, this three-star has benefited from recent renovations, and has reasonably plush en-suite rooms with TV and a/c. Some also have sea-facing balconies. ❺

Park Šetalište Frana Kršninića bb ⓣ020/726-004, ⓕ711-746, ⓔhtp-marketing@etp-korcula.hr. A box-like huddle of buildings on the coastal path just east of town, offering a mix of uninspiring but adequate two-star rooms and recently redecorated three-star rooms. ❺

The Town

Despite recent development, Korčula Town preserves a neat beauty that has few equals on the Adriatic coast. Just up from the quay, cafés, shops and banks line the broad sweep of Plokata 19. travnja, from where an elegant nineteenth-century flight of steps sweeps up to the **Land Gate** (Kopnena vrata), the main entrance to the tiny old town. Begun in 1391, the gate was completed a century later with the addition of the **Revelin**, the hulking defensive tower that looms above it. The northern side of the gate takes the form of a triumphal arch built in 1650 to honour the military governor of Dalmatia, Leonardo Foscolo, who led Venetian forces against the Turks during the Candia War – a struggle for the control of Crete – of 1645–69. Steps to

The Moreška and other sword dances

Korčula Town is famous for its **Moreška**, a traditional sword dance and drama that was once common throughout the Mediterranean. Judging by the name, the dance probably originated in Spain and related to the conflict between the Moors and the Christians, although in Dalmatia its rise was probably connected with the struggles against the Ottoman Turks, in particular the victory over them at the Battle of Lepanto. Whatever its origins, the Moreška has become a major tourist attraction, and its annual performance on St Theodore's Day (July 29) has been transformed into a weekly summer event, held every Thursday evening between May and September at a pitch just outside the Land Gate or – if the weather is bad – in the local cinema near the bus station. Tickets (60Kn) are available from Marko Polo Tours.

Basically the dance tells the story of a conflict between the White King and his followers (actually dressed in red) and the Black King. The heroine, Bula (literally "veiled woman"), is kidnapped by the Black King and his army, and her betrothed tries to win her back in a ritualized sword fight that takes place within a shifting circle of dancers. The adversaries circle each other and clash weapons several times before the evil king is forced to surrender, and Bula is unchained. The strangest thing about the dance is the seemingly incongruous brass band music that invariably accompanies it – a sign that the present-day Moreška falls somewhere between medieval rite and nineteenth-century reinvention.

Similar sword dances are still performed throughout the island, although once outside Korčula Town you're more likely to find them accompanied by traditional instruments such as the *mijeh* (bagpipe). The most important of these are the **Moštra**, performed in Postrana on St Rock's Day (Aug 16), and the **Kumpanjija**, staged in several places at different times of year: Blato on St Vincent's Day (April 28), Čara on St James's Day (July 25), Smokvica on Candlemas (Feb 2), Vela Luka on St Joseph's Day (March 19) and Pupnat on Our Lady of the Snows (Aug 6). Many of these dances are performed in Korčula Town over the summer under the banner of the **Festival of Sword Dances** (Festival viteških igara), with performances running throughout July and August; the tourist office will have details.

In the past many of these dances would have been followed by the beheading of an ox, which was then roasted and divided among the participants. The practice was banned during the communist period, and its revival in Pupnat in 1999 was followed by lurid – and largely negative – reporting in the Croatian press. It's unlikely that ritual slaughter will ever form part of the dances again.

the side of the gate lead up to the terrace of the Revelin (daily 9am–8pm; 10Kn), from which you get a splendid view of Korčula and its surroundings.

Inside the gate lies a well-ordered grid of pale grey stone houses, most dating from before 1800. On the far side of the gate lies Trg braće Radića, a small square bordered on one side by an elegant loggia belonging to the sixteenth-century town hall and, on the other, **St Michael's Church** (Crkva svetog Mihovila). This is connected to a neighbouring building by a small bridge which was used as a private entrance to the church by members of the medieval Brotherhood of St Michael – one of many such charitable brotherhoods formed during the Middle Ages throughout the Adriatic. From here, Korčulanskog statuta 1214 leads on into the town centre, passing the **Church of Our Lady** (Crkva Gospojina; summer daily 9.30am–12.30pm & 7–11pm) on the left, a simple structure whose floor is paved with the tombstones of Korčulan nobles – it's used as a picture gallery selling works by local artists in summer. Above the high altar is a mosaic of the Virgin and Child, a dazzling confection of yellows, blues and pinks completed by Dutchman Louis Schrikkel in 1967.

The cathedral and treasury

Immediately beyond the church lies **St Mark's Cathedral** (Katedrala svetog Marka), squeezed into a diminutive space that passes for a main town square. The cathedral's facade is decorated with a gorgeous fluted rose window and a bizarre cornice frilled with strange beasts. In the centre, a matronly bug-eyed lady gazes earthwards; no one knows for sure who she is – suggestions have ranged from the emperor Diocletian's wife to one of a number of Hungarian queens who helped finance the church. The main figure directly above the porch is St Mark, flanked by lions pawing smaller, more subservient animals, while the door is framed by figures of Adam and Eve, bizarrely depicted in toilet-ready squatting pose.

The **stone carving** on display inside the cathedral is no less exciting, with pillars running along the north side of the nave decorated with extravagant floral squiggles – and writhing goddess-like forms that look anything but Christian in inspiration. There's a pulpit held aloft by griffin-topped pillars, and an elegant ciborium carved by local stonemason Marko Andrijić in the 1490s, its Corinthian columns crowned with statuettes of Archangel Michael and the Virgin. Beneath its pagoda-like canopy hangs a recently-restored Tintoretto altarpiece positively bursting with colour – it depicts St Mark flanked by SS Hieronymus and Bartholomew. There's a wealth of interesting clutter in the south aisle, including some of the pikes used against Uluz Ali, and another Tintoretto (an *Annunciation*, with the Archangel appearing to the Virgin in a shower of sparks). At the end of the south aisle lie the fine Renaissance tomb of Bishop Malumbra and an altar featuring a murky, time-darkened allegory of the Holy Trinity by Venetian painter Leandro Bassano.

Many of the church's treasures have been removed to the **Bishop's Treasury** (riznica; July & Aug: daily 10am–noon & 5–7pm; rest of year apply at the tourist office; 10Kn), next door. This is one of the most charming small art collections in the country, taking in a striking *Portrait of a Man* by Carpaccio, an imposing *Noble with Dog* by Bassano, a tiny *Madonna* by Dalmatian Renaissance artist Blaž Jurjev of Trogir, plus some Tiepolo studies of hands. Oddities include an ivory statuette of Mary Queen of Scots, whose skirts open to reveal kneeling figures in doublet and hose – what it's doing in Korčula remains a mystery. A modest annexe to the treasury, entered just round the corner on Marka Andrijića (same times; 5Kn), displays Roman and Byzantine pottery retrieved from offshore wrecks, and English willow-pattern crockery acquired by nineteenth-century Korčulan ship captains.

The rest of the town

Opposite the cathedral, a Venetian palace houses the **Town Museum** (Gradski muzej; July & Aug: daily 9am–1pm & 5–7pm; rest of year Mon–Sat 9am–1pm; 10Kn), whose modest display includes a copy of a fourth-century BC Greek tablet from Lumbarda – the earliest evidence of civilization on Korčula – and, upstairs, a re-creation of a typical Korčula peasant kitchen, with an open hearth surrounded by cooking pots and bed warmers.

As you move north from the main square, a turning to the right leads to another remnant from Venetian times, the so-called **House of Marco Polo** (Kuća Marka Pola; daily 10am–1pm & 5–7pm; 10Kn). Korčula claims to be the birthplace of Marco Polo – not as extravagant an assertion as it might seem, since there's no record of him being born anywhere else. The Venetians recruited many sea captains from their Adriatic colonies, and the fact that Marco Polo was captured by the Genoese in a sea battle off Korčula in 1298 suggests that he may have had some connection with the place. A family called De Polo have long been resident on the island, adding weight to Korčula's claim. Whatever the truth of the matter, it seems unlikely that Marco Polo had any connection with this seventeenth-century house, which has little of value inside but offers wonderful views of Korčula's terracotta-coloured rooftops from its upper storeys. The building has recently been acquired by Korčula town council, who plan to install a Polo-related display here some time soon.

From here you can descend towards Šetalište Petra Kanavelića, the seafront walkway which leads round the outside of the peninsula. Walk south to the junction with Kaporova to find the **Icon Gallery** (Galerija ikona; July & Aug daily 10am–noon & 5–7pm, rest of year apply at the tourist office), where there's a permanent display of icons in the rooms of the All Saints' Brotherhood. Most of the exhibits were looted from Cretan churches at the end of the Candia War (on the pretence of saving them from falling into infidel hands), when Venice had to hand over the Mediterranean island to the Ottoman Turks. Among the Pantokrators and Virgins emblazoned in gold leaf is a haunting fifteenth-century triptych of the Passion.

From here, a covered bridge similar to the one outside St Michael's Church takes you into **All Saints' Church** (Crkva svih svetih), with its brooding Renaissance interior and one of the most impressive Baroque altarpieces in Dalmatia – an eighteenth-century Pietà carved from walnut wood by Austrian master George Raphael Donner, enclosed by a fifteenth-century ciborium in imitation of the one in the cathedral. On the far side of the altar is another of Blaž Jurjev's fifteenth-century masterpieces, a polyptych centred on a chilling *Deposition*, below which the tiny figures of the All Saints' Brotherhood – identifiable from their trademark white robes – kneel in prayer.

If you're in the mood for more paintings, head west from the old town along Put sv. Nikole to the **Maksimilijan Vanka Gallery** (Galerija Maksimilijana Vanke; July & Aug daily 6–9pm; 5Kn), some five minutes' distant, which hosts summer exhibitions by prominent Croatian artists.

Around town

From behind Korčula's bus station, Šetalište Frane Kršinića heads east towards the package-hotel end of town, passing after some 500m a curious folly in the form of a pair of obelisks and a semicircular stone bench. Known as the **Engleska pjaceta** (English piazzetta), it dates from a short-lived period of British occupation in 1813, when it was built to mark what was then the southeastern boundary of the town. Beyond here the road heads slightly inland and runs along the bottom of a wooded hillside known as **Park Hobner**, where several trails lead up into an enjoyably untamed area of mixed forest. Another popular destination for strollers is **St Anthony's Hill** (Sveti Antun), which lies 1km farther southeast – to get there, continue beyond Park Hobner to the crossroads, go straight over onto the Lumbarda road, then bear left up a residential street at the next junction. A graceful avenue of poplars lines the approach to the hill, an easily scaled affair on top of which you'll find a small chapel and a modest circle of park. Much of Korčula's rippling eastern coast is visible from the summit, with the grey-green mountains of the Pelješac peninsula glowering from across the water.

There's more easy walking on the wooded heights west of town, best reached by heading west along Put svetog Nikole and bearing left up the stepped alleyways that lead through the hillside suburbs. After ten to fifteen minutes you'll emerge onto a plateau where another legacy of British occupation, a simple grey tower known as **Fort Wellington**, rises above the maquis like an abandoned giant chesspiece. Topped by the aerials of a radio relay station, the tower is occasionally open to the public – when you can clamber up onto the parapet for more splendid views.

Beaches and islands

The nearest **beaches** to the old town are on the headland around the *Hotel Marko Polo*, though they're crowded, rocky and uncomfortable. The shingle beach in front of the *Bon Repos* hotel and *Kalac* campsite is marginally preferable, although it can't compare with the sandy beach a short bus ride away in Lumbarda (see opposite). Alternatively, take a water taxi (25Kn) from the harbour on the eastern side of town on the way to the bus station to one of the **Skoji islands** just offshore. The largest and nearest is **Badija**, where boats stop first beside an impressive Franciscan monastery – used as a hotel for many years, it was recently returned to the order and is currently being restored. From here, numerous tracks lead to secluded beaches and a couple of elementary snack bars. Some boats continue onwards to the naturist part of the island round the corner.

The long shingle beaches of Orebić (see p.431) are also only a fifteen-minute ferry ride from Korčula; boats run roughly hourly from the pier opposite the tourist office throughout the day.

Eating and drinking

There are more pizzerias than you can shake a stick at in the old town, and a number of decent **restaurants** serving excellent local seafood. Wherever you eat, try some of the excellent local white wines: Grk from Lumbarda, and Pošip and Rukatac, both from the area around the villages of Čara and Smokvica, are the best. If you're planning a **picnic**, you could head for the fruit and vegetable market just below the Land Gate, where you'll also find the Konzum supermarket.

Daytime **drinking** in Korčula revolves around the cafés on Plokata 19. Travnja, busy with locals and tourists alike. At night, there's a string of cocktail bars on the seafront promenade around the old town, although the bar-choked area around the bus station is marginally more animated.

Snacks

Fresh Hrvatske bratske zajednice bb ⓦ www.igotfresh.com. A kiosk with outdoor seating midway between the bus station and the old town, serving up a tasty range of tortilla wraps, and refreshing fresh fruit drinks. Serves as something of a traveller meeting-point, and has an English-language book exchange to boot.

Restaurants

Adio Mare Svetog Roka. Located just by the alleyway leading down to Marco Polo's House, this is a tourist favourite of long standing, offering top-quality food in an atmospheric, high-ceilinged room of medieval vintage. As well as the obvious seafood, look out for local speciality *Korčulanska pašticada* (braised beef in red wine and prunes). Arrive early to make sure of a table – the queue makes the street outside virtually impassable. Open from 5.30pm.

Buffet Tramonto top of the stairway beside the tourist office. A good choice of pizza and pasta, including a couple of vegetarian options.

Gradski podrum Trg Antuna i Stjepana Radića. Superbly situated, with tables dotted around one of the old town's most atmospheric open spaces, and a very wide-ranging menu, featuring local fish as well as continental-Croatian meat dishes. Open from 5pm.

Kanavelić Šetalište Petra Kanavelića. Surprisingly for a restaurant owned by a hotel chain, *Kanavelić* is actually very good. The fresh fish, mussels and grilled squid are quite delicious, and none too expensive. Open from 7pm.

Komin ul. Don Iva Matijaca. A handful of outdoor tables crammed into a narrow stepped street, and room for a few diners in the teeny interior, serving up consistently good fresh fish grilled over an open hearth. Specialities such as lamb or octopus baked under an ember-covered lid are also well worth trying, although they should ideally be ordered 24 hours in advance.

Konoba Morski konjić/Sea Horse Šetalište Petra Kanavelića. Situated right on the northern tip of the peninsula (and not to be confused with the blander *Morski konjić* restaurant on the eastern side), this is a small and intimate place, although the benches outside are a bit exposed to sea breezes. Good fresh fish, satisfying salads and curiosities like *korčulanski škartoceti* (bacon and cheese wrapped in veal). Open from 6pm.

Maslina on the road to Lumbarda. Two kilometres from the centre in an unpromising area characterized by car repair yards, this family-run place is nevertheless well worth the trip for its top-notch shellfish and grilled fish, as well as old-fashioned island favourites such as lamb goulash with pasta, and various forms of game. Some of the vegetarian dishes we ordered at the last visit were microwave-assisted, but don't let these minor details put you off.

Planjak Plokata 19. travnja. Moderately priced, unpretentious place offering the full range of local grilled-meat fare and plenty of outdoor seating. One of the few restaurants that's open all-year round.

Bars

Dno dna Hrvatske bratske zajednice 102. Characterful café-bar near the bus station whose surreal interior looks like a cross between a submarine and a mermaid's undersea boudoir. Nice outdoor terrace running along a stretch of park.

Dos Locos Šetalište Frana Kršinića Just behind the bus station, this is the one Korčula bar that regularly gets packed out with summer-evening hedonistic drinkers. Lots of outdoor seating, frequent live music and a reasonable range of cocktails.

Massimo Šetalište Petra Kanavelića. Cocktail bar on top of one of Korčula's medieval towers. Choose a comfy chair in the circular main chamber or ascend the wooden ladder to the crenellated terrace. Dependable cocktails at a reasonable price.

Shopping

Alongside the bland souvenir stalls, Korčula can boast a growing number of speciality shops.

Aromatica Depolo Ⓦwww.aromatica.hr. Bricks of soap in all shapes and sizes, made from natural ingredients and aromatic herbs. Also aromatherapy oils and natural cosmetics.

Cukarin ul. Hrvatske bratske zajednice bb. This small shop in the narrow alley running south from Plokata 19. travnja is famous throughout Croatia for its selection of home-baked biscuits and other crispy confections. Prime among these is the *cukarin*, a lemony-orange-flavoured biscuit that looks rather like a croissant with an extra pair of horns (and is best eaten when dipped in sparkling *prošek* wine). Try also the *klašun*, a pastry ball stuffed with walnut filling; and the *Marko Polo*, an asteroid-sized sphere of chocolate, cream and walnuts.

Iridescence Don Iva Matijaca 147 Ⓦwww.sylviagottwald.com. Exquisite jewellery and fashion accessories made from seashells and other naturally occurring materials by designer Sylvia Gottwald. Classy, unique, expensive and worth treasuring.

Vapor Morska Vrata Ⓦwww.vapor-gallery.com. Art gallery selling artist-designed postcards and souvenirs, as well as paintings and limited-edition prints by contemporary Croatian artists.

The beaches at Lumbarda

The best beaches on Korčula island are at **LUMBARDA** (Ⓦwww.lumbarda.hr), 8km south of Korčula Town and accessible by regular buses (Mon–Sat hourly; 5 daily on Sun). Buses terminate at a small chapel on the far side of Lumbarda. From here, the track on the right leads through vineyards to **Pržna bay**, a glorious two-hundred-metre stretch of sand backed by a couple of cafés. Be warned that it soon fills up in July and August. Back at the chapel, the track on the left goes to **Bilin Žal**, a far rockier stretch of shore with brief sandy stretches and dramatic views of the coastal mountains. The half-ruined boathouse right on the shore is home to the atmospheric *Bilin Žal* **konoba**, which serves a memorable *hobotnica na buzara* (bits of octopus in a rich wine sauce) alongside other local seafood favourites.

Once you've seen the beach there are relatively few inducements to stay in Lumbarda itself, although the **tourist office**, in the centre near the bus stop (July

& Aug daily 8am–10pm; June & Sept daily 8am–noon & 4–8pm; Oct–May Mon–Fri 8am–2pm; ⓣ020/712-005, ⓔtz-lumbarda@du.t-com.hr), will help locate private **rooms** (❶) and point you in the direction of the growing number of family-run **pensions** in the suburban villa zone on the north side of town. Of these, *Pansion Lovrić*, Lumbarda bb (ⓣ020/712-052, ⓔsilvana.milina@du.t-com.hr; ❷), offers comfortable en-suite rooms and an excellent restaurant. There's also the *Vela Postrana* **campsite** (ⓣ020/712-067), between the centre and the beaches, although it's in an open field with little shade.

Towards Vela Luka

Heading west from Korčula Town, a single road (served by six buses daily) runs the length of the island to Vela Luka, passing most of the island's major settlements en route. These are a series of attractively weathered villages, many connected by rough road to the nearest strip of coast, where there are usually a few holiday villas and some sort of rocky beach.

At the western end of the island, the ferry port of **VELA LUKA** is totally different in character from Korčula town, with a string of nineteenth-century houses stretching attractively along an expansive, three-fingered bay. There's little in the way of an old town to stroll around, although the bronze-age pots and jewellery displayed in the **town museum** (Mon–Fri 9am–1pm & 8–11pm, Sat 10am–1pm; 10Kn), just behind the sea front, bear sufficient witness to the town's ancient origins. Most of the museum's artefacts are from the nearby **Vela Spila cave**, a major archeological site inhabited continuously from around 18,000 BC until the Roman era. The cave itself (daily 5–8pm; 10Kn) is a twenty-minute walk from town – head down the alleyway behind the *Pod Bore* restaurant on the Riva and follow the fairly obvious (and reasonably well-signed) path uphill. You'll be treated to fantastic views of Vela Luka's bay on the way up. Parts of Vela Spila's limestone roof collapsed several millennia ago, creating an eerie, tunnel-like space with light streaming in from the huge openings above.

Vela Luka's friendly **tourist office** is just behind the seafront at ulica 41 (Mon–Sat 8am–9pm, Sun 9am–noon; ⓣ021/813-619, ⓦwww.tzvelaluka.hr). Mediterano, a few steps along the Riva at Obala 3 (ⓣ020/813-832, 091 534 9889, ⓦwww.mediterano.hr), has the biggest choice of **rooms** and **apartments** in town. *Pod Bore*, Obala 2, is the best place for local seafood, while *Vertigo*, ulica 26, in the courtyard of the town museum, is a good pizzeria with tables set amid some charming modern mosaics. The easy chairs of *Casablanca*, behind the war memorial on the Riva, provide the most stylish venue for daytime coffee and evening drinks.

The **Kumpanjija** – Vela Luka's answer to the Moreška (see p.423) – is performed every Tuesday evening (mid-July to late August) in front of St Joseph's church.

Lastovo

Directly south of Korčula, tiny **LASTOVO** lies at the centre of an archipelago of 45 uninhabited islets some five and a half hours from Split. Remote and virtually self-sufficient in food, Lastovo feels much more isolated than any of the other Adriatic islands, and there's a sense of pride and independence here, most obviously expressed in the annual **Poklad** festival (see box on p.430) at the beginning of Lent. Like Vis, Lastovo was closed to foreigners from 1976 until 1989 owing to its importance as a military outpost, and organized tourism has

Vukodlaci and other vampiric houseguests

Express an interest in **vampires** in today's Croatia and you'll probably be told that you've come to the wrong country – and yet belief in the supernatural creatures was widespread hereabouts until a couple of centuries ago. Europe's first documented case of vampirism took place in an Istrian village in the 1670s, when the nocturnal roamings of Jure Grandi were recorded by Slovenian chronicler J. J. Valvasor. One of the last known outbreaks of vampire mania in Croatia took place on **Lastovo** in 1737, when officials from Dubrovnik had to dissuade the local populace from carrying out mass exhumations of those suspected of walking with the undead.

According to Croatian folk belief, the most common form of vampire was a **vukodlak** (often translated as "werewolf", although it clearly means something quite different), which basically consisted of the skin of a human corpse puffed up with the breath of the devil and further bloated with the blood of its victims. The *vukodlak* was an all-purpose bogeyman whose existence could explain away all manner of crises and conflicts: anything from listlessness among the local livestock to marital problems were blamed on the bloodsuckers (it was said that *vukodlaci* visited the beds of bored wives and pleasured them in the night). A **mora** was a female equivalent of a *vukodlak*, nightly sapping the strength of the menfolk; while **macići** were mischievious young *vukodlaci* who created envy and discord by bringing good luck to some villagers, misfortune to others – if a farmer got rich, neighbours would say that he had a *macić* in the house.

People were said to turn into *vukodlaci* after their death if a dog, cat or mouse passed under their coffin while it was being borne to the grave. The only cure was to dig up the body and cut its hamstrings to prevent it from wandering about at night. Visiting the Dalmatian hinterland as recently as the 1770s, the intrepid Venetian traveller Alberto Fortis discovered that some of the locals asked their families to carry out this operation as soon as they died, just to be on the safe side.

never caught on, but what it lacks in hotels and amenities it more than makes up for in its extraordinary sense of isolation and in its natural, wooded beauty. The island has only one major settlement, **Lastovo Town**, where most of the remaining 800 islanders live.

Ferries leave Split for the island's port at **Ubli** once or twice daily all year, calling at Hvar Town and Vela Luka on Korčula en route. There's a petrol station and a couple of shops opposite the ferry dock, while the *Gušter* **café** on the harbour rents out mountain bikes and scooters, and may have a couple of Internet terminals. You're better off making your way directly to Lastovo Town – all ferries are met by a connecting bus – or to the bay-hugging hamlet of **PASADUR**, 3km north of Ubli, where the island's only **hotel**, the *Ladesta* (Ⓣ020/802-100, Ⓕ802-444; ❹), offers simple en-suite rooms, a restaurant and the Diving Paradise **scuba-diving** school (Ⓣ020/805-179, Ⓦwww.diving-paradise.net).

Lastovo Town and around

Unusually for the capital of a Croatian island, **LASTOVO TOWN** faces away from the sea, spreading itself over the steep banks of a natural amphitheatre with a fertile agricultural plain below. There's a road at the top, a road at the bottom, and a maze of narrow alleys and stone stairways between. The town's buildings date mainly from the fifteenth and sixteenth centuries – although depopulation has left many empty and dilapidated – and are notable for their curious chimneys shaped like miniature minarets, although there's no record of Arab or Turkish raiders ever making it this far.

The Poklad

Lastovo's **carnival** is one of the strangest in Croatia, featuring the ritual humiliation and 'murder' of a straw puppet, the **Poklad**. After a long weekend of preparation things come to a head on Shrove Tuesday, when the Poklad is led through town on a donkey by the men of Lastovo, who dress for the occasion in a uniform of red shirts, black waistcoats and bowler hats. Following this, the Poklad is attached to a long rope and hoisted from one end of town to the other three times while fireworks are let off beneath it. Each transit is met by chanting and the drawing of swords. Finally, the Poklad is put back on the donkey and taken to the square in front of the parish church, to the accompaniment of music and dancing. At the end of the evening, the villagers dance the **Lastovsko kolo**, a sword dance similar to the Moreška in Korčula (see box on p.423), and the Poklad is impaled on a long stake and burned. Drinking and dancing continues in the village hall until dawn.

Local tradition has it that the Poklad symbolizes a young messenger who was sent by Catalan pirates to demand the town's surrender, although it's more likely that the ritual actually derives from ancient fertility rites. Whatever its roots, the islanders take the occasion very seriously, and it's certainly not enacted for the benefit of outsiders. *Lastovčani* from all over the world return to their home village to attend the Poklad, when accommodation is at a premium. If you do want to attend, contact the tourist office well in advance.

The fifteenth-century parish **Church of SS Cosmas and Damian** (Crkva svetog Kuzme i Damjana) in the centre of town is worth a look for its interior, richly adorned with sixteenth- and seventeenth-century paintings and icons, with a dainty fifteenth-century loggia opposite the entrance. Opposite the church, fading propaganda slogans dating from World War II can still be made out on the facade of the village school: *Živili savjeznici SSSR, Engleska i Amerika!* ("Long live the alliance of the USSR, England and America!") is the inspiring message.

Above the town lie the remains of the old French **fort**, built in 1810 above some much older fortifications and now used as a weather station – it's a stiff walk up, but worth it for the views from the top, with Lastovo on one side and the sea on the other. Heading downhill from the main square a road hairpins its way to two tiny harbours: **Lučica**, a tiny hamlet with a mix of derelict houses and renovated holiday homes, and, a little farther over to the west, the quieter **Sveti Mihovil**.

Ask at Lastovo's tourist office whether any local boatmen are offering excursions to **Šaplun**, an uninhabited islet to the south which has a lovely fine shingle beach. Otherwise, you can walk to **Zaklopatica**, a hamlet 3km away on the northern coast of the island which has a yachting harbour and a couple of *konobe*, or to **Skrivena Luka** 7km south, a deep bay backed by sandy hills and cleared of vegetation by forest fires, where there are several rocky places to swim.

Practicalities

The bus from the ferry dock at Ubli stops on the main square right outside the **tourist office** (mid-June to late Aug daily 8am–noon & in the evening when the bus from the ferry arrives; rest of year Mon–Fri 8am–2pm; Ⓣ & Ⓕ020/801-018, Ⓦwww.lastovo-tz.net), where you can pick up a basic map and book **rooms** (❶). **Pansion** *Anica* down the hill in Lučica (Ⓣ020/801-267 or 801-082; ❷) rents out a trio of simple balconied rooms on a half-board basis – the tasty and filling home cooking is more than worth the price.

There are a couple of bars, a bank and a grocery store on the square. Hiding in the back alleys at the bottom end of the village is the town's one **restaurant**, the *Konoba Bačvara*, serving up freshly caught seafood in a snug indoor room or on a terrace hung with fishing nets. For those prepared to wander farther afield, both the *Triton* and the *Augusta Insula* in Zaklopatica are great places for grilled fish. Back in Lastovo Town, there's a **café-bar** down in Sveti Mihovil bay which often stays open until the last customer staggers home.

The Pelješac peninsula

Just across the Pelješac channel (Pelješki kanal) from Korčula is the **PELJEŠAC PENINSULA**, a slim, mountainous finger of land which stretches for some 90km from Lovište in the west to the mainland in the east. Parts of the peninsula are exceptionally beautiful, with tiny villages and sheltered coves rimmed by beaches, but although it's a reasonably popular holiday area, development remains low-key. The downside is that public transport is meagre except along the main Korčula–Orebić–Ston–Dubrovnik route, and most of the smaller places are impossible to get to without a car.

Orebić

A short ferry-hop from Korčula, the small town of **OREBIĆ** was a subsidiary trading outlet of the Dubrovnik Republic for almost five hundred years, and later enjoyed a brief period of extraordinary prosperity during the nineteenth-century revival of Adriatic trade, during which the town's merchants set up a maritime society, built a huge church and constructed their own shipyards to supply an independent merchant fleet. The bubble soon burst, however, and the society and yards were wound up in 1887, after which the town slipped back into obscurity until the emergence of mass tourism. Orebić has featured in the package brochures ever since, largely on account of its long shingle **beaches**.

Today, Orebić straggles along the seashore on either side of its jetties, an aimless but attractive mixture of the old and new. The most attractive part of town is along Obala Pomoraca, just east of the quays, where generations of sea captains built a series of comfortable country villas behind a luscious subtropical screen of palms and cacti. The **Maritime Museum** (Pomorski muzej; Mon–Fri 8am–noon, 1.30–4.30pm & 5–9pm, Sat & Sun 4–9pm; 10Kn) at Trg Mimbeli 12 sports a few crusty amphorae and a dull collection of naval memorabilia relating to the Orebić fleet. Far better to head up to the **Franciscan monastery** (Franjevački samostan; Mon–Sat 9am–noon & 5–7pm, Sun 5–7pm; 10Kn) on a rocky spur twenty minutes' walk out of town – to get there, head west from the ferry quay as far as the *Bellevue* hotel, then bear right onto the road which snakes up the hillside. The monastery was built in the 1480s to house a miraculous icon known as Our Lady of the Angels, brought here by Franciscans from the Bay of Kotor, just south of Dubrovnik. The icon was thought to protect mariners from shipwreck – Orebić ship captains would sound their sirens on passing the monastery on their way into port. The picture still occupies pride of place in the church: a stylized, Byzantine-influenced Madonna and Child surrounded by an oversized frame in which gilded angels cavort in a sky full of bluish cotton-wool clouds. The monastery museum displays votive paintings commissioned by crews who were saved from pirates or storms after offering prayers to the Virgin, and models of ships once owned by Orebić magnates such as the Mimbeli brothers, whose onion-domed mausoleum can be seen in the graveyard outside. There's also a wonderful view of the Pelješac channel from the monastery's terrace.

There are even better views from the 961-metre summit of **Sveti Ilija**, the bare mountain which looms over Orebić to the northwest. A marked path to the summit (4hr walk each way) strikes uphill just before you get to the monastery (look out for the red-and-white paint marks on the rocks). Bear in mind that this is a major expedition, and shouldn't be undertaken without solid footwear, head covering, waterproofs, plenty of liquid – and if possible an accurate weather forecast from Orebić tourist office.

There are some lovely pebble **beaches** stretching west from the ferry terminals in front of Orebić's hotels, although the best of the town's beaches is twenty minutes' walk east from the ferry terminal at Trstenica, where you'll find a crescent of shingle just about fine enough to make sandcastles out of, and views of the distant island of Mljet's ragged coast.

Practicalities

Buses pull up beside the **ferry quay**, from where the **tourist office** is five minutes' walk east on Trg Mimbeli (July & Aug daily 8am–9pm; Sept–June Mon–Fri 9am–1pm; ⓣ020/713-718, ⓦwww.tz-orebic.com); an additional information kiosk right by the quay may be open in summer. The most helpful source of local **rooms** (❶) and **apartments** (two-person studios ❷, four-person apartments from 450Kn) is Orebić Tours, one block back from the seafront boulevard at ul. bana Jelačića 84 (ⓣ020/713-367, ⓦwww.orebic-tours.hr). They also deal with private accommodation in Kučište, Viganj and several other Pelješac villages. Alternatively, there's a string of medium-rise concrete **hotels** spreading out west of the landing stage, looking onto a long stretch of pebble beach. Best of the bunch is the all-inclusive *Orsan* (ⓣ020/713-026, ⓦwww.orebic-htp.hr; ❺), offering cramped but comfy rooms with TV and balcony, and a dinky outdoor pool. Simpler, but still serviceable, is the nearby *Bellevue* (ⓣ020/713-148, ⓦwww.orebic-htp.hr; ❺), a 150-room beachside complex spread over several buildings. There are two **campsites** behind Trstenica beach and several more in private suburban gardens farther east. For **food**, *Pelješki dvori*, on Obala pomoraca, is the best of the mainstream seafood and schnitzel restaurants, and is not too expensive; while the *Bistro Jadran*, on the seafront just beyond the tourist office, does a decent range of pizzas and cheap grill food. *Taverna Mlinica*, midway between the tourist office and Trstenica beach, is more of an acquired taste, with traditional specialities like lamb and octopus baked *ispod sača* (under an ember-covered lid) amid rustic furnishings – expect to pay 200Kn for a slap-up meal.

Kučište and Viganj

West of Orebić, the road follows the coast past the relatively unspoiled villages of Kučište and Viganj, both of which have shingle beaches, a string of shoreside campsites and – in the case of Viganj at least – a burgeoning windsurfing scene. There's little in the way of package holiday development along this stretch of coast but plenty of private rooms (which can be booked through the tourist office in Orebić, see above), making it a laid-back, low-key alternative to the bustle of Orebić and Korčula. There are only three buses a day from Orebić (one on Sundays), but the presence of a privately operated boat service from Kučište and Viganj to Korčula Town ensures that you can still get round and see the sights.

Five kilometres out of Orebić, sleepy **KUČIŠTE** presents a wiggly line of rust-coloured stone houses facing the water. The **tourist office** midway through the village (July & Aug daily 9am–noon & 5–8pm) provides information on boat departures to Korčula and doles out local **rooms** (❶). There's a soothing lack of things to do in Kučište, save for sunbathe on the small-boat jetties strung out along the shoreline, stroll in the scrub-covered foothills of Mount Sveti Ilija above the village, or admire the view of Korčula's woolly tree cover from a brace of waterfront cafés.

It's only a fifteen-minute walk from Kučište to the next village along, **VIGANJ**, which lies on the far side of a pebbly spur of beach from which windsurfers launch themselves into the Pelješac channel. Most of the surfers stay at one of the three **campsites** immediately behind the beach: the straggling and largely unshaded *Ponta* (Ⓣ020/719-060), the large, well-organized *Liberan* (Ⓣ020/719-330, Ⓦwww.liberan-camping.com), or the orchard-like *Antony Boy* (Ⓣ020/719-077, Ⓦwww.antony-boy.com). *Liberan* boasts a **windsurfing** school where it's possible to rent boards (60Kn/hour or 250Kn/day) and sign up for courses (four-day beginners' courses start at around 1000Kn). You can rent out **scooters** at *Antony Boy* for 200Kn/day.

A little farther on in the village itself, the **tourist office** (July & Aug daily 8am–noon & 5–8pm) will sort you out with a **room** (❶). At the eastern end of the village, the *Pansion Mirina* (Ⓣ020/719-033, Ⓦwww.mirina-viganj.com; rooms ❶, studios from ❷) has cute rooms and a handful of apartments, many with sea-facing balconies. The *Kuvenat* **restaurant** in the centre of Viganj is good for fish, mussels and grilled squid; while the plant-filled veranda of the nearby *Bistro Karmela* is the perfect place to relax over a **drink**.

East to Ston

East of Orebić, the main road twists up into the mountains before reaching, after 15km, the turning to the lazy port of **TRPANJ** (served by four buses daily from Orebić), which lies at the end of a ravine on Pelješac's northern coast. It's not a bad place in which to get stuck, with a couple of cafés on the Riva, a tree-shaded pebble beach at the end of the harbour and views of the Makarska Riviera's dramatic mountain backdrop on the other side of the water. The **tourist office** (Mon–Sat 8am–2pm & 4–8pm, Sun 8am–2pm; Ⓣ020/743-433) on the front has plenty of **rooms** (❶), while the seafront *Hotel Faraon* (Ⓣ020/743-408, Ⓦwww.azalea-hotels.com; ❻ all-inclusive, ❺ B&B; April–Oct) offers recently renovated rooms with air conditioning, TV and minibar. There are **ferries** to **Ploče** on the mainland proper, where you can pick up buses north to Split or south to Dubrovnik.

Back on the main road, it's another 18km to the turn-off for **TRSTENIK**, on the peninsula's southern side, a pleasant destination set tight against the hills behind a couple of tiny beaches. It's a wonderfully secluded place to stay, although private accommodation is limited – the tourist office in Orebić (see opposite) will have a list of local landladies. A farther 14km along the main road at Dubrava there's a minor road (not served by bus) down to one of the best pebble beaches on the coast at **Žuljana**, 6km away – a tiny resort built round a sheltered bay at the foot of a steep rocky gorge. There's a **tourist office** (Ⓣ020/756-227) with unreliable opening times right on the beach, plenty of private **rooms** (❶) and three small **campsites** in the centre of the village. For **food**, try one of the unpretentious bar-restaurants on the harbourfront, where you'll also see signs advertising boat trips to even more remote beaches.

Ston and Mali Ston

About 20km beyond Dubrava, the twin settlements of Ston and Mali Ston straddle the neck of land which joins Pelješac to the mainland. **STON** (sometimes called Veliki – or "Great" – Ston to differentiate it from Mali Ston), an important salt-producing town, was swallowed up by Dubrovnik in 1333, becoming the most important fortress along the republic's northern frontier. Ston is still dramatically framed by its fourteenth-century **walls**, built to defend Dubrovnik's northern borders and stretching for some 3km across the rugged hillside above town. Restoration of the bits of wall nearest the town is still ongoing, although there's a V-shaped circuit already open to strollers – it culminates in a stout tower whose parapet affords superb views of a glittering chequerboard of salt pans out to the west. The town itself is also worth a potter, its mix of Renaissance- and Gothic-style houses laid out in a tight gridiron of narrow alleys stuffed with potted plants. If central Ston looks a bit ramshackle it's probably the result of the 1996 earthquake, when almost all of the town's buildings suffered structural damage – many are still in the process of being restored. Just west of Ston, the pre-Romanesque **St Michael's Church** (Crkva svetog Mihovila) squats atop a conical hill overlooking the salt pans and has twelfth-century frescoes inside; however, it's only infrequently open, so ask at the tourist office before making your way up.

Fifteen minutes' walk northeast of Ston, **MALI STON** began life as the outermost bastion of Ston's defensive system, and the line of fortifications linking Ston with Mali Ston can still be seen trailing majestically across the adjacent hillsides. It's now a sleepy little village of old stone houses pressed within its walls, looking out onto Mali Ston bay. In the water the village's **oyster beds** are marked out by wooden poles hung with ropes on which the oysters are encouraged to grow prior to harvesting in May and June. The village's traditional popularity as a seafood centre has been augmented by its growing reputation as a venue for romantic weekend breaks – no doubt something to do with the oysters' aphrodisiac effect. Following the narrow lanes up from the harbour, you'll soon reach a crescent-shaped fortress which marked the northeasternmost extent of Ston's sophisticated network of defences. Nowadays it's an uninhabited shell, though steps do lead up to a parapet from where there are good views – but with sheer drops on either side and no railings, it's not the kind of place you'd want to bring the kids.

There's no **beach** in Mali Ston, but the jetties and rocks around the harbour are pleasant places to sunbathe and the water is clean enough to swim in. Otherwise the nearest pebble beach is by the *Prapratno* campsite (see below) to the southwest.

Practicalities

Buses pull up on Ston's main street, where there's a **tourist office** (Mon–Fri 7am–1pm & 5–7pm, Sat 7am–1pm; ⓣ & ⓕ020/754-452, ⓦwww.tzo-ston.hr), which will give you a list of local rooms (❶) but might not ring them up on your behalf. There are a couple of lovely family-run hotels on Mali Ston's harbour: the *Villa Koruna* (ⓣ020/754-997, ⓦwww.vila-koruna.hr; ❺) is a six-room pension whose small but stylish rooms boast air conditioning and TV, while the slightly grander *Ostrea* (ⓣ020/754-555, ⓕ754-575, ⓦwww.ostrea.hr; ❺) offers posher rooms with a slap-up evening meal included in the price. The nearest campsite is the *Prapratno* (ⓣ020/754-000, ⓦwww.duprimorje.hr), about 4km southwest of town, down a steep side road just off the main route to Orebić. It has its own beach, a couple of grill-restaurants and impressive views of the mountains of Mljet across the water.

Mali Ston also has several upmarket **restaurants** close to the waterfront offering top-quality fish and locally-harvested oysters; *Kapetanova Kuća* (managed by the same people as the *Ostrea*) is one of the longest established and boasts a loyal clientele of local big-spenders, although the next-door *Bota Sare* isn't too far behind in terms of quality and service and has some atmospheric medieval-ish rooms. The restaurant of the *Villa Koruna*, with glass-covered terrace jutting out to sea, is also a worthy contender in the seafood and shellfish stakes. Cheaper food is available in Ston, where *Konoba kod Baće* on the main street has a range of inexpensive *marende* (brunches), as well as meaty grills.

Travel details

Trains

Šibenik to: Split (3 daily with change at Perković; 3hr 30min); Zagreb (3 daily with change at Perković; 5hr 30min).
Knin to: Zagreb (4 daily; 4hr).
Split to: Zagreb (4 daily; 5hr 30min–8hr 30min).
Zadar to: Knin (5 daily; 2hr 10min), Zagreb (5 daily with change at Knin; 6hr 20min–9hr).

Buses

Bol to: Supetar (Mon–Sat 5 daily, Sun 4 daily; 1hr).
Brbinj to: Božava (1–2 daily; 25min).
Hvar Town to: Jelsa (Mon–Sat 5 daily, Sun 2 daily; 55min); Stari Grad (Mon–Sat 8 daily, Sun 4 daily; 35min); Sućuraj (Mon & Fri 1 daily; 1hr 10min); Vrboska (Mon–Sat 5 daily, Sun 2 daily; 45min).
Imotski to: Dubrovnik (1 daily; 4hr); Split (10 daily; 2hr 15min); Zagreb (3 daily; 8hr).
Korčula Town to: Dubrovnik (2 daily; 3hr 30min); Lumbarda (Mon–Sat hourly, Sun 5 daily; 20min); Pupnat (Mon–Sat 7 daily, Sun 4 daily; 20min); Račišće (Mon–Sat 6 daily; 20min); Ston (1 daily; 2hr); Vela Luka (at least 4 daily; 1hr 20min); Zagreb (1 daily; 13hr).
Makarska to: Baška Voda (8 daily; 20min); Brela (8 daily; 30min); Gradac (hourly; 50min); Split (hourly; 1hr 10min); Tučepi (hourly; 15min); Zaostrog (hourly; 40min).
Orebić to: Dubrovnik (2 daily; 2hr 40min); Kućište (Mon–Sat 3 daily, Sun 1 daily; 10min); Lovište (Mon–Sat 3 daily, Sun 1 daily; 35min); Ston (3 daily; 1hr 10min); Trpanj (Mon–Sat 4 daily, Sun 2 daily; 45min); Viganj (Mon–Sat 3 daily, Sun 1 daily; 15min); Zagreb (1 daily; 12hr).
Ploče to: Dubrovnik (hourly; 2hr 15min); Split (hourly; 2hr 30min).
Preko to: Kukljica (10 daily; 10min); Muline (6 daily; 25min); Pašman (8 daily; 20min); Tkon (8 daily; 30min); Ugljan (6 daily; 15min).
Šibenik to: Drniš (10 daily; 40min); Dubrovnik (10 daily; 6hr); Knin (8 daily; 1hr 20min); Murter (8 daily; 1hr); Pula (3 daily; 8hr 30min); Skradin (Mon–Fri 6 daily, Sat & Sun 2 daily; 45min); Split (hourly; 2hr); Rijeka (12 daily; 6hr); Trogir (hourly; 1hr 30min); Vodice (hourly; 25min); Zadar (hourly; 1hr 30min), Zagreb (15 daily; 6hr 30min).
Split to: Dubrovnik (hourly; 4hr 40min); Gradac (hourly; 2hr); Imotski (10 daily; 2hr 15min); Klis (every 30min; 35min); Makarska (hourly; 1hr 10min); Omiš (every 30min; 40min); Plitvice (8 daily; 6hr 30min); Ploče (hourly; 2hr 30min); Rijeka (12 daily; 8–9hr); Šibenik (hourly; 2hr); Sinj (hourly; 1hr); Trsteno (hourly; 4hr); Zadar (hourly; 4hr); Zagreb (8 daily; 9hr); Zaostrog (hourly; 1hr 50min).
Stari Grad to: Hvar Town (Mon–Sat 4 daily, Sun 2; 35min); Jelsa (Mon–Sat 10 daily, Sun 4; 20min); Sućuraj (Mon–Sat 2 daily, Sun 1; 35min); Vrboska (Mon–Sat 10 daily, Sun 4; 10min).
Ston to: Dubrovnik (3 daily; 1hr 30min); Korčula Town (1 daily; 2hr); Orebić (3 daily; 1hr 10min).
Supetar to: Bol (Mon–Sat 5 daily, Sun 4; 1hr); Milna (Mon–Sat 6 daily, Sun 3; 35min); Postira (Mon–Sat 5 daily, Sun 3; 1hr 15min); Povlja (Mon–Sat 4 daily, Sun 3; 1hr 10min); Pučišća (Mon–Sat 5 daily, Sun 3; 45min); Škrip (Mon–Sat 2 daily; Sun 1; 25min); Sumartin (Mon–Sat 3 daily, Sun 2; 1hr 20min).
Trogir to: Šibenik (hourly; 1hr); Split (every 20min; 30–50min); Zadar (hourly; 3hr).
Trsteno to: Dubrovnik (hourly; 40min).
Vela Luka to: Korčula Town (at least 4 daily; 1hr 20min).
Vis Town to: Komiža (5 daily; 25min).
Vodice to: Murter (9 daily; 35min); Šibenik (20 daily; 25min).
Zadar to: Biograd-na-moru (hourly; 40min); Dubrovnik (9 daily; 8hr); Murter (1 daily; 1hr 20min); Nin (Mon–Fri hourly, Sat 13 daily, Sun 10 daily; 30min); Novalja (2 daily; 1hr 40min); Novigrad (Mon–Fri 4 daily, Sat & Sun 1 daily; 1hr); Pag (Mon–Fri 5 daily, Sat & Sun 2 daily; 1hr); Plitvice (hourly; 3hr); Pula (3 daily; 7hr); Rijeka (12 daily; 4hr 40min–5hr); Šibenik (hourly; 1hr 30min); Split (hourly; 3hr 30min); Trogir (hourly; 2hr 30min); Zagreb (20 daily; 3–5hr).

Ferries

Biograd-na-moru to: Tkon (10 daily; 15min).
Drvenik to: Sućuraj (summer 9 daily, winter 4 daily; 20min).
Hvar Town to: Lastovo (daily; 3hr); Split (1–2 daily; 1hr 50min); Vela Luka (daily; 1hr 15min); Vis (weekly; 1hr 15min).
Makarska to: Sumartin (summer 5 daily, winter 3 daily; 30min).
Orebić to: Domince (summer 14 daily, winter 7 daily; 15min); Korčula Town (foot passengers only; summer 8 daily; 15min).
Ploče to: Trpanj (summer 7 daily, winter 3 daily; 1hr).
Šibenik to: Prvić Luka (Mon–Sat 4 daily, Sun 2; 45min); Šepurine (Mon–Sat 4 daily, Sun 2; 55min); Vodice (Mon–Sat 4 daily, Sun 2; 1hr 20min); Zlarin (Mon–Sat 4 daily, Sun 2; 30min).
Split to: Dubrovnik (summer 1 daily, winter 2 weekly; 9hr); Hvar Town (1–2 daily; 1hr 50min); Lastovo (1 daily; 5hr); Rijeka (summer 1 daily, winter 2 weekly; 11hr); Stari Grad (3–5 daily; 2hr); Supetar (summer 13 daily, winter 7 daily; 1hr); Vela Luka (2 daily; 3hr 45min); Vis (1–2 daily; 2hr 30min); Zadar (summer 4 weekly, winter 2 weekly; 5hr 15min).
Stari Grad to: Dubrovnik (July to mid-Sept 1 daily; 7hr); Korčula Town (July to mid-Sept 1 daily; 3hr 30min); Rijeka (July to mid-Sept 1 daily; 11hr 30min); Split (summer 5 daily, winter 3 daily; 2hr); Zadar (July to mid-Sept 4 weekly; 6hr 45min).
Trogir to: Mali Drvenik (2 daily; 50min); Veli Drvenik (2 daily; 1hr 10min).
Vela Luka to: Hvar Town (6 weekly; 1hr 15min); Split (2 daily; 2hr 40min–3hr 45min).
Zadar to: Brbinj (3 daily; 1hr 30min); Ist (5 weekly; 2hr 30min); Iž (Bršanj; 1 daily; 1hr 40min); Iž (Veli Iž; 2 weekly; 1hr 30min); Mali Lošinj (6 weekly; 5hr); Molat (5 weekly; 2hr 30min); Preko (hourly; 30min); Pula (5 weekly; 8hr 10min); Rijeka (1 weekly; 7hr); Sali (2 daily; 1hr 30min); Silba (10 weekly; 2hr 20min or 4hr 20min); Split (1 weekly; 7hr); Zaglav (2 daily; 1hr 45min).

Catamarans and hydrofoils

Hvar Town to: Split (mid-May to mid-Sept 2 daily; 1–2hr); Lastovo (1 daily; 2hr); Vela Luka (1 daily; 1hr); Vis Town (1 daily; 40min).
Lastovo to: Hvar Town (1 daily; 2hr); Split (1 daily; 2hr 45min); Vela Luka (1 daily; 1hr).
Split to: Bol (June–Sept 1 daily; 45min); Hvar Town (mid-May to mid-Sept 2 daily; 1–2hr); Jelsa (June–Sept 1 daily; 1hr); Korčula Town (July & Aug 3 weekly; 2hr 15min); Lastovo (1 daily; 2hr 45min); Vela Luka (1 daily; 2hr); Vis (1 daily; 1hr 40min).
Vela Luka to Hvar (1 daily; 1hr); Lastovo (1 daily; 1hr); Split (1 daily; 2hr).
Vis Town to: Hvar Town (1 daily; 40min); Split (1 daily; 1hr 40min).
Zadar to: Božava (mid-June to mid-Sept 8 weekly; 1hr 15min); Ist (1 direct daily; 1hr 50min; 6 weekly via Sestrinj 2hr 15min); Molat (1 direct daily; 50min); Sali (2 daily; 45min); Silba (1 daily; 1hr 30min).

Domestic flights

Bol to: Zagreb (April–Sept 1 or 2 weekly; 50min).
Split to: Zagreb (April–Sept 4 daily, Oct–March 3 daily; 45min).
Zadar to: Zagreb (April–Sept 2 daily, Oct–March 1 daily; 30min).

International buses

Korčula to: Sarajevo (4 weekly; 12hr)
Split to: Belgrade (1 daily; 15hr); Ljubljana (1 daily; 12hr); Međugorje (3 daily; 5hr); Mostar (8 daily; 5hr); Sarajevo (5 daily; 7hr).
Zadar to: Ljubljana (1 daily; 8hr), Sarajevo (1 daily; 10hr).

International trains

Split to: Ljubljana (July & Aug 1 daily; 10hr 30min).

International ferries

Brbinj to: Ancona (mid-June to mid-Sept 1–2 weekly; 5hr).
Korčula Town to: Bari (mid-June to Sept 1–2 weekly; 11hr); Igoumenitsa (mid-June to Sept 1 weekly; 24hr).
Šibenik to: Ancona (July & Aug 3 weekly, June & Sept 2 weekly; 9hr).
Split to: Ancona (1 daily; 10hr); Bari (mid-June to late Sept 1–2 weekly; 15hr); Igoumenitsa (mid-June to late Sept 1 weekly; 28hr).
Stari Grad to: Ancona (July & Aug 6 weekly, June & Sept 1 weekly; 9hr); Bari (Aug 1–2 weekly; 12hr).
Vis to: Ancona (mid-July to Oct 3 weekly; 9hr).
Zadar to: Ancona (summer 6 weekly; 7hr).

International catamarans

Božava to: Ancona (Miatours/Amatori; June & Sept 1 weekly, July & Aug 3 weekly; 2hr 45min).
Zadar to: Ancona (Miatours/Amatori; June & Sept 1 weekly, July & Aug 3 weekly; 3hr 15min).

International high-speed ferries

Split to: Ancona (Croatia Jet; mid–June to mid–Sept 1 daily; 4hr 30min); Pescara (Pescara Jet; mid-June to mid-Sept 1 daily; 4hr 45min).
Stari Grad to: Pescara (Pescara Jet; mid-June to mid-Sept 1 daily; 3hr 15min).

6

Dubrovnik and around

CHAPTER 6

Highlights

* **Dubrovnik's city walls** A well-trodden walkway follows the full circuit of the battlements, providing the ideal vantage point from which to enjoy the city's medieval and Baroque splendours. See p.449

* **Dominican monastery** Quiet cloister in Dubrovnik's old town, harbouring a small but stunning collection of Renaissance art. See p.456

* **Lokrum** Densely wooded islet a short boat ride from Dubrovnik, the perfect place for a sunbathe or a stroll. See p.459

* **Mount Srđ** Scale the peak overlooking Dubrovnik to enjoy fantastic views of the coast. See p.461

* **Dubrovnik's Summer Festival** The annual cultural shindig brings top-class drama and music to the old town's courtyards, and adds a dash of glamour to the streets. See p.464

* **Trsteno** These Renaissance gardens, perched on a hillside overlooking the sea, provide an ideal excuse for an out-of-town excursion. See p.466

* **The Elaphite Islands** Koločep, Lopud and Šipan are among the most beautiful and unspoilt islands in the Adriatic. See p.471

* **Mljet** Lush, forested island with an easily strollable network of paths beside its two saltwater lakes. See p.475

△ General view of Dubrovnik's old town

Dubrovnik and around

DUBROVNIK's motto, *Libertas* ("liberty"), which is plastered across the sides of buses and the city's tourist literature, speaks volumes about the city's self-image and the idealized way in which it is perceived by others. For several centuries the city-state of Dubrovnik – or **Ragusa** as it was then known – managed to hang on to a modicum of independence while the rest of this coast fell under the sway of foreign powers. The Venetian Lion of St Mark is conspicuously absent, while statues of **St Blaise** (Sveti Vlaho), the symbol of Dubrovnik's independence, fill every conceivable crack and niche in the city.

An essentially medieval city reshaped by Baroque town planners after a disastrous earthquake of 1667, Dubrovnik's **historic core** seems to have been suspended in time ever since. Set-piece churches and public buildings blend seamlessly with the green-shuttered stone houses, to form a perfect ensemble relatively untouched by the twenty-first century. Outside the city walls, modern Dubrovnik is comparatively bereft of sights but exudes a Mediterranean elegance: gardens are an explosion of colourful bougainvillea and oleanders, trees are weighted down with figs, lemons, oranges and peaches.

Few visitors will notice any remaining signs of the 1991–92 **Siege of Dubrovnik**, during which over two thousand enemy shells fell on the old city. Reconstruction has been undertaken with astonishing speed, and the old town is pretty much back to its normal self. The fact that conflict took place here at all only reveals itself through subtle details: the vivacious orange-red hues of brand-new roof tiles, or the contrasting shades of grey where damaged facades have been patched up with freshly quarried stone.

Dubrovnik is worth a visit at any time of year, although late spring and summer – when life spills out onto the streets and café tables remain packed well into the night – bring out the best in the city. Croatia's cultural luminaries visit the town during the **Dubrovnik Summer Festival** in July and August, bringing an added dash of glamour to the streets, while the main event in winter is the **Feast of St Blaise** on February 3, when the patron saint of the city is honoured by a parade and special Mass, followed by much drinking and eating.

The main tourist resorts south of Dubrovnik, **Župa** and **Cavtat**, are within easy reach of the city by public transport. In addition, Dubrovnik's port is the

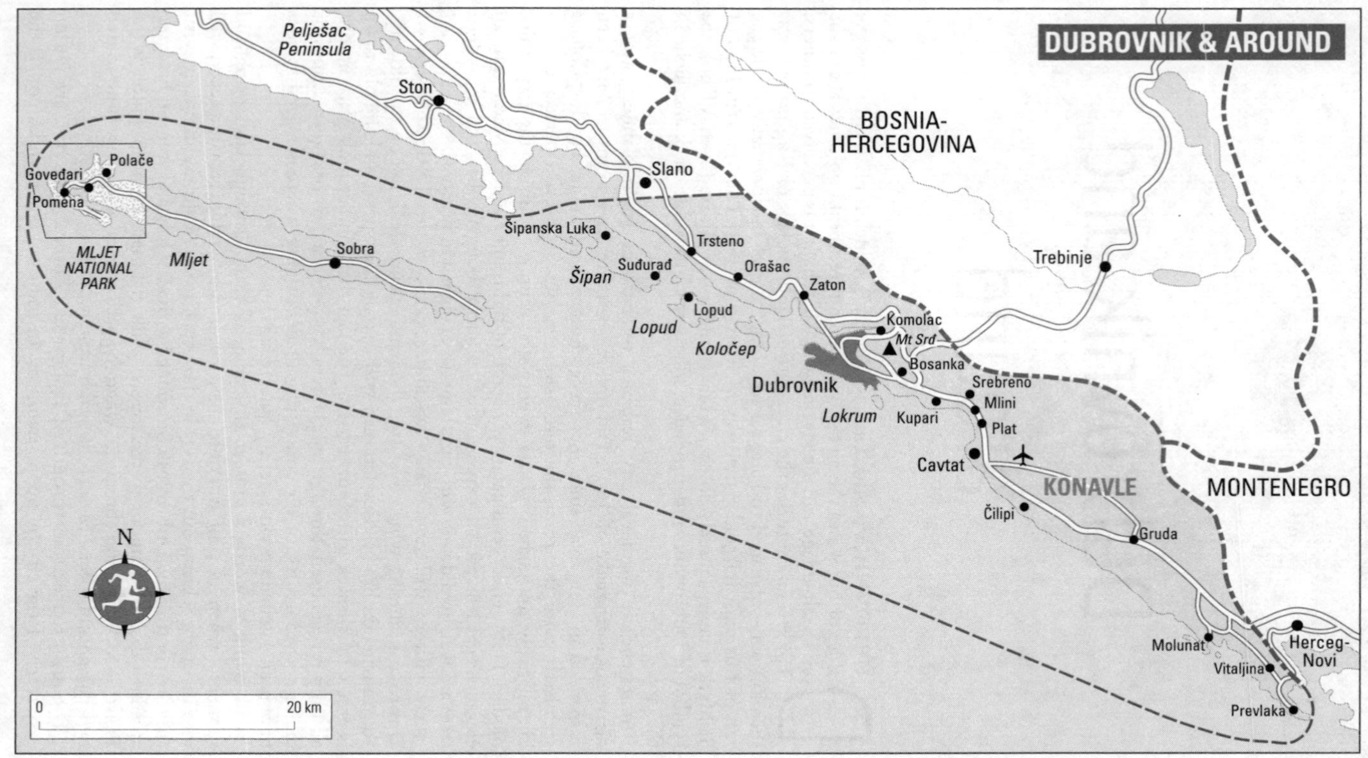
DUBROVNIK & AROUND
Pelješac Peninsula
Ston
BOSNIA-HERCEGOVINA
Slano
Polače
Goveđari
Pomena
MLJET NATIONAL PARK
Mljet
Sobra
Šipanska Luka
Trsteno
Suđurađ
Šipan
Orašac
Zaton
Lopud
Lopud
Koločep
Komolac
Mt Srđ
Bosanka
Dubrovnik
Lokrum
Kupari
Srebreno
Mlini
Plat
Cavtat
Trebinje
KONAVLE
Čilipi
MONTENEGRO
Gruda
Molunat
Vitaljina
Herceg-Novi
Prevlaka
N
0
20 km

natural gateway to the southernmost **islands** of the Croatian Adriatic, with the sparsely populated, semi-wild islands of **Koločep**, **Lopud** and **Šipan** providing beach-hoppers with a wealth of out-of-town bathing opportunities. Slightly farther out to sea, the green island of **Mljet** is one of the most beautiful on the entire coast – you'll need a day or two to do it justice.

Some history

Dubrovnik was first settled in the early seventh century by Greco-Roman refugees from the nearby city of Epidauros (now Cavtat), which was sacked by the Slavs. The refugees took up residence in the southern part of what is now the old town, then an island known as **Laus** – a name which later metamorphosed into **Ragusa**. The Slavs, meanwhile, settled on the wooded mainland opposite, from which the name **Dubrovnik** (from *dubrava*, meaning "glade") comes. Before long the slim channel between the two was filled in and the two sides merged, producing a symbiosis of Latin and Slav cultures unique in the Mediterranean. Ethnically, the city was almost wholly Slav by the fifteenth century, although leading families consistently claimed Roman lineage, and the nobility actively preserved the use of both Latin and Italian in official circles, if not always in everyday speech. They also held on to the name Ragusa, which remained in use until the early twentieth century.

Initially subject to **Byzantium**, the city came under **Venetian** control in 1204. The Venetians stayed until 1358, when they were squeezed out of the southern Adriatic by Louis of Hungary. Officially, Dubrovnik became a vassal of the Hungaro-Croatian kingdom, although it effectively became an independent city-state.

The emergent **Ragusan Republic** was run by an elected senate – fear of dictatorship meant that the nominal head of state, the Rector (*knez*), was virtually a figurehead. However, the republic was by no means a democracy: the city's nobility was the only section of society allowed to vote. Civic peace was ensured by allowing the rest of the citizenry full economic freedom and the chance to grow rich through commerce. Dubrovnik's network of maritime contacts made it one of the major players in Mediterranean trade, but the key to the city's wealth was its unrivalled access to the markets of the Balkan hinterland. The Ottoman Empire, having absorbed the kingdoms of both Serbia and Bosnia, granted Dubrovnik this privileged trading position in return for an annual payment of 1000 ducats, an arrangement that remained essentially unchanged until the Ragusan Republic's fall. Dubrovnik established a network of trading colonies stretching from the Adriatic to the Black Sea, from where wheat, wool, animal hides – and, for a time, slaves – could be shipped back to the mother republic before being re-exported to the West at a fat profit. As commerce grew, so did the need to protect it, and the republic extended its borders to include the whole of the coast from Konavle in the south to Pelješac in the north, as well as the islands of Mljet and Lastovo.

Mercantile wealth underpinned an upsurge in culture, producing a fifteenth- and sixteenth-century **golden age** when the best artists and architects in the Adriatic were drawn to the city. It was during this period that many of the urban landmarks of present-day Dubrovnik were completed: Juraj Dalmatinac and Michelozzo Michelozzi worked on the town **walls**, Paskoje Miličević drew up plans for the **Sponza Palace**, and Onofrio della Cava designed the **Rector's Palace**, as well as the two **fountains** that still bear his name. Florentine styles influenced the work of painters such as Nikola Božidarević, and successive generations of writers – playwright Marin Držić among them – abandoned

Latin in favour of their native tongue, breathing life into the Croatian literary Renaissance in the process.

Suzerainty over Dubrovnik had passed from the Hungaro-Croatian kingdom to the Ottoman Empire by the early sixteenth century, but shrewd diplomacy and the regular **payment of tributes** ensured that the city-state retained its virtual independence. Every year two envoys would visit Istanbul, hand over the agreed cash and stay for a year in fawning acquiescence until someone arrived to relieve them. In the sixteenth and seventeenth centuries Dubrovnik enjoyed the protection of both Spain (Dubrovnik ships sailed with the Armada in 1588) and the papacy, but usually avoided being dragged into explicitly anti-Turkish alliances. In fact, wars between the Ottomans and the West usually led to increased revenues for Dubrovnik, which exploited its position as the only neutral port in the Adriatic.

Decline set in with the **earthquake of 1667**, which killed around five thousand people and destroyed many of the city's buildings. Bandits from the interior looted the ruins, and Kara Mustafa, Pasha of Bosnia, demanded huge tributes in return for keeping the robber bands under control. Kara Mustafa's death during the Siege of Vienna in 1683 allowed the city the chance to rebuild, producing the elegantly planned rows of Baroque town houses which characterize the centre of the city to this day. However, the Austro-Turkish conflict of 1683–1718 seriously affected Dubrovnik's inland trade, a blow from which it never really recovered. By the eighteenth century Dubrovnik's nobility was dying out, and

The siege of Dubrovnik 1991–92

Few thought that Dubrovnik would be directly affected by the **break-up of Yugoslavia**: no significant Serbian minority lived in the city, and its strategic importance was questionable. However, in October 1991 units of the JNA (Yugoslav People's Army), supported by volunteers from Montenegro and Serb-dominated eastern Hercegovina, quickly overran the tourist resorts south of Dubrovnik and occupied the high ground commanding approaches to the city. The **bombardment of Dubrovnik** began in early November and lasted until May 1992. Despite considerable damage to the town's historic core, Dubrovnik's medieval fortifications proved remarkably sturdy, with the fortresses of Revelin and St John (more familiar to tourists as the site of the aquarium) pressed into service as shelters for the civilian population.

The logic behind the attack on Dubrovnik was confused. Belgrade strategists unwisely considered it an easy conquest, the fall of which would damage Croatian morale and break the back of Croatian resistance elsewhere on the Adriatic. The attack on Dubrovnik also presented an effective way of dragging both the Montenegrins and the Serbs of eastern Hercegovina into the conflict, not least because it seemed to promise them ample opportunities for pillage.

Attacking forces employed a mixture of bad history and dubious folklore to justify their actions. Dubrovnik's links with medieval Serbia, and the fact that so many leading Ragusan families had originally come from the Balkan interior, were unconvincingly offered up as evidence that the early republic had been part of the Serbian cultural orbit. In a particularly twisted piece of cultural logic, opportunist Serbian intellectuals painted modern-day Dubrovnik city as a cesspit of Western corruption that could only be purified by the macho values of the Balkan hinterland.

Contrary to Serbian expectations, Dubrovnik's hastily arranged defences held out. In the end, the siege was broken in July 1992 by a Croatian offensive from the north – one of the first big morale-boosting victories of the war. Once Dubrovnik's land links with the rest of Croatia had been re-established, Croatian forces continued their push southwards, liberating Cavtat and Čilipi.

commoners were increasingly elevated to noble rank to make up the numbers; anachronistic **feuds** between the Sorbonnesi (old patricians) and Salamanchesi (newly elevated patricians, named after the universities of Sorbonne and Salamanca, where many young Ragusans studied) weakened the traditional social fabric still further.

The city-state was formally dissolved by Napoleon in 1808. The French occupation of the city provoked a British naval bombardment, while Russian and Montenegrin forces laid waste to surrounding territories, destroying much of suburban Dubrovnik in the process. In 1815 the **Congress of Vienna** awarded Dubrovnik to the Austrians, who incorporated the city into the newly formed province of Dalmatia. Political and economic activity was henceforth concentrated in towns such as Zadar and Split, leaving Dubrovnik on the fringes of Adriatic society.

The symbolic importance of Dubrovnik long outlived the republic itself. For nineteenth-century Croats the city was a **Croatian Athens**, a shining example of what could be achieved – both politically and culturally – by the Slav peoples. It was also increasingly a magnet for foreign travellers, who wrote about the city in glowing terms, save for Rebecca West, for whom it was too perfect and self-satisfied: "I do not like it," she famously wrote. "It reminds me of the worst of England."

Already a society resort in West's time, Dubrovnik enhanced its reputation for cultural chic with the inception in 1949 of the **Dubrovnik Festival**, one of Europe's most prestigious, while the construction of big hotel complexes in Lapad and Babin kuk to the north, and Župa to the south, helped make Dubrovnik one of the most popular tourist destinations in Yugoslavia in the 1970s and 1980s. After repairing the damage done during the **1991–92 siege** with remarkable speed, Dubrovnik is once again fully prepared to welcome the vacationing hordes.

Arrival, information and accommodation

Dubrovnik's **airport** is situated some 22km east of the city, close to the village of Čilipi. Croatia Airlines buses meet all that airline's arrivals (even the late-night ones), dropping off at the main western entrance to the old town, **Pile** (pronounced *pee*-leh) **Gate**, before terminating at the bus station (25min; 35Kn single). If you arrive with another airline you'll either have to wait for the next Croatia Airlines bus or opt for a **taxi**, which will set you back something in the region of 220–260Kn. Buses back to the airport leave the bus station ninety minutes before each Croatia Airlines departure.

The **bus terminal** is located 5km west of the old town in the suburb of Kantafig – buses #1a and #3 run from there to Pile Gate. Both buses pass by the **ferry terminal**, 4km west of the old town in Gruž harbour. Flat-fare **tickets** for local buses can be bought either from the driver (10Kn; exact change only) or from newspaper kiosks (7Kn).

Dubrovnik's tourist association (Ⓦwww.tzdubrovnik.hr) operates **information points** at Stradun bb in the old town (daily: summer 8am–10pm; winter 9am–5pm; Ⓣ020/321-561); Ante Starčevića 7, near the Pile Gate (same times; Ⓣ020/426-253); at Obala Stjepana Radića 27, opposite the ferry dock (same times; Ⓣ020/417-983); and at the bus station (Mon–Fri 8am–8pm, Sat & Sun 5–8pm Ⓣ020/417-851). They offer good advice on local attractions and public

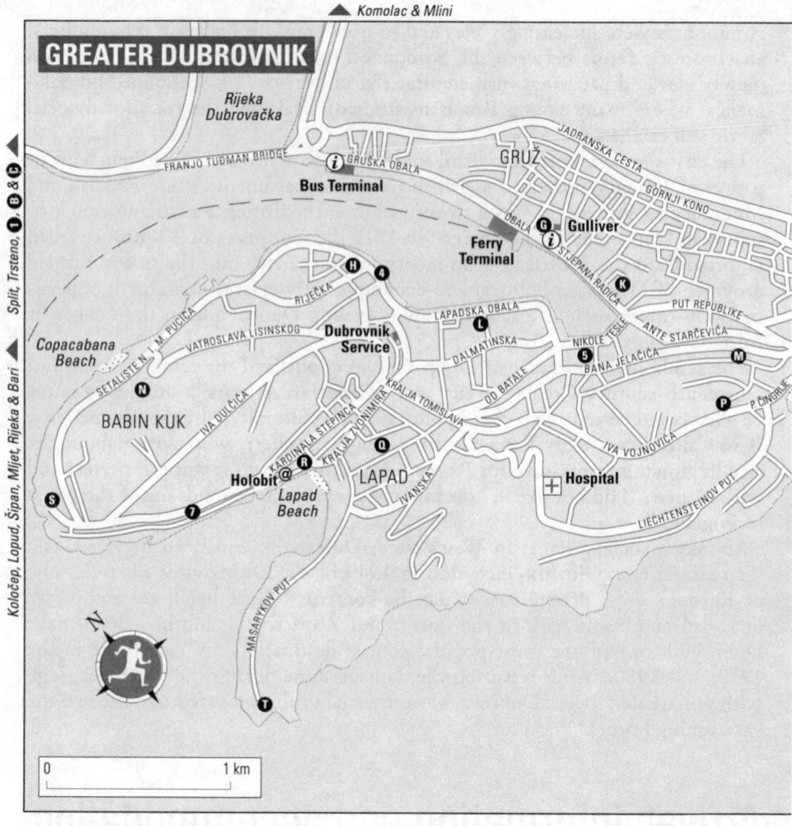

transport details, and give away copies of two useful listings booklets: *Dubrovnik in Your Pocket* (also available from most hotels), a reliable and entertainingly written guide to restaurants, cafés and local services; and *Dubrovnik Guide*, which offers much of the same but in dryer style.

Accommodation

Unless you've opted for a package deal, Dubrovnik's hotels are somewhat overpriced in the high season, leaving budget travellers with little option but to settle for private rooms. Demand for all beds is high in July and August, so you should be prepared to arrive early in the day or reserve in advance.

There are numerous accommodation agencies handling private **rooms** (350–400Kn) and **apartments** (two-person studios from 550 Kn, four-person apartments from 800Kn). Among the most helpful are Gulliver, just opposite the ferry terminal at Obala Stjepana Radića 32 (summer Mon–Sat 7am–7pm, Sun 8am–noon; winter Mon–Sat 7am–7pm; ⓣ020/313-313, ⓦwww.gulliver.hr); Dubrovnik Service, in Lapad at Šetalište kralja Zvonimira 10 (ⓣ020/436-004 or 098 652-870, ⓦwww.dubrovnikservice.com); and Atlas, near Pile Gate at Svetog Đurđa 1 (Mon–Sat 8am–8pm; ⓣ020/442-565, ⓦwww.atlas-croatia.com). For

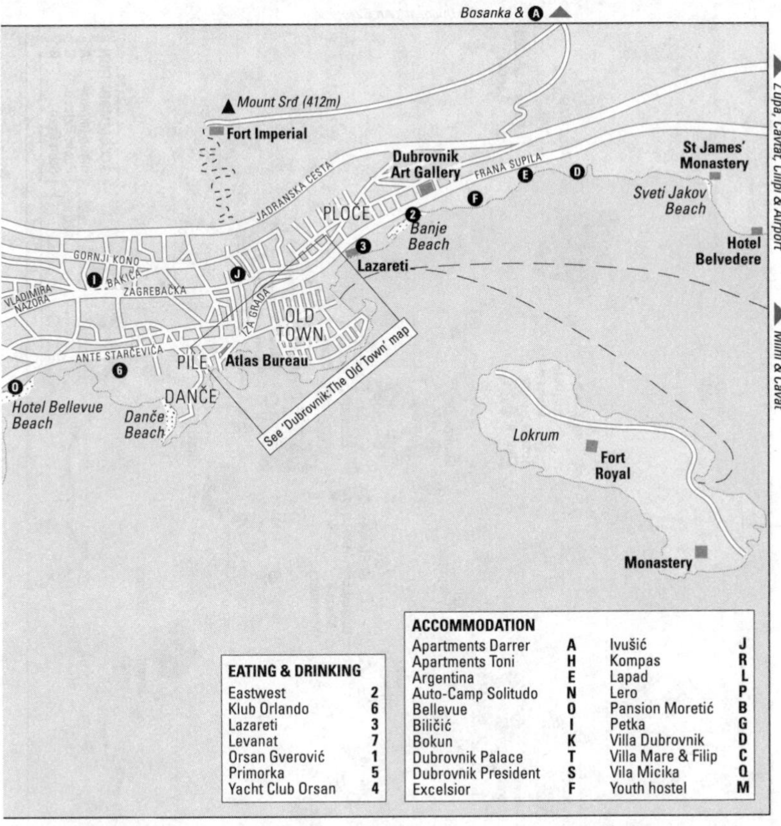

making reservations online, the sites Ⓦwww.dubrovnik-area.com and Ⓦwww.dubrovnik-online.com list hundreds of private rooms and apartments.

Travellers arriving at the bus station may well be besieged by aggressive landladies offering unlicensed rooms, but these are often a long way from the centre, and various "extra costs" may be subsequently added to any price you think you've agreed.

Campsites and youth hostel

Dubrovnik's youth hostel represents a good alternative to private rooms for the budget traveller, as does the large if sometimes crowded campsite; several more campsites are located a short bus ride away in Trsteno (p.466), Kupari (p.467) and Srebreno (p.467).

Auto-Camp Solitudo Babin kuk ⓣ020/448-234, wwww.valamar.com. Roomy and well-organized site on the northern side of Babin kuk peninsula, with modern facilities and a reasonable amount of tree cover. Small shop and a (currently Mexican-style) restaurant on site. It's one of the most expensive sites in Croatia, with prices rising to 110Kn per pitch, 50Kn per person in the high season. Bus #6 (destination Dubrava) from Pile or the bus station.

Youth hostel off bana Jelačića at V. Sagrestana 3 ⓣ020/423-241, ⓕ412-592, ⓔdubrovnik@hfhs.hr. Friendly year-round hostel, perfectly poised between Gruž and the old town. Providing bunk-bed accommodation in neat four- or six-person

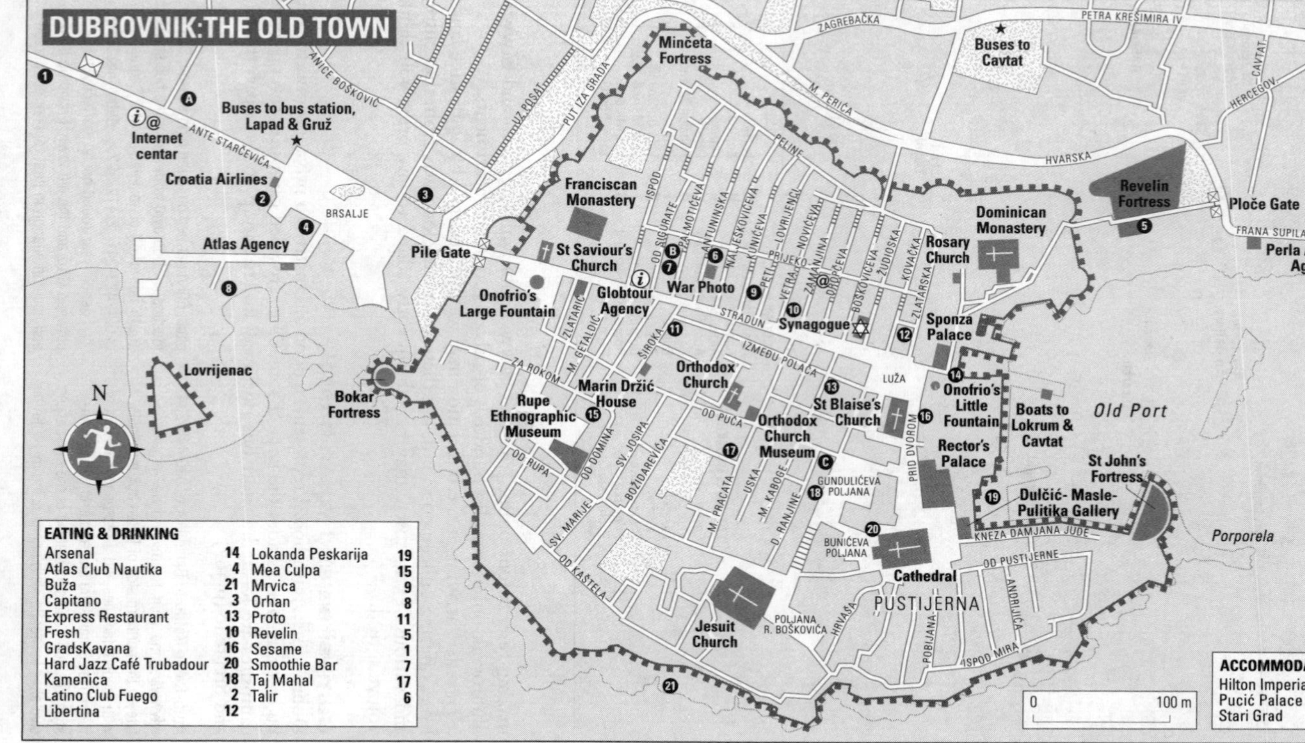
DUBROVNIK: THE OLD TOWN
Lazareti & Dubrovnik Art Gallery
Minčeta Fortress
Buses to Cavtat
Buses to bus station, Lapad & Gruž
Internet centar
Croatia Airlines
Atlas Agency
BRSALJE
Pile Gate
Lovrijenac
Bokar Fortress
Franciscan Monastery
St Saviour's Church
Onofrio's Large Fountain
Globtour Agency
War Photo
Synagogue
Dominican Monastery
Rosary Church
Sponza Palace
Revelin Fortress
Ploče Gate
Perla Adriatica Agency
Onofrio's Little Fountain
Boats to Lokrum & Cavtat
Old Port
St Blaise's Church
Rector's Palace
St John's Fortress
Dulčić- Masle- Pulitika Gallery
Porporela
Orthodox Church
Orthodox Church Museum
Marin Držić House
Rupe Ethnographic Museum
Cathedral
PUSTIJERNA
Jesuit Church
LUŽA
STRADUN
PETRA KREŠIMIRA IV
ZAGREBAČKA
M. PERIĆA
HVARSKA
HERCEGOV.
CAVTAT
FRANA SUPILA
ANICE BOŠKOVIĆ
ANTE STARČEVIĆA
UZ POSAT
PUT IZA GRADA
PELINE
ISPOD
OD SIGURATE
PALMOTIĆEVA
ANTUNINSKA
NALJESKOVIĆEVA
KUNIĆEVA
LOVRIJENCI
NOVIĆEVA
PETILOVRIJENCI
PRIJEKO
VETRA
ZAMANJINA
ODOPĆEVA
BOŠKOVIĆEVA
ŽUDIOSKA
KOVAČKA
ZLATARSKA
ZLATARIĆ
M. GETALDIĆ
ŠIROKA
IZMEĐU POLAČA
ZA ROKOM
OD PUČA
PRID DVOROM
OD DOMINA
SV. JOSIPA
BOŽIDAREVIĆA
OD RUPA
SV. MARIJE
OD KAŠTELA
M. PRACATA
USKA
M. KABOGE
D. RANJINE
GUNDULIĆEVA POLJANA
BUNIĆEVA POLJANA
POLJANA R. BOŠKOVIĆA
HRVAŠA
POBIJANA
ISPOD MIRA
ANDRIJIĆA
OD PUSTIJERNE
KNEZA DAMJANA JUDE
N
0 100 m
EATING & DRINKING
Arsenal 14
Atlas Club Nautika 4
Buža 21
Capitano 3
Express Restaurant 13
Fresh 10
GradsKavana 16
Hard Jazz Café Trubadour 20
Kamenica 18
Latino Club Fuego 2
Libertina 12
Lokanda Peskarija 19
Mea Culpa 15
Mrvica 9
Orhan 8
Proto 11
Revelin 5
Sesame 1
Smoothie Bar 7
Taj Mahal 17
Talir 6
ACCOMMODATION
Hilton Imperial A
Pucić Palace C
Stari Grad B

dorms (some with sinks, some without), it fills up fast in summer, so arrive early or ring in advance. A basic breakfast, available for an additional charge, is served up on an attractive outdoor terrace, and guests have use of a kitchen/dining room in the basement. To get there from the bus station, ride three stops on bus #1a, #3 or #7, head east up Ante Starčevića, and turn uphill to the right after five minutes. 120Kn per person, 2am curfew.

Hotels

There's a dearth of reasonably priced **hotel** accommodation anywhere in Dubrovnik, not least near the old town. The swankiest places are in Ploče, just east of the centre, where you'll be within easy reach of the sights and may even have a view of the medieval walls from your balcony if you're prepared to fork out the extra cash. To the west, there's a brace of mid-range hotels in walking range of the old town. Elsewhere, however, you'll probably be a short bus ride away from the action: there are a couple of hotels handily placed in the Gruž port area, but most of the big package establishments are on the Lapad and Babin kuk peninsulas, 5km west of the Pile Gate, where there are some pleasant, if crowded, beaches. With a car, you could consider the pension-style places in the villages around Dubrovnik. All the places listed below include breakfast, and are open year round unless stated.

Many of the hotels are block-booked by package groups from June to September, so independent travellers should ring well in advance to secure a room. Remember that the high-season prices (July and Aug) expressed in the price codes below can fall by about twenty percent in spring and autumn, thirty percent or more in winter.

All the accommodation reviewed below is marked on the maps on pp.444–445 or p.446.

The old town and around

Argentina Frana Supila 14 ⓣ020/440-555, ⓦwww.gva.hr. Long-established five-star a 10min walk east of the old town, comprising a central building dating from the 1920s, a modern annexe and two characterful *belle-époque* villas: the *Orsula* and the *Sheherezade*. All the creature comforts, including concrete beach and small swimming pool. ❽

Bellevue Pera Čingrije 7 ⓣ020/413-306, ⓦwww.hotel-bellevue.hr. Dramatically situated on a clifftop overlooking Miramare Bay, a 15min walk from Pile Gate, and with a wonderful shingle beach immediately below. Currently being renovated to five-star standard. ❻

Biličić Privezna 2 ⓣ020/417-152 or 098 802-111, ⓦwww.geocities.com/apartments_bilicic. Family-run guesthouse uphill from the centre in the Gornji Konjo district of town, offering doubles with a/c, TV and en-suite bathrooms. It's extremely popular, and is booked up weeks or months in advance in summer. The walled garden is gorgeous – it's no surprise to discover that the owner came third in a local best-kept garden competition in 2006. They'll pick you up from the airport if the family schedule allows. There's no breakfast but you can use the al-fresco kitchen in the porch. ❸

Excelsior Frana Supila 12 ⓣ020/353-353, ⓦwww.hotel-excelsior.hr. Just east of the old town, and recently modernized, this five-star place offers plush en-suite rooms, indoor pool and fitness centre. The terraces of the hotel's bar and restaurants have excellent views back towards the town, as do some of the room balconies. Try and avoid the viewless, north-facing rooms. ❾

Hilton Imperial Marijana Blažića 2 ⓣ020/320-320, ⓦwww.hilton.com/dubrovnik. Originally opened in 1897 and long considered the top address in town, the *Imperial* suffered serious shell damage in 1991 and stood empty for a decade before being laboriously restored by the Hilton chain. Ideally situated next to Pile Gate, and with a guest list that includes George Bernard Shaw and HG Wells. Plush rooms, faultless service and the glass-roofed indoor pool are the main attributes. ❽

Ivušić Bernarda Shawa 1 ⓣ020/432-654, ⓦwww.apartmani-ivusic.hr. Family house in an excellent location on the hillside just above the old town, with a pair of simply decorated doubles with a/c and TV, and two- to four-person apartment with kitchenette. The main selling point is the excellent view down towards the town walls and the Minčeta tower. Breakfast is available on request, and an airport pick-up can be arranged. Three-day minimum stay preferred. ❸

Lero Ive Vojnovića 14 ⓣ020/341-333, ⓦwww.hotel-lero.hr. Modern, functional but comfortable three-star a 20min walk (or a short ride on bus #4) west of Pile Gate. Rooms are neat and contemporary with en-suite shower and TV. ❻

Pucić Palace Od Puča 1 ⓣ020/324-111, ⓦwww.thepucicpalace.com. Five-star boutique hotel in a recently renovated eighteenth-century palace, offering plush, fully equipped – but slightly cramped – doubles. Decor is on the chintzy side, but most rooms come with views of old-town streetlife. Expect to part with upwards of 4000Kn for a double in high season. ❾

Stari Grad Od Sigurate 4 ⓣ020/322-244, ⓦwww.hotelstarigrad.com. Charming old-town building offering small but atmospheric rooms, all with shower and TV. The view from the roof terrace (where breakfast is served in summer) is a major plus. Only eight rooms, so reserve well in advance. ❽

Villa Dubrovnik Vlaha Bukovca 6 ⓣ020/422-933, ⓕ423-465, ⓦwww.villa-dubrovnik.hr. Small, intimate hotel 1km east of the old town with its own gardens and concrete beach. Rooms come with all the usual comforts, plus views of the island of Lokrum. Friendly staff and faultless standards of service complete the picture. Half-board is compulsory in peak season; you're unlikely to be disappointed by the superb food. Doubles from 2100Kn. ❾

Gruž, Lapad and Babin kuk

Apartments Toni Ivana Zajca 5, Lapad ⓣ091/52-94-741 or 098 850 578, ⓔtonitolja@yahoo.com, ⓦwww.apartmanitoni.com. Modern house on the northern side of the Lapad peninsula with a handful of cute two-person studio apartments, each with kitchenette and washing machine, and a beautiful split-level family apartment which can be rented as a whole or as individual double rooms with access to the shared kitchen-diner – which comes with fantastic views of Gruž harbour. Breakfast can be arranged, as can airport transfer. Bus #6 (destination Dubrava) from either Pile or Lapad to the INA petrol station on Lapadska Obala. ❹

Bokun Obala Stjepana Radića 7 ⓣ020/357-290 or 098 9697329, ⓔbonitokun@yahoo.com. Friendly family pension located in the bustling Gruž harbour area but wonderfully secluded behind a walled garden shaded by figs, grapes and kiwi fruit. On offer are a mixture of simply furnished rooms with a/c and TV, some with en-suite facilities, others sharing a WC/shower in the hallway. There are also three two-person apartments, each with a kitchenette. There's an optional continental breakfast (35Kn), and a laundry service (60Kn per load). Rooms ❷, apartments ❹.

Dubrovnik Palace Masarykov put 20, Lapad ⓣ020/430-000, ⓦwww.dubrovnikpalace.hr. Newly renovated five-star on a south-facing headland. All rooms have bathtubs and sea views, and the furnishings look like they're straight out of a lifestyle magazine. There's a gym, wellness centre, sauna and indoor pool on site, and well-tended gardens overlooking a rocky seafront. Bus #4 from Pile to "Hotel Pallace" (*sic*). Rooms from 1800Kn to 2350Kn depending on size. ❾

Dubrovnik President Iva Dulčića 39, Babin kuk ⓣ020/441-100, ⓦwww.valamar.com. The jewel in the crown of the Babin kuk complex, its seven floors ranged across a hillside at the western tip of the peninsula. All rooms have balconies and seaward views, and there's a small pebble beach on site. Standard doubles have 1970s-ish furnishings, so ask for a "superior" room if you want design-studio decor and a garden terrace. Take bus #5 (destination Neptun) from Pile, or bus #6 (destination Dubrava) from Pile or the bus station, and alight at the end of the line. From 1800Kn. ❾

Kompas Šetalište kralja Zvonimira 56, Lapad ⓣ020/352-000, ⓦwww.hotel-kompas.hr. One of the better package-oriented hotels on the Lapad peninsula, this is a well-run place used by German and British tour groups. All rooms are en suite and have cable TV; many also have views of Lapad Bay. Take bus #6 (destination Dubrava) from either Pile or opposite the bus station to Lapad post office, then walk downhill along Šetalište kralja Zvonimira. ❼

Lapad Lapadska obala 37, Lapad ⓣ020/432-922 or 412-436, ⓦwww.hotel-lapad.hr. Large hotel overlooking Gruž harbour and incorporating various architectural styles, from the sixteenth-century reception area to the pre-World War I main building (note the griffin-adorned staircases) and late twentieth-century annexe. All rooms have WC/shower and TV, although those in the modern annexe are bigger and come with a/c. There's a small swimming pool in the courtyard, and Lapad beach is a 15min walk away. Within walking distance of both the bus station and the port, and on the #6 Pile–Dubrava bus route. Easter–Nov only. Old building ❻, new building ❻–❼

Petka Obala Stjepana Radića 38, Gruž ⓣ020/410-500, ⓔhotel-petka@du.t-com.hr. Medium-rise concrete affair opposite the ferry terminal. The rooms are plain and feature furniture that has been around a bit, but they're spick and span, with shower, TV and phone; those at the front have marvellous views of the port. A walkable 1km east of the bus station; otherwise catch bus #1A from Pile. ❻

Vila Micika Mata Vodopica 10, Lapad ⓣ020/437-332, ⓦwww.vilamicika.hr. Family-run pension-style place a short walk uphill from Lapad Bay, offering a handful of cosy doubles and triples, all with en-suite WC/shower and TV. Some have a small balcony. There's no breakfast, but there are plenty of cafés nearby. Bus #6 from Pile or the bus station to Lapad post office. ❸

Outside the city

Apartments Darrer Bosanka 62a ⓣ020/424-127, ⓦwww.dubrovnikportal.com/adriano. Modern house in a village set on a scrub-covered, goat-grazed plateau, high above the city on the shoulder of Mount Srđ. The neat, bright apartments – either two-person studios with kitchenette, or four-person family-sized suites – come with a/c, TV and new furnishings throughout. There's a garden with small swimming pool out front. You'll need a car to get here: head out of town on the Cavtat road and then take the battered side road that leads to Mount Srđ. Once you get settled in, you can walk down to Dubrovnik in under an hour, though getting back up again can be rather more time-consuming. The owners also have a family-sized apartment in the Zlatni potok district of Dubrovnik, a 20min walk from the old town. Two-person studios ❺, four-person apartments 950Kn.

Pansion Moretić na Pržini 10, Orašac ⓣ020/891-507, ⓦwww.i-reception.net/moretic. This bed-and-breakfast in a rustic village 12km west of town, just off the main road to Split, has simple en-suite doubles, some with balconies looking out onto vineyards, olive trees and orange groves. It's a 15min walk from the sea, and handily placed for the botanical gardens at Trsteno (see p.466). The owners speak English, German or Italian, depending on which family member you get hold of. The pension is well signed from the main road, and there's a bus stop (most inter-city buses will pick up and drop off here) nearby. ❸

Villa Mare & Filip Mali Zaton ⓣ020/891-345, ⓦwww.ivana-vojvoda-t.com.hr. Rooms and apartments owned by the Vojvoda family in Zaton in the beautiful, bay-hugging village of Zaton 8km northwest of Dubrovnik. Breakfast and half-board available for a few extra kuna. ❸–❹

The City

With a population of a little over 49,000, Dubrovnik isn't as large a city as you might think, and although it sprawls along the coast for several kilometres, its real heart is the walled and surprisingly compact **old town**. Doing the circuit of the city walls is the one Dubrovnik attraction you really can't miss, and it's worth doing this early on in order to get the feel of the place. The rest of the old town can easily be covered in a day and a half – although once you begin to soak up the atmosphere you'll find it difficult to pull yourself away. Running above the town to the east is the bare ridge of **Mount Srđ**, the summit of which provides expansive views of the town and the coast. The best place for swimming and sunbathing is the islet of **Lokrum**, a short taxi-boat ride from the old town.

The city walls

The **Pile Gate**, where city buses from the ferry and bus terminals arrive, is the logical place to start exploring the old town. The northernmost of the two main entrances to the medieval city, the gate – a simple archway reached through a plain, pillbox-like bastion – is accessible by a stone bridge dating from 1471 which crosses the former moat, now a park full of fruit trees. From here, the best way to get your bearings is by making a tour of the still largely intact **city walls** (Gradske zidine; daily: summer 8am–7.30pm; winter 10am–3pm; 50Kn), 25m high and stretching for some 2km, completely surrounding the old town. The full circuit takes about an hour; longer in high summer when big crowds may slow down your progress. The path along the walls is narrow in places and you're not allowed up there if you're wearing a backpack.

Sea kayaking in Dubrovnik

Sea kayaking has become something of a hit activity in Dubrovnik over the last year or two, and the sight of shoals of orange-bibbed paddlers pulling into Banje beach has become one of the city's most characteristic sights. The activity usually involves a group excursion in one-person kayaks, led by an instructor, and is an exhilarating way of seeing the walled city and its surrounding islands from a maritime perspective. Previous experience is not neccessary, and the pace is gentle enough to suit most people of average health.

The most common kayak trips are a half-day trip round Dubrovnik's walls and the nearby island of Lokrum (around 250Kn per person), or full-day excursions to the slightly more distant islands of Koločep and Lopud (around 400Kn per person). Agencies organizing Kayak trips include Adriatic Kayak Tours, Zrinsko-Frankopanska 6 (Ⓣ020/312-770, Ⓦwww.adriatickayaktours.com); and Laura (Ⓦwww.laura-advenure.com), whose tours can be booked through the Perla Adriatica tourist agency, just outside Ploče gate at Frana Supila 2 (Ⓣ020/422-766).

The walls are encrusted with towers and bastions, and it's impossible not to be struck by their remarkable size and state of preservation. Some parts date back to the tenth century, but most of the original construction was undertaken in the twelfth and thirteenth centuries, with subsequent rebuildings and reinforcements carried out in the mid-fifteenth century when fear of Ottoman expansion was at its height. Once you're on top, the views over the town are of a patchwork sea of terracotta tiles, punctuated by sculpted domes and towers and laid out in an almost uniform grid plan – the Ragusan authorities introduced strict planning regulations to take account of the city's growth as early as the 1270s, and the rebuilding programme which followed the earthquake of 1667 rationalized things still further.

Clockwise around the walls from the Pile Gate, it's a gentle two-hundred-metre climb towards the fat, concentric turrets of the **Minčeta Fortress**, which guards the old town's northern corner. It was begun in 1455 by the Florentine architect Michelozzo Michelozzi and was replaced by Juraj Dalmatinac (see box on p.334), who designed the eye-catching crown of battlements that has made Minčeta such a landmark. From Minčeta it's a farther 500m around the walls to the **Ploče Gate**, where you have an excellent view of the old port area, and another 200m to **St John's Fortress**, a W-shaped curve of thick stone facing out to sea. It's probably as you return towards Pile Gate along the southern, sea-facing walls that you get the best views of old Dubrovnik's tiled roofs and narrow, tunnel-like streets. At the western corner of the old town you'll pass the **Bokar Fortress**, also by Michelozzi and Dalmatinac, a jutting bastion which once guarded sea-borne access to the moat.

Along Stradun

Inside the Pile Gate, **Stradun** (also known as Placa), the city's main street, runs straight across the old town, following the line of the channel that originally separated the island of Ragusa from the mainland. A constant surge of tourists throngs the Stradun in summer, and the evening *korzo* is the busiest in the whole of Croatia – the street's limestone surface has been buffed to a slippery polish by the tramp of thousands of feet. The set-piece uniformity of this thoroughfare is a result of the 1667 earthquake, after which Stradun was reconstructed with the imposing, outwardly unadorned town houses you see today, displaying a civic commitment to purity and order characteristic of a city government that always had a rather disciplinarian streak, and which has been rigorously maintained by subsequent generations. All the houses have identical door and window frames, the latter flanked by uniform green shutters, and though they're nowadays full of tourist shops, laws forbidding conspicuous shop signs mean that the names of boutiques and restaurants are instead inscribed on the lanterns that hang over each doorway.

At the western end of Stradun, the first thing you see is **Onofrio's Large Fountain** of 1444, a circle of water-spouting heads topped by a bulbous dome where, to guard against the plague, visitors to this hygiene-conscious city had to wash themselves before they were admitted. Built by the Italian architect Onofrio de la Cava, the fountain was the culmination of an elaborate water system that delivered water from Mount Srđ to public washing facilities right across town. Across the street is the small **St Saviour's Church** (Crkva svetog Spasa), a simple but harmonious Renaissance structure whose facade – featuring a rose window beneath a trefoil roof line – may have influenced the cathedral at Hvar. The church's bare interior is now used as an exhibition space for contemporary work.

The Franciscan monastery

A narrow passageway leads from St Saviour's Church to the fourteenth-century **Franciscan monastery** (Franjevački samostan) complex, whose intriguing late Romanesque cloister is decorated with rows of double arches topped by a confusion of human heads and fantastic animals. The attached **museum** (daily: summer 9am–6pm; winter unpredictable; 20Kn) is also worth a look, with manuscripts tracing the development of musical notation, together with relics from the apothecary's shop at the entrance to the cloister. Established in 1317, and still in business, it calls itself the oldest pharmacy in Europe. Among the Gothic reliquaries, a smooth, silver-plated fourteenth-century receptacle for St Ursula's head looks far too small and dainty to contain a human skull.

On the Stradun itself, on the right-hand side of the entrance to the monastery cloister, a small stone embellished with a gargoyle-like face juts out of the wall

△ Onofrio's Large Fountain

just above pavement height. For some reason, it has become a test of male endurance to stand on this stone – which is extremely difficult to balance on – and to remove one's shirt while facing the wall before falling off. A few steps beyond is the entrance portal to the monastery church, above which is a moving relief of the Pietà, carved by the Petrović brothers in 1499.

Prijeko and the synagogue

North of the Stradun a succession of alleys filled with potted plants runs uphill towards the city walls, on the way crossing **Prijeko** (literally "across" – a reference to the time when this part of the city was divided from the rest of Dubrovnik by a channel of sea water), which runs parallel to Stradun and contains many of Dubrovnik's more touristy restaurants. One of these steep alleys, Antuninska, is home to the **War Photo Gallery** at no. 6 (daily 9am–9pm; 25Kn), where displays of work by the world's top war photographers are held. Most of the exhibitions here focus on the victims of war rather than the activity itself – powerful, moving stuff for the most part, although the way the gallery views human suffering through glossy travel-magazine aesthetics ultimately leaves a bitter taste in the mouth.

Towards the eastern end of Prijeko, Žudioska ("Jews' Street") leads back down to the Stradun, passing a tiny **synagogue** (summer daily 10am–8pm; winter Mon–Fri 9am–noon; 10Kn) – dating from the fifteenth century and said to be the second oldest in the Balkans. The present-day interior dates from the nineteenth century, its heavy brass lamps and candelabras hanging from a bright-blue ceiling dotted with star of David motifs. Unlike other Christian powers, Dubrovnik welcomed many of the Jews expelled from Spain in 1492, although anti-Semitism was not unknown. Even before their arrival in the city, scapegoating of Jews formed part of Dubrovnik's medieval carnival, most notably in the practice known as the *džudijata*, in which an unfortunate lunatic or criminal was dressed as a Jew before being hauled through the streets in an ox cart and either ritually killed or made to act out a make-believe death – historians are divided on how far things actually went.

Luža Square

The Stradun's far end broadens into the pigeon-choked **Luža Square**, the centre of the medieval town and still today a hub of activity, with its pavement cafés and milling tourists. Overlooking it is the fifteenth-century municipal **bell tower** (*gradski zvonik*), a smooth pillar of pale stone topped by an unassuming pimple-like cupola. On the left, the **Sponza Palace** (daily 8am–1pm; free), once the city's custom house and mint, grew in storeys as Dubrovnik grew in wealth, with a facade that features broad Renaissance arches on the ground floor and florid Venetian Gothic windows on the first floor. It was designed by Paskoje Miličević in 1522, although much of the stone-carving was done by Josip Andrijić, who also worked on Korčula's cathedral as well as Dubrovnik's St Saviour's Church.

Inside, the majestic courtyard is given over to art exhibitions and occasional concerts in summer. A room on the left-hand side contains the **Memorial Room of the Defenders of Dubrovnik** (Spomen soba poginulim dubrovačkim braniteljima), with photographs of those who lost their lives during the 1991–92 siege. Farther on, a couple of rooms belonging to the **Dubrovnik State Archives** (Državni arhiv u Dubrovniku; Mon–Fri 8am–3pm, Sat 8am–1pm; 15Kn) display copies of statues, manuscripts and old photographs. A Latin inscription on the courtyard's northern wall refers to the public scales that once stood here, and puts God firmly on the side of trading standards: "Cheating and tampering with the weights is forbidden, and when I weigh goods God weighs me."

St Blaise's Church and Orlando's Column

Across the square, the Baroque **St Blaise's Church** (Crkva svetog Vlaha), completed in 1714, is in graceful counterpoint to the palace, boasting a fine facade topped by saintly statuettes that seem poised to topple down onto the square below. Twentieth-century stained glass bathes the interior with dappled light, although it's hard to make out the statuette of St Blaise on the high altar, surrounded by a supporting cast of swooning Baroque statuary. Originally an Armenian martyr, Blaise is said to have appeared in a vision to a local priest to warn of impending Venetian attack in 791. Although the whole story is a piece of anti-Venetian propaganda cooked up in around 1000 AD, it was enough to ensure the Saint's adoption as patron of the city.

Outside the church, plumb in the middle of the square, stands the carved figure of an armoured knight on top of a small column, usually referred to as **Orlando's Column**. Surprisingly for such an insignificant-looking object, erected in 1418 as a morale-boosting monument to freedom, this was the focal point of the city-state: it was here that government ordinances were promulgated and punishments carried out. Nowadays, a flag bearing the *libertas* motto flies from atop the column, and the start of the Dubrovnik Summer Festival is formally proclaimed here every July. Orlando's right arm was also the Republic's standard measurement of length (the Ragusan cubit or Dubrovački lakat, equivalent to 51.2cm); at the base of the column you can still see a line of the same length cut in the stone. The medieval cult of Orlando (or Roland) was born in the twelfth century thanks to the popularity of the epic poem, the *Song of Roland*, which told of the knight's heroic defence of a Pyrenean pass during the Arab invasion of Europe in the eighth century. The cult was a predominantly north European affair, brought to Dubrovnik at the time the city was under the protection of the Hungarian king, Sigismund of Luxemburg, who passed through the city after his defeat by the Turks at Nicopolis in 1396. The legend of Orlando was subsequently adapted to Ragusan requirements by making him the saviour of Dubrovnik in battles against the Saracens, during which he fought a duel with a pirate called Spuzente ("Smelly breath") – nobody seemed to mind that the real Saracen siege of Dubrovnik took place almost a century after Orlando's time.

The eastern side of Luža is flanked by a loggia, to the right of which is **Onofrio's Little Fountain**, an altogether more dainty affair than the same sculptor's fountain at the other end of Stradun, decorated with frivolous cherub reliefs courtesy of Onofrio's contemporary, Pietro di Martina of Milan. Along from the fountain, facing the bare southern flank of St Blaise's church, the terrace of **GradsKavana** ("town café") is where Dubrovnik's more stolid burghers traditionally sit to exchange gossip and observe the ebb and flow of tourists below. To the rear of the café, the *Arsenal* bar (see p.463) occupies the city's former **arsenal**, into which galleys were hauled for repairs.

The Rector's Palace and around

From Luža you can head either northeast via the Dominican monastery and Ploče Gate to the Revelin Fortress (see p.458), or south to the **Rector's Palace** (Knežev dvor), the seat of the Ragusan government. The building was effectively a prison: the rector, elected for just one month, had no real power and could only leave on state occasions with the say-so of the nobles who elected him; after the end of his period of duty, he was ineligible for re-election for the next two years. The palace housed all the major offices of state, plus a dungeon and a powder store (which caused the palace to blow up twice in the fifteenth century). Begun in the 1460s after the second of the powder explosions, the current palace, put together by a loose partnership of architects (including Dalmatinac and Michelozzi), is a masterpiece of serene proportion, fringed by an ornate arcaded loggia held up by columns with delicately carved capitals. Farthest to the right as you face them is the so-called **Asclepius Column**, bearing a relief of a bearded figure – presumably the Greco–Roman god of medicine, Asclepius – sitting in a pharmacist's laboratory. Asclepius was thought to be the patron of the ancient city of Epidauros (modern-day Cavtat, 20km south of Dubrovnik), from which the original population of Dubrovnik came, making him something of a distant guardian of the Ragusan state.

The palace's Renaissance atrium is a popular venue for summer recitals. At its centre is a bust of **Miho Pracat** (1522–1607), a rich shipowner and merchant from the island of Lopud who left most of his wealth to the city-state on his death – and was consequently the only citizen the republic ever honoured with a statue. Local folk tales sought to explain how Pracat came by his vast riches. Somewhat improbably, he is said to have robbed Dubrovnik cathedral's treasury to pay for his business ventures, one of which involved exporting the city's cats to North Africa, where he had chanced upon a plague of rodents.

An imposing staircase leads from the atrium to the balcony and, off here, the former state rooms, including the rooms of the city council, the Rector's study and the quarters of the palace guard. Today these are given over to the **City Museum** (Gradski muzej; June–Sept daily 9am–6pm; Oct–May Mon–Sat 9am–1pm; 35Kn), a poorly labelled three-floor collection of furniture and paintings which manifestly fails to tell the story of the republic in any meaningful or accessible way. It works quite well as a picture gallery though, with a respectable hoard of (mostly anonymous) Baroque works amassed by the city's aristocracy, although pride of place goes to a sixteenth-century *Baptism of Christ* by local artist Mihailo Hamzić, clearly showing the impact of Renaissance styles on Ragusan painting. Elsewhere you'll find several imposing portraits of eminent Ragusans to whom moderately interesting stories are attached. On the ground floor, look out for pictures of Nikola Bunić (1635–78), the statesman who died as a hostage in Silistra jail while trying to renegotiate the tribute paid by Dubrovnik to the Turks. Also here is an image of a kaftan-clad Marojica Kaboga (1630–92), who murdered his father-in-law in front of the Rector's Palace but escaped from prison in the chaos following the 1667 earthquake and, finding that there were few other capable nobles left, took charge of the defence and reconstruction of the city.

The Dulčić-Masle-Pulitika Gallery

Immediately south of the Rector's Palace on Poljana Marina Držića, a Baroque townhouse backing onto the city walls is now home to the **Dulčić-Masle-Pulitika Gallery** (Tues–Sun 10am–7pm; 30Kn; same ticket for the Dubrovnik Art Gallery, see p.458), honouring a trio of local painters – Ivo Dulčić (1916–1975), Antun Masle (1919–1967) and Đuro Pulitika (1922–) – who have been dubbed the "Dubrovnik Colourists" for their unabashed enjoyment of bright hues. There's an incendiary display of their expressionistic Mediterranean landscapes on the first floor. The second floor is devoted to Vlaho Bukovac (1855–1922), the Cavtat-born artist whose portrait-painting skills were much sought after in pre-World War I France and England.

The cathedral and St John's Fortress

Across the square from the palace is Dubrovnik's **Cathedral** (Katedrala), a plain but stately Baroque structure designed by Andrea Bufalini of Urbino in 1672, and built under the supervision of a succession of architects imported from Italy (the first three of whom gave up owing either to illness or non-payment) before it was finally completed by local Ilija Kalčić in 1731. According to legend, the original church – destroyed in the 1667 earthquake – was funded by a votive gift from Richard the Lionheart, who may well have been shipwrecked (and saved) off Ragusa on his way back from the Third Crusade, though traces of the original church's foundations have revealed that it actually predated Richard's visit by a couple of decades. Inside the cathedral are a couple of Italian paintings, including Titian's polyptych *The Assumption* behind the main altar, a work originally purchased by the Brotherhood of the Lazarini – a sign of how rich some of Dubrovnik's commoners' associations really were. The west side of the nave holds the icon of Our Lady of the Port, a Veneto-Byzantine Madonna once carried through the streets in time of drought on account of its rain-making powers.

To the left of the altar, the **treasury** (*riznica*; Mon–Sat 8am–7.30pm, Sun 11am–7.30pm; 10Kn) occupies a specially built room hidden behind heavy wooden doors with three locks – the three keys were held separately by the rector, the bishop and a nobleman. Now packed with gilded shelves and small paintings, the treasury originally grew from two collections, one of which was attached to the now destroyed St Stephen's Church, while the other belonged to the old pre-earthquake cathedral. Stored in the Revelin Fortress after the earthquake, both were brought to their current home in a grandiose procession in 1721. One of the prime exhibits is a twelfth-century skull reliquary of St Blaise, fashioned in the shape of a Byzantine crown, studded with portraits of saints and frosted with delicate gold and enamel filigree work. Nearby are both hands and one of the legs of the same saint, the left hand having been brought here from Constantinople by merchant Tomo Vicijan. Even more eye-catching is a bizarre fifteenth-century *Allegory of the Flora and Fauna of Dubrovnik*, a jug and basin festooned with snakes, fish and lizards clambering over thick clumps of seaweed.

From the cathedral, it's a short walk east along Kneza Damjana Jude towards the monolithic hulk of **St John's Fortress**, now refurbished to house a gloomy **aquarium** (*akvarij*; Mon–Sat: summer 9am–8pm; winter 10am–1pm; 30Kn) full of Mediterranean marine life, including a sad-looking sea turtle into whose pool visitors throw coins for good luck. Upstairs, the **Maritime Museum** (Pomorski muzej; summer daily 9am–6pm; winter Tues–Sun 9am–1pm; 35Kn) traces the history of Ragusan sea power through a display of marine artefacts, ranging from the well-stocked medicine chests of nineteenth-century ships' doctors to an excellent collection of models of Dubrovnik boats throughout the ages.

Pustijerna and Gundulićeva poljana

Walking back from St John's Fortress along Pustijerne, you'll find yourself round the back of the cathedral, south of which stretches one of the city's oldest quarters, **Pustijerna**; much of this predates the seventeenth-century earthquake and preserves a medieval feel, with crumbling, ancient houses crowding in on narrow lanes spanned here and there by arches. Dominating the western side of Pustijerna, the **Jesuit Church** (Isusovačka crkva), Dubrovnik's largest, is modelled, like most Jesuit places of worship, on the enormous church of the

Gesù in Rome. It certainly boasts Dubrovnik's most frivolous ecclesiastical interior, with pinks and blues swirling across the ceiling, and a bombastic main altar with scenes from the life of St Ignatius, founder of the Jesuit order – the central panel shows the man renouncing all worldly things (here symbolized by a bevy of comely Baroque ladies).

The steps that lead down from here also had a Roman model – the Spanish Steps – and sweep down to **Gundulićeva poljana**, the square behind the cathedral which is the site of the city's morning fruit and vegetable market. In the middle stands Ivan Rendić's **statue of Ivan Gundulić** (1589–1638), the poet whose cherubic face adorns one side of the 50Kn banknote. Gundulić's epic poem *Osman*, celebrating the victories of the Poles over the Turks, revealed a typical Ragusan paradox: despite growing rich through trade with the Ottoman state, the locals always sympathized with the empire's enemies, especially if they were Slavs. Gundulić's poetry found a nationwide audience in the nineteenth century, when a burgeoning sense of cultural patriotism generated new pride in the literary traditions of the past. The unveiling of the statue in 1893 occasioned one of the biggest demonstrations of solidarity the nation had ever seen, with the cream of Croatian society converging on the city to indulge in what amounted to a week-long street party.

Along Od Puča

Running parallel to Stradun, **Od Puča** leads west from Gundulićeva poljana, with stepped alleys branching off to meet the sea walls. At no. 8 there's an **Orthodox Church Museum** (Muzej pravoslavne crkve; Mon–Sat 9am–2pm; 10Kn), containing a display of icons packed with Virgins, Christ Pantokrators and St Georges, mostly anonymous works hailing from Crete, Greece and the Bay of Kotor in Montenegro. A couple of paces beyond is the **Orthodox Church** itself, whose simple icon screen and functional interior are not of great artistic merit, but nevertheless exude an air of peaceful harmony.

A northward turn off Puča brings you to the **House of Marin Držić** at Široka 7 (Dom Marina Držića; daily 9am–6pm; 35Kn), where Croatia's greatest sixteenth-century playwright (see box opposite) is commemorated in an imaginative audiovisual display (with English commentary). This makes a brave, if not entirely successful, stab at evoking Renaissance Dubrovnik, somewhat hampered by a lack of genuine exhibits – there's not much to actually see apart from a few facsimile manuscripts.

Go a little way south from here up Domina to reach the **Rupe Ethnographic Museum** (Etnografski muzej Rupe; daily 9am–6pm; 35Kn), whose dull display of regional crafts isn't half as interesting as the building itself, a former municipal grain store built in 1548 and featuring fifteen huge storage pits – the *rupe* or "holes" after which the building is named – carved out of bare rock. The Dubrovnik Republic was almost wholly reliant on imported grain, and the city imposed food-carrying responsibilities on shipowners as much as twelve months in advance. On arrival, wheat was dried in the upper storeys of the building before being sent down chutes into the storage pits below.

The Dominican monastery and museum

Back on Luža, a Gothic arch leads off the northeastern corner of the square to the twisting lane which first passes the entrance to the **Old Port** (Stara luka) – nowadays given over to pleasure boats, and the ferries which run across to the island of Lokrum, just offshore (see p.459) – before reaching the **Dominican**

Marin Držić (1508–67)

In many ways **Marin Držić** is to Croatia what William Shakespeare is to the English-speaking world: a seminal figure who transformed the knockabout theatrical entertainments of the day into something approaching modern drama, employing an unprecedented richness of vocabulary and metaphor that helped turn the dialect of sixteenth-century Dubrovnik into a literary medium equal to the other tongues of Renaissance Europe. Držić is an important symbol of Dubrovnik's contribution to Croatian – and European – culture, and his works usually enjoy a central role in the annual Summer Festival.

Born into a family of merchants, Držić was never a member of the aristocratic elite that ran the republic, though the city did award him a scholarship to study at the University of Siena, where his involvement with the theatre began – he was thrown out in 1542 after taking part in a banned theatrical performance. Držić returned to Dubrovnik, and in 1545 entered the service of Graf Rogendorf, an Austrian then working as a diplomat for the Ottoman Empire.

It's not known precisely how and when Držić got involved with the drama troupes active in Dubrovnik. As in other Renaissance cities, satirical, farcical and moralizing performances were put on to entertain the populace at carnival time, or were given at the private parties and wedding feasts of the wealthy. It was in this environment that Držić's bawdy, but subtly plotted, comedies appeared. His first play, the now-lost *Pomet*, was performed in Dubrovnik in 1548. *Dundo Maroje* (1551), a ribald farce set among the expatriate Dubrovnik community in Rome, is the most frequently performed work today. His only tragedy, a reworking of Euripides' *Hecuba*, was interpreted as an anti-aristocratic allegory by the city authorities.

Držić left Dubrovnik for Venice in 1562, where he became an outspoken critic of the Ragusan Republic – his final literary oeuvre took the form of five letters to Cosimo de Medici asking for Florentine help in overthrowing the Dubrovnik aristocracy. The letters went unanswered, and Držić died an embittered and lonely figure. Ragusan men of letters who had rubbished Držić's reputation while he was alive wrote glowing obituaries after his death, and his work was swiftly enshrined as the literary standard against which other Croatian writers were all measured.

monastery. Begun in 1301, the construction of the monastery was very much a communal endeavour: owing to its position hard up against the fortifications, the city authorities provided the Dominicans with extra funds, and ordered the citizenry to contribute labour. The monastery is approached by a grand stairway with a stone balustrade whose columns have been partly mortared in, an ugly modification carried out by the monks themselves in response to the loafers who stood at the bottom of the staircase in order to ogle the bare ankles of women on their way to church. At the top of the steps a doorway leads through to a fifteenth-century Gothic Renaissance cloister, filled with palms and orange trees.

The attached **museum** (daily: summer 9am–6pm; winter 9am–5pm; 15Kn) has some outstanding examples of sixteenth-century religious art from Dubrovnik, including three canvases by **Nikola Božidarević**, the leading figure of the period, who managed to combine Byzantine solemnity with the humanism of the Italian Renaissance. Immediately on the right as you enter, Božidarević's triptych with its central *Madonna and Child* is famous for its depiction of Dubrovnik prior to the earthquake of 1667, when both Franciscan and Dominican monasteries sported soaring Gothic spires. On the panel to the left, St Blaise holds a model of the city, while, on the right, St Dominic (accompanied by St Augustine) brandishes a model of the medieval cathedral. Nearby, Božidarević's *Annunciation* of

1513, commissioned by shipowner Marko Kolendić, contains more local detail in one of its lower panels, showing one of the donor's argosies lying off the port of Lopud. The most Italianate of Božidarević's works is the *Virgin and Child* altarpiece, also of 1513, ordered by the Đorđić family (the bearded donor kneels at the feet of St Martin in the lower right-hand corner) – note the concerted attempt at some serious landscape painting in the background.

Much more statically Byzantine in style is the largest work on display, a polyptych of 1448 in dazzling gold-leaf by Lovro Dobričević Marinov, the most illustrious of Božidarević's predecessors. It shows Christ's Baptism in the River Jordan, flanked from left to right by SS Michael, Nicholas, Blaise and Stephen – the last was put to death by stoning, hence the stylized rock shapes which the artist has rather awkwardly placed on his head and shoulders. Alongside a fine but rather statuesque *St Nicholas* (1512) by Mihajlo Hamzić, there's a smaller, much simpler, but rather more gripping *Martyrdom of St Vincent* by Frano Matkov, in which the saint is roasted on a bed of hot coals. Cabinets full of precious silver follow, including the cross of the Serbian king, Stefan Uroš II Milutin (1282–1321), inscribed with archaic Cyrillic lettering, and a reliquary which claims to contain the skull of King Stephen I of Hungary (975–1038). The Baroque paintings in the next-door room are all fairly second-rate, save for Titian's *St Blaise and St Mary Magdalene* – Blaise holds the inevitable model of Dubrovnik while sinister storm clouds gather in the background. The youth holding a fish on the right of the canvas is St Tobias, here accompanied by the patron, Ragusan noble Damjan Pucić, kneeling in prayer.

The adjoining monastery **church** is an art gallery in its own right, with a dramatic Veneto-Byzantine crucifix, attributed to the fourteenth-century Paolo Veneziano, hanging over the main altar, and a fine pastel *St Dominic*, by the nineteenth-century Cavtat artist Vlaho Bukovac among the highlights.

Right beside the main monastery entrance, an unassuming doorway leads to the **Rosary Church** (Rozarijo), formerly belonging to the Dominicans and nowadays sporadically used as an art gallery. The intimate Renaissance interior, divided by arcades topped by angels' heads, is definitely worth a peek.

The Revelin Fortress to the Dubrovnik Art Gallery

Beyond the monastery, the lane passes beside the **Revelin Fortress**, begun in the mid-1400s but not finished until 1539, when fears of a coming war between the Turks and the Western powers impelled the Ragusans to hastily strengthen their defences. All other building work in the city was cancelled for four months, leaving the city's builders free to concentrate on the fortress; leading families had to send their servants to work as labourers, or pay a fine. The atmospheric, barrel-vaulted armouries inside the fortress are now used as performance venues during the Dubrovnik Summer Festival (see p.464). Immediately beyond the Revelin lies the **Ploče Gate**, the main eastern entrance to the old town. It's larger than the Pile Gate, with another statue of St Blaise in the niche above (the oldest in the city) and a bridge across the moat dating from 1449.

Beyond the gate is the modern suburb of **Ploče**, until the beginning of the twentieth century the scene of a large market where cattle and other goods arrived by caravan from the Balkan interior. Fear that such caravans brought disease prompted the construction in 1590 of a series of quarantine houses, or **Lazareti**, a row of brick-built accommodation blocks and courtyards which can still be seen on the right-hand side of the road. During times of pestilence, visitors entering the Dubrovnik Republic from the Ottoman Empire were obliged to stay here for forty days before proceeding any farther. Ottoman traveller Evliya Çelebi, quarantined here in 1664, likened it to a comfortable and homely inn, although he regretted not being allowed out to enjoy Dubrovnik's nightlife. Sanitary concerns were still uppermost in Ragusan minds in the mid-nineteenth century, when British traveller A.A. Paton reported with satisfaction that the market here was penned in by a chest-high stone partition in order to "permit commerce and conversation without contact".

Nowadays much of the Lazareti complex falls under the aegis of alternative cultural organization Art Radionica Lazareti (Art Workshop Lazareti or AWL), and is one of the city's major venues for non-mainstream rock gigs and club nights (see "Nightlife and entertainment", p.464). AWL's art gallery, **Otok** (daily 10am–5pm), displays challenging contemporary work in one of the former quarantine houses.

Beyond the Lazareti, Frana Supila leads gently uphill to the **Dubrovnik Art Gallery** at no. 23 (Umjetnička galerija; Tues–Sun 10am–6pm; 30Kn; same ticket valid for the Dulčić-Masle-Pulitika Gallery, see p.454), which hosts high-profile contemporary exhibitions – at least one major international artist is usually invited here every summer.

Lokrum

Facing the suburb of Ploče is the wooded island of **LOKRUM**, 1km to the southeast. Reputedly the island where Richard the Lionheart was shipwrecked, it was bought in 1859 by Maximilian von Habsburg, Archduke of Austria (and subsequently ill-fated Emperor of Mexico). He transformed a former Benedictine monastery here into his summer palace, created a botanical garden which he stocked with exotic plants and cacti, and wrote bad verse about the island's beauty. Following Maximilian's execution by Mexican insurgents in 1867, the Habsburgs sold the island to a local businessman eager to turn it into a health resort, only to buy it back on behalf of Emperor Franz Josef's son Rudolf, who wintered here to soothe his bronchial chest.

Boats leave for Lokrum from the old town's port every thirty minutes, and take ten minutes (May–Oct 9am–6pm; 35Kn return). Unfortunately you can't visit the monastery – just up from the island's jetty – although you can look around the cloister (now home to a disappointing restaurant) and wander around Maximilian's **Botanical Garden** next door, where odd varieties of giant triffid-like cactus look as if they could swallow you whole. The best of the (largely rocky) **beaches** are beyond the monastery on the island's southwest side, where you'll find a small salt lake just inland, and a naturist beach at the island's southern tip. Shady paths overhung by pines run round the northern part of the island, with tracks leading uphill towards **Fort Royal**, a gun position left by the Napoleonic French whose grey, menacing ramparts rise rather suddenly from the jungle-like greenery covering the island's central ridge.

North and west of the old town

West of the old town, just outside Pile Gate, steps descend towards a small harbour overlooked by the Bokar Fortress on one side and by the monumental, wedge-shaped fortress of **Lovrijenac** on the other (daily 9am–2pm; 10Kn). Originally built in 1050, but assuming its current shape in the sixteenth century, it was the most important component of the city's south- and west-facing defences, commanding both land and sea approaches from atop a craggy cliff.

In recent times Lovrijenac has become famous as the venue for performances of Shakespeare's *Hamlet* during the Dubrovnik Summer Festival, when it becomes the perfect double for Elsinore castle.

A statue of St Lawrence brandishing a model of the fort watches over the fortress entrance, above which there's a typically proud Ragusan inscription: *Non bene pro toto libertas venditur auro* ("All the gold in the world cannot buy freedom"). There's not much to see inside the fortress, though the triangular courtyard framed by chunky arcades is impressive enough on its own, while the upper level gives a fine view of the city and its walls.

Gruž and the Rijeka Dubrovačka

Spearing westwards from the Pile Gate, Ante Starčevića heads towards the suburb of **Gruž** and Dubrovnik's main port, tucked between the mainland on the eastern side and the Lapad peninsula to the northwest. Dominating the western end of Gruž is the **Franjo Tuđman Bridge** (Most Franja Tuđmana), a breathtakingly elegant suspension bridge spanning the mouth of a four-kilometre inlet known

Dubrovnik beaches

Although the region's most attractive **beaches** are a boat ride away from Dubrovnik on islands like Lokrum and Lopud, there are plenty of places in town worth checking out for their special atmosphere or spectacular views.

For Dubrovnik folk going to the beach on a daily basis is a way of life, and locals discuss their favourite bathing spots in the same way that British people talk about the weather.

Bellevue Hotel A lovely crescent of mixed shingle and sand immediately below the hotel, with good views of rocky Boninovo bay. As an east-facing beach it loses the sun by late afternoon/early evening. Free to residents of the hotel; a small charge for everyone else.

Copacabana Unlike its Brazilian namesake, this is a small crescent comprising pebbles and imported sand on the northwest side of Babin kuk. Owing to its proximity to Gruž's port facilities the water here is not the cleanest, but the combination of enjoyable cafés and good views of coastal mountains make it a good place to hang out if you're in the area.

Danče Boulder-strewn stretch of coast popular with the locals, a few minutes' walk southwest of the Lovrijenac fortress. Great if you like frying on top of a rock.

Banje Busiest of the town's beaches, a mixture of fine shingle and sand just east of the old town, backed by trendy cafés, and with good views of the island of Lokrum. It holds a special place in the heart of Dubrovnik folk, as almost all of them spent at least part of their childhoods here. Sadly, Banje's egalitarian bucket-and-spade nature has been spoiled by the fencing off of a large part of the beach by one of the cafés – but at least you can rent a sun-lounger and order a cocktail if the enclosure takes your fancy.

Lapad Shallow bay on the southwest side of Lapad peninsula, with a shingle beach that soon gets overcrowded owing to the proximity of Lapad's package hotels. The beach-side buildings are somewhat ugly, but it's the safest beach for kids and there are a lot of facilities roundabout.

Sveti Jakov A smallish stretch of pebble at the bottom of a cliff, reached by steps which descend from the coastal path midway between St James' Monastery (Samostan svetog Jakova) and the *Belvedere Hotel* – a good twenty minutes' east of the centre. Fantastic views back towards the old town. West-facing, so catches the afternoon and evening sun.

as the **Rijeka Dubrovačka**. Opened in 2002, the bridge is the first thing that travellers see when approaching the city from the west: as such, it's a marvellously futuristic counterpoint to the historic old town beyond. The Rijeka Dubrovačka itself was once one of the Ragusan Republic's favourite pleasure resorts. Noble families built summer villas here, a number of which still stand – though these days the look of the place has been largely spoiled by the modern city's industrial and residential sprawl. It's not an area you're likely to make a special trip to see (buses #1A and #1B run here from Pile Gate), unless you're heading for the large yachting marina near the suburb of **Komolac** at the end of the inlet, where the slightly unkempt gardens and fishponds of the **Sorkočević Palace** (the interior can't be visited) offer a distant echo of the horticultural splendours of the Ragusan Renaissance.

One kilometre beyond Komolac, on the right-hand side of the road, the inlet itself emerges dramatically from a limestone cliff at **MLINI**, the next settlement along, a slightly scruffy area that seems to have missed out on development as a beauty spot.

Mount Srđ

Towering above the town to the north, **Mount Srđ** was a much-visited attraction until 1991, when Yugoslav forces destroyed the cable car that used to deliver tourists to its 412-metre-high summit. A handful of people still make the trip, either by the winding footpath (the aptly named *serpentina*) which heads up to the top from Jadranska cesta and takes a good two hours to negotiate, or via the badly surfaced road which leaves the Cavtat-bound highway 1km southeast of Dubrovnik, clambering its way to the village of **Bosanka** and thence on to the shoulder of the mountain. If you're walking, bear in mind that the *serpentina* is unshaded, and the ascent can be a hellish experience in hot weather.

Whichever way you get there, you'll be rewarded with a stunning view of the walled town below, with a panorama of the whole coast stretching as far as the Pelješac peninsula to the northwest. The summit-crowning **Fort Imperial** was built by Napoleon's occupying army in 1808 and served as a disco in the 1980s before reverting to its original military purpose in 1991, when it was successfully held by Dubrovnik's defenders. Seriously smashed up by Serbian artillery, however, it's now derelict and can't be visited. The mountain seems a world away from the lush subtropical world of the coastal strip; nothing much grows here apart from sage, which is hungrily devoured by the sheep sent here to graze by the farmers of Bosanka.

Eating, drinking and nightlife

There's no shortage of **places to eat** in Dubrovnik, and culinary standards are reasonably high. The choice of food doesn't significantly differ from what's on offer in the rest of maritime Croatia, with grilled fish, squid and shellfish forming the backbone of local menus. However, certain places have become tourist traps and are worth avoiding: **Prijeko**, the street running parallel to Stradun to the north, is lined with establishments offering identical menus at identical prices, aggressively selling their indifferent fare by sending staff out onto the streets to ambush hungry tourists with dubious offers of free house wine or family discounts. Luckily, there are plenty of other places in the tourist-trodden old town that base their reputation on good cooking rather than the hard sell.

Most **restaurants** reviewed below are open until 11pm unless otherwise stated, although many extend their hours until midnight in season. We've included the telephone numbers of those places where it might be a good idea to reserve in advance. Restaurants in Dubrovnik often charge a cover of 5–10Kn, although you don't always get much in return for this except a few indifferent hunks of bread.

For **snacks**, try the sandwich bars lining the alleys running uphill from Stradun. There are fruit and vegetable **markets** (Mon–Sat mornings) on Gundulićeva poljana and on the waterfront in Gruž, and a pair of **supermarkets** on Gundulićeva poljana. Other supermarkets include Konzum, with branches outside both the Pile and Ploče gates (Mon–Sat 6.30am–8pm, Sun 7am–noon) and the bigger and better-stocked Tommy, on put Republike in Gruž (Mon–Sat 7am–9pm, Sun 7am–8pm).

Snacks and fast food restaurants

Express Restaurant M. Kaboge 1. Self-service canteen food in antiseptic surroundings just off the Stradun, including vegetarian options, filling stews and a salad bar. Tasty fare at rock-bottom prices.

Fresh Vetranovićeva 4. Tortilla wraps with a variety of fillings. Also the site of a great bar (see opposite).

Mrvica Kunićeva. Hole-in-the-wall fast-food bar serving up sandwiches filled with traditional Croatian home-cured meats such as *pršut*, *kulen* and *buđola*.

Restaurants

The old town and around

Atlas Club Nautika Brsalje 3 ⓣ020/442-526. Long considered the best place in town for quality seafood, this is an upmarket environment with two floors of formal dining rooms, each with a small outdoor terrace. Liveried waiters, napkins folded with origami-like precision, and a large list of top international wines complete the picture. Expect to pay around 250–350Kn a head for a full meal.

Kamenica Gundulićeva poljana 8. Unpretentious and cheap seafood restaurant popular with locals and tourists alike, with a cramped, functional interior, and outdoor seating on one of the old town's finest squares. Favourites include *girice* (tiny fish deep fried and eaten whole), *kamenice* (oysters) and *mušule* (mussels).

Lokanda Peskarija Na Ponti. Lively place with outdoor bench seating right beside the old town's port area. Frequently crowded, but somehow succeeds in retaining good standards of food and service, all at moderate prices. Trademark seafood dishes like *kozice* (shrimps) and *crni rižot* (squid risotto) are served in big metal pots. Also good for grilled fish and big, healthy salads.

Mea Culpa za Rokom. Popular pizzeria in the maze of streets south of the Stradun, which manages to combine reasonable quality with cheap prices. Cosy warren of tables inside, plus bench seating on an atmospheric street.

Orhan od Tabakarije 1. Midway between the old town and Lovrijenac fortress, *Orhan* boasts a superbly situated terrace by the side of a wave-battered rocky bay. Reliable if predictable range of grilled fish and grilled meats, and slightly old-fashioned, bow-tie service.

Proto Široka 1 ⓣ020/323-234. Top-notch establishment bang in the heart of old Dubrovnik, with a formal indoor dining room, a rather more relaxed outdoor terrace upstairs, and attention-to-detail service. As usual, fish is the main attraction, although this is one place in Dubrovnik where the meat dishes are prepared to the same level of excellence as the seafood – you can't really go wrong whatever you order. The site has been occupied by a fish restaurant since 1886, and it's claimed that Edward VIII and Wallis Simpson (see p.278) ate here during one of their visits to Dubrovnik in the 1930s. Expect to exceed the 300Kn mark for main course, sweet and drinks.

Sesame Dante Alighieria bb. Relaxing café-restaurant five minutes' west of Pile Gate, with a cramped but atmospheric brick-vaulted interior, and plenty of outdoor seating on the upstairs terrace – although one end of it is subject to traffic noise from the road below. Full range of seafood and an equally appetizing selection of steaks and chicken dishes.

Taj Mahal Nikole Gučetića 2. Bosnian-run restaurant churning out the things that Bosnian cuisine is famous for: grilled *ćevapi* (mincemeat rissoles), *pljeskavice* (mincemeat patties that make Western burgers look like wimp-food), and *burek* (filo-pastry pie filled with meat or cheese). Vegetarians can dine on peppers stuffed with cream cheese, or the excellent spinach *pita* (pie).

Lapad, Babin kuk and outside the city

Levanat Nika i Meda Pucića 15 ⓣ020/435-352. Family-run restaurant on the coastal path between

Lapad and Babin kuk, with chic interior and an outdoor terrace with a marvellous view of jagged offshore outcrops. The extensive seafood menu features excellent shellfish, and the kind of boiled and baked fish recipes that you might not find elsewhere – the *brancin lešo* (sea bass stewed in caper sauce) is well worth trying. A café as well as a restaurant, *Levanat* is one of the most relaxing places in this part of Dubrovnik to stop off for a drink. A full meal will set you back 250–300Kn with drinks.

Orsan Gverović Zaton Mali bb ⓣ020/891-267. Cult seafood restaurant 5km northwest of town, right beside the coastal Magistrala at the entrance to the village of Zaton. The owner adopts a no-nonsense approach: there's little on the menu save for fresh fish and shellfish, grilled to perfection. The Orsan risotto, full of succulent shellfish, squid and prawn, is quite possibly the best combined seafood dish you're likely to find on the Adriatic. The terrace is right on the seashore, so you can order your food and go for a quick dip before the starter arrives. Slightly less expensive than the top-of-the-range seafood places back in town.

Primorka Nikole Tesle 8, Gruž. Unpretentious Dalmatian dishes such as grilled squid, *pržolica* (pork chop smothered in garlic) and fresh grilled fish, in a pleasant garden restaurant opposite Gruž harbour. Cheap and simple.

Yacht Club Orsan Ivana Zajca 2. Situated on the northern side of the Lapad peninsula, right on the marina where Dubrovnik folk are wont to tether their boats, this is as pleasantly peaceful a spot as you will find in this part of town. The menu concentrates on the tried and tested meat and fish favourites, but standards are high and prices a good ten percent lower than in the old town.

Drinking

Drinking in Dubrovnik is for much of the year a question of finding an outside table from which to see and be seen. The pavement cafés of **Stradun** are the best places for daytime and early evening imbibing, providing the classic people-watching and postcard-writing venues. Nearby **Bunićeva poljana**, just behind the cathedral, becomes one vast outdoor bar on summer nights, with rows of tables spread out between the *Hard Jazz Café Trubadour* on one side and *Café Mirage* on the other. You could also try the streets leading uphill from Stradun, where you'll find drinkers sitting on the steps outside tiny bars with blaring music.

Cafés and bars

Arsenal Prid Dvorom 1. Occupying the cavernous stone chamber where sixteenth-century war galleys underwent repairs, this over-designed bar full of ropes, pulleys and other nautical stage decor comes to life on high-season weekends when live bands play rock-pop covers and a hedonistic, high-spending crowd swarm around the bar.

Buža Iza Mira. One of the most atmospheric places to drink in Dubrovnik, this is an unpretentious outdoor bar perched on the rocks just outside the old town's sea-facing walls. It's approached through a hole in the wall – advertised by a sign that simply reads "cold drinks". They don't bother opening if the weather is cold or windy.

Capitano Pile. A few steps north of Pile Gate, this place gets raucous on Fridays, when local youth come to enjoy the crush of bodies inside or to sit on the stone wall outside.

Eastwest Frana Supila bb. Roomy place right on Banje beach offering lounge-bar furnishings and an impressive choice of cocktails. Late-night DJs attract an uninhibited clubby crowd after the sun goes down.

Fresh Vetranovićeva 4. Old-town bar with cool minimalist decor, potent cocktails and pleasantly disorienting video projections on the back wall. Usually spills out onto the neighbouring street.

GradsKavana Prid Dvorom 1. This once staid café with a loyal clientele of older generation, coffee-supping locals, has rejuvenated itself with a recent makeover and is now one of the most inviting places in town to pause for a caffeine-break. There's also a mouth-watering selection of quality cakes and ice cream.

Hard Jazz Café Trubadour Bunićeva poljana. Small and intimate pub-like space which explodes out onto the surrounding square as soon as the weather's warm enough for outdoor drinking. If you're a well-known face in Croatia, you have to be seen drinking here at least once in the summer. Owned by a former member of the Dubrovački Trubaduri (a big-time Sixties beat group that had the dubious honour of representing Yugoslavia in the Eurovision Song Contest), it hosts impromptu live jazz most nights in summer – when drink prices rise according to the status of the performers.

Libertina Zlatarska. Tiny watering hole in a side street next to the Sponza Palace which, despite being located in Dubrovnik's tourist-tramped centre, still has the feel of a neighbourhood bar. A cosy place, stuffed with domestic knick-knacks and garrulous local drinkers.

Revelin Revelin. Cocktails on a terrace overlooking the old town's port. Serves pizzas during the day.

Smoothie Bar Palmotićeva 5. Luscious fruit smoothies to drink in and take away, and a small but lip-smacking list of nicely priced cocktails. And if you missed breakfast, bowls of cereal are also available. The combination of old town location and contemporary, primary-coloured interior is a winner.

Talir Antuninska. Legendary post-performance hangout for actors and musicians during the summer festival – the walls are plastered with photographs of Croatian celebrities past and present. It's a small place, in a side street midway down Stradun, and most people end up sitting on the steps outside.

Nightlife and entertainment

During the summer, the rich cultural diet provided by the **Summer Festival** (see below) is augmented by informal open-air pop and jazz concerts in the old town. At other times, look out for regular performances mounted by the town's two main cultural institutions: the **Marin Držić Theatre** (Ⓣ020/426-437), Prid Dvorom 3, which specializes in serious drama in the Croatian language; and the **Dubrovnik Symphony Orchestra**, which plays in the Revelin fortress and in other venues around town (Ⓣ020/417-101, Ⓦwww.dso.hr). Local folk ensemble Linđo perform in the Lazareti (see p.458) at least twice a week in summer – tourist offices and hotels will have details. The most central **cinema** is Kino Sloboda on Luža.

Most of the **clubbing** venues lack either a regular clientele or a strong identity. *Latino Club Fuego*, near Pile Gate at Brsalje 11, is an enjoyable mainstream disco aimed mostly at tourists. Club nights and **live gigs** (rock, world music and jazz) take place throughout the year at the Lazareti – the Zagreb-based Močvara club (see p.106) takes up residence here for at least one month over the summer. Dubrovnik's other underground hangout is *Klub Orlando* (Ⓦwww.klub-orlando.com), hidden away behind a derelict hospital on Ante Starčevića, with alternative rock bands and non-mainstream DJs performing in a welcoming club space covered in graffiti-style murals, or on a meadow outside. Listings information in the local press is inadequate, so you'll have to look for posters to get an idea of what's on.

Festivals

The **Dubrovnik Summer Festival** (Dubrovačke ljetne igre; July & Aug; Ⓦwww.dubrovnik-festival.hr) stages classical concerts and theatre performances in Dubrovnik's courtyards, squares and bastions in the old town – sometimes offering the only chance to see inside them. The emphasis is very much on high culture: the festival usually includes plays by Shakespeare and Marin Držić (see box on p.457), a major opera, symphonic concerts and a host of smaller chamber-music events. World-renowned violinist Julian Rachlin is one of the regular annual visitors. Seats for some of the more prestigious events often sell out well in advance, but it should be possible to pick up tickets for many performances at fairly short notice. The full programme is usually published in April: for further details and advance tickets contact Dubrovačke ljetne igre, Poljana Paska Miličevića 1, 20000 Dubrovnik (Ⓣ020/412-288 or 426-351, Ⓕ427-944, Ⓔprogram@dubrovnik-festival.hr). Once the festival starts, tickets (30–200Kn) can be bought from festival information points at the Pile Gate and on Stradun.

As a kind of riposte to the festival, the Otok Cultural Centre organizes the **Karantena Festival** of alternative theatre, performance art and happenings in

August, with performances taking place in the Lazareti. Advance information is available from Otok, Pobijana 8, 20000 Dubrovnik (Ⓣ & Ⓕ 020/423-497).

The **Libertas Film Festival** (Ⓦ www.libertasfilmfestival.com; late Aug to early Sept) features non-Hollywood feature films and documentaries, and carries more cultural weight than the Dubrovnik International Film Festival (Ⓦ www.dubrovnikfilmfestival.com; October), which is more of a PR event than an artistic high-point.

Shopping

There's a respectable string of shops selling postcards and souvenirs along the Stradun, and a smattering of high-street clothes and shoe shops in the alleyways nearby. There's little in the way of specific craft products associated with Dubrovnik and its hinterland, save perhaps for the vivid geometric designs featured in **embroidery** from the Konavle region south of the city – tablecloths and napkins bearing Konavle motifs are on sale in the classier gift shops, although they come at a price. The gaggle of **jewellery shops** at the western end of od Puča is the place to look for coral necklaces, filigree earrings and other traditional adornments.

Gifts and souvenirs

Aquarius Poljana Paskala Miličevićca 4. Music shop with decent range of Croatian and international CDs. Usually stocks some of the titles recommended on p.512.

Ivana Bačura Zlatarska 3, Ⓦ www.ivanabacura.com. Beautiful handmade bracelets, earrings and necklaces incorporating silver and enamel, made by a leading jewellery designer.

Dubrovačka kuća Svetog Dominika bb. Big choice of quality souvenirs, from prints and *objets d'art* to olive oil and *rakija*. Try the Lucine Gulozece, strips of candied orange peel which are absolutely delicious.

Franja Coffee & Teahouse od Puča bb. Much more than the title suggests, with local wines, herbal *rakijas*, sweets and soaps.

Sebastian Svetog Dominika 5. Art gallery next to the Dominican monastery with a big collection of prints for sale – most contemporary Croatian artists are represented.

Trinity Palmotićeva 2 Ⓦ www.trinity.hr. Extravagant, expensive jewellery and accessories displayed in a Baroque town house that's an attraction in itself.

Books

Algebra Stradun 9. Everything you ever wanted to read about Dubrovnik will probably be here somewhere. Also sells postcards and souvenirs.

Algoritam Stradun. Good across-the-board choice of English-language books, as well as Dubrovnik-related touristy stuff.

Listings

Airlines Croatia Airlines, Brsalje 9 (Mon–Fri 8am–4pm, Sat 9am–noon; Ⓣ 020/413-777, Ⓦ www.croatiaairlines.hr).

Airport Ⓣ 020/773-333, Ⓦ www.airport-dubrovnik.hr.

Banks and exchange There's a Zagrebačka banka ATM (but no actual bank) next to the Jadrolinija ticket office in the port. In the old town, conveniently situated banks include Nova banka, Stradun (Mon–Fri 7.30am–1pm & 2–7pm, Sat 7.30am–1pm), Gospodarsko-Kreditna banka, just outside Pile Gate (daily 8am–8pm), and Zagrebačka banka, Gundulićeva poljana (Mon–Fri 8.30am–noon & 6–8pm, Sat 8.30am–noon).

Bus station Ⓣ 060/305-070.

Car rental Budget, Obala S. Radića 24, Gruž Ⓣ 020/418-998, Ⓦ www.budget.hr; Gulliver, Obala S. Radića 32, Gruž Ⓣ 020/448-296, Ⓦ www.gulliver.hr.

Diving Blue Planet, at the *Dubrovnik President* hotel (Ⓣ 098 9913621 or 091 8990973, Ⓦ www.blueplanet-diving.com) organize PADI-approved courses (including a half-day beginners' course from 350Kn), and excursions to nearby reefs and wrecks.

Ferries Tickets from Jadrolinija, opposite the ferry terminal, at Obala S. Radića 40, Gruž (Mon, Tues & Thurs–Sat 8am–8pm, Wed 8am–11pm, Sun 8am–10am & 7–8.30pm; ⓣ020/418-000, ⓦwww.jadrolinija.hr).
Hospital Roka Mišetića, Lapad, 4km west of the old town ⓣ020/431-777.
Internet access *Internet Centar*, Ante Starčevića 7, Pile; *Internet*, Prijeko 15; *Netcafé*, Prijeko 21; and *Holobit*, just below the *Hotel Kompas* at Šetalište kralja Zvonimira 56 in Lapad.
Left luggage At the bus station (daily 4.30am–10.30pm).
Pharmacy Kod Zvonika, Stradun (Mon–Sat 7am–8pm); Ljekarna Gruž, Gruška obala (Mon–Sat 7am–8pm). Both take it in turns to be open 24hr.
Post office and telephones Ante Starčevića 2 (Mon–Fri 8am–3pm); put Republike 32 (Mon–Fri 7am–8pm, Sat 8am–4pm).
Taxis There are ranks outside the bus and ferry terminals and at Pile Gate, or call ⓣ970.
Travel agents The Atlas offices at Lučarica 1 or Svetog Đurđa 1 (near the Pile Gate) handle air tickets and excursions (Mon–Sat 8am–9pm, Sun 9am–1pm; ⓣ020/442-222, ⓦwww.atlas-croatia.com).

Northwest of Dubrovnik: Trsteno

Standing on the coastal highway 13km northwest of Dubrovnik, the straggling village of **TRSTENO** is an essential day-trip destination if you're at all interested in things horticultural. It was here in 1502 that Dubrovnik noble Ivan Gučetić built his summer villa, surrounded by formal gardens extending along a terrace overlooking the sea. Such gardens were considered *de rigueur* by the aristocracy of sixteenth-century Dubrovnik – sadly, those of Trsteno are the only ones which can still be enjoyed in something approaching their original form. Maintained by successive generations of the Gučetić family, the villa and its gardens were confiscated in 1948 by a communist regime eager to destroy any latent prestige still enjoyed by the Dubrovnik nobility. The Yugoslav (now Croatian) Academy of Sciences took the place over and expanded it, turning it into an arboretum.

Trsteno is relatively easy to get to, with Dubrovnik–Split **buses** dropping off and picking up in the centre of the village. Standing by the roadside just next to the bus stop is a majestic pair of 400-year-old plane trees, some 50m high and 15m in circumference. From here a path drops you down to the main entrance to the **arboretum** (daily: summer 8am–8pm; winter 8am–5pm; 12Kn), where Gučetić's former villa overlooks the oldest part of the estate, a typical Renaissance garden in which patches of lavender, rosemary, oleander, bougainvillea, myrtle and cyclamen are divided up by lines of box hedge to form a complex geometrical design. A nearby orchard sports bushy grapefruit and mandarin trees, but beyond here the garden has a wonderfully lush, uncontrolled feel, as pathways begin to lose themselves in a dense woodland environment comprising trees from around the world. Amidst it all, a trident-wielding statue of Neptune overlooks a pond packed with goldfish. Running northwest from the villa, beyond a small football pitch, an avenue of palm trees leads to yet more semi-wilderness areas, thick with cypresses and pines. The effects of two recent fires (the first resulting from Yugoslav artillery in 1991, the second starting accidentally in summer 2000), can be seen in the shape of blackened tree trunks and waste ground, dotted here and there with areas of new planting. Overlooking the shore at the northwestern end of the gardens is what looks like a ruined palace – it is in fact a purpose-built nineteenth-century folly – commanding a superb view of the surrounding coastline, with the islands of Lopud and Koločep roughly opposite. From here a staircase with weird stone cactus sculptures adorning its balustrades descends towards a rocky **beach** and tiny harbour perfect for restful sunbathing.

There's an idyllic tree-shaded **campsite** (Ⓣ020/751-060), just below the Magistrala on the approach road to the arboretum; the attached café is the best place in the village for a quick **drink**.

Southeast of Dubrovnik: Župa, Cavtat and the Konavle

Heading southeast from Dubrovnik you soon run into **Župa Dubrovačka**, a group of erstwhile fishing villages which have now merged to form a six-kilometre line of apartment blocks, weekend villas, angular hotels and waterside cafés. The area was occupied by Serb and Montenegrin troops in the winter of 1991–92 and most of the hotels looted, although all but a small proportion have now been spruced up and put back in service. Despite the presence of some nice beaches Župa is overshadowed as a tourist destination by **Cavtat**, a historic town offering plenty in the way of traditional stone architecture fringed by lush Mediterranean vegetation. Beyond Cavtat, the rustic **Konavle** region is a restfully scenic place to drive through, and offers a couple of rewarding village stop-offs to boot. Thirty-five kilometres south of Dubrovnik the road arrives at the border with **Montenegro** (Crna Gora in Croatian and Serbian). Crossing here is relatively problem-free for citizens of the EU, USA, Australia, New Zealand and Canada providing they have a valid passport – nationals of other countries should check visa requirements before leaving home.

Župa Dubrovačka

Ten kilometres out of Dubrovnik, the main Montenegro-bound road descends into **Župa Dubrovačka**, a string of tourism-oriented settlements occupying a verdant coastal strip backed by impressively stark mountains. The name Župa Dubrovačka literally means "parish belonging to Dubrovnik", although the area has recently been awarded the English-language moniker "Dubrovnik Riviera" by a tourist industry eager to give it the requisite amount of summer-holiday appeal. The Župa's westernmost resort is **KUPARI**, a former Yugoslav army-owned holiday settlement which has lain derelict for well over a decade, and your first real taste of the Župa is likely to be the next place along, **SREBRENO**, which sits on the northwestern shoulder of Župa's broad bay. From here an enjoyable promenade runs past well-landscaped stretches of park and an inviting sequence of **beaches** – rough, pebbly affairs at first sight, although the seabed itself is luxuriantly sandy under foot. After a kilometre or two Srebreno fades imperceptibly into **MLINI**, the most attractive of Župa's settlements, boasting a fair number of traditional stone houses, an attractive harbour and a centuries old plane tree that looks as if it could have stepped straight out of the writings of Tolkein. Occupying the southeastern curve of the bay are Župa's remaining resorts, **SOLINE** and **PLAT** – little more than hotel settlements, they're not really worth visiting unless you're actually staying there.

Practicalities

Župa is easily accessible from Dubrovnik, with Dubrovnik–Cavtat **buses** trundling along the main road every thirty minutes or so. The **tourist office** at the northwestern end of the agglomeration in Srebreno, just off the main road (Mon–Fri 8am–3pm, Sat 8am–noon; Ⓣ020/486-254, Ⓦwww.dubrovnik-riviera.com), can direct you towards **rooms** (❷) and **apartments** (two-person studios ❹, four-person apartments from 650Kn), although you may well be offered something a steep walk uphill – most of the waterfront properties are booked up months in advance. The *Astarea* **hotel** in Mlini (April–Oct; ⓣ020/484-020, ⓔhoteli-mlini@du.t-com.hr; ❻) offers three-star comforts in the most attractive part of Župa; the nearby *Mlini* (April–Oct; ⓣ020/486-222, ⓔhoteli-mlini@du.t-com.hr; ❺) represents a frumpy but acceptable two-star alternative. The *Kupari* **campsite** (ⓣ020/485-548, ⓦwww.campkupari.com), by the main road on the border between Kupari and Srebreno, is a big site with a reasonable amount of shade; the *Porto*, a few hundred metres farther on in Srebreno (ⓣ020/487-079), is a bit closer to the waterfront and the beaches.

Cavtat

Twenty kilometres south of Dubrovnik, and 3km off the main coastal highway, **CAVTAT** is a dainty coastal town and package resort which began life in the third century BC as Epidaurum, a colony founded by Greeks from the island of Vis. There's nothing left to see of the antique town: Epidaurum was evacuated in favour of Dubrovnik after a thorough ransacking by the Slavs in the seventh century, and the pretty fishing village of Cavtat subsequently grew up in its place. Discovered by Austro-Hungarian holiday-makers at the beginning of the twentieth century, Cavtat was a favourite haunt of the wealthy until a rash of high-rise hotel building in the 1980s changed the place's profile. Happily, the hotels are set apart from the palm-dotted seafront of the original village, ranged across the neck of a sweet-smelling wooded peninsula.

Arrival, information and accommodation

Bus #10 runs to Cavtat roughly every hour from Dubrovnik. Privately operated **boats** from Dubrovnik's Old Port (see p.456) do the same trip for about 40Kn. Cavtat's **tourist office**, a short walk east of the **bus station** at Tiha 3 (summer Mon–Sat 8am–8pm, Sun 8am–noon; winter Mon–Fri 8am–3pm; ⓣ020/479-025, ⓦwww.tzcavtat-konavle.hr) offers an ocean of town maps and brochures in every conceivable language. Ample private **rooms** (❷) and **apartments** (❸) are available from the Adriatica agency (Mon–Sat 8am–8pm, Sun 9am–noon; ⓣ020/478-713, ⓔadriatica@du.hinet.hr), just by the bus station.

Hotels

Albatross Od žala 2 ⓣ020/471-333, ⓦwww.iberostar.com. One of a trio of package-oriented hotels just northeast of town behind a long shingle beach, the four-star *Albatross* has plush air-conditioned rooms and a large private swimming pool. ❻

Castelletto put od Cavtata 9a ⓣ020/479-547, ⓦwww.dubrovnikexperience.com. Medium-sized, family-run hotel just uphill from the port. Rooms are in creamy pastel colours and come with tiled floors, reconditioned pine furnishings and attractive art prints on the walls. Some have balconies with views towards Dubrovnik; all are equipped with TV, a/c and bathroom. There's a nice garden and a tapas bar on site. Airport pick-up available. ❺

Croatia Frankopanska 10 ⓣ020/475-555, ⓦwww.hoteli-croatia.hr. A vast multi-tiered concrete five-star hogging the ridge of the Sustjepan peninsula. It's easy to get lost in its seemingly endless corridors, but it has modern air-conditioned rooms with TV, and a private beach facing the Cavtat waterfront. The indoor swimming pool is a major feature. ❼

Supetar Obala Ante Starčevića 27 ⓣ020/479-833, ⓦwww.hoteli-croatia.hr A tastefully modernized nineteenth-century building with slightly cramped en suites. Harbourfront position and intimate atmosphere are the main selling points. ❻

Villa Pattiera Trumbićev put 9 ⓣ020/478-800, ⓦwww.villa-pattiera.hr. Twelve-room hotel right on the harbourfront, housed in the former home of inter-war opera singer Tino Pattiera. Peachy and plummy colours, parquet floors, flat-screen TVs. The pricier roms have views of the palm-fringed quay, the others share a large garden terrace at the back of the house. ❼–❽ depending on size and position.

The Town

Much of Cavtat's former charm survives in the old part of town, which straddles the ridge behind the waterfront. Occupying the former Rector's Palace at the southern end of the palm-splashed Riva, the **Baltazar Bogišić Collection** (Zbirka Baltazara Bogišića; Mon–Sat 9.30am–1pm; 10Kn) remembers lawyer and cultural activist Bogišić (1834–1908), who spent a lifetime promoting Croatian literature and learning at a time when Italian was still considered the language of civilized discourse along the coast. Books from Bogišić's collection crowd the display cabinets, although the stand-out exhibit is Vlaho Bukovac's immense canvas of local carnival celebrations in 1901 – with the cream of Cavtat society gamely got up in fancy dress for the occasion. If you're in the mood for more Bukovac, head just uphill to **St Nicholas's Church** (Crkva svetog Nikole), where his paintings of the Four Evangelists look down on the main altar.

Walking north along the Riva and heading up Bukovčeva (a narrow, stepped alleyway rather than a street) brings you to the **Vlaho Bukovac gallery** at no. 5 (Tues–Sat 9am–1pm & 4–8pm, Sun 4–8pm; 20Kn), celebrating the Cavtat-born artist (1855–1922) who painted lucrative society portraits in Paris, London and elsewhere, and ended his career as professor at Prague's Academy of Fine Arts. The building itself once belonged to Bukovac's father, and the artist spent much of his early adulthood here. Vivid frescoes of animals, birds and exotic plants – painted by a sixteen-year-old Bukovac while convalescing after an accident at sea – can still be seen in the hallways and stairwell. The larger rooms contain a thorough overview of Bukovac's oeuvre, ranging from the realistic early portraits of family, friends and high-paying clients to later works influenced by Impressionism and Symbolism – notably the torrid, Dante-inspired canvases depicting Heaven, Purgatory and Hell.

Marking the northern end of the Riva, the rather plain-looking **Monastery of Our Lady of the Snow** (Samostan snježne Gospe) contains a couple of early Renaissance gems in its small church: the first, Vičko Lovrin's triptych of 1509 at the back of the church, shows a gold-clad Archangel Michael slaying a demon while John the Baptist and St Nicholas look on from the wings; the second, Božidar Vlatković's *Madonna and Child* (1494) on the main altar, is a small piece somewhat overpowered by its fussy Baroque frame.

Paths behind the monastery lead up towards the **Račić Mausoleum** (Mon–Sat 10am–noon & 5–7pm, Sun 10am–noon; 4Kn), built on a prime spot high above the town in 1921 by Ivan Meštrović for a local shipowning family. It's one of Meštrović's more successful stabs at architectural eclecticism: a simple, Byzantine-inspired, domed structure guarded by stern, archaic Greek angels and decorated with dog-faced gargoyles, Teutonic-looking eagles and what look like neo-Assyrian winged lambs just below the cupola.

A brace of fine shingle **beaches** lies about 1km east of the town centre in an area known as **žal** (literally, "beach"), although the proximity of the package hotels ensures that they're usually crowded. Quieter spots, if you don't mind perching on rocks, can be found at the far end of the peninsula, ten minutes' walk north from town, or on the Sustjepan peninsula immediately to the west. The latter has a naturist section, just on the other side of the *Croatia Hotel*.

Eating and drinking

There are numerous **restaurants** on or near the waterfront, offering everything from cheap pizza to more expensive local specialities. In addition, a string of cafés along the Riva serve salads, sandwiches and ice cream during the day, potent cocktails at night.

Restaurants

Galija Vuličevićeva 5 ☎020/478-566. Cosy *konoba* in an alleyway behind the monastery, which in summer expands onto a large outdoor terrace with views across the bay. Succulent seafood starters include grilled squid, and salmon with pasta, although the real highlights of the menu are the grilled fresh fish, and the stand-out *riba u pečnici* (a whole fish roasted in a tin together with potatoes and seasonal vegetables).

Ivan Tiha 5. Familiar range of seafood and grilled meats, with tables set out beside a port full of small boats. Good views north towards Župa Dubrovačka.

Konoba Kolona put Tihe 2. Cheap and tasty eats on a small but shady garden terrace just by the bus stop, bordered by bougainvillea and shaded by a palm tree. Stuffed aubergines, swordfish steaks and a host of other reasonably priced goodies.

Leut Trumbićev put 11. A leafy outdoor terrace a few steps back from the seafront, offering top-of-the range grilled fish and a few seafood surprises (the excellent scampi with broccoli and cream sauce is listed as a starter but might suffice as a light lunch).

Toranj Ravnica. A customary range of fish and shellfish backed up with some excellent alternatives, such as stuffed chicken breast and pasta with lobster. Leave room for the excellent home-made cakes. Slightly set back from the Riva, but the charming first-floor terrace is no mean compensation.

The Konavle

Southeast of Cavtat stretches the **Konavle**, a ribbon of fertile agricultural land squeezed between the mountains on one side and the sea on the other. The main road from Dubrovnik to Montenegro heads straight through the region, and its main settlements are also accessible by bus – most usefully the Dubrovnik–Gruda–Molunat service (3 daily; 2 on Sun), and the Cavtat–Molunat–Vitaljina service (3 daily; Mon–Sat only). Traditionally Konavle formed the rural hinterland of the Dubrovnik Republic, keeping the city supplied with fresh victuals – as well as being the major recruiting ground for itinerant labourers and serving girls. The region was also famous for the colourful costumes of its inhabitants, characterized by the small pillbox hats donned by unmarried girls and the enormous white scarves worn by married women. It's a tradition that to some extent lives on in the small village of **ČILIPI**, 6km south of Cavtat and just beyond Dubrovnik's airport, thanks to the **folklore shows** which take place on the village's flagstoned central square every summer Sunday. Organized by the local folklore society, performances are held in the late morning immediately after Mass, when locals and tourists alike perch on the church steps to observe a forty-minute medley of local songs and dances. Foremost among the latter is the *linđo*, which employs rigid, stylized gestures to mimic the rites of courtship, and is accompanied by the *lirica*, an archaic, droning fiddle. **Trips** to Čilipi from Dubrovnik are run by the Atlas agency (see "Listings", p.466), although you can get here independently using the buses which run from Dubrovnik via Čilipi to Molunat. There are a couple of cafés just off the main square, and a largely tourist-oriented Sunday market selling folksy embroidery and textiles.

South of Čilipi the main southeast-bound road continues through a bucolic landscape of vineyards, orchards and sheep pasture, passing after 10km the downbeat village of **Gruda**, notable only for marking the turn-off to the *Konavoski dvori* **restaurant** 3km to the north, a tranquil mill-side spot renowned for its baked lamb, fresh trout, and other Konavle delicacies – although it's frequently swamped by coach parties.

The Konavle's only coastal settlement of any real consequence is **MOLUNAT**, an unspoilt, vegetation-shrouded village at the end of a winding (and well-signed) secondary road 15km southeast of Gruda. A pleasing jumble of houses and holiday villas faces east across a shallow bay which, despite its small size, is one of the most attractive on this part of the coast, boasting a smooth, sandy seabed on one side and a more rocky section on the other – where there are plenty of offshore outcrops perfect for perching on. Tourism in Molunat is limited to an attractive trio of **campsites**, with *Adriatic I* (ⓣ020/796-585) and *Adriatic II* (ⓣ020/794-450) right on the bay, and *Monika* (ⓣ020/794-417), sheltering amid olive trees on a shingle-edged inlet farther south. *Villa Marin*, on the seafront road, is a **café-restaurant** with a pleasant terrace.

The Elaphite Islands

An easy ferry ride away from Dubrovnik's Gruž harbour, the lush, vegetation-carpeted **Elaphite islands** (Elafiti) present the perfect opportunity to savour the Croatian Adriatic at its unspoilt, get-away-from-it-all best. Strung out between Dubrovnik and the Pelješac peninsula to the north, the Elaphites got their name (literally the "deer islands") from first-century AD Roman geographer Pliny the Elder, who mentioned them in his 37-volume *Historia Naturalis*. The Elaphites became part of the Dubrovnik Republic from the fourteenth century, sharing in its prosperity and then its decline – by the middle of the eighteenth century many island villages lay abandoned and depopulation had become a major problem. Today, only three of the islands are inhabited – **Koločep**, **Lopud** and **Šipan** – each of which supports a modest tourist industry. Despite the daily influx of trippers from Dubrovnik, however, tourism on the Elaphites remains reassuringly low key, the almost total absence of cars contributing to the mellow feel (private vehicles are not allowed on any of the islands except Šipan, but almost all the ferries that go there are passenger-only).

All three islands are linked to Dubrovnik by a Jadrolinija **ferry** which runs up to Šipan and back again (up to 4 daily in summer; 1 daily in winter). In addition, the Nova company operates several daily motor launches to the Elaphites from their office in Dubrovnik – they're slightly faster than the ferries, but are more expensive and less comfortable. There's a handful of **hotels** on the islands, but **rooms** and **apartments** are in short supply – few if any Dubrovnik travel agencies bother to deal with accommodation on the Elaphites. Your best bet is to check the apartment listings on websites such as ⓦwww.dubrovnik-area.com and reserve things well in advance.

As you leave Gruž harbour you'll pass the first of the Elaphites, tiny uninhabited **Daksa** – just off Babin kuk, it's notorious as the site of a 1945 massacre when more than two hundred political opponents of the new communist regime were liquidated.

Koločep

Just thirty minutes from Dubrovnik by ferry, the islet of **Koločep** is a little over 2.6 square kilometres in area, and has a population of less than 150 concentrated in two main hamlets: **Donje Čelo**, on the north side of the island where the ferry docks, and **Gornje Čelo** to the southeast. There are no special sights, but Donje Čelo is a pleasant cluster of stone houses with an excellent curving sandy beach. Just uphill from the waterfront, a concreted path strikes inland towards Gornje Čelo, a huddle of vegetation-choked houses overlooking two small bays. From here you can follow innumerable paths into the dense, fragrant pine and deciduous forest that covers the southern part of the island.

Accommodation is limited to the *Hotel Koločep* (ⓣ020/757-025, ⓔhoteli-kolocep@du.t-com.hr; ❺; May–Oct), an ensemble of eight modern blocks ranged across a hillside just above Donje Čelo's beach. There are also a couple of waterfront **café-restaurants** in Donje Čelo, offering simple grills and seafood.

Lopud

In Dubrovnik's heyday, **Lopud**, with a population of some 4000 (today it's less than 350), was the seat of one of the republic's vice-rectors and was the favoured weekend retreat of the city's nobles. A large part of Dubrovnik's merchant fleet was based here, and the ruined palaces of shipowners still occupy crumbling corners of the island's only village. Tourism here dates back to the 1920s, and the island's hotels were used by the Italians to intern Jews from Dubrovnik and Bosnia in 1942. They were shipped off to the notorious concentration camp on Rab the following year, though many managed to escape to join the Partisans after the collapse of Italy in 1943.

Located on the northern side of the island, the village of **LOPUD** is strung around a wide, curving bay, boasting a long, crowded and reasonably sandy **beach**. Its most prominent monument is the fortified **monastery** which overlooks the village from a promontory just east of the quay where ferries dock. Built by the Franciscans (and funded by Lopud merchants) in 1483, it's now mostly derelict, although there's long been talk of inviting a foreign investor to take the place over and put it to some use. For the time being all that can be visited is the erstwhile monastery (and now parish) **Church of Our Lady of the Rocks** (Crkva Gospe od Špilice), which boasts a rich collection of altar paintings. Among these is a triptych (to the right as you face the main altar) by Nikola Božidarević or his workshop, depicting the Virgin and Child accompanied by a bevy of saints, the ubiquitous St Blaise among them. The main altar is separated from the main body of the church by a delicately carved stone screen, on which small mammals munch away happily on berries, and are in turn menaced by snarling dragons.

West along the seafront from the quay, steps lead up to the ruined palace and private chapel of **Miho Pracat**, the sixteenth-century merchant and shipowner

△ Lopud

whose bust stands in the Rector's Palace in Dubrovnik. A few steps beyond, the **Đorđić-Mayner Park** (Perivoj Đorđić-Mayner) is one of the nicest in the region, with trees from around the world grouped beneath soaring pines, with roses, cacti and other ornamental plantings basking beneath. Paths at the back of the village lead up onto the high ground at the centre of the island, one of which (look for signs reading "Kaštio" or "Tvrđava") climbs towards the Ragusan **fortress**, a forty-minute walk away, which looms above Lopud village to the southeast. It's a complete ruin nowadays, but the view from its crumbling ramparts is magnificent, with stark grey coastal mountains to the east, and the green, cone-shaped hills of Šipan and Pelješac to the north. The best of Lopud's beaches is **Šunj Bay** (Uvala Šunj), the only truly sandy beach in the area and highly popular in summer; it's 2km south of Lopud village and easily reached via an asphalt path.

Practicalities

Lopud's **tourist office** on the seafront (May to mid-Oct Mon–Thurs, Sat & Sun 8am–1pm & 5–7pm; ⓣ020/759-086) can provide a list of rooms and apartments on the island, though won't make bookings. The main seafront promenade is full of hotels and guesthouses, for which it's wise to book well in advance.

For **eating**, *Obala*, on the main strip at Obala Iva Kuljevana 17, offers good-quality seafood on a terrace overlooking the beach; while *Konoba Peggy*, a well-signed five-minute walk uphill from the seafront, has a large terrace overlooking the town and fresh fish and squid cooked on an open hearth.

Hotels and guesthouses

Glavović Obala Iva Kuljevana bb ⓣ020/759-359, ⓦwww.hotel-glavovic.hr. A family-run, fourteen-room hotel with neat en-suite rooms, centrally positioned at the heart of the bay. May–Oct. ❻

La Villa Obala Iva Kuljevana ⓣ020/759-259 or 091 322 0126, ⓦwww.lavilla.com.hr. Six-room guesthouse whose rooms come with tiled floors, Mediterranean colours, vivaciously tiled bathrooms and a/c. There's a shady breakfast terrace, an Internet corner and library, and bikes and kayaks for rent. Open April–Oct. Three-day minimum stay preferred. ❻

Villa Vilina Obala Iva Kuljevana 5 ⓣ020/759-333, ⓦwww.villa-vilina.hr. Intimate and luxurious small hotel in an old stone house near the Franciscan monastery, offering a handful of tastefully furnished, plush-carpeted rooms with TV. The same company runs the *Lopudski Dvori* (same number), another stone building comprising seven well-appointed two-person apartments with shared garden and swimming pool. May–Oct. Both *Lopudski Dvori* apartments and *Villa Vilina* rooms. ❼

Lafodia Obala Iva Kuljevana bb ⓣ020/759-022, ⓔhotel-lafodia@du.htnet.hr. Ungainly, overpriced two-hundred-room concrete package hotel at the southern end of Lopud's bay. The bland en-suite rooms do at least have small balconies, many with excellent views towards the harbour. May–Oct. ❼

Šipan

The largest of the populated Elaphites, the island of **Šipan** is a delightful combination of craggy hills strung out around a long, fertile plain dotted with the occasional hamlet. There are few special sights and there's certainly no nightlife, but if you're after some peace and quiet and gentle hikes, this is one of the best places to be on the coast.

The first port of call for the ferry is **SUĐURAĐ**, a bay-hugging clump of houses overlooked by an imposing pair of stone **towers**, built to guard the walled summer villa of sixteenth-century Dubrovnik shipowner Vice Stjepović Skočibuha. Parts of the villa have been lovingly restored but, somewhat frustratingly, they're only open to pre-booked groups. Running round the side of the palace, the village's main alleyway ascends towards the blockhouse-shaped

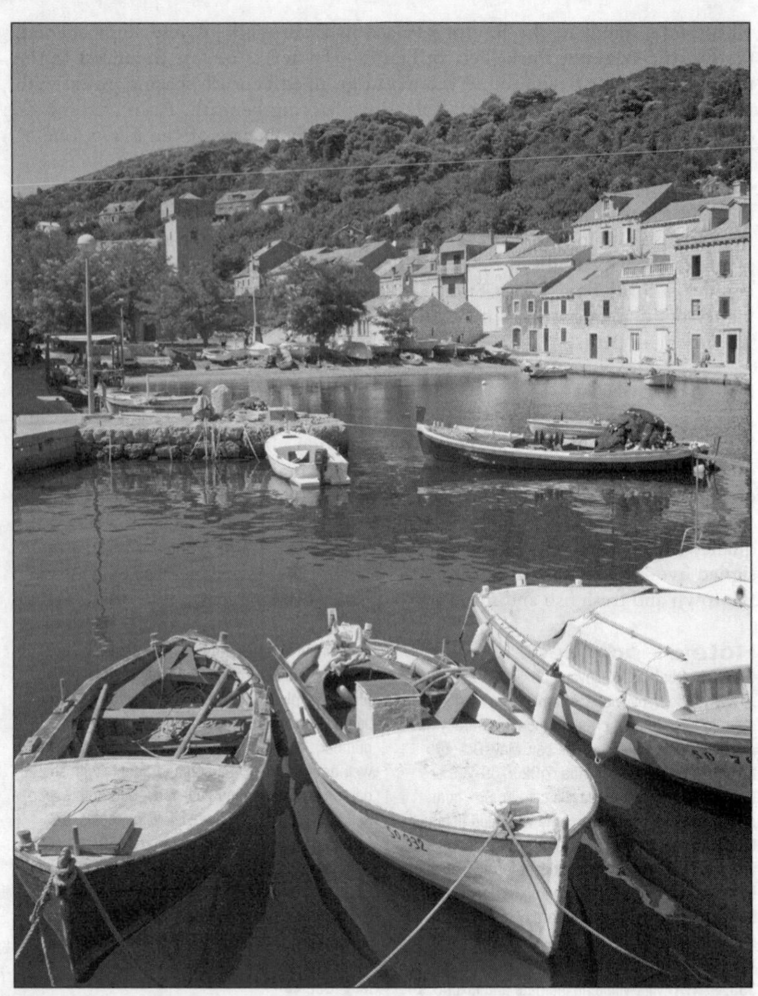

△ Šipan

Church of the Holy Spirit (Crkva svetog Duha), a fortified structure built to serve as a refuge for the locals in the event of pirate attack. Bearing right at the church, and following the road that winds its way round the hillside hamlet of Pakljena, will take you towards one of the most attractive corners of the island – an area of dense maquis broken up by agaves, olive groves and pines. After about 2km you'll chance upon the fortified **Church of Our Lady** (Crkva velike Gospe), a former monastic foundation whose crumbling outbuildings appear to be sinking into the undergrowth. The church is hardly ever open, but the sight of its crenellated sixteenth-century tower peeking above the greenery provides a convenient excuse to wander this far.

Heading north from the Church of the Holy Spirit along the island's only properly paved road, the seven-kilometre **walk to Šipanska Luka** (see opposite) takes you past some lovely inland scenery. Vineyards and olive groves cover the island's central plain, which is edged by the ruined summer houses of the Dubrovnik nobility, and perfumed by wild fennel, rosemary and other herbs.

Šipanska Luka

Ferries terminate at **ŠIPANSKA LUKA**, a pretty little place buried at the end of a deep inlet at the island's northern end. Grouped around an enormous plane tree that's thought to be as old as those in Trsteno, the settlement contains the odd relic of former glories: best is the neglected Stjepančić villa on the harbourfront, which boasts a balcony supported by carved lions, and seems to be crying out for restoration. Šipanska Luka's most attractive **beach** is about 500m away from the harbourfront, a tiny strip of sand pressed against a thread of rock that separates the western side of the bay from the sea. More isolated spots for bathing can be found by following the path which extends beyond the ferry jetty on the opposite side of the bay, threading its way between rocky shoreline and shady olive groves before petering out in dense undergrowth after a couple of kilometres.

The small tourist office at the apex of Šipan's bay (June–Sept Mon–Sat 8am–noon & 5–8pm; ⓣ020/758-084) will provide addresses of local private **rooms** (❷) but will not book them on your behalf. The harbourfront **hotel**, the *Šipan* (ⓣ020/758-000, ⓕ758-004, ⓦwww.hotel-sipan.hr; mid-April to Oct; ❺), offers standard en-suite rooms – the attic rooms on the top floor are the cosiest – and also rents out **bikes**. There's a growing number of **eating** and **drinking** possibilities: *Tauris*, set back from the shore behind Šipan's plane tree, prepares deliciously succulent *lignje* (squid), fried or grilled, as well as excellent fish; while *Kod Marka*, on the southern side of the bay, has earned cult status with the local yachting fraternity with its fresh seafood, although it's eccentric with it – you might receive attentive service or simply be left waiting for hours. *Barka*, occupying one half of the *Hotel Šipan*'s restaurant, offers coffee and cakes during the daytime and cocktails after nightfall, with tables strewn across a palm-shaded lawn.

Mljet

The westernmost of the islands accessible by local ferry from Dubrovnik is **MLJET**, a thin strip of land some 32km long and never more than 3km wide, running roughly parallel to the Pelješac peninsula. The most visited part of the island is the green and unspoilt west, where untouched Mediterranean forest and two saltwater lakes provide the focus of the **Mljet National Park**, an area of arcadian beauty within which lie the villages of **Polače** and **Pomena**. Despite a nascent package-holiday industry in the village of Pomena, the region remains invitingly quiet, and there are few shopping or nightlife opportunities.

According to legend, Odysseus holed up here for some time with the nymph Calypso, and Mljet also has fair claim to being the island of Melita, where St Paul ran aground on his way to Italy and was bitten by a viper before he set sail again. (Mljet's snake problem was once so bad that a colony of mongooses had to be imported from India to get rid of them, and the fat-tailed creatures are still very much in evidence in the national park.) The Romans used the island as a place of exile, and it was briefly owned by the kings of Bosnia, who sold it to Dubrovnik in 1333. The republic sent an emissary on May 1 every year to rule the island for a year, and many of Dubrovnik's admirals built summer houses here.

Coming **from Dubrovnik**, there are two ways of getting to the island. The easier option is the passenger-only *Nona Maria* catamaran (May–Sept; information and tickets from Atlantagent, Obala Stjepana Radića 26; ⓣ020/313-355, ⓦwww.atlantagent.com), which sails daily to Polače in the morning, and leaves you with several hours to look round the park before returning to Dubrovnik in the evening. The year-round Jadrolinija car ferry sails to Sobra in the eastern part of the island (it's a good 20km short of the park; Sobra–Polače–Pomena buses await incoming ferries), and doesn't return to Dubrovnik until early the following morning, making an overnight stay on the island unavoidable. If you come here by car, be sure to fill your tank before you cross the water – there's nowhere to get petrol on the island. Approaching **from Korčula** or **Orebić**, you can reach Mljet on the regular hydrofoil excursions (arriving at either Polače or Pomena) run by local travel agents – expect to pay 250–280Kn per person, including the park entrance fee.

Sobra to Pomena

Jadrolinija ferries from Dubrovnik dock 3km south of **SOBRA**, an insignificant settlement roughly halfway along the island. After winding its way over to the west the road descends to **POLAČE**, little more than a row of houses along a small harbour – whose waters are clean enough to swim in. The harbour is bordered to the north by the impressively lofty walls of a fourth-century AD **Roman palace**, the inner courtyard of which is now home to a couple of lemon trees. A small white house on the harbour contains a **tourist office** (mid-June to mid-Sept Mon–Sat 8am–noon & 4–6pm; mid-Sept to mid-June Mon–Fri 8am–1pm; ⓣ020/745-125), which can point you in the direction of locals offering **rooms** (❷). For **food and drink**, there are a couple of café-restaurants along the front, and a small provisions store open mornings and evenings.

Sheltering in a bay at the western tip of Mljet, **POMENA** is a seaside hamlet similar to Polače – save for the presence of a large modern hotel and a harbour which is becoming increasingly popular with touring yachtspeople. The *Odisej* **hotel** (ⓣ020/362-111, ⓦwww.hotelodisej.hr; ❺) is a prim collection of whitewashed modern blocks and has **exchange** facilities. Room quality varies from one part of the complex to the other – insist on a room with air conditioning and TV. For **food**, the restaurant of the *Odisej* is respectable, and the nearby *Pansion Pomena* offers excellent-value set lunches and a more elaborate range of pricey seafood in the evening. Regular taxi boats (check the lobby of the *Odisej* for details) run to the naturist islet of **Pomeštak**, just offshore.

The Mljet National Park

There's no official entrance point to the **Mljet National Park** (ⓦwww.np-mljet.hr), and by the time you arrive in Polače or Pomena you're already well inside it. However, you're expected to buy a ticket (June–Sept 65Kn; Oct–May 45Kn) from one of the kiosks in Pomena, Polače or just outside Goveđari once you've settled in, and certainly before you start exploring. The kiosks also have park information and **maps** (50Kn).

The park's main attractions are its two forest-shrouded "lakes" (actually inlets connected to the sea by narrow channels), **Malo jezero** ("Small Lake") and **Veliko jezero** ("Big Lake"), which together form a stretch of water some 4km long. Both are encircled by foot- and cycle paths, and the clear, blue-green waters are perfect for bathing. If you're staying in Polače, it's possible to walk over to the lakes by road or by a well-signed forest path (via the 253-metre Montokuc hill) in about 45 minutes. From Pomena, Malo jezero is ten minutes' walk south, by way of a stone-paved footpath that heads over a wooded ridge just up from the port. Once you hit the shore of Malo jezero, it's another ten-minute walk to **Mali most** ("Little Bridge"), spanning the channel feeding into Veliko jezero, edged by magnificently soothing, tree-shaded pathways.

Mali most is the departure point for an hourly boat service (vouchers for the trip are included with the entrance ticket) down Veliko jezero to **St Mary's Island** (Otok svete Marije), where the Benedictines established a monastery in the twelfth century. Overlooked by a sturdy defensive tower, the monastery church features unusually chunky altarpieces carved from local stone and exuberantly coloured. The central dome is enclosed in a squat quadrangular tower, whose dog-tooth-patterned exterior can be admired from the neighbouring courtyard. There's a **café-restaurant** in the monastery grounds.

Bikes are a handy way to get around the lakes: they can be rented from Mali most, the national park kiosk in Polače, or in front of the *Odisej* hotel in Pomena (30Kn/hour, 90Kn/day). **Kayaks** (same price) can also be rented at Mali most.

Travel details

Buses

Dubrovnik to: Cavtat (every 30–45min; 40min); Čilipi (Mon–Sat 3 daily, Sun 2 daily; 45min); Korčula (1 daily; 4hr); Makarska (18 daily; 3hr); Molunat (Mon–Sat 3 daily, Sun 2 daily; 1hr 10min); Orebić (2 daily; 3hr); Plitvice (3 daily; 10hr); Ploče (hourly; 2hr); Pula (1 daily; 16hr); Rijeka (Mon–Sat 4 daily; Sun 3 daily; 13hr); Šibenik (9 daily; 6hr 30min); Split (18 daily; 5hr); Ston (3 daily; 1hr 30min); Trsteno (hourly; 40min); Vela Luka (1 daily; 5hr); Zadar (7 daily; 9hr); Zagreb (8 daily; 12hr).

Šipanska Luka to: Suđurađ (Mon–Fri 5 daily, Sat 2 daily; 15min).

Sobra to: Pomena (2 daily; 1hr 10min).

Ferries

Dubrovnik to: Koločep (1–4 daily; 30min); Korčula (summer 1 daily, winter 4 weekly; 3hr); Lopud (1–4 daily; 50min); Polače (1 daily; 1hr 40min); Rijeka (summer 1 daily, winter 4 weekly; 22hr); Sobra (1–2 daily; 2hr 15min); Šipanska Luka (1–2 daily; 1hr 45min); Split (summer 1 daily, winter 4 weekly; 10hr); Suđurađ (1–4 daily; 1hr); Stari Grad (summer 1 daily, winter 4 weekly; 7hr); Zadar (summer 1 daily, winter 4 weekly; 15hr).

Motor boats

Dubrovnik to: Koločep (May & Oct 2 daily; June–Sept 6 daily; 25min), Lopud (May & Oct 2 daily; June–Sept 6 daily; 1hr 5min), Suđurađ (May & Oct 2 daily; June–Sept 6 daily; 1hr 20min).

Domestic flights

Dubrovnik to: Zagreb (2–3 daily; 1hr).

International buses

Dubrovnik to: Međugorje (1 daily; 4hr); Mostar (2 daily; 5hr); Sarajevo (2 daily; 7hr).

International ferries

Dubrovnik to: Bari (2–4 weekly; 8hr).

half in about 45 minutes (return journey. [illegible]) walk south by way of a stone-paved [illegible] path that leads down [illegible] to [illegible] port. Once you hit the shore of Malo jezero [illegible] walk to Mali most ("Little Bridge") [illegible] the channel leading into Veliko jezero, [illegible] by magnificently [illegible] pathways.

Mali most [illegible] departure [illegible] hourly boat service [illegible] the trip [illegible] included with the entrance ticket) [illegible] Veliko jezero to St Mary's Island [illegible] where the Benedictines established a monastery in the twelfth century [illegible] by a sturdy [illegible] tower, the [illegible] church [illegible] unusually [illegible] altar [illegible] carved from local stone and [illegible]. The [illegible] is enclosed in a square quadrangle tower, whose [illegible] excellent [illegible] from [illegible] the courtyard. There's a café-restaurant in the [illegible] grounds.

Bikes are a handy way to get around the lakes: they can be [illegible] from [illegible] near the national park [illegible] or in front of the [illegible] (90Kn/day) [illegible] can also be rented at [illegible].

Travel details

[illegible]

Dubrovnik to: Cavtat (every 30min; 30min); [illegible] daily; Split 2 daily; 45min); Korčula ([illegible] daily; 3hr); Makarska ([illegible] daily; 3hr); Orebić (2 daily; 2hr); [illegible] Ploče; [illegible] (daily; [illegible]); Rijeka ([illegible] daily; [illegible]); Split ([illegible] daily; 4hr30min); [illegible] daily; Zagreb (3 daily; 11hr).

[illegible] to [illegible] 2 daily; [illegible].

[illegible]

Dubrovnik to Korčula ([illegible] daily; [illegible]); Korčula ([illegible] summer); [illegible] daily, winter 4 weekly; [illegible] daily; [illegible]; Rijeka ([illegible] daily; [illegible]); [illegible] daily; winter 4 weekly; [illegible] daily; [illegible].

[illegible] to [illegible] daily; [illegible]. Ancona ([illegible] summer) daily, winter weekly; [illegible] daily; [illegible] daily; winter 4 weekly; 10hr).

[illegible]

Dubrovnik to Korčula ([illegible] daily; [illegible]); [illegible] ([illegible] daily; [illegible]); [illegible] daily; [illegible]; [illegible] daily; [illegible].

[illegible]

Dubrovnik to Zagreb (2–3 daily; 1hr).

[illegible]

Dubrovnik to [illegible] ([illegible] daily; [illegible]).

[illegible]

Dubrovnik to Bari (2–4 weekly; 8hr).

Contexts

Contexts

A brief history of Croatia

History is a serious business in a country which has spent so much of its past under the sway of foreign powers. It's also exceedingly complicated, as the history of Croatia is interlinked, for lengthy periods, with the histories of Hungary, Austria and Venice, not to mention that of the former Yugoslavia.

Croatia before the Croatians

Our knowledge of the first humans to inhabit Croatia is patchy, although a form of Neanderthal – named **Krapina Man** after the town in which remains have been found (see p.126) – is known to have roamed the hills north of Zagreb some thirty millennia ago. By about the seventh millennium BC, Neolithic farmers had spread out along the coast, and were increasingly using the islands as stepping stones to cross the Adriatic. Advanced Neolithic cultures certainly existed on Hvar, where 5000-year-old painted pottery offers evidence of the so-called Hvar Culture, and beside the River Danube in eastern Slavonia, where similarly rich ceramics have been unearthed at Vučedol near Vukovar.

By the first millennium BC the indigenous peoples of the region now covered by Croatia, Bosnia, Albania and Serbia had begun to coalesce into a group of tribes subsequently known as the **Illyrians**. Although they were united by common styles of fortress-building and burial-mound construction, it's not clear whether the Illyrians ever existed as a culturally homogenous group, and they were never politically united. They did, however, produce some powerful tribal states: the Histri in Istria and the Liburnians in the Kvarner and northern Dalmatia were minor maritime powers, building towns whose names – in modified, Slavonic form – still survive, like Aenona (Nin) and Jadera (Zadar).

Greeks, Romans and Byzantines

Greek city-states, led by Syracuse in Sicily, began dispatching trade missions and settlers to the Adriatic coast from the fourth century BC onwards, founding colonies such as Issa (on present-day Vis) and Paros (on Hvar). There were various attempts by the Illyrians to drive the new colonists out, the most serious coming from King Agron and his queen and successor Teuta, whose territory stretched from present-day Zadar in the north to what is now Albania in the south.

In 229 BC the Greeks asked for Roman help against Teuta, beginning a period of **Roman expansion** that continued until 9 AD, when the eastern Adriatic and its hinterland were annexed by the future emperor Tiberius. The seaboard was reorganized into the Roman province of Dalmatia, while northern and eastern Croatia were divided between the provinces of Noricum (which covered much of present-day Austria) and Pannonia (which stretched into modern Hungary). The older Greek settlements continued to flourish, but were outshone as political and cultural centres by new Roman cities, often founded on or near sites that had previously served as power bases for the Illyrian tribes. The main Roman centres were Salona (Solin, near Split) and Jadera (Zadar), although the vast amphitheatre at Pula attests to the prosperity of Istria during this period. The Illyrians were either romanized or absorbed by later immigrants like the Slavs.

Roman power in the Adriatic ended temporarily in 493, when the region fell to King Teodoric of the Ostrogoths, although Justinian, emperor of the eastern half of the Roman Empire, whose capital was at **Byzantium**, reconquered the area in 544. Inland, things were more chaotic: the **Avars**, a warlike central Asian people, briefly forged a central European empire at the beginning of the seventh century, and even reached the coast, sacking Salona and Epidaurum in 614. Refugees from these cities went on to found Split and Dubrovnik.

The arrival of the Croats

Precisely when the **Croats** – a Slav tribe who came to southeastern Europe from an area north of the Carpathians – arrived in the territories they now inhabit is a bit of a mystery, although the Byzantine emperor Constantine Porphyrogenitus (writing three hundred years after the event) stated that they were invited by one of his predecessors, Heraclius, in the early seventh century in order to serve as a counterweight to the Avars.

One problem in tracking the movement of the Croats before their arrival in southeast Europe is that the name "Croat" (Hrvat) is thought to be of Persian rather than Slav origin, suggesting that the Croats were subject to Persian-speaking tribes before moving towards southeastern Europe, or even that the Croats were themselves of Iranian origin and picked up the Slav tongue from neighbours as they migrated. The latter theory has always been popular among Croatian nationalists keen to emphasize the uniqueness of their people, athough it's disputed by more mainstream scholars.

The Croats probably migrated to southeastern Europe at the same time as the **Serbs**, who settled in the middle of the Balkan peninsula. The fact that the groups share a common language suggests that they originated in the same area, and Serbs and Croats – along with other tribes speaking similar Slav dialects such as the Slovenes, Bulgarians and Macedonians – were subsequently to be known collectively as the **South Slavs**.

The medieval Croatian state

The Croats who settled along the Dalmatian seaboard established a tribal state ruled by a **knez** (prince or duke), who assumed leadership of other Slav tribes already settled in the region, as well as of sundry Avars and surviving remnants of the Illyrian and Roman populations. Inland areas to the north, such as present-day Slavonia, fell under independent chieftains loosely allied to the Croats on the Adriatic. The existence of two Croatian heartlands – a southern one oriented towards the Mediterranean and a northern one looking towards central Europe – has had a profound effect on Croatian culture ever since.

Both areas maintained a tenuous independence until squeezed by powerful neighbouring empires: the Byzantines, who still held several Adriatic towns and islands, and the Carolingian Empire of the Franks, which was expanding into central Europe by the late 700s. Croat leaders boosted their legitimacy in the eyes of their more advanced western neighbours by accepting **Christianity**, and although the northern Croatian state became subject to the Franks in the 790s, the southern state played one predator off against another and prospered. Ruling from their citadel at Klis (see p.376), princes such as Mislav (ruled 835–845), Trpimir (845–864) and Domagoj (864–876) paid homage to either Byzantines or Franks as necessary, while preserving *de facto* independence and simultaneously beating off two newcomers to the Adriatic: the Venetians and the Arabs.

With the Croatian state growing stronger militarily, Branimir (879–892) threw off Byzantine vassalage once and for all, and was recognized by Pope John VIII as an independent ruler, definitively tying Croatia to the Roman rather than the Byzantine Church. His successor-but-one, **Tomislav** (910–928), pushed things further, defeating the Hungarians to gain control of northern Croatia and battling the Bulgarians to win northwestern Bosnia. Eager to secure an alliance with Tomislav, the Byzantines ceded sovereignty over Split, Trogir, Osor, Rab and Krk. Declaring himself king in 925 (previous Croatian leaders had kept to the title "knez"), Tomislav reorganized the Croatian Church, placing all his lands under the control of a Croatian archbishop at Split, thereby lessening papal influence without actually questioning his ultimate loyalty to the pope.

For the seventy years following Tomislav's death Croatia was financially, militarily and dynastically stable, until a succession crisis in the early eleventh century allowed both Venice and Byzantium to regain footholds on the Adriatic coast, while northern Croatia was lost to the Hungarians. **Petar Krešimir IV** (1058–75) presided over a revival of fortunes, and reunion with northern Croatia was achieved by weaning the ruler of Slavonia, **Dimitr Zvonimir**, away from Hungary and appointing him co-ruler (though Zvonimir's marriage to Princess Jelena of Hungary would later complicate the dynastic picture). Petar Krešimir died childless, and power passed to Zvonimir (1075–89), though he too died without issue, leaving the nobles to chose Stjepan II (1089–91), who also failed to produce an heir.

The kingdom began to disintegrate, leaving Zvonimir's brother-in-law, King Ladislas of Hungary, free to secure control of the north, while a group of nobles in the south regrouped under King Petar (1093–97). Independent Croatia's last monarch was defeated by a Hungarian army under Ladislas's successor Koloman at **Gvozd** (subsequently named Petrova gora or Peter's Mountain), the highland region south of Zagreb.

Hungarian control of Croatia was confirmed by the **Pacta Conventa** of 1102, according to the terms of which Croatia and Hungary remained separate states united by the same royal family. Croatia retained its own institutions – a **Ban** (governor) appointed by the king, and the **Sabor** (parliament) representing the nobility – but, despite these provisions, the Hungarian crown steadily reduced the power of the Croatian aristocracy in the years that followed, speeding Croatia's demise as a united and distinct state.

Croatia under the Hungarians

Life in what became known as the **Hungaro-Croatian kingdom** was characterized by a strengthening of the feudal order, with the landed nobility growing stronger at the expense of a rural population overloaded with feudal obligations. Town life, especially in northern Croatia, underwent rapid development as Varaždin, Vukovar, Samobor and Zagreb were earmarked as centres of trade.

The Croatian lands were overrun by the **Tatars** in 1242, but King Bela IV managed to keep royal authority alive by moving from one coastal stronghold to the next (innumerable Adriatic towns were subsequently given special privileges for assisting Bela in his flight). The material damage was enormous, however, and much medieval Croatian architecture was lost. The Hungarian monarchy was strengthened under **Charles Robert of Anjou** (1301–42), who further weakened the remaining independence of the south Croatian nobles. Hungarian control of the Adriatic seaboard – slowly eroded by Venetian penetration during the previous century – was reasserted by Charles Robert and his son **Louis of Anjou** (1342–82), who threw the Venetians out of Dalmatia in 1358. Louis died without a male heir, and his inheritance was disputed by Sigismund of Luxembourg (Louis's son-in-law) and Charles III of Naples. The nobles of southern Croatia appointed Charles's son, **Ladislas of Naples**, king of Croatia in 1403, but his armies were no match for those of Sigismund. In 1409, Ladislas fled, selling his rights over Dalmatia to the Venetians for the sum of 100,000 ducats.

Venice was now in command of almost all of Istria and Dalmatia apart from a few Habsburg territories and **Dubrovnik**, an independent city-state owing nominal allegiance to the Hungarian crown. The Venetians were to stay for over 350 years, flooding the Adriatic seaboard with Italianate art and architecture, but taking away the traditional autonomy of the towns at the same time.

Cut off from the Adriatic, the Croatian lands in the Dalmatian hinterland and the north were also being squeezed from another direction. Croatia's immediate neighbour to the southeast was **Bosnia**, a mountainous inland region which had long been a buffer zone between Croatia, the Byzantine Empire and, more recently, Serbia, which had emerged as a unified and independent state at the end of the twelfth century. The inhabitants of Bosnia were the ethnic kin of the Serbs and Croats, and both the Croatian and Serbian churches had made inroads into the region. Large parts of Bosnia – especially the north and west – had long been in the Hungaro-Croatian sphere of influence, and from 1138 Bosnia had been a vassal of Hungary ruled by its own Ban. Powerful and resourceful rulers like Kulin (1180–1204), Stjepan II Kotromanić (1322–53) and Tvrtko I (1353–91) were nevertheless able to expand their territory at the expense of the south Croatian aristocracy, though by the fifteenth century the northward expansion of the **Ottoman Turks** had begun to threaten Bosnia, something which would have grave consequences for the Croats.

The Ottoman threat

From their heartland in Anatolia, the Ottoman Turks had gained a foothold in southeastern Europe in the early 1300s and soon expanded their territory, fatally weakening Byzantium, swallowing Bulgaria and reducing Serbia to vassal status within a century. Staving off the Ottoman advance was a major preoccupation of Sigismund and his successors, although the mid-fifteenth-century victories of Transylvanian warlord **János Hunyadi** initially made it look as if central Europe might be saved from the Turks. However, the conquest of Bosnia by the Ottomans in the 1460s and 1470s left Croatia in an extremely vulnerable position.

In 1493, a large Hungarian-Croatian force assembled at **Krbavsko polje** (in the Lika, just south of Plitvice) was decisively beaten by the Turks, leaving the Adriatic open to Ottoman raids. In 1517, Pope Leo X called Croatia *antemurale christianitatis* ("the ramparts of Christendom") in recognition of its front-line status. To the east, the defeat of Hungary at the **Battle of Mohács** in 1526 left the Turks in command of much of Pannonia, with Slavonia and northwestern Croatia at their mercy.

The Hungarian King Louis II had died childless at Mohács, leaving the throne to his designated successor, the Austrian **Ferdinand I of Habsburg**. The Hungarian state was thus absorbed into the growing Habsburg Empire, taking inland Croatia with it. Despite the resources of his vast central European empire, however, Ferdinand could do little to stem the Ottoman advance. Klis, the last Croatian fortress in middle Dalmatia, fell in 1537, and by the 1540s the Turks had overrun the whole of Slavonia as far as Sisak, only 50km south of Zagreb. By the end of the century Croatia had been reduced by the Turks and Venetians to a belt of territory running from the Kvarner Gulf in the southwest to the Međimurje in the northeast, with Zagreb at its centre. The Venetians continued to hold Istria and the Dalmatian coastal strip, and the city-state of Dubrovnik further south retained its independence by paying tribute to the Ottoman Empire. The rest of Croatia was occupied by the Ottomans.

The expansion of Turkish power had also set in train a sequence of population movements, with refugees fleeing to areas that were still under the control of Christian powers. Areas depopulated by war and migration were often filled by itinerant stockbreeders, or **Vlachs**, many of whom were descended from the romanized inhabitants of ancient Illyria and still spoke a dialect of Latin akin to modern Romanian. A mixture of Catholic and Orthodox Christians, the Vlachs fell under the influence of the Croatian and Serbian churches, and were soon slavicized, coming to identify themselves as Croats or Serbs as time went on.

Vlach tribes had already served both Ottoman and Christian rulers as border guards, experience which was put to good use by the Habsburgs. The Vlachs were settled in a belt running along Croatia's borders with Ottoman territory and given lands in return for military service. This belt became known as the **Military Frontier** (Vojna krajina), a defensive cordon ruled directly from either Graz or Vienna. It was to remain in existence until the mid-nineteenth century, by which time the Ottoman threat had long receded.

The seventeenth and eighteenth centuries

Habsburg forces – with many Croats in their ranks – scored an important victory over the Turks at the **Battle of Sisak** in 1593, ending the myth of Ottoman invincibility and stabilizing the Habsburg–Ottoman frontier. A further Ottoman attack on Vienna in 1683 was thrown back by a combined force of Austrians, Germans and Poles. In the decades that followed, Habsburg armies led by **Prince Eugene of Savoy** gradually drove the Ottomans out of central Europe. The Venetians, who had often avoided all-out war with the Turks owing to the precariousness of their position in Dalmatia, exploited Austrian gains by winning back parts of the Dalmatian hinterland. By the time of the **Peace of Passarowitz** in 1718, the Habsburgs had won back the whole of Slavonia, while the Venetians gained control of a belt of highland territory running from Knin to Imotski. Significantly, the Turks retained Bosnia and Hercegovina (the latter a belt of territory along southwest Bosnia), and the frontiers agreed at Passarowitz are very close to those still dividing Bosnia-Hercegovina from Croatia today.

Because the Habsburg lands were made up of a multitude of states – its rulers were simultaneously Duke of Austria, Holy Roman Emperor and King of Hungary – political authority within the empire was often confused. In Croatia, the Military Frontier (considerably enlarged after the capture of Slavonia) was still under the direct control of Vienna, while the nobles in the rest of Croatia enjoyed a semblance of autonomy through the Croatian Sabor, which met in Zagreb and (briefly) in Varaždin. However Croatia still nominally belonged to the Hungarian Crown, making the Hungarian parliament in Buda the real focus of political power and intrigue. The Croatian aristocracy had been progressively hungarianized from the late seventeenth century on (when its last great magnates, **Petar Zrinski** and **Fran Krsto Frankopan**, were executed for treason; see box on p.137), and took little interest in the Croatian language or culture.

Agriculturally rich areas of northwestern Croatia and Slavonia were reasonably prosperous in the eighteenth century, but little was done to develop town life, trade or industry. Most official deliberations took part in either German or Latin (the official language of Hungary) rather than Croat, and few of society's leading figures took an interest in promoting indigenous culture. Venetian-controlled Dalmatia was increasingly impoverished due to a fall-off in trade, and Dubrovnik had been in slow decline since suffering a catastrophic earthquake in 1667.

The nineteenth century

In 1797 the Venetian Republic was dissolved by **Napoleon**. Its possessions in Istria and Dalmatia were initially awarded to the Habsburgs in compensation for territories they had lost to the French in northern Italy, but after another bout of fighting between 1806 and 1808, Napoleon gained control of the whole of the eastern Adriatic seaboard. Stretching from Villach in Austria to the Bay of Kotor (now part of Montenegro) in southern Dalmatia, this new French protectorate was named the **Illyrian Provinces** and placed under a French governor, Marshal Marmont. He set about building roads, developing the education system and promoting Slav-language publishing, although the provinces were soon abandoned to the Austrians in 1813 following Napoleon's defeat at the hands of the Russians.

Habsburg dominance of Dalmatia was confirmed by the **Treaty of Vienna** in 1815, and the economic fortunes of the Adriatic began to revive under Austrian stewardship. The main language of the Adriatic sea trade, however, was Italian, and economic development went hand-in-hand with the italianization of maritime Croatia, disappointing many who had seen the return of Austrian power as an opportunity to renew links between the Croats of Dalmatia and the Croats of the north.

The Croatian national revival

One of Napoleon's aims in the creation of the Illyrian Provinces had been to encourage the growth of South Slav consciousness, in the hope that Croats, Slovenes and Serbs could be weaned away from other great powers that might pose as their protectors, notably Austria and Russia. For the Croatian elite, the example of Serbia itself was increasingly important. Subject to the Ottoman empire since the fifteenth century, the Serbs had risen up against the Turks in

1804 and 1815, and the emergence of an **autonomous Serbian principality** in 1830 was greeted by many Croat intellectuals as an example of what South Slavs could achieve. Apart from an undercurrent of distrust between the Catholic and Orthodox churches, the Serbs had never been regarded as historic enemies, and the development of common links between Serbs and Croats became a popular intellectual theme.

The closeness of the Croat and Serb languages sparked a renewed interest in the orally transmitted folk poems – often speaking of heroic resistance to the Turks or some other common foe – that characterized both Serbian and Croatian popular culture, especially in mountainous areas like the Dalmatian hinterland, where the two communities lived side by side. The interest in folk poems led to a new awareness of the languages themselves: a literary form of written Serbian was established by Vuk Stefanović Karađić, whose example was followed by the Croatian writer **Ljudevit Gaj** (1809–72). Gaj set about developing a form of literary Croatian close enough to Serbian for the two to be mutually intelligible, basing it on the Štokavski dialect used by Croats in Slavonia, Hercegovina and Dubrovnik. *Danica*, the cultural supplement of his own newspaper, *Novine Hrvatske*, changed over to the new, Štokavski-based written language in 1835.

The movement which grew out of Gaj's reforming zeal was known as **Illyrianism** (*Ilirizam*) – a name which harked back to the ancient Roman province of Illyria and therefore avoided too close an identification with any single ethnic group. Illyrianism contributed enormously to the flowering of Croatian language and culture in the mid-nineteenth century known as the **Croatian National Revival**. Although the movement was originally intended to provide a bridge between Croats and Serbs, it remained a purely Croatian affair: the fact that the Croats used the Roman alphabet and the Serbs wrote in Cyrillic characters made it unlikely that the two languages and cultures would ever be harmonized. The infant Serbian state was in any case much more interested in expansion than in co-operation with its Slav neighbours.

Vienna initially tolerated Illyrianism as a politically useful counterweight against the boisterous nationalism of the Hungarians, but eventually took fright and came down heavily, banning any mention of the word "Illyria" in 1843. The movement lived on, however, with the formation of the Narodna stranka – the "National Party", whose members were known as the **Narodnjaci** – which from now on was to be the country's main pro-Croat, anti-Hungarian force.

1848 and after

With the outbreak of **revolution in Paris** in February 1848, a wave of reforming fervour spread through Europe. In Hungary, the fiery Lajos Kossuth agitated for the introduction of a constitutional monarchy, while mobs on the streets of Vienna demanded democratic reforms. The fall of the Austrian chancellor Metternich, who had been right-hand man to a succession of emperors for nearly forty years, produced a power vacuum throughout the Habsburg Empire which new organizations and personalities rushed to fill. Croatian opinion saw the 1848 revolution as a means of winning autonomy from the Hungarians and forging a new Croatian or South Slav unit within the Austrian Empire. This conflict of national interests pitched Croatian radicals against the Hungarian radicals under Kossuth who, despite their liberal credentials, continued to regard Croatia as a junior partner in a reinvigorated Hungary.

Fast losing control of a complex situation, the Habsburg court had no choice but to tolerate the emergence of Croatian national sentiment, in the hope that it would serve to counterbalance the Hungarians. Vienna succumbed to popular pressure and elevated Colonel **Josip Jelačić**, a popular garrison commander in the Military Frontier and a well-known supporter of the Narodnjaci, to the position of Ban of Croatia. Jelačić immediately called elections to the Croatian Sabor in order to provide himself with a popular mandate. The Narodnjaci won a sweeping victory and, armed with the Sabor's support, Jelačić first broke off relations with the Hungarians, then declared war on them. Ultimately, however, he became a pawn in a wider game: after relying on his support to crush the revolutionaries in Hungary and Austria, reactionaries at the Viennese court gradually forgot about Croatian demands for autonomy and reintroduced centralized rule.

The late nineteenth century

Revolution was followed by the era of **Bach's Absolutism**, named after the Austrian interior minister, Alexander Bach. Under Bach's stewardship, the Habsburg Empire, headed by arch-conservative **Franz Josef I** (1848–1916), attempted to reorganize itself as a centralized state in which all regionalist aspirations were suppressed in favour of loyalty to the Habsburg dynasty. Bach was dispensed with in 1860, but continuing tension between Vienna and Budapest forced another reorganization of the empire in 1867. According to the terms of the **Ausgleich** ("Compromise"), the Habsburg state became the **Dual Monarchy of Austria-Hungary**. Franz Josef was to be emperor of Austria and king of Hungary simultaneously, and Vienna was to retain overall control of defence and foreign policy, but in all other respects the Austrian and Hungarian halves of the empire were to run their own affairs. This had serious consequences for the Croats: while Dalmatia was to remain in the Austrian half, the bulk of Croatia found itself in a semi-independent Hungary, thereby preventing the emergence of a unified Croatian national movement with clear goals.

Political life in **Dalmatia** after the Ausgleich was characterized by a struggle between the local branch of the Narodnjaci, who promoted Croat rights and called for the unification of Dalmatia and the rest of Croatia, and the pro-Italian Autonomaši, who argued that Dalmatia was not wholly Croat and had a distinct Latin–Slav identity of its own. The Serbs of the Dalmatian hinterland sided with the Autonomaši after the 1870s to prevent the Narodnjaci from gaining the upper hand, but by the end of the century fear of Italian designs on Dalmatia was beginning to unite Serbs and Croats of all political persuasions.

In the territories ruled by the Hungarians, there were two strands to Croatian nationalism in the second half of the nineteenth century: one emphasized the cultural similarities between all South Slavs, while the other had a more exclusively Croat perspective. The principal representative of the former strand was **Juraj Strossmayer** (1815–1905), Bishop of Đakovo and leader of the Narodnjaci, who thought that Croats and Serbs within the Habsburg Empire could unite to form a South Slav state within a federal Austria-Hungary. Strossmayer also seriously considered the possibility of Austria-Hungary's collapse, concluding that an independent Yugoslav (which literally means "South Slav" in Croatian and Serbian) state, including all Croats and Serbs and supported by Russia, would be the best solution. Strossmayer used the income from his episcopal estates to fund cultural projects, founding the Yugoslav Academy of Science and Arts in Zagreb in 1867. Opposition to Strossmayer's nascent Yugoslavism was supplied by **Ante Starčević** (1823–96), who formed the **Croatian Party of Rights** in 1861. Starčević favoured the formation of an independent Croatian state under Habsburg auspices and was suspicious of any deal with the Serbs, believing that they would never treat the Croats as equals.

Party politics in Croatia after 1867 were largely manipulated by the Ban, who was responsible to the Hungarian government in Budapest. The worst offender in this regard was Ban **Károly Khuen-Hédervàry** (1883–1903), who promoted Hungarian language and culture at the expense of Croatian, and indulged in electoral gerrymandering to secure a docile Sabor. Hédervàry was especially adept at playing off Croats against Serbs. Austria-Hungary had occupied the Ottoman province of Bosnia-Hercegovina in 1878, thus ending the *raison d'être* of the Military Frontier, which was abolished in 1881 and absorbed into Croatia, and thereby increasing the number of Orthodox Serbs in the country. The majority of these Serbs had been living peacefully with Catholic Croats for centuries, but the existence of a youthful and expanding Serbian state to the southeast gave the Serbs of Croatia a new focus of loyalty, and they increasingly turned to political parties of their own. The Hédervàry administration supported the publication of a Serb newspaper, *Srbobran*, which in 1901 ran an article which claimed that neither the Croat nation nor language really existed, and that the Serb national agenda was the only one with any future. Although by no means a reflection of what most Serbs felt, it led to anti-Serb riots in Zagreb.

A wave of anti-Hungarian protests in northern Croatia in 1903 provoked the breakdown of the Hédervàry regime, creating new political opportunities. The first sign of the so-called **New Course** in Croatian politics came with 1905's **Rijeka Resolution**, when Croatian deputies joined with the Hungarian opposition in calling for democratic reforms and the unification of Dalmatia with the rest of Croatia. Almost immediately, Serb politicians from northern Croatia and Dalmatia followed with the **Zadar Resolution**, which promised support for the aims of the Rijeka Resolution providing that the equality of Serbs in Croatia could be guaranteed. The two sides came together to form the **Croat–Serb Coalition**, which scored a resounding success in the 1906 elections to the Croatian Sabor. Faced by a hostile Sabor, successive Bans found it difficult to form a workable government. Vienna's attempts to split the Croat–Serb Coalition by accusing 53 Croatian Serbs of working secretly for the creation of a Greater Serbia merely produced the opposite effect, and became the subject of international outrage. Croatia rapidly became ungovernable after Ban Nikola Tomašić's failed attempts to manipulate the elections of 1911, and the Sabor was suspended later that year by his successor, Slavko Cuvaj.

World War I and the creation of Yugoslavia

After forty years of occupation, Austria-Hungary formally annexed Bosnia-Hercegovina in 1908, assuming responsibility for its mixed population of Catholic Croats, Orthodox Serbs and Muslim Slavs of both Serbian and Croatian stock. The annexation went down badly in Serbia, which viewed Bosnia-Hercegovina as a potential area for Serbian expansion. The ultimate goal of Serbian foreign policy – to forge a state which would include all Serbs wherever they lived, was a serious challenge to Austria-Hungary, which had a large Serbian population within its own borders. Serbian successes in the **Balkan Wars** of 1912–13, when Ottoman forces were driven out of Macedonia, increased

THE AUSTRO-HUNGARIAN EMPIRE AND THE SUCCESSOR STATES (1914-1918)

Serbian prestige, especially among those Croats who saw Serbia as the potential nucleus of a future South Slav state.

Tension between Austria-Hungary and Serbia was therefore high when Franz Josef's nephew and heir **Archduke Franz Ferdinand** was assassinated in the Bosnian capital Sarajevo on June 28, 1914, by **Gavrilo Princip**, a young Bosnian Serb who had been supplied with weapons by Serbia's chief of military intelligence. The anti-Serbian mood in Viennese court circles had achieved critical mass, and Austria-Hungary declared war on Serbia on July 28. Germany was pulled in on the Austrian side, making a response from the anti-German alliance of Russia, France and Great Britain inevitable, and **World War I** was under way.

Initially Croats fought loyally on the Habsburg side, but the longer the war went on, the clearer it became that Austria-Hungary might not survive. Faced with the possibility of a future without the Habsburgs, few Croatian politicians considered it practical to work for the establishment of an independent Croatia – such a state would be vulnerable to predatory Hungarian, Italian and Serbian neighbours. Instead they increasingly embraced the idea of **Yugoslavia** – a South Slav state which would include Serbs, Croats and Slovenes and be strong enough to stand up to outside powers. With Italy joining the Triple Entente in the hope of gaining a foothold in Dalmatia, the need to promote the Yugoslav ideal was paramount.

In 1915, veteran Dalmatian politicians Frano Supilo and Ante Trumbić, joined by sculptor Ivan Meštrović and other exiles, formed the **Yugoslav Committee** in Paris in order to lobby foreign governments and make contacts with Serbian leaders. The Serbs were initially unwilling to treat the committee as an equal partner, but negotiations culminated in the signing of the **Corfu Declaration** of

July 1917, in which both sides agreed that any future South Slav state would be a constitutional monarchy in which Serbs, Croats and Slovenes would enjoy equal rights, but which would be headed by Serbia's Karađorđević dynasty. In October 1918 the political leaders of Austria-Hungary's Serbs, Croats and Slovenes formed the **National Council** in Zagreb and declared their independence from Budapest and Vienna.

Austria-Hungary collapsed on November 3, and Italian troops landed in Dalmatia ready to stake a claim to the parts they coveted. The territory ruled by the National Council was in chaos: they had no army, bands of deserting soldiers were roaming the countryside, and fear of social revolution was rife. Desperate to restore order and keep the Italians out, the National Council rushed to declare union with Serbia on the basis of the Corfu Declaration, and the Serbian Prince Aleksandar Karađorđević declared the creation of the **Kingdom of Serbs, Croats and Slovenes** on December 1, 1918. The name "Yugoslavia" had been quietly dropped because Belgrade didn't think it sounded Serbian enough. The other areas incorporated into the new state were the Principality of Montenegro (Crna gora), which had strong ties to Serbia, and Macedonia, which had been conquered by Serbia during the Balkan Wars.

The first Yugoslavia

Many Croats entered the new state on the assumption that it would have a federal constitution which would guarantee each of its constituent peoples a degree of autonomy. Unfortunately, the leading Serb politicians of the time had other ideas. Nikola Pašić (Serbia's wartime prime minister) and Svetozar Pribićević (leader of those Serbs who had hitherto lived in Habsburg territory) were both keen to draw Croats and Slovenes into a state controlled by Serbian politicians, arguing that because large numbers of Serbs were scattered throughout Croatia and Bosnia, only a unitary state could protect their interests.

The Croats were against the idea of a unitary state because they feared that they would always be outvoted by the numerically superior Serbs, and they gravitated towards the **Croatian Republican Peasant Party (HRSS)**, a republican movement that backed the interests of farmers against the urban bourgeoisie and which was also suspicious of Serbian centralism. When elections to the new kingdom's constituent assembly took place on November 28, 1920, the HRSS won 50 of the 93 seats allocated to Croatia. HRSS leader **Stjepan Radić** claimed that the party's victory had given him a mandate to declare Croatia an independent republic, and spoke enthusiastically of replacing the Kingdom of Serbs, Croats and Slovenes with a Balkan peasant federation comprising Slovenia, Croatia, Serbia and Bulgaria (where a democratically elected pro-peasant government under Alexander Stamboliiski was already in power). Belgrade kept a lid on the situation by packing Radić off to prison and sending in the troops, but the HRSS's reputation as the main defender of Croat interests was secured.

Croatian deputies were unable to prevent the Constituent Assembly from passing the 1921 **Vidovdan Constitution**, which declared the new kingdom a unitary state and convinced many Croats that their new homeland was merely Greater Serbia under a different name. Radić immediately withdrew the HRSS from parliament and tried to raise support for the Croatian cause abroad, although Great Britain, France and the US were far too committed to the idea of a strong Yugoslavia to aid those hostile to the central government in Belgrade.

By the mid-1920s the complete freeze in relations between Belgrade and the Croatian political elite had persuaded Radić to change tack. He dropped the "R" for "Republican" from the party's name, ended the boycott of parliament and began working for Croatian autonomy rather than outright independence. He briefly served as a government minister before joining his old adversary, the Serbian Svetozar Pribićević, in forming a new opposition bloc, the **Peasant–Democratic Coalition**. The Radić–Pribićević alliance was a serious threat to the Belgrade establishment, and passions were already running high when Stjepan Radić was shot in the parliamentary chamber by the pro-Belgrade Montenegrin deputy Puniša Račić on June 20, 1928. Radić died two months later; his funeral in Zagreb was attended by 100,000 people. Fearful of further inter-ethnic violence, King Aleksandar suspended parliament and launched the **Sixth of January Dictatorship** at the beginning of 1929. The name of the state was changed to **Yugoslavia** later the same year, in the hope that an appeal to South Slav idealism might help paper over the country's cracks.

The 1930s

Radić was succeeded as leader of the HSS by **Vlatko Maček**, who broadened the party's appeal to make it a national movement representing all classes of Croats. Banned from political activity, the HSS sponsored various front organizations such as the Peasant Accord, which supported cultural activities in rural areas, and the Croatian Peasant Defence Force, a paramilitary organization which was tolerated by the government because its members occasionally beat up socialists.

One other organization that opposed the unitary nature of the Yugoslav state was the **Communist Party of Yugoslavia (KPJ)**, which despite being banned in 1920 continued to exert a strong influence over the intelligentsia. Initially the KPJ had envisaged Croatia as part of either a federal Yugoslavia or a wider Balkan confederation. In the mid-1920s it became communist policy to encourage the break-up of Yugoslavia into independent states, but by the mid-1930s the Comintern had ordered a return to the idea of a federal Yugoslavia as a potential bulwark against the rise of Nazism. It was this concept that was inherited by **Josip Broz Tito**, whom Moscow appointed leader of the KPJ in December 1937.

Diametrically opposed to communism was the **Ustaše** – a right-wing Croatian separatist organization inspired by Italian fascism and dedicated to the violent overthrow of the Yugoslav state – which had been founded by **Ante Pavelić** in 1929. Together with the similarly inclined Internal Macedonian Revolutionary Organization (IMRO), the Ustaše orchestrated the assassination of the Yugoslav King Aleksandar in Marseilles in October 1934.

Fearful that the Croat question would tear Yugoslavia apart, prime minister Milan Stojadinović tried to reach an accommodation with the HSS, relaxing the ban on its activities. Maček, however, turned to the Serbian opposition instead, joining up with the Serbian Radical and Peasant parties to put together the **Alliance for National Agreement**, which won 37.5 percent of the vote in the government-manipulated elections of 1935, rising to 44.9 percent in 1938. New Yugoslav prime minister Dragiša Cvetković was charged with the task of making a deal with the Croats amid a worsening international situation and the fear that Yugoslavia's internal weaknesses could be exploited by predatory neighbours. The result was the Cvetković–Maček Agreement, or **Sporazum**, signed on August 26, 1939, according to which an autonomous Croatian territory, the **Banovina**, was created within the borders of Yugoslavia, including all of present-day Croatia as well as those portions of western Bosnia inhabited by large numbers of Croats. Maček became deputy prime minister in the Yugoslav government, while fellow HSS leader **Ivan Šubašić** became Ban of Croatia. Inside the Banovina the HSS became the party of government, although they were supported by the Serbian Democratic Party (SDS), which represented Serbs in Croatia.

World War II

Yugoslavia initially opted for a policy of neutrality when **World War II** broke out in September 1939, although German pressure eventually forced Cvetković to sign up to the Tripartite Pact (the alliance forged by Germany, Italy and Japan) on March 25, 1941. Pro-British officers in the Yugoslav Army launched a successful coup on March 27 and denounced the pact, but most of the leading figures in the coup were Serbs, and the new regime didn't enjoy the loyalty of Croats. When the Germans declared war on Yugoslavia on April 6, resistance quickly melted away.

German troops entered Zagreb on April 10, 1941, and quickly established a puppet government, with the Ustaše declaring the formation of the **Independent State of Croatia** (**NDH**). Ustaše exiles returned home to usher in a new order on the Nazi model, with Ante Pavelić styling himself the "Poglavnik" (a Croatian rendering of "Führer") in imitation of Hitler. The rest of Yugoslavia was carved up between Germany and her allies, although a rump of Serbia was allowed to survive under German occupation. Bosnia was awarded to the NDH, although large chunks of northern and middle Dalmatia, together with the islands, were given to Italy, something for which many Croats never forgave the Ustaše. Even the NDH's own territory was split into German and Italian spheres of influence, and NDH military commanders were under the supervision of their German and Italian colleagues.

As a result of the inclusion of Bosnia, the NDH now included large numbers of Serbs and Bosnian Muslims. The Muslims were regarded as allies (some Croat historians have always regarded the Bosnian Muslims as ethnic Croats who abandoned the Catholic faith in the sixteenth century), while the Serbs were regarded as a potentially traitorous element which had to be eliminated. It soon became clear that the Ustaše's attitude to Serbs was little different from the Nazi Party's attitude to Jews. The NDH immediately embarked on three main **anti-Serbian policies**: the deportation of Croatian and Bosnian Serbs to Serbia proper, their mass conversion to Catholicism or their mass murder. It's estimated that one in six Croatian Serbs died between 1941 and 1945, many of them killed in concentration camps like Jasenovac (see p.145), where Jews, Gypsies and anti-fascist Croats were also murdered.

The sheer ferocity of the Ustaše campaign against the Serbs led to an immediate increase of resistance activity. The most important group early on were the **četniks**, Serbs loyal to the Yugoslav government in exile, who often carried out vicious revenge attacks upon Croats and Muslims, but they were soon eclipsed by Tito's communist **Partisans**, who played down ethnic differences in order to forge a popular anti-fascist movement that drew support from all races and areas of society. The collapse of Italy in September 1943 allowed the Partisans to capture weaponry and take command of large chunks of territory in Istria and Dalmatia, although they were soon chased out by the Germans. In 1944 the

Partisans were recognized by the British, who withdrew all remaining support from the četniks and persuaded the Yugoslav government in exile in London to sign an agreement recognizing Tito's authority.

The Partisans entered Zagreb on May 8, 1945. Thousands of Croatian **Domobrani** (home guardsmen), the majority of whom were no great supporters of the Ustaše, had been mobilized by Pavelić in the preceding weeks and ordered to retreat to Austria – in the hope that they could surrender to the Allies and preserve themselves as the nucleus of some future anti-communist force. The British unit that received them at the town of Bleiburg shipped them back across the border to the waiting Partisans. As many as fifty thousand of these Croatian prisoners were murdered in the weeks that followed: some were shot immediately and thrown into mass graves; others were marched to internment camps in the deep south of Yugoslavia – a journey subsequently dubbed the *Križni put* or Way of the Cross. Pavelić himself escaped to South America, and then to Spain, where he died in 1959.

Tito's Yugoslavia

The British had hoped that Tito's agreement with the Yugoslav government in exile would help preserve a degree of democracy in Yugoslavia after the war, but Tito acted swiftly to quash dissent. As the country moved towards democratic elections, most of the political parties were encouraged to join the **People's Front**, an organization dominated by the communists; those that declined were effectively prevented from campaigning. Although the ballot was nominally secret, anyone voting against the People's Front had to place their ballot papers in a separate box – sufficiently intimidating to ensure that few people took the risk. Packed with the communists and their supporters, the resulting National Assembly voted unanimously to declare Yugoslavia a republic on November 29, 1945. A new Soviet-inspired constitution was adopted, creating a federation of six national republics – Slovenia, Croatia, Bosnia-Hercegovina, Serbia, Montenegro and Macedonia. The rigid discipline of the Communist Party was to hold the whole structure together.

In Croatia, the communists' elimination of political opponents went hand in hand with an attack on the **Catholic Church**. Some members of the church hierarchy had been enthusiastic supporters of the NDH, and it wasn't difficult to discredit the whole organization using the charge of collaboration. Archbishop Stepinac (see p.82) was offered a role in the new order if he broke off links with the Vatican – and was rewarded with a sixteen-year prison sentence when he refused.

The birth of Yugoslav socialism

The Yugoslav economy was in a state of ruin in 1945, and the new government used the need for speedy reconstruction as an excuse to rush ahead with wholesale revolutionary change. Large estates were confiscated, businesses were nationalized, and a five-year plan, with the emphasis on heavy industry, was instituted. Yugoslavia's efforts to ape the USSR made it look like the model pupil, but in June 1948 Soviet leader **Josef Stalin** denounced the Yugoslav party for indulging in ideological deviations, expecting the Yugoslavs to ditch Tito and appoint a more pliant leader. With cold-war tensions rising in Europe,

it's likely that Stalin wanted to enforce unity among the communist states of Eastern Europe by making an example of Tito, the only Eastern European leader who had risen to power more or less independently of the Red Army. Yugoslavia was expelled from the Cominform, the Soviet-controlled organization of European communist countries, and the Soviets made an unsuccessful appeal to Yugoslav communists to overthrow Tito.

A period of acute tension between the two countries followed, with a very real threat of Soviet invasion. Tito responded to the crisis by protesting his loyalty to the Soviet Union, while at the same time purging members of his circle whom he suspected of being Soviet agents. On the whole, however, Tito's wartime Partisan colleagues stood by their leader, and Yugoslavia's resistance to Soviet pressure won Tito new levels of popularity both at home and abroad. Party

△ President Tito with Indian Prime Minister Jawaharlal Nehru and Egyptian President Gamal Nasser

members who sided with Stalin were dubbed "Cominformists" and shipped off to endure years of harsh treatment on the infamous Goli otok, or "Bare Island" (see box on p.286).

Stalin's economic blockade, coupled with a string of bad harvests brought about by bungled attempts at collectivization, led Yugoslavia to the brink of economic collapse. Aid from the capitalist West was gratefully received, and a drastic rethink of the country's political objectives followed. The support of industrial workers was cultivated by introducing a system of **workers' self-management**, in which all enterprises would be controlled not by the state but by the people who worked in them – on the surface, a decisive move away from Stalinism. The Communist Party itself was renamed the **Yugoslav League of Communists**, in a (largely cosmetic) attempt to suggest that it would play a less overbearing role in the country's future. The League of Communists in each republic was allowed increasing autonomy, with the personal authority of Tito and his wartime comrades holding the whole thing together. Meanwhile, Tito joined Nehru and Nasser to form the **Non-Aligned Movement** in 1961 and, although the movement itself was largely ineffective, Tito's delicate balancing act between East and West gained Yugoslavia international credibility far in excess of its size or power.

The liberalization of Yugoslav communism had its limits, however. The Montenegrin **Milovan Đilas**, federal vice-president and one of Tito's closest Partisan colleagues, was forced out of office in 1954 for suggesting that the introduction of self-management should be followed by a gradual abdication of the entire communist bureaucracy. He remained Yugoslavia's most notorious dissident – whenever Tito felt the need to improve relations with the USSR, he packed Đilas off to jail as a sign of Yugoslavia's continuing communist orthodoxy.

Throughout this period **Croatia** was in the firm grip of Tito's trusted sidekick Vladimir Bakarić, who did his best to protect Croatian interests in the Yugoslav federation without going too far. Above all, the break with the Soviet Union removed the Stalinist straitjacket, allowing Croatia to renew its spiritual and cultural links with the West. As one of the more developed republics in the federation Croatia was well placed to profit from the economic boom of the 1960s, a decade which saw real wages almost double. The relaxation of visa requirements for visitors from capitalist countries led to a **tourism explosion** on the Adriatic – although the role of Belgrade-based travel companies in creaming off the profits was always resented.

The Croatian spring

During the 1960s the quickening pace of economic liberalization created a rift between the conservative communists and their more reform-minded colleagues. Tito initially sided with the reformists, moving in 1966 to oust another of his wartime comrades, the Serb **Aleksandar Ranković**, the feared head of the secret police. Ranković was in favour of a unitary state in which the autonomy enjoyed by the republics would be strictly limited, and most non-Serb Yugoslavs were pleased to see him go. However, the expected democratization never really materialized, petering out in a morass of inter-republican disputes. The phenomenal economic growth of the 1960s also created tensions within the federation, with the developed northern republics of Slovenia and Croatia anxious to exploit their prosperity without the interference of central government.

In Croatia, growing national sentiment first expressed itself in the cultural sphere. In 1967, 130 writers and intellectuals, worried by attempts to create a single Serbo-Croatian literary language, issued a declaration – supported by the country's leading cultural organization, the **Matica Hrvatska** – stating the unique nature of the Croatian tongue. A group of Serbian intellectuals responded by saying that, if that was the case, then the Serbian minority in Croatia had the right to use their own language together with the Cyrillic script. Official bodies denounced the two declarations as being provocative, and the leaders of the Matica Hrvatska were forced to resign.

By the beginning of the 1970s, the leaders of the **Croatian League of Communists** (the Yugoslav League of Communists was divided into six republican parties) were increasingly keen to play the nationalist card, hoping to gain domestic support in bargaining with central institutions for more republican autonomy. The Matica Hrvatska itself re-emerged as a mouthpiece of nationalist opinion in 1971, drawing on the support of thousands of ordinary Croats, and when nationalists won control of the Zagreb university students' union in April 1971 the republican authorities pointedly failed to take action against them. Mixing demands for economic liberalization with calls for more republican autonomy, the ferment of ideas and debate that characterized Croatia throughout 1971 came to be dubbed the "**Croatian Spring**". In November 1971 Zagreb students went on strike, calling for opponents of reform to be sacked from the party, but Tito was by this time seriously worried that things were getting out of hand, and in December accused the Croatian leadership of not taking effective steps against nationalism and chauvinism. The leaders of the Croatian League of

Communists were forced to resign, Matica Hrvatska leaders were put on trial, and the short-lived Spring was at an end.

The 1970s

The crackdown on the Croats sounded the death-knell for liberalization all over Yugoslavia. The silencing of reformists in Serbia soon followed, and Yugoslav socialism entered a period of ideological stagnation from which it never really recovered. Tito's personal authority kept the lid on any further outbreaks of inter-republican animosity; in Croatia itself, nationalism was once more a taboo subject, while a disproportionate number of Serbs were appointed to top posts, storing up more resentment for the future. The Croatian patriotic song *Ljepa naša domovino* (Our Beautiful Homeland) was made the official hymn of the republic in 1972, but could only be performed in certain circumstances, and was never allowed to take precedence over the Yugoslav national anthem, *Hej slaveni*. Unofficial performances of the song were rewarded with a prison sentence of sixty days. Outside the country, Croatian exiles assassinated the Yugoslav ambassador to Sweden in 1971 and hijacked a TWA airliner in 1976, giving Western observers the impression that Croatian nationalism was a volatile and dangerous political force which was not to be encouraged. Tolerated by Western governments, the Yugoslav secret services sent hit squads abroad to silence the state's critics.

The 1980s

Tito died on May 4, 1980, leaving the country without an effective leader. He was replaced by an eight-man presidency in which each republic took turns to supply a head of state. The federal government was relatively weak compared with those of the individual republics, making it difficult to adopt nationwide policies capable of dealing with Yugoslavia's worsening economic problems. The economic boom of the 1960s had been financed by Western loans, but the oil-crisis-ridden 1970s had seen a drying-up of credit, leaving Yugoslavia with crippling foreign debt, galloping inflation and high unemployment.

Problems began in Kosovo, a province of southwestern Serbia which had been given autonomous status because the majority of its inhabitants were ethnic Albanians. In 1981, Albanian demonstrations in Kosovo demanding that the province be upgraded to a full republic had been put down by the army. In 1986, the Serbian Academy of Sciences issued a **Memorandum** which stated that the Serbian minority in Kosovo was under threat from Albanian nationalists, adding (without much supporting evidence) that the Serbian community in Croatia was also under pressure from Croatian cultural hegemony. The Memorandum was eagerly seized upon by Serbian intellectuals who argued that the constitution of Yugoslavia should be re-centralized in order to give the Serbs (numerically superior to the other nations) more power.

The Serbian League of Communists, loyal to the federalist ideal, was initially against the Memorandum. Then, on April 24, 1987, **Slobodan Milošević**, a little-known apparatchik recently installed as Serbian party chairman, visited the town of Kosovo Polje to meet leaders of the Serbian minority in Kosovo. When local police started jostling Serb demonstrators, Milošević intervened with the now famous words "Niko ne sme da vas bije!" ("Nobody has the right to beat you!"). Propelled to national prominence as a defender of Serbian rights, Milošević realized that nationalism was the tool with which he could remould Yugoslav communism in his own image. Using support for the Serbs in Kosovo as the issue on which all other politicians should be judged, he soon drove liberal communists out of the Serbian League of Communists, purged the Serbian media and overthrew the leadership of Vojvodina, the other province of Serbia that had been given autonomy in 1974.

Many of the Serbs who joined the mass meetings in support of Milošević mistakenly thought that they were taking part in some kind of democratic revolution: in fact, they were accessories to a neo-Stalinist putsch. In March 1989 a new Serbian constitution ended the autonomy of Kosovo and Vojvodina, while shortly afterwards Milošević supporters succeeded in winning control of the leadership of another republic, Montenegro; he also found allies in the Macedonian and Bosnian parties. Milošević hoped that this growing bloc of support would be sufficient to outvote his remaining opponents in federal institutions, thereby making it possible to recast Yugoslavia in a new and more centralized form.

In November 1989 the Berlin Wall came down. As the rest of Eastern Europe prepared for multi-party rule, the biggest republic in Yugoslavia was reverting to hardline communism. The Slovenes and Croats had to assert themselves before it was too late.

The break-up of Yugoslavia

By 1989, Slovenia, the most westernized and liberal of Yugoslavia's republics, was moving inexorably towards multi-party elections. Croatia was initially slow to follow this lead, and by the late 1980s the phrase **Hrvatska šutnja** ("Croatian silence") had been coined to describe the unwillingness of the republic's politicians to discuss the future of Yugoslavia or to champion Croatian interests. The crunch came when the Slovenes insisted on changes to the Yugoslav constitution which would guarantee the autonomy of individual republics: the Croats had to choose between supporting Slovenia or being left to the mercy of Milošević. At the last-ever congress of the Yugoslav League of Communists in January 1990, the Slovenes called for complete independence for each of the republican communist parties, a move rejected by the Serbs and their allies. The Slovene delegates walked out of the congress, followed by the Croats, who were now led by the reform-oriented **Ivica Račan**, effectively burying the Yugoslav League of Communists for good.

Democratization was moving at different speeds in different republics, however, making a smooth, pan-Yugoslav transition to non-communist rule impossible. May 1989 saw the creation of Croatia's first non-communist political organizations, among them the Croatian Democratic Union, or **HDZ**, led by former army general and dissident historian **Franjo Tuđman**. The HDZ held their first congress in February 1990, calling for Croatia's right to secede from Yugoslavia and for a reduction in the number of Serbs in Croatia's police force and state bureaucracy. This anti-Yugoslav tone caught the mood of a country increasingly frustrated by the state's failure to offer any resistance to Milošević, and the HDZ easily won Croatian **elections** in April 1990. On May 13, a football match between Dinamo Zagreb and Red Star Belgrade was abandoned on account of a three-way fight between the two sets of fans and the Serb-dominated police, worsening relations between Croatia and Serbia still further. When the Sabor met on May 30, Tuđman was sworn in as president, and Croatian "statehood" (a potential step to full independence) was declared. The HDZ's **Stipe Mešić** became Croatia's first post-communist prime minister. The Sabor immediately began work on a new **constitution**, which contained one highly controversial passage: the Serbs who lived in Croatia were no longer to be classified as one of the constituent nations of the republic, but as a national minority – a wording which caused understandable anxiety among the Serbs themselves.

The rebellion of Croatia's Serbs

Ever since Milošević's rise to power, the Serbs of Croatia (numbering 580,000 according to the 1991 census, most living in the arc of territory which ran alongside Croatia's border with Bosnia-Hercegovina) had been subjected to a Belgrade media campaign designed to make them feel endangered by their Croatian neighbours. In February 1990, the Serbian Democratic Party, or **SDS**, was formed in the largely Serbian town of Knin, just inland from Šibenik, and they soon assumed leadership of a community fearful of what might happen to them in a Croatia increasingly independent of Belgrade. On June 2 the SDS organized a referendum on autonomy for Serbs living in Croatia. The Croatian authorities banned the referendum, but weren't able to prevent it. Not surprisingly, the vote was massively in favour of autonomy.

Throughout the spring and summer of 1990 the Knin Serbs had been arming themselves with the connivance of the intelligence services in Serbia proper, aided by pro-Serb officers in the Yugoslav People's Army, the **JNA**. In July of that year the SDS declared the autonomy of the Knin region, creating the so-called **Kninska Krajina**. Barricades went up on the roads around the town, policed by paramilitary units organized by Milan Martić, the Knin police chief. Croatian authorities sent police helicopters to restore order, but they were forced back to Zagreb by Yugoslav airforce MIGs. The Krajina declared its independence from Croatia in February 1991, seeking union with Serbia. The rebellion now spread to other areas of the republic: in March, the Serb-dominated town council of Pakrac in Slavonia stated that it no longer recognized the Croatian authorities, provoking the latter to send in the police to re-establish control of the town. The JNA moved in to keep the peace. The resulting stand-off didn't produce any casualties, but Belgrade Radio reported 11 Serb deaths all the same.

The drift to war

Despite the installation of democratically elected governments in Croatia and Slovenia, the state of Yugoslavia still existed at the end of 1990, and many feared that the JNA – possibly with the connivance of Milošević – would launch a military coup to prevent its break-up. However the JNA surprised everyone by failing to act, despite numerous promptings from the Serbian leader. Sensing that the break-up of Yugoslavia was now inevitable, Milošević began instead to plan for the next best thing: the creation of a **Greater Serbia** which would include all the parts of Croatia and Bosnia-Hercegovina where Serbs lived.

Belgrade subsequently stepped up aid and encouragement to the Knin Serbs, and in March 1991 Knin paramilitaries took control of the Plitvice National Park. Croatian police units were dispatched to arrest them, and the resulting shoot-out produced the first casualties of the Serb–Croat conflict, with two Serbs and one Croat killed. The JNA moved in, ostensibly to keep the two factions apart, but in reality sealing off the area from Croatian civilian control, a pattern to be repeated elsewhere as the spring and summer progressed. On April 29 the Croat village of Kijevo near Knin was surrounded by Serb irregulars and its inhabitants were either forced to leave or shot – the first step in a campaign to **ethnically cleanse** the Serb-held parts of Croatia of any remaining Croats.

On May 17 the head of Yugoslavia's presidency, the Serb Borislav Jović, came to the end of his one-year term. The next incumbent was due to be Croatia's delegate, Stipe Mesić. Other members of the presidency were split on whether to endorse his accession: four members voted for Mesić and four against, leaving Yugoslavia without a head of state.

The Slovenes had voted for full independence from Yugoslavia in a referendum in December 1990; on May 19, 1991, the Croats followed suit. Co-ordinating their actions, both Slovenia and Croatia declared their **independence** on June 26. Yugoslav Prime Minister Ante Marković, still believing that the federation could be saved, ordered the JNA to secure the country's borders, but Slovene territorial units quickly surrounded and neutralized JNA columns, and the "war" came to an end ten days later with the EU offering to mediate. The Slovenes and Croats agreed to place a three-month moratorium on independence, while the JNA withdrew from Slovenia, and the Serbs and their allies agreed to recognize Stipe Mesić as Yugoslav president. In terms of injecting new life into Yugoslavia the agreement was meaningless – Slovenia had won de facto independence if not outright recognition, while the fate of Croatia was left to be fought over.

The war in Croatia

The withdrawal of the JNA from Slovenia meant that military strength could now be concentrated in the Serb-inhabited areas of Croatia, where low-level conflict – largely waged by Serbian irregulars against the Croatian police – dragged on through the summer. In late August the JNA and Serb irregulars launched a major offensive to gain control of eastern Slavonia, beginning with air bombardments of Vukovar and Vinkovci. In response, the newly formed Croatian National Guard began a blockade of all JNA barracks in Croatia. Areas under firm JNA and Serb control – a chain running from Knin in the southwest through the Plitvice area, Slunj, Glina and Petrinja to the environs of Pakrac in the west – were organized into the **Republic of the Serbian Krajina** (**RSK**), and Croats who lived in the region were expelled, creating almost half a million refugees. An attempt was made to cut northern Croatia off from Dalmatia by advancing towards the ports of Zadar and Šibenik, but neither city fell. In October, JNA and Montenegrin forces began the siege of **Dubrovnik**, an operation designed to weaken Croatian morale and reward Montenegro for its support of the Serbs with opportunities for territorial aggrandizement and plunder.

The Serb advance in eastern Slavonia was held up by the defenders of **Vukovar**, who displayed incredible heroism against vastly superior odds. Many believe that Zagreb could have done more to aid Vukovar's defenders, but saw a prolonged siege as a useful way of gaining international sympathy for the Croatian cause. Vukovar fell on November 18, after which the Serb–JNA forces began the bombardment of the next big city to the north, **Osijek**.

The defence of Croatia had initially been a hastily improvised affair, but as fighting continued, the Croats gradually assembled a highly motivated military force armed with weapons captured from JNA barracks. Serb advances were halted, while a counteroffensive won back portions of western Slavonia in December. Both Croatian paramilitaries and regular forces committed acts of revenge: the murder of civilians, torture of prisoners and dynamiting of Serb-owned houses was widespread throughout Croatia.

The EU made consistent attempts to bring the two warring sides to the table, however, and agreement became possible once it became clear that the Serb–JNA offensive had been stalled by tenacious Croatian defence. The **Geneva Agreement** brokered a ceasefire: the Croats agreed to end the siege of all remaining JNA barracks, and the JNA agreed to withdraw from Croatia. At the same time, a UN peace mission headed by Cyrus Vance secured the deployment of an international peacekeeping force, UNPROFOR, to police the ceasefire line. The Serbs were happy to accept this because it froze the front line at its current position, apparently confirming their territorial gains. The peacekeepers were deployed in March 1992 and the JNA departed as agreed, but gave most of its weaponry to the forces of the RSK.

Meanwhile, Croatia was emerging from its diplomatic isolation. The Germans believed that EU recognition of Slovenia and Croatia would dissuade the JNA from further aggression, and despite initial opposition from the French and British, **Croatian statehood** was recognized by all the EU countries on January 15, 1992.

The ceasefire wasn't perfect, and shells continued to fall on Osijek, Dubrovnik and other Croatian towns. Summer 1992 saw a Croatian counter-attack break the siege of Dubrovnik, and in January 1993 the Croats recaptured the area around Maslenica in northern Dalmatia, taking the pressure off Zadar. When the Croats took the Medak Pocket (Medački džep) near Gospić in September, irregular troops allegedly murdered more than 100 Serb civilians and prisoners. The international community protested at Croatia's breaches of the truce, but was too preoccupied with events in neighbouring **Bosnia** to take action.

The war in Bosnia

The ethnic balance in **Bosnia-Hercegovina** was more delicate than that of any other Yugoslav republic, with a three-way split between Serbs, Croats and Muslims. The Croats, who made up about twenty percent of the population, lived in western Hercegovina near the border with Dalmatia, where they were in the majority, and scattered among Serbs and Muslims throughout central Bosnia.

Bosnia-Hercegovina had received international recognition as an independent state at the same time as Croatia in the hope that it would discourage any attempts to partition it. In fact it had the opposite effect, and a Serbian community which wanted no part in an independent Bosnia gradually moved towards armed rebellion in spring 1992. A familiar pattern of events ensued: Serbian irregulars aided by the JNA quickly gained control of areas where Serbs lived, together with any strategic towns that potentially stood in their way, ejecting or murdering a large portion of the non-Serb population.

Initially, Bosnian Croats and Bosnian Muslims cooperated in the struggle against the Serbs, although the highly organized Bosnian-Croat army – the Croatian Defence Council or **HVO** – remained independent of the largely Muslim army of the Bosnian government in Sarajevo. With Croats and Muslims in central Bosnia increasingly squeezed by Serbian successes, the two sides started fighting each other for territory, beginning a vicious Croat–Bosnian war which began in spring 1993 and continued sporadically for a year. The conflict

△ Franjo Tuđman

was disastrous for the Croats of central Bosnia, who were forced to flee towards Hercegovina or Croatia proper. It was also disastrous for the international reputation of the Croatian state, whose support for the HVO in Bosnia led to accusations that Tuđman was as cynical as Milošević in his attempts to destroy multinational Bosnia by carving it up into ethnically pure units. Indeed, Tuđman and Milošević had discussed the possibility of dividing up Bosnia between them as early as spring 1991, and it seemed that the Croatian president – in league with the hardline Croats of Hercegovina – was prepared to sacrifice the Croats of central Bosnia in order to achieve his goal. Croatian atrocities in Bosnia – the massacre of at least 104 Muslim civilians in the village of Ahmići, the internment of Muslim men in Dretelj concentration camp and the destruction of the 500-year-old Turkish bridge at Mostar – were propaganda disasters for the Croatian cause.

The road to Dayton

In the end the Croat–Muslim conflict was brought to an end by the US, which had adopted a harder line against the Serbs since the election of President Clinton in 1992. US sympathies were primarily with the Bosnian Muslims and their besieged capital of Sarajevo, but it was widely recognized that Croat military power would have to play a part in any solution. The US-sponsored **Washington Agreement** of March 1994 created a federation of Croats and Muslims in Bosnia-Hercegovina, and an alliance between this Croat–Muslim

Federation and the state of Croatia. The Croats of western Hercegovina continued to run their territory (so-called "**Herceg-Bosna**") as if it was an independent statelet, although this was overlooked in the interests of unity.

Changes on the battlefield pushed all sides nearer to a settlement in 1995. In Croatia proper, the Croats overran the remaining portions of western Slavonia in the operation known as **Blijesak** ("Flash") on May 1–2, allowing the Croatian army to liberate Serb-held parts of Bosnia near the Croatian border. On August 4, the **Oluja** ("Storm") offensive was launched with an artillery bombardment of Knin, and the Serbian Krajina collapsed within three days. Fearing reprisals, the Serbian population fled through Serb-controlled Bosnian territory into Serbia proper. Oluja was followed by successful Croat–Muslim operations in Bosnia which, combined with NATO air strikes in September, persuaded both the Bosnian Serbs and their masters in Belgrade to seek a negotiated peace.

The war in Croatia had virtually ended with the Oluja campaign, although the Serbs remained in control of eastern Slavonia. According to the US-sponsored **Erdut Agreement**, eastern Slavonia would be governed by the UN for a transitional period before being returned to Croatia in January 1998. The war in Bosnia was formally brought to an end by the **Dayton Accords** of November 10, 1995, which created a unified Bosnian state comprising two so-called "entities": one Serbian and one Croat–Muslim. On paper, Dayton brought an end to the existence of Herceg-Bosna, but in practice it continued to lead a life quite separate from the rest of Bosnia-Hercegovina, flying Croatian flags from its public buildings and using the Croatian currency as legal tender.

Croatia after the war

The HDZ, which had come to power in 1990, was a broad movement which aimed to unify all Croats in the face of an outside menace. If it had any ideology at all, it was right-of-centre, preaching traditional family values, respect for the Catholic Church and national solidarity. The movement's creator, and Croatia's first president, **Franjo Tuđman**, was not a great admirer of Western democracy and did not want to be constrained by a strong parliament. From the start, the advisory bodies assembled by the president had more power than the Sabor or the prime minister, and policy was usually decided by Tuđman's inner circle of confidants.

The HDZ's authoritarian streak was seen as a necessary evil while the nation was fighting for its survival in 1991, but began to look increasingly anachronistic as the years progressed, while the government's actions at home and in Bosnia helped significantly to tarnish the reputation of the new nation. After 1995, Croatia dragged its feet in helping Serbs who had fled the country to return and, worse still, seemed to be providing the Croats of Hercegovina with moral support in their attempts to frustrate full implementation of the Dayton Accords, something which led the West to believe that Tuđman was still secretly working for the partition of Bosnia-Hercegovina. Croatia was threatened with UN sanctions in 1996 and again in 1999 following her refusal to extradite suspects to the Hague war crimes tribunal, while the country's unsatisfactory state of democracy – with free and fair elections rendered impossible by the fact that the state-owned TV network was a blatant government mouthpiece – ensured that Croatia was held at arm's length by the EU.

Franjo Tuđman

Franjo Tuđman was born on May 14, 1922, to a peasant family in the Zagorje village of Veliko Trgovišće, just 15km south of Kumrovec, birthplace of Tito. His father was local leader of the Croatian Peasant Party (HSS), and Franjo involved himself in left-wing politics from an early age before joining the Partisans in 1941, rising to become a political commissar in liberated territories in eastern Croatia.

After the war, Tuđman went to the Yugoslav Defence Ministry in Belgrade, working his way through the ranks before being elevated to the rank of **general** – the youngest in the army – in 1960. He also began to make his name as a **historian**, graduating in 1957 and publishing the first of his theoretical works, *Rat protiv rata* (War Against War). Resigning from the army in 1961 to concentrate on academic research, Tuđman was appointed to head the Institute for the History of the Workers' Movement. His thoughts were moving away from party orthodoxy, however, and while researching into Ustaše war crimes he became convinced that the numbers of their victims had been deliberately inflated by a regime eager to discredit Croatian nationalism.

Expelled from the Yugoslav League of Communists Central Committee and forced to leave the Institute on account of his work and views, Tuđman began to establish a reputation as a prominent **dissident** which would make him ideally placed to take advantage of the communist system's decline in the late 1980s. He was briefly imprisoned following the collapse of the Croatian Spring, and again in 1981 after giving an interview to French radio in which he spoke of Yugoslavia's need to move towards political pluralism.

Tuđman emerged from nowhere to become the leader of Croatia's anti-communist opposition in 1989. His big idea was the **Pomirba** (best translated as a "setting aside of old scores"), which emphasized the coming together of all strands of Croatian opinion – from Partisan to Ustaše – to build a new patriotic consensus that could stand up to Belgrade. In part this was a pragmatic move which allowed Tuđman to tap the financial resources of right-wing exiles, but it also reflected his own personal journey from left-wing idealist to **social conservative**. An over-readiness to accommodate the far right was a weakness of the Tuđman regime from beginning to end. At the HDZ's first congress in 1990 Tuđman described the NDH (the fascist puppet regime which ruled Croatia during World War II), as an authentic expression of Croatia's yearning for independent statehood, and during the 1990 election campaign notoriously stated "Thank God my wife is neither a Serb nor a Jew", an opinion he never retracted.

Tuđman's other major hobby horse was the unviability of Bosnia-Hercegovina as an independent state. He had always regarded the **division of Bosnia** between himself and Milošević as a potential way of settling Serbian and Croatian differences, and even had negotiations with the Serb leader to this effect in March 1991. Many people in Croatia proper opposed Tuđman's support for the Hercegovinian Croats in the Bosnian Croat–Muslim war of 1993–94, and Croats from Hercegovina – where Croatian nationalism was traditionally purer than anywhere else – rose to positions of prominence and power under Tuđman far out of proportion with their actual numbers.

Tuđman demanded deference from his subjects, donning a red, white and blue sash whenever attending official functions, and appearing in a white uniform to receive the salute at military parades – prompting criticisms that he was becoming another Tito. Debate about whether members of his family personally profited from the kind of dodgy business deals that characterized the Croatian economy in the 1990s still continues.

When Tuđman **died**, however, thousands of ordinary Croats headed for the presidential palace to file past the coffin. He was still seen as the man who had stiffened Croatian resolve during the dark days of 1991–92, winning the country international recognition as an independent state for the first time since the Middle Ages. The final, damning verdict on the political system he had built was delivered at the general election barely one month later.

In the meantime, daily life for many Croats was becoming increasingly hard. The country ended the decade with twenty percent unemployment, an average wage of around $400 a month and many companies unable to pay salaries with any regularity.

The January 2000 elections

It had been an open secret that Tuđman had been ill with cancer since 1996, but he chose not to designate a successor, preferring to remain in sole charge until the end. The HDZ – by now lacking any coherent political ideology – began to resemble a collection of warring factions rather than a party. The opposition parties on the other hand were beginning to unite around the need to defeat the HDZ at the next elections, which were scheduled for December 1999. By the autumn of that year, an anti-HDZ grouping led by the SDP (former communists who had re-branded themselves as Social Democrats) and the HSLS (right-of-centre liberals) had banded together to form a coalition.

Tuđman entered hospital at the beginning of November 1999, and died on December 10. A genuine outpouring of popular grief ensued, but the HDZ had lost the one talismanic figure who could persuade Croats, out of a sense of loyalty if nothing else, to keep the party in power. The elections were put off until January 4, 2000, in the hope that the festive season would knock the wind out of the opposition's sails, with Croatian national television unleashing hitherto unseen levels of pro-HDZ bias. It was all to no avail however, as the SDP–HSLS coalition won a staggering 52 percent of the vote, against the HDZ's 24 percent. The SDP's **Ivica Račan,** the uninspiring technocrat who had previously served as reformist head of the Croatian League of Communists, became prime minister, while HSLS leader **Dražen Budiša** (student leader during the Croatian Spring; see p.497) set his sights on the presidential elections due in three weeks' time. In the event he was surprisingly beaten by another centrist candidate **Stipe Mesić**, the jocular charmer who had once served as the unenthusiastic president of a dying Yugoslavia. A former HDZ leader who had split with Tuđman over the latter's policies in Bosnia-Hercegovina, Mesić had spent the intervening years amassing solid liberal-democratic credentials. His election was received with glee by an international community eager for proof that Croatia was moving in a decidedly pro-Western direction.

Croatia's diplomatic position began to improve almost overnight. The HDZ defeat seemed to mark the end of the Croatian government's support for the hardline nationalists of Hercegovina, and also held out the possibility of a more conciliatory attitude towards Croatia's Serbs. Mesić seemed keen to strip himself of some of the presidential trappings adopted by Tuđman, giving the Sabor and the prime minister more real power.

The post-Tuđman era

Despite an increase in foreign investment and a boom in sectors of the economy such as tourism and real estate, the vast majority of Croats didn't experience any appreciable rise in living standards during the Račan administration's four-year term. Agriculture and heavy industry still struggled to pay their way, especially with the country opening up to more and more outside competition. However the biggest strain on the government came from the demands made on it by the **International War Crimes Tribunal** in the Hague – an institution with which

Croatia had to cooperate in order to be accepted as a candidate for EU and NATO membership. Most Croats accepted that individuals had committed atrocities during the 1991–95 war, but expected the Hague to concentrate on rounding up prominent Serbian perpetrators rather than focusing attention on Croatian suspects.

The first signs of a crisis came in February 2001, when international warrants were issued for the arrest of General **Mirko Norac**, suspected of overseeing the murder of Serbs in Gospić in 1991. The government's eagerness to extradite Norac (who initially evaded arrest by going into hiding) split Croatian society down the middle, with some arguing that the honour of the country would be best served by complying with international demands, others claiming that the memory of Croatia's wartime struggle would be irreparably tarnished by subjecting decorated officers to the jurisdiction of foreign courts. Things got worse in July of that year, when the Hague put popular general **Ante Gotovina** on its wanted list – Gotovina was an officer-in-charge during the Oluja campaigns of 1995, when numerous atrocities are alleged to have taken place. Gotovina promptly went into hiding. Prime minister Račan and President Mesić were left with the awkward task of reassuring the international community of Croatia's long-term commitment to the Hague court, while at the same time retaining the support of patriotic opinion at home.

The Hague controversy left Račan in charge of a coalition seriously weakened by defections to the opposition, and played into the hands of the HDZ – who denounced Mesić and Račan as traitors and presented themselves as the true guardians of patriotic values. However, HDZ leaders studiously avoided direct links with the right-wing groups who organized mass demonstrations in Norac and Gotovina's defence, preferring instead to project a moderate image more in keeping with the modern conservative parties of Western Europe than the HDZ of old. Aware that Croatian voters were more interested in managerial competence than ideological extremes, new HDZ leader **Ivo Sanader** ditched many of the hard-liners of the Tuđman era and promoted competent technocrats in their place.

The HDZ emerged from the **parliamentary elections** of November 2003 as the single largest party in the Sabor. A coalition agreement with smaller centrist parties soon confirmed Sanader as the new prime minister. Despite a few changes of emphasis however, the main themes of post-Tuđman politics – economic reform at home and candidature for both the EU and NATO – remained essentially unchanged. Despite its earlier support for war crimes suspects, the HDZ in government showed more willingness in cooperating with the Hague tribunal than anyone expected. Croatia's relations with the outside world followed a relatively problem-free course as a result, a petty dispute with Slovenia over maritime borders being the only exception.

The peaceful post-Tuđman changeover from HDZ to SDP and back again seemed to confirm that Croatia was becoming an ordinary European democracy. In January 2005 the popular centrist Stipe Mesić won another five-year term in **presidential elections** that were only half-heartedly contested by the SDP and HDZ – further evidence of Croatia's entry into a post-ideological era of consensus politics.

Runaway General Ante Gotovina was apprehended and delivered to the Hague Tribunal in 2005, removing the last major obstacle to Croatia's full integration into Western organizations. Negotiations with the EU are picking up speed, although a concrete timetable for Croatia's accession is yet to be set. Croatian membership of NATO is also a realistic goal by the end of the decade.

Croatian folk music

Croatian folk music (*narodna glazba or narodna muzika*) is as diverse as you would expect from a country poised between the cultural worlds of the Mediterranean, central Europe and the Balkans. Traditional music still forms a part of everyday life in many towns and villages, with local folklore societies preserving knowledge of songs and dances long associated with weddings, feasts and seasonal merrymaking. A good deal of folk culture has filtered through into the commercial mainstream, producing a style of pop in some ways similar to country and western in the US – many of the tunes hark back to traditional melodies, but everything else is pure showbiz.

One of the best ways to hear folk music in Croatia is to catch one of the concerts given by the various folklore societies. **Lado**, based in Zagreb, is the state's one professional troupe, performing songs and dances from all over Croatia. All the other folklore ensembles comprise amateur enthusiasts and are likely to concentrate on a more regional repertoire. The biggest of these regional ensembles, Dubrovnik's **Linđo**, has a reputation comparable with that of Lado, and often plays a part in the city's annual arts festival.

There's quite a range of folk-related festivals (see p.50), but the biggest single folk event is Zagreb's **International Folklore Festival** (Međunarodna smotra folklora; ⓦwww.msf.hr), which brings together an array of performers from all over the country alongside international guests. The cultural happenings arranged in tourist resorts throughout the summer always include at least some traditional music, and package hotels often lay on performances for their guests. Otherwise, look out for Croatian **weddings**, which usually take place on Saturdays and often involve celebrants gathering in a town park or square to be serenaded by traditional musicians.

Slavonia and the tamburica

The indigenous folk music of eastern Croatia, particularly Slavonia, has grown to dominate Croatian music over the last century and a half. It's characterized by the tambura (more commonly known by its diminutive form, **tamburica**), a lute-like instrument which is plucked or strummed to produce a sound not dissimilar to that of a mandolin.

Originally of Anatolian origin, the tamburica was brought to southeastern Europe by the Ottoman Turks in the fourteenth and fifteenth centuries. The instrument was gradually taken up by the local Slav population, whose frequent migrations (often between Ottoman and Habsburg lands) helped spread it still further. By the nineteenth century, the tamburica was the most common folk instrument throughout both eastern Croatia and the northern Serb province of Vojvodina.

Because the instrument was popular with both Croats and Serbs, it was championed in the mid-nineteenth century by the Illyrian movement (see p.487), a Zagreb-based group of intellectuals who aimed to promote South Slav unity. As the nineteenth century progressed, the tamburica was increasingly seen as a symbol of an indigenous culture under threat from the dominant Germanic and Hungarian influences of the Habsburg Empire. Tamburica orchestras were

△ Dubrovnik Folk Music Festival

formed in Croatian towns and cities to play popular folk tunes, concentrating on the jolly, rhythmic melodies that often accompanied rural merrymaking. These orchestras often featured a lot of tamburica players playing in unison, creating a wall of thrumming sound which has remained a feature of tamburica music ever since; they also regularly provided the music for village dances at which locals performed the *kolo* – a local variant of the circle dances found throughout south-eastern Europe.

In the twentieth century the Slavonian sound increasingly came to symbolize Croatia as a whole. The Croatian Peasant Party, the main voice for Croatian aspirations during the 1920s and 1930s, promoted the music as a way of renewing village cultural life, and it also grew in significance among the many Croatian émigrés in North America, for whom it was an important link with the homeland.

Remaining popular through the Yugoslav period, tamburica music was increasingly dragged into the commercial mainstream in the 1980s, when a new generation of tamburica bands began to mix folk melodies with a modern pop sound. Foremost among these were **Zlatni Dukati** (The Golden Ducats), who mixed tamburicas with electric bass and guitar and were initially popular with Serbs in Vojvodina as well as Croats throughout Croatia. Other tamburica-pop bands have followed in Zlatni Dukati's footsteps, most notably **Gazde** (The Bosses), who ditched the folksy costumes traditionally associated with the tamburica scene in favour of a leather-clad rockabilly image, and developed a similarly modified, pop-rock-influenced sound.

The need for morale-boosting popular music heavily flavoured with indigenous folk motifs led to an explosion of tamburica music during the early 1990s. A decade and a half later, tamburica music is no longer the ever-present force it once was, although it still forms the staple diet of radio stations in the east of the country. Performances by traditional-style tamburica orchestras remains a major feature of big Slavonian folk festivals such as Brodsko Kolo (see p.160), Đakovački vezovi (p.162) and Vinkovačka jesen.

Other inland Croatian music

The ubiquity of tamburica music has tended to overshadow the other musical traditions of inland Croatia, especially in Slavonia itself, where many local instruments (such as the *gajde* and *dude*, both local types of bagpipe) have almost totally died out.

The music of the **Zagreb region** and the **Zagorje** centres on the polkas and waltzes common to central Europe. There's a strong tradition of brass-band music here too, although more common are the four- or five-piece string bands that you'll see playing at weddings or in restaurants, usually featuring double bass, a couple of violins and a guitar or tamburica.

The traditional sounds of the area **southwest of Zagreb** couldn't be more different, having more in common with the Balkan south than with any part of central Europe. Arid mountain regions such as Lika and Hercegovina (the latter, although forming part of Bosnia-Hercegovina, is predominantly populated by Croats) are home to a harsh and dissonant form of polyphonic singing known as *ojkanje* (characterized by the ululating "oy" sound at the end of every line) or *gange*. Unaccompanied *gange* songs are traditionally performed at village festivities, and even now are rarely performed in concerts. As in Slavonia, the *kolo* is more popular in these highland areas than dancing in pairs. A form of *kolo* typical to the region is the *nijemo kolo*, or "dumb kolo", a dance performed without music, the only sound coming from the whirling and stamping of the dancers themselves. A particularly acrobatic form of this is the **Vrlićko** *kolo* from Vrlika, a town inland from Šibenik, in which dancers hang onto each other by their belts and swing each other into the air.

The music of the **Međimurje**, in the far northeast of Croatia, has much in common with the music of neighbouring Hungary, with lilting melodies accompanied by a string band and occasionally a zither or a cimbalom. There's also a strong tradition of unaccompanied narrative songs sung by women, including many tales of unrequited love featuring, oddly enough, railway stations, at which village boys waved goodbye to their sweethearts before going off to serve with the Austro-Hungarian army. Many of these were rediscovered in the early twentieth century, when the folklorist Vinko Žganec started systematically transcribing them. The songbooks produced by Žganec were plundered by a new generation of folk singers in the 1980s and 1990s, although there's always been a question mark about their authenticity: Žganec asked local organist Florijan Andrašec to help him collect traditional tunes, paying him for every new song he came up with – it's believed Andrašec made up many songs himself to earn extra cash.

The coast

Traditionally, the music of rural **Dalmatia** revolved around two-part songs on heroic or tragic themes, mostly sung by women. Although these still survive in some places, the tradition was superseded in the last century by the growth of the male-voice choir, or **klapa**. Today almost every town or village has a *klapa*, which usually consists of up to ten members and performs smoothly harmonized songs of a sentimental nature. Some *klape* sound like barbershop quartets;

others have a raw feeling reminiscent of male polyphonic singing from Corsica or Georgia. Many Dalmatian towns hold *klapa* festivals in the summer – the most famous is at Omiš, just south of Split, in July. Farther south, towards **Dubrovnik**, a three-string fiddle known as the *lirica* provides droning accompaniment to dances such as the *linđo* (an ancient courtship dance), which you'll still see performed outside Čilipi church on Sunday mornings.

Utterly different is the startling music of the **Istrian peninsula**, which uses a distinctive local scale (the *istarska ljestvica*). A lot of Istrian songs employ two-part harmonies which sound discordant to the average non-Istrian ear, and this singing style has given rise to an entire body of instruments dedicated to reproducing such harmonies. Prominent among these are the *sopila*, a large oboe which is always played in pairs; the *šurla*, which consists of two pipes with a single mouthpiece, allowing a single musician to play two parts; and the *mijeh* (also known as *meh* or *mih*), a bagpipe made from the bladder of a young goat. Istrian styles of singing and bagpipe playing are also found on the **Kvarner Gulf** islands of Cres, Krk and Rab. The most exciting exponent of Istrian music today is the *sopila* player Dario Marušić, who brings a modern-jazz sensibility to bear on a selection of raucous, uneasy-listening traditional tunes. His albums are hard to get hold of, but he does feature on the *Ethno Ambient Live: Salona 98* CD (see opposite).

New sounds

The last decade or so has seen an increasing hybridization of Croatian roots music, with a string of performers attempting to breathe new life into traditional forms with studio technology or new musical styles. Most of them have drawn inspiration from the fringe areas of Croatian folk (notably Međimurje and Istria), as if consciously offering an alternative to the monopoly of mainstream tamburica-pop.

First off the mark were **Vještice** (The Witches), formed in 1988 by veterans of the Zagreb New Wave scene, who created a whole new audience for traditional music by performing Međimurje folk songs in alternative rock style. This interest in the music of northeastern Croatia was picked up in the early 1990s by **Dunja Knebl** (Ⓦwww.dunjaknebl.com), a Zagreb woman who didn't start singing professionally until already in her mid-40s, fired by enthusiasm for the newly fashionable Međimurje songs. Around the same time, the younger Međimurje-born singer-songwriter **Lidija Bajuk** was moving in a similar direction. Both Knebl and Bajuk had grown up listening to acoustic-guitar-wielding folkies from Joan Baez onwards, and their interpretations of traditional Croatian songs have an uncomplicated accessibility – without losing too much of the other-worldly strangeness of the originals.

The mid-1990s also saw the emergence of **Legen**, an ambitious techno-folk crossover act using synthesizers and samples to soup up folk in the manner of Transglobal Underground or Loop Guru, though with less danceable results. Legen tried to put the mystery back into Croatian folk, building their repertoire around songs celebrating seasonal rites with pagan undertones – such as St George's Day fertility rituals, or the St John's Day bonfires which still take place in many parts of the country. Legen broke up in 2001, and lead singer Mojmir Novaković took his ethno-electronic obsessions one step further with new band **Kries** (Ⓦwww.kries.info) – their 2004 album *Ivo i Mara* is the most successful

Discography

Many of the Croatia-only releases listed below are available from the **online record store** at ⓦwww.croart.com.

Afion *Afion* (Aquarius, Croatia). Traditional songs from Croatia, Macedonia and farther afield, given a startlingly successful jazz-folk makeover by Croatia's best young band. Not as gutsy as their live performances, but an exceedingly promising debut all the same.

Miroslav Evačić *Čardaš Blues* (Scardona, Croatia). Country-and-southeastern music from the Pannonian plain, with a bittersweet collection of traditional standards and folk-influenced songs, delivered with lashings of slide guitar and cimbalom.

• **Gustafi** *Freak Folk* (Dancing Bear, Croatia). Infectious Istrian-Reggae-Latino fiesta music from Croatia's most exhilarating band. The 2003 album *Na minimumu*, and 1999's **Vračamo** *se odmah* (both Dancing Bear) are worth checking out too.

• **Dunja Knebl** *Iz globline srca/From the Heart of Hearts* (Dancing Bear, Croatia). Haunting, mysterious folk songs from Međimurje performed by the angelic-sounding Knebl mostly to simple acoustic-guitar backing. Decent English–Croatian sleeve-notes too. If you like what you hear, then subsequent albums *Da sam barem guska/Over There*, *Četiri Frtalji* and *Polje široko, nebo visoko* (all Dancing Bear) feature more of the same.

• **Mojmir Novaković i Kries** *Ivo i Mara* (Kopito, Croatia). Stentorian-voiced former Legen frontman Novaković returns with a rousing collection of bittersweet traditional melodies, eerie vocal harmonies and bone-crunching rhythms.

• **Tamara Obrovac** *Sve pasiva* (Crno Bijeli Svijet, Croatia). Multilayered collection of songs released in 2003 by the Pula-based Obrovac, blending jazzy textures with the folk music of the Istrian interior. Her other releases *Daleko is faraway* (2005), *Transhistria* (2001) and *Ulika* (1998) bring together some of the best folk and jazz musicians in central Europe.

Compilations

• *Croatian Folksongs and Dances* (Harmonia Mundi/Quintana, France). Music from Croatian communities in south Hungary in archive recordings made mostly in the 1950s and 1960s. Some really archaic songs are included, alongside excellent fiddle playing from renowned virtuoso Stipan Pavkovics and lots of good tamburica bands, notably the Pavo Yimora Baraban orchestra from Felsöszentmárton, still a centre of tamburica music today. Most of the bands have a vital raw sound, rather than showy glitz.

• *Croatie: musiques d'autrefois* (Ocora, France). Survey of traditional songs and instrumental music taken from Croatian radio archives between 1958 and 1993. Divided into regional areas, it begins with some Međimurje songs and includes plenty of good tamburica bands and Dalmatian *klapa* singing.

• *Croatie: musiques traditionelles d'aujourd'hui* (Auvidis/Unesco, France). This excellent record, compiled with the help of the Institute of Ethnology and Folklore Research in Zagreb, documents practically the whole range of Croatian music, from obscure offerings that you would be fortunate ever to hear to the sort of commercial and sentimental songs you'd be lucky to avoid. Featuring music from Istria, Međimurje, Slavonia and Dalmatia, this is undoubtedly the best place to start exploring Croatia's music, while the informative sleeve notes can point those interested in learning more in the right direction.

• *Village Music from Yugoslavia* (Elektra-Nonesuch, US). Despite the misleading subtitle "Songs and Dances from Bosnia-Hercegovina, Croatia and Macedonia", this is all Croatian music, except for one Macedonian track. Excellent songs from village performers and dance music from typical tamburica bands.

combination of traditional culture and computer programming yet to come out of the country.

One not-so-traditional vocalist who found her way onto *Ethno Ambient Live: Salona 98* was jazz siren **Tamara Obrovac**, who draws inspiration from Istrian melodies – lullabies and harvest-time songs rather than the ear-bending stuff – to produce an intriguing folk-jazz hybrid, featuring rolling, part-improvised songs sung in Istrian dialect. As well as launching the annual Istria Ethno Jazz festival, Obrovac has released a string of critically acclaimed albums, with 2003's *Sve Pasiva*, a seamlessly accomplished exercise in jazz-roots fusion, winning Obrovac a nomination for Best European Act in the 2004 BBC World Music Awards.

Also picking up international attention is **Miroslav Evačić**, whose blend of blues and Croatian-Hungarian borderland music is currently one of central Europe's most intriguing hybrids. One of Croatia's more maverick groups is Pula-based **Gustafi**, who began as a new wave rock band before metamorphosing into an accordion-driven Mexican–Istrian crossover act that defies categorization. Their irreverent, eclectic approach seems to have rubbed off on other acts such as the Zagreb group **Cinkuši**, who perform traditional north Croatian songs with a wilfully non-traditional choice of instruments, including Mediterranean mandolin and African djembe drums. Cinkuši were influential in bringing self-taught Međimurje singer **Teta Liza** ("Auntie Liza") to a wider audience, serving as backing band on her traditional-leaning CD *Moje Međimurje*.

Evidence that Croatian roots music is showing interest in other world-music traditions is provided by young Zagreb group **Afion**, who perform Croatian, Macedonian and Armenian songs using an alchemic blend of double bass, jazzy flute, muscular percussion and strong vocal harmonies. Already packing out clubs in Zagreb, they seemed destined to become Croatia's most exportable musical product.

Books

There's a dearth of good books about Croatia in the English language. Many of the most entertaining accounts are by nineteenth-century travellers to the Adriatic though, sadly, their books are often only available from larger public libraries or specialist book dealers. The number of publications devoted to the break-up of the former Yugoslavia is considerable: we've listed the best of them, rather than trying to offer an exhaustive survey of the entire field. In the reviews that follow, "o/p" means out of print; titles marked ★ are especially recommended.

Travel writing

Abbé Alberto Fortis *Travels into Dalmatia* (o/p). Classic eighteenth-century travelogue written by an Italian priest and containing a mine of historical anecdote and observations. Fortis's tendency to romanticize the simple and brutish lifestyles of the locals exerted a strong influence over subsequent generations of travel writers.

T.G. Jackson *Dalmatia, the Quarnero and Istria* (o/p). First published in 1887, this is an illuminating and exhaustive three-volume guide to the architecture of the Adriatic coast, with sizeable dollops of history and reportage en route.

A.A. Paton *Highlands and Islands of the Adriatic* (o/p). Record of a journey made in 1846–47 with the usual mixture of historical anecdote and firsthand description. Very good for local colour, and especially strong on social life in nineteenth-century Split and Dubrovnik. Paton finished his life as the British consul in Dubrovnik – his grave can still be seen in the cemetery on Liechtensteinov put.

★ **Rebecca West** *Black Lamb and Grey Falcon*. Classic travel book based on West's journey through Yugoslavia in the 1930s. Mixing opinionated observations with character sketches and extensive forays into history, this is definitely an acquired taste, particularly the sweeping generalizations about the Balkan Slavs, about whom West has a tendency to be over-rhapsodic. The first quarter of the book covers Croatia, after which the intrepid author moves on to Bosnia, Serbia, Macedonia and Montenegro.

Sonia Wild Bićanić *British Travellers in Dalmatia* 1757–1935 (Fraktura, Zagreb). Lively account of the intrepid Adriatic expeditions of A.A. Paton, T.G Jackson and others, including many insightful observations from an author who knows the territory well. Available from bookshops in Croatia.

History and politics

Phyllis Auty *Tito* (o/p). Originally researched when the dictator was still alive, this book is over-deferential towards its subject and offers little in the way of salacious gossip. However it's still the best available chronology of the man and his career, and works quite well as a general history of twentieth-century Yugoslavia.

Ivo Banac *The National Question in Yugoslavia*. Absorbing history of the competing currents of Croatian nationalism, Serbian nationalism and Yugoslavism, culminating with the Vidovdan Constitution of 1921.

Catherine Wendy Bracewell *The Uskoks of Senj: Piracy, Banditry and Holy War in the Sixteenth-century Adriatic*. Definitive and scholarly account of the Uskoks, which lays to rest some of the more romantic myths surrounding their freebooting activities. It's also an excellent introduction to sixteenth-century Adriatic life in general.

Milovan Djilas *Tito: the Story from Inside* (o/p). Montenegrin communist Djilas was Tito's right-hand man in the 1940s, before falling foul of the regime and becoming Yugoslavia's most celebrated dissident. As lighthearted as it is bitter, this is an entertaining series of digressions on the nature of power rather than a straightforward biography. The same author's *Conversations with Stalin* and *The New Class* offer further insights into the workings of the communist mind.

Ivo Goldstein *Croatia*. Sober, impartial overview of Croatian history from the earliest times to the present day, written by a leading medievalist at Zagreb University.

Tim Judah *The Serbs*. Excellent analysis of the main themes in Serbian history, providing illuminating background to Serbia's central role in all the Balkan conflicts of the 1990s. The same author's *Kosovo: War and Revenge* takes the story up to NATO's campaign against Belgrade in 1999.

Bariša Krekić *Dubrovnik in the 14th and 15th Centuries: a city between east and west* (o/p). Probably the best English-language introduction to Dubrovnik's golden age, if you can find it.

John R. Lampe *Yugoslavia as History*. If a general account of Yugoslavia and its peoples is what you're looking for, then this is the best place to start – the author has carefully sifted all the existing scholarship on the subject to produce an objective, accessible history.

Michael McConville *A Small War in the Balkans* (o/p). Chapter and verse on British commando campaigns in the former Yugoslavia during World War II, written – with an eye for telling detail rather than dewy-eyed nostalgia – by one of the old soldiers themselves.

Marcus Tanner *Croatia: a Nation Forged in War*. The best general history of Croatia currently available. Balanced, thorough, and written with enthusiasm and verve by an *Independent* journalist who observed Yugoslavia's disintegration at first hand.

The break-up of Yugoslavia

Mark Almond *Europe's Backyard War*. Well-informed analysis of Yugoslavia's break-up written by an academic historian. It's broadly sympathetic to the Croatian cause, and Almond's most forceful prose is directed against the cynicism of Serbian policy and the hapless blundering of the Western powers.

Christopher Bennett *Yugoslavia's Bloody Collapse*. Scholarly and informed account from a journalist who was in Yugoslavia when war broke out. His central thesis – that Yugoslavia's break-up was far from inevitable until the rise of Serbian national communism under Milošević – is convincingly argued.

Misha Glenny *The Fall of Yugoslavia*. Vivid and often moving front-line reportage of the conflict by the BBC's former central Europe correspondent. The book is regarded by some Croat observers as being pro-Serb – a tribute to Glenny's impassioned objectivity. The same author's *The Balkans* is a compendious account of southeastern European history from the early nineteenth century onwards, in which Croatia plays a walk-on part. It's sometimes too wide-ranging for its own good, but Glenny's attempt to explain the history of the Balkans – and the outside world's meddling in Balkan affairs – is consistently readable and thought-provoking.

Brian Hall *The Impossible Country*. Hall travelled through Croatia, Serbia and other parts of Yugoslavia during the summer of 1991, just as the country was beginning to fall apart. As well as being a studiously impartial observer, he is an excellent writer, historically informed, witty and humane, and the result is one of the most compelling accounts of the last days of Yugoslavia you will find.

Branka Magaš *The Destruction of Yugoslavia: Tracking the Break-up 1980–1992* (o/p). Collection of essays and articles written by a veteran Yugoslavia-watcher. Not much on Croatia, but excellent analysis of Milošević's rise and his single-handed demolition of Yugoslav federalism.

Alec Russell *Prejudice and Plum Brandy*. Wide-ranging Balkan reportage from the Romanian revolution to the Yugoslav break-up, including a revealing eye-witness account of the siege of Dubrovnik, when the author was holed up in the *Hotel Argentina*.

Louis Sell *Slobodan Milošević and the Destruction of Yugoslavia*. Incisive biography of the man who single-handedly destroyed the Yugoslav ideal while blithely claiming to defend it. Written by a former US diplomat who observed Milošević at close quarters.

Brendan Simms *Unfinest Hour: Britain and the Destruction of Bosnia*. Masterly dissection of the cynicism, incompetence and pure intellectual cowardice that characterized British policy towards the former Yugoslavia in the 1990s. Simms convincingly argues that British dithering was crucial in prolonging the Bosnian war (and the misery of its inhabitants), although he rejects the theory – popular among Croatian nationalists – that the British secret services deliberately stoked the conflict between Bosnia's Croats and Muslims.

Laura Silber and Alan Little *The Death of Yugoslavia* (UK)/ *Yugoslavia: Death of a Nation* (US). Combining journalistic immediacy with prodigious research, this is by far the best blow-by-blow account of the war, although it sheds little light on the long-term causes of Yugoslavia's demise. The authors had access to many of the key players in the events described, resulting in a wealth of revealing quotes.

Mark Thompson *A Paper House*. Thompson travelled throughout Yugoslavia on the eve of its break-up to produce this insightful book, part travelogue, part analysis of a fragmenting society. The same author's *Forging War: the Media in Croatia, Serbia, Bosnia and Hercegovina* examines the role of the Yugoslav press in stoking ethnic hatred.

Croatian literature

Ivo Andrić *The Bridge on the Drina*. A Croat who grew up in Bosnia and wrote in the Serbian literary language, Andrić left a vast body of work which currently lies unclaimed by any of Yugoslavia's successor states – despite the fact that he won the Nobel Prize for Literature in 1960. A complex, generation-spanning narrative set in Bosnia under the Ottoman Empire, this book is typical of Andrić's oeuvre.

Slavenka Drakulić *As If I Was Not There* (UK)/*A Novel About the Balkans* (US). Unflinching, often harrowing novel about a Bosnian woman's experience of life in a Serbian internment camp, written by one of Croatia's leading novelists. Drakulić's previous novel, *The Taste of a Man*, couldn't be more different, dealing with love and cannibalism in New York. Earlier works *Marble Skin* and *Holograms of Fear* are short on plot, but offer powerful meditations on sensuality and mortality respectively. Drakulić's book of essays, *Café Europa*, eloquently captures the author's dismay at the flowering of nationalism in the former Yugoslavia.

Miljenko Jergović *Sarajevo Marlboro*. A Bosnian Croat who grew up in Sarajevo and currently lives in Zagreb, Jergović is one of Croatia's most productive novelists, essayists and magazine feature-writers. This sparkling collection of short stories recounts Balkan lives, loves and tragedies with the kind of wry, self-deprecating humour that's typical of the city in the title.

Miroslav Krleža *The Return of Philip Latinowicz*. The best-known novel by Croatia's leading twentieth-century writer, in which a painter returns home to a provincial Slavonian town sometime in the 1920s and embarks on an affair which ends in tragedy. Intended as a dissection of Croatia's directionless upper classes in the wake of World War I, it's not as powerful as his *On the Edge of Reason*, set in the same period, which convincingly preaches the message that bourgeois society is a form of self-deluding madness, but to rebel against it drives you insane.

Slobodan Novak *Gold, Frankincense and Myrrh* (o/p). A difficult but rewarding read, this sombre, meditative study of a man looking after his sick and elderly mother one winter on the island of Rab was highly regarded in Yugoslavia when it was first published in the 1970s.

Dubravka Ugrešić *The Museum of Unconditional Surrender*. Dismayed by Croatia's descent into right-wing authoritarianism, Ugrešić spent most of the 1990s living outside Croatia, and this largely autobiographical novel is a powerful meditation on memory and exile. By the same author, the heavyweight collection of essays *Culture of Lies* is an essential read for anyone interested in the negative side of Croatian culture and nationalism in the 1990s.

Language

Language

Croatian

Croatian is a difficult language to learn, and the locals rarely expect anyone to bother, making them all the more pleasantly surprised if you make the effort to learn a few phrases. The vast majority of Croatians speak at least one foreign language: most people – especially the young – understand some English, while German and Italian are also widely spoken on the coast.

Croats, Serbs and Bosnians can understand one another perfectly well, despite developing separate literary languages at different times in their history; Croatian, Serbian and Bosnian are usually regarded as dialects of a single Slavonic language described by linguists as **Croato-Serbian** or **Serbo-Croat** (although native speakers hardly ever use either description themselves). That said, each community has preserved its own linguistic idiosyncracies, even in areas where they have lived side by side for generations.

You'll find variations in **dialect** all over Croatia itself, the principal ones being named after the three different ways of saying "what?" – *kaj?*, *ča?* and *što?* In Zagreb and the Zagorje people speak *kajkavski*, because of their use of the word *kaj* for "what", while on the Adriatic coast people speak *čakavski*, and in Hercegovina and Slavonia *štokavski*. The literary language is based on *štokavski*, and although the other dialects are heard on the streets, they don't feature on the radio, TV or in newspapers – except in a humorous context.

The best of the **self-study courses** available are *Colloquial Croatian and Serbian* by Celia Hawkesworth (Routledge), closely followed by *Teach Yourself Serbo-Croat* by David Norris (Hodder Headline). Both books concentrate on the Croatian variant of the language, although Serbian reading passages are also included.

Grammar and pronunciation

There are three **genders** in Croatian – masculine, feminine and neuter. Masculine nouns usually end with a consonant, feminine nouns with *-a*, neuter nouns with *-o* or *-e*. Plurals are usually formed by adding *-i*, *-ovi* or *-evi* to masculine nouns (*autobus*, bus, becomes *autobusi*, buses; *vlak*, train, becomes *vlakovi*, trains); *-e* to feminine nouns (*plaža*, beach, becomes *plaže*, beaches); and *-a* to neuter nouns (*auto*, car, becomes *auta*, cars) – although there are plenty of irregular nouns which don't follow these rules exactly. It's also worth bearing in mind that there are six noun **cases** in Croatian, ensuring that each noun (and any adjectives qualifying it) changes its ending according to what part of the sentence it occupies. Travelling around the coast, for example, you'll notice that "*u Dubrovnik*" means "to Dubrovnik", "*u Dubrovniku*" means "in Dubrovnik", and "*od Dubrovnika*" means "from Dubrovnik". Similarly, look out for *u Pulu* (to Pula), *u Puli* (in Pula), and *od Pule* (from Pula).

Pronunciation is not as difficult as it first appears. Every word is spoken exactly as it's written, and each letter represents an individual sound. The only letters you're likely to have problems with are the following consonants, which differ from their English equivalents.

c "ts" as in cats
č "ch" as in church
ć a softer version of č; similar to the "t" in future
đ somewhere between the "d" in endure and the "j" in jam
g always hard, as in get
j "y" as in youth
r always rolled; fulfils the function of a vowel in words like Hrvatska ("Croatia")
š "sh" as in shoe
ž "s" as in pleasure

There are no hard-and-fast rules governing **stress** in Croatian, save to say that it hardly ever falls on the last syllable of a word, and quite frequently falls on the first.

Useful words and phrases

Greetings and civilities

dobar dan	hello/good day
bog!	hi!/bye!
kako ste?	how are you? (polite)
kako si?	how are you? (informal)
dobro, hvala	fine, thanks
gdje si? (literally: "where are you?")	whassup?/where have you been?
što radiš? (literally: "what are you doing?")	what have you been up to?/what's new?
dobro jutro	good morning
dobra večer	good evening
laku noć	good night
do viđenja	goodbye
molim	please
hvala (lijepo)	thank you (very much)
izvinite	excuse me
oprostite or **sorry**	sorry
izvolite	here you are
hajdemo!	let's go!

Basic terms and phrases

da	yes
ne	no
kada?	when?
gdje?	where?
zašto?	why?
koliko?	how much?
veliko	large
malo	small
više	more
manje	less
dobro	good
loše	bad
jeftino	cheap
skupo	expensive
otvoreno	open
zatvoreno	closed
toplo	hot
hladno	cold
sa/bez	with/without
govorite li engleski?	do you speak English?
ne razumijem	I don't understand
ne znam	I don't know
kako se zove ovo na hrvatskom?	what is this called in Croatian?
Hrvatska	Croatia
Hrvat	Croatian person (m)
Hrvatica	Croatian person (f)
Hrvatski	Croatian language
odakle ste?	where are you from (polite)?
odakle si?	where are you from (familiar)?
Ja sam iz . . .	I am from . . .
Australije	Australia
Kanade	Canada
Velike Britanije	Great Britain
Irske	Ireland
Nove Zelandije	New Zealand
Amerike	the US

Directions and getting around

kamo?/kuda?	where to?
gdje je?/gdje se nalazi . . . ?	where is . . . ?
najbliža banka	the nearest bank
najbliži hotel	the nearest hotel
ovdje	here
tamo	there
lijevo	left
desno	right
pravo	straight on
natrag	backwards
gore	above; upstairs
dolje	below; downstairs
sjever	north
jug	south
istok	east
zapad	west
Izgubio sam se	I'm lost (m)
Igubila sam se	I'm lost (f)
je li to blizu?	is it nearby?
koliko je daleko?	how far is it?
zračna luka	airport
(autobusni/željeznički) kolodvor	(bus/train) station
kolosijek	platform
stajalište autobusa	bus stop
tramvajsko stajalište	tram stop
luka	port
trajektna luka	ferry terminal
gat	pier
vez	mooring
garderoba	left-luggage office
polazak	arrival
odlazak	departure
u koliko sati polazi vlak/autobus/ trajekt?	what time does the train/bus/ferry leave?
kada polazi sljedeći autobus/ trajekt/ vlak za . . . ?	when does the next bus/ferry/train leave for . . . ?
ima li zakašnenja?	is it running late?
jednu kartu za . . . molim	a ticket for . . . please
u jednom pravcu	single
povratnu kartu	return
mogu li rezervirati sjedište?	can I reserve a seat?
zabranjeno pušenje	no smoking
ulaz	entrance
izlaz	exit
plaža	beach
parkiralište	car park
kino	cinema
veleposlanstvo	embassy
galerija	gallery
bolnica	hospital
tržnica	market
muzej	museum
optičar	optician
benzinska stanica	petrol station/gas station
ljekarna	pharmacy
policijska stanica	police station
pošta	post office
dućan	shop
stadion	stadium
samoposluga	supermarket
bazen	swimming pool
kazalište	theatre
turistički ured or turistički informativni centar	tourist office

Accommodation

imate li . . .	do you have ...
(jednokrevetnu/ dvokrevetnu) sobu?	a (single/double) room?
apartman	an apartment
privatnu sobu	a private room
sa . . .	with . . .
francuskim ležajem	a double bed
tušem/banjom	a shower/bath
pogledom na more	a sea view
mogu li pogledati sobu?	can I see the room?

imate li nešto jeftinije?	do you have anything cheaper?
noćenje i doručak	bed and breakfast
pansion/polupansion	full board/half board
imam rezervaciju	I have a reservation
mogu li rezervirati sobu?	can I book a room?
slavina/svijetlo/telefon/televizor/klimatizacija ne radi	the tap/light/telephone/TV/air conditioning doesn't work
ključ	key
gdje je najbliži autokamp?	where's the nearest campsite?
šator	tent
prikolica	caravan
vreća za spavanje	sleeping bag

Shopping

gdje mogu kupiti . . . ?	where can I buy . . . ?
kupaći kostim	bathing costume
baterije	batteries
cigarete	cigarettes
upaljač	cigarette lighter
vadičep	corkscrew
hranu	food
šibice	matches
telekartu	phonecard
poštanske marke	postage stamps
razglednice	postcards
sapun	soap
toaletni papir	toilet paper
pastu za zube	toothpaste
ručnik	towel
prašak za pranje	washing powder
koliko stoji/koliko košta?	how much does it cost?
to je skupo	that's expensive

Numbers

jedan	1
dva	2
tri	3
četiri	4
pet	5
šest	6
sedam	7
osam	8
devet	9
deset	10
jedanaest	11
dvanaest	12
trinaest	13
četrnaest	14
petnaest	15
šesnaest	16
sedamnaest	17
osamnaest	18
devetnaest	19
dvadeset	20
dvadeset i jedan	21
trideset	30
četrdeset	40
pedeset	50
šezdeset	60
sedamdeset	70
osamdeset	80
devedeset	90
sto	100
dvjesta	200
trista	300
tisuća	1000

Times and dates

dan	day
tjedan	week
mjesec	month
godina	year
danas	today
sutra	tomorrow
jučer	yesterday
prekosutra	the day after tomorrow
prekjučer	the day before yesterday

ujutro	in the morning
popodne	in the afternoon
uvečer	in the evening
rano	early
kasno	late
koliko je sati?	what time is it?
sat	hour
minuta	minute
deset sati	10 o'clock
deset i petnaest	10.15
deset i trideset or **pola jedanaest**	10.30
petnaest do jedanaest	10.45
ponedjeljak	Monday
utorak	Tuesday
srijeda	Wednesday
četvrtak	Thursday
petak	Friday
subota	Saturday
nedjelja	Sunday
praznik	holiday
blagdan	church holiday, saint's day
siječanj	January
veljača	February
ožujak	March
travanj	April
svibanj	May
lipanj	June
srpanj	July
kolovoz	August
rujan	September
listopad	October
studeni	November
prosinac	December
proljeće	spring
ljeto	summer
jesen	autumn
zima	winter

Food and drink

Basic terms

čaša	glass
dobar tek!	bon appetit!
doručak	breakfast
gableci	brunch
hrana	food
ispod peke or **pod pekom**	baked under a lid covered with hot embers
jelovnik	menu
konoba	inn, tavern, folksy restaurant
kuhano	boiled
marenda	brunch
lešo	boiled
na ražnju	spit roasted
na roštilju/na žaru	grilled
nazdravje!	cheers!
nož	knife
pečeno or **u pećnici**	baked
pekarna or **pekarnica**	bakery
pladanj	platter
pohani	fried in breadcrumbs
prženo	fried
račun	bill
ručak	lunch
slastičarnica	patisserie
šalica	cup
tanjur	plate
večera	dinner
viljuška	fork
zajutrak	breakfast
živjeli!	cheers!
žlica	spoon

Basic foods

burek	greasy pastry, usually filled with cheese
jaje	egg
jogurt	yogurt
kifla	breakfast pastry, croissant

kruh	bread	**pekmez**	jam
maslac	butter	**riža**	rice
masline	olives	**salata**	salad
maslinovo ulje	olive oil	**salsa**	tomato sauce
med	honey	**šećer**	sugar
mlijeko	milk	**sir**	cheese
ocat	vinegar	**sol**	salt
omlet	omelette	**umak**	sauce
papar	pepper	**vrhnje**	cream
pašteta	paté		

Soups (juhe) and starters (predjela)

fažol	bean soup from Istria	**paški sir**	hard piquant cheese from the island of Pag
grah	soup made from haricot beans	**pršut**	home-cured ham similar to Italian prosciutto
jota	bean-and-sauerkraut soup	**sir iz ulja**	hard yellow cheese with piquant rind, kept under vegetable or olive oil
kobasica	sausage	**sir s vrhnjem**	cream cheese
kozji sir	goat's cheese	**škripavac**	mild hard cheese from Lika
kulen	spicy paprika-flavoured pork and beef salami from Slavonia	**šunka**	ham
maneštra	bean-and-vegetable soup from Istria	**vrat**	cured pork neck
punjene paprike	stuffed peppers		
ovčji sir	sheep's cheese		

Vegetables (povrće) and pasta (tjestenine)

ajvar	spicy relish made from puréed aubergines and peppers	**grašak**	peas
bijeli luk	garlic	**hren**	horseradish
blitva	spinach-like leaves of mangelwurzel (eaten with fish)	**kapulica**	spring onion
češnjak	garlic	**kiseli kupus**	sauerkraut
đuveč or **đuveđ**	ratatouille-style mixture of vegetables and rice, heavily flavoured with paprika	**krastavac**	cucumber, gherkin
fuži	pasta twirls	**krumpir**	potato
gljiva	mushroom	**kukuruz**	corn on the cob
grah	beans; also bean soup	**kupus**	cabbage
		luk	onion
		mlinci	ragged sheets of baked pasta dough
		mrkva	carrot
		njoki	gnocchi
		paprika	pepper, paprika
		paradajz, pomadora or **rajčica**	tomato
		patlidžan	aubergine

repa turnip
šampinjoni champignon mushrooms
šparoga asparagus
šurlice pasta twirls
tartufi truffle

Fish (riba)

bakalar cod (often dried)
barbun mullet
brancin sea bass
brodet fish stew
cipal golden grey mullet
crni rižot squid risotto
dagnje mussels
girice small fish like whitebait, usually deep fried whole
grdobina frogfish
hobotnica octopus
iglica garfish
inćun anchovy
jakopove kapice scallops
jastog lobster
jegulja eel
kalamari squid
kamenice oysters
kapica clam
kovač John Dory
lignje squid
list sole
lubin sea perch
mušule mussels
orada gilthead sea bream
oslić hake
ostrige oysters
pastrva trout
rak crab
ribice whitebait, sprats
riblja salata literally "fish salad", usually octopus
šaran carp
sipa cuttlefish
škampi scampi
školjke mussels
škrpan/škrpina groper, sea scorpion
skuša mackerel
smuđ pike-perch
som catfish
srdele anchovies
štuka pike
trilja striped or red mullet
žablji kraci frogs' legs
zubatac dentex

Meat (meso) and poultry (perjad)

arambašica cabbage leaves stuffed with meat and rice
bečki odrezak Wiener schnitzel
bubrezi kidneys
buncek pork hock
ćevapčići or **ćevapi** grilled mincemeat rissoles
čobanec paprika-flavoured meat stew
govedina beef
gulaš goulash
guska goose
janjetina lamb
jetra liver
koljenica pork knuckle
kotlet cutlet, chop
kunić rabbit
lungić lean, boneless and tender pork chop
mućkalica paprika-flavoured meat stew
nogice pigs' trotters
odrezak escalope of veal or pork
ombolo Istrian pork chop
panceta bacon
pašticada beef cooked in wine, vinegar and prunes
patka duck
piletina chicken
pljeskavica hamburger-style minced-meat patty

pulić	donkey
purica	turkey
purica s mlincima	turkey with baked pasta sheets
ražnjići	pieces of pork grilled on a skewer; kebab
sarma	cabbage leaves stuffed with rice
slanina	bacon
srneći gulaš	venison goulash
srnetina	venison
svinjetina	pork
teletina	veal
tuka	turkey
zagrebački odrezak	schnitzel stuffed with ham and cheese and fried in breadcrumbs

Desserts (deserti)

fritule or **uštipci**	deep-fried dough balls dusted with icing sugar
kolač	cake
kremšnita	cream cake or custard slice
krofna	doughnut
kroštule	deep-fried twists of pastry
makovnjača	poppy seed cake
orehnjača	walnut cake
palačinke	pancakes
rožata	creme-caramel-style custard from Dubrovnik
savijača or **štrudla**	strudel
štrukli	dough blobs stuffed with cheese
sladoled	ice cream
torta	gateau

Fruit (voće)

ananas	pineapple
banana	banana
breskva	peach
dinja	melon
grožđe	grapes
jabuka	apple
jagoda	strawberry
kajsija	apricot
kruška	pear
limun	lemon
lubenica	watermelon
naranča	orange
šljiva	plum
smokva	fig
trešnja	cherry
višnja	sour cherry

Drinks (pića)

bambus	red wine and cola
bermet	bitter stomach-settling spirit from Samobor
bevanda	wine mixed with water
bijelo vino	white wine
biska	mistletoe-flavoured brandy
borovnica	bilberry juice
čaj	tea
crno vino	red wine
crveno vino	rosé wine
džus or **đus**	juice
gemišt	white wine and mineral water
kava	coffee
limunada	lemonade
loza/lozovača	grape brandy
medenica/ medovina	honey-flavoured brandy
mineralna voda	mineral water
orahovača	walnut-flavoured brandy

pelinkovac	bitter juniper-based aperitif
penjušac	sparkling wine
pivo	beer
rakija	brandy
šljivovica	plum brandy
sok	juice
špricer	white wine and soda
svjetlo pivo	light, lager-style beer
topla čokolada	hot chocolate
travarica	herb-based spirit similar to Italian grappa
viljamovka	pear brandy
voda	water
vodka	vodka
led	ice
s ledom	with ice
bez leda	without ice

Glossary

General terms

Autocesta Motorway.

Beč Vienna.

Beograd Belgrade.

Brdo/Brijeg Hill.

Buk Waterfall.

Bura Strong wind which often blows in northern Adriatic.

Centar Centre.

Cesta Road.

Crkva Church.

Dolac Dell (in karst areas, a small cultivable area enclosed by wall).

Dolina Valley.

Donji grad Lower town.

Draga Vale, bay.

Dvor Palace, court, courtyard.

Dvorac Castle.

Dvorište Yard, courtyard.

Fortica Fortress.

Gaj Grove.

Gat Quay.

Gornji grad Upper town.

Grad Town.

Gradska vijećnica Town hall.

Groblje Graveyard.

Hram Temple, church.

Jadran Adriatic Sea.

Jama Pit, cave.

Jezero Lake.

Kamenjar Stony, infertile land; used to describe the arid areas of Hercegovina and inland Dalmatia.

Kaštel Castle, fortress.

Kavana Café.

Kolo Folk dance.

Kolodvor Station.

Konoba Inn, tavern, folksy restaurant.

Korzo Evening promenade.

Krčma Inn, tavern.

Kuća House.

Lučka kapetanija Harbourmaster's office.

Luka Port.

Lungomare Shoreline road or promenade.

Maestral North wind.

Magistrala Highway running the length of the Adriatic coast.

Mandrać Inner harbour for small boats.

Mleci Venice.

More Sea.

Most Bridge.

Obala Shore, quayside.

Oluja Storm.

Otok Island.

Palača Palace.

Park prirode Nature park, nature reserve.

Perivoj Park, public garden.

Plaža Beach.

Poljana/Polje Field, square.

Poluotok Peninsula.

Put Road, way.

Rat/Rt Cape.

Rijeka River.

Riva Seafront.

Riznica Treasury.

Samostan Monastery.

Selo Village.

Stajalište Bus stop.

Stari grad (i) Old town; (ii) Castle.

Staza Path.

Šetalište Walkway, promenade.

Školj Small island.

Škor/Škver Shipyard or part of fishing village where boats are repaired.

Špilja Cave.

Šuma Forest, wood.

Toranj Tower.

Trg Square.

Tržnica Market.

Tvrđava Fortress.

Ulica Street.

Uvala Bay.

Varoš Central residential quarter of an old town.

Vijećnica Council chamber, town hall.

Vikendica Holiday house or cottage.

Vodopad Waterfall.

Vrata Gate, door.

Vrh Peak.

Vrt Garden.

Žal Beach.

Zaljev Bay, gulf.

Zdenac Well.

Ždrilo Gorge.

Zidine Walls.

Županija County.

Zvonik Bell-tower, campanile.

Artistic and architectural terms

Apse Semicircular recess at the altar (usually eastern) end of a church.

Baldachin Canopy, often resting on columns, above main altar.

Cardo Principal north–south street in a Roman town.

Caryatid Pillars in the form of women, often decorating the facade of a building.

Ciborium See "Baldachin".

Decumanus Principal east–west street in a Roman town.

Incunabula Books printed before 1500.

Lapidarium Collection of sculpture.

Loggia Arcaded porch – often in front of the town hall – intended to provide Renaissance citizenry with a place to meet and talk.

Lunette Semicircular niche above a doorway or portal.

Peristyle Colonnade surrounding a courtyard or building.

Plutej Pleatwork design characteristic of early medieval Croatian stone carving.

Polyptych Painting on several joined wooden panels.

Revelin Bastion; defensive tower.

Secession Movement of artists who split from Vienna's Academy of Arts in 1897. Also used more generally as a term roughly synonymous with Art Nouveau.

Political and historical terms

Austria-Hungary Official name adopted by the Habsburg Empire in 1867, designed to make the Hungarians feel that they were equal partners with the Austrians in the imperial enterprise.

AVNOJ Literally "anti-fascist council of national liberation of Yugoslavia", a provisional parliament established by the Partisans during World War II, first convened in Jajce, Bosnia-Hercegovina, in 1943.

Ban Governor or viceroy. Title given to rulers of Croatia appointed by Hungarian (later Austrian) monarchs.

Blijesak "Flash". Name given to the Croatian Army offensive which drove Serbian forces out of western Slavonia in 1995.

Bošnjak Bosnian Muslim.

Četnik Serbian irregular fighter. The term was first coined during the anti-Turkish struggles of the nineteenth century and subsequently used to describe nationalist anti-communists in World War II, then Serbian forces active in Croatia and Bosnia in 1991–95.

Domovinski rat "Homeland War". Official Croatian name for the 1991–95 conflict.

Dragovoljac Croatian volunteer in the Domovinski rat (see above).

Frankopans Aristocratic family long associated with the island of Krk.

Glagolitic The script used by the Croatian church in the early Middle Ages. Survived in some areas of Istria and the Kvarner region until the early nineteenth century, when it was replaced by the Latin script.

Habsburg Empire The central European state ruled by the Habsburg family, who first gained control of parts of Austria in the early thirteenth century, and went on to control an empire comprising – among others – Germans, Italians, Czechs, Slovaks, Hungarians, Slovenes and Croats. The empire was broken up in 1918.

Hajduk Brigand. Romantically associated with popular struggles against the Turks, the term has positive connotations for Croats, Serbs, Bulgarians and other southeast European peoples.

HDZ Croatian Democratic Union. Right-of-centre pro-independence political movement formed in 1989 and led by Franjo Tuđman. The governing party in Croatia from 1990 to 2000.

HRT Croatian Radio and Television. The main state-owned broadcasting network.

Hrvatski narodni preporod Croatian National Renaissance. Name given to the mid-nineteenth-century upsurge in Croatian culture, language and consciousness.

HSLS Croatian Social Liberal Party. Croatia's main centre party; in opposition 1991–2000, briefly shared power with the SDP (see below) 2000–02.

HVO Croatian Defence Council. Formed by Croats in Bosnia-Hercegovina to organize themselves militarily against the Serbs (and subsequently Muslims) in the Bosnian war of 1992–95.

Illyria Roman name for the territories which are nowadays roughly covered by the states of Croatia, Bosnia-Hercegovina, Serbia and Albania. The term was resurrected by Napoleon in 1805 with the creation of the Illyrian Provinces, which stretched from Villach in southern Austria to Dubrovnik in Dalmatia. Some Western writers continued to use the term "Illyria" to describe the South Slav lands throughout the nineteenth century.

Illyrianism Early nineteenth-century Croatian cultural movement which stressed the linguistic affinities of Croats and Serbs.

JNA Yugoslav People's Army. Official title of Yugoslavia's army from 1945 to 1991. Generally sided with the Serbs during the 1991–92 conflict.

Knez Prince, duke or (in Dubrovnik and other Dalmatian towns) city governor or rector.

Kralj King.

Military frontier (Vojna krajina in Croatian; Militärgrenze in German). Belt of territory running along Croatia's border with Ottoman-controlled Bosnia-Hercegovina, created in the early sixteenth century and finally dismantled in the mid-nineteenth. Designed to prevent Ottoman expansion, it was under the direct rule of Habsburg military bodies in Graz or Vienna.

NDH Puppet Croatian state established under Nazi auspices 1941–45.

Non-Aligned Movement Created by Tito, Nehru and Nasser to give a voice to countries which existed outside the East–West divisions of the Cold War.

Oluja "Storm". The Croatian offensive of August 1995 which finally defeated secessionist Serb forces and brought an end to the war in Croatia.

Partisan Anti-fascist fighter in World War II.

Ragusa Old name for Dubrovnik.

RS Serbian Republic. Name adopted by Serbian-controlled areas of Bosnia after 1992.

RSK Republic of the Serbian Krajina. Serbian name for the territories controlled by Serbian secessionists in Croatia 1991–95.

Sabor Assembly, parliament.

SDP Social Democratic Party. Successor to the SKH. Principal opposition party from 1990 to 2000, and leading partner in the coalition elected to power in January 2000. Developed in the 1950s to distinguish Yugoslav communism from the Soviet model.

SKH Croatian League of Communists.

SKJ Yugoslav League of Communists.

Uskok Sixteenth-century freebooters operating out of the port of Senj; see p.227.

Ustaša (plural Ustaše). Croatian nazi movement formed by Ante Pavelić which came to power with German help in 1941, forming the NDH.

Travel store

ROUGH GUIDES Complete Listing

UK & Ireland
Britain
Devon & Cornwall
Dublin **D**
Edinburgh **D**
England
Ireland
The Lake District
London
London **D**
London Mini Guide
Scotland
Scottish Highlands & Islands
Wales

Europe
Algarve **D**
Amsterdam
Amsterdam **D**
Andalucía
Athens **D**
Austria
Baltic States
Barcelona
Barcelona **D**
Belgium & Luxembourg
Berlin
Brittany & Normandy
Bruges **D**
Brussels
Budapest
Bulgaria
Copenhagen
Corfu
Corsica
Costa Brava **D**
Crete
Croatia
Cyprus
Czech & Slovak Republics
Denmark
Dodecanese & East Aegean Islands
Dordogne & The Lot
Europe
Florence & Siena
Florence **D**
France
Germany
Gran Canaria **D**
Greece
Greek Islands
Hungary
Ibiza & Formentera **D**
Iceland
Ionian Islands
Italy
The Italian Lakes
Languedoc & Roussillon
Lanzarote & Fuerteventura **D**
Lisbon **D**
The Loire Valley
Madeira **D**
Madrid **D**
Mallorca **D**
Mallorca & Menorca
Malta & Gozo **D**
Menorca
Moscow
The Netherlands
Norway
Paris
Paris **D**
Paris Mini Guide
Poland
Portugal
Prague
Prague **D**
Provence & the Côte D'Azur
Pyrenees
Romania
Rome
Rome **D**
Sardinia
Scandinavia
Sicily
Slovenia
Spain
St Petersburg
Sweden
Switzerland
Tenerife & La Gomera **D**
Turkey
Tuscany & Umbria
Venice & The Veneto
Venice **D**
Vienna

Asia
Bali & Lombok
Bangkok
Beijing
Cambodia
China
Goa
Hong Kong & Macau
Hong Kong & Macau **D**
India
Indonesia
Japan
Kerala
Laos
Malaysia, Singapore & Brunei
Nepal
The Philippines
Rajasthan, Dehli & Agra
Singapore
Singapore **D**
South India
Southeast Asia
Sri Lanka
Taiwan
Thailand
Thailand's Beaches & Islands
Tokyo
Vietnam

Australasia
Australia
Melbourne
New Zealand
Sydney

North America
Alaska
Baja California
Boston
California
Canada
Chicago
Colorado
Florida
The Grand Canyon
Hawaii
Honolulu **D**
Las Vegas **D**
Los Angeles
Maui **D**
Miami & South Florida
Montréal
New England
New Orleans **D**
New York City
New York City **D**
New York City Mini Guide
Orlando & Walt Disney World® **D**
Pacific Northwest
San Francisco
San Francisco **D**
Seattle
Southwest USA
Toronto
USA
Vancouver
Washington DC
Washington DC **D**
Yellowstone & The Grand Tetons
Yosemite

Caribbean & Latin America
Antigua & Barbuda **D**
Argentina
Bahamas
Barbados **D**
Belize
Bolivia
Brazil
Cancùn & Cozumel **D**
Caribbean
Central America
Chile
Costa Rica
Cuba
Dominican Republic
Dominican Republic **D**
Ecuador
Guatemala
Jamaica
Mexico
Peru
St Lucia **D**
South America
Trinidad & Tobago
Yúcatan

Africa & Middle East
Cape Town & the Garden Route
Dubai **D**
Egypt
Gambia
Jordan

D: Rough Guide **DIRECTIONS** for short breaks

Available from all good bookstores

Kenya
Marrakesh **D**
Morocco
South Africa, Lesotho & Swaziland
Syria
Tanzania
Tunisia
West Africa
Zanzibar

Travel Specials
First-Time Africa
First-Time Around the World
First-Time Asia
First-Time Europe
First-Time Latin America
Travel Health
Travel Online
Travel Survival
Walks in London & SE England
Women Travel
World Party

Maps
Algarve
Amsterdam
Andalucia & Costa del Sol
Argentina
Athens
Australia
Barcelona
Berlin
Boston & Cambridge
Brittany
Brussels
California
Chicago
Chile
Corsica
Costa Rica & Panama
Crete
Croatia
Cuba
Cyprus
Czech Republic
Dominican Republic
Dubai & UAE
Dublin
Egypt
Florence & Siena
Florida
France
Frankfurt
Germany
Greece
Guatemala & Belize
Iceland
India
Ireland
Italy
Kenya & Northern Tanzania
Lisbon
London
Los Angeles
Madrid
Malaysia
Mallorca
Marrakesh
Mexico
Miami & Key West
Morocco
New England
New York City
New Zealand
Northern Spain
Paris
Peru
Portugal
Prague
Pyrenees & Andorra
Rome
San Francisco
Sicily
South Africa
South India
Spain & Portugal
Sri Lanka
Tenerife
Thailand
Toronto
Trinidad & Tobago
Tunisia
Turkey
Tuscany
Venice
Vietnam, Laos & Cambodia
Washington DC
Yucatán Peninsula

Dictionary Phrasebooks
Croatian
Czech
Dutch
Egyptian Arabic
French
German
Greek
Hindi & Urdu
Italian
Japanese
Latin American Spanish
Mandarin Chinese
Mexican Spanish
Polish
Portuguese
Russian
Spanish
Swahili
Thai
Turkish
Vietnamese

Computers
Blogging
eBay
iPhone
iPods, iTunes & music online
The Internet
Macs & OS X
MySpace
PCs and Windows
PlayStation Portable
Website Directory

Film & TV
American Independent Film
British Cult Comedy
Chick Flicks
Comedy Movies
Cult Movies
Film
Film Musicals
Film Noir
Gangster Movies
Horror Movies
Kids' Movies
Sci-Fi Movies
Westerns

Lifestyle
Babies
Ethical Living
Pregnancy & Birth
Running

Music Guides
The Beatles
Blues
Bob Dylan
Book of Playlists
Classical Music
Elvis
Frank Sinatra
Heavy Metal
Hip-Hop
Jazz
Led Zeppelin
Opera
Pink Floyd
Punk
Reggae
Rock
The Rolling Stones
Soul and R&B
Velvet Underground
World Music (2 vols)

Popular Culture
Books for Teenagers
Children's Books, 5-11
Conspiracy Theories
Crime Fiction
Cult Fiction
The Da Vinci Code
His Dark Materials
Lord of the Rings
Shakespeare
Superheroes
The Templars
Unexplained Phenomena

Science
The Brain
Climate Change
The Earth
Genes & Cloning
The Universe
Weather

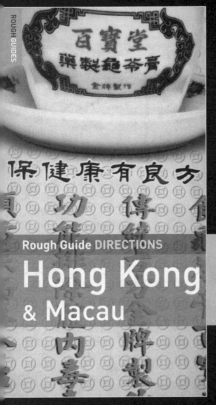

Small print and Index

A Rough Guide to Rough Guides

Published in 1982, the first Rough Guide – to Greece – was a student scheme that became a publishing phenomenon. Mark Ellingham, a recent graduate in English from Bristol University, had been travelling in Greece the previous summer and couldn't find the right guidebook. With a small group of friends he wrote his own guide, combining a highly contemporary, journalistic style with a thoroughly practical approach to travellers' needs.

The immediate success of the book spawned a series that rapidly covered dozens of destinations. And, in addition to impecunious backpackers, Rough Guides soon acquired a much broader and older readership that relished the guides' wit and inquisitiveness as much as their enthusiastic, critical approach and value-for-money ethos.

These days, Rough Guides include recommendations from shoestring to luxury and cover more than 200 destinations around the globe, including almost every country in the Americas and Europe, more than half of Africa and most of Asia and Australasia. Our ever-growing team of authors and photographers is spread all over the world, particularly in Europe, the USA and Australia.

In the early 1990s, Rough Guides branched out of travel, with the publication of Rough Guides to World Music, Classical Music and the Internet. All three have become benchmark titles in their fields, spearheading the publication of a wide range of books under the Rough Guide name.

Including the travel series, Rough Guides now number more than 350 titles, covering: phrasebooks, waterproof maps, music guides from Opera to Heavy Metal, reference works as diverse as Conspiracy Theories and Shakespeare, and popular culture books from iPods to Poker. Rough Guides also produce a series of more than 120 World Music CDs in partnership with World Music Network.

Visit www.roughguides.com to see our latest publications.

Rough Guide travel images are available for commercial licensing at www.roughguidespictures.com

Rough Guide credits

Text editor: Helen Marsden and Ruth Blackmore
Layout: Sachin Tanwar
Cartography: Alakananda Bhattacharya
Picture editor: Sarah Cummins
Production: Aimee Hampson
Proofreader: Serena Stephenson
Cover design: Chloë Roberts
Photographer: Martin Richardson
Editorial: **London** Kate Berens, Claire Saunders, Polly Thomas, Richard Lim, Alison Murchie, Karoline Densley, Andy Turner, Keith Drew, Edward Aves, Nikki Birrell, Alice Park, Sarah Eno, Lucy White, Jo Kirby, Samantha Cook, James Smart, Natasha Foges, Roisin Cameron, Joe Staines, Duncan Clark, Peter Buckley, Matthew Milton, Tracy Hopkins, Ruth Tidball; **New York** Andrew Rosenberg, Steven Horak, AnneLise Sorensen, Amy Hegarty, April Isaacs, Ella Steim, Anna Owens, Joseph Petta, Sean Mahoney
Design & Pictures: **London** Scott Stickland, Dan May, Diana Jarvis, Mark Thomas, Jj Luck, Harriet Mills, Nicole Newman; **Delhi** Umesh Aggarwal, Ajay Verma, Jessica Subramanian, Ankur Guha, Pradeep Thapliyal, Anita Singh, Madhavi Singh, Karen D'Souza
Production: Katherine Owers
Cartography: **London** Maxine Repath, Ed Wright, Katie Lloyd-Jones; **Delhi** Jai Prakash Mishra, Rajesh Chhibber, Ashutosh Bharti, Rajesh Mishra, Animesh Pathak, Jasbir Sandhu, Karobi Gogoi, Amod Singh, Athokpam Jotinkumar
Online: **New York** Jennifer Gold, Kristin Mingrone; **Delhi** Manik Chauhan, Narender Kumar, Rakesh Kumar, Amit Kumar, Amit Verma, Rahul Kumar, Ganesh Sharma, Debojit Borah
Marketing & Publicity: **London** Liz Statham, Niki Hanmer, Louise Maher, Jess Carter, Vanessa Godden, Vivienne Watton, Anna Paynton, Rachel Sprackett; **New York** Geoff Colquitt, Megan Kennedy, Katy Ball; **Delhi** Reem Khokhar
Special Projects Editor: Philippa Hopkins
Manager India: Punita Singh
Series Editor: Mark Ellingham
Reference Director: Andrew Lockett
Publishing Coordinator: Megan McIntyre
Publishing Director: Martin Dunford
Commercial Manager: Gino Magnotta
Managing Director: John Duhigg

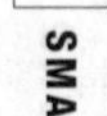

SMALL PRINT

Publishing information

This fourth edition published May 2007 by
Rough Guides Ltd,
80 Strand, London WC2R 0RL
345 Hudson St, 4th Floor,
New York, NY 10014, USA
14 Local Shopping Centre, Panchsheel Park,
New Delhi 110017, India
Distributed by the Penguin Group
Penguin Books Ltd,
80 Strand, London WC2R 0RL
Penguin Group (USA)
375 Hudson Street, NY 10014, USA
Penguin Group (Australia)
250 Camberwell Road, Camberwell,
Victoria 3124, Australia
Penguin Books Canada Ltd,
10 Alcorn Avenue, Toronto, Ontario,
Canada M4V 1E4
Penguin Group (NZ)
67 Apollo Drive, Mairangi Bay, Auckland 1310,
New Zealand

Cover concept by Peter Dyer.

Typeset in Bembo and Helvetica to an original design by Henry Iles.

Printed in Itlay by Legoprint S.p.A

552pp includes index

A catalogue record for this book is available from the British Library

ISBN: 978-1-84353-783-0

The publishers and authors have done their best to ensure the accuracy and currency of all the information in **The Rough Guide to Croatia**, however, they can accept no responsibility for any loss, injury, or inconvenience sustained by any traveller as a result of information or advice contained in the guide.

1 3 5 7 9 8 6 4 2

Help us update

We've gone to a lot of effort to ensure that the fouth edition of **The Rough Guide to Croatia** is accurate and up to date. However, things change – places get "discovered", opening hours are notoriously fickle, restaurants and rooms raise prices or lower standards. If you feel we've got it wrong or left something out, we'd like to know, and if you can remember the address, the price, the time, the phone number, so much the better.

We'll credit all contributions, and send a copy of the next edition (or any other Rough Guide if you prefer) for the best letters. Everyone who writes to us and isn't already a subscriber will receive a copy of our full-colour thrice-yearly newsletter. Please mark letters: **"Rough Guide Croatia Update"** and send to: Rough Guides, 80 Strand, London WC2R 0RL, or Rough Guides, 345 Hudson St, 4th Floor, New York, NY 10014. Or send an email to **mail@roughguides.com**

Have your questions answered and tell others about your trip at **www.roughguides.atinfopop.com**

Acknowledgements

Jonathan Bousfield would like to thank: Plamenko Anzulović, Višnja Arambašić, Marijana Biondić, the Blagaić sisters, Martina Csiffary, Mirjana Darrer, Vesna Jovičić, Mihaela Kadija, Dubravko Kavčić, Sanja & Jonathan Kawaguchi, Dunja Knebl, Kristina Kovač, Silvija Lučevnjak, Marin Matošić, Maja Milovčić, Ivana Mirković, Lidija Mišćin, Andrea Petrov, Vesna Petrović, Andrea Pisac, Adriana Piteša, Igor Prikaski, Stanka Kraljevic, Nada Prodan Mraković, Andrija Rudić, Sara Salamunić, Kornel Šeper, Đurđica Šimičić, Nina Štohera and Tonči Šurjak.

SMALL PRINT

Readers' letters

Thanks to the following readers who took the time to write in with their comments and suggestions (and apologies to anyone whose name we've misspelt or omitted).

Michael Bardeaux, Dr Chris Brockwell, Jeniffer Carey, Debbie Carnegie, Jane Chesters, Euseka, Bruce Evans, Cathy Fowler, Chris Fudge, Robert Green, Simon Hartley, Alison J Kempenaar, Michael Levin, Jonas F Ludvigsson, John Messenger, Marius Mollersen, Mike Nevin, Barry Newsome, Michael Plunkett, Ian Reid, Chris Scott & Lucy Ridout, Laura Selan, Andrew Sides, John & Angela Thompson, Antonela Vogranic, Sue Wall, Tony Walton, David White.

Photo credits

All photos © Rough Guides except the following:

Introduction
Zagreb church © Alamy
Bellringers in traditional clothing, Rijeka © Alamy
Korcula from the ferry © Sarah Cummins
Hvar Town © Sarah Cummins

Things not to miss
01 Amphitheatre, Pula © Croatian tourist board
03 Café society, Split © Alamy A8JEF8
05 Skradinski buk, Krka National Park © Alamy
06 The Zagorje, Veliki Tabor © Alamy
07 Boat trips to the Kornati Islands © Croatian tourist board
13 Tower of the Church of St Martin, Mali Losinj © Alamy
14 Krk folk dancing, Omisalj © Corbis
15 Coastal ferry © Alamy
16 Trsteno, fountain in botanical gardens © Alamy
18 Paklenica National Park © Alamy AHFECE
20 Scuba-diving © Alamy
27 Truffle omelette © Jon Bousfield
30 Walking Dubrovnik's walls © Corbis

Croatian Cuisine colour section
Ispod Peke © Croatian Tourist Board

Croatia's islands colour section
Dolphin © Alamy AY4X10k

Black and whites
p.68 Tram, Zagreb © Travel Ink
p.122 Satue of Josip Broz Tito © Alamy
p.153 Lonjsko village © Alamy
p.259 Olives © Alamy
p.342 Primošten © Croatia tourist board
p.420 Korčula © Croatia tourist board

Contexts
1956: Indian Prime Minister Jawaharlal Nehru (1889–1964) (left), Yugoslav President Josip Broz Tito (1892–1980), (centre), and Egyptian President Gamal Nasser (1918–1970) sit around a coffee table during a meeting of the Non-Aligned Countries, Brionu, Croatia (Photo by Hulton Archive/Getty Images) © Getty (p.496)
President Franjo Tuđjman © Getty (p.503)
Dubrovnik Folk music festival © Alamy (p.509)

Index

Map entries are in colour.

INDEX

E

F

G

H

I

INDEX

INDEX

INDEX

INDEX

Map symbols

maps are listed in the full index using coloured text

International boundary
Chapter boundary
Motorway
Major road
Minor road
Steps
Tunnel
Pedestrianised road
Unpaved road
Railway
Funicular
Cable car
Footpath
Wall
River
Ferry route
Mountain peak
Mountain range
Cave
Waterfall
Marsh
Bridge
Gate
British cemetery

Campsite
Fortress
Castle
Church (regional maps)
Monastery
Synagogue
Place of interest
Hotel
Information office
Internet access
Bus stop
Airport
Parking
Post office
Hospital
Swimming pool
Building
Church (town maps)
Market
Stadium
Park
Beach
Beach fill
Cemetery